Welcome to London

History and tradition greet you at every turn in London; it's also one of the coolest, most modern cities in the world. If London contained only landmarks such as Westminster Abbey and Buckingham Palace, it would still rank as one of the world's great destinations, but Britain's capital is much more. People come to glimpse the royals and stop by hot galleries; to take in theater and trendy shops; to sample tea and scones or cutting-edge cuisine. When you need a break from the action, pop into a pub, relax in a park—or take a walk and make London your own.

TOP REASONS

★ **Architectural Icons:** The Tower of London and Big Ben are quintessential London.

★ **Art Museums:** From the National Gallery to the Tate Modern, a visual feast awaits.

★ **Top Theater:** Whether it's Shakespeare or avant-garde drama, the play's the thing.

★ **City of Villages:** Unique neighborhoods from Mayfair to the East End invite discovery.

★ **Shopping:** Fun markets, famous flagship department stores, chic boutiques.

★ **Parks and Squares:** Distinctive green spaces large and small are civilized retreats.

Contents

MAPS

Fodor's Features

Chapter 1

EXPERIENCE LONDON

20 ULTIMATE EXPERIENCES

London offers terrific experiences that should be on every traveler's list. Here are Fodor's top picks for a memorable trip.

1 Big Ben and Houses of Parliament

The neo-Gothic Houses of Parliament contains the Houses of Commons and Lords (the legislative bodies of the United Kingdom's government) and the giant clock tower known as Big Ben (one of London's most beloved icons). *(Ch. 3)*

2 Drinking in Historic Pubs

The history of London's taverns and pubs is the history of the city itself. Grab a pint or a gin cocktail, and get to know how the locals live. *(Ch. 3–14)*

3 British Museum

It would take a lifetime to do justice to the extraordinary collection (spanning 8 million artifacts from over 2 million years) at Britain's most visited museum. *(Ch. 6)*

4 Hampton Court Palace

One of Britain's grandest royal palaces, Hampton Court contains some of the finest Tudor architecture in the world and is imbued with an overwhelming sense of history. *(Ch. 14)*

5 Gallery Hopping in East London

With one of the highest concentrations of artists in Europe, East London is fertile ground for some serious contemporary art gallery hopping, from Whitechapel to Hackney. *(Ch. 8)*

6 Hyde Park & Kensington Gardens

London is famous for its awesome Royal Parks, and the contiguous Hyde Park and Kensington Gardens are perfect for escaping the hustle and bustle of the city. *(Ch. 10)*

7 The Markets

From gourmet food to antiques, you can find nearly everything at London's most famous street markets, Portobello Market in Notting Hill and Borough Market on Southbank. *(Ch. 9, 11)*

8 London Eye

For an unrivaled bird's-eye view of the metropolis and beyond, take a ride on one of the world's tallest observation wheels. *(Ch. 9)*

9 Afternoon Tea

For a quintessential English ritual, enjoy a pot of tea served in bone china alongside finger sandwiches, fruit scones, and cakes at one of the city's fanciest hotels. *(Ch. 1)*

10 Shakespeare's Globe

A replica of the original Globe Theatre just yards from where Shakespeare's Elizabethan playhouse stood, the modern-day Globe still hosts open-air performances of the Bard's plays. *(Ch. 9)*

11 Indian Food in Brick Lane

Thanks to successive waves of immigrants, Whitechapel's Brick Lane is famous for London's highest concentration of curry houses and some of the best Indian food outside India. *(Ch. 8)*

12 Victoria & Albert Museum

With a vast collection of 2.3 million objects, the V&A is one of the world's greatest museums of decorative arts and design. *(Ch. 10)*

13 Tate Modern

A must-visit for global art lovers, the Tate Modern wows with its extensive collection of constantly rotating modern art. *(Ch. 9)*

14 St. Paul's Cathedral

With the second largest cathedral dome in the world, St. Paul's is a towering masterpiece of English Baroque design, both inside and out. *(Ch. 7)*

15 Covent Garden

Covent Garden is considered the heart of London, thanks to its markets, pubs, restaurants, museums, theaters, boutique shops, street entertainers, and more. *(Ch. 5)*

16 Buckingham Palace

The official residence of the British monarch is opulently filled with priceless tapestries, artwork, and marble and gilt galore. *(Ch. 3)*

17 Theater in the West End

Thanks to some of the world's best actors and directors (and the most historic theaters), London's contributions to the theater world give Broadway a run for its money. *(Ch. 5)*

18 National Gallery

With more than 2,300 of the world's masterpieces, this museum is considered Britain's greatest art collection. *(Ch. 3)*

19 Tower of London

With a gory 950-year history of beheadings, imprisonments, and torture, myths and legends shroud England's most perfect medieval fortress and home of the Crown Jewels. *(Ch. 7)*

20 Westminster Abbey

The site of all but two royal coronations since 1066, the Abbey is steeped in history—from tombs of monarchs to monuments for nobles, statesmen, and poets. *(Ch. 3)*

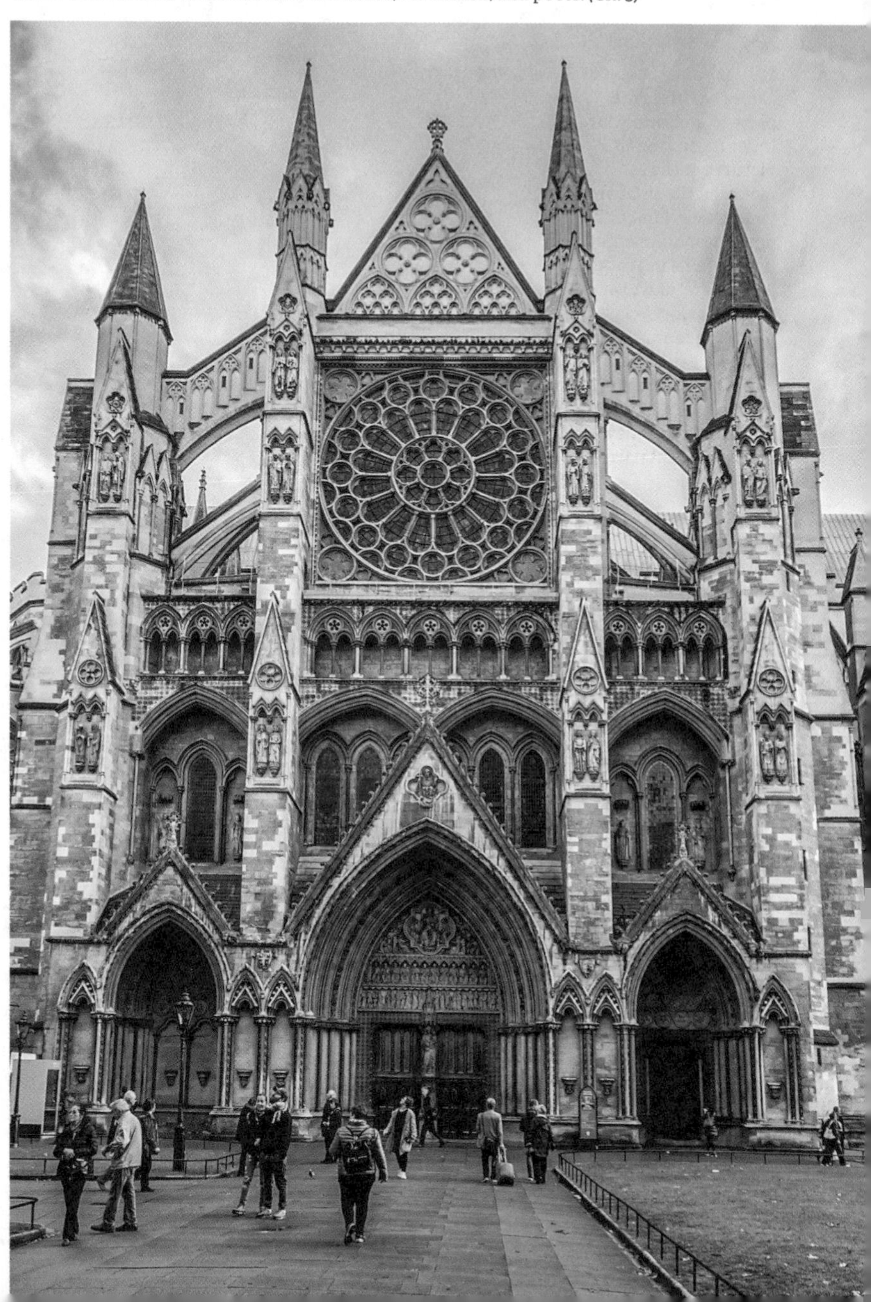

WHAT'S WHERE

1 Westminster and St. James's. This is the place to embrace your inner tourist. Snap pictures of the mounted Horse Guards, watch kids clambering onto the monumental bronze lions in Trafalgar Square, and visit stacks of world-class art in the fantastic national galleries. Brave the crowds to peruse historic Westminster Abbey and its ancient narrative in stone.

2 Mayfair and Marylebone. You may not have the wallet for London's most prestigious shops, but remember window-shopping in historic Mayfair is free. Meanwhile, chic boutiques in Marylebone are a refreshing change from gaudy Oxford Street a few blocks south.

3 Soho and Covent Garden. More sophisticated than seedy these days, the heart of London puts Theatreland, strip joints, Chinatown, burger boîtes, and the trendiest of film studios side by side. Hold tight through the hectic hordes in Leicester Square. Covent Garden's historic paved piazza is one of the

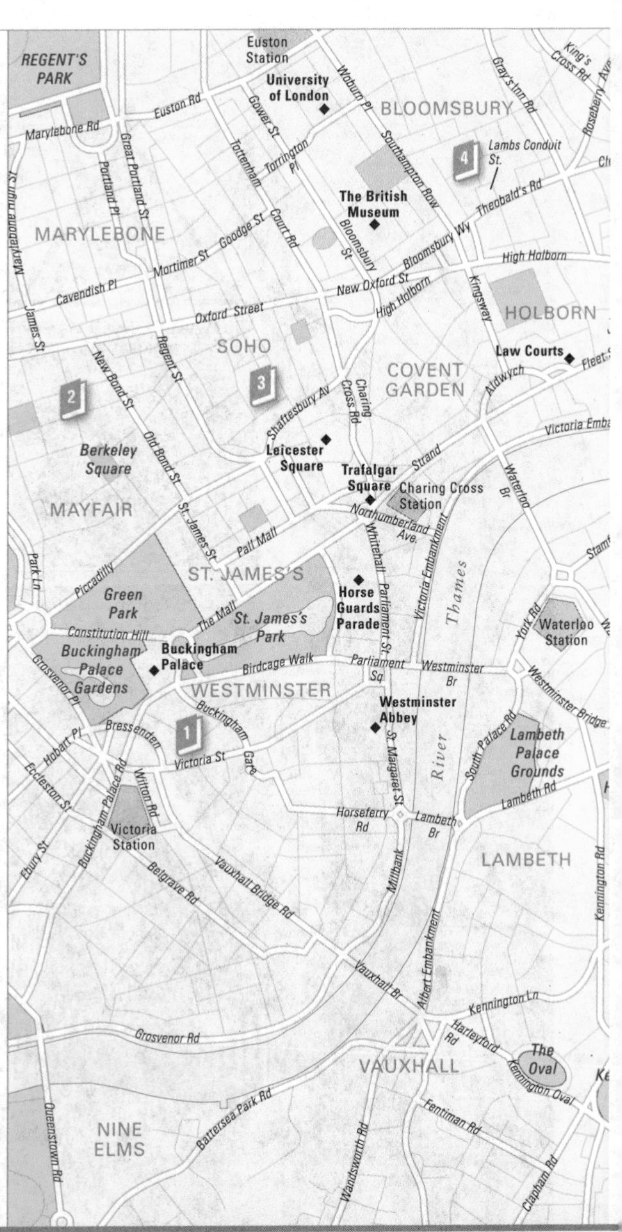

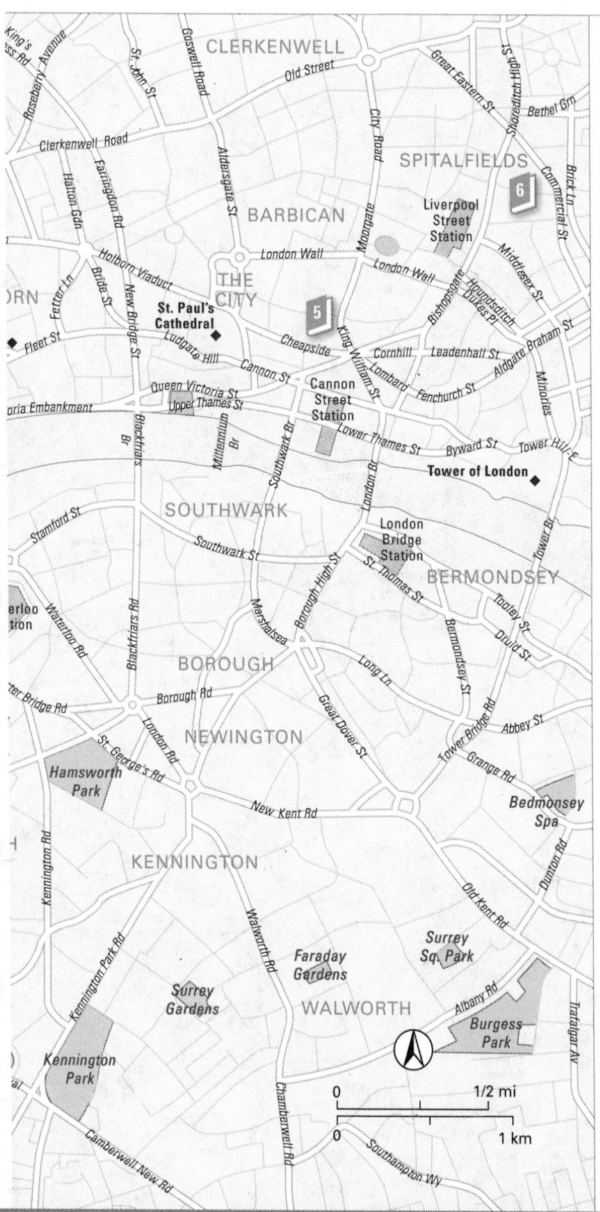

most raffishly enjoyable parts of the city.

4 Bloomsbury and Holborn. Once the bluestocking and intellectual center of London, elegant 17th- and 18th-century Bloomsbury is now also a mixed business district. The British Museum has enough amazing objets d'art and artifacts to keep you busy for a month; the Law Courts, University of London, and quaint, trendy Lamb's Conduit Street are worth a gander. Clerkenwell, meanwhile, is a hotbed of history and culinary reinvention.

5 The City. London's Wall Street might be the oldest part of the capital, but thanks to new skyscrapers and a sleek Millennium Bridge, it also looks like the newest. History fans won't be short-changed, however: head for St. Paul's Cathedral, Tower Bridge, and the Tower of London.

6 East London. Once famed for the 19th-century slums immortalized by Charles Dickens and Jack the Ripper, today the area is a fulcrum of London's contemporary art scene and a hip party zone. Dive headfirst into the eclectic wares at Spitalfields, Brick Lane, and Columbia Road's much-loved early-morning flower market.

WHAT'S WHERE

7 South of the Thames. The Southbank Centre—including the National Theatre and Royal Festival Hall, plus nearby Shakespeare's Globe and Tate Modern—showcases the capital's crowning artistic glories. Or put it all in aerial perspective from the 72nd floor of the Shard.

8 Kensington, Chelsea, Knightsbridge, and Belgravia. Although the many boutiques of King's Road have lost much of their heady '60s swagger, the free museums are as awe-inspiring as ever. Kensington High Street is slightly more affordable than King's Road; otherwise, flash your cash at London's snazziest department stores, Harrods and Harvey Nichols.

9 Notting Hill and Bayswater. North of Kensington, around Portobello Road, Notting Hill Gate is a trendsetting couple of square miles of photographers' galleries, indie bookshops, fashionable boutiques, and hip restaurants. Nearby, Bayswater mixes eclectic fashions, organic fresh food shops, and gaudy Middle Eastern and Chinese restaurants.

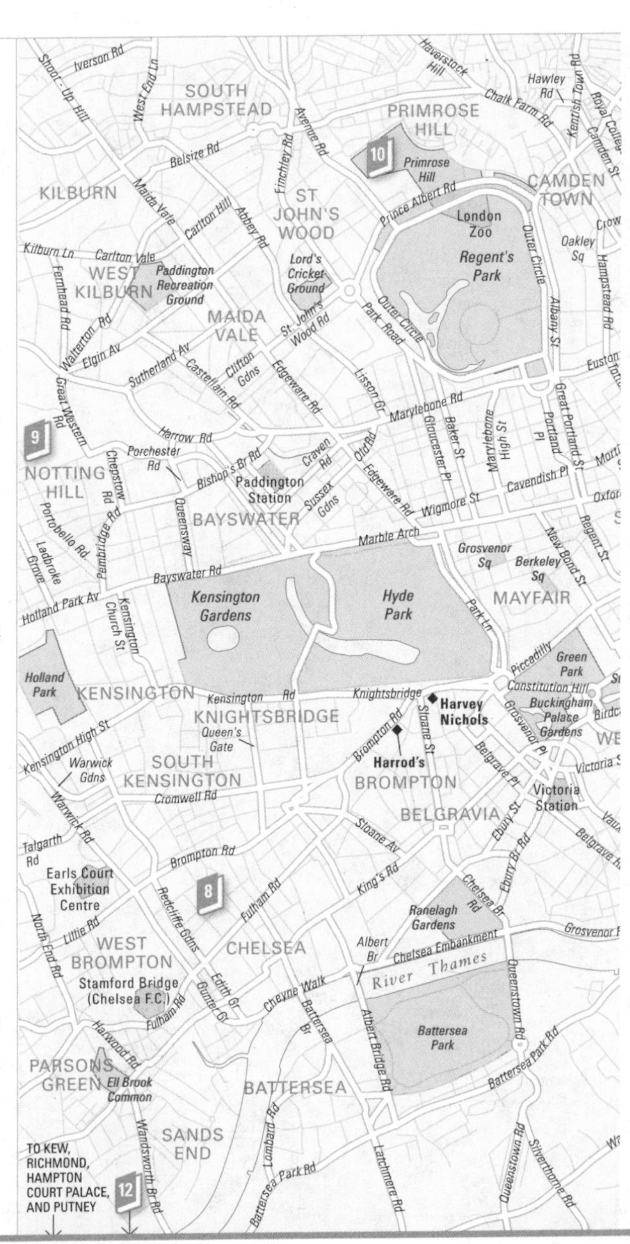

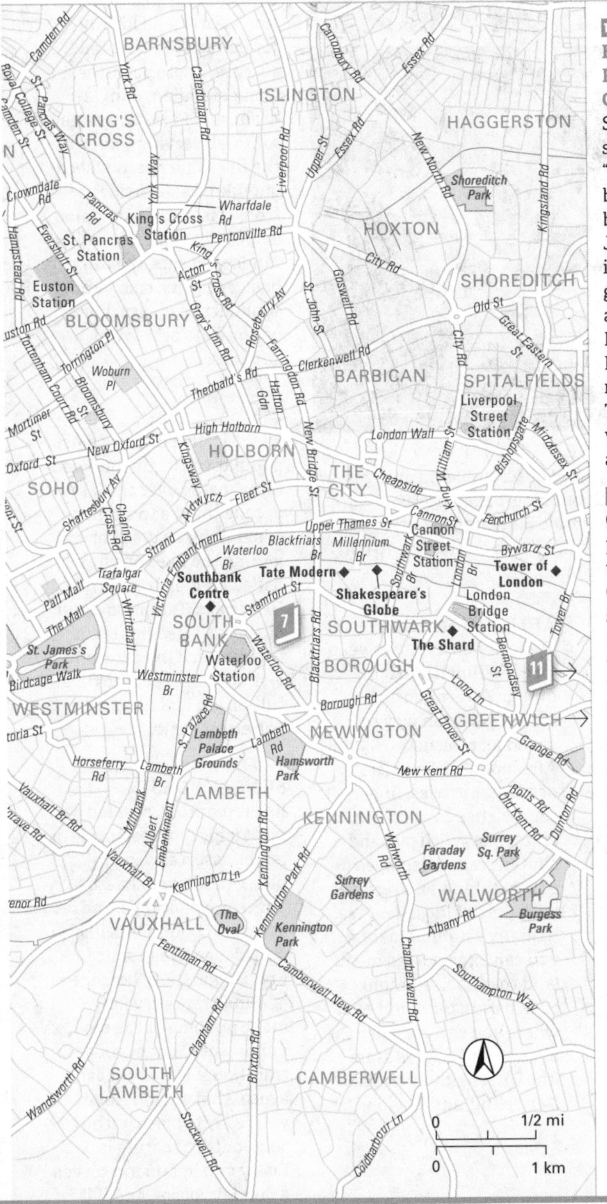

10 Regent's Park and Hampstead with Primrose Hill and Camden Town. Surrounded by elegant, stucco-fronted "terraces"—mansions as big as palaces—designed by 19th-century architect John Nash, Regent's Park is a Regency extravaganza. The nearby ancient hilltop villages of Hampstead and Primrose Hill attract celebrity residents while Camden Town provides the area with a much needed hip, alternative bent.

11 Greenwich. The Royal Observatory, Sir Christopher Wren's architecture, the Old Royal Naval College, British clipper ship *Cutty Sark*, and the Prime Meridian all add up to one of the best Thames-side excursions beyond central London.

12 The Thames Upstream. As an idyllic retreat from the city, stroll around London's historic gardens and enjoy the stately homes of Kew, Richmond, and Putney. Better yet, take a gentle river cruise and end up at the famous Hampton Court Palace.

What to Eat and Drink in London

FULL ENGLISH BREAKFAST
Consisting of eggs (usually fried or scrambled), sausages, bacon, fried tomatoes, black pudding, baked beans, mushrooms, and toast, the classic Full English breakfast is best enjoyed with a classic builder's tea on the side to cut through the greasy, calorific mass.

FISH-AND-CHIPS
England's most famous dish is available throughout the city and comes in many shapes and sizes. Best enjoyed out of a hot paper wrap from a typical fish-and-chip shop aka a chipper (and generally takeaway only), the meal should be eaten with a miniature wooden fork for extra authenticity. The fish is usually cod (but haddock, skate, and rock are not uncommon), covered in a crispy deep-fried batter. Chips are thick-cut fried potatoes and sides can include anything from pickles and pickled eggs to mushy peas and curry sauce.

AFTERNOON TEA
Typically enjoyed between an early lunch and late dinner, Afternoon Tea is a very British way to spend an afternoon. A true Afternoon Tea consists of cakes, pastries, finger sandwiches sans crusts, and scones with jam and clotted cream displayed on a tiered stand and served with pots of loose-leaf tea. In many establishments, you can expect a tea menu (and the fanciest might even have a tea sommelier) where you can consider the likes of Earl Grey, Assam (the Queen's favorite teas), Darjeeling, and Ceylon.

CURRY
The 1970s saw a wave of Bangladeshi immigrants arriving in London and setting up restaurants along Brick Lane and the surrounding area; competition clearly (and luckily for London diners) bred success. These days, there's a mix of Indian, Bangladeshi, and Pakistani restaurants, all serving some of the finest curry anywhere outside of Asia. Aside from classics like vindaloo (super-hot), madras, and tandoori meats, the range of sweet, salty, spicy, and sour curries makes it one of London's best-loved cuisines.

GIN
Historically London's most popular spirit, gin has been rejuvenated over the last decade thanks to a range of small-batch distilleries joining the likes of established London brands like Hendricks, Tanqueray, and Sipsmith. The "ginaissance" is very much in vogue and visitors can expect to find full-on gin menus and a variety of tonics.

SUNDAY ROAST
Roast potatoes, roasted meat (chicken, beef, pork, or lamb), assorted vegetables, cauliflower cheese, Yorkshire puddings, and assorted condiments like mint sauce, bread sauce, English mustard, horseradish, and cranberry jelly make up some of the most important elements of a traditional Sunday roast, a meal that should leave you ready to sleep within 30 minutes of eating it. Every pub in London serves a Sunday roast—and if it

doesn't, then it can hardly call itself a pub—and the quality ranges dramatically depending on the establishment.

PIMM'S CUP
Best enjoyed while outside in the sun, Pimm's is a gin-based liqueur typically mixed with lemonade and ice, then filled with sliced strawberries, cucumber, and mint (and orange if you're feeling fancy). Popular at weddings, regattas, Wimbledon, horse-racing tracks, and cricket matches, it is the British version of the Aperol Spritz and even more refreshing than water.

SRI LANKAN HOPPERS
A relatively new craze in London, the Sri Lankan hopper was always destined for great things in the city—who could resist the concept of a rice and coconut pancake filled with curry, relish, and fried eggs? Find them in Hoppers, the hip Soho restaurant that played a large part in exposing the Sri Lankan classic to the masses; just expect long lines at this no-reservations spot.

DIM SUM DUMPLINGS
While Soho has lost much of its independent dining scene, next-door Chinatown is much the same as it has always been, aside from the odd new bubble tea shop or Sichuan joint. That means reliably good dim sum can be found throughout the neighborhood in any one of Gerard Street's litany of restaurants; look out for the ubiquitous all-day dumpling menu.

SALT BEEF BEIGELS
Cured in brine and slow-boiled for hours, the delicacy of salt beef belongs sandwiched between two beigels (yes, that's bagel to you Americans) halves, slathered in hot English mustard, and topped with pickles. The sandwich is available throughout the city in locations like the famous Brass Rail in Selfridges department store or at Brick Lane's historic 24-hour Beigel Bake, where every beigel comes with a dollop of East London charm.

PASTA FROM PADELLA
While pasta in London is well-regarded, it's unusual to see huge crowds lining up for the chance to sample well-crafted ravioli. But that's the story at Padella, the Borough Market restaurant whose legendary pasta inspired levels of hysteria not seen on the city since the dawn of the no-reservations, walk-in burger joints of 2012. After trying the beef shin pappardelle and simple tagliarini with garlic and chilli, you'll be ready and willing to line up to try out the rest of the menu in no time.

TURKISH FOOD
London's huge Turkish community is responsible for gifting the city one of its favorite dishes—the doner kebab, a huge hunk of meat roasted on a revolving spit. While Londoners love stopping off for late-night doner after a night of drinking , that's just one way to consume Turkish food. For those with more sophisticated palettes, head to one of the city's many excellent

Gin

Turkish ocakbasi and opt for shish (large cubes of chicken or lamb cooked on the grill), beyti (ground lamb or beef wrapped in lavash bread and topped with yogurt), and plenty of roasted red onions and pomegranate.

CRAFT BEER
While real ale (which is relatively flat and warm) still has its fans, the craft beer revolution has been the heart of London's beer scene for the last decade. Inspiration from American IPAs and pale ales' heady hops awakened London's senses, leading to a mass of new breweries supplying the demand for these eclectic ales.

What to Buy in London

Vintage shopping at Camden and Spitalfields Markets

BESPOKE SUITS

Arguably the most famous road in men's fashion, Savile Row in Mayfair is the classic destination for all your bespoke suiting needs. A made-to-measure suit from the likes of Gieves and Hawkes or Oswald Boateng might be quite the investment, but the quality and craftsmanship ensure a purchase that will stand the test of time.

VINTAGE SHOPPING

The booming London vintage scene is proof that one person's trash is another's treasure with plenty of shops, markets, and warehouses set-up around the city selling preloved clothing, shoes, and accessories. Head to Camden Market, Spitalfields Market, and best of all, Brick Lane and adjoining Cheshire Street, for the finest vintage finds in the city.

ANTIQUE BOOKS

The famous bookshop Foyles might have once used its old books in place of sandbags to protect its roof during the Blitz, but today the city has nothing but respect for the treasures found in its many rare and used book shops. Still an exceptional bookshop, Foyles has left antiquarian titles behind, but bibliophiles can source rare treasures in the likes of

James Smith & Sons

Hatchards, Maggs Bros. Ltd, and Peter Harrington Rare Books.

TOYS FROM BENJAMIN POLLOCK'S TOYSHOP
While no child can say no to a visit to toy megastore Hamley's, adults will prefer the vintage appeal of Benjamin Pollocks Toyshop. This boutique shop is all about beautiful pop-up books, wooden yo-yos, and classic games.

UMBRELLAS FROM JAMES SMITH & SONS
While stories of relentless London rainfall are exaggerated, it's fair to say an umbrella will still come in handy on a trip here. If you'd rather skip the flimsy hotel parasol for a refined brolly, perhaps with a chic polished elm handle and a sturdy steel frame, you'll find the iconic James Smith & Sons a dream come true. The Smith family have been keeping Londoners dry since 1830.

BOROUGH MARKET
There is nowhere quite like Borough Market in London and the most important thing to remember before visiting is to arrive on an empty stomach. Between the coffee, deli meats, exotic vegetables, fresh bread, oysters, and cheese stands, you can almost fill up on samples alone. There's also plenty of condiments, jams, spices, and snacks to bring home with you.

PORTOBELLO MARKET
Portobello Market is a hodgepodge street sale selling everything from vintage clothes to fruit and vegetables, but the glue that holds it all together is the always interesting antiques section that commands big crowds. Every Saturday, a parade of stalls line up to sell antique goods with a sometimes dramatic range in quality—the fun is finding the best bits and engaging in a little haggling.

TEA FROM FORTNUM & MASON
If it's good enough for the Queen, then the tea selection at Fortnum and Mason should suffice for everyone else. The range of loose leaf teas at this gourmet department store can seem endless, but keep in mind Her Majesty loves the assam and Earl Grey. Available in tin boxes, hampers, and selection packs, tea from Fortnum and Mason makes the perfect gift.

Best Museums in London

THE NATURAL HISTORY MUSEUM
Undoubtedly the museum to have inspired more future paleontologists than any other, the Natural History Museum is the spiritual home of dinosaurs in London. The star attractions among the dino collection include a full fossil of a tyrannosaurus rex and the skull of a triceratops.

THE V&A MUSEUM
As the largest museum of art and design in the world, the V&A Museum will greet you with intricate ceramic staircases, marble vaulted ceilings, and frescoed walls, all before you even begin thinking about the museum's collection of decorative arts.

TATE BRITAIN
All regal grandeur and impressive portico architecture, the classy—not to mention super old—Tate Britain was opened in 1897 and owns a collection spanning 500 years, with some works dating back to 1500.

THE BRITISH MUSEUM
The biggest museum in London, the British Museum is also the most popular thanks to its eclectic collection of art, curiosities, and artifacts from around the world. Covering nearly 19 acres, the space contains everything from the riches of the Roman Empire to the largest collection of Egyptian artifacts outside of Egypt—and yes, that includes a 5,000-year-old mummy.

TATE MODERN
Housed in a vast former power station on the south bank of the Thames, the towering structure of Tate Modern dominates its particular section of riverfront real estate. On top of the impressive collection of modern and contemporary artists—like Picasso, Francis Bacon, David Hockney, and Duchamp—on display in the main gallery, there's the grand Turbine Hall and its interactive installations.

THE NATIONAL GALLERY
Instantly recognizable by its portico pillars overlooking Trafalgar Square, the National Gallery is probably the square's second most popular cultural attraction—placing close behind its handsome lions, of course. A grand gallery that shuns contemporary art in favor of masterpieces dating from the 1300s to the 1900s, the museum's permanent collection includes paintings by Da Vinci, Caravaggio, Titian, Michelangelo, Raphael, and Van Gogh.

Imperial War Museum

THE NATIONAL PORTRAIT GALLERY
It may reside in the physical shadow of the larger National Gallery just around the corner, but the National Portrait Gallery is no less of a draw. Start in the Tudor and Stewart rooms, where you'll find a line-up of all the kings and queens of England and Scotland. Don't miss Graham Sutherland's Churchill, the Darnley portrait of Queen Elizabeth I, or the only portrait of Shakespeare ever painted from life.

SIR JOHN SOANE'S MUSEUM
A cult institution that has gained mainstream popularity in recent years, the Sir John Soane's Museum is a museum with a difference, in that it's a loving memorial to the late great British architect in the shape of the perfect preservation of his former home in the heart of Holborn. A four-story townhouse, the home has been left untouched in accordance with the wishes of Sir John Soane upon his death in 1837.

SCIENCE MUSEUM
Between learning about the amazing intricacies of super viruses, embarking on a journey into space via VR, and tracing back the history of flight, there's not a lot left uncovered by the Science Museum.

IMPERIAL WAR MUSEUM
Consisting of Churchill's War Rooms; the decommissioned HMS *Belfast* battleship on the Thames; and the original Imperial War Museum, with exhibits featuring everything from Holocaust remembrance tours to war photography, the collection creates a comprehensive and thoughtful take on the theme of modern conflict without necessarily celebrating war.

Best Royal Sights in London

THE TOWER OF LONDON
A royal residence, long-time vault for the Crown Jewels, and gory location of more beheadings than you could count, the Tower of London has been a little bit of everything over the years.

BUCKINGHAM PALACE
Originally built in 1703, the palace has had significant upgrades over the last 300 years to make it fit for lavish royal living. Synonymous with both Queen Victoria (the first monarch to live here) and its current resident, Queen Elizabeth II, Buckingham Palace remains a working palace, although visitors can book guided tours of the State Rooms in summer.

HAMPTON COURT PALACE
One of only two surviving palaces owned by Henry VIII, Hampton Court Palace was the home of Tudor royalty. The palace's serene location on the Thames, amazing gardens (including the famous maze), and dramatic interiors (be sure to see the famous Great Hall) make the short trip to Hampton well worth taking.

WESTMINSTER ABBEY
Royals never have to worry about securing a wedding venue because Westminster Abbey is ready and waiting with 16 royal weddings since the first in 1100, thanks to the stained-glass windows, weathered oil paintings, and incredible Gothic interior stonework. The Abbey has also been the site of all but two royal coronations since 1066.

HOUSEHOLD CAVALRY MUSEUM
If you miss the Changing of the Guard, the next best thing is a visit to the Household Cavalry Museum. Here you can see the living, working routines of the Queen's Household Cavalry—the commissioned soldiers in full ceremonial regalia that you see at Changing of the Guard—as they go about their day.

KENSINGTON PALACE
Kensington Palace has had some of the royal family's biggest names as residents, with William, Kate, and their three children continuing to call it home today. You can explore the Sunken Garden, the Queen's Apartments, and the King's State Apartments on a visit.

ST. JAMES'S PALACE
While no king or queen has lived in St. James's Palace since King William IV in the 1830s, the Tudor palace is older than Buckingham Palace and represents the most senior royal residence in the country.

Kew Palace

THE QUEEN'S GALLERY
Housed within Buckingham Palace, the Queen's Gallery displays the royal family's downright huge and important collection of art, held in trust for the nation. The gallery is an amassed assortment of paintings, photography, antique furniture, and decorative arts that span the ages.

KEW PALACE
Once home to King George III and Queen Charlotte, Key Palace has been restored to its former glory and the private redbrick retreat makes for a picturesque sight surrounded by the manicured hedges and bucolic gardens of Kew. It may be the smallest of the royal palaces, but the English country house interiors are nothing short of charming.

CLARENCE HOUSE
Built by John Nash, Clarence House is today home to the Prince of Wales and the Duchess of Cornwall, Charles and Camilla. The impressive whitewashed facade of the aristocratic town house mansion stands out from the crowd in its picturesque location beside St James's Palace and The Mall.

Best Parks and Gardens in London

ST. JAMES'S PARK
Bordered by Buckingham Palace, the Mall and Horse Guards, St. James's Park is London's most whimsical royal green space. Roam the gardens, tour the lakes, and spy their own lively pod of pelicans (residents here for more than 400 years).

KEW GARDENS
Home to some of the world's rarest threatened species and most elusive plants, the Royal Botanic Gardens are more than just an attraction, they are a sanctuary, with a historic Victorian glasshouse at their heart. The range of exhibitions, installations, themed gardens, tropical greenhouses, and treetop walkways are way more than you can fit into a day, so start your explorations early.

RICHMOND PARK
Once a favorite hunting ground of Henry VIII, Richmond Park covers close to 2,500 acres of grasslands and forest, making it the biggest of London's Royal parks. Any given weekend sees a rush of cyclists pushing themselves around the undulating 6.7-mile road that circles the park's perimeter, while others enjoy walking, running, and all manner of group activities across the meadows.

HAMPSTEAD HEATH
It's the sign of a good London summer day when the bathing ponds of Hampstead Heath are packed with fair-weather locals and tourists alike, mixing it up with the ducks. But the real allure of Hampstead Heath is its wild, roaming grassland, wooded copses, and stunning views of the city, which combine to lend the heath an unmistakable literary quality.

KENSINGTON GARDENS
Annexed from Hyde Park by the Serpentine Lake, Kensington Gardens have a quieter, more intimate appeal compared to their larger neighbors. Here you'll find the Diana Princess of Wales Memorial Playground; the iconic bronze statue of Peter Pan; and, of course, the historic royal residence of Kensington Palace.

HYDE PARK
London's most popular park, Hyde Park is home to the Serpentine Galleries and the annual Pavilion art installation, plus boating lakes, the Albert Memorial, and the Speakers' Corner.

REGENT'S PARK
On top of the gorgeous gardens, the picturesque lake and its pedalo boats, and an impressive collection of fountains and statues, Regent's Park is also home to London Zoo.

Greenwich Park

HOLLAND PARK
A grand expanse of manicured lawns, nature trails, paths, and woodland surround the proud remains of a Jacobean mansion at the heart of Holland Park. The building suffered bomb damage during World War II, but the remaining front terrace provides a spectacular backdrop to the summertime open-air plays staged in the park. Be sure to check out the stunning Kyoto Garden, where Japanese maple trees, dahlias, and a tiered waterfall with a koi carp pond are some of the highlights.

GREENWICH PARK
There's no park in London like Greenwich Park—after all, this is the only one of the city's green spaces that gives visitors the chance to pose with legs astride the Prime Meridian Line. Located outside the Royal Observatory and its planetarium, the Prime Meridian establishes the reference for Greenwich Mean Time and the area's maritime history. In addition, there are green fields, orchards, stunning gardens, and some truly spectacular views of London and its Docklands.

Best Historic Pubs in London

THE DOG AND DUCK, SOHO
Elbow room is scant at this cramped Soho pub, but it's well worth pushing inside to take a look around. The beautiful Victorian tiles, plush red leather banquets, imposing double-decker bar, polished chessboard floor, and vintage mirrors will appeal to literary history hunters looking for the spirit of George Orwell's "down and out in London."

THE SPANIARDS INN, HAMPSTEAD
Hampstead Heath has a smattering of pubs surrounding its boundaries, but none carry the history of the Spaniards Inn, where poets Byron and Keats were once locals. There's also a resident ghost.

THE LAMB, BLOOMSBURY
Close enough to the West End that it can form a part of any day trip around the major sites of Central London, The Lamb on Lamb's Conduit Street is one of Bloomsbury's finest. Walking through the door here is like entering a time warp that transports you to a simpler time when the cell phone was but a twinkle in the eye of its inventor and the art of conversation ruled.

THE GEORGE INN, SOUTH BANK
The only pub in London owned by the National Trust, The George Inn is a fully functioning historic relic, dating back to somewhere around 1543. Not only is it one of the oldest pubs in London, but the George Inn is also the only original galleried coach house left in the city.

YE OLDE CHESHIRE CHEESE, THE CITY
Rebuilt after the 1666 Great Fire of London, the Ye Olde Cheshire Cheese is so old that it actually deserves its "Ye Olde" moniker. And with age comes beauty in this pub that attracted a literary crowd centuries before it became a home away from home to Fleet Street's journalists.

THE HARP, COVENT GARDEN
A traditional West End pub that has changed with the times is The Harp, which supplements its physical charms with a range of about 20 real ales and craft beers on tap. There is an upstairs lounge here, but the cramped bar space below is way more fun.

Lamb & Flag

THE DOVE, HAMMERSMITH
London's oldest riverside pub north of the Thames is one of the city's finest and perfect for a whimsical wander along the river path west of central London. With low-beamed ceilings, grand brick fireplaces, and secret rooms, The Dove couldn't be cozier if it tried.

LAMB & FLAG, COVENT GARDEN
Tucked away in a hidden courtyard in the heart of Covent Garden, The Lamb & Flag is a beautiful old pub established in 1772 and once nicknamed "The Bucket of Blood" on account of the bare-knuckle fights it hosted in its upstairs room.

THE BLACKFRIAR, THE CITY
This is a quirky wedge of a local pub filled with religious iconography, art nouveau flourishes, and a roaring fire. A touch Bavarian in theme, it dates back to 1875 and sits on the site of a former friary, hence the name.

Under-the-Radar Things to Do in London

THE 1714 GEFFYRE MUSEUM
A museum of many facets, the 1714 Geffrye Museum in Hoxton is a nostalgic exploration of home life through the ages from 1600 to the present day. Preserved rooms fill the quaint building, and include a 1745 parlor, a re-created living room from 1935, an 1890 drawing room, and a 1630 hallway.

HORNIMAN MUSEUM WALRUS
A resident of the Horniman Museum for more than a century, London's favorite walrus is a taxidermy specimen who doesn't quite live up to his real-life counterparts. Prepared in the 19th century when taxidermists didn't have the luxury of the Internet for reference, the lovingly idiosyncratic and overstuffed walrus is synonymous with this charming natural history museum that sits at the top of Forest Hill. Full of educational and evocative pieces, the permanent collection features everything from ancient tribal art to man-made mermaids.

BERMONDSEY BEER MILE
More than 10 independent craft breweries and bottle shops are housed in the old brick railway arches of Bermondsey, and their close proximity and the decision to synchronize opening times on Saturday has led to the birth of the Bermondsey Beer Mile. Start at Fourpure Brewery in South Bermondsey.

PRINCE CHARLES CINEMA
Surrounded by the multiplexes of Leicester Square, the Prince Charles caters to cinephiles who pine for the old, the odd, and the iconic, showing classic double-billings, quote-along screenings, all-night movie marathons, and cult movies in their original 35 mm formats.

REGENTS CANAL
Dotted with stylish cafés, pubs, breweries, and one whimsical floating bookshop, the length of the Regents Canal between Angel and Hackney Wick is an ideal way to explore the East End.

Barbican Centre

HIGHGATE CEMETERY
Highgate Cemetery is the most famous of London's Victorian cemeteries, and locals love exploring its flora and fauna and finding an appealingly atmospheric—not to mention beautiful—place to wander. It's the final resting place for the likes of Karl Marx, Malcolm McLaren, and George Eliot.

BARBICAN CENTRE
Having recently enjoyed something of a renaissance, it's now acceptable to enjoy the bold, rigid lines of this Brutalist masterpiece, which houses Europe's largest performing arts center. With a cinema, theater, library, and exhibition spaces, the Barbican Centre is a haven of creativity and artistic expression.

VICTORIA & ALBERT MUSEUM AFTER-HOURS
The V&A was one of the first museums in London to host regular after-hours events. The Friday Late series runs on the last Friday of every month, when DJs, pop-up cocktail bars, artists, and designers help create one of the best free nights out in town.

London Today

Majestic London has always been a great city in flux, and these days it's hard to turn a corner without stumbling into some work-in-progress crater so vast you can only imagine what was there before. New neighborhoods continually bubble up and burst to the fore—for example, a visit to Shoreditch at the eastern edge of The City should provide you with your quotient of London hipness. The anything-goes creative fervor that swirls through London like a fog shows up in DIY art galleries, cutting-edge boutiques, pop-up restaurants, nighttime street-food markets, and slick hipster hotels.

Discovery can take a bit of work, however. Modern London still largely reflects its medieval layout, a difficult tangle of streets and alleys. Even Londoners get lost in their own city. But London's bewildering street pattern will be a plus for the visitor who wants to experience its indefinable historic atmosphere. London is a walker's city and will repay every moment you spend exploring on foot.

Although many images are seared on your consciousness before you arrive—the guards at Buckingham Palace, the big red double-decker buses, Big Ben, and the River Thames—time never stands still in this ancient and yet gloriously modern city. Instead, London is in permanent revolution, and evolves, organically, mysteriously, historically through time.

ARCHITECTURE

With the exceptions of Canary Wharf, the former Swiss Re HQ ("the Gherkin"), the Lloyd's of London building, and the London Eye, London's skyline has traditionally been low-key, with little of the sky-scraping swagger of, say, Manhattan, Hong Kong, or Shanghai. But a spectacular crop of soaring new office towers with wonderful monikers—the Quill, the Shard, the Pinnacle, the Cheese Grater, and the Walkie-Talkie—is taking over the city skyline. With an astonishing 250-odd new skyscrapers being planned or built, opinions are split. Not everyone loves Renzo Piano's spire-like Shard and its 95-floor cloud-piercing "Vertical City" at London Bridge, which has stunning viewing galleries on the 68th, 69th, and 72nd floors. However, once you whiz up and enjoy the 40-mile views, your take on the vast immensity of London is transformed forever.

IMMIGRATION

There's no doubt that London was built on immigration and is now one of the most diverse cities on Earth, with 300 languages spoken on the streets and nearly every world religion practiced at its places of worship. Immigrants make up over a third of the population and "white Britons" are in the minority for the first time, representing 45% of London's population of 8.2 million. The largest first-generation immigrant communities are from India, Poland, Ireland, Nigeria, Pakistan, Bangladesh, and Jamaica. To Londoners, this is no big deal, as this has always been a city of immigrants—from invaders like the Romans, Anglo-Saxons, Vikings, and Normans to those seeking sanctuary like the French Huguenots and east European Jews, along with those seeking their postwar fortunes from Caribbean islands, the Indian subcontinent, and the rest of the British Commonwealth. Despite the populist tendencies sprouting up in other parts of the United Kingdom and Europe (and a new anti-immigration Prime Minister in the form of Boris Johnson), London remains proud of its immigrant heritage, and welcoming to any who wish to call themselves a Londoner.

ARTS AND CULTURE

Have you scanned a free copy of the daily London *Evening Standard* newspaper lately? They're full of world-class shows, plays, jazz performances, readings, recitals, concerts, fashion follies, lectures, talks, tastings, cabarets, burlesque, and art auctions and exhibitions. Whether it's modern art and rare Old Master paintings at Frieze London art fair in Regents Park or a Dinerama nighttime vinyl-and-food-truck feast in Hoxton, London is one of the most happening places on the planet.

PUBLIC TRANSPORTATION

Despite being horribly expensive, you'll notice that the public transport in London is generally nicer and more reliable than mass transit in other major cities. The much-delayed, £15 billion high-speed Crossrail underground railway—known as the Elizabeth Line, after Queen Elizabeth II—is an epic feat of engineering that will shorten the journey time for east to west trips. With 10 new stations and quick trips linking Paddington Station with Heathrow Airport and Canary Wharf in the east, even the notorious over-congestion will be eased when it finally opens in 2021. In addition, the Night Tube now runs 24-hours a day on weekends on five key Underground lines. Don't miss London's popular bike-sharing program, Santander Cycles, which has more than 11,000 bikes at some 700-odd central London docking stations, with unlimited short rides costing just £2 over a 24-hour period.

POLITICS

With its heady mix of modernity, migrants, and money, London is historically a pretty liberal city. It elected its first Muslim mayor in 2016, Sadiq Khan, a former London MP, human rights lawyer, and son of a London bus driver, but the city keeps adjusting to the fallout from the 2016 Brexit vote. The majority of Londoners voted to remain in the European Union, and many of the city's E.U.-origin residents, students, and workers are nervous about what leaving the E.U. means for them and their legal rights to live, work, and study in the United Kingdom. Most Londoners were not pleased when pro-Brexit, anti-immigration former mayor Boris Johnson became Prime Minister in 2019 following Theresa May's resignation. But whatever the final agreed terms of Brexit are (discussions are still in progress), London carries on as ever—vibrant, vital, diverse, and open for business.

NEW UPGRADES AND EXHIBITS

Some of London's top cultural attractions seem to be caught in an arts upgrade arms race and are investing heavily in new galleries, exhibits, extensions, and assorted shiny new bells and whistles. Look for the major £56 million revamp of the eminent Royal Academy of Arts in Piccadilly, which includes extended public galleries and a slick new bridge, or enjoy the recently sprung-to-life Granary Square at King's Cross, where 1,080 choreographed water jets are the buzzy area's answer to an Italian piazza. Tate Modern has added a £50 million modern brick extension, but look for the city's quirkier historic openings such as the 670-year-old Charterhouse in Smithfield, which you can now tour with residents of this Wolf Hall–like former Carthusian monastery, mansion, boys' school, and latter-day almshouse.

London's Royal Legacy

THE ROCKY MONARCHY

From medieval castles and keeps, to Royal Parks, palaces, pageants, ceremonies and processions, London has had a tumultuous and sometimes bloody royal history, which can still be encountered at practically every turn. London has been the royal capital of England since 1066, when the Norman king William the Conqueror began the tradition of royal coronations at Westminster Abbey. All but two reigning monarchs since then—from Richard I (the "Coeur de Lion") in 1189 to the current Queen Elizabeth II in 1953—have been crowned at the Abbey. Many of England's illustrious—and sometimes downright notorious—kings and queens have left a legacy or their majestic mark on the city. You'll find many of the finest places have royal associations: William I subjugated London with the imposing Tower of London; Henry VIII hunted deer at Hampton Court; Elizabeth I enjoyed bear baiting in Southwark; and Charles I was publicly executed on Whitehall. Tyrannical but weak monarchs like King John (1199–1216) granted the City of London extra power under the Magna Carta, while the first "Parliament" sat at the royal Palace of Westminster in 1265 under Henry III. The late medieval Tudors, however, rarely brooked dissent: Elizabeth I's half-sister, "Bloody" Mary I (1553–58), burned heretic Protestant bishops at the stake, and traitors were hung, drawn, and quartered, with their heads stuck on pikes on London Bridge.

A CULTURAL RENAISSANCE

From 1558 to 1601, peace under Elizabeth I ("the Virgin Queen") led to a cultural renaissance and the great flowering of English theater, poetry, letters, music, and drama, centered on Shakespeare's Globe and the open-air playhouses of Southwark. Charles I was later captured by the formidable Puritan Oliver Cromwell during the English Civil War, and beheaded on a freezing day outside Banqueting House in Westminster in 1649. Although the Interregnum lasted only 16 years (outlawing simple pleasures, such as dancing and theater), the Restoration of Charles II in 1660 and subsequent monarchs saw London grow and transform into a teeming metropolis. These monarchs included the Dutch Protestant William III and Mary II—who moved into Kensington Palace, now the current home of the Duke and Duchess of Cambridge—and the House of Hanover's four Georgian kings and later Queen Victoria.

THE MODERN ROYALS

These days you might spot the Duke and Duchess of Sussex (Prince Harry and Meghan Markle) and baby Archie walking on a London visit (they currently live in Windsor) or the Duke and Duchess of Cambridge (Prince William and Kate Middleton) walking in Kensington Gardens with their three young children. Besides the color, pageantry, and marching bands of the Changing of the Guard ceremony at Buckingham Palace, there's also a rich calendar of royal ceremonies. The Ceremony of the Keys to lock up the Tower of London has taken place at 9:53 pm each night for more than 700 years (bar the odd bombing during the Blitz), and you can see the Monarch take the Royal Salute from the Household Division at the annual Trooping the Colour march from Horse Guards Parade to St. James's Park. The Queen is also drawn by four horses in the dazzling Irish State Coach from Buckingham Palace to the Palace of Westminster in a huge royal procession for the State Opening of Parliament each autumn, and you can see her pay homage to the war dead at the Cenotaph on Remembrance Sunday.

Sports in London

Sports in the capital are probably best watched rather than participated in. If you're lucky enough to score a ticket for a Premier League football match, you'll experience a seething mass of jeering, mockery, and tribal chanting. Rugby, tennis, horse-racing, and cricket also impinge on Londoners' horizons at crucial times of the year, but you're unlikely to see grown men crying at the outcome of the Wimbledon Men's Final.

CRICKET

At its best, cricket can be a slow build of smoldering tension and unexpected high-wire excitement. At its worst, it can be too slow and uneventful for the casual observer, as five-day games crawl toward a draw or as rain stops play. But try to visit Lord's—known as the home of cricket—on match days, just to hear the *thwack* of leather on willow and to see the English aristocracy and upper middle classes on full display.

Lord's Lord's Cricket Ground, home of the venerable 1787 Marylebone Cricket Club (MCC), has been hallowed cricketing turf since 1814, and MCC rules codified the game. Tickets for major Test matches are hard to come by: obtain an application form online and enter the ballot (lottery) to purchase them. ✉ *Marylebone Cricket Club, Lord's Cricket Ground, St. John's Wood Rd., St. John's Wood* ☎ *020/7432–1000* 🌐 *www.lords.org* Ⓜ *St. John's Wood.*

FOOTBALL

London's top soccer teams—Chelsea, Tottenham Hotspur, Arsenal, and West Ham—are top-class outfits and the first three often progress in the Europe-wide Champions League. It's unlikely you'll get tickets for anything except the least popular Premier League games during the August–May season, despite the high ticket prices—£50 for a walk-up match-day seat at Chelsea, and £95.50 for the most expensive tickets at Arsenal.

ROWING

The Boat Race Join more than a quarter of a million merry devotees along the banks of the River Thames between Putney and Mortlake for a glimpse of the annual Oxford and Cambridge University Boat Race, held on the last Saturday of March or the first Saturday of April. Sink a few pints and soak up the tweed-cap-and-Barbour-clad atmosphere as these heavyweight eight-man university crews clash oars and tussle head-to-head for supremacy. First raced in 1829, the 4-mile route is a picturesque stretch between Putney and Chiswick bridges. The equally exciting women's eight Boat Race is also held the same day. ✉ *Putney Bridge, Putney* 🌐 *www.theboatraces.org.*

TENNIS

Wimbledon Lawn Tennis Championships The All England Club's Wimbledon Lawn Tennis Championships are famous for Centre Court, strawberries and cream, a gentle spot of rain, and a nostalgic old-school insistence on players wearing white. Thankfully, the rain has been banished on Centre Court by the nifty retractable roof, but whether you can get tickets for Centre Court all comes down to the luck of the draw—there's a ballot system for advance purchase (see website for more details). ✉ *The All England Lawn Tennis Club, Church Rd.* ☎ *020/8971–2473 for general inquiries* 🌐 *www.wimbledon.com.*

Free and Cheap

The exchange rate may vary, but there is one conversion that will never change: £0 = $0. Here are our picks for the top free (and cheap) things to do in London.

CONCERTS

St. Martin-in-the-Fields, St. Stephen Walbrook, St. Olaves in The City, and St. James's Church Piccadilly all host free lunchtime concerts and recitals, as does St. George in Bloomsbury on Sunday afternoons. There are also regular organ recitals at Westminster Abbey.

Of the elite music colleges, the Royal Academy of Music, the Royal College of Music, the Guildhall, Trinity College, and the Royal Opera House offer free recitals. For contemporary ears, there's free jazz and classical music on an exquisite 1897 Bechstein on the first Sunday of the month at the Dysart Petersham restaurant (✉ *135 Petersham Rd.* ☎ *07967/481–625*) in Richmond and live jazz at the Blue Posts (✉ *28 Rupert St.* ☎ *07921/336-010*) in Soho, starting at 3 pm every Sunday. For free blues Sunday–Thursday or before 8:30 pm on Friday and Saturday, head to the Ain't Nothin But ... honky-tonk blues bar in Soho (✉ *20 Kingly St.* ☎ *020/7287–0514*).

FILM, THEATER, AND OPERA

If all seats have been sold, the National Theatre sells unobstructed-view £5 standing-room tickets on the day of performances at their Olivier, Lyttleton, and Dorfman theaters. Standing-room tickets are £3–£15 at the Royal Opera House, with 49 cheap tickets available each Friday at 1 pm for sold-out performances. If you're under 30 or a student, becoming an "Access all Arias" member of the English National Opera is free and allows you to buy £10–£30 tickets. There are 500 £5 standing-room tickets available for every performance at the Shakespeare's Globe theater, as well as £10 standing-room tickets for magical candlelit plays and concerts at the adjacent indoor Sam Wanamaker Playhouse. At Sloane Square, the Royal Court Theatre has a limited number of standing-room tickets for 10 pence each at the Jerwood Theatre Downstairs, available an hour before performances.

SIGHTSEEING

Prop yourself on the top deck of a red double-decker bus for a fantastic sightseeing tour through the most scenic parts of the city. Route15 operates a Heritage route on the traditional 1950s Routemaster buses on select weekends. With all buses now cashless, you can instead use your Oyster card or buy tickets from machines at bus stops for the following routes:

Bus 11: King's Road, Sloane Square, Victoria Station, Westminster Abbey, Houses of Parliament and Big Ben, Whitehall, Trafalgar Square, the Strand, Royal Courts of Justice, Fleet Street, and St. Paul's Cathedral.

Bus 19: Sloane Square, Knightsbridge, Hyde Park Corner, Green Park, Piccadilly Circus, Shaftsbury Avenue, Bloomsbury, Angel, and Islington.

Bus 88: Oxford Circus, Conduit Street, Piccadilly Circus, Haymarket, Trafalgar Square, Whitehall, Horse Guards Parade, Westminster Station, Westminster Abbey, Horseferry Road, and Tate Britain.

London With Kids

ACTIVITIES

Ride the London Eye. Europe's largest observation wheel looks like a giant fairground ride, and you can see across what seems like half of London from the top.

Pose with a Queen's Horse Guard. There's always the Queen's mounted guards in uniform by the entrance to Horse Guards on the Trafalgar Square end of Whitehall. They don't mind posing for pictures, but they're not allowed to smile.

Ice-skating at Somerset House. Send your kids whizzing, arms whirling, across ice mid-November–January at this spotlighted open-air ice rink in a former Renaissance royal palace.

Pedalo on the Serpentine. Pack a picnic and take a blue pedalo out into the middle of Hyde Park's famed Serpentine lake; settle back and tuck in to lunch.

Lose the kids at Hampton Court Maze. The topiary might be more than 300 years old, but the quest to reach the middle of Hampton Court's world-famous trapezoid-shape yew hedge maze remains as challenging as ever.

West End musicals. Foot-stompingly good West End musicals and shows like *Les Misérables, Billy Elliot, Matilda, Mamma Mia!, The Lion King, Oliver!, Grease,* and *Harry Potter and the Cursed Child* will captivate the over-seven crowd.

EDUCATION WITHOUT YAWNS

Kew Gardens. The Royal Botanic Gardens in Kew is great for young ones, and the huge Children's Garden features a 60-foot high treetop Sky Walk, trampolines, scramble slides, and children's trails; it's free for kids under four.

The London Dungeon. It's guts and gore galore at this top South Bank attraction that plunges you into the blood-soaked depths of London history, with tales from a gruesome Jack the Ripper pub, Sweeney Todd barbers, and Mrs. Lovett's infamous pie shop.

London Zoo. Disappear into the animal kingdom among the enclosures, complete with sessions for kids about all kinds of bugs and spiders in this popular animal retreat in Regent's Park.

Natural History Museum. It doesn't get more awe-inspiring than bloodsucking bats, a cabinet of hummingbirds, simulated Kobe earthquakes, and a life-size blue whale. Just make sure you know your dodo from your *daspletosaurus.*

Science Museum. Special effects, virtual space voyages, 800 interactive exhibits, puzzles, and mysteries from the world of science can keep kids effortlessly engaged all day.

Tower of London. Perfect for playing prince and princess in front of the Crown Jewels, but not so perfect for imagining what becomes of the fairy tale—watch your royal necks.

PERFORMANCES

Covent Garden street performers. You can't beat the open-air gaggle of jugglers, fire-eaters, unicyclists, mime artists, and human statues tantalizing crowds at Covent Garden piazza.

Regent's Park Open-Air Theatre. Welcome to the land of fairy dust and magic. Don't miss an evening performance under the stars of *A Midsummer Night's Dream* in high summer.

Best Festivals in London

World renowned for its thriving culture scene, London unsurprisingly keeps a packed annual arts calendar filled with festivals of all shapes and sizes, many of which include free events that are open to everyone. From movies on the Southbank to dance at Sadler's Wells, London's parade of festivals takes over swaths of the city's most interesting and eclectic venues throughout the year. Attending one is a great way to step out of your comfort zone and experience something new that you'll likely only find in London.

SPRING

Underbelly Festival Southbank Running April through September, the Underbelly Festival Southbank offers a packed calendar of stand-up comedy, cabaret, and circus from its pop-up location at the edge of the Thames. The range of shows are tailored to cater to all ages, from family-friendly daytime events to risque after-hours parties. Shows take place in the self-contained, inflatable cow-shape venue (hence the name of the festival). Tickets can be purchased in advance or you can stop in and see what's available on any given day, which can be part of the fun. ✉ *Belvedere Road Coach Park, South Bank* ☎ *084/4545–8252* 🌐 *www.underbellyfestival.com* 🎫 *Free–£25* Ⓜ *Waterloo.*

SUMMER

Film4 Summer Screen Every year, Film4 Summer Screen gives Londoners the chance to watch a collection of classic movies and exclusive premieres under the stars in the Somerset House courtyard, cocooned by the handsome exterior walls of one of the city's most beautiful neoclassical buildings. Pack a blanket and an umbrella (this is London after all) and enjoy fine film, food, and wine on select dates throughout August. ✉ *Somerset House, Strand, Covent Garden* ☎ *020/7845-4600* 🌐 *www.somersethouse.org* 🎫 *From £18* Ⓜ *Charing Cross.*

Meltdown The wildly eclectic and very cool Meltdown Festival generally takes place in June at the Southbank Centre. It's curated by a different big-name artist each year (e.g., Robert Smith in 2018 and Nile Rodgers in 2019), so you never have any idea what to expect until the program comes out. ✉ *Belvedere Rd., South Bank* ☎ *020/3879–9555* 🌐 *www.southbankcentre.co.uk* 🎫 *Free–£90* Ⓜ *Waterloo, Embankment.*

The Proms Hosted predominantly in the epic Royal Albert Hall, The Proms is an eight-week long festival of classical concerts that takes place every summer. More than 100 years old, the festival is considered an institution but the line-up doesn't shy away from embracing the new and quirky aspects of classical music. Expect to find the likes of children's concerts, classic film scores, and avant-garde African salsa on the bill. Standing tickets of £6 are available for most performances. ✉ *Royal Albert Hall, Kensington Gore, South Kensington* ☎ *020/7589–8212* 🌐 *www.royalalberthall.com* 🎫 *From £6.*

FALL

BFI London Film Festival More than 200 feature films, many of them world or European premieres, plus shorts and artist talks, grace the program of the BFI London Film Festival, which takes place over 12 days every October. The big movie theaters in Leicester Square are the focus for the galas and major releases, but you can catch screenings at a total of 14 other venues across town, including locations like the ICA. Booking ahead advised. ✉ *London* ☎ *020/7928–3232* 🌐 *whatson.bfi.org.uk/lff* 🎟 *From £10.*

Dance Umbrella The biggest annual performing arts event in London is Dance Umbrella, a 20-day festival in October that hosts international and British-based artists at venues across the city. ✉ *London* ☎ *020/7257–9380* 🌐 *www.danceumbrella.co.uk* 🎟 *Free–£35.*

Frieze London A glamorous contemporary art fair, Frieze London brings the crème de la crème of the international art world to London each October. Its sister show, Frieze Masters, is a 15-minute walk across Regent's Park and focuses on art from the ancient world through the late 20th century. For the two events combined, hundreds of galleries exhibiting thousands of artworks—everything from Old Masters to Rachel Whiteread—fill two huge pop-up spaces in the park. The food and drink available on-site is pricey but excellent, and there's a compelling program of artist and curator talks. Catch the free Frieze Sculpture Park in Regent's Park between July and October. ✉ *Regent's Park, Regent's Park* ☎ *020/3372–6111* 🌐 *www.frieze.com/fairs/frieze-london* 🎟 *Combined ticket £65* Ⓜ *Regent's Park, Baker St., Great Portland St.*

London Jazz Festival Come November, international jazz superstars rub shoulders with upcoming local talent and cutting-edge bands at more than 50 venues across the city during the 10 days of the London Jazz Festival. A varied program of around 350 performances, including free concerts and gigs for toddlers, means both jazz connoisseurs and those new to the genre will find plenty to enjoy. ✉ *London* 🌐 *www.efglondonjazzfestival.org.uk* 🎟 *Free–£65.*

WINTER

Vault Festival This six-week extravaganza of fringe theater and stand-up comedy is a chance to see some of the U.K.'s most innovative and engaging performers. The atmosphere in the eerie tunnels beneath Waterloo Station (where the Vault Festival takes place) is always buzzing. ✉ *The Vaults, Leake St., South Bank* ☎ *07598/676–202* 🌐 *www.vaultfestival.com* 🎟 *From £5* Ⓜ *Waterloo.*

Afternoon Tea

AN AGE-OLD TRADITION

So what is Afternoon Tea, *exactly*? Well, it is real loose-leaf tea—Earl Grey, English Breakfast, Ceylon, Darjeeling, or Assam—brewed in a silver or porcelain pot and served with fine bone china cups and saucers, milk or lemon, and silver spoons, taken between noon and 6 pm. For the traditional full English experience, there should be elegant finger foods on a three-tier silver cake stand: finely cut crustless finger sandwiches on the bottom; scones with Cornish clotted cream and strawberry preserve in the middle; and rich English fruitcake, shortbread, patisseries, macarons, and dainty *petits gateaux* on top.

CLASSIC CHOICES

The Savoy on the Strand offers one of the most beautiful settings for Afternoon Tea. The Thames Foyer, a symphony of grays and golds centered on a winter garden wrought-iron gazebo and great glass cupola, is just the place for the house pianist to accompany you as you enjoy 72 rare house teas along with finger sandwiches, homemade scones, and pastries. A traditional Afternoon Tea here is £65.

Setting the standard in its English Tea Room for some of London's best-known traditional teas, **Brown's Hotel** in Mayfair offers Afternoon Tea for £55 in an Agatha Christie–esque wood-paneled salon or, if you wish to splurge, Champagne Afternoon Tea for £65.

If you seek timeless chic, the art deco dining room at **The Delaunay** grand café at the Aldwych remains a deeply fashionable hangout. The silver service teas here—light Cream Tea is £9.50, Viennese Tea is £19.75, and Champagne Tea, £29.75—come with wheat-free poppyseed *Gugelhupf* cakes and are among the best in town.

SOMETHING DIFFERENT

Add spice to your tea time by trying a popular Moroccan-style Afternoon Tea (£32 or £42) at the souk-chic tearoom at **Momo** off Regent Street, where you'll enjoy sweet mint tea plus scones with fig jam, Maghrebian pastries, Moroccan chicken wraps, and honey-and-nut-rich Berber-style crepes.

Alternatively, you can sample finger sandwiches and sip fine English sparkling wine while looking out onto the immaculate lawns of **The Kensington Palace Pavilion,** the sight of William and Kate's marriage proposal within resplendent Kensington Gardens. Afternoon Tea is £34, and a suitably Royal Afternoon Tea (with a glass of English sparkling wine) is £45.

Covent Garden's grand French brasserie **Balthazar** has a fabulous New York City-inspired Afternoon Tea, for those who want to instill a little Americana into the British custom. Inspired by the Big Apple, the tea menu features pastrami buns and mustard, baked cheesecake, and cookies 'n' cream tarts for a twist on the classic; prices start at £30.

AN EDWARDIAN ESCAPE

For some gilt-edged Rococo grandeur, few can compete with Afternoon Tea at **The Ritz** on Piccadilly. It's served in the stunning Palm Court, replete with linen-draped tables, Louis XIV chaise longues, sparkling chandeliers, resplendent bouquets, and discrete musical accompaniment; it's a true taste of Edwardian London in the 21st century. Afternoon Tea is £58, and Celebration Champagne Tea is £88. There are five sittings from 11:30 am to 7:30 pm; be sure to book three months ahead, and men should wear a jacket and tie.

Chapter 2

TRAVEL SMART LONDON

Updated by James O'Neill

★ **CAPITAL:**
London

POPULATION:
8,787,800

LANGUAGE:
English

$ CURRENCY:
Pound sterling

COUNTRY CODE:
44

EMERGENCIES:
999

DRIVING:
On the left

ELECTRICITY:
220–240V/50Hz; Continental-style plugs, with two or three round prongs

TIME:
5 hours ahead of New York

WEB RESOURCES:
www.visitbritain.com
www.visitlondon.com
www.standard.co.uk
www.timeout.com/london

What You Need to Know Before Going to London

As one of the largest cities in the world, London can be overwhelming for a first time visitor. Here are some key tips to help you navigate your trip, whether it's your first time visiting or your twentieth.

LONDON IS ONE OF THE MOST DIVERSE CITIES IN THE WORLD.
With 300 languages spoken on the streets and nearly every world religion practiced at its places of worship, immigrants make up over a third of the population, and "white Britons" are now in the minority for the first time in history. You'll find most Londoners embrace this diversity, and indeed some of the best neighborhoods to visit are thriving immigrant communities. The highest population of immigrants come from India, Pakistan, Bangladesh, China, Nigeria, Ghana, and Turkey.

THE CHAOS OF BREXIT IS STILL IN FULL-FORCE.
While London continues to be as multicultural as ever (the city elected its first Muslim mayor, Sadiq Khan in 2016), fall-out from the 2016 Brexit vote is still ongoing. The majority of Londoners voted to remain in the European Union and tensions are still high as the U.K. prepares to exit the European Union. The withdrawal date is currently set for October 2019, but Boris Johnson's ascension to prime minister in July 2019 has only added to the chaos. He's widely reviled by Londoners and with Parliament located in the center of the city, it's impossible to escape politics talk these days.

THE ROYAL FAMILY IS A MUCH BIGGER DEAL IN AMERICA.
The Royal Family is as prevalent as ever in England, although not all Londoners have the affinity for the Queen and her brood as Americans seem to. Some continue to be quite critical of the monarchy, but it always makes for a lively topic, especially as the Crown continues to modernize and stay relevant. The biggest complaint from Londoners tends to concern taxpayers paying the cost of the royal lifestyle, but there's no denying that the continued fascination for the royal family has caused tourism numbers to swell. From Prince Harry and Meghan Markle to Netflix's *The Crown*, tourism interest in the royal family both past and present is as high as ever. Just don't expect a local to gush over Prince George as much as you do.

LEARNING SOME BRITISH SLANG CAN BE HELPFUL.
Nearly everyone knows that Brits have different words for certain things than Americans do. But some slang knowledge is essential for a trip to London: a lift is an elevator, instead of waiting in line you queue, the bathroom is known as the toilet, the loo, or the water-closet (in public spaces looking for a W/C sign instead of a restroom sign), pants are actually underpants (they call them trousers), chips are french fries, and crisps are potato chips. Do say "cheers" when toasting with drinks; it can also be used while saying good-bye and saying thank you. The list can go on forever, so if something a local is saying doesn't quite make sense to you, it's probably a matter of slang.

CHECK TO SEE IF YOUR TRIP FALLS DURING A BANK HOLIDAY.
Several national "bank" holidays are celebrated throughout the year in the U.K: May Day (first Monday in May), the last Monday in May, the last Monday in August, and Boxing Day (December 26). Many stores and some attractions might be closed, and other restaurants and museums might be much busier than usual.

LEARN SOME TIPS FOR SAVING MONEY.
There's no denying London is an expensive city, but there are plenty of ways to save money. Most major museums in London are free, and those that aren't are often covered under The

London Pass. With a variety of prices and durations (from 1 day for £75 to 10 days for £199), you'll get access to nearly every major London attraction.

THE PUB IS A HUGE PART OF LIFE FOR LONDONERS.
The drinking age in England is 18, and pub life is a huge part of culture in London. Expect rowdy after work crowds, especially on days of soccer or rugby matches. While not explicitly legal *everywhere*, alcohol can be consumed in public areas within reason, so don't be afraid to put together a gin-heavy Pimms punch for your picnic. Smoking is banned in all indoor public spaces in London, although you will see that many Londoners still smoke cigarettes. Currently marijuana is not legal in the United Kingdom.

TAKE PUBLIC TRANSIT.
Renting a car during your time in London is a downright horrible idea. Both taxis and ride-share programs are widely available, although these can get pricey and the traffic in the city can be notoriously bad depending on the time of day (Uber is indeed still up-and-running in the city after a 2018 lawsuit from London cabbies almost banned the ride-share app from the city). But the best way to get around London during your trip is by using the buses and underground Tube system. The Tube now runs for 24 hours a day on weekends on five major lines: Piccadilly, Victoria, Northern, Central, and Jubilee. For other times and destinations, the Night-buses (which run midnight to 5 am) are the way to get home late. When traveling the city via public transportation, be sure to purchase an Oyster card, a smart card that can be charged with a cash value and then used for discounted travel throughout the city. Buy your Oyster card for £5 when you first arrive in the city, and then prepay any amount you wish for your expected travel in the city.

Two important things to remember when traveling on the city's public transit; first, always stand to the right on escalators; second, alcohol is banned within London's TFL network (think Underground and buses), but not on national rail lines that link to the city.

LONDON CAN BE HARD TO NAVIGATE.
London is a confusing city to navigate, even for people who've visited it a few times. Its streets are arranged in medieval patterns that no longer make much sense, meaning that you can't always use logic to find your way around. A good map is essential, and public transportation can be a lifesaver: buses will take you magically from point A to point B, and the Tube is often the quickest way to reach your destination. Although free tourist maps can be handy, they're usually quite basic and include only major streets. If you're going to be doing lots of wandering around, buy the pocket-size map book *London A–Z*, which is sold in bookstores and Tube and train stations throughout the city. Its detailed maps are invaluable. To find your way, look for tall landmarks near where you are headed: the London Eye, for example, or the cross atop St. Paul's Cathedral—or the most obvious of all, Big Ben. If you get properly lost, the best people to ask are the Londoners hustling by you, who know the area like nobody else.

Central London and its surrounding districts are divided into 32 boroughs (33, counting the City of London). More useful for finding your way around, however, are the subdivisions of London into postal districts. The first one or two letters give the location: N means north, NW means northwest, and so on. Don't expect the numbering to be logical, however. You won't, for example, find W2 next to W3. The general rule is that the lower numbers, such as W1 or SW1, are closest to Buckingham Palace, but it is not consistent—SE17 is closer to the city center than E4, for example.

Getting Here and Around

Air Travel

Flying time to London is about 6½ hours from New York, 7½ hours from Chicago, 11 hours from San Francisco, and 21½ hours from Sydney.

For flights out of London, the general rule is that you should be at the airport at least one hour before your scheduled departure time for domestic flights and two to three hours before international flights.

AIRPORTS

Most international flights to London arrive at either Heathrow Airport (LHR), 15 miles west of London, or at Gatwick Airport (LGW), 27 miles south of the capital. Most flights from the United States go to Heathrow, which is divided into five terminals, with Terminals 3–5 handling transatlantic flights. Gatwick is London's second gateway. It has grown from a European airport into an airport that also serves dozens of U.S. destinations. A third airport, Stansted (STN), is 35 miles northeast of the city; it handles European and domestic traffic. Three smaller airports, Luton (LTN), 30 miles north of town, Southend (SEN), 40 miles to the east, and business-oriented London City (in east London E16) mainly handle flights to Europe.

GROUND TRANSPORTATION

London has excellent if pricey bus and train connections between its airports and central London. If you're arriving at Heathrow, you can pick up a map and fare schedule at the Transport for London (TfL) Information Centre, in the Underground station serving Terminals 2–3. Train service can be quick, but the downside (for trains from all airports) is that you must get yourself and your luggage to the train via a series of escalators and connecting trams. Airport link buses (generally National Express airport buses) may ease the luggage factor and drop you off closer to central hotels, but they're subject to London traffic, which can be horrendous and make the trip drag on for hours. Taxis can be more convenient than buses, but beware that prices can go through the roof. Airport Travel Line has additional transfer information and takes advance booking for transfers between airports and into London.

From Heathrow to Central London

TRAVEL MODE	TIME	COST
Taxi	1 hour-plus	£48–£90 (depending on traffic)
Heathrow Express Train	15 minutes	From £22 (£37 round-trip), £32 for first class
Underground	50 minutes	£6 one-way (less with Oyster card)
National Express Bus	1 hour	From £6 one-way

Heathrow by Bus: National Express buses take one hour to reach the city center (Victoria) and cost from £6 one-way and £12 round-trip (book online for best prices). The National Express Hotel Hoppa service runs from all airports to 25 hotels near the airport (from £4.50). Heathrow Shuttle offers a shared minibus service between Heathrow and more than 500 London hotels starting from £15. The N9 night bus runs to Aldwych every 20 minutes midnight–5 am; it takes just over an hour and costs £1.50 (you need to pay with an Oyster card or a contactless debit/credit card). Please note: the N9 doesn't stop at Terminal 4; take Bus Nos. 490 or 482 to Terminal 5 and catch it there.

Heathrow by Tube and Train: The cheap, direct route into London is via the Piccadilly Line of the Underground (London's extensive subway system, or "Tube"). Trains normally run every four to eight minutes from all terminals from early morning until just before midnight. The 50-minute trip into central London costs £6 one-way and connects with other central Tube lines. The Heathrow Express train is comfortable and convenient, if costly, speeding into London's Paddington Station in 15 minutes. Standard one-way tickets cost £22 (£37 round-trip) and £32 for first class. Tickets are more expensive to buy on board, so book ahead (online is the cheapest option; at a counter/kiosk, less so). There's daily service 5:10 am (6:10 am on Sunday)–11:25 pm, with departures usually every 15 minutes. Local trains to Paddington are a cheaper alternative to the Heathrow Express (one-way tickets start from £10.50). However, these trains take a little longer (28 minutes), are less frequent (two per hour), and make five stops en-route. They also have no first class carriages.

Heathrow by Taxi: Taking a taxi from the airport into the city is an expensive and time-consuming option. The city's congestion charge (£11.50) may be added to the bill if your hotel is in the charging zone; you run the risk of getting stuck in traffic; and if you take a taxi from the stand, the price will be even more expensive (whereas a minicab booked ahead is a set price). The trip can take more than an hour and can cost in the region of £70, depending on time of day.

Gatwick by Bus: An hourly bus service runs from Gatwick's north and south terminals to London's Victoria Station, with stops at Hooley, Coulsdon, Mitcham, Streatham, Stockwell, and Pimlico. The journey takes upward of 90 minutes (depending on time of day) and costs from £5 one-way. The easyBus service runs to west London (Earl's Court) or Waterloo from as little as £2 if booked in advance; the later the ticket is booked online, the higher the price (up to £11 on board).

Gatwick by Train: The fast, nonstop Gatwick Express leaves for Victoria Station every 15 minutes, 6 am–11:10 pm. The 30-minute trip costs from £19.90 one-way, and £35 round-trip (cheapest tickets are available online). The Thameslink Great Northern rail company runs nonexpress services that are cheaper; Thameslink trains run regularly throughout the day to St. Pancras International, London Bridge, and Blackfriars stations; departures are every 15 minutes (hourly during the night), and the journey takes 45–55 minutes. Tickets are from £9.70 one-way to St. Pancras International.

Stansted by Bus: Hourly service on National Express Airport bus A6 (24 hours a day) to Victoria Coach Station costs from £5 one-way, £10 round-trip, and takes about 1 hour 45 minutes (again, the cheapest tickets are only available online and in advance). Stops include Golders Green, Finchley Road, St. John's Wood, Baker Street, Marble Arch, and Hyde Park Corner. The easyBus service to Victoria via Baker Street costs from £2 one-way, but book early and online for best prices.

Stansted by Train: The Stansted Express to Liverpool Street Station (with a stop at Tottenham Hale) runs daily every 15 minutes, 5:30 am–12:30 am. If booked online, the 50-minute trip costs from £7 one-way and £14 round-trip; tickets cost more when purchased on board or nearer travel time.

Luton by Bus and Train: An airport shuttle runs from Luton Airport to the nearby Luton Airport Parkway Station, from which you can take a train or bus into London (this shuttle is free if you have bought a rail ticket in advance; otherwise it's £2.40 one-way). From there, the Thameslink Great Northern train service runs to St. Pancras, Farringdon, Blackfriars, and London Bridge. The journey takes about 30 minutes. Trains leave every 10 minutes or so during the day, and hourly during the night. Single tickets cost from £13 one-way, if booked in advance. The Green Line 757 bus service from Luton to Victoria Station runs three times an hour, takes about 90 minutes, and costs from £11 one-way, if booked in advance.

TRANSFERS BETWEEN AIRPORTS

Allow at least two to three hours for an interairport transfer. The cheapest option—but most complicated—is public transportation: from Gatwick to Stansted, for instance, you can catch the nonexpress commuter train from Gatwick to Victoria Station, take the Tube to Liverpool Street Station, then catch the train to Stansted from there. To get from Heathrow to Gatwick by public transportation, take the Tube to King's Cross, then change to the Victoria Line, get to Victoria Station, and then take the commuter train to Gatwick.

The National Express airport bus is the most direct option. Between Gatwick and Heathrow, buses pick up passengers every 15–20 minutes 3.15 am–midnight from both airports. The trip takes around 75 minutes, and the fare is from £27 one-way, but it's advisable to book tickets in advance. National Express buses between Stansted and Gatwick depart every 30–45 minutes and can take 3–4½ hours, depending on traffic. The adult one-way fare is from £19. Some airlines may offer shuttle services as well—check with your travel agent in advance of your journey.

 Bicycle Travel

Nicknamed "Boris bikes" after the former mayor, dedicated cyclist, and current Prime Minister Boris Johnson, a 24-hour bike-rental program called Santander Cycles enables Londoners to pick up a bicycle at one of more than 750 docking stations and return it at another. The first 30 minutes are free, then it's £2 for every 30-minute period thereafter. There is also a £2-per-day access charge. You pay at the docking station, using credit or debit cards only (cash is not accepted)—simply follow the instructions on the touch screen and away you go.

 Bus Travel

ARRIVING AND DEPARTING

National Express is the biggest British long-distance bus operator and the nearest equivalent to Greyhound. It's not as fast as traveling by train, but it's comfortable (with bathrooms on board). Services depart mainly from Victoria Coach Station, a well-signposted short walk behind the Victoria mainline train station. The departures point is on the corner of Buckingham Palace Road; this is also the main information point. The arrivals point is opposite, at Elizabeth Bridge. National Express buses travel to all large and midsize cities in southern England and the midlands. Scotland and the north are not as well served. The station is extremely busy around holidays and weekends. Arrive at least 30 minutes before departure so you can find the correct exit gate.

Another bus company, Megabus, offers cross-country fares for as little as £1 per person. The company's single- and double-decker buses serve an extensive array of cities across Great Britain with a cheerful budget attitude. In London, buses for all destinations depart from the Green Line bus stand at Victoria Station. Megabus does not accommodate wheelchairs, and the company strictly limits luggage to one piece per person checked, and one piece of hand luggage.

Green Line serves the counties surrounding London, as well as airports. Bus stops (there's no central bus station) are on Buckingham Palace Road, between the Victoria train station and Victoria Coach Station.

Tickets on many long-distance routes are cheaper if purchased in advance, and traveling midweek costs less than over weekends and at holiday periods.

GETTING AROUND LONDON

Private, as opposed to municipal, buses are known as coaches. Although London is famous for its double-decker buses, the old beloved rattletrap Routemasters, with the jump-on, jump-off back platforms, now only serve a single "heritage" route (No. 15H) and *only* on summer weekends and bank holidays. That route takes you from Trafalgar Square down Fleet Street and on to St. Paul's Cathedral and the Tower of London. Modernized Routemaster buses have taken to the streets on other routes.

Bus stops are clearly indicated; signs at bus stops feature a red TfL symbol on a plain white background. You must flag the bus down at some stops. Each numbered route is listed on the main stop, and buses have a large number on the front with their end destination. Not all buses run the full route at all times; check with the driver to be sure. You can pick up a free bus guide at a TfL Travel Information Centre (at Euston, Liverpool Street, Piccadilly Circus, King's Cross, and Victoria Tube stations; and at Heathrow Airport).

Buses are a good way of seeing the town, particularly if you plan to hop on and off to cover many sights, but don't take a bus if you're in a hurry, as traffic can really slow them down. To get off, press the red "Stop" buttons mounted on poles near the doors. You will usually see a "Bus Stopping" sign light up. Expect to get sardined during rush hour, 8–9:30 am and 4:30–6:30 pm.

Night buses, denoted by an "N" before their route numbers, run midnight–5 am on a more restricted route than day buses. However, some night-bus routes should be approached with caution, and the top deck avoided (the danger is that muggings are most likely to occur there, since it's farthest from both the exit doors and the driver). All night buses run by request stop, so flag them down if you're waiting, or push the button if you want to alight.

All London buses are now cash-free, which means you must buy your ticket *before* you board the bus. There are a number of ways to do this. One-day paper bus passes are available at underground and rail stations as well as London Transport Visitor Centres and cost £5. An easier, and cheaper, option is to pay by prepaid Oyster card or "contactless" bank card. Visitor Oyster cards must be purchased before you arrive; they cost £5 (plus postage), but a day's bus travel is capped at £4.40. Normal Oyster cards (also £5) are available from ticket desks at all major airports or at any Tube station and are transferable if you have money left over. Contactless cards are increasingly being used for London travel: you touch a compatible debit or credit card on a bus or Tube-station's reader, and the fare is automatically debited from your bank account.

One alternative is to buy a one- or seven-day Travelcard, which is good for both Tube and bus travel. Travelcards can be bought at Tube stations, rail stations, and travel information centers. However, note that seven-day Travelcards bought in London *must be loaded onto an Oyster card.* Although using a Travelcard may save you some money, it might be easier to just add additional money to your Oyster card as needed, since there are machines at all Tube stations and at lots of London newsagents. A seven-day paper Travelcard can only be purchased in advance, online. However you buy your ticket, just make sure you have one: traveling without a valid ticket makes you liable for a significant fine (£80). Buses are supposed to swing by most stops every five or six minutes, but in reality you often end up waiting a bit longer, although those in the city center are quite reliable.

Car Travel

The best advice on driving in London is this: don't. London's streets are a winding mass of chaos, made worse by one-way roads. Parking is also restrictive and expensive, and traffic is tediously slow at most times of the day; during rush hours (8–9:30 am and 4:30–6:30 pm) it often grinds to a standstill, particularly on Friday, when everyone wants to leave town. Avoid city-center shopping areas, including the roads feeding Oxford Street, Kensington, and Knightsbridge. Other main roads into the city center are also busy, such as King's Cross and Euston in the north. Watch out also for cyclists and motorcycle couriers, who weave between cars and pedestrians that seem to come out of nowhere, and you may get a heavy fine for straying into a bus lane during its operating hours—check the signs.

If you are staying in London for the duration of your trip, there's virtually no reason to rent a car, because the city and its suburbs are widely covered by public transportation. However, you may want a car for day trips to castles or stately homes out in the countryside. Consider renting your car in a medium-size town in the area where you'll be traveling, and then journeying there by train and picking up the car once you arrive. Rental rates are generally reasonable, and insurance costs are lower than in comparable U.S. cities. Rates generally begin at £20 per day for a small economy car (such as a subcompact General Motors Vauxhall Corsa, or Renault Clio), usually with manual transmission. Air-conditioning and unlimited mileage generally come with the larger-size automatic cars.

In London your U.S. driver's license is acceptable (as long as you are over 23 years old, with no driving convictions). If you have a driver's license from a country other than the United States, it may not be recognized in the United Kingdom. An International Driver's Permit is a good idea no matter what; it's available from the American or Canadian Automobile Association (AAA and CAA, respectively) and, in the United Kingdom, from the Automobile Association (AA) or Royal Automobile Club (RAC). International permits are universally recognized, and having one may save you a problem with the local authorities.

Remember that Britain drives on the left, and the rest of Europe on the right. Therefore, if you cross the Channel into Britain in a right-side rental, you may want to leave it there and pick up a left-side rental.

CONGESTION CHARGE

Designed to reduce traffic through central London, a congestion charge has been instituted. Vehicles (with some exemptions) entering central London on weekdays 7 am–6 pm (excluding public holidays) have to pay £11.50 per day; it can be paid up to 90 days in advance, or on the day of travel, or on the following "charging day," when the fee goes up to £14. Day-, month-, and yearlong passes are available on the Congestion Charging page of the Transport for London website, at gas stations, parking lots (car parks), by mail, by phone, and by SMS text message. Traffic signs designate the entrance to congestion areas, and cameras read car license plates and send the information to a database. Drivers who don't pay the congestion charge by midnight of the next charging day following the day of driving are penalized £160, which is reduced to £80 if paid within 14 days. On top of the congestion charge, the entire Greater London area has been designated a Low Emissions Zone which means that all older and pollution-heavy vehicles will be levied with an extra daily charge of £12.50. However, this will almost certainly not apply to rented cars (which tend to be newer and therefore greener), but it's smart to check with the rental company first.

GASOLINE

Gasoline (petrol) is sold in liters and is expensive (at this writing about £1.30 per liter—around $5.90 per gallon). Unleaded petrol, denoted by green pump lines, is predominant. Premium and Super Premium are the two varieties, and most cars run on regular Premium. Supermarket pumps usually offer the best value. You won't find many service stations in the center of town; these are generally on main, multilane trunk roads away from the city center. Service is self-serve, except in small villages, where gas stations are likely to be closed on Sunday and late evening. Most stations accept major credit cards.

PARKING

During the day—and probably at all times—it's safest to believe that you can park nowhere except at a meter, in a pay-and-display bay, or in a garage; otherwise, you run the risk of an expensive ticket, plus possibly even more expensive clamping and towing fees (some boroughs are clamp-free). Restrictions are indicated by the "No Waiting" parking signpost on the sidewalk (these restrictions vary from street to street), and restricted areas include single yellow lines or double yellow lines, and Residents' Parking bays. Parking at a bus stop is prohibited, and parking in bus lanes is restricted. On Red Routes, indicated by red lines, you are not allowed to park or even stop. It's illegal to park on the sidewalk, across entrances, or on white zigzag lines approaching a pedestrian crossing.

Meters have an insatiable hunger in the inner city—20p may buy you just three minutes—and many will permit only a maximum two-hour stay. Coin meters (which take 10p, 20p, 50p, £1, and £2 coins) are being phased out. Some meters take payment by credit card, but increasingly meters in central London are pay-and-display machines that require payment by cell phone. You will need to set up an account to do this (🌐 *www.westminster.gov.uk*). Meter parking is free after 6:30 or 8:30 in the evening, on Sunday, and on holidays; always check the sign. In the evening, after restrictions end, meter bays are free. After meters are free, you also can park on single yellow lines—but not double yellow lines. In the daytime, take advantage of the many NCP parking lots in the center of town (from about £8 per hour, but cheaper prices are available if booked in advance).

Getting Here and Around

RULES OF THE ROAD

London is a mass of narrow, one-way roads and narrow, two-way streets no bigger than the one-way roads. The speed limit is either 20 or 30 mph—unless you see the large 40 mph signs found only in the suburbs. Speed bumps are sprinkled about with abandon in case you forget. Speed is strictly controlled and cameras, mounted on occasional lampposts, photograph speeders for ticketing.

Medium-size circular intersections are often designed as "roundabouts" (marked by signs in which three curved arrows form a circle). On these, cars travel left in a circle and incoming cars must yield to those already on their way around from the right. Make sure you're in the correct lane when approaching a roundabout—this will make leaving the roundabout at your desired exit easier. Stay in the left lane if you wish to go left, the middle lane for going straight ahead, and the right-hand lane for turning right. Signal when about to leave the roundabout.

Jaywalking is not illegal in London and everybody does it, despite the fact that striped crossings with blinking yellow lights mounted on poles at either end—called "zebra crossings"—give pedestrians the right-of-way to cross. Cars should treat zebra crossings like stop signs if a pedestrian is waiting to cross or already starting to cross. It's illegal to pass another vehicle at a zebra crossing. At other crossings (including intersections) pedestrians must yield to traffic, but they do have the right-of-way over traffic turning left at controlled crossings.

Traffic lights sometimes have arrows directing left or right turns; try to catch a glimpse of the road markings in time, and don't get into the turn lane if you mean to go straight ahead. Turning on a red light is not permitted. Signs at the beginning and end of designated bus lanes give the time restrictions for use (usually during peak hours); if you're caught driving on bus lanes during restricted hours, you will be fined. By law, seat belts must be worn in the front and back seats. Drunk-driving laws are strictly enforced, and it's safest to avoid alcohol altogether if you'll be driving. The legal limit is 80 milligrams of alcohol per 100 milliliters of blood, which roughly translated means two units of alcohol—two small glasses of wine, one pint of beer, or one glass of whiskey.

DLR: Docklands Light Railway

For reaching destinations in east London, the quiet, driverless Docklands Light Railway (DLR) is a good alternative, with interesting views of the area.

The DLR connects with the Tube network at Bank and Tower Hill stations as well as at Canary Wharf. It goes to London City Airport, the Docklands financial district, and Greenwich, running 5:30 am–12:30 am Monday–Saturday, 7 am–11:30 pm Sunday. The DLR takes Oyster cards, contactless bank cards, and Travelcards, and fares are the same as those on the Tube.

River Bus Travel

One legacy of the 2012 Olympics was a new push to develop river travel as part of London's overall public transportation system. The service, operated by Thames Clippers, stops at eight piers between London Eye/Waterloo and Greenwich, with peak-time extensions to Putney in the west and Woolwich Arsenal in the east. The Waterloo–Woolwich commuter service runs 7 am–11:05 pm on weekdays, 9:45 am–11:40 pm on weekends (peak-time frequency: every 20 minutes). Tickets are £7.30, with a one-third discount for Travelcard holders and a 20% discount for Oyster card holders. When there are events at the O2 (North Greenwich Arena), a half-hourly express service runs to and from Waterloo starting three hours before the event. Thames Clippers also operate the special Tate to Tate Boat, a 15-minute trip between Tate Modern and Tate Britain that costs £8.70 one-way. Boats run every 20–30 minutes, from 10 to 4 on weekdays and 9 to 7 on weekends. A River Roamer ticket (from £17.80 per day if booked online) offers unlimited river travel after 9 am.

Taxi Travel

Universally known as "black cabs" (even though many of them now come in other colors), the traditional big black London taxicabs are as much a part of the city's streetscape as red double-decker buses, and for good reason: the unique, spacious taxis easily hold five people, plus luggage. To earn a taxi license, drivers must undergo intensive training on the history and geography of London. The course, and all that the drivers have learned in it, is known simply as "the Knowledge." There's almost nothing your taxi driver won't know about the city. Partly because of lobbying efforts by the black cab industry, companies such as Uber have yet to make significant inroads into the London market, although the battle is ongoing.

Hotels and main tourist areas have cabstands (just take the first in line), but you can also flag one down from the roadside. If the orange "For Hire" sign on the top is lighted, the taxi is available. Cab drivers sometimes cruise at night with their signs unlighted so that they can choose their passengers and avoid those they think might cause trouble. If you see an unlighted, passengerless cab, hail it: you might be lucky.

Fares start at £3 and charge by the minute—a journey of a mile (which might take 6–13 minutes) will cost £6–£9.40 (the fare goes up 10 pm–5 am—a system designed to persuade more taxi drivers to work at night). A surcharge of £2 is applied to a telephone booking and £2.80 for journeys that start from the Heathrow Airport taxi ranks. At Christmas and New Year, there is an additional surcharge of £4. You may, but do not have to, tip taxi drivers 10% of the tab. Usually passengers round up to the nearest pound.

Minicabs, which operate out of small, curbside offices throughout the city, are generally cheaper than black cabs, but they are less reliable and less trustworthy. These are usually unmarked passenger cars, and their drivers are often not native Londoners, and do not have to take or pass "the Knowledge" test. Still, Londoners use them in droves because they are plentiful and cheap. If you choose to use them, do not ever take an unlicensed cab: anyone who curb-crawls looking for customers is likely to be unlicensed. Unlicensed cabs have been associated with many crimes and can be dangerous. All cab companies with proper dispatch offices are likely to be licensed. Look for a small purple version of the Underground logo on the front or rear window with "private hire" written across it.

There are plenty of trustworthy and licensed minicab firms. For London-wide service try Lady's and Gent's MiniCabs, or Addison Lee, which uses comfortable minivans but requires that you know the full postal code for both your pickup location and your destination. When using a minicab, always ask the price in advance when you phone for the car, then verify with the driver before the journey begins.

Train Travel

The National Rail Enquiries website is the clearinghouse for information on train times and fares as well as the main place for booking rail journeys around Britain—and the earlier the better. Tickets bought two to three weeks in advance can cost a quarter of the price of tickets bought on the day of travel. However, journeys within commuting distance of city centers are sold at unvarying set prices, and those can be purchased on the day you expect to make your journey without any financial penalty. You may also be able to purchase a PlusBus ticket, which adds unlimited bus travel at your destination. Note that, in busy city centers such as London, all travel costs more during morning rush hour. You can purchase tickets online, by phone, or at any train station in the United Kingdom. Check the website or call the National Rail Enquiries line to get details of the train company responsible for your journey and have them give you a breakdown of available ticket prices. Regardless of which train company is involved, many discount passes are available, such as the 16–25 Railcard (for which you must be under 26 and provide a passport-size photo), the Senior Railcard, and the Family & Friends Travelcard, which can be bought from most mainline stations. But if you intend to make several long-distance rail journeys, it can be a good idea to invest in a BritRail Pass, available to non-U.K. residents (which you must buy before you leave home).

You can get a BritRail Pass valid for London and the surrounding counties, for England, for Scotland, or for all of Britain. Discounts (usually 20%–25%) are offered if you're between 16 and 25, over 60, traveling as a family or a group, or accompanied by a British citizen. The pass includes discounts on the Heathrow Express and Gatwick Express. BritRail Passes come in two basic varieties. The Consecutive Pass allows travel on consecutive days, and the FlexiPass allows a number of travel days within a set period of time. The cost (in U.S. dollars) of a BritRail Consecutive Pass adult ticket for 8 days is $327 standard and $487 first-class; for 15 days, $487 and $719; and for 22 days, $609 and $914. The cost of a BritRail FlexiPass adult ticket for 4 days' travel within one month is $289 standard and $420 first-class; for 8 days' travel within one month, $414 and $618; and for 15 days' travel within *two* months, $623 and $923. Prices drop by about 20% for off-peak travel passes November–February.

Most long-distance trains have refreshment carriages, called buffet cars. Most trains these days also have "quiet cars," where the use of cell phones and music devices is banned. Smoking is forbidden in all railcars.

Generally speaking, rail travel in the United Kingdom is expensive and the ticketing system unnecessarily convoluted: for instance, a round-trip ticket to Bath from London can cost more than £150 per person at peak times, although for an off-peak ticket purchased far enough in advance, that price can drop to £20 or even less. It's best to avoid the frantic business commuter rush (before 9:30 am and 4:30–7 pm). Credit cards are accepted for train fares paid in person, by phone, and online.

Delays are not uncommon, but they're rarely long. You almost always have to go to the station to find out if there's going to be one (because delays tend to happen at the last minute). Luckily, most stations have coffee shops, restaurants, and pubs where you can cool your heels while you wait for the train to get rolling. National Rail Enquiries provides an up-to-date state-of-the-railroads schedule.

Most of the time, first-class train travel in England isn't particularly first class. Some train companies don't offer at-seat service, so you still have to get up and go to the buffet car for food or drinks. First class is generally booked by business travelers on expense accounts because crying babies and noisy families are quite rare in first class and quite common in standard class.

Short of flying, taking the Eurostar train through the Channel Tunnel is the fastest way to reach the continent: it's 2 hours 15 minutes from London's St. Pancras International Station to Paris's Gare du Nord. You can also go from St. Pancras to Midi Station in Brussels in just under two hours, or to Amsterdam in 3 hours 40 minutes. If purchased in advance, round-trip tickets from London to Belgium, Holland, or France cost from as little as £39, especially if you travel in the very early or very late hours of the day. If you want to bring your car over to France (ask the rental company if this is permitted), you can use the Eurotunnel Shuttle, which takes 35 minutes from Folkestone to Calais, plus at least 30 minutes to check in. The Belgian border is just a short drive northeast of Calais.

Underground Travel: The Tube

London's extensive Underground train system (the Tube) has color-coded routes, clear signage, and many connections. Trains run out into the suburbs, and all stations are marked with the London Underground circular symbol. (Do not be confused by similar-looking signs reading "subway," which is British for "pedestrian underpass.") Trains are all one class; smoking isn't allowed on board or in the stations. There is also an Overground network serving the farther reaches of Inner London.

Some lines have multiple branches (Central, Circle, District, Northern, Metropolitan, and Piccadilly), so be sure to note which branch is needed for your particular destination. Do this by noting the end destination on the lighted sign on the platform, which also tells you how long you'll have to wait until the train arrives. Compare that with the end destination of the branch you want. When the two match, that's your train.

London is divided into six concentric zones (ask at Underground ticket booths for a map and booklet, which give details of the ticket options), so be sure to buy a ticket for the correct zone or you may be liable for an on-the-spot fine of £80. Don't panic if you do forget to buy a ticket for the right zone: just tell a station attendant that you need to buy an "extension" to your ticket. Although you're meant to do that in advance, if you're an out-of-towner, they generally don't give you a hard time. You also can pay your fare using an Oyster card or a contactless debit or credit card.

Oyster cards are "smart cards" that can be charged with a cash value and then used for discounted travel throughout the city. A Visitor Oyster card, which you must buy before arriving in the United Kingdom, costs £5. Normal Oyster cards also cost £5 and you can open an Oyster account online or pick up an Oyster card at any London Underground station, and then prepay any amount you wish for your expected travel while in the city. Each time you take the Tube or bus, you

Getting Here and Around

place the blue card on the yellow readers at the entrance and the amount of your fare is deducted.

Passengers using Oyster cards pay lower rates. For one-way Tube fares paid in cash, a flat £4.90 price per journey now applies across all central zones (1–2), whether you're traveling 1 stop or 12. However, the corresponding Oyster card fare is £2.40 off-peak, £2.90 peak. One-day Travelcards used to be a good value for the money, but now, costing from £12.70 per card, they're a much less attractive option. If you're planning several trips in one day, it's much cheaper to buy an Oyster card: because of the system's daily "cap," you can make as many journeys as you want in Zones 1–2 for just £7 (or, in Zones 1–3 for £8.20). If you're going to be in town for several days, a seven-day Travelcard gives you the same value as an Oyster card (£35.10 for Zones 1–2, £64.20 for Zones 1–6). Children aged 11–15 can travel at discounted rates on the Tube and travel free on buses and trams with an Oyster photocard (must be ordered online at least four weeks before date of travel), while those under 11 travel free on all buses, and on the Tube if accompanied by an adult or with an Oyster photocard. Young people aged 16–18 and students over 18 get discounted Tube fares with an Oyster photocard. Oyster card Tube fares start at £2 and go up depending on the number of zones you're covering, the time of day, and whether you're traveling into Zone 1.

However, although Oyster cards sound like the way of the future, they will soon be a thing of the past. Moves are underway to gradually phase out Oyster cards and to encourage passengers to move to a system of direct payments using their bank debit or credit cards instead. In practice, this means swiping a "contactless" bank card instead of your Oyster card at ticket barriers. The cheaper fares available to Oyster card holders are the same as those who pay by contactless cards.

Tube trains now run for 24 hours a day on weekends on five major lines: Piccadilly, Victoria, Northern, Central, and Jubilee. On all other lines the usual timetable still applies, with trains running from just after 5 am Monday to Saturday, and with the last services leaving central London between midnight and 12:30 am. On Sunday, trains start an hour later and finish about an hour earlier. The frequency of trains depends on the route and the time of day, but normally you should not have to wait more than 10 minutes in central areas.

There are TfL Travel Information Centres at the following Tube stations and travel locations: Liverpool Street, King's Cross and Victoria (Monday–Sunday 9 am–5 pm); Piccadilly Circus and Paddington (9:30 am–4 pm); Gatwick Airport, North & South terminals (8 am–4 pm); and at Heathrow Airport, Terminals 2 and 3 and Underground stations (8 am–6pm).

Important note: you need to have your ticket (Oyster card, Travelcard, regular ticket, or contactless debit/credit card) handy in order to exit the turnstiles of the Tube system, not just to enter them.

Before You Go

Passport

U.S. citizens need only a valid passport to enter Great Britain for stays of up to six months.

Visa

U.S. citizens do not require a tourist visa for entry into Great Britain for visits under 90 days.

Immunizations

There are currently no required immunizations or vaccinations for entry into Great Britain.

When to Go

The heaviest tourist season runs April through September, with another peak around Christmas. Late spring is the time to see the Royal Parks and gardens at their freshest; fall brings autumnal beauty and fewer people. Summer gives the best chance of good weather, although the crowds are intense. Winter can be dismal—it's dark by 5—but all the theaters, concerts, and exhibitions go full speed ahead, and Christmas lights bring a major touch of festive magic. Weather-wise, winter is cold and wet with occasional light snow and spring is colorful and fair. June through August can range from a total washout to a long hot summer and anything in between. Autumn ranges from warm to cool to mild. It's impossible to forecast London weather, but you can be certain that it will not be what you expect.

The October "half-term," when schools in the capital take a break for a week or two, results in most attractions being overrun by children. The start of August can be a very busy time, and hot weather makes Tube travel a sweltering and sweaty nightmare. Air-conditioning is far from the norm in London, even in hotels; although it rarely tops 90°F, it can feel much hotter. And festive shopping in central London just before Christmas borders on the insane.

Safety

The rules for safety in London are the same as in New York City or any big metropolis. The most important rule is to use common sense. In central London, nobody will raise an eyebrow at tourists studying maps on street corners, and don't hesitate to ask for directions. However, outside of the center, exercise general caution about the neighborhoods you walk in: if they don't look safe, take a cab. After midnight, outside of the center, take cabs rather than wait for a night bus. Although London has plenty of so-called minicabs—normal cars driven by self-employed drivers in a cab service—don't ever get into an unmarked car that pulls up offering you "cab service." Take a licensed minicab only from a cab office, or, preferably, a normal London "black cab," which you flag down on the street.

London is one of the most diverse cities in the world and, as such, is a safe and attractive destination for LGBTQ travelers. Popular gay-friendly neighborhoods include slap-bang-in-the-middle-of-things Soho as well as just-south-of-the-river Vauxhall, which is a mile or so west of the London Eye. With the usual precautions (avoid deserted ill-lit sidestreets and less central neighborhoods altogether after dark), solo females travelers will also find London safe and welcoming.

Essentials

If your invitation from Queen Elizabeth still hasn't shown up in the mail, no worries—staying at one of London's grande dame hotels is the next best thing to being a guest at the palace—and some say it's even better. Luckily there is no dearth of options where friendliness outdistances luxe; London has plenty of atmospheric places that won't cost a king's ransom.

That noted, until fairly recently it was extremely difficult to find a decent hotel in the center of town for less than £150 per night. Things have improved, thanks to a flurry of new mid-priced hotels that have sprung up in recent years. You'll still have to shop around for deals—never assume you'll be able to find somewhere good *and* cheap on short notice.

Of course, it's very different if money is no object. London has some of the very best and most luxurious hotels in the world. Freshly minted millionaires favor the rash of supertrendy hot spots like the Corinthia or ME London, while fashionistas gravitate toward Kit Kemp's superstylish hotels like the Covent Garden and the Charlotte Street. But even these places have deals, and you can sometimes snag a bargain within reach of mere mortals, particularly in the off-season, or just be a spectator to all the glamour by visiting for afternoon tea, the most traditional of high-society treats.

Meanwhile, several mid-range hotels have dropped their average prices in response to the choppy waters of the global economy, which has pulled some fantastic places, such as Hazlitt's, the Rookery, and Town Hall, back into the affordable category. There's also a clutch of new, stylish, and supercheap hotels that are a real step forward for the city. The downside is that these places tend to be a little out of the way, but that's often a price worth paying. Another attractive alternative includes hotels in the Premier and Millennium chains, which offer sleek, modern rooms, lots of up-to-date conveniences, and sales that frequently bring room prices well below £100 a night.

At the budget level, London has come a long way in the last couple of years, with a familiar catch: to find a good, reasonably priced bed-and-breakfast, you must be prepared to look outside the very center of town. This means that you have to weigh the city's notoriously high transport costs against any savings—but on the plus side, the Tube can shuttle you out to even some far-flung suburbs in less than 20 minutes. If you're prepared to be just a little adventurous with your London base, you will be rewarded by a collection of unique and interesting B&Bs and small boutiques, in the kinds of neighborhoods real Londoners live in—places like the Cable Street Inn, the Main House, and the Church Street Hotel. If you're willing to fend for yourself, the city also has some great rental options.

But if you are interested in luxury, London is just the place. Although the image we love to harbor about Olde London Towne may be fast fading in the light of today's glittering city, when it comes time to rest your head, the old-fashioned clichés remain enticing. Choose one of London's heritage-rich hotels—Claridge's supplies perfect parlors; the Savoy has that river view—and you'll find that these fantasies can, and always will, be fulfilled.

RESERVATIONS

Yes, hotel reservations are an absolute necessity when planning your trip to London, so book your room as far in advance as possible. The further in advance you can book, the better a deal you're likely to get. Just watch out if you change your mind—cancellation fees can be hefty. On the other hand, it is possible to find some amazing last-minute deals at mid- to high-range places, but this is a real gamble, as you could just as easily end up paying full rate. Fierce competition means properties undergo frequent improvements, so when booking inquire about any ongoing renovations that may interrupt your stay.

What It Costs in Pounds

$	$$	$$$	$$$$
HOTELS			
Under £125	£125–£250	£251–£400	Over £400

Dining

British food hasn't always had the best reputation, but nowhere in the country is that reputation being completely upturned more than in London. The city has zoomed up the global gastro charts, and can now seriously compete with the world's top culinary heavyweights. The truth is that no other city—barring New York—has the immense range of global cuisines that London has to offer. Standards have rocketed at all price points, and every year it seems like the London restaurant scene is better than ever.

To appreciate how far London has risen in the food game, just look back to the days of Somerset Maugham, who was once justified in warning, "To eat well in England you should have breakfast three times a day." Change was slow after World War II, when it was understood that the British ate to live, while the French lived to eat. When people thought of British cuisine, fish-and-chips—a greasy grab-and-gulp dish that tasted best wrapped in yesterday's newspaper—first came to mind. Then there was always shepherd's pie, ubiquitously found in smoke-filled pubs, though not made, according to *Sweeney Todd,* "with real shepherd in it."

These days, standards are miles higher and shepherd's pie has been largely replaced by the city's unofficial dish, Indian curry. London's restaurant revolution is built on its extraordinary ethnic diversity, and you'll find the quality of other global cuisines has grown immeasurably in recent years, with London becoming known for its Chinese, Japanese, Indian, Thai, Spanish, Italian, French, Peruvian, and west African restaurants. Thankfully, pride in the best of British food—local, seasonal, wild, and foraged—is enjoying quite the renaissance, too.

What it Costs

$	$$	$$$	$$$$
RESTAURANTS			
Under £16	£16–£23	£24–£31	Over £31

Nightlife

There isn't *a* London nightlife scene—there is a multitude of them. As long as there are crowds for obscure teenage rock bands, Dickensian-style pubs, comedy cabarets, cocktail lounges, and swing dance nights, someone will create clubs and venues for them in London. The result? London has become a veritable utopia for excitement junkies, culture fiends, and those who—simply put—like to party.

Nearly everyone who visits London these days is mesmerized by the city's energy, which reveals itself in layers. Whether

Where Should I Stay?

	NEIGHBORHOOD VIBE	PROS	CONS
Westminster and St. James's	Historic and home to major tourist attractions.	Central area; easy Tube access; safe.	Expensive lodging; few good restaurants and entertainment venues.
Mayfair and Marylebone	Traditional, old money; a mixture of the business and financial set with fashionable shops.	In the heart of the action; excellent hotels.	Pricey; peace and quiet hard to come by.
Soho and Covent Garden	A tourist hub with endless entertainment.	Buzzing area with plenty to see and do; late-night entertainment abounds; wonderful shopping district.	London's busiest (and noisiest) district after dark; few budget hotels.
Bloomsbury and Holborn	Diverse area that is part bustling business center and part tranquil respite.	Easy access to Tube; major sights like the British Museum.	Busy and noisy streets; the area around King's Cross can be sketchy—particularly at night.
The City	London's financial district.	Extremely central with easy transportation access and great hotel deals.	Can be as quiet as a tomb on weekends—even the pubs close.
East London	One of London's trendiest areas, with a great arts scene.	Great for art lovers, shoppers, and business execs with meetings in Canary Wharf.	Parts can be a bit dodgy at night; 20-minute Tube ride from central London.
South of the Thames	A vibrant cultural hub.	London's unofficial cultural quarter, walking distance from the West End theaters.	Close to some sketchy areas.
Kensington, Chelsea, Knightsbridge, and Belgravia	Upscale neighborhoods and a hub of London's tourist universe.	Diverse hotel selection; great area for meandering urban walks; London's capital of high-end shopping.	Depending on where you are, the nearest Tube might be a hike; might be too quiet for some.
Notting Hill and Bayswater	An upscale, trendy area favored by locals.	Affordable; gorgeous greenery.	Not all hotels are great; residential area may be quiet.
Regent's Park and Hampstead	A mix of arty, fashionable districts with a villagelike feel.	Some of London's most fashionable neighborhoods.	Some distance from center; lack of hotel options.

you prefer rhythm and blues with fine French food, the gritty guitar-riff music of Camden Town, the craft beers of East London, a pint and a gourmet pizza at a local gastro-pub, or swanky heritage cocktails and sushi at London's sexiest subterranean lair, London is sure to feed your fancy.

London's nightlife has been given a big boost with five Night Tube lines serving central London (see 🌐 *www.tfl.gov.uk* for details) that run all night on Friday and Saturday, making getting home after a night out cheaper and easier than ever before. The rest of the network stops running around 12:30 am Monday through Saturday and midnight on Sunday. Night buses are largely safe and reliable but far slower than taxis, as you'd expect. The best place to hail a black taxi is at the front door of one of the major hotels; or find a licensed local minicab firm on the Transport for London website. Avoid unlicensed taxis or minicabs that tout for business around closing time.

PUBS

Pubs are where Londoners go to hang out, see and be seen, act out the drama of life, and, for some, drink themselves into varying degrees of oblivion. The pub is still a vital part of London life, though many of the traditions of the pub experience are evolving. There are few better places to meet Londoners in their local habitat. There are somewhere around 4,000 pubs in London; some are dark and woody, others plain and functional, a few still have original Victorian etched glass, Edwardian panels, and art nouveau carvings.

Not long ago, before the smoking ban, pubs tended to be smoky, male-dominated places with a couple of ubiquitous beers on tap and the only available food a packet of salt-and-vinegar-flavor crisps (potato chips). All that has changed.

Gastropub fever swept through London around the turn of the 21st century and at many places, char grills are installed in the kitchen and inventive pub grub is on the menu. A new wave of enthusiasm for craft beers and microbreweries is now having a similar effect on the liquid offerings.

The big decision is what to drink. The beer of choice among Britons has traditionally been **"bitter,"** lightly fermented, with an amber color, and getting its bitterness from hops. It's usually served at cellar temperature (that is, cooler than room temperature but neither chilled, nor, as common misconception would have it, warm). **Real ales,** served from wooden kegs and made without chilling, filtering, or pasteurization, are flatter than other bitters and are enjoying a renaissance. Many small London breweries have sprung up in recent years, and bottled designer and American beers can be found in most bars across London. **Stouts,** like Guinness, are a meal in themselves and something of an acquired taste—they have a dark, caramel-infused flavor and look like thickened flat Coke with a frothy top. Chilled continental **lagers,** most familiar to American drinkers, are light in color and carbonated. ■ **TIP→ The most commonly served lagers in Britain are from continental Europe.**

Many English pubs are owned by chains such as Fullers, Nicholson's, or Samuel Smith, and are tenanted, meaning that they are run on a sort of franchise basis. Most are not obviously branded and retain at least some independence. Independently owned pubs, sometimes called "free houses," tend to offer a more extensive selection of beer. Other potations available include apple-based **ciders,** ranging from sweet to dry and from alcoholic to very alcoholic (Irish cider, served over ice, is now also ubiquitous), and **shandies,** a refreshing mix of beer and lemonade. Friendly pubs will usually be happy to give you a taste of the brew of your choice before you order.

Because today's cool spot is often tomorrow's forgotten or closed venue, check the weekly listings in the *Evening Standard* (*www.standard.co.uk*) and especially *Time Out* (*www.timeout.com/london*). Other websites to consult are *www.londontown.com* or *www.allinlondon.co.uk*. Although most clubs are frequented by those under 30, there are plenty of others that are popular with patrons of all ages and types. One particularly useful website for clubs and club nights is *www.residentadvisor.net*.

Performing Arts

"All the world's a stage," said Shakespeare, immortal words heard for the first time right here in London. And whether you prefer your theater, music, and art classical or modern, or as contemporary twists on time-honored classics, you'll find that London's vibrant cultural scene more than holds its own on the world stage.

Divas sing original-language librettos at the Royal Opera House, Shakespeare's plays are brought to life at the reconstructed Globe Theatre, and challenging new writing is produced at the Royal Court. Whether you feel like basking in the lighthearted extravagance of a West End musical or taking in the next shark-in-formaldehyde at the White Cube gallery, the choice is yours.

There are international theater festivals, innovative music festivals, and critically acclaimed seasons of postmodern dance. Short trip or long, you'll find the cultural scene in London is ever-changing, ever-expanding, and ever-exciting.

The website *www.whatsonstage.com* is an invaluable resource for theater listings.

Shopping

The keyword of London shopping has always been "individuality," whether expressed in the superb custom tailoring of Savile Row, the nonconformist punk roots of quintessential British designer Vivienne Westwood, or the unique small stores that purvey their owners' private passions—be they paper theaters, toy soldiers, or buttons. This tradition is under threat from the influx of chains (global luxury, domestic mid-market, and international youth), but the distinctively British mix of quality and originality, tradition, and character remains.

You can try on underwear fit for a queen at Her Majesty's lingerie supplier, track down a leather-bound Brontë classic at an antiquarian bookseller, or find a bargain antique on Portobello Road. Whether you're just browsing—there's nothing like the size, variety, and sheer theater of London's street markets to stimulate the acquisitive instinct—or on a fashion-seeking mission, London shopping offers something for all tastes and budgets.

Although it's impossible to pin down one particular look that defines the city, London style tends to fall into two camps: one is the quirky, somewhat romantic look exemplified by homegrown designers like Matthew Williamson, Jenny Packham, Vivienne Westwood, and Lulu Guinness; the other reflects Britain's celebrated tradition of classic knitwear and suiting, with labels like Jaeger, Pringle, and Brora, while Oswald Boateng, Paul Smith, and Richard James take tradition and give it a very modern twist. Traditional bespoke men's tailoring can be found in the upscale gentlemen's shops of Jermyn Street and Savile Row—there's no better place in the city to buy custom-made shirts and suits—while the handbags at Mulberry, Asprey, and Anya Hindmarch are pure classic quality. If your budget can't stretch that far, no problem; the city's chain stores like Topshop, Zara, and H&M, aimed at the younger end of the market, are excellent places to pick up designs copied straight from the catwalk at a fraction of the price, while mid-market chains like Reiss, Jigsaw, and L.K. Bennett offer smart design and better quality for the more sophisticated shopper.

If there's anything that unites London's designers, it's a commitment to creativity and originality, underpinned by a strong sense of heritage. This combination of posh and rock 'n' roll sensibilities turns up in everyone from Terence Conran, who revolutionized product and houseware design in the '60s (and is still going strong), to Alexander McQueen, who combined the punk aesthetic with the rigor of couture. You'll see it in fanciful millinery creations by Philip Treacy and Stephen Jones, and in the work of imaginative shoemakers Nicholas Kirkwood, United Nude, and Terry de Havilland—and it keeps going, right through to current hot designers Erdem, Christopher Kane, Victoria Beckham, and up-and-coming names like Shrimps, Duro Olowu, and Molly Goddard.

One reason for London's design supremacy is the strength of local fashion college Central St. Martin's, whose graduates include Conran, Kane, McQueen, his successor at his eponymous label—and designer of the Duchess of Cambridge's wedding dress—Sarah Burton, and Stella McCartney's equally acclaimed successor at Céline, Phoebe Philo.

To find the McQueens and McCartneys of tomorrow, head for the independent boutiques of the East End and Bermondsey. If anything, London is even better known for its vibrant street fashion than for its high-end designers. Stock up from the stalls at Portobello, Camden, and Spitalfields markets.

Aside from bankrupting yourself, the only problem you may encounter is exhaustion. London's shopping districts are spread out over the city, so do as savvy locals do: plan your excursion with military precision, taking in only one or two areas in a day, and stopping for lunch with a glass of wine or for a pint at a pub.

$ Customs and Duties

You're always allowed to bring goods of a certain value back home without having to pay any duty or import tax. But there's a limit on the amount of tobacco and liquor you can bring back duty-free, and some countries have separate limits for perfumes; for exact figures, check with your customs department. The values of so-called "duty-free" goods are included in these amounts. When you shop abroad, save all your receipts, as customs inspectors may ask to see them as well as the items you purchased. If the total value of your goods is more than the duty-free limit, you'll have to pay a tax (most often a flat percentage) on the value of everything beyond that limit.

There are currently two levels of duty-free allowance for entering Britain: one for goods bought outside the European Union (EU) and the other for goods bought within the EU.

Of goods bought outside the EU you may import the following duty-free: 200 cigarettes or 100 cigarillos or 50 cigars or 250 grams of tobacco; 4 liters of still wine and 16 liters of beer and, in addition, either 1 liter of alcohol over 22% by volume (most spirits), or 2 liters of alcohol under 22% by volume (fortified or sparkling wine or liqueurs).

Of goods bought within the EU, you should not exceed the following (unless you can prove they are for personal use): 800 cigarettes, 400 cigarillos, 200 cigars, or 1 kilo of tobacco, plus 10 liters of spirits, 20 liters of fortified wine such as port or sherry, 90 liters of wine, or 110 liters of beer.

Pets (dogs and cats) can be brought into the United Kingdom from the United States without six months' quarantine, provided that the animal meets all the PETS (Pet Travel Scheme) requirements, including microchipping and vaccination. Other pets have to undergo a lengthy quarantine, and penalties for breaking this law are severe and strictly enforced.

Fresh meats, vegetables, plants, and dairy products may be imported from within the EU. Controlled drugs, switchblades (aka flick knives), obscene material, counterfeit or pirated goods, and self-defense sprays may not be brought into the United Kingdom; firearms (both real and imitation) and ammunition, as well as souvenirs made from endangered plants or animals, are barred except with relevant permits.

Holidays

Standard holidays are New Year's Day, Good Friday, Easter Monday, May Day (first Monday in May), spring and summer bank holidays (last Monday in May and August, respectively), Christmas, and Boxing Day (December 26). On Christmas Eve and New Year's Eve, some shops, restaurants, and businesses close early. Some museums and tourist attractions may close for at least a week around Christmas, or operate on restricted hours—call to verify.

 Taxes

Departure taxes are divided into two bands. The Band A tax on a per-person economy fare for flights of under 2,000 miles is £13; Band B, for everything over, is £80. The fee is subject to government tax increases.

The British sales tax (V.A.T., value-added tax) is 20%. The tax is almost always included in quoted prices in shops, hotels, and restaurants.

Most travelers can get a V.A.T. refund (no minimum amount is required) by either the Retail Export or the more cumbersome Direct Export method. Many, but not all, large stores provide these services, but only if you request them; they will handle the paperwork. For the Retail Export method, you must ask the store for Form VAT 407 when making a purchase (you must have identification—passports are best). Some retailers will refund the amount on the spot, but others will use a refund company or the refund booth at the point when you leave the country. For the latter, have the form stamped like any customs form by U.K. customs officials when you leave the country, or, if you're visiting several European Union countries, when you leave the EU. After you're through passport control, take the form to a refund-service counter for an on-the-spot refund (which is usually the quickest and easiest option), or mail it to the address on the form (or the envelope with it) after you arrive home. You receive the total refund stated on the form (the retailer or refund company may deduct a handling fee), but the processing time can be long, especially if you request a credit-card adjustment. This may be preferable to a check, however, as U.S. banks will charge a fee for depositing a check in a foreign currency.

With the Direct Export method, the goods are shipped directly to your home. You must have a Form VAT 407 certified by customs, the police, or a notary public when you get home and then send it back to the store, which will refund your money. For inquiries, contact Her Majesty's Revenue & Customs office.

Global Blue (formerly, Global Refund) is a worldwide service with 270,000 affiliated stores and more than 200 Refund Offices. Its refund form, called a Tax Free Check, is the most common across the European continent. The service issues refunds in the form of cash, check, or credit-card adjustment.

Tipping

Tipping is done in Britain just as in the United States, but at a lower level. Tipping less than you would back home in restaurants—and not tipping at all in pubs—is not only accepted, but standard. Do not tip movie or theater ushers, elevator operators, or bar staff in pubs—although you can always offer to buy the latter a drink.

Visitor Information

You can get good information at the Travel Information Centre near the Eurostar arrivals area at St. Pancras International train station and at Victoria and Liverpool Street stations. The Visitor Information Center at Heathrow Airport (Terminals 2 and 3, Tube Station) is open daily from 8 am–6 pm while the center at Gatwick Airport (North and South Terminals, arrivals hall) is open daily from 8 am–4 pm.

Tipping Guidelines for London

Bartender	In cocktail bars, if you see a tip plate, it's fine to leave £1–£2. For table service, tip 10% of the cost of the bill. However, the gratuity is often included in the check at more expensive bars.
Bellhop	£1 per bag, depending on the level of the hotel.
Hotel Concierge	£5 or more, if a service is performed for you.
Hotel Housekeeper	It's extremely rare housekeepers to be tipped; £1–£2 would be generous.
Porter at Airport or Train Station	£1 per bag
Taxi Driver	Optional 10%–12%, perhaps a little more for a short ride.
Tour Guide	Tipping optional; £1–£2 would be generous.
Server	10%–15%, with 15% being the norm at high-end restaurants; nothing additional if a service charge is added to the bill.

Great Itineraries

London in 1 Day

Do a giant best-of loop of the city by open-top boat and bus through six key districts, with a stop at the 953-year-old Tower of London and fun in Soho at the end. Start early, with the first ride of the London Eye at 10 am; you'll have the rest of the day to explore at whatever pace you wish, but be sure to get to Buckingham Palace before the sun sets or you'll miss out on some great photo opportunities.

On your morning ride on the **London Eye,** you'll be able to get an unrivaled bird's-eye view of the city. Then launch from the Eye's namesake pier for a swivel-eyed Thames River cruise past four famous bridges and Traitors' Gate before landing in front of the iconic **Tower of London.**

Once inside the Tower, take in the Crown Jewels and gory royal history on a Yeoman Warder's tour, before jumping on a double-decker bus over **Tower Bridge,** past Monument, the Embankment, Park Lane, Oxford, and Piccadilly circuses and stopping at **Trafalgar Square,** where you can glimpse **Big Ben** and the **Houses of Parliament,** before stopping for lunch at a historic Westminster pub. Then take a walk over to **Westminster Abbey,** where a self-guided tour will take you through centuries of British history within one awe-inspiring building (note that the Abbey closes early on Saturday). Then take another short stroll through **St. James's Park** to **Buckingham Palace**; you'll have missed the daily Changing of the Guard, but that means the palace grounds will be less crowded, with more photo ops. End the day by meandering over to the hip Soho neighborhood, where foodies will find endless eclectic restaurants for dinner, and partygoers will find some of the city's best nightlife.

London in 5 Days

DAY 1: BUCKINGHAM PALACE, TRAFALGAR SQUARE, AND THE NATIONAL PORTRAIT GALLERY

Start day one with coffee in a Dickensian alleyway just north of **St. James's Palace,** before being first into the 19 impossibly grand State Rooms at **Buckingham Palace.** Afterward, join the crowds outside the palace to watch a sea of bearskin Foot Guards perform the **Changing of the Guard** ceremony, held 11:30 am most days. Some Palace tickets include tours of the **Queen's Gallery,** which showcases top Old Masters art from the Royal Collection. Then take a stroll through **St. James's Park** before lunch at a historic Pall Mall pub. It's a short walk to the **National Gallery** at **Trafalgar Square.** Hit its quieter Sainsbury Wing, pick up an audio guide, and hunt down a few choice early Renaissance masterpieces. Enjoy stern portraits of Tudor monarchs at the **National Portrait Gallery** next door, before browsing the antiquarian booksellers on Charing Cross Road or Cecil Court and enjoying fresh handmade dim sum in **Chinatown.**

DAY 2: WESTMINSTER ABBEY, HOUSES OF PARLIAMENT, AND THE EAST END

Devote the early morning of day two to a 90-minute verger guided tour of solemn **Westminster Abbey.** Then investigate the **Houses of Parliament.** If in session, you can attend debate in the Public Galleries or take a 75-minute tour of both houses. The stately **Members' and Strangers' Dining Rooms** in the House of Commons are occasionally open to the public for lunch; otherwise have a ploughman's lunch at a historic pub. Take pics of **Big Ben** and walk up Whitehall to the gates of **No 10. Downing Street,** the Prime Minister's residence. For a complete change of tune, take the Tube over to the gritty yet hip East End and Bangladeshi-influenced Brick Lane, where you can stroll along the art galleries and have a classic Indian curry for dinner.

DAY 3: THE SOUTH BANK

Start with a ride on the **London Eye** for eye-popping city panoramas. Take a long walk along the Thames, popping into any galleries, cinemas, or shops that catch your eye, like the excellent **Hayward Gallery.** Eventually meander along to **Tate Modern** for a modern art fix, stopping for lunch nearby. Then enjoy a Shakespeare hit with tours of the replica Elizabethan **Shakespeare's Globe.** Wiggle along for venison burgers and foodie stall heaven at **Borough Market** before backtracking over the pedestrian **Millennium Bridge** for a stunning approach to **St. Paul's Cathedral.** Hopefully you'll catch Choral Evensong there at 5 pm, then head east toward Bow Lane alleyway for a customary City pub fish-and-chips dinner.

DAY 4: THE BRITISH MUSEUM AND SOHO

On day four, start early at the **British Museum** in Bloomsbury and leave a few hours to explore hits like the Egyptian mummies, Rosetta Stone, and 7th-century Anglo-Saxon Sutton Hoo treasures. Afterward, Tube it to restaurant-mad **Soho** where you can stop for Sri Lankan rice-and-curry at Hoppers, before browsing **Carnaby Street** and the surrounding indie fashion boutiques. Cut across Regent Street via the dapper gentlemen's tailors of **Savile Row** and head south for **Fortnum & Mason** and the old-world gentlemen's outfitters and bespoke shoe shops on Jermyn Street. Work back through the twinkly Regency red-carpet **Burlington Arcade** and pop into the **Royal Academy** gallery before taking Afternoon Tea at the cozy Brown's Hotel in Mayfair.

DAY 5: KENSINGTON'S MUSEUMS, PICCADILLY, AND THE WEST END

Finally on day five, start with a one-hour tour of the **V&A Museum** of decorative arts and design, whose collection ranges from rare Persian rugs to Tudor chalices. Once out, refuel with a crêpe on pedestrianized Exhibition Road near the South Kensington Tube, then choose either all things science at the **Science Museum,** or the *T. rex* dinosaur trail at the **Natural History Museum.** Then stroll up Knightsbridge to **Harrods** famous Food Hall, where you can drool over salamis and people-watch to your heart's content. Either duck in for the ace fashion at **Harvey Nichols** or sip early cocktails at **The Ritz** at Green Park. Then enjoy the giant neon lights of **Piccadilly Circus** and **Leicester Square** before having a pretheater dinner in **Covent Garden** and then catching a West End play or musical.

Best Tours in London

With its crooked medieval streets, layers of history, and atmospheric buildings, London is a true walking city often best explored on a guided tour. Tours are a great way to investigate out-of-the-way, hidden, historic, and secret districts; to get an insider's eye on where locals like to eat, drink, and be merry; and to learn all the interesting and infamous aspects of London's history, architecture, and inhabitants.

BOAT TOURS

City Cruises. In nice weather, an open top-deck ride from Westminster, the London Eye, or Tower Piers to the ancient royal romping ground of Greenwich along the Thames River is one of the best ways to get acquainted with the city. You'll pass sights like Tower Bridge, the Tower of London, and St. Paul's Cathedral, all with a chirpy Cockney boatman running commentary. Lunch, Afternoon Tea, and nighttime cruises are also available. ✉ *Cherry Garden Pier, Cherry Garden St.* ☎ *020/7740–0400* 🌐 *www.citycruises.com* 🎫 *From £11.*

Thames RIB Experience. Make like James Bond in an exhilarating special forces–style inflatable speedboat as you whiz past the MI6 building, Shakespeare's Globe, and Tower Bridge on a high-speed 50-minute round-trip to Canary Wharf. There are also 40-minute roller-coaster blasts to the O2 Arena in Greenwich and 75-minute round-trips from Tower Pier to the Thames Barrier. ✉ *Embankment Pier* ☎ *020/3613–7838* 🌐 *www.thamesribexperience.com* 🎫 *From £27.*

BUS TOURS

Golden Tours. Various hop-on, hop-off open-top double-decker tours with this company take in the main sites on three key loops. With 60 drop-off points and 48-hour passes, they also offer discount tickets to attractions like the Tower of London and the London Dungeon, as well as nighttime tours, free walking tours, and boat rides on the Thames. ✉ *London* ☎ *020/7630–2028* 🌐 *www.goldentours.com* 🎫 *From £28.*

The Original London Sightseeing Tour. Like its double-decker competitors, the Original London Sightseeing Tour offers various hop-on, hop-off open-top tours of the city, but its most popular feature is its 48-hour pass that includes loops of the main historic sites, The City, Westminster, and the South Kensington museum district. They also throw in free tickets for a Thames boat cruise, plus Jack the Ripper, Changing of the Guard, and Rock 'n' Roll walking tours. ✉ *London* ☎ *020/8877–1722* 🌐 *www.theoriginaltour.com* 🎫 *From £33.*

FREE TOURS

City Tours. The City of London City Guides offer a small program of top-quality daily walks, including an insider tour of Guildhall, Mansion House, the Bank of England, and Royal Exchange, plus others focusing on topics like The City's gardens, Charles Dickens, Dr. Samuel Johnson, and famed architect Sir Christopher Wren's churches. 🌐 *www.cityoflondonguides.com* 🎫 *from £7.*

Sandemans New Europe London. It seems almost too good to be true: Sandemans offers an excellent free, 2½-hour Royal London walking tour daily, which winds from Buckingham Palace to Big Ben. Led by wisecracking actors, poets, and esteemed art historians, other paid walks include a boozy five-stop pub crawl and spooky East End's Dark Secrets tours. Tours are also available in Spanish and while free, tips are the expected way to show your appreciation (along with a round of applause at the finish). ☎ *30/5105–0030* 🌐 *www.neweuropetours.eu/london* 🎫 *Free.*

SPECIALTY TOURS

Brit Movie Tours. See the exterior of Grantham House and the spot where Branson first confesses his love for Lady Sybil on this insiders' central London tour of *Downton Abbey* filming locations. Other tours focusing on James Bond, *Sherlock, The Da Vinci Code,* and Harry Potter filming locations, among many others, are also available. ☎ *0844/247–1007* 🌐 *www.britmovietours.com* 🎟 *From £12.*

London Food Lovers Food Tours. London's a top global foodie city now, and the London Food Lovers walking tour of Soho is a fascinating way to explore the capital's gastro delights. The four-hour walk kicks off with Hawaiian blueberry pancakes at burger bar Kua'Aina and takes in offbeat stops for truffle pumpkin ravioli at Soho's retro Italian delicatessen Lina Stores, a hot chocolate tasting at SAID artisanal Roman chocolatiers, and a sit-down lunch of fish-and-chips and Indian pale ale in quaint Soho pub the Dog and Duck. Well led and synchronized throughout, you'll also stop in Chinatown to sample steamed prawn dim sum at Beijing Dumpling, and spot celebrities amid the Afternoon Tea crowds at the Maison Bertaux French patisserie and tearoom. The tour ends with a dessert and wine pairing in the Dickensian underground cellar vaults of the 1890s Gordon's Wine Bar. There are various versions of the Soho tour, as well as a Jack the Ripper Happy Hour Tasting Tour and a Borough Market tour. ✉ *Islington* ☎ *0777/4099–306* 🌐 *www.londonfoodlovers.com* 🎟 *£60.*

WALKING TOURS

Context Travel. This company takes a highbrow approach to its intellectually curious small-group walks program, providing PhD- and MA-level scholars, authors, architects, and historians to lead walks of no more than six people. Lasting up to three hours, walks include the evolution of London theater to Charles Dickens and Victorian London. ☎ *800/691–6036* 🌐 *www.contexttravel.com/cities/london* 🎟 *From £90.*

London Walks. With London's oldest established walking tours, there's no need to book ahead; instead, just turn up at the meeting point at the allotted hour and pay £10 for a first-rate, guided two-hour walk with themes like Secret London, Literary London, Harry Potter film locations, Haunted London, and much more. Top crime historian and leading Ripper authority Donald Rumbelow often leads the 7:30 pm Jack the Ripper walk in Whitechapel. As a bonus bargain, kids can come along for free. ☎ *020/7624–3978* 🌐 *www.walks.com* 🎟 *From £10.*

Sophie Campbell. Travel journalist and former BBC *Travel Show* broadcaster Sophie Campbell specializes in superlong London walks. Full-day walks include Old Church Chelsea (by the river) to St. Michael's Highgate (high on a north London hill); or Hampton Court Palace to Richmond Palace via the noble palazzi of the nontidal Thames. Half-day hikes include a forensic examination of Fleet Street journalism and James Bond's London. ☎ *07743/566–323* 🌐 *www.sophiecampbell.london* 🎟 *From £220.*

Contacts

Air Travel

AIRPORTS Gatwick Airport. ☎ *0344/892–0322* 🌐 *www.gatwickairport.com.* **Heathrow Airport.** ☎ *0844/335–1801* 🌐 *www.heathrow.com.* **London City Airport.** ☎ *020/7646–0088* 🌐 *www.londoncityairport.com.* **Luton Airport.** ☎ *01582/405100* 🌐 *www.london-luton.co.uk.* **Southend Airport.** ☎ *01702/538500* 🌐 *www.southendairport.com.* **Stansted Airport.** ☎ *0808/169–7031* 🌐 *www.stanstedairport.com.*

GROUND TRANSPORTATION Airport Travel Line. ☎ *0871/200–2233* 🌐 *www.traveline.info.* **easyBus.** 🌐 *www.easybus.com.* **Gatwick Express.** ☎ *0345/850–1530* 🌐 *www.gatwickexpress.com.* **Heathrow Express.** ☎ *0345/600–1515* 🌐 *www.heathrowexpress.com.* **Heathrow Shuttle.** ☎ *0845/415–4268* 🌐 *www.heathrowshuttle.com.* **National Express.** ☎ *0871/781–8181* 🌐 *www.nationalexpress.com.* **Stansted Express.** ☎ *0345/600–7245* 🌐 *www.stanstedexpress.com.* **Thameslink.** ☎ *0345/026–4700* 🌐 *www.thameslinkrailway.com.*

Boat Travel

Thames Clippers. 🌐 *www.thamesclippers.com.* **Transport for London.** ☎ *0343/222–1234* 🌐 *www.tfl.gov.uk.*

Bus Travel

LONG-DISTANCE BUS CONTACTS easyBus. 🌐 *www.easybus.co.uk.* **Green Line.** ☎ *0344/801–7261* 🌐 *www.greenline.co.uk.* **Megabus.** ☎ *0900/160–0900* 🌐 *www.megabus.com.* **National Express.** ☎ *0871/781–8181* 🌐 *www.nationalexpress.com.* **Transport for London.** ☎ *0343/222–1234* 🌐 *www.tfl.gov.uk.* **Victoria Coach Station.** ✉ *164 Buckingham Palace Rd., Victoria* ☎ *0343/222–1234* Ⓜ *Victoria.*

Taxi Travel

Addison Lee. ☎ *020/7387–8888* 🌐 *www.addisonlee.com.* **Dial-a-Cab.** ☎ *020/7253–5000 for cash bookings, 020/7251–0581 for inquiries* 🌐 *www.dialacab.co.uk.* **Lady's and Gent's MiniCabs.** ☎ *020/8888–9999* 🌐 *www.ladysandgentsminicabs.com.*

Train Travel

BritRail Travel. ☎ *866/938–7245 in U.S. and Canada* 🌐 *www.britrail.net.* **Eurostar.** ☎ *03432/186186* 🌐 *www.eurostar.com.* **Eurotunnel.** ☎ *0844/335–3535 in U.K., +33/3–21–00–20–61 from outside Europe* 🌐 *www.eurotunnel.com.* **National Rail Enquiries.** ☎ *0345/748–4950* 🌐 *www.nationalrail.co.uk.*

Tube Travel

Transport for London. ☎ *0343/222–1234* 🌐 *www.tfl.gov.uk.*

Visitor Information

Official Websites:
🌐 *www.visitbritain.com*
🌐 *www.visitlondon.com*

Other Websites:
🌐 *www.londontown.com*
🌐 *www.standard.co.uk*
🌐 *www.bbc.co.uk*

Entertainment Information:
🌐 *www.timeout.com/london* 🌐 *www.officiallondontheatre.co.uk*

Chapter 3

WESTMINSTER AND ST. JAMES'S

Updated by
Jo Caird

Sights	Restaurants	Hotels	Shopping	Nightlife
★★★★★	★★★☆☆	★★☆☆☆	★★☆☆☆	★★☆☆☆

WESTMINSTER AND ST. JAMES'S SNAPSHOT

TOP REASONS TO GO

Westminster Abbey: This Gothic church was not only the site of William and Kate's marriage in 2011 but also has seen 38 coronations, starting with William the Conqueror in 1066.

Buckingham Palace: Even if you miss the palace's summer opening, keep pace with the marching soldiers as they enact the time-honored Changing the Guard.

The National Gallery: Leonardo, Raphael, Van Eyck, Rembrandt, and many other artistic greats are shown off in the gorgeous rooms at the National Gallery.

Churchill War Rooms: Listen to Churchill's radio addresses to the British people as you explore this atmospheric underground wartime hideout.

Trafalgar Square: With London's most famous photo op (the 315-foot-high clock tower Big Ben) under scaffolding until 2021, head to Trafalgar Square for a snap with the enormous bronze lions at the base of Nelson's Column.

GETTING THERE

Trafalgar Square is in the center of the action. Take the Tube to Embankment (Northern, Bakerloo, District, and Circle lines) and walk north until you cross the Strand, or exit to Northumberland Avenue at Charing Cross (Bakerloo and Northern lines). Buses are another great option, as almost all roads lead to Trafalgar Square.

Two Tube stations are right in the heart of St. James's: Piccadilly Circus (Piccadilly and Bakerloo lines) and Green Park (Piccadilly, Victoria, and Jubilee lines).

MAKING THE MOST OF YOUR TIME

For royal pageantry, begin with Buckingham Palace, Westminster Abbey, and the Household Cavalry Museum, followed by the Houses of Parliament and Big Ben. For art, the National Gallery, Tate Britain, and the Queen's Gallery top anyone's list.

QUICK BITES

■ **Iris & June** The area between Victoria and Westminster is something of a wasteland in terms of quick-bite eateries, but this minimalist café serves excellent coffee, salads, wraps, and more. ✉ *1 Howick Pl., Victoria* 🌐 *www.irisandjune.com* ⏲ *No dinner* Ⓜ *Victoria.*

■ **Notes Music and Coffee** Next door to the London Coliseum (home of the English National Opera), this hip café serves some of the best sandwiches, salads, and coffee in the neighborhood. ✉ *31 St. Martin's La., Westminster* ☎ *020/7240–0424* 🌐 *www.notescoffee.com* Ⓜ *Charing Cross.*

NEAREST PUBLIC RESTROOMS

■ Paid restrooms (50 p) are across the street from Westminster Abbey at the bottom of Victoria Street. Banqueting House and the Queen's Gallery have elegant restrooms.

This is postcard London at its best. Crammed with historic churches, grand state buildings, and some of the world's best art collections, Royal London and Westminster unite politics and high culture. (Oh, and the Queen lives here, too.) The places you'll want to explore are grouped into four distinct areas—Trafalgar Square, Whitehall, St. James's, and Buckingham Palace—each nudging a corner of triangular St. James's Park. There is as much history in these acres as in many whole cities, so yourself—this is concentrated seeing.

inster

Home to London's most photogenic pigeons, **Trafalgar Square** is the official center of the district known as **Westminster,** nominally a separate city but in fact the official center of London. What will bring you here are the two magnificent museums on the northern edge of the square, the **National Gallery** and the **National Portrait Gallery.** From the square, two boulevards lead to the seats of different areas of governance. The avenue called **Whitehall** drops south to the neo-Gothic **Houses of Parliament,** where members of both (Commons and Lords) hold debates and vote on pending legislation. Just opposite, **Westminster Abbey** is a monument to the nation's history and for centuries the scene of daily worship, coronations, and royal weddings. Poets, political leaders, and 17 monarchs are buried in this world-famous, 13th-century Gothic building. Sandwiched between the two is the **Jewel Tower,** the only surviving part of the medieval Palace of Westminster (a name still given to Parliament and its environs). Halfway down Whitehall, **10 Downing Street** is both the residence and the office of the prime minister. One of the most celebrated occupants, Winston Churchill, is commemorated in the **Churchill War Rooms,** his underground wartime headquarters off Whitehall. Just down the road is the **Cenotaph,** built for

A Brief History Of Westminster

The Romans may have shaped The City, but England's royals created Westminster. Indeed, it's still technically a separate city—notice it reads "City of Westminster" on street signs, not "City of London"—although any formal divide between the two vanished centuries ago, along with the open countryside that once lay between them. Edward the Confessor started the first Palace of Westminster in the 11th century; in the 1040s, he also founded Westminster Abbey, where every British coronation has taken place. The district became the focus of political power in England after the construction of Whitehall Palace in the 16th century; a vast and opulent building, it was the official residence of the monarch until it burned down in 1698. It survives both as the name of Westminster's most important road, and as a term still used in Britain to refer to the seat of government in general. The first Parliament building was part of the same complex; it, too, was nearly destroyed by the Gunpowder Plot of 1605 (the foiling of which is still commemorated annually on November 5, Guy Fawkes Day) and eventually succumbed to fire in 1834. The Westminster we see today took shape during the Georgian and Victorian periods, as Britain reached the zenith of its imperial power. Grand architecture sprang up, and Buckingham Palace became the principal royal residence in 1837, when Victoria acceded to the throne. Trafalgar Square and Nelson's Column were built in 1843, to commemorate Britain's most famous naval victory, and the Houses of Parliament were rebuilt in the 1840s in the trendy neo-Gothic style of the time. The illustrious Clarence House, built in 1825 for the Duke of Clarence (later William IV), is now the home of Prince Charles and Camilla, Duchess of Cornwall.

the dead of World War I and since then a focal point for the annual remembrance of those lost in war.

The Mall, a wide elegant avenue beyond the stone curtain of **Admiralty Arch,** heads southwest from Trafalgar Square toward the **Queen Victoria Memorial** and **Buckingham Palace,** the sovereign's official London residence. The building is open to the public only in summer (and for tours on select dates throughout the year), but you can see highlights of the royal art collection in the **Queen's Gallery** and spectacular ceremonial coaches in the **Royal Mews,** both open all year. Farther south toward Pimlico, **Tate Britain** focuses on prominent British artists from 1500 to today.

The main drawback to sightseeing here is that half the world is doing it at the same time. So, for a large part of the year a lot of Royal London is floodlit at night (when there's more elbow room), adding to the theatricality of the experience.

Sights

Banqueting House

CASTLE/PALACE | James I commissioned Inigo Jones, one of England's great architects, to undertake a grand building on the site of the original Tudor Palace of Whitehall, which was (according to one foreign visitor) "ill-built, and nothing but a heap of houses." Jones's Banqueting House, finished in 1622 and the first building in England to be completed in the neoclassical style, bears all the hallmarks of the Palladian sophistication and purity that so influenced Jones during his time in Italy. James's son, Charles I, enhanced the interior by employing the Flemish painter Peter Paul Rubens to glorify his father and himself (naturally) in a series of vibrant painted ceiling panels called *The Apotheosis of James I.* As it turned out, these allegorical paintings, depicting a wise monarch being received into heaven, were the last thing Charles saw before he stepped through the open first-floor window onto the scaffold, which had been erected directly outside for his execution by Cromwell's Parliamentarians in 1649. Twenty years later, his son, Charles II, would celebrate the restoration of the monarchy in the exact same place. ✉ *Whitehall, Westminster* ☎ *084/4482–7777* 🌐 *www.hrp.org.uk/BanquetingHouse* 🎟 *£7* Ⓜ *Charing Cross, Embankment, Westminster.*

★ Churchill War Rooms

MUSEUM | FAMILY | It was from this small warren of underground rooms—beneath the vast government buildings of the Treasury—that Winston Churchill and his team directed troops in World War II. Designed to be bombproof, the whole complex has been preserved almost exactly as it was when the last light was turned off at the end of the war. Every clock shows almost 5 pm, and the furniture, fittings, and paraphernalia of a busy, round-the-clock war office are still in situ, down to the colored map pins.

During air raids, the leading government ministers met here, and the Cabinet Room is arranged as if a meeting were about to convene. In the Map Room, the Allied campaign is charted on wall-to-wall maps with a rash of pinholes showing the movements of convoys. In the hub of the room, a bank of differently colored phones known as the "Beauty Chorus" linked the War Rooms to control rooms around the nation. The Prime Minister's Room holds the desk from which Churchill made his morale-boosting broadcasts; the Telephone Room (a converted broom cupboard) has his hotline to FDR. You can also see the restored rooms that the PM used for dining and sleeping. Telephonists (switchboard operators) and clerks who worked 16-hour shifts slept in lesser quarters in unenviable conditions.

An excellent addition to the War Rooms is the Churchill Museum, a tribute to the great wartime leader himself. ✉ *Clive Steps, King Charles St., Westminster* ☎ *020/7416–5000* 🌐 *www.iwm.org.uk/visits/churchill-war-rooms* 🎟 *£22* Ⓜ *Westminster.*

Downing Street

GOVERNMENT BUILDING | Were it not for the wrought-iron gates and armed guards that block the entrance, you'd probably miss this otherwise unassuming Georgian side street off Whitehall—but this is the location of the famous **No. 10,** London's modest equivalent of the White House. The Georgian entrance to the mid-17th-century mansion is deceptive; it's actually a huge complex of discreetly linked buildings. Since 1732 it has been the official home and office of the prime minister—the last private resident was the magnificently named Mr. Chicken (the current prime minister actually lives in the private apartments above No. 11, traditionally the residence of the Chancellor of the Exchequer, the head of the Treasury). There are no public tours, but the famous black front door to No. 10 is clearly visible from Whitehall. Keep your eyes peeled for Larry the cat, whose official title is Chief Mouser to the Cabinet Office. Just south of Downing Street, in the middle of Whitehall, is the **Cenotaph,** a stark white monolith built to commemorate the 1918 armistice. On Remembrance Day (the Sunday nearest November 11), it's strewn with red poppy wreaths to honor the dead of both world wars and all British and Commonwealth soldiers killed in action since; the first wreath is always laid by the Queen. A

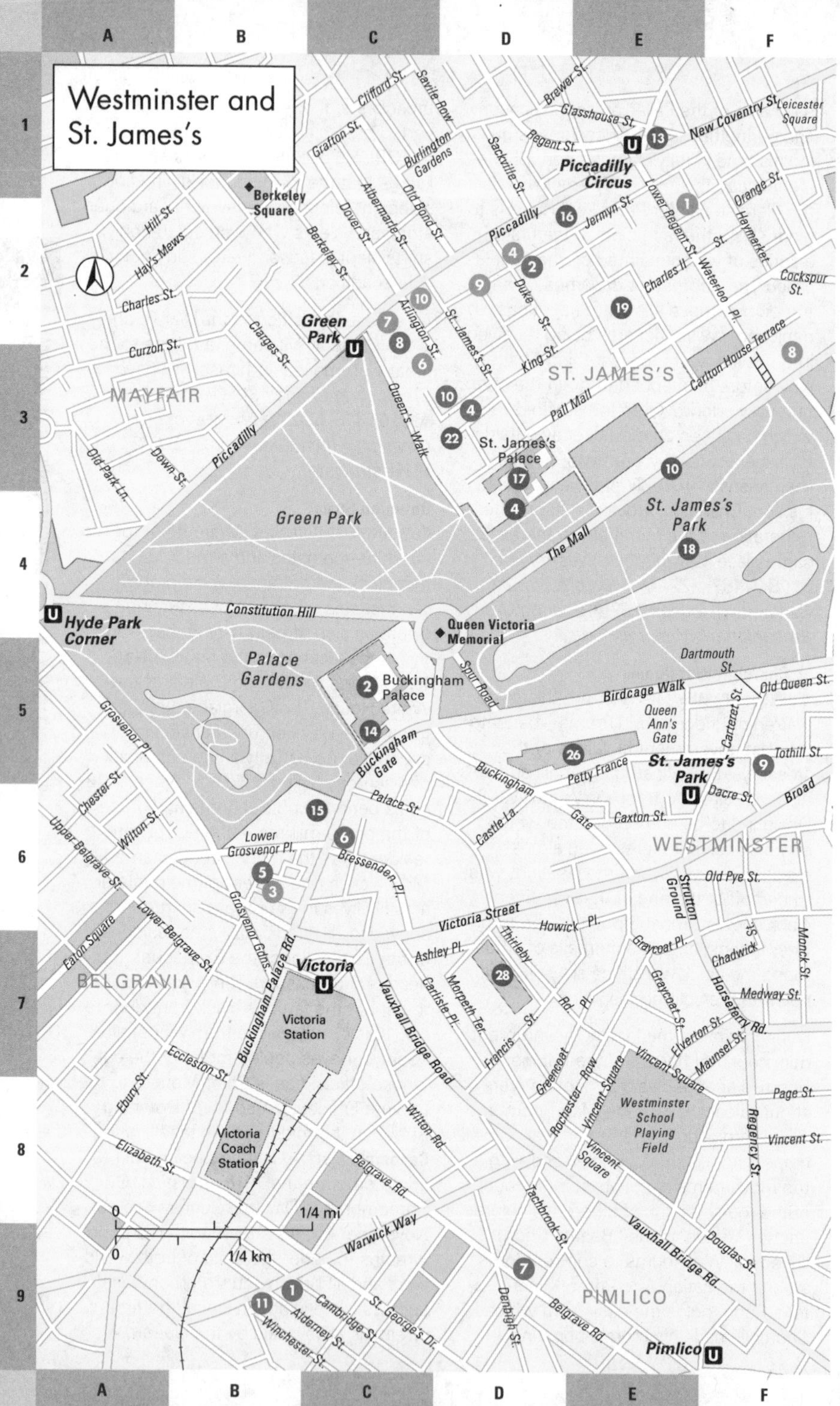
Westminster and St. James's
A
B
C
D
E
F
1
2
3
4
5
6
7
8
9
Berkeley Square
Green Park
Piccadilly Circus
Hyde Park Corner
St. James's Park
Victoria
Pimlico
MAYFAIR
ST. JAMES'S
WESTMINSTER
BELGRAVIA
PIMLICO
Green Park
St. James's Park
Palace Gardens
St. James's Palace
Buckingham Palace
Queen Victoria Memorial
Victoria Station
Victoria Coach Station
Westminster School Playing Field
Queen Ann's Gate
0
1/4 mi
0
1/4 km

Sights

1 Banqueting House...... G3
2 Buckingham Palace..... C5
3 Churchill War Rooms... G4
4 Clarence House......... D4
5 Downing Street......... G4
6 Horse Guards Parade.. G3
7 Household Cavalry Museum................ G3
8 Houses of Parliament.. H5
9 The Jewel Tower....... G6
10 The Mall.................. E3
11 National Gallery......... G2
12 National Portrait Gallery.................. G1
13 Piccadilly Circus......... E1
14 The Queen's Gallery..... C5
15 Royal Mews............. C6
16 St. James's Church..... D2
17 St. James's Palace..... D3
18 St. James's Park......... E4
19 St. James's Square...... E2
20 St. Margaret's Church.................. G5
21 St. Martin-in-the-Fields..................... G1
22 Spencer House......... D3
23 The Supreme Court..... G5
24 Tate Britain............. G9
25 Trafalgar Square........ G2
26 Wellington Barracks and the Guards Museum..... E5
27 Westminster Abbey.... G5
28 Westminster Cathedral................ D7

Restaurants

1 Aquavit.................... E1
2 Boyds Grill and Wine Bar................. G2
3 The Dining Room at The Goring............... B6
4 45 Jermyn St............ D2
5 Kerridge's Bar & Grill... H2
6 Le Caprice................. C3
7 The Ritz Restaurant...... C2
8 Rochelle Canteen at the Institute of Contemporary Arts...... F3
9 Wiltons.................. D2
10 The Wolseley............ C2

Hotels

1 Artist Residence........ B9
2 The Cavendish.......... D2
3 The Corinthia........... H2
4 Dukes Hotel............. D3
5 The Goring............... B6
6 Hotel 41.................. C6
7 The Luna Simone Hotel........... D9
8 The Ritz.................. C2
9 Sanctuary House Hotel.............. F5
10 The Stafford London.... D3
11 Windermere Hotel...... B9

KEY
Sights
Restaurants
Hotels

hundred yards farther, toward Parliament, is the **Monument to the Women of World War II.** The prominent black marble sculpture uses a string of empty uniforms to symbolize the vital service of women in then-traditionally male jobs during the war, as well as in frontline roles, such as medics and auxiliary officers. ✉ *Whitehall* Ⓜ *Westminster.*

Horse Guards Parade

PLAZA | FAMILY | Once the tiltyard for jousting tournaments, Horse Guards Parade is best known for the annual Trooping the Colour ceremony, in which the Queen takes the salute on her official birthday, on the second Saturday in June. (Though it's called a birthday it's actually the anniversary of her coronation—her real birthday is April 21.) It's a must-see if you're around, with marching bands and throngs of onlookers. Throughout the rest of the year, the changing of two mounted sentries known as the **Queen's Life Guard** at the Whitehall facade of Horse Guards provides what may be London's most popular photo opportunity. The ceremony takes place daily from April to July, and on alternate days from August to March (usually odd numbered days, but check the monthly schedule at 🌐 *www.householddivision.org.uk/changing-the-guard-calendar*). It starts at 10:30 am at St. James's Palace, where the guard begins its march to Buckingham Palace, and the new guards take up their posts in a ceremony at 11. (It's sometimes cancelled in bad weather.) At 4 pm daily is the dismounting ceremony, aka the 4 O'Clock Parade, during which sentries are posted and horses are returned to their stables. It began in 1894, when Queen Victoria discovered the guards on duty drinking and gambling. As a punishment she decreed that the regiment should be inspected every day at 4 pm for the next 100 years—by the time 1994 swung around they decided to continue the tradition indefinitely. ✉ *Whitehall* 🌐 *www.householddivision.org.uk/changing-the-guard* 🎫 *Free* Ⓜ *Westminster.*

Household Cavalry Museum

MUSEUM | FAMILY | Hang around Horse Guards for even a short time and you'll see a member of the Household Cavalry on guard, or trotting past on horseback, resplendent in a bright crimson uniform with polished brass armor. Made up of soldiers from the British Army's most senior regiments, the Life Guards and the Blues and Royals, membership is considered a great honor; they act as the Queen's official bodyguards and play a key role in state occasions (they also perform the famed Changing the Guard ceremony). Housed in the cavalry's original 17th-century stables, the museum has displays of uniforms and weapons going back to 1661 as well as interactive exhibits on the regiments' current operational roles. In the tack room you can handle saddles and bridles, and try on a trooper's uniform, including a distinctive brass helmet with horsehair plume. You can also observe the working horses being tended to in their stable block behind a glass wall. ✉ *Horse Guards Parade, Whitehall* ☎ *020/7930–3070* 🌐 *www.householdcavalrymuseum.co.uk* 🎫 *£9* Ⓜ *Charing Cross, Westminster.*

★ **Houses of Parliament**

GOVERNMENT BUILDING | The Palace of Westminster, as the complex is called, was first established on this site by Edward the Confessor in the 11th century. William II built a new palace in 1097, and this became the seat of English power. A fire destroyed most of the palace in 1834, and the current complex dates largely from the mid-19th century. The best view is from the opposite (south) bank of the Thames, across Lambeth Bridge. It is most dramatic at night when lighted green and gold.

The **Visitors' Galleries** of the House of Commons provide a view of democracy in action when the benches are filled by opposing MPs (members of Parliament). Debates are formal but raucous, especially during the **Prime Minister's**

Questions (PMQs), when any MP can put a question to the nation's leader. Tickets to PMQs are free but highly sought after, so the only way for non-U.K. citizens to gain access is by lining up on the day and hoping for returns or no-shows. The action starts at noon every Wednesday when Parliament is sitting, and the whole shebang is broadcast live on television. For non-PMQ debates, Embassies and High Commissions have a quota of tickets available to their citizens, which can help you avoid long lines. The easiest time to get into the Commons is during an evening session—Parliament is still sitting if the top of the Clock Tower is illuminated. There are also Visitors Galleries for the House of Lords. The Clock Tower—renamed **Elizabeth Tower** in 2012, in honor of the Queen's Diamond Jubilee—was completed in 1858, and contains the 13-ton bell known as **Big Ben.** ⚠ **Renovations of the tower and clock will be taking place throughout 2020, with scaffolding getting in the way of photo ops during this period.** At the southwest end of the main Parliament building is the 323-foot-high Victoria Tower.

Engaging guided and audio tours of Parliament are available on Saturday and weekdays when Parliament isn't sitting, but sell out six months in advance. Other tours, including afternoon tea in a riverside room, are also available. ✉ *St. Stephen's Entrance, St. Margaret St., Westminster* ☎ *020/7219–4114 for public tours* 🌐 *www.parliament.uk/visiting* 🎫 *Free; tours from £20* 🕒 *Closed Sun.* Ⓜ *Westminster.*

The Jewel Tower

BUILDING | Overshadowed by the big-ticket attractions of Parliament to one side and Westminster Abbey to the other, this is the only significant portion of the Palace of Westminster complex to have survived intact from medieval times. Built in the 1360s to contain treasures belonging to Edward III, it once formed part of the palace's defensive walls—hence the fortresslike appearance. Check out the original ribbed stone ceiling on the ground floor; look up to see the carved stone images of men and beasts. The Jewel Tower was later used as a records office for the House of Lords, but hasn't served any official function since the rest of the old palace was destroyed by fire in 1834 and the ancient documents were moved to the greater safety of the Tower of London. Today it contains an exhibition on the history of the building. ✉ *Abingdon St., Westminster* ☎ *020/7222–2219* 🌐 *www.english-heritage.org.uk/visit/places/jewel-tower* 🎫 *£6* Ⓜ *Westminster.*

★ National Gallery

MUSEUM | **FAMILY** | Anyone with even a passing interest in art will want to put this near the top of their to-do lists while visiting London, for it is truly one of the world's great art museums. More than 2,300 masterpieces are on show here, including works by Michelangelo, Leonardo, Turner, Monet, Van Gogh, Picasso, and more. Enter through the grand portico overlooking the north side of Trafalgar Square to delve headlong into the highlights of the collection, although the Sainsbury Wing (the modern building immediately to the left), which focuses mainly on medieval art, is invariably less crowded. You could easily spend all day discovering what the National Gallery has to offer, but among the best-known highlights are: in Room 4, *The Ambassadors* by Hans Holbein (1497–1543), a portrait of two wealthy visitors from France, surrounded by objects laden with enough symbolism to fill a book—including, most beguilingly, a giant skull at the base, which only takes shape when viewed from an angle; in Room 63, the *Arnolfini Portrait* by Van Eyck (1390–1441), in which a solemn couple holds hands, the fish-eye mirror behind them mysteriously illuminating what can't be seen from the front view; in Room 66, *The Virgin of the Rocks* by Leonardo da Vinci (1452–1519), a magnificent sculpted altarpiece commissioned in 1480; and in Room 34, *Rain,*

Did You Know?

After an 1834 fire, Parliament was rebuilt, combining Renaissance and Gothic styles. Then, when the bomb-damaged House of Commons was rebuilt after World War II, some of its ornamental flourishes were toned down.

Steam and Speed–The Great Western Railway by J.M.W. Turner (1775–1851), which seems, in its mad whirl of rain, steam, and mist, to embody the mystical dynamism of the steam age (spot the fleeing hare). Special exhibitions, of which there are several every year, tend to be major events. Generally they're ticketed, so booking is advisable if it's a big name. The permanent collection, however, is always free. Also free are weekday lunchtime lectures and Ten Minute Talks, which illuminate the story behind a key work of art. Hour-long free guided tours start at the Sainsbury Wing at 2 pm on weekdays. ✉ *Trafalgar Sq., Westminster* ☎ *020/7747–2885* 🌐 *www.nationalgallery.org.uk* 🎫 *Free; special exhibitions from £7; audio guide £5* Ⓜ *Charing Cross, Embankment, Leicester Sq.*

★ National Portrait Gallery

MUSEUM | **FAMILY** | The National Portrait Gallery was founded in 1856 with a single aim: to gather together portraits of famous (and infamous) Britons throughout history. More than 150 years and 200,000 portraits later, it is an essential stop for all history and literature buffs. If you visit with kids, ask at the desk about the excellent Family Trails, which make exploring the galleries with children much more fun. Galleries are arranged clearly and chronologically, from Tudor times to contemporary Britain. The enormous portrait of Elizabeth I—bejeweled and literally astride the world in a powerful display of imperial intent—may be the most impressive image in the Tudor Gallery, but there are plenty of contenders for that title. The huge permanent collections include portraits of Shakespeare, the Brontë sisters, and Jane Austen. Look for Stuart Pearson Wright's portrait of a seated J.K. Rowling and Annie Leibovitz's striking photograph of Queen Elizabeth II. Temporary exhibitions can be explored on the first three floors, particularly in the Wolfson and Porter galleries on the ground floor. **TIP→ On the top floor, the Portrait Restaurant has one of the best views in London—a panoramic vista of Nelson's Column and the backdrop along Whitehall to the Houses of Parliament.** ✉ *St. Martin's Pl., Westminster* ☎ *020/7306–0055* 🌐 *www.npg.org.uk* 🎫 *Free; special exhibitions from £6; audiovisual guide £3* Ⓜ *Charing Cross, Leicester Sq.*

St. Margaret's Church

RELIGIOUS SITE | Dwarfed by its neighbor, Westminster Abbey, St. Margaret's was probably founded in the 11th century and rebuilt between 1482 and 1523. It's the unofficial parish church of the House of Commons—Winston Churchill tied the knot here in 1908, and since 1681, a pew off the south aisle has been set aside for the Speaker of the House (look for the carved portcullis). Samuel Pepys and John Milton also worshipped here. The stained glass in the north windows is classically Victorian, facing abstract glass from John Piper in the south, while the east windows date from the early 16th century. These were to replace the originals, which were ruined in World War II. ✉ *St. Margaret's St., Parliament Sq., Westminster* ☎ *020/7222–5152* 🌐 *www.westminster-abbey.org/st-margarets-church* 🎫 *Free* Ⓜ *Westminster.*

St. Martin-in-the-Fields

RELIGIOUS SITE | **FAMILY** | One of London's best-loved and most welcoming of churches is more than just a place of worship. Named after St. Martin of Tours, known for the help he gave to beggars, this parish has long been a welcome sight for the homeless, who have been given soup and shelter at the church since 1914. The church is also a haven for music lovers; the internationally known Academy of St. Martin-in-the-Fields Chamber Ensemble was founded here, and a popular program of concerts continues today (many of the shows are free, although some do charge an entry fee). The crypt is a hive of activity, with a popular café and shop. Here you can also make your own life-size souvenir knight,

The Tate Britain showcases British art from the last 500 years, including contemporary works.

lady, or monarch from replica tomb brasses, with metallic waxes, paper, and instructions. ✉ *Trafalgar Sq., Westminster* ☎ *020/7766–1100* 🌐 *www.smitf.org* 🎫 *Free; brass rubbing from £5* Ⓜ *Charing Cross, Leicester Sq.*

The Supreme Court

GOVERNMENT BUILDING | The highest court of appeal in the United Kingdom is a surprisingly young institution, only having heard its first cases in 2009. Visitors are welcome to drop by and look at the three courtrooms, housed in the carefully restored Middlesex Guildhall, including the impressive Court Room 1, with its magnificent carved wood ceiling. Court is in session Monday through Thursday and since space in the public galleries is limited, you'll want to arrive early. The Court's art collection, on permanent display, includes portraits by Thomas Gainsborough and Joshua Reynolds. Guided tours are available on Friday. There is a café downstairs. The library is open on selected dates. ✉ *Parliament Sq., Westminster* ☎ *020/7960–1500* 🌐 *www.supremecourt.uk* 🎫 *Free; guided tour £7* 🕒 *Closed weekends* Ⓜ *Westminster.*

★ Tate Britain

MUSEUM | FAMILY | First opened in 1897, and funded by the sugar magnate Sir Henry Tate, this stately neoclassical institution may not be as ambitious as its Bankside sibling, Tate Modern, but its bright galleries lure only a fraction of the Modern's overwhelming crowds and are a great place to explore British art from 1500 to the present. The museum includes the Linbury Galleries on the lower floors, which stage temporary exhibitions, and a permanent collection on the upper floors. And what a collection it is—with classic works by John Constáble, Thomas Gainsborough, Francis Bacon, and an outstanding display from J.M.W. Turner in the Clore Gallery. Sumptuous Pre-Raphaelite pieces are a major draw, while more recent art historical periods are represented by works by artists such as Rachel Whiteread, L.S. Lowry, Vanessa Bell, Duncan Grant, Barbara Hepworth, and David Hockney. The Tate Britain also hosts the annual Turner Prize exhibition, with its accompanying furor over the state of contemporary art, from about October to January each year. There's a good little café, and the excellent Rex Whistler Restaurant has been something of an institution since it first opened in 1927. Look out for semiregular Late at Tate Friday evening events, when the gallery is open late for talks or performances; check the website for details.

TIP→ Craving more art? Head down the river on the Tate Boat (£8.60 one-way) to the Tate Modern; it runs between the two museums every 40 minutes. A River Roamer ticket (£19.80) permits a day's travel, with stops including the London Eye and the Tower of London. You get a discount of roughly a third if you have a Travelcard. ✉ *Millbank, Westminster* ☎ *020/7887–8888* 🌐 *www.tate.org.uk/britain* 💷 *Free; special exhibitions from £13; audio guide £5* Ⓜ *Pimlico.*

★ Trafalgar Square

PLAZA | This is officially the center of London: a plaque on the corner of the Strand and Charing Cross Road marks the spot from which distances on U.K. signposts are measured. (London's *actual* geographic center is a rather dull bench on the Victoria Embankment.) Medieval kings once kept their aviaries of hawks and falcons here; today the humbler gray pigeons flock en masse to the open spaces around the ornate fountains (feeding them is banned). The square was designed in 1830 by John Nash, who envisaged a new public space with striking views of the Thames, the Houses of Parliament, and Buckingham Palace. Of those, only Parliament is still clearly visible from the square, but it remains an important spot for open-air concerts, political demonstrations, and national celebrations, such as New Year's Eve. Dominating the square is 168-foot **Nelson's Column,** erected as a monument to the great admiral in 1843. Note that the lampposts on the south side, heading down Whitehall, are topped with ships—they all face Portsmouth, home of the British navy. The column is flanked on either side by enormous bronze lions. Climbing them is a very popular photo op, but be extremely careful, as there are no guardrails and it's a long fall onto concrete if you slip. Four plinths border the square; three contain militaristic statues, but one was left empty—it's now used for contemporary art installations, often with a wry and controversial edge. Surprisingly enough, given that this was a square built to honor British military victories, the lawn at the north side, by the National Gallery, contains a statue of George Washington—a gift from the state of Virginia in 1921. At the southern point of the square is the **equestrian statue of Charles I.** After the Civil War and the king's execution, Oliver Cromwell, the antiroyalist leader, commissioned a brazier, John Rivett, to melt the statue down. The story goes that Rivett instead merely buried it in his garden. He made a fortune peddling knickknacks wrought, he claimed, from its metal, only to produce the statue miraculously unscathed after the restoration of the monarchy—and then made another fortune reselling it. In 1675 Charles II had it placed where it stands today, near the spot where his father was executed in 1649. Each year, on January 30, the day of the king's death, the Royal Stuart Society lays a wreath at the foot of the statue. ✉ *Westminster* Ⓜ *Charing Cross.*

Wellington Barracks and the Guards Museum

MUSEUM | **FAMILY** | These are the headquarters of the Guards Division, the Queen's five regiments of elite foot guards (Grenadier, Coldstream, Scots, Irish, and Welsh), who protect the sovereign and, dressed in tunics of gold-purled scarlet and tall bearskin caps, patrol her palaces. Guardsmen alternate these ceremonial postings with serving in current conflicts, for which they wear more practical uniforms. If you want to learn more about the guards, visit the

Guards Museum, which has displays on all aspects of a guardsman's life in conflicts dating back to 1642; the entrance is next to the Guards Chapel. Next door is the **Guards Toy Soldier Centre,** a great place for a souvenir. ✉ *Birdcage Walk, Westminster* ☎ *020/7414–3428* 🌐 *www.theguardsmuseum.com* 🎫 *£8* Ⓜ *St. James's Park, Green Park.*

★ Westminster Abbey

RELIGIOUS SITE | Steeped in hundreds of years of rich and occasionally bloody history, Westminster Abbey is one of England's most iconic buildings. An abbey has stood here since the 10th century, although the current building mostly dates to the 1240s. It has hosted 38 coronations—beginning in 1066 with William the Conqueror—and no fewer than 16 royal weddings, the latest being that of Prince William and Kate Middleton in 2011. But be warned: there's only one way around the abbey, and it gets very crowded, so you'll need to be alert to catch the highlights. The **Coronation Chair,** which you'll find in St. George's Chapel by the east door, has been used for nearly every coronation since Edward II's in 1308, right up to Queen Elizabeth II's in 1953. Farther along, the exquisite confection of the Henry VII's **Lady Chapel** is topped by a magnificent fan-vaulted ceiling. The tomb of Henry VII lies behind the altar. Elizabeth I is buried above her sister "Bloody" Mary I in the tomb in a chapel on the north side, while her arch enemy, Mary Queen of Scots, rests in the tomb to the south. The **Chapel of St. Edward the Confessor** contains the shrine of the pre-Norman king, who reigned from 1042 to 1066. Because of its great age, you must join the verger-guided tours to be admitted to the chapel (£7; book at the admission desk). To the left, you'll find **Poets' Corner.** Geoffrey Chaucer was the first poet to be buried here, and other statues and memorials include those to William Shakespeare, D. H. Lawrence, T. S. Eliot, and Oscar Wilde. The medieval **Chapter House** is adorned with 14th-century frescoes and a magnificent 13th-century tiled floor, one of the finest in the country. Near the entrance is Britain's oldest door, dating from the 1050s. If you walk toward the West Entrance, you'll see a plaque to Franklin D. Roosevelt—one of the abbey's very few tributes to a foreigner. The poppy-wreathed **Grave of the Unknown Warrior** commemorates soldiers who lost their lives in both world wars. With a separate timed ticket (£5), you can visit the Queen's Diamond Jubilee Galleries located 52 feet above the Abbey floor; it's worth it for the views onto the Abbey's interior below alone, but it also gets you access to a remarkable collection of historical objects that tell the story of the building, including its construction and relationship to the monarchy. Exact hours for the various parts of the abbey are frustratingly long and complicated, and can change daily, so it's important to check before setting out, particularly if you're visiting early or late in the day, or off-season. The full schedule is posted online daily (or you can call). Certain areas of the abbey are completely inaccessible to wheelchair users; however, you will get free entry for yourself and one other. ✉ *Broad Sanctuary, Westminster* ☎ *020/7222–5152* 🌐 *www.westminster-abbey.org* 🎫 *£22* ⏲ *Closed Sun., except for worship* Ⓜ *Westminster, St. James's Park.*

Westminster Cathedral

RELIGIOUS SITE | Tucked away on traffic-clogged Victoria Street lies this remarkable neo-Byzantine gem, seat of the Archbishop of Westminster, head of the Roman Catholic Church in England and Wales. Faced with building a church with Westminster Abbey as a neighbor, architect John Francis Bentley looked to the east for inspiration, to the basilicas of St. Mark's in Venice and the Hagia Sofia in Istanbul. The asymmetrical redbrick edifice, dating to 1903, is banded with stripes of Portland stone and abutted by a 272-foot bell tower at the northwest corner, ascendable by elevator for sterling

One of London's most iconic sites, Westminster Abbey contains more than 600 monuments and memorials, and serves as the final resting place of some of England's most famous citizens.

views. The interior remains incomplete, the unfinished overhead brickwork of the ceiling lending the church a dark brooding intensity. The side chapels, including the Chapel of the Blessed Sacrament and the Holy Souls Chapel, are beautifully finished in glittering mosaics. The Lady Chapel—dedicated to the Virgin Mary—is also sumptuously decorated. Look out for the Stations of the Cross, done here by Eric Gill, and the striking baldachin—the enormous stone canopy standing over the altar with a giant cross suspended in front of it. The nave, the widest in the country, is constructed in green marble, which also has a Byzantine connection—it was cut from the same place as the marble used in the Hagia Sofia, and was almost confiscated by warring Turks as it traveled west. All told, more than 100 different types of marble can be found within the cathedral's interior. There's a café in the crypt. ✉ *Ashley Pl., off Victoria St., Westminster* ☎ *020/7798–9055* 🌐 *www.westminstercathedral.org.uk* 🎟 *Bell Tower and viewing gallery £6, Treasures of the Cathedral exhibition £5; combination ticket £9* Ⓜ *Victoria.*

Restaurants

Given the huge range of excellent dining options in nearby St. James's and Covent Garden, Westminster itself has surprisingly few restaurants of note, with mostly chain sandwich and quick bite joints dominating the busy touristy landscape. The good news is that the handful that do exist can be relied upon to serve up high quality ingredients in often rather chic surroundings.

Boyds Grill and Wine Bar
$$ | **INTERNATIONAL** | One of those restaurants you could never hope to find unless you were looking for it, Boyds occupies a ravishing, marble-clad dining room on the premises of an otherwise nondescript Northumberland Avenue business hotel. Steak is the focus, although other British meat and fish does make an appearance on an international menu that puts simplicity over innovation, with satisfying

results. **Known for:** comfort food such as burgers and sausages; excellent location within spitting distance of Trafalgar Square; wide range of wines, including English wines, available by the glass. *Average main: £19 8 Northumberland Ave., Trafalgar Sq. 020/7808–3344 www.boydsgrillandwinebar.co.uk No lunch weekends, no dinner Sun. Charing Cross, Embankment.*

★ **The Dining Room at The Goring**
$$$$ | BRITISH | *Downton Abbey* meets *The Crown* at this quintessentially English, old-school dining salon located within an Edwardian-era hotel down the road from Buckingham Palace. A favorite with royalty and courtiers, here you can enjoy daily specials like traditional beef Wellington or antediluvian quirks such as Eggs Drumkilbo (a hard-boiled egg/lobster seafood cocktail with caviar)—a onetime favorite of the late Queen Mother. **Known for:** plush salon designed by Viscount David Linley; glazed lobster omelet with duck fat chips; royal history and pedigree. *Average main: £34 The Goring, Beeston Pl., Victoria 020/7396–9000 www.thegoring.com No lunch Sat. Victoria.*

Kerridge's Bar & Grill
$$$$ | BRITISH | Tom Kerridge made his name earning Michelin stars at rural gastropubs and there's still a sense of pub grub about the menu here, his first London restaurant, despite the glamorous high-ceilinged dining room, flawless service, and rather steep prices. That's no bad thing, however, when you've got a chef as skilled as Kerridge—think rich, meat-focused dishes served up alongside unusual twists such as gherkin ketchup or black cabbage purée. **Known for:** inventive use of rotisserie cooking, from steak to cauliflower; playful presentation, from irreverant pastry additions to pour-it-yourself sauces; atmospheric views of Northumberland Avenue. *Average main: £37 10 Northumberland Ave., Trafalgar Sq. 020/7321–3244 www.kerridgesbarandgrill.co.uk Embankment, Charing Cross.*

Hotels

Staying in the capital's most central neighborhood is ideal if you like stepping out of the lobby onto more or less the doorstep of fantastic galleries, government buildings, and green spaces.

★ **Artist Residence**
$$ | HOTEL | As packed with bohemian character as they come, this small boutique hotel, more in Pimlico than Belgravia, oozes retro charm. **Pros:** quirky charm; excellent breakfasts; great staff. **Cons:** some rooms on the small side; stairs to upper floors; most rooms have a shower only. *Rooms from: £200 52 Cambridge St., Pimlico 020/7931–8946 www.artistresidencelondon.co.uk 10 rooms Free breakfast Victoria, Pimlico.*

★ **The Corinthia**
$$$$ | HOTEL | The London outpost of the exclusive Corinthia chain is design heaven-on-earth, with levels of service that make anyone feel like a VIP. **Pros:** so much luxury and elegance you'll feel like royalty; exceptional spa with indoor pool; excellent fine dining options. **Cons:** prices jump to the stratosphere once the least expensive rooms sell out; not many special offers; air-conditioning and lighting is difficult to use. *Rooms from: £540 Whitehall Pl., Westminster 020/7930–8181 www.corinthia.com 283 rooms No meals Embankment.*

The Goring
$$$$ | HOTEL | With Buckingham Palace just around the corner, this hotel, built in 1910 and now run by third-generation Gorings, has always been a favorite among discreet VIPs—including Kate Middleton's family on the night before her marriage to Prince William in 2011. **Pros:** elegant spacious rooms; overlooks Buckingham Palace; great attention to detail. **Cons:** price is still too high for what you get; interior's a bit fussy; the basic gym is small. *Rooms from:*

£615 ✉ 15 Beeston Pl., Grosvenor Gardens, Westminster ☎ 020/7396–9000 🌐 www.thegoring.com 69 rooms 🍽 No meals Ⓜ Victoria.

★ Hotel 41

$$$$ | HOTEL | With faultless service, sumptuous designer furnishings, and a sense of fun to boot, this impeccable hotel breathes new life into the cliché "thinks of everything," yet the epithet is really quite apt. **Pros:** impeccable service; beautiful and stylish; Buckingham Palace is on your doorstep. **Cons:** unusual design is not for everyone; expensive; the private bar can feel stuffy. *$ Rooms from: £497 ✉ 41 Buckingham Palace Rd., Westminster ☎ 020/7300–0041 🌐 www.41hotel.com 30 rooms 🍽 No meals Ⓜ Victoria.*

The Luna Simone Hotel

$$ | HOTEL | FAMILY | This delightful and friendly family-run hotel in Pimlico, a short stroll from Buckingham Palace, is a real find for the price in central London. **Pros:** friendly and well run; family rooms are outstanding value; superb central location. **Cons:** tiny bathrooms; thin walls; no elevator. *$ Rooms from: £139 ✉ 47–49 Belgrave Rd., Pimlico ☎ 020/7834–5897 🌐 www.lunasimone-hotel.com 36 rooms 🍽 Free breakfast Ⓜ Pimlico, Victoria.*

Sanctuary House Hotel

$$ | B&B/INN | This is a classic example of what the British mean when they refer to an "inn"—a pub with bedrooms, albeit one of better-than-average quality for London. **Pros:** cozy, authentic London feel; friendly staff; "wow" location right in the heart of Westminster. **Cons:** noise from pub; after-work crowd keeps the pub busy; dining options are limited. *$ Rooms from: £229 ✉ 33 Tothill St., Westminster ☎ 020/7799–4044 🌐 www.sanctuaryhousehotel.co.uk 35 rooms 🍽 Free breakfast Ⓜ St. James's Park.*

Windermere Hotel

$$ | HOTEL | FAMILY | This sweet and rather elegant old hotel, on the premises of one of London's first B&Bs (1881), is a decent, well-situated option. **Pros:** good location close to Victoria Station; free Wi-Fi; good amenities for an old hotel of this size, including air-conditioning and an elevator. **Cons:** rooms and bathrooms are tiny; traditional decor might not suit all tastes; many major attractions are a 20-minute walk away. *$ Rooms from: £185 ✉ 142–144 Warwick Way, Pimlico ☎ 020/7834–5163 🌐 www.windermere-hotel.co.uk 19 rooms 🍽 Free breakfast Ⓜ Victoria.*

Nightlife

BARS

Cinnamon Club

BARS/PUBS | FAMILY | On the ground floor of what was once the Reading Room of the old Westminster Library, the book-lined Library Bar of this contemporary Indian restaurant (the curries are superb) has Indian-theme cocktails (mango mojitos, "Delhi mules"), delicious bar snacks, and a clientele that includes young politicos. The bar is sometimes used for private events so it can be a good idea to call before you visit. *✉ The Old Westminster Library, 30–32 Great Smith St., Westminster ☎ 020/7222–2555 🌐 www.cinnamonclub.com Ⓜ St James's, Westminster.*

★ Gordon's Wine Bar

BARS/PUBS | Nab a rickety candelit table in the atmospheric, 1890s low-slung brick vaulted cellar interior of what claims to be the oldest wine bar in London, or fight for standing room in the long pedestrian-only alley garden that runs alongside it. Either way, the mood is always cheery as a diverse crowd sips on more than 60 different wines, ports, and sherries. Tempting cheese and meat plates are great for sharing. *✉ 47 Villiers St., Westminster ☎ 020/7930–1408 🌐 gordonswinebar.com Ⓜ Charing Cross, Embankment.*

PUBS

The Red Lion

BARS/PUBS | Given its proximity to both the Houses of Parliament and Downing Street, it's no surprise that this traditional old boozer should be so popular with politicos of all stripes. Portraits of former prime ministers—several of whom also drank here—line the walls, and the bar room is one of a handful of premises outside the Palace of Westminster fitted with a "division bell" that recalls members of Parliament to the chamber for important votes. ✉ *48 Parliament St., Westminster* ☎ *020/7930–5826* 🌐 *www.redlionwestminster.co.uk* Ⓜ *Westminster.*

Performing Arts

St. John's Smith Square

CONCERTS | Chamber music, organ recitals, and orchestral concerts are held at this baroque church behind Westminster Abbey. There are three or four lunchtime recitals a month. ✉ *Smith Sq., Westminster* ☎ *020/7222–1061* 🌐 *www.sjss.org.uk* Ⓜ *Westminster.*

St. James's

As a fitting coda to all of Westminster's pomp and circumstance, St. James's—packed with old-money galleries, restaurants, and gentlemen's clubs that embody the history and privilege of traditional London—is found to the south of Piccadilly and north of the Mall.

When Whitehall Palace burned down in 1698, all of London turned its attention to St. James's Palace, the new royal residence. In the 18th and 19th centuries, the area around the palace became the place to live, and many of the estates surrounding the palace disappeared in a building frenzy, as mansions were built and streets laid out. Most of the homes here are privately owned and therefore closed to visitors, but there are some treasure houses that you can explore (such as Spencer House), as well as many fancy shops that have catered to the great and good for centuries.

Today, St. James contains some interesting art galleries and antiques shops. In one corner is St. James's Park, framed on its western side by the biggest monument in the area: Buckingham Palace, the official London residence of the Queen. The smaller St. James's Palace is where much of the office work for the House of Windsor gets done; nearby is Clarence House, London home of Prince Charles and his wife, Camilla.

Sights

★ **Buckingham Palace**

CASTLE/PALACE | If Buckingham Palace were open year-round, it would be by far the most visited tourist attraction in Britain; as it is, the Queen's main residence, home to every British monarch since Victoria in 1837, opens its doors to the public only in the summertime, with a handful of other dates throughout the year. The Queen is almost never there at the time—traditionally she heads off to Scotland for a couple of months every summer, where she takes up residence at Balmoral Castle. (Here's a quick way to tell if the Queen's at home: if she's in residence, the Royal Standard flies above the palace; if not, it's the more famous red, white, and blue Union Jack.) The tour covers the palace's 19 State Rooms, with their fabulous gilt moldings and walls adorned with Old Masters. The **Grand Hall,** followed by the **Grand Staircase** and **Guard Room,** are visions in marble and gold leaf, filled with massive, twinkling chandeliers. Don't miss the theatrical **Throne Room,** with the original 1953 coronation throne, or the sword in the Ballroom, used by the Queen to bestow knighthoods and other honors with a touch on the recipient's shoulders. Royal portraits line the **State Dining Room,** and the **Blue Drawing Room** is dazzling in

A classic photo op: cavalry from the Queen's Life Guard at Buckingham Palace

its splendor. The bow-shape **Music Room** features lapis lazuli columns between arched floor-to-ceiling windows, and the alabaster-and-gold plasterwork of the **White Drawing Room** is a dramatic statement of wealth and power. Admission is by timed-entry ticket every 15 minutes throughout the day. It's also worth adding a guided tour of the sprawling gardens to your visit. Allow up to two hours to take it all in. **Changing the Guard** remains one of London's best free shows and culminates in front of the palace. Marching to live military bands, the old guard proceed up the Mall from St. James's Palace to Buckingham Palace. Shortly afterward, the new guard approach from Wellington Barracks. Then within the forecourt, the captains of the old and new guards symbolically transfer the keys to the palace. Get there early for the best view. ✉ *Buckingham Palace Rd., St. James's* ☎ *030/3123–7300* 🌐 *www.royalcollection.org.uk/visit* 🎫 *From £25* ⏲ *Closed Oct.–July except on selected dates* Ⓜ *Victoria, St. James's Park, Green Park.*

Clarence House

HOUSE | The London home of the Queen Mother for nearly 50 years until her death in 2002, Clarence House is now the residence of Charles, the Prince of Wales and his wife, Camilla, the Duchess of Cornwall. The Regency mansion was built in 1828 by John Nash for the Duke of Clarence (later to become William IV) who considered next-door St. James's Palace to be too cramped for his liking, although postwar renovation work means that little remains of Nash's original. Since then it has remained a royal home for princesses, dukes, and duchesses, including the present monarch, Queen Elizabeth II, as a newlywed before her coronation. The rooms have been sensitively preserved to reflect the Queen Mother's taste, with the addition of many works of art from the Royal Collection, including works by Winterhalter, Augustus John, and Sickert. Clarence House is usually open only for the month of August, and tickets must be booked in advance. ✉ *St. James's Palace, The Mall, St. James's* ☎ *030/3123–7300* 🌐 *www.*

Royalty Watching

You've seen Big Ben, the Tower, and Westminster Abbey. But somehow you feel something is missing: a close encounter with Britain's most famous attraction—Her Royal Majesty, Elizabeth II. The Queen and the Royal Family attend hundreds of functions a year, and if you want to know what they are doing on any given date, turn to the Court Circular, printed in the major London dailies, or check out the Royal Family website (*www.royal.uk*) for the latest events on the Royal Diary. Trooping the Colour is usually held on the second Saturday in June, to celebrate the Queen's official birthday. This spectacular parade begins when she leaves Buckingham Palace in her carriage and rides down the Mall to arrive at Horse Guards Parade at 11 exactly. To watch, just line up along the Mall with your binoculars.

Another time you can catch the Queen in all her regalia is when she and the Duke of Edinburgh ride in state to open the Houses of Parliament. The famous black and gilt-trimmed Irish State Coach travels from Buckingham Palace—on a clear day, it's to be hoped, for this ceremony takes place in late October or early November. The Gold State Coach, an icon of fairy-tale glamour, is used for coronations and jubilees only.

But perhaps the most relaxed, least formal time to see the Queen is during Royal Ascot, held at the famous racetrack near Windsor Castle—a short train ride out of London—usually during the third week of June (Tuesday–Saturday). The Queen and members of the Royal Family are driven down the track to the Royal Box in an open carriage, giving spectators a chance to see them. After several races, the famously horse-loving Queen invariably walks down to the paddock, greeting racegoers as she proceeds. If you meet her, the official etiquette is to first make a short bow or curtsy, and then to address her first as "Your Majesty," and then "Ma'am" thereafter.

royalcollection.org.uk *£11* *Closed Sept.–July* *Green Park.*

The Mall

NEIGHBORHOOD | This stately, 115-foot-wide processional route sweeping towards Trafalgar Square from the Queen Victoria Memorial at Buckingham Palace is an updated 1911 version of a promenade laid out around 1660 for the game of *paille-maille* (a type of croquet crossed with golf), which also gave the parallel road Pall Mall its name. (That's why Mall is pronounced to rhyme with "pal," not "ball.") The tarmac is colored red to represent a ceremonial red carpet. During state visits, several times a year, the Mall is traditionally bedecked with the flag of the visiting nation, alongside the Union Jack. The **Duke of York Memorial** up the steps toward stately John Nash-designed Carlton House Terrace (worth a look in itself) is a towering column dedicated to George III's second son, who was further immortalized in the English nursery rhyme "The Grand Old Duke of York." Be sure to stroll along the Mall on Sunday when the road is closed to traffic, or catch the bands and troops of the Household Division on their way from St. James's Palace to Buckingham Palace for the Changing the Guard. At the northernmost end of the Mall is Admiralty Arch, a stately gateway named after the adjacent Royal Navy headquarters. It was designed by Sir Aston Webb and built in

1910 as a memorial to Queen Victoria. Actually comprising five arches—two for pedestrians, two for traffic, and the central arch, which is only opened for state occasions—it was a government building until 2012, and has even served as an alternative residence for the Prime Minister while Downing Street was under renovation. It is currently being transformed into a luxury hotel. Look out for the bronze nose grafted onto the inside wall of the right-hand traffic arch (when facing the Mall); it was placed there in secret by a mischievous artist in 1997 and has been allowed to remain. ✉ *St. James's* Ⓜ *Charing Cross, Green Park.*

Piccadilly Circus

NEIGHBORHOOD | The origins of the name "Piccadilly" relate to a humble 17th-century tailor from the Strand named Robert Baker who sold piccadills—stiff ruffled collars all the rage in courtly circles—and built a house with the proceeds. Snobs dubbed his new-money mansion Piccadilly Hall, and the name stuck. Pride of place in the circus—a circular junction until the construction of Shaftesbury Avenue in 1886—belongs to the statue universally referred to as Eros, dating to 1893 (although even most Londoners don't know that it is, in reality, a representation of Eros's brother Anteros, the Greek God of requited love). The other instantly recognizable feature of Piccadilly Circus is the enormous bank of lit-up billboards on the north side; if you're passing at night, frame them behind the Tube entrance sign on the corner of Regent Street for a classic photograph. ✉ *St. James's* Ⓜ *Piccadilly Circus.*

The Queen's Gallery

MUSEUM | Technically speaking, the sovereign doesn't "own" the rare and exquisite works of art in the Royal Collection: she merely holds them in trust for the nation—and what a collection it is. Only a selection is on view at any one time, presented in themed exhibitions. Let the excellent (and free) audio guide take you through the elegant galleries filled with some of the world's greatest artworks.

A rough timeline of the major royal collectors starts with Charles I (who also commissioned Rubens to paint the Banqueting House ceiling). An avid art enthusiast, Charles established the basis of the Royal Collection, purchasing works by Raphael, Titian, Caravaggio, and Dürer. During the Civil War and in the aftermath of Charles's execution, many masterpieces were sold abroad and subsequently repatriated by Charles II. George III, who bought Buckingham House and converted it into a palace, scooped up a notable collection of Venetian (including Canaletto), Renaissance (Bellini and Raphael), and Dutch (Vermeer) art, and a large number of baroque drawings, in addition to patronizing English contemporary artists such as Gainsborough and Beechey. The Prince Regent, later George IV, had a particularly good eye for Rembrandt, equestrian works by Stubbs, and lavish portraits by Lawrence. Queen Victoria had a penchant for Landseer animals and landscapes, and Frith's contemporary scenes. Later, Edward VII indulged Queen Alexandra's love of Fabergé, and many royal tours around the empire produced gifts of gorgeous caliber, such as the Cullinan diamond from South Africa and an emerald-studded belt from India. Tickets are valid for one year from the date of entry. ✉ *Buckingham Palace, Buckingham Palace Rd., St. James's* ☎ *030/3123–7300* 🌐 *www.royalcollection.org.uk* 🎫 *From £14* Ⓜ *Victoria, St. James's Park, Green Park.*

Royal Mews

MUSEUM | **FAMILY** | Fairy-tale gold-and-glass coaches and sleek Rolls-Royce state cars emanate from the Royal Mews, next door to the Queen's Gallery. Designed by John Nash, the Mews serves as the headquarters for Her Majesty's travel department (so beware of closures for state visits), complete with the Queen's own special breed of horses, ridden by wigged postilions decked in red-and-gold regalia. Between the stables and the riding school arena are exhibits of polished saddlery and riding tack. The highlight of the Mews is the splendid Gold State Coach, a piece of art on wheels, with its sculpted tritons and sea gods. There are activities for children, and free guided tours are available April through October (daily at 10:15, then hourly 11–4). ✉ *Buckingham Palace, Buckingham Palace Rd., St. James's* ☎ *030/3123–7300* 🌐 *www.royalcollection.org.uk* 🎫 *From £12* ⏲ *Closed Dec. and Jan.* Ⓜ *Victoria, St. James's Park.*

Spencer House

HOUSE | Ancestral abode of the Spencers—Princess Diana's family—this is perhaps the finest extant example of an elegant 18th-century London town house. Reflecting his passion for the Grand Tour and classical antiquities, the first Earl Spencer commissioned architect John Vardy to adapt designs from ancient Rome for a magnificent private palace. Vardy was responsible for the exteriors, including the gorgeous west-facing Palladian facade, its pediment adorned with classical statues, and the ground-floor interiors, notably the lavish Palm Room, with its spectacular screen of columns covered in gilded carvings that resemble gold palm trees. The lavish style was meant not only to attest to Spencer's power and wealth but also to celebrate his marriage, a love match then rare in aristocratic circles (the palms are a symbol of marital fertility). Midway through construction—the house was built between 1756 and 1766—Spencer changed architects and hired James "Athenian" Stuart, whose designs were based on a classical Greek aesthetic, to decorate the gilded State Rooms on the first floor. These include the Painted Room, the first completely neoclassical room in Europe. Since the 1940s, the house has been leased by the Spencers to a succession of wealthy residents. Entry is by tours only, which occur on Sundays only. ■ **TIP→ Note that children under 10 are not allowed inside.** ✉ *27 St. James's Pl., St. James's* ☎ *020/7514–1958* 🌐 *www.spencerhouse.co.uk* 🎫 *£15* ⏲ *Closed Mon.–Sat. and Aug.* Ⓜ *Green Park.*

St. James's Church

RELIGIOUS SITE | Bombed by the German Luftwaffe in 1940 and not restored until 1954, this was one of the last of Sir Christopher Wren's London churches—and his favorite. Completed in 1684, it contains one of the finest works by the master carver Grinling Gibbons (1648–1721): an ornate limewood *reredos* (the screen behind the altar). The church is a lively place, with all manner of lectures and concerts (some are free). A café occupies a fine location right alongside the church, while a small sedate garden is tucked away at the rear. The market out front is full of surprises; come Monday and Tuesday for food stalls, and Wednesday through Saturday for arts and crafts. ✉ *197 Piccadilly, St. James's* ☎ *020/7734–4511* 🌐 *www.sjp.org.uk* 🎫 *Free* Ⓜ *Piccadilly Circus, Green Park.*

St. James's Palace

CASTLE/PALACE | Commissioned by Henry VIII, this Tudor brick palace was the residence of kings and queens for more than 300 years; indeed, while all monarchs have actually lived at Buckingham Palace since Queen Victoria's day, it is still one of the official residences of the Royal Family. (This is why foreign ambassadors are received by the "Court of St. James.") Today it contains various royal apartments and offices, including the working office of Prince Charles. The palace is not open to the public, but the surprisingly low-key Tudor exterior is well worth the short detour from the Mall. Friary Court out front is a splendid setting for Trooping the Colour, part of the Queen's official birthday celebrations. Everyone loves to take a snapshot of the scarlet-coated guardsman standing sentry outside the imposing Tudor gateway. Note that the Changing the Guard ceremony at

St. James's Palace occurs only on days when the guard at Buckingham Palace is changed. ✉ *Friary Ct., St. James's* Ⓜ *Green Park.*

★ St. James's Park

CITY PARK | FAMILY | There is a story that, many years ago, a royal once inquired of a courtier how much it would cost to close St. James's Park to the public. "Only your crown, ma'am," came the reply. Bordered by three palaces—Buckingham, St. James's, and the governmental complex of the Palace of Westminster—this is one of London's loveliest public parks. It's also the oldest; the former marshland was acquired by Henry VIII in 1532 as a nursery for his deer. Later, James I drained the land and installed an aviary, which gave Birdcage Walk its name, and a zoo (complete with crocodiles, camels, and an elephant). When Charles II returned from exile in France, where he had been hugely impressed by the splendor of the gardens at the Palace of Versailles, he transformed the park into formal gardens, with avenues, fruit orchards, and a canal. Lawns were grazed by goats, sheep, and deer, and in the 18th century the park became a different kind of hunting ground, for wealthy lotharios looking to pick up nighttime escorts. A century later, John Nash redesigned the landscape in a more naturalistic, romantic style, and if you gaze down the lake toward Buckingham Palace, you could easily believe yourself to be on a country estate.

A large population of waterfowl—including pelicans, geese, ducks, and swans (which belong to the Queen)—breed on and around Duck Island at the east end of the lake. The pelicans are fed at 2:30 daily. From March to October, the deck chairs (charge levied) come out, crammed with office workers at midday, eating lunch while being serenaded by music from the bandstands. One of the best times to stroll the leafy walkways is after dark, with Westminster Abbey and the Houses of Parliament rising above the floodlit lake. ✉ *The Mall or Horse Guards approach or Birdcage Walk, St. James's* 🌐 *www.royalparks.org.uk* Ⓜ *St. James's Park, Westminster.*

St. James's Square

PLAZA | One of London's oldest squares, St. James's was first laid out in the 1660s. It soon became the capital's most fashionable address; by 1720, it was home to 14 dukes and earls. These days you're more likely to find it populated with office workers eating their lunches under the shade of its leafy old trees on a warm summer's day, but it still has some prestigious residents. Most famous among them is the **London Library** at No. 14, one of the several 18th-century residences spared by World War II bombs. Founded by Thomas Carlyle, it contains a million or so volumes, making it the world's largest independent lending library, and is also considered the best private humanities library in the land. Nonmembers can take a free evening tour of the library on alternate Mondays at 6 pm, although reservations must be made in advance. ✉ *St. James's* Ⓜ *Piccadilly Circus.*

Restaurants

It's no surprise, given the illustrious royal residents of this neighborhood, that so many of its restaurants feel fit for a future king. This is where you'll find London's top-end eateries—dining experiences that are geared toward a well-heeled, deep-pocketed clientele. You should make reservations well in advance to dine at any of these restaurants for dinner (or reserve a table for the earlier or later parts of the evening, when demand is lower). Keep in mind that no-shows mean last-minute tables often crop up, and having lunch here can be a great money-saving strategy. Dress codes are usually stricter than elsewhere in town; if in doubt, men should opt for a jacket and tie.

Aquavit

$$$ | **SCANDINAVIAN** | **FAMILY** | There's a *hygge*-style glow at this ritzy New Nordic emporium off Piccadilly Circus. Swedish designer Martin Brudnizki pulls out all the best Scandinavian design stops, while a hip, upscale crowd dish over the pickled Matjes herring from the small-jars *smörgåsbord* and pair Swedish meatballs with mash and lingonberries. **Known for:** nifty Nordic smorgasbord starters; soaring Scandinavian design showcase; sea bass with creamy Sandefjord sauce. *$ Average main: £27 ✉ St. James's Market, 1 Carlton St., Piccadilly Circus ☎ 020/7024–9848 🌐 www.aquavitrestaurants.com ⏲ No dinner Sun. Ⓜ Piccadilly Circus.*

45 Jermyn St

$$$ | **BRASSERIE** | **FAMILY** | A sophisticated crowd enjoys the clubhouse vibe at this classic brasserie at the back of the Queen's grocer Fortnum & Mason. An old-school trolley trundles up table-side to serve Siberian Sturgeon caviar with scrambled eggs, baked new potatoes, and blinis, while creamy beef Stroganoff and whole duck with elderberry sauce gets the full table-side *flambé* treatment. **Known for:** unique caviar trolley; glamorous decor; collection of boozy ice-cream floats. *$ Average main: £28 ✉ 45 Jermyn St., St. James's ☎ 020/7205–4545 🌐 www.45jermynst.com Ⓜ Green Park.*

Le Caprice

$$$ | **MODERN EUROPEAN** | **FAMILY** | Celebrity hot spot Le Caprice commands the deepest loyalty of any restaurant in London. It must be the 40-odd-year history of famous diners (think Liz Taylor, Joan Collins, Lady Di, and Victoria Beckham), the pitch-perfect service, and the long-standing menu that sits somewhere between Euro peasant and trendy fashion plate. **Known for:** celebrity sightings galore; classic fish-and-chips with minted pea puree; live jazz on Sunday night. *$ Average main: £26 ✉ Arlington House, 20 Arlington St., St. James's ☎ 020/7629–2239 🌐 www.le-caprice.co.uk Ⓜ Green Park.*

The Ritz Restaurant

$$$$ | **BRITISH** | **FAMILY** | London's most opulent dining salon here at the Ritz would impress even Marie Antoinette with its sumptuous Gilded Age Rocco Revival trompe-l'oeil frescoes, tasseled silk drapery, and towering marble columns. Sit at the late Margaret Thatcher's favorite seat overlooking Green Park (Table 1) and luxuriate in unreconstructed British haute cuisine such as Bresse chicken with black Périgord truffles or beef Wellington carved table-side. **Known for:** luxurious dining made for the British elite; possibly London's best beef Wellington; legendary traditional Afternoon Tea in the Palm Court. *$ Average main: £47 ✉ The Ritz, 150 Piccadilly, St. James's ☎ 020/7493–8181 🌐 www.theritzlondon.com 👔 Jacket and tie Ⓜ Green Park.*

Rochelle Canteen at the Institute of Contemporary Arts

$$ | **BRITISH** | Foodies, fashionistas, and art scene insiders flock to the hearty, low-key Modern British fare at the Institute of Contemporary Arts, one of the city's biggest art and cultural centers. In the uncluttered, all-white space, opt for the slab of braised ox tongue with a single broomstick carrot, or the rustic slow-poached chicken with grilled leeks and a punchy green sauce. **Known for:** pared-back Modern British dishes; relaxed arty environment; suet-rich rabbit and smoked bacon pie. *$ Average main: £17 ✉ The Institute of Contemporary Arts, 12 Carlton House Terr., St. James's ☎ 020/7930–3647 🌐 www.ica.art/rochelle-canteen ⏲ Closed Mon. Ⓜ Piccadilly Circus, Charring Cross.*

Wiltons

$$$$ | **BRITISH** | Lords, ladies, and other assorted aristocrats blow the family bank at this Edwardian bastion of traditional English fine dining on Jermyn Street (the

place first opened near the Haymarket as a shellfish stall in 1742). Posh patrons tend to order half a dozen oysters, followed by grilled Dover sole, Blythburgh pork from the carving trolley, or fabulous native game, such as roast partridge, grouse, or teal. **Known for:** traditional English dining focused on shellfish and game; waiter service that would put Jeeves to shame; Bordeaux-heavy wine menu. *Average main: £38* *55 Jermyn St., St. James's* *020/7629–9955* *www.wiltons.co.uk* *Closed Sun. and bank holidays. No lunch Sat.* *Jacket required* *Green Park.*

The Wolseley

$$$ | AUSTRIAN | FAMILY | A glitzy procession of famous faces, media moguls, and hedge-funders comes for the spectacle, swish service, and soaring elegance at this bustling Viennese-style grand café on Piccadilly. Located in a former Wolseley Motors luxury-car showroom, this brasserie begins its long decadent days with breakfast at 7 am (8 am at weekends) and serves Dual Monarchy delights until 11:30 pm. **Known for:** old-country Austrian and Hungarian delights; Afternoon Tea with a Viennese twist; classic grand café ambience. *Average main: £25* *160 Piccadilly, St. James's* *020/7499–6996* *www.thewolseley.com* *Green Park.*

Hotels

Some of the best, most discreet, and (unsurprisingly) most expensive hotels in London can be found in St. James's. As with restaurants in this area, think traditional, service-oriented establishments with a timeless feel and plenty of luxurious touches.

The Cavendish

$$$ | HOTEL | Located next door to Fortnum and Mason (one of the most luxurious department stores in the world), it seems appropriate that the Cavendish comes with a touch of Gilded Age history, a whiff of historical scandal, and a pleasant air of joie de vivre. **Pros:** sophisticated yet relaxed; great service; unbeatable location. **Cons:** guest rooms are small; some street noise; rooms near the elevator can be particularly noisy. *Rooms from: £260* *81 Jermyn St., St. James's* *020/7930–2111* *www.thecavendish-london.co.uk* *230 rooms* *Free breakfast* *Piccadilly.*

Dukes Hotel

$$$$ | HOTEL | At this small exclusive hotel in a discreet cul-de-sac, ample natural light brightens the classically elegant rooms. **Pros:** famous martini bar; peaceful setting in a central location; excellent restaurant. **Cons:** maybe a bit too quiet for some; price is still rather high for what's available; the price of breakfast is steep. *Rooms from: £643* *35 St. James's Pl., St. James's* *020/7941–4840, 800/381–4702 in U.S.* *www.dukeshotel.com* *87 rooms* *No meals* *Green Park.*

The Ritz

$$$$ | HOTEL | If you're wondering if the *Downton Abbey*–style world of the old British upper class still exists, look no further than here; the Ritz is as synonymous with London's high society and decadence today as it was when it opened in 1906. **Pros:** historic luxury hotel; service at every turn; iconic restaurant and bar. **Cons:** sometimes snooty service; tediously old-fashioned dress code; located on a congested road. *Rooms from: £555* *150 Piccadilly, St. James's* *020/7493–8181* *www.theritzlondon.com* *136 rooms* *No meals* *Piccadilly Circus.*

★ **The Stafford London**

$$$$ | HOTEL | This is a rare find: a posh hotel that's equal parts elegance and friendliness, and located in one of the few peaceful spots in the area, down a small lane behind Piccadilly. **Pros:** great staff; home to one of London's original "American Bars"; quiet location. **Cons:** traditional style of majority of the rooms may not be to all tastes; perks in the more expensive rooms could be more generous (free airport transfer, but one-way only; free clothes pressing, but only one item per day); some rooms can feel small. *Rooms from: £450* ✉ *16–18 St. James's Pl., St. James's* ☎ *020/7493–0111* 🌐 *www.thestaffordlondon.com* *107 rooms* *No meals* Ⓜ *Green Park.*

Nightlife

BARS

★ American Bar

BARS/PUBS | FAMILY | Festooned with a chin-dropping array of old club ties, vintage signed celebrity photographs, sporting mementos, model airplanes, and baseball caps, this sensational hotel cocktail bar has superb martinis and Manhattans. The name dates from the 1930s, when hotel bars in London started to cater to growing numbers of Americans crossing the Atlantic in ocean liners. The collection of paraphernalia was started in the 1970s when a customer left a small carved wooden eagle. ✉ *The Stafford, 16–18 St. James's Pl., St. James's* ☎ *020/7493–0111* 🌐 *www.thestaffordlondon.com* Ⓜ *Green Park.*

Performing Arts

Institute of Contemporary Arts (*ICA*)

ARTS VENUE | You would never suspect that behind the stately white John Nash–designed stucco facade in the heart of Establishment London, you'll find a champion of the avant-garde. Since 1947, the ICA has been pushing boundaries in visual arts, performance, theater, dance, and music. There are two movie theaters, a performance theater, three galleries, a high-brow bookstore, a reading room, a restaurant run by top chef Margot Henderson, and a café/bar. ✉ *The Mall, St. James's* ☎ *020/7930–3647* 🌐 *www.ica.org.uk* *Exhibitions £3, cinema tickets from £8* Ⓜ *Charing Cross, Piccadilly Circus.*

White Cube

MUSEUM | The English role in the exploding contemporary art scene has been major, thanks in good portion to Jay Joplin's influential gallery, which has regularly moved around London since 1993. This striking modern concrete structure was the first freestanding building to be built in the area for 30 years when it opened in 2006. It is home base for an array of British artists who have won the Turner Prize, including Damien Hirst, Tracey Emin, and Antony Gormley. ✉ *25–26 Mason's Yard, St. James's* ☎ *020/7930–5373* 🌐 *www.whitecube.com* *Free* *Closed Sun. and Mon.* Ⓜ *Green Park, Piccadilly Circus.*

Shopping

ACCESSORIES

★ Lock & Co. Hatters

SPECIALTY STORES | Need a silk top hat, a flat-weave Panama, or a traditional tweed flat cap? Or, for ladies, an occasion hat? James Lock of St. James's has been providing hats from this wood-paneled shop since 1676 for customers ranging from Admiral Lord Nelson, Oscar Wilde, and Frank Sinatra to, more recently, Robert Downey Jr., Guy Ritchie, and Kate Middleton, as well as trendsetting musicians and models. ✉ *6 St. James's St., St. James's* ☎ *020/7930–8874* 🌐 *www.lockhatters.co.uk* *Closed Sun.* Ⓜ *Green Park.*

★ Swaine Adeney Brigg

SPECIALTY STORES | Providing practical supplies for country pursuits since 1750, Swaine Adeney Brigg carries beautifully crafted umbrellas, walking sticks, and hip flasks, or ingenious combinations, such as the umbrella with a slim tipple-holding flask secreted inside the stem. The same level of quality and craftsmanship applies to the store's leather goods, which include attaché cases (you can buy the "Q Branch" model that James Bond carried in *From Russia with Love*) and wallets. You'll find scarves, caps, and the

Herbert Johnson "Poet Hat," the iconic headgear (stocked since 1890) worn by Harrison Ford in every Indiana Jones film. ✉ *7 Piccadilly Arcade, St. James's* ☎ *020/7409–7277* 🌐 *www.swaineadeney-brigg.com* ⏲ *Closed Sun.* Ⓜ *Green Park.*

ANTIQUES AND COLLECTIBLES

The Armoury of St. James's

ANTIQUES/COLLECTIBLES | Besides fine toy soldiers in lead or tin representing conflicts ranging from the Crusades through World War II with prices starting at £15 and going into four figures, the shop has regimental brooches and drums, historic orders and medals, royal memorabilia, and military antiques. ✉ *17 Piccadilly Arcade, St. James's* ☎ *020/7493–5082* 🌐 *www.armoury.co.uk* ⏲ *Closed Sun.* Ⓜ *Piccadilly Circus.*

BEAUTY

Floris

PERFUME/COSMETICS | What did Queen Victoria, Mary Shelley, and Marilyn Monroe have in common? They all used products from Floris, one of the most beautiful shops in London, with gleaming glass-and-Spanish-mahogany showcases salvaged from the Great Exhibition of 1851. In addition to scents for both men and women (including the current queen), Floris has been making its own shaving products—plus combs, brushes, and fragrances—since 1730 (and is still owned by the same family), reflecting its origins as a barbershop. Other gift possibilities include a famous rose-scented mouthwash and beautifully packaged soaps and bath essences. ✉ *89 Jermyn St., St. James's* ☎ *0330/134–0180* 🌐 *www.florislondon.com* Ⓜ *Piccadilly Circus, Green Park.*

BOOKS

★ Hatchards

BOOKS/STATIONERY | This is the United Kingdom's oldest bookshop, open since 1797 and beloved by writers themselves—customers have included Oscar Wilde, Rudyard Kipling, and Lord Byron. Despite its wood-paneled, "gentleman's library" atmosphere and eclectic selection of books, Hatchards is now owned by the large Waterstone's chain. Nevertheless, the shop still retains its period charm, aided by the staff's old-fashioned helpfulness and expertise. Look for the substantial number of books signed by notable contemporary authors on the well-stocked shelves. There's another branch in the St. Pancras International train station. ✉ *187 Piccadilly, St. James's* ☎ *020/7439–9921* 🌐 *www.hatchards.co.uk* Ⓜ *Piccadilly Circus.*

CLOTHING

Dover Street Market

CLOTHING | With its creative displays and eclectic, well-chosen mix of merchandise, this four-floor emporium is as much art installation as store. The merchandise and its configuration change every six months, so you never know what you will find, which is half the fun. The creation of Comme des Garçons' Rei Kawakubo, Dover Street Market showcases all of the label's collections for men and women alongside a changing roster of other ultrafashionable designers, including Gucci, Raf Simons, Balenciaga, Ambush, Loewe, Wales Bonner, and Molly Goddard, all of whom have their own customized miniboutiques—plus sneaker and denim collaborations, eyeglass frames, and jewelry. An outpost of the Rose Bakery on the top floor makes for a good break. ✉ *18–22 Haymarket, St. James's* ☎ *020/7518–0680* 🌐 *london.doverstreetmarket.com* Ⓜ *Piccadilly Circus.*

Turnbull & Asser

CLOTHING | The Jermyn Street store sells luxurious jackets, cashmere sweaters, suits, ties, pajamas, ready-to-wear shirts, and accessories perfect for the billionaire who has everything. The brand is best known for its superb custom-made shirts—worn by Prince Charles and every James Bond to appear in film, to name a few. These can be ordered at the nearby Bury Street or Davies Street branches, which are devoted to bespoke wear.

At least 18 separate measurements are taken, and the cloth, woven to the company's specifications, comes in 1,000 different patterns—the cottons feel as good as silk. The first order must be for a minimum of four shirts, which start at £275 each. ✉ *71–72 Jermyn St., St. James's* ☎ *020/7808–3000* 🌐 *www.turnbullandasser.co.uk* ⏲ *Closed Sun.* Ⓜ *Green Park.*

FOOD

★ Berry Bros. & Rudd

WINE/SPIRITS | Nothing matches Berry Bros. & Rudd for rare offerings and a unique shopping experience. A family-run wine business since 1698 (Lord Byron was a customer), BBR stores more than 4,000 vintage bottles and casks in vaulted cellars that are more than 300 years old. The in-house wine school offers educational tasting sessions, while the dedicated spirits room also has an excellent selection of whiskeys, cognacs, rums, and more. The shop has a quirky charm, and the staff are extremely knowledgeable—and not snooty if you're on a budget. ✉ *63 Pall Mall, St. James's* ☎ *800/280–2440* 🌐 *www.bbr.com* ⏲ *Closed Sun.* Ⓜ *Green Park.*

★ Fortnum & Mason

DEPARTMENT STORES | Although F&M is jokingly known as "the Queen's grocer" and the impeccably mannered staff still wear traditional tailcoats, its celebrated food hall stocks gifts for all budgets, including irresistibly packaged luxury foods stamped with the gold "By Appointment" crest for under £5. Try the teas, preserves (including the unusual rose-petal jelly), condiments, or Gentleman's Relish (anchovy paste). The store's famous hampers are always a welcome gift. The gleaming food hall spans two floors and incorporates a sleek wine bar, with the rest of the store devoted to upscale housewares, men's and women's accessories and toiletries, a dedicated candle room, and a jewelry department featuring exclusive designs by breakthrough talent. If you start to flag, take a break in the tea salon, the Gallery café offering tastes of the food hall, the contemporary 45 Jermyn St. restaurant (the three-course set menu is good value), or an indulgent ice-cream parlor, where you can find decadent treats like a banana split or a less-traditional gin-and-tonic float. Gentlemen also can kick back at the traditional barbershop on the fourth floor. There's another branch at St. Pancras International train station. ✉ *181 Piccadilly, St. James's* ☎ *020/7734–8040* 🌐 *www.fortnumandmason.com* Ⓜ *Green Park, Piccadilly Circus.*

Paxton & Whitfield

FOOD/CANDY | In business for more than 200 years, this venerable and aromatic London shop stocks hundreds of the world's greatest artisanal cheeses, particularly British and French varieties (a homesick General de Gaulle shopped here during World War II). The cheeses are laid on straw on refrigerated shelves, with tasting samples set out on a marble-top counter. You can pick up some ham, pâté, condiments, preserves, wine, or port, as well as cheese-related accessories like boards or knives. There's another branch in Chelsea. ✉ *93 Jermyn St., St. James's* ☎ *020/7930–0259* 🌐 *www.paxtonandwhitfield.co.uk* Ⓜ *Piccadilly Circus, Green Park.*

JEWELRY

Wartski

ANTIQUES/COLLECTIBLES | This family-run specialist in antique jewelry and precious objects boosted its fortunes when the founder's canny son-in-law snapped up confiscated treasures from the Bolshevik government after the Russian Revolution of 1917. As a result, this is the place to come if you're looking for a miniature carved Fabergé Easter Bunny, a 1920s Cartier stickpin, art nouveau necklace by Lalique, or 17th-century gold signet ring. Even if you're not in the market to buy but are just interested in the history of jewelry, it's worth a visit. You can also order handmade wedding rings—Wartski created the engagement ring Prince William gave Kate Middleton. ✉ *60 St. James's St., St. James's* ☎ *0207/493–1141* 🌐 *www.wartski.com* 🕓 *Closed weekends* Ⓜ *Piccadilly.*

SHOES

Loake Shoemakers

SHOES/LUGGAGE/LEATHER GOODS | Long established in England's Midlands and a provider of boots to the British armed forces in both world wars, this family-run firm specializes in classic handcrafted men's shoes. Whether you're after brogues, loafers, or deck shoes, the staff will take the time to ensure you have the right fit. In terms of quality and service, Loake represents real value for money, though they definitely aren't inexpensive. There are other branches in London: one in The City, on Bow Lane and Lime Street, and one by Old Spitalfields Market.. ✉ *39C Jermyn St., St. James's* ☎ *020/7734–8643* 🌐 *www.loake.co.uk* Ⓜ *Piccadilly.*

SPECIALTY STORES

Geo F. Trumper

SPECIALTY STORES | If you don't have the time for an old-fashioned hot-towel shave at this "traditional gentlemen's barbers" established in 1875, pick up a razor, a shaving brush, or other men's grooming accessories to take home for yourself or as a gift. The Extract of Limes Skin Food is a popular, zingy aftershave, and the Coconut Oil Hard Shaving Soap, which comes in a hand-turned wooden bowl, is a classic. There is also a store at 9 Curzon Street in Mayfair. ✉ *1 Duke of York St., St. James's* ☎ *020/7734–6553* 🌐 *www.trumpers.com* 🕓 *Closed Sun.* Ⓜ *Piccadilly Circus.*

Chapter 4

MAYFAIR AND MARYLEBONE

Updated by
Toby Orton

Sights
★★★★☆

Restaurants
★★★★☆

Hotels
★★★★☆

Shopping
★★★★☆

Nightlife
★☆☆☆☆

MAYFAIR AND MARYLEBONE SNAPSHOT

TOP REASONS TO GO

The Duke of Wellington's home: The Iron Duke's Apsley House is filled with splendid salons lined with grand Old Master paintings.

Fashion galore: There's great shopping aplenty on Bond and Mount streets, where the likes of McQueen and McCartney will keep your credit card occupied, but don't forget stylish, gigantic Selfridges.

London's most charming shopping arcade: Built for Lord Cavendish in 1819, the beautiful Burlington Arcade is right out of a Victorian daguerreotype.

The Wallace Collection: Savor room after room of magnificent furniture, porcelain, silver, and top Old Master paintings, in the former residence of the marquesses of Hertford.

Claridge's: Afternoon tea at this sumptuous art deco gem is the perfect end to a shopping spree in Mayfair.

GETTING THERE

Three Tube stations on the Central Line are handy for reaching these neighborhoods: Marble Arch, Bond Street (also on the Jubilee Line), and Oxford Circus (also on the Victoria and Bakerloo lines).

You can also take the Piccadilly or Bakerloo Line to the Piccadilly Circus Tube Station, the Piccadilly Line to the Hyde Park Corner Station, or the Piccadilly, Victoria, or Jubilee Line to the Green Park Station.

The best buses are the 22, which takes in Green Park, Berkeley Square, and New Bond Street, and the 9—London's oldest existing bus route—which runs along Piccadilly.

FEELING PECKISH?

■ **Crussh** This successful chain serves up delicious juices and smoothies, as well as sandwiches, soups, and wraps. ✉ *1 Curzon St., Mayfair* ☎ *020/7629–2554* 🌐 *www.crussh.com* ⏲ *Closed weekends* Ⓜ *Green Park.*

■ **Richoux** This has been an affordable refuge from busy Piccadilly for more than a century. Simple but well-executed French bistro food and assorted classic British dishes are served all day, as is scrumptious afternoon tea. ✉ *172 Piccadilly, Mayfair* ☎ *020/7493–2204* 🌐 *www.richoux.co.uk* Ⓜ *Green Park, Piccadilly Circus.*

MAKING THE MOST OF YOUR TIME

■ Set aside at least a day to experience Mayfair and Marylebone. Leave enough time for shopping and also to wander casually through the streets and squares. The only areas to avoid are the Tube stations at rush hour, and Oxford Street if you don't like crowds. At all costs, stay away from Oxford Circus around 5 pm, when the commuter rush can, at times, resemble an East African wildebeest migration—but without the charm. The area becomes quiet at night, so plan to party elsewhere.

Mayfair forms the core of London's West End, the city's most stylish central area. This neighborhood oozes class and old-school style. The sense of being in one of the world's most wealthy and powerful cities is palpable as you wander along its grand and graceful streets. Scoot across the district's one exception to all this elegance—Oxford Street—and you'll discover the pleasant thoroughfares of Marylebone, the most central of London's many "villages."

Mayfair

Ultraritzy Mayfair, lined with beautiful 18th-century mansions (along with Edwardian apartment buildings made of deep-red brick), is the address of choice for many of London's wealthiest residents—note the number of Rolls-Royces, Bentleys, and Jaguars on the streets. Even the delivery vans all seem to bear some royal coat of arms, advertising that they've been purveyors of fine goods for as long as anyone can remember.

The district can't claim to be stuffed with must-sees, but that is part of its appeal. There is no shortage of history and gorgeous architecture; the streets here are custom-built for window-shopping, expansive strolling, and getting a peek into the lifestyles of London's rich and famous, past and present. Mayfair is primarily residential, so its homes are off-limits except for one satisfyingly grand example: **Apsley House,** the Duke of Wellington's home, built by Robert Adam in 1771, and once known as No. 1, London; the nearby **Wellington Arch** also commemorates the great hero.

Despite being bordered by four of the busiest streets in London—the busy budget-shopping mecca Oxford Street (to the north), the major traffic artery Park Lane (to the west), and the bustling Regent Street and Piccadilly (to the east and south, respectively)—Mayfair itself is remarkably traffic-free and a delight to explore. Starting at **Selfridges,** on Oxford Street, a southward stroll will take you through quiet streets lined with Georgian town houses (the area was largely developed in the 17th and 18th centuries). From there, with a bit of artful navigating, you can reach four pleasant patches of green: **Grosvenor Square, Berkeley Square, Hanover Square,** with

Each June for the past 240 years, the iconic Royal Academy of Arts has put on its Summer Exhibition, a huge draw for art-loving visitors and Londoners alike.

its splendid **St. George's Church** where Handel worshipped, and the quiet **St. George's Gardens,** bounded by a maze of streets and mews. Some of London's most exclusive shopping destinations are here, including **Mount Street, Bruton Street, Savile Row,** and the **Burlington Arcade.** The **Royal Academy of Arts** is at the southern fringe of Mayfair on Piccadilly, beyond which begins the more sedate St. James's.

Sights

★ Apsley House

HOUSE | Apsley House was built by Robert Adam in the 1770s and was bought by the Duke of Wellington two years after his famous victory over Napoléon at the Battle of Waterloo in 1815. Long known simply as No. 1, London, on account of its being the first mansion at the old tollgate from Knightsbridge village, the Duke's old regency abode continues to look quite grand. Victory over the French made Wellington the greatest soldier and statesman in the land. The so-called Iron Duke lived here from 1817 until his death in 1852, and, although the 7th Duke of Wellington gave the house to the nation, the family retained some residential rights. As you'd expect, the mansion has many uniforms and weapons on display, but it also houses a celebrated art collection, the bulk of which was once owned by Joseph Bonaparte, onetime King of Spain and older brother of Napoléon. With works by Brueghel, Van Dyck, and Rubens, as well as the Spanish masters Velázquez and Murillo (note the former's famous portrait of Pope Innocent X), the collection also includes a Goya portrait of the duke himself on horseback. An 11-foot-tall statue of a nude (fig-leafed) Napoléon looms over you as you approach the grand central staircase. The statue was taken from the Louvre and given as a gift to Wellington from the grateful British government in 1816. ✉ *149 Piccadilly, Hyde Park Corner, Mayfair* ☎ *0370/333–1181* 🌐 *www.english-heritage.org.uk* 🎫 *From £11* 🕑 *Closed Mon. and Tues.* Ⓜ *Hyde Park Corner.*

Bond Street

NEIGHBORHOOD | This world-class shopping haunt is divided into northern "New" (1710) and southern "Old" (1690) halves. You can spot the juncture by a bronzed bench on which Franklin D. Roosevelt sits companionably next to Winston Churchill. At No. 34–35, on New Bond Street, you'll find **Sotheby's,** the world-famous auction house, as well as upscale retailers like Asprey's, Burberry, Louis Vuitton, and Church's. You'll find even more opportunities to flirt with financial ruin on Old Bond Street, with flagship boutiques of top-end designers like Prada, Gucci, and Yves Saint Laurent; an array of fine jewelers including Tiffany & Co.; and art dealers Richard Green, Richard Nagy, and Trinity Fine Art. **Cork Street,** which parallels the top half of Old Bond Street, is where many top dealers in contemporary art have their galleries. ✉ *Mayfair* 🌐 *www.bondstreet.co.uk* Ⓜ *Bond St., Green Park.*

★ **Burlington Arcade**

NEIGHBORHOOD | With ceilings and lights now restored to how they would have looked when it was built in 1819, Burlington Arcade is the finest of Mayfair's enchanting covered shopping alleys. Originally built for Lord Cavendish, it was meant to stop commoners from flinging garbage into his garden at next-door Burlington House. Top-hatted watchmen called beadles—the world's smallest private police force—still patrol, preserving decorum by preventing you from singing, running, or carrying an open umbrella. The arcade is also the main link between the Royal Academy of Arts and its extended galleries at 6 Burlington Gardens. ✉ *Piccadilly, Mayfair* ☎ *020/7493–1764* 🌐 *www.burlingtonarcade.com* Ⓜ *Green Park, Piccadilly Circus.*

David Zwirner

MUSEUM | This is just one of several influential New York gallerists to open a London space in Mayfair in recent years, a trend that has revitalized an area that's been losing ground to edgier neighborhoods like Bethnal Green. Zwirner's roster contains the likes of Bridget Riley and Jeff Koons, and modern masters such as Piet Mondrian are exhibited in this grand converted town house, too. ✉ *24 Grafton St., Mayfair* ☎ *020/3538–3165* 🌐 *www.davidzwirner.com* 🎫 *Free* 🕐 *Closed Sun.* Ⓜ *Green Park.*

Grosvenor Square

PLAZA | Pronounced "*Grove*-na," this leafy square was laid out in 1721–31 and is as desirable an address today as it was then. Americans have certainly always thought so—from John Adams, the second president, who as ambassador lived at No. 38, to Dwight D. Eisenhower, whose wartime headquarters was at No. 20. The entire west side of the square was home to the U.S. Embassy for more than 50 years until its relocation south of the river. In the square itself stand memorials to Franklin D. Roosevelt and those who died on September 11, 2001. Grosvenor Chapel, completed in 1730 and used by Eisenhower's men during World War II, stands a couple of blocks south of the square on South Audley Street, with the entrance to pretty **St. George's Gardens** to its left. ✉ *Mayfair* 🌐 *www.royalparks.org.uk* Ⓜ *Bond St.*

Handel and Hendrix in London

MUSEUM | This fascinating museum celebrates the lives of not one, but two, musical geniuses: classical composer George Frederick Handel and rock guitar legend Jimi Hendrix. Comprising two adjoining buildings, the bulk of the museum centers on the life and works of Handel who lived at No. 25 for more than 30 years until his death in 1759. In rooms decorated in fine Georgian style, you can linger over original manuscripts and gaze at portraits. Some of the composer's most famous pieces were created here, including the *Messiah* and *Music for the Royal Fireworks.* Fast-forward 200 years or so, and the apartment on the upper floors of No. 23 housed one of rock's great innovators, Jimi Hendrix, for a short

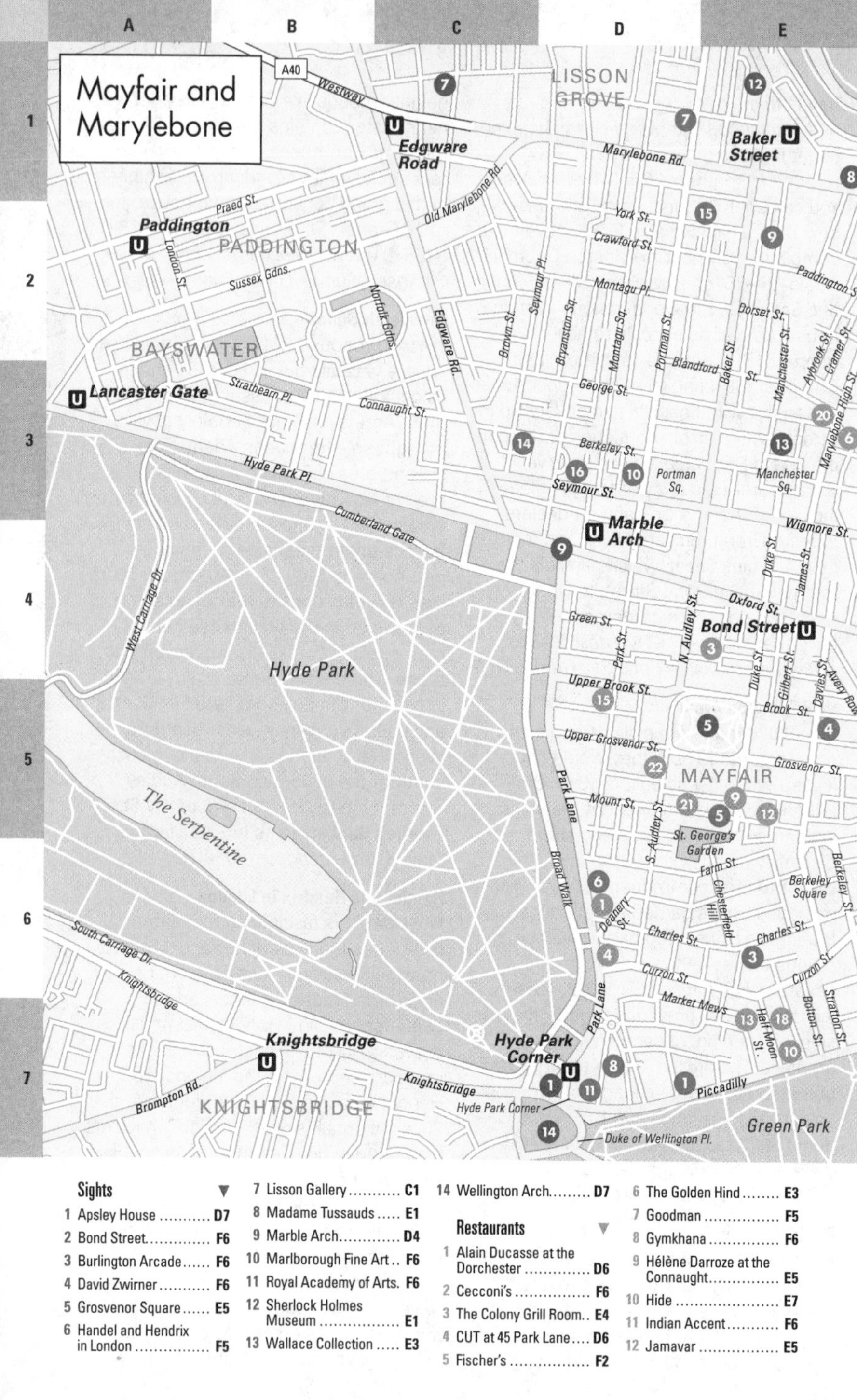
A
B
C
D
E
1
2
3
4
5
6
7
Mayfair and Marylebone
A40
Westway
Edgware Road
LISSON GROVE
Marylebone Rd.
Baker Street
Old Marylebone Rd.
Praed St.
Paddington
PADDINGTON
London St.
Sussex Gdns.
York St.
Crawford St.
Paddington St.
Montagu Pl.
Norfolk Gdns.
Edgware Rd.
Brown St.
Seymour Pl.
Bryanston Sq.
Montagu Sq.
Portman St.
Dorset St.
Blandford St.
Baker St.
Manchester St.
Aybrook St.
Cramer St.
BAYSWATER
Lancaster Gate
Strathearn Pl.
Connaught St.
George St.
Marylebone High St.
Berkeley St.
Portman Sq.
Manchester Sq.
Hyde Park Pl.
Seymour St.
Cumberland Gate
Marble Arch
Wigmore St.
Duke St.
James St.
Oxford St.
West Carriage Dr.
Green St.
Park St.
N. Audley St.
Bond Street
Hyde Park
Upper Brook St.
Duke St.
Gilbert St.
Davies St.
Avery Row
Brook St.
Upper Grosvenor St.
Grosvenor St.
MAYFAIR
Park Lane
Mount St.
The Serpentine
S. Audley St.
St. George's Garden
Broad Walk
Farm St.
Chesterfield Hill
Berkeley Square
Berkeley St.
Deanery St.
Charles St.
South Carriage Dr.
Curzon St.
Knightsbridge
Park Lane
Market Mews
Half Moon St.
Bolton St.
Stratton St.
Knightsbridge
Hyde Park Corner
Brompton Rd.
Knightsbridge
Piccadilly
KNIGHTSBRIDGE
Hyde Park Corner
Green Park
Duke of Wellington Pl.
Sights
1 Apsley House D7
2 Bond Street F6
3 Burlington Arcade F6
4 David Zwirner F6
5 Grosvenor Square E5
6 Handel and Hendrix in London F5
7 Lisson Gallery C1
8 Madame Tussauds E1
9 Marble Arch D4
10 Marlborough Fine Art .. F6
11 Royal Academy of Arts. F6
12 Sherlock Holmes Museum E1
13 Wallace Collection E3
14 Wellington Arch D7
Restaurants
1 Alain Ducasse at the Dorchester D6
2 Cecconi's F6
3 The Colony Grill Room.. E4
4 CUT at 45 Park Lane D6
5 Fischer's F2
6 The Golden Hind E3
7 Goodman F5
8 Gymkhana F6
9 Hélène Darroze at the Connaught E5
10 Hide E7
11 Indian Accent F6
12 Jamavar E5

13 Kitty Fisher's............ E7
14 La Petite Maison........ F5
15 Le Gavroche............ D5
16 Les 110 de Taillevent ... F4
17 No. 5 Social............. F5
18 Ormer Mayfair E7
19 Pollen Street Social F5
20 Roganic................. E3
21 Scott's.................... E5
22 34......................... D5

Hotels ▼

1 Athenaeum Hotel and Apartments.............. D7
2 Brown's Hotel F6
3 Chesterfield Mayfair Hotel............ E6
4 Claridge's E5
5 The Connaught.......... E5
6 The Dorchester D6
7 Dorset Square Hotel.... D1
8 Four Seasons Park Lane................ D7
9 Holmes Hotel............ E2
10 Hyatt Regency London—The Churchill D3
11 InterContinental London Park Lane................ D7
12 The Langham............ G4
13 No. 5 Maddox Street ... F5
14 The Sumner C3
15 22 York Street........... E2
16 Zetter Townhouse Marylebone D3

Marble Arch was originally a gateway to Buckingham Palace before it was moved to the corner of Hyde Park.

but creative period in the late 1960s. The apartment has been lovingly restored, complete with replica furniture, fixtures, and fittings from Hendrix's heyday. ✉ *23–25 Brook St., entrance in Lancashire Court, Mayfair* ☎ *020/7495–1685* 🌐 *www.handelhendrix.org* 🎫 *£10* ⏲ *Closed Sun.* Ⓜ *Bond St.*

Marble Arch

BUILDING | John Nash's 1827 arch, moved here from Buckingham Palace in 1851, stands amid the traffic whirlpool where Bayswater Road segues into Oxford Street, at the top of Park Lane. The arch actually contains three small chambers, which served as a police station until the mid-20th century. Search the sidewalk on the traffic island opposite the movie theater for the stone plaque recalling the Tyburn Tree, an elaborately designed gallows that stood here for 400 years, until 1783. The condemned would be conveyed here in their finest clothes from Newgate Prison in The City, and were expected to affect a casual indifference or face a merciless heckling from the crowds. Towering across the grass from the arch toward Tyburn Way is *Still Water,* a vast patina-green statue of a horse's head by sculptor Nic Fiddian-Green. Cross over (or under) to the northeastern corner of Hyde Park for Speakers' Corner, a parcel of land long-dedicated to the principle of free speech. On Sunday, people of all views—or none at all—come to pontificate, listen, and debate about everything under the sun. ✉ *Park La., Mayfair* Ⓜ *Marble Arch.*

Marlborough Fine Art

MUSEUM | This veteran of the Mayfair art scene has been presenting exhibitions by masters old and new since it was founded in 1946. Great living artists like Paula Rego and Frank Auerbach, plus exhibitions of graphic works from a whole host of starry names, are showcased in the main first floor space, while the contemporary gallery on the second floor puts the spotlight on a younger generation of artists from the U.K. and abroad. ✉ *6 Albermarle St., Mayfair* ☎ *020/7629–5161* 🌐 *www.marlboroughlondon.com* 🎫 *Free*

Closed Sun. and Mon. Green Park, Piccadilly Circus.

★ Royal Academy of Arts

MUSEUM | Burlington House was built in 1664, with later Palladian additions for the 3rd Earl of Burlington in 1720. The piazza in front dates from 1873, when the Renaissance-style buildings around the courtyard were designed by Banks and Barry to house a gaggle of noble scientific societies, including the Royal Society of Chemistry and the Royal Astronomical Society.

The house itself is home to the Royal Academy of Arts and an ambitious redevelopment for the academy's 250th anniversary in 2018 has meant that even more of its 46,000 treasures are now on display. The statue of the academy's first president, Sir Joshua Reynolds, palette in hand, stands prominently in the piazza. Free tours show off part of the collection and the excellent temporary exhibitions. Every June through August, the RA puts on its Summer Exhibition, a huge and eclectic collection of art by living Royal Academicians and many other contemporary artists. *Burlington House, Piccadilly, Mayfair* *020/7300–8000* *www.royalacademy.org.uk* *Free –£18* *Piccadilly Circus, Green Park.*

Wellington Arch

BUILDING | Opposite the Duke of Wellington's mansion, Apsley House, this majestic stone arch surveys the traffic rushing around Hyde Park Corner. Designed by Decimus Burton and completed in 1828, it was created as a grand entrance to the west side of London and echoes the design of that other landmark gate, Marble Arch. Both were triumphal arches commemorating Britain's victory against France in the Napoleonic Wars. Atop the building, the Angel of Peace descends on the *quadriga*, or four-horse chariot of war. Inside the arch, three floors of permanent and temporary exhibits reveal the monument's history. From the balconies at the top of the arch you can peek into the Queen's back garden at across-the-road Buckingham Palace. *Hyde Park Corner, Mayfair* *020/7930–2726* *www.english-heritage.org.uk* *From £6* *Hyde Park Corner.*

Restaurants

Between its grand dame institutions, deluxe steakhouses, and contemporary A-list eateries, Mayfair's restaurant scene is all about fine dining with something to suit all tastes—provided you are willing to pay big for it. With more Michelin stars than any other neighborhood in the city, Mayfair is the epicenter of London dining royalty.

★ Alain Ducasse at the Dorchester

$$$$ | **FRENCH** | One of only three three-Michelin-starred restaurants in the city, Alain Ducasse at the Dorchester achieves the pinnacle of classical French haute cuisine in a surprisingly fun, lively, and unstuffy salon. Diners feast on a blizzard of beautifully choreographed dishes including classic rum baba with Chantilly cream, sliced open and served in a silver domed tureen. **Known for:** impeccable five-star service; surprisingly unstarchy vibe; signature sauté lobster with chicken quenelles. *Average main: £45* *The Dorchester, 53 Park La., Mayfair* *020/7629–8866 for reservations only* *www.alainducasse-dorchester.com* *Closed Sun. and Mon. No lunch Sat.* *Marble Arch, Green Park.*

Cecconi's

$$$ | **MODERN ITALIAN** | Revel with the A-listers in the glamorous buzz at this upscale Italian brasserie wedged between Cork Street, Savile Row, and the Royal Academy of Arts. Perfect for a pit stop during a West End shopping spree or after browsing the nearby Mayfair galleries and auction houses, diners spill out onto pavement tables for breakfast, brunch, and *cicchetti* (Italian tapas), and return later in the day for something more substantial. **Known for:** favorite of nearby Vogue House staff and Sotheby's clientele; popular veal Milanese; all-day jet-setter hangout. *Average main: £29 5A Burlington Gardens, Mayfair 020/7434–1500 www.cecconis.co.uk Green Park, Piccadilly Circus.*

The Colony Grill Room

$$$ | **AMERICAN** | Glide past the parked royal blue Armstrong Siddeley, through the foyer of the five-star Beaumont hotel, and into the swank art deco–inspired dining salon of the Colony Grill Room. Fans of 1920s New York will admire the throwback decor, before digging into throwbacks like the mock turtle soup, clam chowder, and the flambé bananas Foster. **Known for:** evocative American 1920s panache and glamour; bespoke sundae menu; classic buttermilk fried chicken. *Average main: £26 The Beaumont, 8 Balderton St., Brown Hart Gardens, Mayfair 020/7499–9499 www.colonygrillroom.com Marble Arch.*

CUT at 45 Park Lane

$$$$ | **STEAKHOUSE** | Austrian-born star chef Wolfgang Puck amps up the stakes at this ultraexpensive steak house on Park Lane. Set against a luxe backdrop of Damien Hirst artwork and globe lights, carnivores go crazy for the pricey prime cuts from England, Australia, Japan, and the United States. **Known for:** rare Kagoshima Wagyu beef steaks; celebrity chef hot spot; art gallery-like interior. *Average main: £50 45 Park La., Mayfair 020/7493–4545 for reservations only www.dorchestercollection.com Marble Arch, Hyde Park Corner.*

Goodman

$$$$ | **STEAKHOUSE** | This Manhattan-themed, Russian-owned swanky steak house, named after Chicago jazz legend Benny Goodman, has everyone in agreement: these truly are some of the best steaks in town. USDA-certified, 150-day corn-fed, and on-site dry-aged Black Angus T-bones, rib eye, porterhouse, and New York bone-in sirloins compete for taste and tenderness with heavily marbled grass-fed prime cuts from Scotland and the Lake District. **Known for:** truly impressive steaks; whole king crab available on request; long list of classy Coravin-extracted red wines by the glass. *Average main: £40 24–26 Maddox St., Mayfair 020/7499–3776 www.goodmanrestaurants.com Closed Sun. Oxford Circus, Piccadilly Circus.*

★ Gymkhana

$$$ | **MODERN INDIAN** | The last days of the Raj are invoked here at one of London's finest Indian curry emporiums, where top choices include dosas with fennel-rich Chettinad duck or the famed suckling pig vindaloo. Diners admire the whirring ceiling fans, rattan chairs, and other decor inspired by the colonial-era gymkhana sporting clubs of yesteryear. **Known for:** unusual game curries; Indian punches in the basement private dining booths; signature kid goat methi keema. *Average main: £28 42 Albemarle St., Mayfair 020/3011–5900 www.gymkhanalondon.com Closed Sun. Green Park.*

Hélène Darroze at the Connaught

$$$$ | **FRENCH** | The city's wealthy flock to French virtuoso Hélène Darroze's restaurant at the Connaught for her dazzling regional French haute cuisine, served up in a stylish Edwardian wood-paneled dining salon. Taking inspiration from Les Landes in southwestern France, Darroze sallies forth with a procession of magnificent dishes, like Robert Dupérier foie gras with fig and port or Limousin sweetbreads with Jerusalem artichokes. **Known for:** sumptuous dining salon; classy French haute dishes; relatively affordable three-course set lunch. *Average main: £38 The Connaught, Carlos Pl., Mayfair 020/3147–7200 for reservations only www.the-connaught.co.uk Jacket required Green Park.*

Hide

$$$$ | **MODERN BRITISH** | Mayfair is home to more than its share of fussy fine dining restaurants, so Hide is a welcome alternative, charming with experimental dishes that make the new-Nordic, produce-focused modern European menu shine. Look out for art-like dishes strewn with wildflowers on the seasonal eight-course tasting menus served in a fairy tale–like setting. **Known for:** signature coddled hens' eggs served in shell with mushrooms and smoked butter; vast wine collection is the largest of any restaurant in the country; bespoke interiors including a gorgeous spiral oak staircase. *Average main: £39 ✉ 85 Piccadilly, Mayfair ☎ 020/3146–8666 🌐 www.hide.co.uk Ⓜ Green Park.*

Indian Accent

$$$ | **MODERN INDIAN** | The bar for high-end Indian food in London has been raised at this praised New Delhi import. Unusual but homey Indian cuisine is presented in a modern, decidedly non-Indian fashion, from mini-naan stuffed with black pudding to spiced ghee roast lamb served Peking-duck style. **Known for:** mid-century Rajput palace setting; adventurous and experimental Indian fusion cuisine; playful dishes like Bombay minced soya keema with quail eggs. *Average main: £26 ✉ 16 Albemarle St., Mayfair ☎ 020/7629–9802 🌐 www.indianaccent.com/london Ⓜ Green Park.*

Jamavar

$$ | **INDIAN** | There is no finer fish dish in town than the Malai stone bass *tikka* at this upmarket Indian restaurant. The food and spices here are so authentic that it regularly buzzes with Bollywood stars, wealthy Mayfair moguls, and the entire well-heeled Indian diaspora. **Known for:** stunning interior of dark wood, marble, and Indian artwork; unmissable Malai stone bass tikka; glossy, luxurious Indian crowd. *Average main: £25 ✉ 8 Mount St., Mayfair ☎ 020/7499–1800 🌐 www.jamavarrestaurants.com Ⓜ Bond St., Green Park.*

Kitty Fisher's

$$$ | **MODERN BRITISH** | Named after an infamous 18th-century courtesan, Kitty Fisher's is situated in a tiny, creaky Georgian town house in Mayfair's Shepherd Market. Crammed with antique prints, portraits, and silver candelabras, here you can sample some of the finest wood-grill and smokehouse fare around. **Known for:** cozy and candlelit town-house setting; incredible steaks from the grill; high-end showbiz and politico diners. *Average main: £29 ✉ 10 Shepherd Market, Mayfair ☎ 020/3302–1661 🌐 www.kittyfishers.com ⏲ Closed Sun. Ⓜ Green Park.*

La Petite Maison

$$$$ | **FRENCH** | **FAMILY** | With the legend "*Tous Célèbres Ici*" ("All Famous Here") boldly etched on the front doors, the delightful Petite Maison boasts an impressively well-sourced and balanced French Mediterranean, Ligurian, and Provençal menu. Based on the relaxed Riviera style of the original La Petite Maison in Nice, try the soft burrata cheese with sweet Datterini-tomato-and-basil spread, or aromatic baked turbot with artichokes, chorizo, five spices, and white wine sauce. **Known for:** light French Riviera-inspired dining; excellent selection of rosé wines; whole roast black leg chicken. *Average main: £35 ✉ 53–54 Brook's Mews, Mayfair ☎ 020/7495–4774 🌐 www.lpmlondon.co.uk Ⓜ Bond St., Oxford Circus.*

Le Gavroche

$$$$ | **FRENCH** | Masterchef Michel Roux Jr. works the floor in the old-fashioned proprietorial way at this old-school Mayfair basement institution—established by his father and uncle in 1967—which many still rate as the best formal dining in London. Roux's mastery of classical French haute cuisine hypnotizes with signature dishes like foie gras with cinnamon-scented crispy duck pancake or saddle of rabbit with Parmesan cheese. **Known for:** swanky Mayfair basement setting; relatively affordable three-course

set lunch menus; tasty souffle Suissesse. *Average main: £44 43 Upper Brook St., Mayfair 020/7408–0881 www.le-gavroche.co.uk Closed Sun. and Mon. No lunch Sat. Jacket required Bond St., Marble Arch.*

No. 5 Social

$$$ | **MODERN BRITISH** | Part of Michelin-starred chef Jason Atherton's dining dynasty, No. 5 Social (formerly Little Social) backs its elegant, modernist dining room with a menu of adventurous dishes celebrating the joy of British produce. Expect to find a range of prime cuts straight from the Josper grill, and pay special attention to the Herdwick lamb chops and braised neck with mint, peas, and Jersey Royals to enjoy an elevated experience of a stone-cold British classic. **Known for:** relaxed mid-century modern setting; great value set menu; chic cocktail bar. *Average main: £27 5 Pollen St., Mayfair 020/7870–3730 www.no5social.com Closed Sun. Oxford Circus, Piccadilly Circus.*

Ormer Mayfair

$$$$ | **BRITISH** | Hidden away in the depths of a Mayfair hotel is famed chef Shaun Rankin's triumphant ode to all things Jersey (in the Channel Islands, that is). In the art deco–inspired basement haven, indulge on world-class dishes all caught, reared, and foraged from the Jersey seashore. **Known for:** standout Jersey crab and lobster ravioli; top English wine selection; great vegetarian and vegan fine dining options. *Average main: £34 Flemings Hotel, 7–12 Half Moon St., Mayfair 020/7016–5601 for reservations only www.flemings-mayfair.co.uk/fine-dining-london/ormer-mayfair-restaurant Closed Sun. and Mon. Green Park.*

Pollen Street Social

$$$$ | **MODERN EUROPEAN** | Gastro god Jason Atherton may not man the stoves here anymore, but his flagship in a cute Dickensian alleyway off Regent Street still knocks the London dining scene for a loop. Fans can enjoy refined small and large dishes ranging from a " Fruite of the Sea" appetizer to sublime suckling pig belly with Spanish peach. **Known for:** Michelin-star riffs on classic British dishes; dedicated dessert bar; vegan and vegetarian tasting menus. *Average main: £35 8–10 Pollen St., Mayfair 020/7290–7600 www.pollenstreetsocial.com Closed Sun. Oxford Circus, Piccadilly Circus.*

Scott's

$$$$ | **SEAFOOD** | Imposing doormen in bowler hats greet visitors with a wee nod at this ever-fashionable seafood haven on Mount Street in Mayfair. Originally founded in 1851 in the Haymarket, and a former haunt of James Bond author Ian Fleming (he apparently enjoyed the potted shrimps), Scott's draws the wealthiest of London, who enjoy the fresh Lindisfarne oysters, Dover sole, and tasty shrimp burgers. **Known for:** possibly London's most magnificent crustacean bar; huge platters of fresh fruits de mer; extravagant prices. *Average main: £37 20 Mount St., Mayfair 020/7495–7309 for reservations only www.scotts-restaurant.com Green Park, Bond St.*

34

$$$ | **INTERNATIONAL** | A-listers head straight for 34, off Grosvenor Square in Mayfair, simply because all the other celebrities seem to hang out here, too. It must be the plush Edwardian and art deco dining salon, the neat fish, game, and steak-focused menu, and the smooth Upper Manhattan–style service. **Known for:** an endless procession of Hollywood stars; impressive global meats off an Argentine-inspired grill; live jazz. *Average main: £30 34 Grosvenor Sq., entrance on S. Audley St., Mayfair 020/3350–3434 www.34-restaurant.co.uk Marble Arch.*

Hotels

Athenaeum Hotel and Apartments

$$$$ | **HOTEL** | This grand hotel overlooking Green Park offers plenty for the money: rooms are both comfortable and lavishly decorated, with deeply comfortable Hypnos beds, plasma-screen TVs, luxurious fabrics, and original contemporary artworks. **Pros:** peaceful park views; central location; an excellent afternoon tea. **Cons:** bathrooms are almost all small; some rooms can feel tiny; only some rooms come with park views. *Rooms from: £405 116 Piccadilly, Mayfair 020/7499–3464 www.athenaeumhotel.com 164 rooms No meals Green Park.*

Brown's Hotel

$$$$ | **HOTEL** | Founded in 1837 by James Brown, Lord Byron's "gentleman's gentleman," this hotel occupying 11 Georgian town houses holds a treasured place in London society. **Pros:** elegant spaces; attentive service; good afternoon tea. **Cons:** even the most basic room is very pricey; renovation detracted from the hotel's historic atmosphere; low availability for the most basic rooms. *Rooms from: £600 34 Albemarle St., Mayfair 020/7493–6020, 888/667–9477 in U.S. www.roccofortehotels.com 148 rooms No meals Green Park.*

Chesterfield Mayfair Hotel

$$$ | **HOTEL** | Deep in the heart of Mayfair, the former town house of the Earl of Chesterfield welcomes guests in wood-and-leather public rooms that match the dark-wood furnishings in the bedrooms—small but looking like fashion magazine spreads, with bold designer wallpaper or tones of fawn and gray. **Pros:** laid-back atmosphere; attentive service; great afternoon tea. **Cons:** prices rise sharply if you don't get the cheapest rooms; some rooms are tiny; restaurant is very expensive. *Rooms from: £290 35 Charles St., Mayfair 020/7491–2622, 877/955–1515 in U.S. www.chesterfieldmayfair.com 107 rooms No meals Green Park.*

★ **Claridge's**

$$$$ | **HOTEL** | **FAMILY** | The well-heeled have been meeting—and eating—at Claridge's for generations, and the tradition continues in the original art deco public spaces of this superglamorous London institution. **Pros:** see-and-be-seen dining and drinking; serious luxury everywhere—this is an old-money hotel; famed history. **Cons:** better pack your designer wardrobe if you want to fit in with the locals; all that luxury means an expensive price tag; to protect the privacy of guests, photographs are prohibited in some areas. *Rooms from: £650 Brook St., Mayfair 020/7629–8860, 866/599–6991 in U.S. www.claridges.co.uk 203 rooms No meals Bond St.*

★ **The Connaught**

$$$$ | **HOTEL** | **FAMILY** | A huge favorite of the "we wouldn't dream of staying anywhere else" monied set since its opening in 1917, the Connaught has many dazzlingly modern compliments to its famously historic delights. **Pros:** legendary hotel; great for star-spotting; Michelin-starred dining. **Cons:** history comes at a price; bathrooms are small; the superior king room is small for the price. *Rooms from: £650 Carlos Pl., Mayfair 020/7499–7070, 866/599–6991 in U.S. www.the-connaught.co.uk 121 rooms No meals Bond St.*

★ **The Dorchester**

$$$$ | **HOTEL** | Few hotels this opulent manage to be as personable as the Dorchester, which opened in 1939 and boasts a prime Park Lane location with unparalleled glamour; gold leaf and marble adorn the public spaces, and guest quarters are awash in English country house–meets–art deco style. **Pros:** historic luxury in 1930s building; lovely views of Hyde Park; excellent spa. **Cons:** traditional look is not to all tastes; prices are sky-high; some rooms are disappointingly

One of Mayfair's most famous and historic hotels, Claridge's also offers one of the city's most authentic high-class Afternoon Teas.

small. $ *Rooms from: £640* ✉ *53 Park La., Mayfair* ☎ *020/7629–8888* 🌐 *www.dorchestercollection.com* 🛏 *250 rooms* 🍽 *No meals* Ⓜ *Marble Arch, Hyde Park Corner.*

Four Seasons Park Lane

$$$$ | **HOTEL** | A racy departure for the Four Seasons, this hotel has an English clubhouse look with a dose of boudoir. **Pros:** highly elegant rooms; excellent spa; lovely location next to Hyde Park. **Cons:** not for strict traditionalists; haute design comes with high prices; breakfast is an additional fee. $ *Rooms from: £750* ✉ *Hamilton Pl., Park La., Mayfair* ☎ *020/7499–0888* 🌐 *www.fourseasons.com/london* 🛏 *193 rooms* 🍽 *No meals* Ⓜ *Hyde Park Corner.*

InterContinental London Park Lane

$$$$ | **HOTEL** | Overlooking busy Hyde Park Corner and the grounds of Buckingham Palace (much to the Queen's chagrin, allegedly), this hotel's luxurious rooms are aimed at high-end business travelers. **Pros:** great location; feel-like-a-million-dollars service; good business facilities. **Cons:** no park views with standard rooms; prices sky-high in midsummer; without the wow factor or history of some similarly priced Park Lane hotels. $ *Rooms from: £400* ✉ *1 Hamilton Pl., Park La., Mayfair* ☎ *020/7409–3131* 🌐 *parklane.intercontinental.com* 🛏 *447 rooms* 🍽 *No meals* Ⓜ *Hyde Park Corner.*

★ The Langham

$$$$ | **HOTEL** | Hotel pedigrees don't come much greater than this one; built in 1865, the Langham was *the* original luxury hotel in the city, all but inventing the very image of what a great London hotel looked like. **Pros:** beautiful historic building; gorgeous and peaceful pool; great restaurant and bar. **Cons:** price rises considerably once cheapest rooms sell out; need to book ahead for the wildly popular Artesian Bar; some modernized rooms don't share the building's historic charm. $ *Rooms from: £475* ✉ *1C Portland Pl., Mayfair* ☎ *020/7636–1000* 🌐 *www.langhamhotels.co.uk* 🛏 *380 rooms* 🍽 *No meals* Ⓜ *Oxford Circus.*

No. 5 Maddox Street

$$$ | **RENTAL** | **FAMILY** | Just five minutes' walk from Oxford Street, this is a great option for those who tire of traditional hotels: 12 luxury suites—some with balconies and working fireplaces—filled with everything you could ever need, including a handy kitchen. **Pros:** cozy and private; room service will deliver meals from local restaurants; guests have access to nearby health club. **Cons:** no elevator; no communal lobby can make you feel isolated; central location can (predictably) be noisy. *Rooms from: £329* ✉ *5 Maddox St., Mayfair* ☎ *020/7647–0200* 🌐 *www.living-rooms.co.uk/hotel/no5maddoxstreet* *12 suites* *No meals* Ⓜ *Oxford Circus.*

Nightlife

Bars in this upscale central neighborhood—many of which can be found within luxury hotels—attract a polished crowd. Cocktails, fine wines, and rare aged spirits are the tipples of choice. Even the pubs tend to be as upscale as the people who frequent them, but you'll also find plenty of informal establishments with a lot of character.

BARS

Claridge's Bar

BARS/PUBS | This elegant Mayfair meeting place remains unpretentious even when it brims with beautiful people. The bar has an art deco heritage made hip by the sophisticated touch of designer David Collins. A library of rare Champagnes and brandies as well as a delicious choice of traditional and exotic cocktails—try the Flapper or the Black Pearl—will occupy your taste buds. Request a glass of vintage Cristal in the darkly moody leather-walled 36-seat Fumoir. ✉ *Claridge's, 55 Brook St., Mayfair* ☎ *020/7629–8860* 🌐 *www.claridges.co.uk* Ⓜ *Bond St.*

★ **Connaught Bar**

BARS/PUBS | The walls are platinum silver leaf and everything's all buffed and burnished at this glamorous David Collins–designed 1920s cocktail lounge at the Connaught. Hail the famous martini trolley for a classic dry martini or sip signatures like a Ron Zacapa rum-based Vieux Connaught, which is presented on a mirrored tray with a swirl of saffron smoke. ✉ *The Connaught, Carlos Place, Mayfair* ☎ *020/7314–3419* 🌐 *www.the-connaught.co.uk* ☞ *No reservations* Ⓜ *Green Park, Marble Arch.*

★ **Mr Fogg's Residence**

BARS/PUBS | Explorers of all stripes will be captivated by this Jules Verne–inspired cocktail parlor, which is chock-full of the weathered maps, hunting trophies, taxidermy, suspended penny-farthings, and *Around the World in 80 Days* globe-trotting items of eccentric fictional Victorian British adventurer, Phileas J Fogg. Expect Victorian tipples and gin-based Afternoon "Tipsy teas" from staff in bow ties and other old-fashioned get-ups. ✉ *15 Bruton La., Mayfair* ☎ *020/7036–0608* 🌐 *www.mr-foggs.com* Ⓜ *Green Park, Oxford Circus.*

Sketch

BARS/PUBS | **FAMILY** | One seat never looks like the next at this downright extraordinary collection of esoteric living-room bars off Savile Row. The exclusive Parlour, a pâtisserie during the day, exudes plenty of rarefied charm; the intimate East Bar at the back is reminiscent of a sci-fi film set; the Gallery is a shocking pink wonderland; and in the Glade it's permanently sunset in an enchanted forest. The space-age dinosaur egg-pod-shape restrooms are definitely London's quirkiest. ✉ *9 Conduit St., Mayfair* ☎ *020/7659–4500* 🌐 *www.sketch.london* Ⓜ *Oxford Circus.*

PUBS

The Punch Bowl

BARS/PUBS | In a quiet corner of Mayfair, the cozy little Punch Bowl dates to 1729 and the interior remains steadfastly old-fashioned, with a painting of Churchill, candles, polished dark wood, and engraved windows. Try the place's own ale, made specially in Scotland by Caledonian. A dining area at the rear buzzes at lunchtime with locals who come for the upscale English pub food, and there's a fancier restaurant upstairs. ✉ *41 Farm St., Mayfair* ☎ *020/7493–6841* 🌐 *www.punchbowllondon.com* Ⓜ *Green Park, Bond St.*

Shopping

ACCESSORIES

Mulberry

CLOTHING | Staying true to its rural Somerset roots, this luxury goods company epitomizes *le style anglais,* a sophisticated take on the earth tones and practicality of English country style. Best known for highly desirable luxury handbags—such as the Lily, Chiltern, and Bayswater models—the company also produces gorgeous leather accessories, from wallets to luggage, as well as shoes and clothing for men and women. Aside from the New Bond Street flagship, there are branches in Knightsbridge, Covent Garden, Heathrow, and the Westfield centers, along with Mulberry concessions in most of the major upscale department stores. The small store on St. Christopher's Place in Marylebone stocks accessories only. ✉ *50 New Bond St., Mayfair* ☎ *020/7491–3900* 🌐 *www.mulberry.com* Ⓜ *Bond St.*

William & Son

JEWELRY/ACCESSORIES | William Asprey, scion of a jewelry dynasty, sells his carefully chosen, British-made luxury goods using a friendlier and less formal approach. You'll find all sorts of items here that you didn't know you needed, like Pininfarina brushed aluminum retractable pencils, green crocodile backgammon sets, or a silver champagne bottle stopper. The jewelry is tasteful and subtle rather than knock-your-eyes-out, and the store will also do custom work. ✉ *34–36 Bruton St., Mayfair* ☎ *020/7493–8385* 🌐 *www.williamandson.com* ⏲ *Closed Sun.* Ⓜ *Bond St.*

ANTIQUES

Grays Antique Centre

ANTIQUES/COLLECTIBLES | There are approximately 200 dealers here, specializing in everything from Bakelite items to Mughal art. The majority focus on jewelry, ranging from contemporary to antique. Bargains are not out of the question, and proper pedigrees are guaranteed. Go on a weekday for the most choice; the store is closed Sunday and not all stalls are open on Saturday. ✉ *58 Davies St., Mayfair* ☎ *020/7629–7034* 🌐 *www.graysantiques.com* Ⓜ *Bond St.*

BOOKS AND STATIONERY

★ **Heywood Hill**

BOOKS/STATIONERY | Open since 1936, this is considered by some to be the best small bookstore in the English-speaking world—John Le Carré, who set a scene in *Tinker Tailor Soldier Spy* here, is a long-standing customer. Browse for a leather-bound volume on architecture, gardening, natural history, or topography—just some of the topics in which the antiquarian collection specializes. The contemporary selection emphasizes literature, history, biography, travel, architecture, and children's books, and the knowledgeable staff are happy to provide advice. During World War II, author Nancy Mitford helped keep the bookstore going. Today, the 12th Duke of Devonshire, a descendant of her brother-in-law, the 11th Duke, is the owner. It's closed on weekends. ✉ *10 Curzon St., Mayfair* ☎ *020/7629–0647* 🌐 *www.heywoodhill.com* Ⓜ *Green Park.*

Smythson of Bond Street

BOOKS/STATIONERY | No hostess of any standing would consider having a leather-bound guest book made by anyone besides this elegant stationer, and the shop's social stationery and distinctive diaries with their pale-blue pages are the epitome of British good taste. These, along with other made-in-Britain leather goods including a small line of handbags, backpacks, and luggage tags, can be personalized. There are branches in Chelsea, Notting Hill, and Heathrow, plus concessions in leading department stores. ✉ *131–132 New Bond St., Mayfair* ☎ *020/3535–8009* 🌐 *www.smythson.com* Ⓜ *Bond St., Oxford Circus.*

Waterstone's

BOOKS/STATIONERY | At this megabookshop (Europe's largest, with more than 8 miles of bookshelves) in a former art deco department store near Piccadilly Circus, browse for your latest purchase, attend one of the frequent meet-the-author events, or admire the view with a glass of wine at the 5th View Bar and Restaurant (open until 9.30); there's also a café in the basement. Waterstone's is the country's leading book chain, and it's pulled out all the stops to make its flagship as welcoming as a bookstore can be. There are several smaller branches throughout the city. ✉ *203–206 Piccadilly, Mayfair* ☎ *0207/851–2400* 🌐 *www.waterstones.com* Ⓜ *Piccadilly Circus.*

CLOTHING

Alexander McQueen

CLOTHING | Since the legendary designer's untimely death in 2010, his right-hand woman, Sarah Burton, has been at the helm, receiving raves for continuing his tradition of theatrical, darkly romantic, and beautifully cut clothes incorporating corsetry, lace, embroidery, and hourglass silhouettes, all of which were exemplified in Burton's celebrated wedding dress for Kate Middleton. Can't afford a gala gown? Go home with a skull-print silk scarf. ✉ *27 Old Bond St., Mayfair* ☎ *020/7355–0088* 🌐 *www.alexandermcqueen.com* Ⓜ *Bond St.*

Belstaff

CLOTHING | For years the purveyors of Britain's coolest motorcycle leathers, Belstaff has expanded into dresses, skirts, and handbags, as well as knitwear, boots, tops, and trousers for men, women, and children. Outerwear in general and leather jackets in particular remain a strength. All the items reflect the brand's functional yet unconventional heritage. Previous customers include Lawrence of Arabia, Amelia Earhart, Steve McQueen, and Che Guevara. There's another branch in Spitalfields. ✉ *135–137 New Bond St., Mayfair* ☎ *020/7495–5897* 🌐 *www.belstaff.co.uk* Ⓜ *Bond St.*

Burberry

CLOTHING | Known for its trademark tartan, this company has cultivated an edgy, high-fashion image in recent years, and creative director and former Givenchy designer Riccardo Tisci is pushing the boundaries even more, bringing in a street-style influence. For those who prefer the traditional Burberry look, the raincoats are still a classic buy, along with handbags and plaid scarves in every color imaginable. If you're up for a trek, there's a huge factory outlet in Hackney on Chatham Place that has clothes and accessories for men, women, and children at half price or less. There are also branches in Knightsbridge, Covent Garden, and the Westfield shopping center in addition to this spectacular flagship store. ✉ *121 Regent St., Mayfair* ☎ *020/7806–8904* 🌐 *uk.burberry.com* Ⓜ *Piccadilly Circus.*

★ Fenwick

DEPARTMENT STORES | A manageably sized department store, Fenwick is a welcome haven of affordability in a shopping area where stratospheric prices are the norm. The store is particularly strong on accessories (notably lingerie, wraps, and hats), cosmetics, perfumes, and chic, wearable fashion by both big names and more niche designers such as Goat, J Brand, and Tory Burch. There are also three small spas (Chantecaille, La Prairie, and a Blink waxing room), various beauty services (including a hair salon, nail bar, and Blink brow bar), and three restaurants plus a men's department in the basement. ✉ *63 New Bond St., Mayfair* ☎ *020/7629–9161* 🌐 *www.fenwick.co.uk* Ⓜ *Bond St.*

Isabel Marant London

CLOTHING | The first London store from Marant, a favorite of French fashion editors, this airy skylit space is full of her signature slim-cut pants, slouchy knits, wedge sneakers, and rock-chick miniskirts, all exuding Left Bank boho cool. ✉ *29 Bruton St., Mayfair* ☎ *020/7499–7887* 🌐 *www.isabelmarant.com* ⏲ *Closed Sun.* Ⓜ *Bond St.*

Matches Fashion

CLOTHING | Housed within a beautiful six-story Mayfair town house, Matches Fashion's flagship store is so much more than just a retail destination. Designed to create a bricks-and-mortar location that delivers the ultimate contemporary shopping experience, this is a multifaceted emporium in which the ground floor fashion retail space is complemented by an in-house garden, exhibition spaces, multimedia studios, and a calendar of curated talks and events. Whether this is the future of fashion retail is still to be seen, but at the very least it's a lovely place to shop for brands from Gucci to Jil Sander. ✉ *5 Carlos Pl., Mayfair* ☎ *020/3907–8590* 🌐 *www.matchesfashion.com* ⏲ *Closed Sun.* Ⓜ *Green Park.*

Stella McCartney

CLOTHING | It's not easy emerging from the shadow of a Beatle father, but Stella McCartney is a major force in fashion in her own right. Her signature jumpsuits and tuxedo pantsuits embody her design philosophy, combining minimalist tailoring with femininity and sophistication with ease of wear. Her love of functionality and clean lines has led to her branching off into lingerie, accessories, swimwear, and sportswear, designing a line for Adidas. A vegetarian like her parents, she refuses to use fur or leather, making her a favorite with similarly minded fashionistas. There's another boutique in South Kensington. ✉ *23 Old Bond St., Mayfair* ☎ *020/7518–3100* 🌐 *www.stellamccartney.com* Ⓜ *Bond St.*

Victoria Beckham

CLOTHING | Many were dubious when the former Spice Girl launched herself as a high-end designer, but her elegant yet wearable clothes soon made her a favorite with influencers and customers alike. This, her only stand-alone boutique, carries all the Beckham lines: the VVB diffusion line, the main collection, and accessories like bags, shoes, and eyewear, all displayed like artwork in the gallery-like space. ✉ *36 Dover St., Mayfair* ☎ *0207/042–0700* 🌐 *www.victoriabeckham.com* Ⓜ *Green Park, Piccadilly.*

Vivienne Westwood

CLOTHING | From her beginnings as the most shocking and outré designer around, Westwood (now Dame Vivienne) has become a standard-bearer for high-style British couture. At the Chelsea boutique where she first sold the lavish corseted ball gowns, dandified nipped-waist jackets, and tartan-meets-punk daywear that formed the core of her signature look, you can still buy ready-to-wear—mainly items from the more casual Anglomania diffusion line and the exclusive Worlds End label, which draws from her archives. The small Davies Street boutique is devoted to couture (plus bridal), while the flagship Conduit Street store carries all of the above. There's also a men's collection at 18 Conduit Street. ✉ *44 Conduit St., Mayfair* ☎ *020/7439–1109* 🌐 *www.viviennewestwood.com* Ⓜ *Oxford Circus.*

DEPARTMENT STORES

Thomas Goode

CERAMICS/GLASSWARE | This spacious luxury housewares shop has been at the same smart Mayfair address since 1845. The china, silver, crystal, and linen, whether from the store's own line or from luxury brands like Christofle and Puiforcat, are simply the best that money can buy, a legacy of its original customer base of international royals and heads of state. The store still holds two royal warrants, but anyone who can afford it can commission their own bespoke set of china. If such luxury is beyond you, visit anyway for the shop's small museum of plates, either antique or designed for royalty, including some created for Princess Diana's wedding. ✉ *19 S. Audley St., Mayfair* ☎ *020/7499–2823* 🌐 *www.thomasgoode.co.uk* Ⓜ *Green Park.*

FOOD

Charbonnel et Walker

FOOD/CANDY | Established in 1875, this master chocolatier's Mayfair shop specializes in traditional handmade chocolates (rose-petal creams and Champagne truffles, for example) and has been creating these beautifully packaged, high-quality candies from long before most of today's fashionable brands appeared. Their drinking chocolate—coarsely grated fine chocolate in a tin—is worth carrying home in a suitcase. ✉ *One The Royal Arcade, 28 Old Bond St., Mayfair* ☎ *020/7318–2075* 🌐 *www.charbonnel.co.uk* Ⓜ *Green Park.*

JEWELRY

Asprey

JEWELRY/ACCESSORIES | The company's "global flagship" store displays exquisite jewelry—as well as silver and leather goods, watches, china, and crystal—in a discreet, very British setting that oozes quality, expensive good taste, and hushed comfort. If you're in the market for an immaculate 1930s cigarette case, a silver cocktail shaker, a pair of pavé diamond and sapphire earrings, or a ladylike handbag, you won't likely be disappointed. And, for the really well-heeled, there's custom service available as well (Ringo Starr had a chess set made here). This store has occupied the premises since 1847, some 66 years after Asprey was established in 1781. ✉ *167 New Bond St., Mayfair* ☎ *020/7493–6767* 🌐 *www.asprey.com* Ⓜ *Green Park.*

Garrard

JEWELRY/ACCESSORIES | The oldest jewelry house in the world, Garrard has been in business since 1735. Between 1843 and 2007, the company was responsible for the upkeep of the Crown Jewels in the Tower of London and for creating several royal crowns (you can see some on display in the Tower). Today the focus is on precious gems in simple, classic settings, along with silver accessories. Although some collections are definitely contemporary (with items like minimalist hoop earrings or two-finger rings), many of the designs are traditional and impressive—which will be handy should you be in the market for an old-school diamond tiara. ✉ *24 Albemarle St., Mayfair* ☎ *207/518–1070* 🌐 *www.garrard.com* Ⓜ *Green Park.*

MEN'S CLOTHING

Alfred Dunhill

CLOTHING | For more than 100 years, Dunhill has been synonymous with the most luxurious and sophisticated men's goods, including accessories, briefcases, and superbly tailored clothes. This Georgian mansion, their flagship, also features a barbershop, cellar bar, courtyard restaurant, and bespoke services, where you can order custom-fitted menswear or unique versions of the brand's celebrated leather goods. The smaller, original St. James's shop has been on Jermyn Street since 1906. ✉ *Bourdon House, 2 Davies St., Mayfair* ☎ *020/3425–7300* 🌐 *www.dunhill.com* 🕓 *Closed Sun.* Ⓜ *Bond St.*

Gieves and Hawkes

CLOTHING | One of the grand men's tailoring houses of Savile Row, this company made its name outfitting British royals who served as officers in the armed forces. The company still supplies custom-made military uniforms, as well as beautifully tailored formal and civilian wear for clients who have included Winston Churchill and Ian Fleming. Prices for a bespoke suit start around £5,000 and made to measure at £1,150, but you can find ready-made versions from around £900 (separates from £200), while a new line of casualwear has several items under £200. Custom-made shoes are also available. ✉ *1 Savile Row, Mayfair* ☎ *020/7434–2001* 🌐 *www.gievesandhawkes.com* Ⓜ *Piccadilly Circus.*

Ozwald Boateng

CLOTHING | The dapper menswear by Ozwald Boateng (pronounced "Bwateng") combines contemporary funky style with traditional Savile Row quality. His made-to-measure suits have been worn by the dandyish likes of Jamie Foxx, Mick Jagger, and Laurence Fishburne, who appreciate the sharp cuts, luxurious fabrics, and occasionally vibrant colors (even the more conservative choices have jacket linings in bright silk). ✉ *30 Savile Row, Mayfair* ☎ *020/7437–2030* 🌐 *www.ozwaldboateng.co.uk* ⏲ *Closed Sun.* Ⓜ *Piccadilly Circus.*

SHOES

Nicholas Kirkwood

SHOES/LUGGAGE/LEATHER GOODS | Kirkwood is one of Britain's most fashionable shoe designers, and this is his only retail boutique. You won't be able to hike in his imaginative, elegant, sky-high stilettos (be warned: prices are similarly high), but you will be able to make quite an entrance. There are also more wearable styles that are equally flattering and gorgeous. ✉ *5 Mount St., Mayfair* ☎ *020/7290–1404* 🌐 *www.nicholaskirkwood.com* ⏲ *Closed Sun.* Ⓜ *Green Park.*

Rupert Sanderson

SHOES/LUGGAGE/LEATHER GOODS | Designed in London and made in Italy, Sanderson's elegant shoes have been a huge hit in fashion circles with their lavish ornamentation on heels and flats alike. Red-carpet-ready high heels—worn by celebs including Claire Danes, Nicole Kidman, and Sandra Bullock—come in gorgeous colors and prints; peep toes are signature elements. The high prices reflect the impeccable craftsmanship. ✉ *19 Bruton Pl., Mayfair* ☎ *0207/491–2260* 🌐 *www.rupertsanderson.com* ⏲ *Closed Sun.* Ⓜ *Bond St., Green Park.*

Sophia Webster

SHOES/LUGGAGE/LEATHER GOODS | Gorgeous, fanciful shoes embellished with jeweled flowers, sequins, butterflies, and trademark wings at the heel fill Webster's first stand-alone boutique. This stylists' favorite is best known for her open-toed stilettos, but there are plenty of flat sandals, mid-height heels, platforms, and even clogs, as well as a sneaker collaboration with Puma. ✉ *Mount Street Mews, 124 Mount St., Mayfair* ☎ *0203/150–2960* 🌐 *www.sophiawebster.co.uk* ⏲ *Closed Sun.* Ⓜ *Bond St.*

Marylebone

A favorite of newspaper style sections everywhere, Marylebone High Street forms the heart of Marylebone Village (pronounced "Marr-le-bone"), a vibrant, upscale neighborhood that encompasses the squares and streets around High Street and nearby Marylebone Lane. The district took its name from a church dedicated to St. Mary and the bourne (another word for "stream") that ran through the original village. Nowadays, it's hard to believe you're just a few blocks north of gaudy Oxford Street as you wander in and out of Marylebone's small shops and boutiques, the best of which include Cadenheads Whisky Shop and Tasting Room (26 Chiltern Street); La Fromagerie (2–6 Moxon Street), an excellent cheese shop; Daunt Books (Nos. 83–84 Marylebone High Street), a superlative travel bookshop; the "Cabbages and Frocks" market (Saturday 11–5) on the grounds of the St. Marylebone Parish Church, purveying specialty foods and vintage clothing; and a large farmers' and

At 221B Baker Street, you can immerse yourself in the world of one Mr. Sherlock Holmes.

artisanal-food market (Sunday 10–2) in a parking lot on Cramer Street, just behind High Street. But some memorable sights await, too, including the best remnant of *ancien régime* France in London, the fabled Wallace Collection.

Sights

Lisson Gallery
MUSEUM | Owner Nicholas Logsdail represents about 50 blue-chip artists, including the minimalist Sol LeWitt and performance artist Marina Abramović, at one of the most respected art galleries in London. The gallery is most associated with New Object sculptors like Anish Kapoor and Richard Deacon, many of whom have won the Turner Prize. There's another branch down the road at 27 Bell Street. ✉ *67 Lisson St., Marylebone* ☎ *020/7724–2739* 🌐 *www.lissongallery.com* 🎫 *Free* ⏲ *Closed Sun.* Ⓜ *Edgware Rd., Marylebone.*

Madame Tussauds
MUSEUM | **FAMILY** | One of London's busiest tourist attractions, this is nothing less than the world's most famous exhibition of lifelike waxwork models of celebrities. Madame T. learned her craft while making death masks of French Revolution victims, and in 1835 she set up her first show of the famous ones near this spot. Top billing still goes to the murderers in the Chamber of Horrors, who stare glassy-eyed at visitors—one from an electric chair, one sitting next to the tin bath where he dissolved several wives in quicklime. ■ **TIP→ Beat the crowds by booking timed-entry tickets in advance. You can also buy nondated, "priority access" tickets via the website (at a premium).** ✉ *Marylebone Rd., Regent's Park* ☎ *0844/248–2624 for timed-entry tickets* 🌐 *www.madametussauds.com* 🎫 *From £29* Ⓜ *Baker St.*

Sherlock Holmes Museum
MUSEUM | **FAMILY** | Outside Baker Street Station, by the Marylebone Road exit, is a 9-foot-high bronze statue of Arthur Conan

Doyle's celebrated detective, who "lived" around the corner at number 221B Baker Street—now a museum to all things Sherlock. Inside, Mrs. Hudson, Holmes's housekeeper, guides you into a series of Victorian rooms where the great man lived, worked, and played the violin. It's all carried off with such genuine enthusiasm and attention to detail that you could be forgiven for thinking that Mr. Holmes actually *did* exist. ✉ *221B Baker St., Regent's Park* ☎ *020/7224–3688* 🌐 *www.sherlock-holmes.co.uk* 🎫 *£15* Ⓜ *Baker St.*

★ Wallace Collection

MUSEUM | FAMILY | With its Great Gallery stunningly refurbished, there's even more reason to visit this exquisite gem of an art gallery—although housing one of the world's finest collections of Old Master paintings is reason enough. This glorious collection and the 18th-century mansion in which it's located were bequeathed to the nation by Lady Julie-Amélie-Charlotte Wallace, the widow of Sir Richard Wallace (1818–90). Wallace's father, the 4th Marquess of Hertford, took a house in Paris after the French Revolution and set about snapping up paintings by what were then dangerously unpopular artists. Frans Hals's *Laughing Cavalier* is probably the most famous painting here, or perhaps Jean-Honoré Fragonard's *The Swing*. The full list of painters in the collection reads like a "who's who" of classical European art—from Rubens, Rembrandt, and Van Dyck to Canaletto, Titian, and Velázquez. English works include paintings by Gainsborough and Turner. There are also fine collections of furniture, porcelain, Renaissance gold, and *majolica* (15th- and 16th-century Italian tin-glazed pottery). With craft activities, hands-on sessions, and the "Little Draw" drawing workshops, as well as the chance to try on a suit of armor in the "Arms and Armour" collection, there's plenty to keep kids occupied, too. The conditions of the bequest mean that no part of the collection can leave the building; this is the only place in the world you'll ever be able to see these works. ✉ *Hertford House, Manchester Sq., Marylebone* ☎ *020/7563–9500* 🌐 *www.wallacecollection.org* 🎫 *Free* Ⓜ *Bond St.*

Restaurants

If you're looking for something more wallet-friendly, head north to Marylebone, formerly dowdy but now prized for its uberchic, villagelike feel. Here you'll find an array of low-key little cafés, boîtes, and tapas bars, Champagne-and-hot-dog joints, and the odd world-class sizzler, offering everything from Moroccan and Spanish to Thai and Japanese.

Fischer's

$$ | AUSTRIAN | FAMILY | It almost feels like Sigmund Freud or Gustav Klimt might doff their Homburg hats and shuffle into a dark leather banquette at this evocative, early-20th-century–style Viennese neighborhood café on Marylebone High Street. Savor the antique light fittings and distressed wallpaper before diving into *brötchen*chopped chicken livers with dill on rye bread. **Known for:** evocative turn-of-the-20th-century Old Vienna café decor; some of London's best breaded Wiener schnitzel; decadent strudels and ice cream coupes. $ *Average main: £21* ✉ *50 Marylebone High St., Marylebone* ☎ *020/7466–5501* 🌐 *www.fischers.co.uk* Ⓜ *Baker St., Bond St.*

The Golden Hind

$ | SEAFOOD | FAMILY | You'll land some of the best fish-and-chips in town at this British chippy in a retro 1914 art deco café. Marylebone locals and satisfied tourists alike hunker down for the neatly prepared and decidedly nongreasy deep-fried or steamed battered cod, haddock, and plaice, the classic hand-cut Maris Piper chips, and the traditional mushy peas and homemade tartare sauce. **Known for:** some of the city's best deep-fried battered cod and chips; hard-to-find traditional mushy peas; huge portions. *Average main: £14 71A–73 Marylebone La., Marylebone 020/7486–3644 www.goldenhindrestaurant.com Closed Sun. No lunch Sat. Bond St.*

Les 110 de Taillevent

$$$ | FRENCH | Dazzling classic French dishes mark out Les 110 de Taillevent as the city's top French *brasserie de luxe.* Housed in a chic former Coutts bank on Cavendish Square, diners and oenophiles delight in the exquisite cuisine and accompanying master list of 110 fine wines by the glass. **Known for:** soaring traditional dining salon; brilliant list of paired fine wines by the glass; haunt for wine experts and merchants. *Average main: £28 16 Cavendish Sq., Marylebone 020/3141–6016 www.les-110-taillevent-london.com Closed Sun. Bond St., Oxford Circus.*

★ Roganic

$$$$ | MODERN BRITISH | Field-to-fork, New Nordic chef Simon Rogan takes diners on a madcap journey with his bonkers 4- to 17-course tasting menu here at Roganic. Hold on tight for a cyclone of minibites and highly technical dishes, ranging from salt-baked celeriac with enoki mushroom and whey cream to burnt hispi cabbage, crab, and crispy chicken skins. **Known for:** extravagant tasting menus; fresh, local-based produce; smoked juniper fudge for dessert. *Average main: £35 5–7 Blandford St., Marylebone 020/3370–6260 www.roganic.uk Closed Sun. and Mon. Bond St.*

Hotels

★ Dorset Square Hotel

$$$ | HOTEL | This fashionable boutique hotel occupies a charming old town house in one of London's most upscale neighborhoods. **Pros:** ideal location; lovely design; good afternoon tea. **Cons:** some rooms are small; no bathtub in some rooms; no gym. *Rooms from: £252 39 Dorset Sq., Marylebone 020/7723–7874 www.firmdalehotels.com 38 rooms No meals Baker St.*

Holmes Hotel

$$$ | HOTEL | Named in honor of the fictional detective who had his home on Baker Street, rooms here have a masculine edge with plenty of nods to Mr. Holmes himself (along with hypermodern bathrooms stocked with fluffy bathrobes). **Pros:** chic decor; international electrical outlets, including those that work with American equipment; fun literary theme that doesn't go overboard. **Cons:** have to walk through the bar to get to reception; not well soundproofed from the noisy street; rooms on the small side. *Rooms from: £240 108 Baker St., Marylebone 0333/400–6136 www.parkplazasherlockholmes.com 118 rooms No meals Baker St.*

Hyatt Regency London—The Churchill

$$$ | HOTEL | Even though it's one of London's largest hotels, the Churchill is always abuzz with guests smiling at the perfection they find here, including warmly personalized service and calmly alluring guest rooms. **Pros:** comfortable and stylish; great dining and drinking, including a bottomless brunch; central location. **Cons:** feels more geared to business than leisure travelers; lots of renovations going on; prices are steep. *Rooms from: £369 30 Portman Sq., Marylebone 020/7486–5800 www.hyatt.com/en-US/hotel/england-united-kingdom/hyatt-regency-london-the-churchill/lonch 440 rooms No meals Marble Arch.*

The Sumner

$$ | HOTEL | You can feel yourself relaxing the minute you enter this elegant Georgian town house. **Pros:** excellent location for shopping; small enough that the staff know your name; attractive conservatory and garden. **Cons:** services are limited; high prices; street noise can be a minor issue. *Rooms from: £170* *54 Upper Berkley St., Marble Arch, Marylebone* *020/7723–2244* *www.thesumner.com* *20 rooms* *Free breakfast* *Marble Arch.*

22 York Street
$$ | **B&B/INN** | **FAMILY** | This lovely Georgian town house has a cozy family feel, with polished pine floors and fetching antiques decorating the homey, individually furnished guest rooms. **Pros:** live out your London town-house fantasy; flexible check-in times; good location for shoppers. **Cons:** if you take away the great location, you're paying a lot for a B&B; not everyone enjoys socializing with strangers over breakfast; some guests won't enjoy the lack of anonymity. *Rooms from: £165* *22 York St., Marylebone* *020/7224–2990* *www.22yorkstreet.co.uk* *10 rooms* *Free breakfast* *Baker St.*

★ **Zetter Townhouse Marylebone**
$$$ | **HOTEL** | No matter how hip the crowd here gets, the clientele is never likely to distract from the sumptuous decor of this boutique hotel that is equal parts Tudor-style and Georgian flair, with a pinch of steampunk for good measure. **Pros:** beautiful interior design; cocktail bar that makes repeat visits a must; gorgeous rooms that feel like you're on a movie set. **Cons:** atmosphere can feel too trendy at times; prices are high considering the amenities; neighborhood can be too quiet on weekends. *Rooms from: £265* *28–30 Seymour St., Marylebone* *020/7324–4544* *www.thezettertownhouse.com/marylebone* *24 rooms* *No meals* *Marylebone.*

Performing Arts

CLASSICAL MUSIC

★ **Wigmore Hall**
CONCERTS | **FAMILY** | London's most beautiful venue for chamber music also happens to boast near-perfect acoustics. The hall has a rich history, including hosting the premieres of a number of works by the British composer Benjamin Britten, and today attracts leading ensembles from all over the world. The varied program contains lunchtime and Sunday morning concerts, plus workshops and concerts for babies and toddlers. *36 Wigmore St., Marylebone* *020/7935–2141* *www.wigmore-hall.org.uk* *From £18* *Bond St.*

Shopping

ANTIQUES

Alfies Antique Market
ANTIQUES/COLLECTIBLES | This four-story, bohemian-chic labyrinth is London's largest indoor antiques market, housing more than 75 dealers specializing in art, lighting, glassware, textiles, jewelry, furniture, and collectibles, with a particular strength in vintage clothing and 20th-century design. Come here to pick up vintage (1900–70) clothing, accessories, and luggage from Tin Tin Collectables, antique and vintage glassware and vases at Robinson Antiques, or a spectacular mid-20th-century Italian lighting fixture at Vincenzo Caffarella. The atmosphere may be funky, but the prices are not. There's also a rooftop café with free Wi-Fi if you need a coffee break. In addition to the market, this end of Church Street is lined with excellent antiques shops. *13–25 Church St., Marylebone* *020/7723–6066* *www.alfiesantiques.com* *Closed Sun. and Mon.* *Marylebone.*

BOOKS

★ Daunt Books

BOOKS/STATIONERY | An independent bookstore chain (there are additional branches in Belsize Park, Chelsea, Hampstead, Holland Park, and Cheapside), Daunt favors a thoughtful selection of contemporary and classic fiction and nonfiction. The striking Marylebone branch is an original Edwardian bookstore, where a dramatic room with a long oak-paneled gallery under lofty skylights houses the noted travel section, which includes not only guidebooks but also related literature and poetry. The Hampstead branch is strong on children's books. ✉ *83 Marylebone High St., Marylebone* ☎ *020/7224–2295* 🌐 *www.dauntbooks.co.uk* Ⓜ *Baker St.*

CLOTHING

Matches Fashion

CLOTHING | This carefully curated boutique carries fashion from a selection of 400 designers both rising and established, including Christopher Kane, Erdem, J.W. Anderson, Proenza Schouler, Vetements, McCartney, McQueen, Balenciaga, Balmain, Valentino, Saint Laurent, Marni, and Duro Olowu. There's also an equally stylish menswear department, plus jewelry, lingerie, footwear, and accessories. Other branches can be found in Mayfair, Notting Hill, and southwest London. ✉ *87 Marylebone High St., Marylebone* ☎ *020/7487–5400* 🌐 *www.matchesfashion.com* Ⓜ *Regent's Park, Baker St.*

Reiss

CLOTHING | With an in-house design team whose experience includes stints at Gucci and Calvin Klein and customers like Beyoncé and the Duchess of Cambridge, who wore a Reiss dress for her official engagement picture, this reliable chain brings luxury standards of tailoring and details to mass-market womens- and menswear. The sleek and contemporary style doesn't come cheap, but does offer value for money. There are branches in Knightsbridge, The City, Covent Garden, Chelsea, Hampstead, Islington, Soho, Kensington, and basically all over London. ✉ *10 Barrett St., Marylebone* ☎ *020/7486–6557* 🌐 *www.reiss.com* Ⓜ *Oxford St.*

DEPARTMENT STORES

Marks & Spencer

DEPARTMENT STORES | You'd be hard-pressed to find a Brit who doesn't have something in the closet from Marks & Spencer (or M&S, as it's popularly known). This major chain is famed for its classic dependable clothing for men, women, and children—affordable cashmere and lamb's wool sweaters are particularly good buys—and occasionally scores a fashion hit. The food department at M&S is consistently good, especially for frozen food, and a great place to pick up a sandwich or premade salad on the go (look for M&S Simply Food stores all over town). The flagship branch at Marble Arch and the Pantheon location at 173 Oxford Street have extensive fashion departments. ✉ *458 Oxford St., Marylebone* ☎ *020/7935–7954* 🌐 *www.marksandspencer.com* Ⓜ *Marble Arch.*

★ Selfridges

DEPARTMENT STORES | This giant bustling store (the second largest in the United Kingdom after Harrods) gives Harvey Nichols a run for its money as London's most fashionable department store. Packed to the rafters with clothes ranging from mid-price lines to the latest catwalk names, the store continues to break ground with its innovative retail schemes, especially the ground-floor Wonder Room (for extravagant jewelry and luxury watches), a dedicated Denim Studio, a Fragrance Bar where you can create custom perfume, an array of pop-ups ranging from spaces for designers such as Jil Sander to a healthy shot bar (if you need some colloidal silver to keep you going) or a collaboration with boutique boxing club BXR. The giant accessories hall has miniboutiques dedicated to top-end designers such as Chanel, Gucci, and Vuitton while the new Corner Shop offers U.K.-theme gifts and souvenirs at all price points. There are so many zones that merge into one another—from youth-oriented Miss Selfridge to audio equipment to the large, comprehensive cosmetics department—that you practically need a map. Don't miss the Shoe Galleries, the world's largest shoe department, which is filled with more than 5,000 pairs from 120 brands, displayed like works of art under spotlights. Take a break with a glass of wine at the rooftop restaurant or pick up some tea in the Food Hall as a gift. ✉ *400 Oxford St., Marylebone* ☎ *0800/123400* 🌐 *www.selfridges.com* Ⓜ *Bond St.*

JEWELRY

Kabiri

JEWELRY/ACCESSORIES | A carefully curated array of exciting contemporary jewelry by emerging and established designers from around the world is packed into this small shop. There is something to suit most budgets and tastes, though understated minimalism predominates. You can score an elegant, one-of-a-kind piece here for a very reasonable price. ✉ *94 Marylebone La., Marylebone* ☎ *020/7317–2150* 🌐 *www.kabiri.co.uk* Ⓜ *Baker St.*

Chapter 5

SOHO AND COVENT GARDEN

Updated by
Alex Wijeratna

Sights ★★★☆☆ | Restaurants ★★★★☆ | Hotels ★★☆☆☆ | Shopping ★★★☆☆ | Nightlife ★★★★★

SOHO AND COVENT GARDEN SNAPSHOT

TOP REASONS TO GO

Newburgh Quarter: Head to this adorable warren of cobblestone streets for stylish boutiques, edgy stores, and young indie upstarts.

Dining: London has fallen in love with its chefs, and Soho is home to many of the most talked-about restaurants in town.

Covent Garden Piazza: Eliza Doolittle's former backyard has been taken over by boutiques and street performers who play to the crowds from morning to night.

Royal Opera House: Even if you're not going to the opera or ballet, take in the beautiful architecture and sense of history.

West End Theater: Shaftesbury Avenue is the heart of London's theater district, where more than 50 West End theaters pull in the crowds with a mix of extravagant musicals, plays, and performances.

GETTING THERE

Almost all Tube lines cross the Covent Garden and Soho areas, so it's easy to hop off for dinner or a show in one of the hippest parts of London. For Soho, take any train to Piccadilly Circus, Leicester Square, Oxford Circus, or Tottenham Court Road. For Covent Garden, get off at Covent Garden Station on the Piccadilly Line. (It may be easier to exit the Tube at Leicester Square or Holborn and walk.) Thirty buses connect to the Covent Garden area from all over London; check out the area's website (🌐 *www.coventgarden.london*).

MAKING THE MOST OF YOUR TIME

You can comfortably tour all the sights around Soho and Covent Garden in a day. Make sure to leave plenty of time to watch street entertainment or shop at the stalls around Covent Garden Piazza or in the fashion boutiques of Soho in the afternoon. Save some energy for a night on the town in Soho.

QUICK BITES

■ **Canela** Bright and casual by day, intimate and atmospheric by night, this is a great spot for refueling mid–shopping trip, grabbing a bite before a show (think filling dishes like pork and clam stew or salted cod, plus charcuterie and sandwiches), or lingering over a glass of reasonably priced Portuguese wine. ✉ *33 Earlham St., Covent Garden* ☎ *020/7240–6926* 🌐 *www.canelacafe.com* Ⓜ *Covent Garden, Leicester Sq.*

■ **Maison Bertaux** This eccentric French pâtisserie (London's oldest) has been around since 1871. Not the finest coffee around, but a nice range of teas and glasses of wine, plus fab French cakes, tarts, and savory quiches more than make up for that. ✉ *28 Greek St., Soho* ☎ *020/7437–6007* 🌐 *www.maisonbertaux.com* Ⓜ *Tottenham Court Rd., Leicester Sq.*

LGBT LONDON

■ Old Compton Street in Soho is the epicenter of London's affluent, stylish gay scene. There are some fun nightclubs in the area, with crowds forming in Soho Square, south of Oxford Street. Some of the more well-known clubs and bars in the area include the Friendly Society, Ku Bar, and She.

A red-light district no more, today's Soho is more stylish than seedy and offers some of London's best bars, live music venues, restaurants, and theaters. By day, this hotbed of media production reverts to the business side of its late-night scene. If Soho is all about showbiz, neighboring Covent Garden is devoted to culture. Both districts offer an abundance of narrow streets packed with one-of-a-kind shops and lots of antique character.

Soho

Soho, which, along with Covent Garden, is loosely known as "the West End," has long been known as the entertainment and arts quarter of London's center. Bordered to the north by Oxford Street, Regent Street to the west, and Chinatown and Leicester Square to the south, the narrow streets of Soho are unabashedly devoted to pleasure. Wardour Street bisects the neighborhood, with lots of interesting boutiques and some of London's best-value restaurants to the west (especially around Foubert's Place and on Brewer and Lexington streets). Most nightlife lies to the east—including the gay clubs of Old Compton Street—and beyond that is the city's densest collection of theaters, on Shaftesbury Avenue. London's compact Chinatown is wedged between Soho and Leicester Square.

A bit of erudition surfaces to the east of the square on Charing Cross Road, famous for its secondhand bookshops, and on tiny Cecil Court, a pedestrianized passage lined with small antiquarian booksellers and curiosity shops specializing in vintage film posters, maps, and theater paraphernalia.

Sights

★ Newburgh Quarter

PEDESTRIAN MALL | Want to see the hip style of today's London? Find it one block east of Carnaby Street—where the look of the '60s "Swinging London" was born—in an adorable warren of cobblestone streets now lined with specialty boutiques, edgy stores, and young indie upstarts. A check of the ingredients reveals one part '60s London, one part futuristic fetishism, one part steampunk, and one part British street swagger. The new-bohemian look best flourishes in shops like Peckham Rye, a tiny boutique crowded with rockers and fashionistas who adore its grunge–meets- *Brideshead Revisited* vibe. Quality coffee shops abound—take a break at Department of Coffee and Social Affairs, where you can also browse for home coffee-making equipment. ✉ *Newburgh St., Foubert's Pl., Ganton St., and Carnaby St., Soho* 🌐 *www.carnaby.co.uk.*

★ The Photographers' Gallery

MUSEUM | Britain's first and foremost public photography gallery programs cutting-edge and provocative exhibitions. The prestigious Deutsche Börse Photography Prize is exhibited and awarded here annually. The gallery also has a print sales room, a bookstore, an archive, and a café-bar—a great spot to escape the bustle of nearby Oxford Street. ✉ *16–18 Ramillies St., Soho* ☎ *020/7087–9300* 🌐 *www.thephotographersgallery.org.uk* 🎟 *£5 for exhibitions* Ⓜ *Oxford Circus.*

Sadie Coles HQ

MUSEUM | Containing the work of important British and international artists such as Sarah Lucas and Martine Syms, this all white and light-filled art space overlooking busy Regent Street marked a major expansion for respected British gallerist Sadie Coles when it opened in fall 2013. A second Sadie Coles exhibition space operates nearby at Davies St. in Mayfair. ✉ *62 Kingly St., Soho* ☎ *020/7493–8611* 🌐 *www.sadiecoles.com* ☞ *Closed Sun. and Mon.* Ⓜ *Oxford Circus, Piccadilly Circus.*

Restaurants

Soho and Covent Garden are the city's historic playground and pleasure zone, an all-day, all-night jostling neon wonderland of glitz, glamour, grime, and greasepaint. This area is London's cultural heart, with old and new media companies, late-night dive bars, cabaret, street performers, West End musicals, and world-class theater, ballet, and opera houses. Rising rents have recently forced out many of Soho's seedier red-light businesses and ushered in more edgy, top-notch restaurants. Just follow your nose in Covent Garden and Theatreland to find copious and increasingly excellent options for pre and posttheater dining.

Andrew Edmunds

$$ | **MEDITERRANEAN** | Candlelit at night, with a haunting Dickensian vibe, Andrew Edmunds is a permanently packed, old-school dining institution. Tucked away behind Carnaby Street in an 18th-century Soho town house, it's a cozy favorite whose unpretentious and keenly priced dishes draw on the tastes of Ireland, the Mediterranean, and Middle East. **Known for:** deeply romantic, Georgian-era town-house setting; unpretentious daily changing handwritten menus; bargains galore on the acclaimed wine list. Ⓢ *Average main: £18* ✉ *46 Lexington St., Soho* ☎ *020/7437–5708* 🌐 *www.andrewedmunds.com* Ⓜ *Oxford Circus, Piccadilly Circus.*

BAO

$ | **TAIWANESE** | Lines form daily to secure a prized seat, perch, or stool at this no-reservations 32-seater from a crack team of Taiwanese steamed bao-bun specialists. The gloriously soft and plump milk-based, rice-flour bao buns—skillfully stuffed with organic Cornish braised pork, peanut powder, and fermented greens—are the undisputed stars of the show. **Known for:** long lines for the steamed, stuffed bao buns; highly Instagramable pig's blood cake; bao bun with Horlicks ice cream for dessert. Ⓢ *Average main: £6* ✉ *53 Lexington St., Soho* 🌐 *www.baolondon.com* ⏲ *No dinner Sun.* Ⓜ *Oxford Circus, Piccadilly Circus, Tottenham Court Rd.*

★ Bar Italia

$ | **CAFÉ** | This legendary Italian coffee bar on Frith Street is Soho's unofficial beating heart and a 22-hours-a-day classic institution. Established in 1949 during the postwar Italian coffee bar craze and still run by the founding Polledri family, today most regulars grab an espresso or frothy cappuccino made from the vintage Gaggia coffee machine, and wolf down a snack at one of the mirrored bar counters. **Known for:** tiny hole-in-the-wall setting; old-school Italian espresso; sturdy sausage or bacon sandwiches. *$ Average main: £6 ✉ 22 Frith St., Soho ☎ 020/7734–4737 🌐 www.baritaliasoho.co.uk Ⓜ Leicester Sq.*

Blacklock

$ | STEAKHOUSE | FAMILY | Set in a former basement brothel, this Soho meatopia cranks out £20 platters of delectable char-grilled lamb, beef, and pork skinny chops and juice-soaked flat bread, all served on retro antique pearlware. Supplied by master butchers Philip Warren from Cornwall, Blacklock's killer chops are charcoal-grilled under heavy antique blacklock irons from Tennessee. **Known for:** young and bubbly service with top '80s tunes; huge platters of skinny chops and flat bread; £18 Sunday roasts with all the trimmings. *$ Average main: £12 ✉ The Basement, 24 Great Windmill St., Soho ☎ 020/3441–6996 🌐 www.theblacklock.com ⏲ No dinner Sun. Ⓜ Piccadilly Circus, Oxford Circus.*

Blanchette

$$ | FRENCH | French tapas may sound sacrilegious, but Blanchette hits the spot at this rustic hipster headquarters where a dreamy French sound track complements the charming candlelit interior. Visually feast on the Paris flea market bric-a-brac and order a few small plates to share, like the crispy frogs' legs and truffle saucisson or baked scallops with Café de Paris sauce. **Known for:** unusual French tapas-style dishes and shared plates; cool Soho crowd with jazzy sound track; crunchy French frogs' legs. *$ Average main: £18 ✉ 9 D'Arblay St., Soho ☎ 020/7439–8100 🌐 www.blanchettesoho.co.uk Ⓜ Tottenham Court Rd.*

★ Bob Bob Ricard

$$$ | RUSSIAN | At this flashy, Russian-owned palace known for its steak and Oscietra caviar, all you have to do is press a tableside button to order more Champagne. And money is no object for the high-rollers that buzz away for vintage Dom Pérignon and Cristal Rosé Champagne while enjoying rich Russian hits like chicken Kiev, baked oysters Brezhnev, and sole goujons à la Ivan. **Known for:** glitzy interiors crammed with polished brass and burnished ceilings; pricey comfort food like lobster mac and cheese; after-dinner partying in the basement Club Room. *$ Average main: £29 ✉ 1 Upper James St., Soho ☎ 020/3145–1000 🌐 www.bobbobricard.com Ⓜ Oxford Circus, Piccadilly Circus, Tottenham Court Rd.*

★ Bocca di Lupo

$$ | ITALIAN | This upscale Italian restaurant is always crammed and the tables are jammed too close together, but everyone still comes for the glorious spread of regional Italian small plates. Located off Theatreland's Shaftesbury Avenue, the family-run trattoria offers a magnificent menu featuring peasant-based pastas, stews, roasts, and crudités from Piedmont to Bologna. **Known for:** open kitchen counter serving a medley of rustic small plates; enticing all-Italian wine list; crowd-pleasing lobster spaghettini. *$ Average main: £22 ✉ 12 Archer St., Soho ☎ 020/7734–2223 🌐 www.boccadilupo.com Ⓜ Piccadilly Circus.*

Brasserie Zédel

$ | FRENCH | Enjoy great value, prix-fixe menus of classic French dishes at Piccadilly's bustling subterranean Parisian brasserie. Dripping with Beaux-Arts gilt mirrors and monumental marble pillars, you can enjoy French standards like steak haché, choucroute, Niçoise salad, and crème brûleé. **Known for:** London's largest and most spectacular Beaux-Arts basement brasserie; fantastically cheap set meal deals; nightly live music, cabaret, and comedy. *$ Average main: £14 ✉ 20 Sherwood St., Piccadilly Circus*

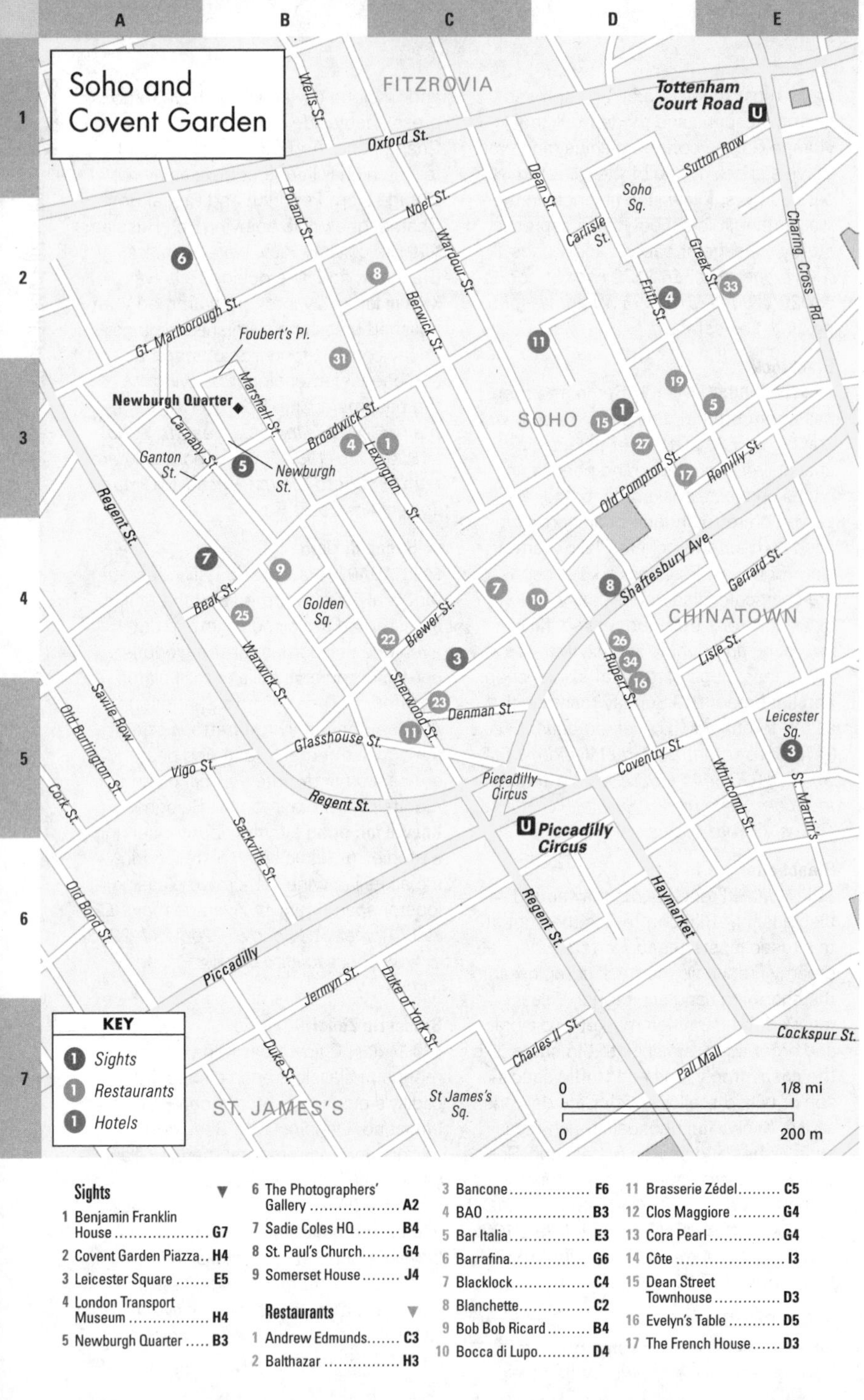

Sights ▼

1 Benjamin Franklin House G7
2 Covent Garden Piazza.. H4
3 Leicester Square E5
4 London Transport Museum H4
5 Newburgh Quarter B3
6 The Photographers' Gallery A2
7 Sadie Coles HQ B4
8 St. Paul's Church........ G4
9 Somerset House J4

Restaurants ▼

1 Andrew Edmunds....... C3
2 Balthazar H3
3 Bancone................. F6
4 BAO B3
5 Bar Italia.................. E3
6 Barrafina................ G6
7 Blacklock................ C4
8 Blanchette............... C2
9 Bob Bob Ricard B4
10 Bocca di Lupo........... D4
11 Brasserie Zédel......... C5
12 Clos Maggiore G4
13 Cora Pearl G4
14 Côte I3
15 Dean Street Townhouse D3
16 Evelyn's Table D5
17 The French House...... D3

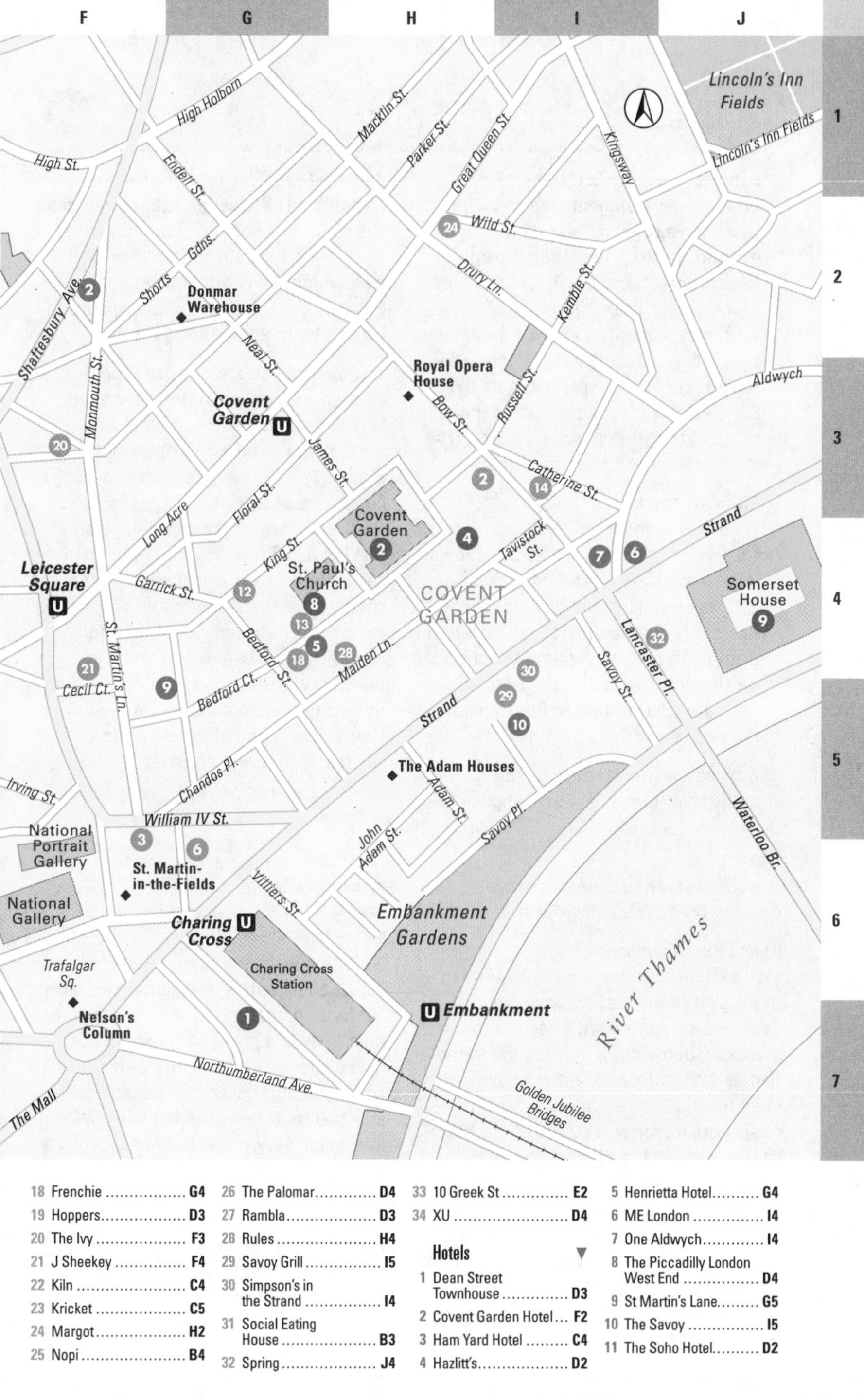

18 Frenchie G4
19 Hoppers................. D3
20 The Ivy F3
21 J Sheekey F4
22 Kiln C4
23 Kricket C5
24 Margot.................. H2
25 Nopi B4
26 The Palomar............ D4
27 Rambla.................. D3
28 Rules H4
29 Savoy Grill I5
30 Simpson's in the Strand I4
31 Social Eating House B3
32 Spring J4
33 10 Greek St E2
34 XU D4

Hotels ▼

1 Dean Street Townhouse D3
2 Covent Garden Hotel ... F2
3 Ham Yard Hotel C4
4 Hazlitt's.................. D2
5 Henrietta Hotel......... G4
6 ME London I4
7 One Aldwych............. I4
8 The Piccadilly London West End D4
9 St Martin's Lane......... G5
10 The Savoy I5
11 The Soho Hotel.......... D2

A Brief History of Soho

Almost as soon as a 17th-century housing development covered what had been a royal park and hunting ground, Soho earned a reputation for louche entertainment, bohemianism, and cosmopolitan liberality. When the authorities adopted a zero-tolerance policy towards soliciting in 1991 (the most recent of several attempts to end Soho's sex trade), they cracked down on an old neighborhood tradition that still resurfaces from time to time.

Successive waves of refugees—French Huguenots in the 1680s, followed by Germans, Russians, Jews, Poles, Greeks, Maltese, Italians, and Chinese—settled and brought their national cuisines with them. So when dining out became fashionable after World War I, Soho was the natural place for restaurants to flourish (as they continue to do today).

Among the luminaries who have made their home here are landscape painter John Constable; Casanova; Canaletto, the great painter of Venice; the visionary poet William Blake; and Karl Marx. In the 1950s and '60s, Soho was London's artists' (and gangsters') quarter and the place to find the top jazz clubs, brothels, and galleries.

The outlines of present-day Covent Garden took shape in the 1630s, when Inigo Jones turned what had been agricultural land into Britain's first planned public square. After the Great Fire of 1666, it became the site of England's largest fruit-and-vegetable market (the flower market arrived in the 19th century). The district's many theaters, taverns, and coffee shops gave the area a somewhat dubious reputation, and after the produce market relocated in 1973, the surviving buildings were scheduled for demolition. A local campaign saved them, and the restored market opened in 1980.

☎ *020/7734–4888* 🌐 *www.brasseriezedel.com* Ⓜ *Piccadilly Circus.*

Dean Street Townhouse

$$$ | **BRITISH** | Everyone feels 10 times more glamorous just stepping inside this candlelit restaurant attached to the swanky Georgian-era hotel of the same name. Straightforward retro-British favorites include pea and ham soup, old-school mince and potatoes, smoked haddock soufflé, and tasty sherry trifle. **Known for:** classy candlelit dining salon with British art on the walls; super professional service; cheery High Tea and Afternoon Tea. $ *Average main: £24* ✉ *69–70 Dean St., Soho* ☎ *020/7434–1775* 🌐 *www.deanstreettownhouse.com* Ⓜ *Oxford Circus, Tottenham Court Rd.*

★ **Evelyn's Table**

$$$ | **ITALIAN** | Hidden in a former beer cellar underneath a 280-year-old pub, there's a sultry speakeasy vibe at Evelyn's Table, a tiny eatery specializing in Italian seafood. A secret door with a peephole reveals a small but bustling open galley kitchen where three deft chefs serve modern Italian fish-based marvels sourced from Looe market in Cornwall. **Known for:** secret and cozy cellar venue; wonderfully fresh Cornish day boat fish; superb soundtracks curated by ex-DJ and current co-owner Layo Paskin. $ *Average main: £26* ✉ *The Blue Posts , 28 Rupert St., Soho* ☎ *07921/336–010* 🌐 *www.theblueposts.co.uk* ⏲ *Closed Sun. No lunch* Ⓜ *Piccadilly Circus, Leicester Sq.*

★ The French House

$$$ | **FRENCH** | Black and white photos of legendary French House regulars like artists Lucian Freud and Francis Bacon beam down at this old-school Soho hangout. Set above a tiny pub run by a former cabaret artist, you can sip Ricard pastis or bargains from the all-French wine list before embracing classics like salt cod beignets, calves brain with brown butter, or slow-braised Naravin of lamb with cheesy aligot mash. **Known for:** iconic home to Soho's artists, writers, and bohemians; French classics like whole roast garlic bulb on toast; no online bookings, no mobile phones, no laptops, and no music. *Average main: £24 49 Dean St., Soho 020/7437–2477 www.frenchhousesoho.com Restaurant closed weekends. No dinner Mon. and Fri. Piccadilly Circus, Tottenham Court Rd.*

★ Hoppers

$ | **SRI LANKAN** | Sri Lankan curry fans have gone mad for the fermented rice-flour egg pancakes (a Sri Lankan specialty known as hoppers) and paper-thin griddled dosas at this highly spiced Frith Street snuggery. Diners gorge on chili mutton rolls, curried duck hearts, bone marrow curry, and piles of steamed string hoppers dipped in spicy broth, coconut chutney, or onion-and-Maldives-fish-flakes relish. **Known for:** crispy egg hopper pancakes with coconut sambol; authentic Colombo-style cabin atmosphere; signature goat or black pork kari curry. *Average main: £9 49 Frith St., Soho www.hopperslondon.com Closed Sun. Oxford Circus, Tottenham Court Rd.*

Kiln

$ | **THAI** | Earthy northern Thai cuisine bursts out of the charcoal-fired kiln and clay pots at this BBQ-focused wonderland in Soho. Overlook the open kitchen and you'll see sizzling cumin-dusted hogget skewers and charcoal-grilled chicken thigh bites, along with other village-style dishes that show influences from Laos, Myanmar, and the Yunnan province of China. **Known for:** open kitchen counter setup with charcoal grill and hot clay pots; array of Cornish grown Thai, Burmese, and other Asian herbs and spices; popular cumin-dusted aged hogget skewers. *Average main: £10 58 Brewer St., Soho www.kilnsoho.com Oxford Circus, Piccadilly Circus.*

Kricket

$ | **INDIAN** | Upsized dishes of zingy Indian street food fly from the open kitchen at this Piccadilly party spot. Sit at the L-shaped, lava-topped counter and watch the chefs haul out bone marrow-smeared *kulcha* breads from the blazing clay tandoor alongside other funky dishes. **Known for:** pepped-up Indian street food faves; colonial cocktails in the raucous downstairs dining den; hip, young crowds. *Average main: £11 12 Denman St., Piccadilly Circus No phone www.kricket.co.uk/soho Closed Sun. Piccadilly Circus.*

Nopi

$$$ | **MODERN ISRAELI** | Israeli star chef and global cookbook sensation Yotam Ottolenghi cleans up at his flagship vegetable-centric restaurant off Regent Street. Mixing densely flavored small dishes from the Middle East, Asia, and the Mediterranean, diners here can jump around from courgette (zucchini) and manouri cheese fritters to harissa-marinated octopus and Persian love rice to carob and coconut ice cream. **Known for:** veg-focused classics like roast eggplant, pomegranate seeds, and feta yogurt; healthy offerings like rainbow trout with koji and sheep's labneh; popular shakshuka and scrambled tofu-laden breakfasts. *Average main: £26 21–22 Warwick St., Soho 020/7494–9584 www.ottolenghi.co.uk Oxford Circus, Piccadilly Circus.*

The Palomar

$$ | **MIDDLE EASTERN** | It's Jerusalem meets Palestine meets Beirut meets a funky scenester vibe at this Arab-Israeli spot off Chinatown. Sit at the open-kitchen zinc counter and down shots of *arak* while trading quips with the Middle Eastern chefs, who offer a medley of Levantine delights, including Yemeni-Jewish *kubaneh* bread, Palestinian steak tartare, Jerusalem truffled mushroom polenta, and tangy paprika-rich pork belly tagine with Israeli couscous. **Known for:** fun, Middle Eastern party atmosphere and free arak shots; lively pork pie–hatted chefs brigade in the open kitchen; popular Persian oxtail stew. *Average main: £16 ✉ 34 Rupert St., Piccadilly Circus ☎ 020/7439–8777 🌐 www.thepalomar.co.uk Ⓜ Piccadilly Circus, Leicester Sq.*

Rambla

$$ | **TAPAS** | Dine curbside on Soho's busy Dean Street or lean in at the open kitchen counter at this popular elegant but casual tapas joint. Brilliantly cheap and exceptionally tasty Catalan-inspired small plates like spinach croquettas or velvetted hake are complemented by a fine all-Spanish wine list, which focuses on sherry, Cava, and wines from Catalunya. **Known for:** seafood and mountain-based Catalan small plates; braised oxtail canelones with Nevat goat cheese sauce; Catalan puddings for dessert. *Average main: £18 ✉ 64 Dean St., Soho ☎ 020/7734–8428 🌐 www.ramblalondon.com ⏲ No dinner Sun. Ⓜ Piccadilly Circus, Tottenham Court Rd.*

Social Eating House

$$$ | **FRENCH** | At Jason Atherton's underrated but brilliant French *bistronomie* Soho hangout, witty dishes like smoked duck's ham (made from cured duck's breast) and Scotch egg-and-chips are served alongside complex classics like charred Cumbrian pork with mustard jelly. The moodily lit bare-brick salon is decorated with dark parquet floors, antique mirrored ceilings, and red leather banquettes. **Known for:** extravagant tasting menus at the open chef's table; popular set lunch menu; vintage cocktails at the speakeasy lounge upstairs. *Average main: £29 ✉ 58 Poland St., Soho ☎ 020/7993–3251 🌐 www.socialeatinghouse.com ⏲ Closed Sun. Ⓜ Oxford Circus, Tottenham Court Rd.*

10 Greek Street

$$ | **MODERN EUROPEAN** | There may only be 28 table seats and nine counter stools at this stripped-down Modern European humdinger, but the consistently great food, cheap wine, affable prices, and excellent service more than make up for it. Once seated, expect simple starters and mains like butternut ravioli with sage or slip sole with lemon butter. **Known for:** buzzed-up foodie atmosphere in a pared-back dining space; gutsy seasonal Modern European mains; generous platters of house-cured charcuterie. *Average main: £22 ✉ 10 Greek St., Soho ☎ 020/7734–4677 🌐 www.10greekstreet.com Ⓜ Tottenham Court Rd.*

★ XU

$$ | **TAIWANESE** | It feels like a cinematic reinterpretation of 1930s Taipei at this glamorous jewel box on the edge of Chinatown. Peerless dishes like tomato and smoked eel cold soup and marinated *Shou Pa* chicken with rice, ginger, and white pepper are complemented by a tea kiosk, a tea master, railway clocks, two hidden mahjong rooms, and a collection of cute solo dining seats. **Known for:** Taiwanese classics like Char Siu Iberico pork with grilled cucumber; sparkling Hong Yu cold brew tea; Taiwanese whisky. *Average main: £19 ✉ 30 Rupert St., Piccadilly ☎ 020/3319–8147 🌐 www.xulondon.com Ⓜ Piccadilly Circus, Leicester Sq.*

Hotels

Dean Street Townhouse

$$$ | **HOTEL** | Discreet and unpretentious—and right in the heart of Soho—this oh-so-stylish Georgian town house has a

bohemian vibe and an excellent Modern British restaurant, hung with pieces by renowned artists like Peter Blake and Tracy Emin. **Pros:** ultracool vibe; resembles an upper-class pied-à-terre; great location in the heart of Soho. **Cons:** some rooms are extremely small; rooms at the front of the building can be noisy, especially on weekends; the crowd can often feel cooler-than-thou. *Rooms from: £330 69–71 Dean St., Soho 020/7434–1775 www.deanstreettownhouse.com 39 rooms Free breakfast Leicester Sq., Tottenham Court Rd.*

★ Ham Yard Hotel
$$$ | HOTEL | Luxurious, playful, and riotously good fun, the Ham Yard Hotel is another property from the stable of London hotel designer extraordinaire, Kit Kemp. **Pros:** great modern British design; excellent service; fun facilities, including a bowling alley. **Cons:** rates can get very pricey; some will find the scene at the hotel a little too trendy; with a cinema, bowling alley, and spa on-site, you might not leave the hotel. *Rooms from: £400 1 Ham Yard, Soho 020/3642–2000 www.firmdalehotels.com/hotels/london/ham-yard-hotel 91 rooms No meals Piccadilly Circus.*

★ Hazlitt's
$$$ | HOTEL | This disarmingly friendly place, full of personality, robust antiques, Old Masters portraits, and claw-foot tubs, occupies three connected early 18th-century town houses, one of which was the last home of critic and essayist William Hazlitt (1778–1830). **Pros:** great for lovers of antiques and Old Masters art; historic atmosphere with lots of small sitting rooms and wooden staircases; truly beautiful and relaxed. **Cons:** no in-house restaurant; breakfast costs extra; no elevators. *Rooms from: £255 6 Frith St., Soho 020/7434–1771 www.hazlittshotel.com 30 rooms No meals Tottenham Court Rd.*

The Piccadilly London West End
$$$ | HOTEL | FAMILY | This hotel couldn't be better situated for theater lovers; it's right in the famed West End district with three such venues within sight of the front door alone. **Pros:** unbeatable location; some thoughtful extras; attentive staff. **Cons:** noise is unavoidable; you're paying for the location rather than the amenities, and it shows; rooms are compact. *Rooms from: £295 65–73 Shaftesbury Ave., Soho 020/7871–6000, 877/898–1586 in U.S. www.piccadillypremierlondon.co.uk 67 rooms No meals Piccadilly Circus.*

The Soho Hotel
$$$ | HOTEL | A mecca for film, media, and fashion folk, this supertrendy hotel personifies Soho's enduring hipness with its artsy, urban chic vibe. **Pros:** small and sophisticated; excellent service; great restaurant. **Cons:** bar can be crowded and noisy on weeknights; some lower-level rooms lack the amenities of pricier rooms; expensive for a boutique hotel. *Rooms from: £340 4 Richmond Mews, off Dean St., Soho 020/7559–3000 www.firmdalehotels.com/hotels/london/the-soho-hotel 96 rooms No meals Tottenham Court Rd.*

Nightlife

The center of town is famous for its vibrant gay scene, atmospheric music, cabaret venues, and acclaimed comedy clubs. Traditional British "boozers" stand side by side with informal continental-style drinking dens. Drop in for a late drink and you may find yourself rubbing shoulders with musicians and actors from the West End's 50-odd theaters. In Covent Garden, recent bar openings have also added extra buzz.

BARS

★ Bar Américain
BARS/PUBS | The Beaux-Arts interior of this underground bar just north of Piccadilly Circus is so opulent and glamorous that

you'd be forgiven for thinking it had been here since the 1930s. In fact it's a relatively new arrival and has been a hit since it opened in 2012, along with Brasserie Zédel and racy The Crazy Coqs cabaret and floor show that share the premises. The charming cocktails pay homage to post–World War I America and France, with wonderful names like Jack Rose, Paloma, and Hemingway Daiquiri. ✉ *20 Sherwood St., Soho* ☎ *020/7734–4888* 🌐 *www.brasseriezedel.com* Ⓜ *Piccadilly Circus.*

★ The Blind Pig

BARS/PUBS | Chances are you won't have heard of half the ingredients on the cocktail menu at this dark and sultry bar above Jason Atherton's smart casual restaurant, Social Eating House in Soho, but the sense of mystery only adds to the experience. So, too, do the antique mirrored ceilings and copper-topped bar, the delectable small plates (like black pepper prawn crackers and macaroni and cheese with shaved mushroom)—and the knowledge that you've nabbed a seat at one of the coolest spots in Soho. ✉ *58 Poland St., Soho* ☎ *020/7993–3251* 🌐 *www.socialeatinghouse.com* Ⓜ *Oxford Circus, Tottenham Court Rd.*

Mark's Bar

BARS/PUBS | At bon vivant Mark Hix's relaxed basement Soho haunt, you can knock back decidedly British cocktails (from age-old recipes) like the Britz Spritz or a Full English Negroni or stick to the resplendent Punch Bowls, perfectly executed classic cocktails, and British ales. The bar is tucked below the modern British restaurant Hix Soho. The atmosphere is clubby, with kilim rugs, suede poufs, a low sunken bar, and worn large leather Chesterfields. For food, there are first-rate bar snacks, including oysters, Scotch quail eggs, and pork crackling with rhubarb sauce. ✉ *66–70 Brewer St., Soho* ☎ *020/7292–3518* 🌐 *www.hixrestaurants.co.uk* Ⓜ *Oxford Circus, Piccadilly Circus.*

COMEDY

Amused Moose Comedy

CABARET | This roving West End comedy night group is often considered the best place to see breaking talent as well as household names doing "secret" shows. Comedians Ricky Gervais, Eddie Izzard, and Russell Brand are among those who have graced the Amused Moose stage, and every summer a handful of the Edinburgh Fringe comedians preview here. The bar is open late (and serves food), and there's a DJ and dancing after the show. Tickets are often discounted with a printout from their website, and shows are mainly on Monday, Wednesday, and weekends. ✉ *Townsend House, 22–25 Dean St., Soho* ☎ *020/7287–3727* 🌐 *www.amusedmoose.com* 🎟 *From £12* Ⓜ *Oxford Circus, Tottenham Court Rd.*

★ The Comedy Store

COMEDY CLUBS | Before heading off to prime time, some of the United Kingdom's funniest stand-ups cut their teeth here, at what's considered the birthplace of alternative comedy. The Comedy Store Players, a team with six comedians doing improvisation with audience suggestions, entertain on Wednesday and Sunday; The Cutting Edge steps in with a topical take every Tuesday; Thursday, Friday, and Saturday have the best stand-up acts. There's also a bar with food. Note you must be over 18 to enter. ✉ *1A Oxendon St., Soho* ☎ *020/7024–2060 for tickets and booking* 🌐 *www.thecomedystore.co.uk* 🎟 *From £12* Ⓜ *Leicester Sq., Piccadilly Circus.*

ECLECTIC MUSIC

The 100 Club

MUSIC CLUBS | Since this small club opened in 1942, many of the greats have played here, from Glenn Miller and Louis Armstrong to The Who, The Clash, The Buzzcocks, and The Sex Pistols. Saved from closure in 2010 by a campaign led by Sir Paul McCartney, the legendary space now reverberates to jazz, ska, '60s R&B, and northern soul. ✉ *100*

Oxford St., Soho ☎ No phone 🌐 www.the100club.co.uk 🎫 From £10 Ⓜ Oxford Circus, Tottenham Court Rd.

Phoenix Artist Club

THEMED ENTERTAINMENT | Thankfully nonmembers can gain free entry before 9 pm at this legendary West End open-mike musical theater, cabaret, impromptu arts review, brasserie, and late-night private members' club of thespians, writers, and critics. You might catch a raunchy cabaret, see a Theaterland star belt it at the Thursday night open-mike sessions, or be transported by the anecdotes of a one-time movie star. ✉ *1 Phoenix St., Soho ☎ 020/7836–1077 🌐 www.phoenixartistclub.com Ⓜ Covent Garden, Tottenham Court Rd.*

GAY AND LESBIAN

The Friendly Society

BARS/PUBS | An unremarkable-looking door in a Soho alleyway leads down some dingy steps into one of the most fun LGBTQ+ joints in the neighborhood. Hopping with activity almost any night of the week, the place is known for its welcoming atmosphere to everyone—gay, trans, questioning, or straight. The interior alone—including garden gnome stools and a ceiling covered in Barbie dolls and disco balls—is enough to lift the spirits. ✉ *79 Wardour St., Soho ☎ 020/7434–3804 Ⓜ Leicester Sq., Tottenham Court Rd.*

Ku Bar

BARS/PUBS | A deliciously camp vibe, toned bar staff, and a friendly atmosphere make this one of Soho's most popular gay bars. The crowd is mostly male, but women are very welcome. Head to the quieter upstairs lounge bar for a more laid-back mood, or dance the night away at Ku Klub in the basement. There's a second branch around the corner on Lisle Street, near Leicester Square. ✉ *25 Frith St., Soho ☎ 020/7437–4303 🌐 www.ku-bar.co.uk Ⓜ Leicester Sq., Tottenham Court Rd.*

She

DANCE CLUBS | This basement club, part of the popular Ku group of gay venues, is a recent arrival on the Soho scene. It welcomes a mostly young lesbian crowd for informal cocktails early in the evening followed by dancing—of the pop and house variety—later on. The vibe is fun and friendly, especially on the last Thursday of each month, when She hosts London's only drag-king open-mike night. ✉ *23A Old Compton St., Soho ☎ 020/7437–4303 🌐 www.she-soho.com 🎫 £6 cover weekends after 9 pm Ⓜ Leicester Sq., Piccadilly Circus.*

JAZZ AND BLUES

Ain't Nothin' But...

MUSIC CLUBS | This sweaty fun place off Carnaby Street does exactly what its name suggests. Local blues musicians, as well as some notable names, squeeze onto the tiny stage and there's good bar food of the chili-and-gumbo variety. Most weekday nights there's no cover. ✉ *20 Kingly St., Soho ☎ 020/7287–0514 🌐 www.aintnothinbut.co.uk 🎫 £7 cover weekends after 8:30 pm Ⓜ Oxford Circus, Piccadilly Circus.*

Pizza Express Jazz Club

MUSIC CLUBS | One of the United Kingdom's most ubiquitous pizza chains also runs a leading Soho jazz venue. Established in 1976, the dimly lit restaurant hosts both established and emerging top-quality international jazz acts every night, with food available in the downstairs venue (as opposed to the upstairs restaurant) around 90 minutes before stage time. The Italian-style thin-crust pizzas are popular, but about what you'd expect from a major chain. ✉ *10 Dean St., Soho ☎ 020/7439–4962 for jazz club, 020/7437–9595 for restaurant 🌐 www.pizzaexpresslive.com 🎫 From £16 Ⓜ Tottenham Court Rd.*

★ **Ronnie Scott's**

MUSIC CLUBS | London's best-known jazz club has attracted the biggest names—from Ella Fitzgerald and Count Basie and Stan Getz—since opening nearby in 1959. It's usually dark, hot, and crowded, but the food and table service are better than they used to be. The ultracool mood can't be beat, even since the sad departure of the eponymous founder and saxophonist. Jazz sets and shows take place every night, with additional late gigs on Friday and Saturday. Reservations are recommended. ✉ *47 Frith St., Soho* ☎ *020/7439–0747* 🌐 *www.ronniescotts.co.uk* 🎫 *From £24* Ⓜ *Leicester Sq., Tottenham Court Rd.*

PUBS

The Dog and Duck

BARS/PUBS | FAMILY | A beautiful example of a late-19th-century London pub, the Dog and Duck has a well-preserved Heritage-listed interior furnished with glazed tiles, cut glass mirrors, and polished wood, though it's often so packed that it's hard to get a good look. There's a decent selection of real ales at the bar and a restaurant serving outstanding pale ale-battered fish-and-chips with mushy peas. Originally built in 1734 and patronized by artists John Constable and Dante Rossetti, the cozy upstairs dining room is named for writer George Orwell, who also frequented this spot. ✉ *18 Bateman St., Soho* ☎ *020/7494–0697* 🌐 *www.nicholsonspubs.co.uk* Ⓜ *Oxford Circus, Tottenham Court Rd.*

Performing Arts

London's hip center has it all, from multiplexes playing the biggest blockbuster movies to niche contemporary art galleries tucked away in backstreets, and from world-famous opera houses to sultry cabaret joints.

FILM

★ Curzon Soho

FILM | FAMILY | This popular independent movie theater opposite Chinatown runs a vibrant and artsy program of mixed repertoire and mainstream films, with a good calendar of director talks, Q&As, and other events. The bar is great for a quiet drink, even when Soho is crawling with people. There are further Curzon branches in Mayfair, Bloomsbury, Aldgate, Victoria, Wimbledon, and Richmond. ✉ *99 Shaftesbury Ave., Soho* ☎ *0333/321–0104* 🌐 *www.curzoncinemas.com* 🎫 *From £11* Ⓜ *Piccadilly Circus, Leicester Sq.*

The Prince Charles Cinema

FILM | FAMILY | This cult repertory movie theater right off Leicester Square offers you a chance to catch up with independent features, documentaries, and even blockbusters you may have missed. A second screen upstairs shows newer movies at more usual West End prices. This is where the "Sing-along screening" took off; come in character and warble along to *The Sound of Music, Grease, The Rocky Horror Picture Show,* and others. ✉ *7 Leicester Pl., Soho* ☎ *020/7494–3654* 🌐 *www.princecharlescinema.com* 🎫 *From £5; sing-alongs £17* Ⓜ *Leicester Sq., Piccadilly Circus.*

THEATER

Soho Theatre

DANCE | This sleek theater in the heart of Soho is devoted to fostering new work and is a prolific presenter of plays by young and emerging writers, comedy performances, cabaret shows, dance, and other entertainment. The bar is always buzzing. ✉ *21 Dean St., Soho* ☎ *020/7478–0100* 🌐 *www.sohotheatre.com* 🎫 *From £5* Ⓜ *Oxford Circus, Tottenham Court Rd.*

Shopping

ACCESSORIES

Peckham Rye

CLOTHING | On the small cobblestone streets leading off Carnaby Street, among other little specialty shops, the family-run Peckham Rye sells heritage-style men's accessories: handmade silk and twill ties, bow ties, and scarves, all using traditional patterns drawn from the archives going back to 1799. Embodying the

Ralph Lauren aesthetic even more than Ralph Lauren, the socks, striped shirts, and handkerchiefs attract modern-day dandies like Mark Ronson and David Beckham. Bespoke tailoring for men is also offered. ✉ *11 Newburgh St., Soho* ☎ *020/7734–5181* 🌐 *www.peckhamrye.com* Ⓜ *Oxford St., Tottenham Court Rd.*

BOOKS

★ Foyles

BOOKS/STATIONERY | FAMILY | Founded in 1903 by the Foyle brothers after they failed the Civil Service exams, this family-owned bookstore is in a 1930s art deco building, once the home of the renowned art college Central Saint Martins. One of London's best sources for textbooks and the United Kingdom's largest retailer of foreign language books, with more than 200,000 titles on its four miles of bookshelves, Foyles also stocks everything from popular fiction to military history, sheet music, medical tomes, graphic novels, and handsome, illustrated fine arts books. It also offers the store-within-a-store Ray's Jazz (one of London's better outlets for music) and a cool café. Foyles also has branches in the Royal Festival Hall at the Southbank Centre and at Waterloo Station. ✉ *107 Charing Cross Rd., Soho* ☎ *020/7437–5660* 🌐 *www.foyles.co.uk* Ⓜ *Leicester Sq., Tottenham Court Rd.*

CLOTHING

Agent Provocateur

CLOTHING | Created by fashion designer Vivienne Westwood's son and daughter-in-law, this line of lingerie in gorgeous fabrics, silks, latex, and lace tends toward the kind of risqué underwear that is both provocative and practical. The original boudoir-like shop is staffed by assistants in prim pink uniforms in what was Soho's red-light district, but the brand has gone a bit more mainstream and now sells bathing suits, nightwear, jewelry and luggage in multiple locations in Knightsbridge, Mayfair, Victoria, Notting Hill, and the City. ✉ *6 Broadwick St., Soho* ☎ *020/7439–0229* 🌐 *www.agentprovocateur.com* Ⓜ *Oxford Circus, Tottenham Court Rd.*

Wolsey

CLOTHING | Specializing in men's knitwear since 1755, this long-established company now sells rugged but stylish outerwear, sweaters, shirts, hats, scarves, socks, T-shirts, sweatshirts, sleepwear, and underwear (the undies of choice for polar explorers Roald Amundsen, Captain Robert Scott, and Ernest Shackleton). The company also supplied woolen garments to British troops in 1914. It's not all heritage, though; Wolsey makes hoodies as well, and its padded jackets and vests employ the latest in thermalwear technology. The interior reflects this blend of the traditional and the contemporary, with exposed brick walls, brushed steel beams, and photographs of expeditions the brand has outfitted. There's another branch in Covent Garden. ✉ *83A Brewer St., Soho* ☎ *020/7434–4257* 🌐 *www.wolsey.com* Ⓜ *Piccadilly Circus.*

DEPARTMENT STORES

★ Liberty

DEPARTMENT STORES | FAMILY | The wonderful black-and-white mock-Tudor facade, created from the timbers of two Royal Navy ships, reflects this store's origins in the late-19th-century Arts and Crafts movement. Leading designers were recruited to create the classic art nouveau Liberty prints that are still a centerpiece of the brand, gracing everything from cushions and silk kimonos to embossed leather bags and photo albums. Inside, Liberty is a labyrinth of nooks and crannies stuffed with thoughtfully chosen merchandise, including niche beauty, perfume, footwear, and housewares lines such as Soho Home, which features furniture and textiles from the membership clubs. Clothes for both men and women focus on high quality and high fashion, with labels like Rixo and Roland Mouret. The store regularly commissions new prints from contemporary designers, and sells both these and its classic patterns by the yard. If you're not so handy with a needle, an interior design service will create soft furnishings for you. There's also a florist, a hair salon, a traditional men's barber, branded beauty treatment rooms, a brow bar, a piercing studio, and a foot spa. ✉ *Regent St., Soho* ☎ *020/7734–1234* 🌐 *www.libertylondon.com* Ⓜ *Oxford Circus.*

FOOD

★ SAID dal 1923

FOOD/CANDY | **FAMILY** | Sip some of London's best hot chocolate from a chocolate cup and with a chocolate spoon at this cult chocolate shop and café in Soho. Three cauldrons of white, milk, and dark hot chocolate bubble away behind the counter, which is decked with wall-mounted vintage chocolate molds. Trawl the fine truffle selection and head out with grand cru chocolate bars, beans, buttons, and jars of hazelnut chocolate spread. ✉ *41 Broadwick St., Soho* ☎ *020/7437–1584* 🌐 *www.said.it/en/london-soho* Ⓜ *Oxford Circus, Piccadilly Circus, Tottenham Court Rd.*

The Vintage House

WINE/SPIRITS | If whiskey is more to your taste than wine, visit the family-run Vintage House, which has the country's largest selection of single malts (more than 1,350), including many rare bottles and some exclusive to the shop. You'll also find more than 100 tequilas, plus rums, liqueurs, and Armagnacs, as well as Cuban cigars. The shop is open until 11 pm (10 pm on Sunday). ✉ *42 Old Compton St., Soho* ☎ *020/7437–2592* 🌐 *www.vintagehouse.london* Ⓜ *Leicester Sq.*

MUSIC

Reckless Records

MUSIC STORES | Open since 1984, this legendary Soho secondhand vinyl store has seen the reigns of cassette tapes, CDs, Napster, and Spotify, and arguably has helped contribute to vinyl's recent resurgence. Featured on the cover of Oasis's 1995 hit album *(What's The Story) Morning Glory?*, come here for rare vinyl finds and classic albums, spanning everything from jazz and blues to drum 'n' bass. ✉ *30 Berwick St., Soho* ☎ *020/7437–4271* 🌐 *www.reckless.co.uk* Ⓜ *Oxford Circus, Piccadilly Circus, Tottenham Court Rd.*

TOYS

Hamleys

TOYS | **FAMILY** | When British children visit London, this institution—the oldest toy store in the world—is at the top of their agenda. Its six floors hold the latest dolls, soft toys, video games, and technological devices, as well as old-fashioned pleasures like train sets, drum kits, and magic tricks, plus every must-have on the preteen shopping list (some parents may find the offerings to be overly commercialized, as they're heavy on movie and TV tie-ins). Hamleys is a madhouse at Christmastime, but the Santa's grotto is one of the best in town. There's a smaller branch in St. Pancras International train station and one near the Shard in south London. ✉ *188–196 Regent St., Soho* ☎ *0371/704–1977* 🌐 *www.hamleys.com* Ⓜ *Oxford Circus, Piccadilly Circus.*

Covent Garden

To the east of Charing Cross Road lies Covent Garden, the famous marketplace–turned–shopping mall. Although boutiques and haute fashion shops line the surrounding streets, many Londoners come to Covent Garden for its two outposts of culture: the **Royal Opera House** and the **Donmar Warehouse,** one of London's best and most innovative theaters. The area becomes more sedate just to the east, at the end of Wellington Street, where semicircular Aldwych is lined with grand buildings, and from there the Strand leads to the huge stately piazza of **Somerset House,** a vibrant center of contemporary arts and

Leicester Square is home to many movie theaters and a half-price theater ticket booth.

home to the many masterpieces on view at the **Courtauld Gallery.** You'll get a sense of old-fashioned London just behind the Strand, where small lanes are little changed since the 18th century. On the way to the verdant **Embankment Gardens** bordering the Thames, you may pass the **Benjamin Franklin House,** where the noted statesman lived in the years leading up to the American Revolution.

Covent Garden joins Soho as an arts-and-entertainment center in the city, popularly referred to as "the West End." The neighborhood centers on the Piazza, site of the original Covent Garden market. High Holborn to the north, Kingsway to the east, and the Strand to the south form its other boundaries.

Sights

★ Benjamin Franklin House

HOUSE | FAMILY | This architecturally significant 1730 house is the only surviving residence of American statesman, scientist, writer, and inventor Benjamin Franklin, who lived and worked here for 16 years preceding the American Revolution. The restored Georgian town house has been left unfurnished, the better to show off the original features: 18th-century paneling, stoves, beams, bricks, and windows. Visitors are led around the house by the costumed character of Polly Hewson, the daughter of Franklin's landlady, who interacts with engaging video projections and recorded voices (Wednesday–Sunday). On Monday you can take a guided tour focusing on the architectural details of the building, and a walking tour of the surrounding area lasting up to 90 minutes sets off from the house every morning at noon. ✉ *36 Craven St., Covent Garden* ☎ *020/7839–2006* 🌐 *www.benjaminfranklinhouse.org* 🎫 *Historical experience £8; architectural tour £6* 🕓 *Closed Tues.* Ⓜ *Charing Cross, Embankment.*

★ Covent Garden Piazza

HISTORIC SITE | FAMILY | Once home to London's main flower market, where *My Fair Lady's* Eliza Doolittle peddled

Did You Know?

Somerset House was lapped by the River Thames before the Victoria Embankment was built in the 19th century. The neoclassical building's grand courtyard is home to ice-skating in winter and dancing fountains in summer.

her blooms, the square around which Covent Garden pivots is known as the Piazza. In the center, the fine old market building now houses stalls and shops selling expensive clothing, plus several restaurants and cafés, and knickknack stores that are good for gifts. One particular gem is Benjamin Pollock's Toyshop at No. 44 in the market. Established in the 1880s, it sells delightful toy theaters. The superior **Apple Market** has good crafts stalls on most days, too. On the south side of the Piazza, the indoor **Jubilee Market,** with its stalls of clothing, army-surplus gear, and more crafts and knickknacks, feels a bit like a flea market. In summer it may seem that everyone in the huge crowds around you in the Piazza is a fellow tourist, but there's still plenty of office life in the area. Londoners who shop here tend to head for Neal Street and the area to the north of Covent Garden Tube station, rather than the market itself. In the Piazza, street performers—from global musicians to jugglers and mimes—play to the crowds, as they have done since the first English Punch and Judy Show, staged here in the 17th century. ✉ *Covent Garden* 🌐 *www.coventgarden.london* Ⓜ *Covent Garden.*

Ice-Skating

It's hard to beat the skating experience at Somerset House, where from mid-November to mid-January a rink is set up in the grand courtyard of this central London palace. Check the website for current prices; its popularity is enormous, and if you can't get a ticket, other atmospheric venues such as Hampton Court, the Tower of London, the London Eye, and the Natural History Museum are following Somerset House's lead in having temporary winter rinks. ☎ *0333/320–2836* 🌐 *www.somersethouse.org.uk.*

Leicester Square

PLAZA | FAMILY | Looking at the neon of the major movie houses, the fast-food outlets, and the casino and disco entrances, you'd never guess that this square (pronounced "Lester") was a model of formality and refinement when it was first laid out around 1670. By the 19th century, the square was already bustling and disreputable, and although it's not a threatening place, you should still be on your guard, especially at night—any space so full of people is bound to attract pickpockets, and Leicester Square certainly does. Although there's a bit of residual glamour (major red-carpet film premieres often happen here), Londoners generally tend to avoid the place, though it's worth a visit for its hustle and bustle, its mime artists, and the pleasant modern fountain at its center. Also in the middle is a famous statue of a sulking Shakespeare, perhaps remembering the days when the movie houses were live theaters—burlesque houses, but live all the same. On the northeast corner, in Leicester Place, stands the church of **Notre Dame de France,** with a wonderful mural by Jean Cocteau in one of its side chapels. For more in the way of atmosphere, head north and west from here, through Chinatown and the narrow streets of Soho. ✉ *Covent Garden* Ⓜ *Leicester Sq.*

London Transport Museum

MUSEUM | FAMILY | Housed in the old flower market at the southeast corner of Covent Garden, this stimulating museum is filled with impressive vehicle, poster, and photograph collections. As you watch the crowds drive a Tube-train simulation and gawk at the early Victorian steam locomotives and horse-drawn trams (and the piles of detritus that remained behind), it's unclear who's enjoying it more: children or adults. Best of all, the kid-friendly museum (under 18 admitted free, and there's a play area) has a multilevel approach to education, including information for the youngest visitor and the most advanced transit aficionado alike. Food and drink are available at the Upper Deck café, and the shop has lots of good options for gift-buying. ■ **TIP→ Tickets are valid for unlimited entry for 12 months.** ✉ *Covent Garden Piazza, Covent Garden* ☎ *0343/222–5000* 🌐 *www.ltmuseum.co.uk* 🎫 *£18* Ⓜ *Covent Garden, Leicester Sq.*

★ Somerset House

MUSEUM | FAMILY | This huge complex—the work of Sir William Chambers (1723–96), and built during the reign of George III to house offices of the Navy Board—has been transformed from dusty government offices to one of the capital's most buzzing centers of culture and the arts, often hosting several interesting exhibitions at one time. The cobblestone Italianate courtyard, where Admiral Nelson used to walk, makes a great setting for 55 playful fountains and is transformed into a romantic ice rink in winter; the grand space is the venue for music and outdoor movie screenings in summer. **The Courtauld Gallery** (currently closed for renovations) occupies most of the north building, facing the busy Strand. Across the courtyard are the barrell-vaulted Embankment Galleries, with a vibrant calendar of design, fashion, architecture, and photography exhibitions. The East Wing has another fine exhibition space, and events are sometimes also held in the atmospherically gloomy cellars below the Fountain Court. Fernandez & Wells is a great spot for an informal meal or snack. In summer eating and drinking spills out onto the large terrace next to the Thames. ✉ *Strand, Covent Garden* ☎ *020/7845–4600* 🌐 *www.somersethouse.org.uk* 🎫 *Embankment Galleries price varies, other areas free* Ⓜ *Charing Cross, Covent Garden, Holborn, Temple.*

St. Paul's Church

RELIGIOUS SITE | If you want to commune with the spirits of Vivien Leigh, Noël Coward, Gracie Fields, and Charlie Chaplin, this might be just the place. Memorials to them and many other theater greats are found in this 1633 work of the renowned Inigo Jones, who, as Surveyor of the King's Works, designed the whole of Covent Garden Piazza. St. Paul's Church has been known as "the actors' church" since the Restoration, thanks to the neighboring theater district and St. Paul's prominent parishioners. (Well-known actors often read the lessons at services, and the church still hosts concerts and small-scale productions.) Fittingly, the opening scene of Shaw's *Pygmalion* takes place under its Tuscan portico. The western end of the Piazza is a prime pitch for street entertainers, but if they're not to your liking, you can repair to the serenity of the garden entered from King or Bedford streets. Charming open-air theater performances of Shakespeare plays and other works are staged there in the summertime. ✉ *Bedford St., Covent Garden* ☎ *020/7836–5221* 🌐 *www.actorschurch.org* Ⓜ *Covent Garden.*

Restaurants

Balthazar

$$$ | BRASSERIE | FAMILY | British restaurateur Keith McNally re-creates his famed New York Parisian brasserie at this busy corner spot just off Covent Garden. The decor creates an enchanting backdrop to enjoy a classic French brasserie menu of few surprises, including flavor-packed dishes like macaroni and Gruyère cheese or ox cheek bourguignon. **Known for:** Parisian-style grand café; handy prix fixe, brunch, children's, and Afternoon Tea menus; vegan and vegetarian options. Ⓢ *Average main: £24* ✉ *4–7 Russell St., Covent Garden* ☎ *020/3301–1155* 🌐 *www.balthazarlondon.com* Ⓜ *Covent Garden, Charing Cross, Holborn.*

★ Bancone

$ | ITALIAN | London's awash with New Wave, affordable, and fresh pasta joints, but Bancone in Covent Garden is one of the best options . Diners regularly pitch up at the white marble, porcelain, and bronze bar counter and marvel at the silkiness of the pastas and the outstandingly low prices. All antipasti are under £10, while popular fresh pastas, like 10-hour oxtail ragu mafalde or "silk handkerchiefs" sheets with walnut butter, weigh in under £15. **Known for:** high-end pasta at cheap prices; slick urban Italian setting of olive greens, earth tones, and natural stones; location close to the National Portrait Gallery. *Average main: £12 39 William IV St., Covent Garden 020/7240–8786 www.bancone.co.uk Charing Cross, Covent Garden, Leicester Sq.*

Barrafina

$$$ | TAPAS | One of London's favorite Spanish tapas bars is modeled after Cal Pep in Barcelona, and has only a few raised bar stools within the bright open kitchen off St. Martin's Lane. Lunchtime lines form starting at noon for a succession of brilliantly sourced small plates, ranging from giant Spanish *carabineros* (red prawns) to black squid-ink risotto with cuttlefish. **Known for:** long lines starting at noon; intriguing offal dishes like milk-fed lamb's kidneys; top Cava and Spanish sherry selection. *Average main: £26 10 Adelaide St., Covent Garden www.barrafina.co.uk Charing Cross, Covent Garden, Leicester Sq.*

Clos Maggiore

$$$ | FRENCH | FAMILY | Insist on a seat in the dreamy, white blossom–filled conservatory at this warm, cozy, and seriously romantic Provençal country-style inn in the heart of Covent Garden. Once inside, you'll be wooed by old-fashioned and refined French cuisine. **Known for:** one of London's most romantic restaurants; warren of blossom-filled conservatories and open wood-fired hideaways; lunch and pre- and posttheater meal deals. *Average main: £26 33 King St., Covent Garden 020/7379–9696 www.closmaggiore.com Covent Garden.*

Cora Pearl

$$$ | MODERN BRITISH | Famous British standbys like ham and cheese toasties, bubble and squeak, and even the mighty chip are turned into showstoppers at this classy Covent Garden act. Triple-cooked chips are squeezed, sliced, buttered, and deep-fried to perfection, while those crustless toasties are all succulent ham hock, Montgomery cheddar, and tangy house pickle. Jazz and blues music plays amid the elegant decor, from the antique table glasses and French linen napkins to the tarnished mirrors and deep green velvet banquettes. **Known for:** elegant decor and atmosphere; buffed-up British dishes; classy pretheater option. *Average main: £25 30 Henrietta St., Covent Garden 020/7324–7722 www.corapearl.co.uk No dinner Sun. Covent Garden, Holborn.*

Côte

$ | BISTRO | Where else can you find an amazing three-course French meal in Covent Garden for £17? The Côte brasserie chain does the trick, and offers a menu loaded with classic French favorites: crêpes with mushrooms and Gruyère cheese, boeuf bourguignon, *moules marinières* (mussels with white wine), and iced berries and white chocolate sauce. **Known for:** part of a dependable chain of French brasseries; very reasonable pre- and posttheater deals; reliable French classics like moules marinères. *Average main: £14 17–21 Tavistock St., Covent Garden 020/7379–9991 www.cote.co.uk Covent Garden.*

Frenchie

$$$$ | FRENCH | With three popular restaurants in Paris, French chef Grégory Marchand brings his daring dishes to London at this sleek standout not far from the historic Covent Garden piazza. Everyone loves the effortlessly ebullient offerings like stone bass, bisque, and borlotti beans or Welsh lamb with sweetcorn three ways served in a modern brasserie setting. **Known for:** eclectic dishes like duck foie gras pressé with sour black cherries, almonds, and elderflower; flavor-packed puddings like lemon curd, olive shortbread, and rosemary ice cream; adventurous wine list stacked with small, artisanal, and eco-friendly producers. *Average main: £34 ✉ 30 Henrietta St., Covent Garden ☎ 020/7836–4422 🌐 www.frenchiec-oventgarden.com Ⓜ Charring Cross, Embankment.*

★ The Ivy

$$$ | **MODERN BRITISH** | London's one-time most famous celebrity haunt and West End landmark is still so popular it receives over a thousand calls a day. Established as an Italian café in 1917, today it's still where London's wealthiest dine on haddock and chips, Thai-baked sea bass, and good ol' English classics like Shepherd's pie and sticky toffee pudding. **Known for:** celebrity-filled history; famed house staples like grilled calf's liver; great people-watching. *Average main: £26 ✉ 1–5 West St., Covent Garden ☎ 020/7836–4751 🌐 www.the-ivy.co.uk Ⓜ Covent Garden, Tottenham Court Rd.*

J Sheekey

$$$ | **SEAFOOD** | This timelessly chic 1896 seafood haven is a discreet alternative to the more celebrity-focused eateries in the neighborhood. J Sheekey charms with an inviting menu of snappingly fresh Atlantic prawns, pickled Arctic herring, scallop, shrimp, and salmon burgers, or the famous Sheekey fish pie. Better yet, sip Gaston Chiquet Champagne and down half a dozen Fine de Claire rock oysters at the antique mirrored oyster bar for the ultimate in true romance. **Known for:** low-key celebrity hideaway; old-school seafood menu and discreet service; glamorous art deco oyster bar. *Average main: £27 ✉ 28–35 St. Martin's Ct., Covent Garden ☎ 020/7240–2565 🌐 www.j-sheekey.co.uk Ⓜ Charing Cross, Leicester Sq.*

Margot

$$$ | **ITALIAN** | Served by seriously suave staff in bow ties and tuxedos, enjoy some of London's finest service at this effortlessly elegant Italian restaurant. Diners come for top pastas like *tagliolini* with Sicilian red prawns or roast octopus with *'nduja* and Umbrian lentils. **Known for:** unrivaled service; classic Milanese veal osso buco with saffron risotto; glitzy Covent Garden setting. *Average main: £25 ✉ 45 Great Queen St., Covent Garden ☎ 020/3409–4777 🌐 www.margotrestaurant.com Ⓜ Covent Garden, Holborn.*

★ Rules

$$$ | **BRITISH** | Opened by Thomas Rule in 1798, London's oldest restaurant is still arguably its most beautiful. Resembling a High Victoriana bordello, here you can dig into classic traditional British fare like jugged hare, steak-and-kidney pie, or roast beef and Yorkshire pudding. **Known for:** the oldest restaurant in London; fancy, high-class game-focused menu; famous diners from Charles Dickens to the Prince of Wales. *Average main: £30 ✉ 35 Maiden La., Covent Garden ☎ 020/7836–5314 🌐 www.rules.co.uk Jacket required Ⓜ Covent Garden.*

Savoy Grill

$$$$ | **BRITISH** | You can feel the history at this 1889 art deco hotel-dining powerhouse, which has wined and dined everyone from Oscar Wilde and Sir Winston Churchill to Elizabeth Taylor and Marilyn Monroe. Nowadays it caters to CEOs and wealthy West End tourists who come for the Grill's famed table-side serving trolley, which might trundle up laden with hulking great roasts like beef Wellington, Suffolk rack of pork, or saddle of lamb. **Known for:** ravishing old-school dining salon; beef Wellington from the daily carvery trolley service; signature glazed omelet Arnold Bennett. *Average main: £40 ✉ The Savoy, 100 Strand, Covent Garden ☎ 020/7592–1600 for*

reservations only ⊕ *www.gordonramsay-restaurants.com/savoy-grill* Ⓜ *Charing Cross, Covent Garden.*

Simpson's in the Strand

$$$ | **BRITISH** | Head straight for the 30-day roast rib of Scottish beef and Yorkshire puddings carved table-side at this magnificent 1828 dining institution. Originally a cigar lounge, coffeehouse, and later a famed chess venue, it was once frequented by the likes of Sir Arthur Conan Doyle, Charles Dickens, and Vincent van Gogh. **Known for:** one of the city's most grand and historic taverns; traditional Sunday roast dinner; roast beef and Welsh lamb served from the silver domed carving trolley. $ *Average main: £28* ✉ *100 Strand, Charing Cross* ☎ *020/7420–2111 restaurant reservations only* ⊕ *www.simpsonsinthestrand.co.uk* Ⓜ *Charing Cross.*

★ **Spring**

$$$ | **ITALIAN** | Australian chef Skye Gyngell worships the four seasons at her wildflower-filled dining salon in majestic Somerset House off the Strand. Housed in the building's 1865 neoclassical New Wing, Spring offers healthy root-to-stem, produce-driven Italian dishes in a light-drenched room. **Known for:** homemade bread, butter, and ice cream; highly seasonal, sustainable, and ingredient-driven dishes; biodynamic Fern Verrow Farm salads. $ *Average main: £30* ✉ *Somerset House, New Wing, Lancaster Pl., Covent Garden* ✣ *Turn right on entering courtyard at Somerset House from the Strand* ☎ *020/3011–0115* ⊕ *www.springrestaurant.co.uk* ⊗ *Closed Sun.* Ⓜ *Charing Cross, Holborn.*

Hotels

★ **Covent Garden Hotel**

$$$ | **HOTEL** | It's little wonder this is now the London home-away-from-home for off-duty celebrities, actors, and style mavens, with its Covent Garden location and guest rooms that are design-magazine stylish, using mix-and-match couture fabrics to stunning effect. **Pros:** great for star-spotting; supertrendy; basement cinema for movie buffs. **Cons:** you can feel you don't matter if you're not famous; location in Covent Garden can be a bit boisterous; only some rooms come with balcony views. $ *Rooms from: £320* ✉ *10 Monmouth St., Covent Garden* ☎ *020/7806–1000, 888/559–5508 in U.S.* ⊕ *www.firmdalehotels.com/hotels/london/covent-garden-hotel* *58 rooms* *No meals* Ⓜ *Covent Garden.*

Henrietta Hotel

$$ | **HOTEL** | The stylish and hip will fit right in at this beautifully refined Covent Garden property. **Pros:** amazing bar and restaurant; beautiful boutique interiors; great location in the heart of Covent Garden. **Cons:** hip atmosphere and slick interiors won't be for everyone; standard rooms are on the small side; street noise can be a minor irritant. $ *Rooms from: £213* ✉ *14–15 Henrietta St., Covent Garden* ☎ *020/3794–5313* ⊕ *www.henriettahotel.com* *18 rooms* *No meals* Ⓜ *Covent Garden.*

★ **ME London**

$$$ | **HOTEL** | A shiny fortress of luxury, the ME brings a splash of modern cool to a rather stuffy patch of the Strand. **Pros:** sleek and fashionable; full of high-tech comforts; stunning views from rooftop bar. **Cons:** design can sometimes verge on form over function; very small closets and in-room storage areas; the rooftop bar can get uncomfortably busy. $ *Rooms from: £280* ✉ *336–337 The Strand, Covent Garden* ☎ *020/7395–3400* ⊕ *www.melia.com* *157 rooms* *No meals* Ⓜ *Covent Garden, Charing Cross, Holborn.*

One Aldwych

$$$ | **HOTEL** | **FAMILY** | An Edwardian building, with an artsy lobby and understated blend of contemporary and classic, provides pure modern luxury in a great location for theaters and shopping. **Pros:** understated luxury; ultracool

atmosphere; good deals and special offers, including big advance-booking discounts. **Cons:** all this luxury doesn't come cheap; fashionable ambience is not always relaxing; rooms are relatively plain. *Rooms from: £378* *1 Aldwych, Covent Garden* *020/7300–1000* *www.onealdwych.com* *105 rooms* *Free breakfast* *Charing Cross, Covent Garden.*

★ The Savoy

$$$$ | HOTEL | One of London's most iconic hotels maintains its status at the top with winning attributes of impeccable service, stunning decor, and a desirable location on the Strand. **Pros:** one of the top hotels in Europe; iconic pedigree; Thames-side location. **Cons:** everything comes with a price tag; street noise is surprisingly problematic, particularly on lower floors; street can be too busy for some. *Rooms from: £504* *The Strand, Covent Garden* *020/7836–4343, 888/265–0533 in U.S.* *www.thesavoylondon.com* *268 rooms* *Free breakfast* *Covent Garden, Charing Cross.*

★ St Martin's Lane

$$$ | HOTEL | Hip travelers come to this Philippe Starck–designed spot positioned right between Trafalgar Square and Covent Garden. **Pros:** hyper cool lobby, restaurant, bar, and secret speakeasy; funky color-your-mood bedroom lighting system; guests enjoy free entry to adjacent Gymbox gym. **Cons:** rooms can be small; noise from St Martin's Lane inevitable; some find it a bit cooler-than-thou. *Rooms from: £280* *45 St. Martin's Ln., Covent Garden* *020/7300–5500* *www.stmartinslane.com* *204 rooms* *No meals* *Charing Cross, Leicester Sq.*

Nightlife

BARS

★ Beaufort Bar

PIANO BARS/LOUNGES | Things could hardly get more glamorous than at the Savoy's lesser-known Beaufort Bar—a black-and-gold art deco master class with dramatic lighting that has vintage champagne and a spread of heritage cocktails. Dark and sultry and with a rising cabaret stage once graced by Gershwin and Josephine Baker, this venue has nightly live jazz piano music beginning at 7 pm. *The Savoy, Strand, Covent Garden* *020/7420–2111 for reservations only* *www.fairmont.com/savoy-london* *Charing Cross, Covent Garden.*

Terroirs

WINE BARS—NIGHTLIFE | Specializing in low-intervention "natural wines" (organic, unfiltered, biodynamic, and sustainably produced with minimal added ingredients), Terroirs wine bar has an unusually large selection of 290 wines from small French and artisan winemakers. Red, white, sparkling and macerated orange and amber wines are served along with delicious, relatively simple wine-friendly dishes—charcuterie, tapas, cheese, and more substantial French-inspired dishes—at a bar and bare oak tables surrounded by whitewashed walls and wooden floors. *5 William IV St., Covent Garden* *020/7036–0660* *www.terroirswinebar.com* *Charing Cross.*

Upstairs at Rules

BARS/PUBS | Discretion's the word at this under-the-radar cocktail lounge above Rules in Covent Garden, London's oldest restaurant. In rooms where Edward VII used to dine with his socialite mistress Lillie Langtry, old-school bartenders serve traditional cocktails (martinis are stirred, never shaken). The decor reflects a more bygone era, with royal portraits, antler's horns, and Edwardian hunting scenes. *Rules, 34–35 Maiden La., Covent Garden* *020/7836–5314* *www.rules.co.uk* *Covent Garden, Leicester Sq., Holborn.*

GAY AND LESBIAN

Heaven

MUSIC CLUBS | With the best light show on any London dance floor, Heaven is unpretentious, loud, and huge, with a labyrinth of rooms, bars, and live-music parlors. Thursday through Saturday nights it's all about the G-A-Y club and comedy nights. Check in advance about live performances—they can take place any night of the week. If you go to just one gay club in London, Heaven should be it. ✉ *Under the Arches, Villiers St., Covent Garden* ☎ *0844/847–2351 24-hr ticket line* 🌐 *www.heavenlive.co.uk* 🎫 *From £15* Ⓜ *Charing Cross, Embankment.*

PUBS

The Harp

BARS/PUBS | FAMILY | This is the sort of friendly flower-decked locale you might find on some out-of-the-way backstreet, except that it's right in the middle of town, between Trafalgar Square and Covent Garden. As a result, The Harp can get crowded, especially because it was recently named British pub of the year by the Campaign for Real Ale, but the squeeze is worth it for the excellent beer and cider (there are usually 10 carefully chosen ales, often including a London microbrew, plus 10 ciders and perries) and a no-frills menu of high-quality British sausages, cooked behind the bar. ✉ *47 Chandos Pl., Covent Garden* ☎ *020/7836–0291* 🌐 *www.harpcoventgarden.com* Ⓜ *Charing Cross.*

The Lamb & Flag

BARS/PUBS | This refreshingly ungentrified 17th-century pub was once known as the Bucket of Blood because the upstairs room and front yard were used as a ring for winner-takes-all bare-knuckle boxing contests. Now it's a much friendlier place, serving food and real ale. It's on the edge of Covent Garden, up a hidden alley off Garrick Street. ✉ *33 Rose St., Covent Garden* ☎ *020/7497–9504* 🌐 *www.lambandflagcoventgarden.co.uk* Ⓜ *Covent Garden.*

Performing Arts

OPERA

★ Royal Opera House

DANCE | Along with Milan's La Scala, New York's Metropolitan, and the Palais Garnier in Paris, this is one of the world's great opera houses. The resident troupe has mounted spectacular productions in the past, while recent productions have tended toward more contemporary operas. Whatever the style of the performance, the extravagant theater delivers a full dose of opulence. The famed Royal Ballet performs classical and contemporary repertoire here, too, and smaller-scale works of both opera and dance are presented in the Linbury Theatre and Clore Studio Upstairs. A small allocation of tickets for each performance of main stage productions for the week ahead—even those that are sold out—goes on sale online at 1 pm every Friday. **TIP→ If you wish to see the famed auditorium but are not able to procure a ticket, you can join a backstage tour or one of the less frequent tours of the auditorium; they book up several weeks in advance.** BP Big Screens is the ROH's summer series of live relays of its opera and ballet productions; screenings are free and take place outdoors in public spaces all over the country, including Trafalgar Square. ✉ *Bow St., Covent Garden* ☎ *020/7304–4000* 🌐 *www.roh.org.uk* 🎫 *Performances from £4; tours from £10* Ⓜ *Covent Garden.*

PERFORMING ARTS CENTERS

The London Coliseum

CONCERTS | FAMILY | A veritable architectural extravaganza of Edwardian exoticism, the baroque-style theater has a magnificent auditorium and a rooftop glass dome with a bar and great views. As one of the city's most venerable theaters, the Coliseum functions mainly as the home of the English National Opera, which produces innovative opera, sung in English, for lower prices than the Royal Opera House. In recent years the company also has presented musicals, sometimes featuring star opera singers. During opera's off-season (including summertime and during winter holidays), the house hosts the English National Ballet (🌐 *www.ballet.org.uk*) and other troupes. Guided tours offering fascinating insights into the architecture and history of the building take place on selected dates at 11 am. ✉ *St. Martin's La., Covent Garden* ☎ *020/7845–9300* 🌐 *www.eno.org* 🎫 *Opera from £10, ballet from £14, tours £10* Ⓜ *Charing Cross, Leicester Sq.*

Shopping

BOOKS AND PRINTS

Grosvenor Prints

ART GALLERIES | London's largest collection of 17th- to early-20th-century prints emphasizes views of the city and architecture as well as royal, sporting, and decorative motifs. The selection is hugely eclectic, with prices ranging from £10 to the thousands. It's closed on weekends. ✉ *19 Shelton St., Covent Garden* ☎ *020/7836–1979* 🌐 *www.grosvenorprints.com* Ⓜ *Covent Garden, Leicester Sq.*

★ **Stanfords**

BOOKS/STATIONERY | **FAMILY** | When it comes to encyclopedic coverage, there is simply no better map and travel shop on the planet. Trading in Covent Garden since 1853, Stanfords is packed with a comprehensive selection of travel books and travel accessories, as well as ordinance surveys, cycle route maps, travel adaptors, globes, replicas of antique maps, mosquito nets, and more. Even the floor is decorated with giant maps. Whether you're planning a day trip to Surrey or an adventure to the Kalahari Desert, this should be your first stop. ✉ *7 Mercer Walk, Covent Garden* ☎ *020/7836–1321* 🌐 *www.stanfords.co.uk* Ⓜ *Covent Garden.*

CLOTHING

Jack Wills

CLOTHING | The heritage and country sports-inspired styles here have a fresh, sexy edge. Crowds of lithe teens don't mind the pumping music while they browse the collection—trench coats, jeans, and dresses (LBDs, floral sundresses, rugby stripe jerseys) for the girls, and sweatshirts, athleisure jackets, chinos, and polo shirts for the boys. The store also carries backpacks, baseball hats, holdalls, branded water bottles, and other youthful lifestyle items. Other branches are in Soho and Westfield White City. ✉ *136 Long Acre, Covent Garden* ☎ *020/7240–8946* 🌐 *www.jackwills.com* Ⓜ *Leicester Sq., Covent Garden.*

★ **Paul Smith**

CLOTHING | British classics with an irreverent twist define Paul Smith's collections for women, men, and children. Beautifully tailored suits for men and women take hallmarks of traditional British style and turn them on their heads with humor and color, combining exceptional fabrics with flamboyant linings or unusual detailing. Gift ideas abound—wallets, scarves, phone cases, and distinctive belts and socks—all in Smith's signature rainbow stripes. There are several branches throughout London, in Notting Hill, Soho, Marylebone, Southwark, and Canary Wharf, plus a Mayfair shop that includes vintage furniture. ✉ *40–44 Floral St., Covent Garden* ☎ *020/7379–7133* 🌐 *www.paulsmith.com* Ⓜ *Covent Garden.*

The Vintage Showroom

CLOTHING | It's all rare one-off pieces and benchmark examples at London's top men's vintage clothes emporium. Everything's at least over 50 years old here, where rummaging might lead you to anything from a 1940s North American hunting jacket to paratrooper jumpsuits or a purple Edwardian high break sports blazer and matching striped cap. ✉ *14 Earlham St., Covent Garden*

☎ *020/7836–3964* 🌐 *www.thevintage-showroom.com* Ⓜ *Covent Garden, Holborn, Leicester Sq.*

Walker Slater

CLOTHING | Edinburgh tailor and heritage tweed specialists Walker Slater step back in time at this men and women's tweed cornucopia near the Royal Opera House. The myriad selection of Border and hand-woven Harris tweed from Scotland's Outer Hebrides ranges from three-piece turn-up suits and riding jacket-inspired tail coats to over-the-knee herringbone, plus Williamsburg, Kintyre, and Kirk caps. ✉ *38 Green Queen St., Covent Garden* ☎ *020/3754–9787* 🌐 *www.walkerslater.com* Ⓜ *Covent Garden, Holborn, Leicester Sq.*

FOOD

★ Neal's Yard Dairy

FOOD/CANDY | Great towers of Britain's finest farmhouse cheeses fill the shelves at this star cheesemonger and artisanal cheese lovers' paradise off Seven Dials. Ever pungent and matured on-site, browse the rare raw milk Stilton-esque Stichelton from Welbeck in Nottinghamshire or the 65 other small batch creations like Montgomery cheddar, Camembert-style Tunworth, or a lactic goat's cheese Innes Log. ✉ *17 Shorts Gardens, Covent Garden* ☎ *020/7500–7520* 🌐 *www.nealsyarddairy.co.uk* Ⓜ *Covent Garden, Holborn.*

MARKETS

Covent Garden Market

OUTDOOR/FLEA/GREEN MARKETS | **FAMILY** | This popular destination includes three separate market areas: the Apple Market, the East Colonnade Market, and the Jubilee Market. In the covered area originally designed by Inigo Jones and known as the Apple Market, 40 stalls sell handcrafted jewelry, prints, clothes (such as hand-painted dancewear), ceramics, and crafts Tuesday through Sunday, while Monday is given over to antiques, curios, and collectables. The East Colonnade Market has stalls with mostly handmade specialty items that include handmade soaps and jewelry, as well as housewares, accessories, and magic tricks. The Jubilee Market, in Jubilee Hall toward Southampton Street, tends toward the more pedestrian (kitschy T-shirts, unremarkable household goods, and the like) Tuesday through Friday, but has vintage collectibles and antiques on Monday and worthwhile handmade goods on weekends. Largely aimed at the tourist trade in the past, Covent Garden Market continues its ascent, introducing a more sophisticated image (and correspondingly high prices) with the opening of upscale restaurants and chains in the surrounding arcades, including the world's second largest Apple Store ; beauty outlets for Chanel, M.A.C., and Dior; and boutiques for brands like Tumi, Mulberry and N. Peal. ■ **TIP→ Don't miss the magicians, musicians, jugglers, and escape artists who perform in the open-air piazza; the performances are free (though contributions are welcome).** ✉ *The Piazza, off Wellington St., Covent Garden* 🌐 *www.coventgarden.london* Ⓜ *Covent Garden.*

SHOES

The Shop at Bluebird

CERAMICS/GLASSWARE | The brainchild of the couple behind popular womenswear brand Jigsaw, this 15,000-square-foot space over three floors brings together men's and women's fashion from of-the-moment designers like Alexander Wang, Shrimps, and Peter Pilotto, as well as numerous hip denim lines like Acne Studios and Citizens of Humanity. There's also furniture, beauty products, art, homewares, and designer tech accessories—all chosen for style and originality—and an expansive restaurant on the second floor. It's worth visiting for the displays alone, which change regularly. ✉ *Carriage Hall, 29 Floral St., Covent Garden* ☎ *020/7351–3873* 🌐 *www.theshopatbluebird.com* Ⓜ *Covent Garden.*

TOYS

★ Benjamin Pollock's Toyshop

TOYS | **FAMILY** | This landmark shop still carries on the tradition of its founder, who sold miniature theater stages made from richly detailed paper from the late 19th century until his death in 1937. Among his admirers was Robert Louis Stevenson, who wrote, "If you love art, folly, or the bright eyes of children, speed to Pollock's." Today the antique model theaters are expensive, but there are plenty of magical reproductions for less than £10. There's also an extensive selection of new but nostalgic puppets, marionettes, teddy bears, spinning tops, jack-in-the-boxes, and similar traditional children's toys from the days before batteries were required (or toys were even run on them). ✉ *44 The Market Bldg., Covent Garden* ☎ *020/7379–7866* 🌐 *www.pollocks-coventgarden.co.uk* Ⓜ *Covent Garden.*

The Tintin Shop

TOYS | Before there was Harry Potter, there was Tintin. Created by the Belgian cartoonist Hergé, the story of the fictional boy detective and his intrepid dog Snowy has been a cult favorite for generations. At this namesake shop devotees can find Tintin-related books, posters, T-shirts, metal and resin figurines, diecast model airplane, alarm clocks, and more. ✉ *34 Floral St., Covent Garden* ☎ *020/7836–1131* 🌐 *thetintinshop.uk.com* Ⓜ *Covent Garden.*

Chapter 6

BLOOMSBURY AND HOLBORN

Updated by
James O'Neill

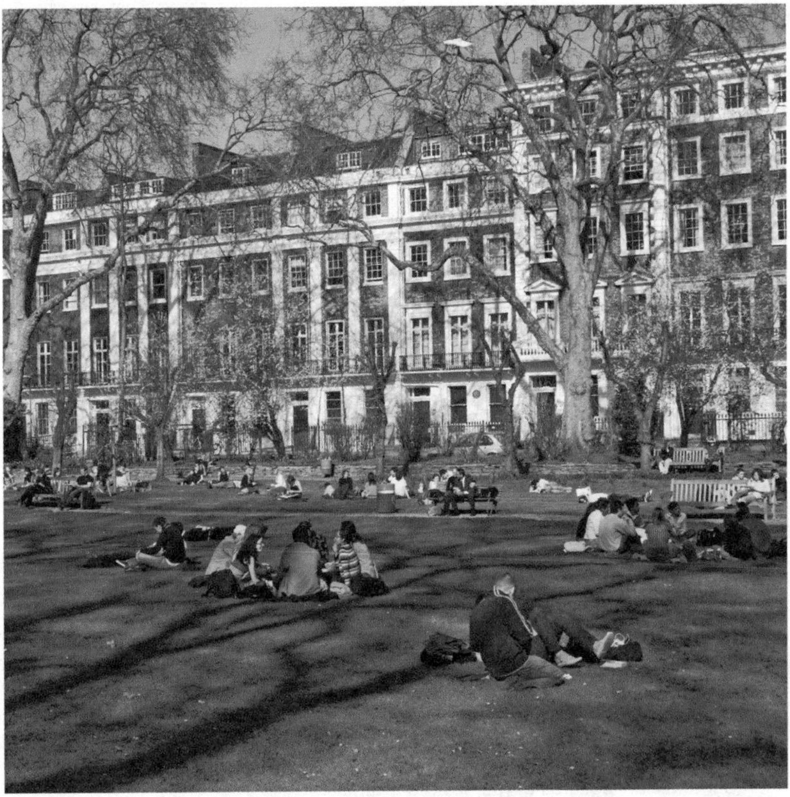

Sights ★★★☆☆ Restaurants ★★☆☆☆ Hotels ★★★★☆ Shopping ★★☆☆☆ Nightlife ★★☆☆☆

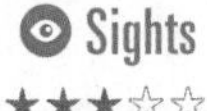

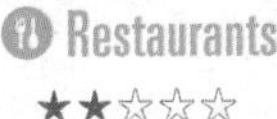

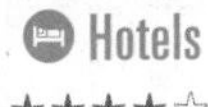

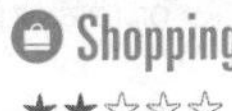

BLOOMSBURY AND HOLBORN SNAPSHOT

TOP REASONS TO GO

The British Museum: From the Rosetta Stone to the Elgin Marbles, the British Museum is a wondrous vault of priceless treasures seized over centuries by the British Empire.

The Inns of Court: The quiet courts, leafy gardens, and magnificent halls that make up the heart of Holborn are the closest thing to the spirit of Oxbridge in London.

Sir John Soane's Museum: Quirky and enchanting, the former home of the celebrated 19th-century architect is a delightful treasure trove of antiquities and oddities.

The British Library: In keeping with Bloomsbury's literary spirit, this world-renowned archive holds everything from the Magna Carta to Shakespeare's First Folio.

Charles Dickens: The famed author's former residence—he wrote *Oliver Twist* while living here—is now a fascinating museum.

GETTING THERE

The Russell Square Tube stop on the Piccadilly Line leaves you right at the corner of Russell Square. The best Tube stops for the Inns of Court are Holborn on the Central and Piccadilly lines or Chancery Lane on the Central Line. Tottenham Court Road on the Northern and Central lines is best for the British Museum. Once you're in Bloomsbury, you can easily get around on foot.

MAKING THE MOST OF YOUR TIME

If you plan to visit the Inns of Court as well as the British Museum, and you'd like to get a feel for the neighborhood, devote an entire day to this literary and legal enclave. An alternative scenario is to set aside a separate day for a visit to the British Museum, which can easily consume as many hours as you have to spare. It's a pleasure to wander through the leafy squares at your leisure, examining historic Blue Plaques or relaxing at a street-side café.

QUICK BITES

■ **The Betjeman Arms** Inside St. Pancras International's renovated Victorian station, this pub is the perfect place to grab a pint and some classic pub fare. ✉ *Pancras Rd., Unit 53, King's Cross* ☎ *020/7923–5440* 🌐 *www.thebetjemanarms.co.uk* Ⓜ *King's Cross St. Pancras.*

■ **The Hare and Tortoise Dumpling & Noodle Bar** This informal eatery serves scrumptious Asian fast food in generous portions at reasonable prices. ✉ *11–13 Brunswick Shopping Centre, Brunswick Sq., Bloomsbury* ☎ *020/7278–9799* 🌐 *www.hareandtortoise.co.uk/bloomsbury* Ⓜ *Russell Sq.*

■ **Truckles of Pied Bull Yard** This wine bar and café serves up tasty modern British food within a stone's throw of the British Museum. Weather permitting, sit in its pretty Georgian courtyard. ✉ *Off Bury Pl., Bloomsbury* ☎ *020/7404–5338* 🌐 *www.davy.co.uk/truckles* ⊙ *Closed Sun.*

With the British Library, the British Museum, and countless colleges of the University of London among its residents, Bloomsbury might appear all bookish and cerebral—but fear not, it's much more than that. There's a youthfulness about its buzzing thoroughfares, and this vitality extends from down-by-the-Thames Holborn—once Dickens territory, now the heartbeat of legal London—way up to revamped King's Cross and classy Islington to the north, and cool Clerkenwell out east.

Bloomsbury

Fundamental to the region's spirit of open expression and scholarly debate is the legacy of the Bloomsbury Group, an elite corps of artists and writers who lived in this neighborhood during the first part of the 20th century. **Gordon Square** was at one point home to Virginia Woolf, John Maynard Keynes (both at No. 46), and Lytton Strachey (at No. 51). But perhaps the best-known square in Bloomsbury is the large, centrally located **Russell Square,** with its handsome gardens. Scattered around the **University of London** campus are Woburn Square, Torrington Square, and Tavistock Square. The **British Library,** with its vast treasures, is a few blocks north, across busy Euston Road.

Bloomsbury is bordered by Tottenham Court Road on the west, Euston Road on the north, Woburn Place (which becomes Southampton Row) on the east, and New Oxford Street on the south.

The area from Somerset House on the Strand, all the way up Kingsway to the Euston Road, is known as London's **Museum Mile** for the myriad historic houses and museums that dot the area. The **Charles Dickens Museum,** in the house where the author wrote *Oliver Twist,* pays homage to the master, and artists' studios and design shops share space near the majestic **British Museum.** And guaranteed to raise a smile from the most blasé and footsore tourist is **Sir John Soane's Museum,** where the colorful collection reflects the eclectic interests of the namesake founder.

Bloomsbury's liveliness extends north to the exciting redevelopment of King's Cross, now fast becoming a cultural and culinary destination in its own right. Newly polished King's Cross merges seamlessly into upscale Islington, with its bustling streets and elegant squares. Due south of Islington, and east of Bloomsbury, don't miss out on the charms of easygoing, fashionable Clerkenwell.

Sights

British Library

LIBRARY | FAMILY | With a collection totaling more than 150 million items, plus 3 million new additions every year, the British Library is a world-class repository of knowledge. Its greatest treasures are on view to the general public in the Sir John Ritblat Gallery: the Magna Carta, the Codex Sinaiticus (an ancient bible containing the oldest complete copy of the New Testament), Jane Austen's writings, and Shakespeare's First Folio, as well as musical manuscripts by Handel and Beethoven and original handwritten lyrics by the Beatles. ✉ *96 Euston Rd., Bloomsbury* ☎ *0330/333–1144* 🌐 *www.bl.uk* 🎫 *Free, donations appreciated; charge for special exhibitions* Ⓜ *Euston, Euston Sq., King's Cross St. Pancras.*

★ **British Museum**

MUSEUM | FAMILY | The sheer scale and importance of the British Museum's many treasures is impossible to overstate or exaggerate; it truly is one of the world's great repositories of human civilization. Established in 1753 and initially based on the library and "cabinet of curiosities" of the Royal Physician Sir Hans Sloane, the collection grew exponentially over the following decades, partly due to bequests and acquisitions, but also as a result of plundering by the burgeoning British Empire.

The neoclassical grandeur of the museum's Great Russell Street entrance befits what lies in wait inside. Here you'll find the **Rosetta Stone,** whose inscriptions were key to deciphering hieroglyphics (Room 4); the controversial but exquisite **Elgin Marbles** (aka the Parthenon Sculptures) that once stood on the Acropolis in Athens (Room 18); the remarkable 7th century BC masterpieces of Assyrian sculpted reliefs, the **Lion Hunts** (Room 10a); and stunning fragments and friezes from the **Mausoleum of Halikarnassos** (aka one of the Seven Wonders of the Ancient World; Room 21).

Other perennial favorites include the **Egyptian mummies** (Rooms 62–63); the colossal **Statue of Ramesses II,** dating to circa 1270 BC and weighing in at just over 7 tons (Room 4); and the splendid 8th-century Anglo-Saxon **Sutton Hoo Treasure** with magnificent helmets and jewelry aplenty (Room 41).

Leave time for exploring the glass-covered **Great Court** designed by celebrated architect Norman Foster at the turn of the present millennium—it has become a focal point of the museum. Likewise, don't miss the revered circular **Reading Room** where Karl Marx wrote *Das Kapital* under the room's beautiful blue-and-gold papier-mâché dome. If it all seems a little overwhelming or if you're pushed for time, try one of the excellent museum tours. Eye-opener Tours (free; 30–40 minutes) focus on 14 individual galleries each day, while the 90-minute Highlights Tour covers all the major exhibits plus a few lesser-known ones, and begins at 11:30 am and 2 pm on Friday and weekends (£14; book online or at the ticket desk in the Great Court). Alternatively, Audio Guides can be rented from the information desk for £7. ✉ *Great Russell St., Bloomsbury* ☎ *020/7323–8000* 🌐 *www.britishmuseum.org* 🎫 *Free; donations encouraged* Ⓜ *Russell Sq., Holborn, Tottenham Court Rd.*

Charles Dickens Museum

MUSEUM | This is one of the few London houses Charles Dickens (1812–70) inhabited that is still standing, and it's the place where he wrote *Oliver Twist* and *Nicholas Nickleby*. The house looks exactly as it would have in Dickens's day, complete with first editions, letters, and a tall clerk's desk (Dickens wrote standing up). Catch the fascinating Housemaid's Tour (£15) in which you're taken back in time to 1839 by Dickens's housemaid who reveals the private lives of the great author and his family; note that it's only available select Sunday mornings and must be booked in advance. ✉ *48 Doughty St., Bloomsbury* ☎ *020/7405–2127* 🌐 *www.dickensmuseum.com* 🎫 *£10* ⏲ *Closed Mon.* Ⓜ *Chancery La., Russell Sq.*

Lamb's Conduit Street

NEIGHBORHOOD | If you think Bloomsbury is about all things intellectual, then think again. Lamb's Conduit Street, a pedestrian-only street of gorgeous Georgian town houses nestled to the east of Russell Square, is building a reputation as one of the capital's most charming—and fashionable—shopping thoroughfares. Avail yourself of what the boutiques have to offer, from fashion to ceramics, books to jewelry, fine art to flowers; there's even an excellent run-by-locals food cooperative called the People's Supermarket. Alternatively, you could just window-shop your way down to **The Lamb,** a Victorian-era pub whose patrons have included Ted Hughes, Sylvia Plath, and Mr. Dickens himself. ✉ *Bloomsbury* Ⓜ *Russell Sq.*

Petrie Museum

MUSEUM | If you don't get your fill of Egyptian artifacts at the British Museum, you can see more in the neighboring Petrie Museum, located on the first floor of the DMS Watson library. The museum houses an outstanding collection of Egyptian, Sudanese, and Greco-Roman archaeological objects, including jewelry, art, toys, and some of the world's oldest garments. ✉ *Malet Pl., Bloomsbury* ☎ *020/7679–2884* 🌐 *www.ucl.ac.uk/museums/petrie* 🎫 *Free, donations appreciated* ⏲ *Closed Sun. and Mon.* Ⓜ *Euston Sq., Goodge St.*

★ **Sir John Soane's Museum**

HOUSE | Sir John (1753–1837), architect of the Bank of England, bequeathed his eccentric house to the nation on one condition: that nothing be changed. It's a house full of surprises. In the Picture Room, two of Hogarth's famous *Rake's Progress* paintings swing away to reveal secret gallery recesses where you can find works by Canaletto and Turner. Everywhere, mirrors play tricks with light and space, and split-level floors worthy of a fairground fun house disorient you. Soane's lovingly restored private apartments are also open to the public, but they can only be viewed as part of a first-come, first-serve tour at 1:15 pm and 2 pm, daily. While entry to the house is free (with a suggested donation), you must book timed tickets at least a day in advance online or over the phone. ✉ *13 Lincoln's Inn Fields, Bloomsbury* ☎ *020/7405–2107* 🌐 *www.soane.org* 🎫 *Free; guided tours £15* ⏲ *Closed Mon. and Tues.* Ⓜ *Holborn.*

Wellcome Collection

MUSEUM | If you fancy something unconventional, sample this collection by U.S. pharmaceutical millionaire and philanthropist Henry Wellcome (1853–1936). Styled as "the free destination for the incurably curious," this museum explores the connections between medicine, life, and art (some exhibits may not be suitable for younger children). Comprising an estimated 1 million items, the collection includes Napoléon's toothbrush, Horatio Nelson's razor, and Charles Darwin's walking stick. There are also anatomical models, Peruvian mummies, and Japanese sex toys as well a fascinating permanent exhibition called Medicine Man. Free half-hour tours run at 11:30 am, 2:30 pm, and 3:30 pm, daily. Watch out for an original Picasso artwork in the lobby just above the entrance when you enter. ✉ *183 Euston Rd., Bloomsbury*

Continued on page 170

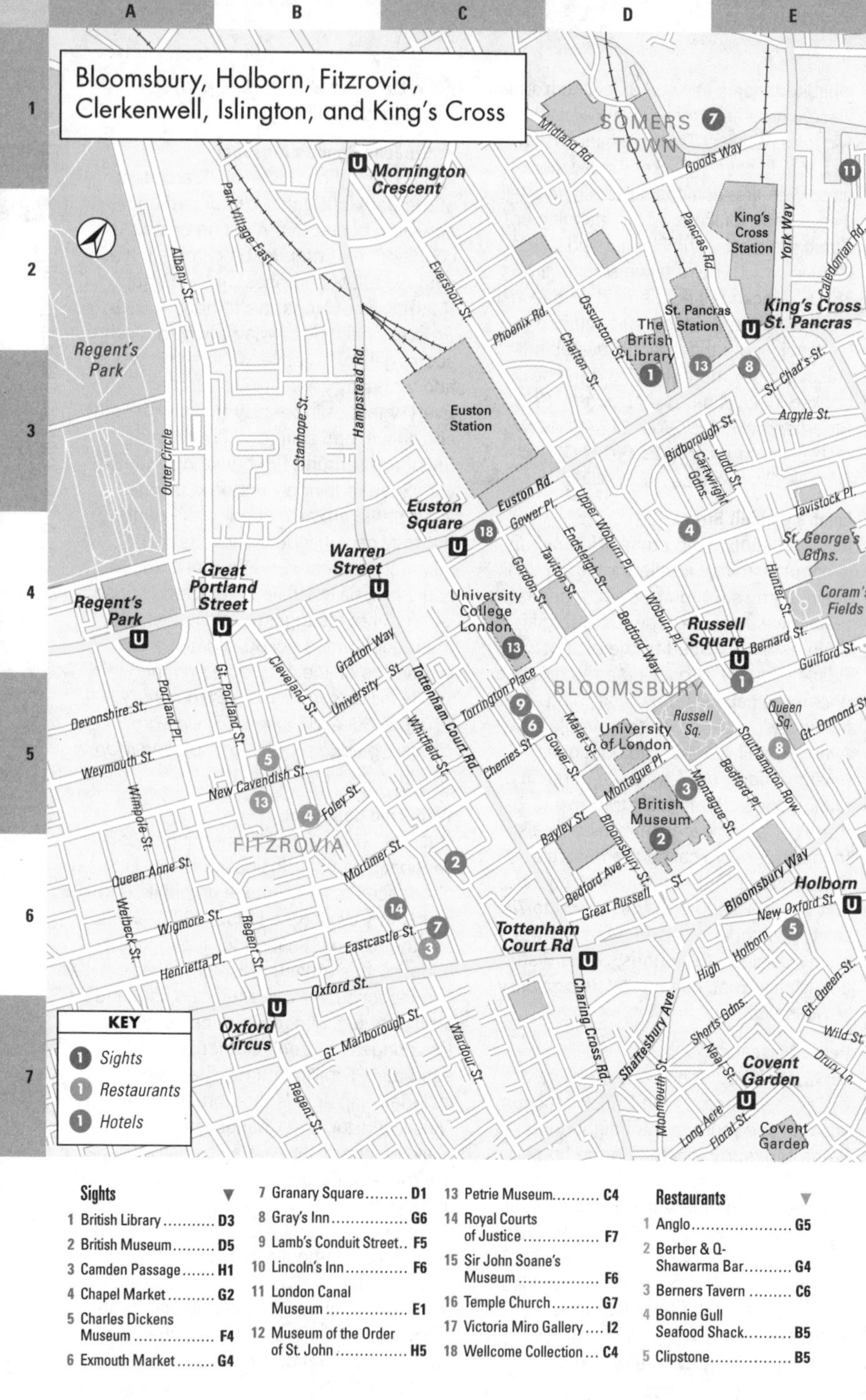

Sights

1 British Library D3
2 British Museum D5
3 Camden Passage H1
4 Chapel Market G2
5 Charles Dickens Museum F4
6 Exmouth Market G4
7 Granary Square D1
8 Gray's Inn G6
9 Lamb's Conduit Street.. F5
10 Lincoln's Inn F6
11 London Canal Museum E1
12 Museum of the Order of St. John H5
13 Petrie Museum.......... C4
14 Royal Courts of Justice F7
15 Sir John Soane's Museum F6
16 Temple Church.......... G7
17 Victoria Miro Gallery I2
18 Wellcome Collection ... C4

Restaurants

1 Anglo...................... G5
2 Berber & Q-Shawarma Bar.......... G4
3 Berners Tavern C6
4 Bonnie Gull Seafood Shack.......... B5
5 Clipstone.................. B5

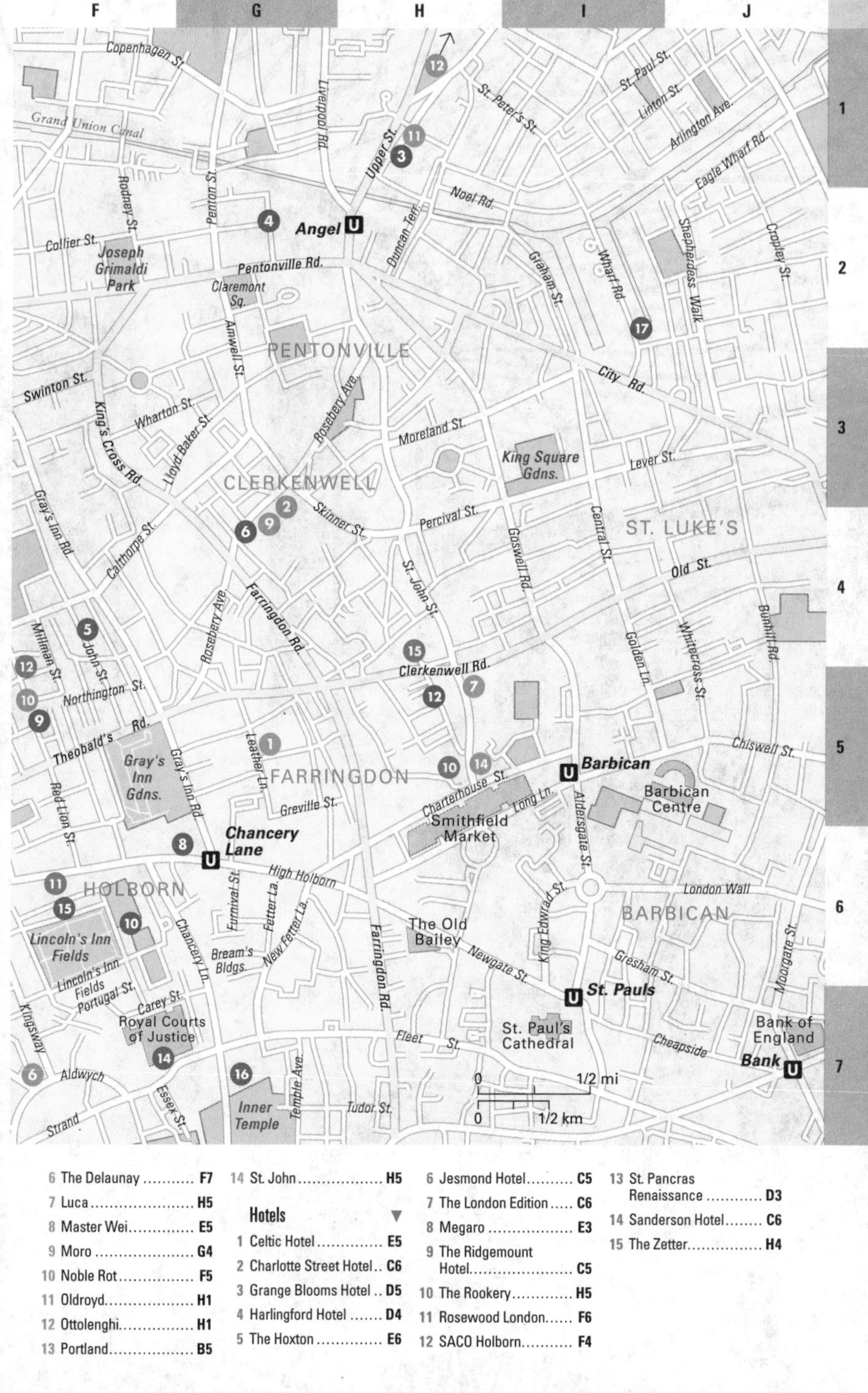

6 The Delaunay F7
7 Luca H5
8 Master Wei.............. E5
9 Moro G4
10 Noble Rot................ F5
11 Oldroyd.................... H1
12 Ottolenghi................ H1
13 Portland................... B5
14 St. John H5

Hotels ▼

1 Celtic Hotel E5
2 Charlotte Street Hotel.. C6
3 Grange Blooms Hotel .. D5
4 Harlingford Hotel D4
5 The Hoxton E6
6 Jesmond Hotel.......... C5
7 The London Edition..... C6
8 Megaro E3
9 The Ridgemount Hotel...................... C5
10 The Rookery............. H5
11 Rosewood London...... F6
12 SACO Holborn........... F4
13 St. Pancras Renaissance D3
14 Sanderson Hotel........ C6
15 The Zetter................ H4

MAJESTY QUEEN ELIZABET

THE BRITISH MUSEUM

Anybody writing about the British Museum had better have a large stack of superlatives close at hand: most, biggest, earliest, finest. This is the golden hoard of nearly three centuries of the Empire, the booty brought from Britain's far-flung colonies.

The first major pieces, among them the Rosetta Stone and the Parthenon Sculptures (Elgin Marbles), were "acquired" from the French, who "found" them in Egypt and Greece. The museum has since collected countless goodies of worldwide historical significance: the Black Obelisk, some of the Dead Sea Scrolls, the Lindow Man. And that only begins the list.

The British Museum is a vast space split into 94 galleries, generally divided by continent or period of history, with some areas spanning more than one level. There are marvels wherever you go, and—while we don't like to be pessimistic—it is, yes, impossible to fully appreciate everything in a day. So make the most of the tours, activity trails, and visitors guides that are available.

The following is a highly edited overview of the museum's greatest hits, organized by area. Pick one or two that whet your appetite, then branch out from there, or spend two straight hours indulging in the company of a single favorite sculpture. There's no wrong way to experience the British Museum, just make sure you do!

⊠ Great Russell St., Bloomsbury WC1

☎ 020/7323–8299

🌐 www.britishmuseum.org

🎫 Free; donations encouraged. Tickets for special exhibits vary in price.

Ⓤ Russell Square, Holborn, Tottenham Court Rd.

(left) The Great Court
(top) Cradle to Grave by Pharmacopoeia

MUSEUM HIGHLIGHTS

Ancient Civilizations

The Rosetta Stone. Found in 1799 and carved in 196 BC by decree of Ptolemy V in Egyptian hieroglyphics, demotic, and Greek, it was this multilingual inscription that provided French Egyptologist Jean-François Champollion with the key to deciphering hieroglyphics. *Room 4.*

Colossal statue of Ramesses II. A member of the 19th dynasty (ca. 1270 BC), Ramesses II commissioned innumerable statues of himself—more than any other preceding or succeeding king. This one, a 7-ton likeness of his perfectly posed upper half, comes from his mortuary temple, the Ramesseum, in western Thebes. *Room 4.*

The Parthenon Sculptures. Perhaps these marvelous treasures of Greece shouldn't be here—but while the debate rages on, you can steal your own moment with the Elgin Marbles. Carved in about 440 BC, these graceful decorations are displayed along with an in-depth, high-tech exhibit of the Acropolis; the handless, footless Dionysus who used to recline along its east pediment is especially well known. *Room 18.*

Mausoleum of Halikarnassos. All that remains of this, one of the Seven Wonders of the Ancient World, is a fragmented form of the original "mausoleum," the 4th-century tomb of Maussollos, King of Karia. The highlight of this gallery is the marble forepart of the colossal chariot horse from the *quadriga. Room 21.*

The Egyptian mummies. Another short flight of stairs takes you to the museum's most popular galleries, especially beloved by children: the Roxie Walker Galleries of Egyptian Funerary Archaeology have a fascinating collection of relics from the Egyptian realm of the dead. In addition to real corpses, wrapped mummies, and mummy cases, there's a menagerie of animal companions and curious items that were buried alongside them. *Rooms 62–63.*

Portland Vase. Made in Italy from cameo glass at the turn of the first century, it is named after the Dukes of Portland, who owned it from 1785 to 1945. It is considered a technical masterpiece—opaque white mythological figures cut by a gem-cutter are set on cobalt-blue background. *Room 70.*

(top) Portland vase
(bottom) Colossal statue of Ramesses II

The **Enlightenment Gallery** should be visited purely for the fact that its antiquarian cases hold the contents of the British Museum's first collections—Sir Hans Sloane's natural-history loot, as well as that of Sir Joseph Banks, who acquired specimens of everything from giant shells to fossils to rare plants to exotic beasts during his voyage to the Pacific aboard Captain Cook's *Endeavour. Room 1.*

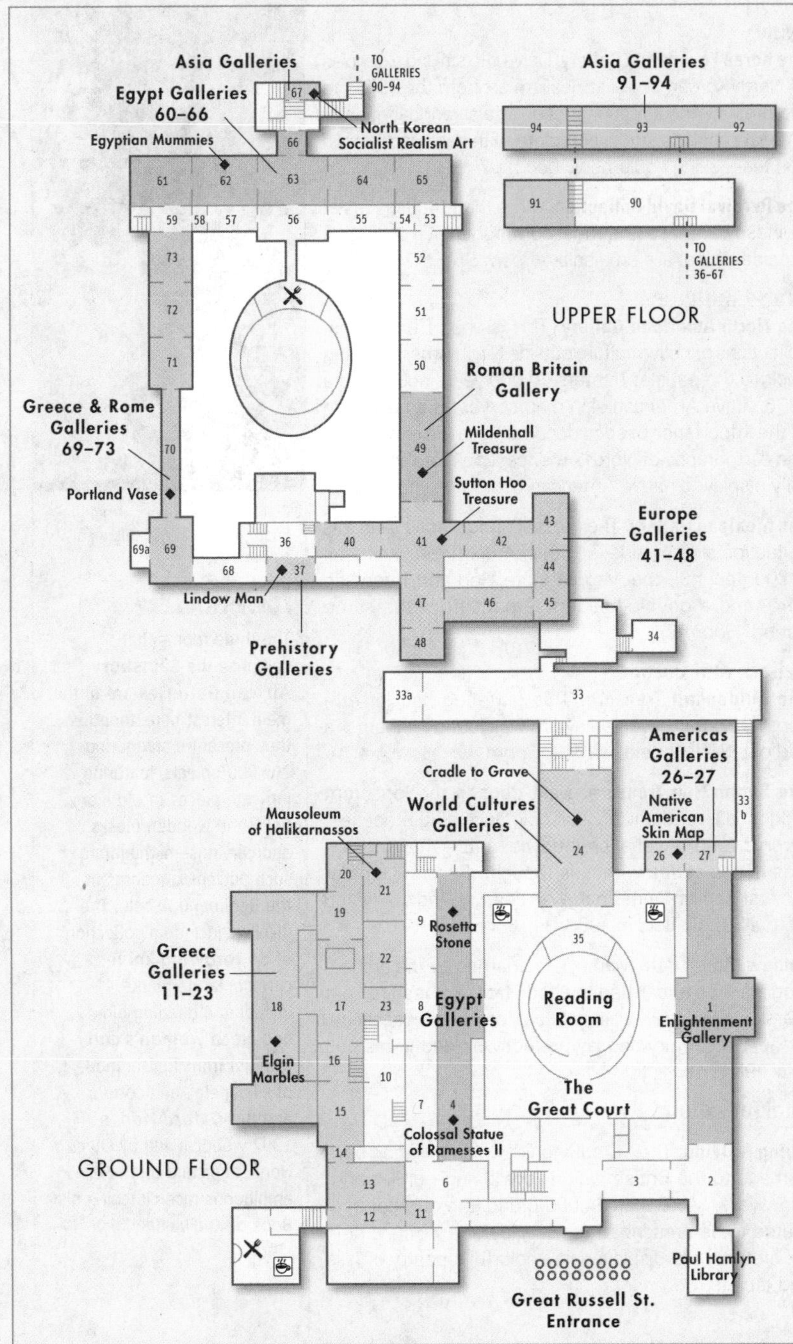
Asia Galleries
TO GALLERIES 90–94
Egypt Galleries 60–66
North Korean Socialist Realism Art
Egyptian Mummies
Asia Galleries 91–94
TO GALLERIES 36–67
UPPER FLOOR
Roman Britain Gallery
Mildenhall Treasure
Greece & Rome Galleries 69–73
Portland Vase
Sutton Hoo Treasure
Europe Galleries 41–48
Lindow Man
Prehistory Galleries
Americas Galleries 26–27
Cradle to Grave
World Cultures Galleries
Native American Skin Map
Mausoleum of Halikarnassos
Rosetta Stone
Greece Galleries 11–23
Egypt Galleries
Reading Room
Enlightenment Gallery
Elgin Marbles
The Great Court
Colossal Statue of Ramesses II
GROUND FLOOR
Paul Hamlyn Library
Great Russell St. Entrance

Asia

The Korea Foundation Gallery. Delve into striking examples of North Korean Socialist Realism art from the 1950s to the present and a reconstruction of a sarangbang, a traditional scholar's study, complete with hanji paper walls and tea-making equipment. *Room 67.*

The Percival David Collection. More than 1400 pieces of Chinese ceramics (the most comprehensive collection outside China) are on display. *Room 95.*

World Cultures

The North American Gallery. This is one of the largest collections of native culture outside North America, going back to the earliest hunters 10,000 years ago. Here a 1775 native American skin map serves as an example of the importance of such documents in the exploration and cartography of North America. Look for the beautifully displayed native American costumes. *Room 26.*

The Mexican Gallery. The most alluring pieces sit in this collection side by side: a 15th-century turquoise mask of Xiuhtecuhtli, the Mexican Fire God and Turquoise Lord, and a double-headed serpent from the same period. *Room 27.*

Britain and Europe

The Mildenhall Treasure. This glittering haul of 4th-century Roman silver tableware was found beneath the sod of a Suffolk field in 1942. *Room 49.*

The Sutton Hoo Treasure. Next door to the loot from Mildenhall—and equally splendid, including brooches, swords, and jewel-encrusted helmets—the treasure was buried at sea with (it is thought) Redwald, one of the first English kings, in the 7th century, and excavated from a Suffolk field in 1938–39. *Room 41.*

Lindow Man. "Pete Marsh"—so named by the archaeologists who unearthed the body from a Cheshire peat marsh—was ritually slain, probably as a human sacrifice, in the 1st century and lay perfectly pickled in his bog until 1984. *Room 50.*

Theme Galleries

Living & Dying. The "Cradle to Grave" installation pays homage to the British nation's wellbeing—or ill-being, as it were. More than 14,000 drugs (the number estimated to be prescribed to every person in the U.K. in his lifetime) are displayed in a colorful tapestry of pills and tablets. *Room 24.*

Colossal chariot horse from the quadriga of the Mausoleum at Halikarnassos

LOWER GALLERY

The three rooms that comprise the **Sainsbury African Galleries** are of the main interest here: together they present a staggering 200,000 objects, featuring intricate pieces of old ivory, gold, and wooden masks and carvings—highlighting such ancient kingdoms as the Benin and Asante. The displays include a collection of **55 throwing knives**; ceremonial garments including a dazzling pink and green **woman's coif** (*qufiya*) from Tunisia made of silk, metal, and cotton; and the ***Oxford Man***, *a* 1992 woodcarving by Owen Ndou, depicting a man of ambiguous race clutching his Book of Knowledge.

DID YOU KNOW?

Galleries help divide this sprawling space into manageable sizes for visitors. The Sainsbury African Galleries are just some of the 94 galleries; the British Museum's collection totals more than 7 million objects.

THE NATION'S ATTIC: A HISTORY OF THE MUSEUM

The collection began when Sir Hans Sloane, physician to Queen Anne and George II, bequeathed his personal collection of curiosities and antiquities to the nation. The collection quickly grew, thanks to enthusiastic kleptomaniacs after the Napoleonic Wars—most notoriously the seventh Earl of Elgin, who obtained the marbles from the Parthenon and Erechtheion on the Acropolis in Athens during his term as British ambassador in Constantinople.

Soon thereafter, it seemed everyone had something to donate—George II gave the old Royal Library, Sir William Hamilton gave antique vases, Charles Townley gave sculptures, the Bank of England gave coins. When the first exhibition galleries opened to visitors in 1759, the trustees agreed to admit only small groups guided by curators. The British Museum quickly became one of the most fashionable places to be seen in the capital, and tickets, which had to be booked in advance, were treated like gold dust.

The museum's holdings quickly outgrew their original space in Montague House. After the addition of such major pieces as the Rosetta Stone, other Egyptian antiquities (spoils of the Napoleonic War), and the Parthenon sculptures, Robert Smirke was commissioned to build an appropriately large and monumental building on the same site. It's still a hot ticket: the British Museum now receives more than 6 million visitors every year.

THE GREAT COURT & THE READING ROOM

The museum's classical Greek-style facade features figures representing the progress of civilization, and the focal point is the awesome Great Court, a massive glass-roofed space. Here is the museum's inner courtyard (now the largest covered square in Europe) that, for more than 150 years, had been used for storage.

The 19th-century Reading Room, an impressive 106-foot-high blue-and-gold-domed library, forms the centerpiece of the Great Court. H.G. Wells, Thomas Hardy, Lord Tennyson, Oscar Wilde, George Orwell, T.S. Elliot, and Beatrix Potter are just a few writers who have used this space as a literary and academic sanctuary over the past 150 years or so.

(above) Reading Room

PLANNING YOUR VISIT

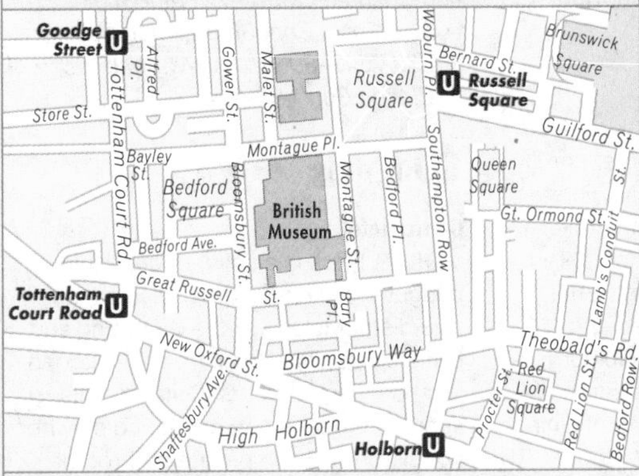

Tours

The **30–40 minute eye Opener tour (free)** by Museum Guides does just what it says; ask for details at the information desk. After this tour, you can then dip back into the collections that most captured your imagination at your leisure.

An excellent **multimedia guide** is a good way to explore the galleries at your own pace, via a series of differently-themed tours.

Alternatively, the **Visitor's Guide** gives a brief but informative overview of the museum's history and is, again, divided into self-guided themed tours.

Before you go, take a look at the online **COMPASS tour** using the museum's navigation tool (www.thebritishmuseum.org/compass), which allows users to browse past and present exhibits as well as search for specific objects. A children's version can also be found here. Computer stations in the Reading Room offer onsite access to COMPASS.

■ TIP→ The closest underground station to the British Museum is Russell Square on the Piccadilly line. However, since you will be entering via the back entrance on Montague Place, you will not experience the full impact of the museum's grand facade. To do so, alight at Holborn on the Central and Piccadilly lines or Tottenham Court Road on the Central and Northern lines. The walk from these stations is about 10 minutes.

WITH KIDS

- Take a look at the "Family Visits" page online for the top 12 objects to see with children.
- The Families Desk in the Great Court has trails for kids ages 3 to 5 and 6 to 11. The Ford Centre for Young Visitors has free activity backpacks.
- Art materials are available for free from information points, where you can also find out about workshops, performances, storytelling sessions, and other free events.
- Around the museum, there are Hands On desks open daily 11–4, which let visitors handle objects from the collections.

WHERE TO REFUEL

The British Museum's self-service **Gallery Café** gets very crowded but serves an acceptable menu beneath a plaster cast of a part of the Parthenon frieze that Lord Elgin didn't remove. It's open daily, but isn't particularly family friendly.

The **café in the Great Court** keeps longer hours and is a great place to people-watch and admire the spectacular glass roof while you eat your salad and sandwich.

If the weather is nice, exit the museum via the back entrance on Montague Place and amble over to **Russell Square**, which has grassy lawns, water fountains, and a glass-fronted café for post-sandwich coffee and ice cream.

020/7611–2222 *www.wellcome-collection.org* *Free* *Closed Mon.* *Euston Sq., Euston.*

Restaurants

The literary giants of the Bloomsbury set—from Virginia Woolf to E.M. Forster and Vanessa Bell—may be long gone but this bluestocking enclave (centered on the University of London and British Library) still excels at a cultured and pleasure-loving dining scene. Holborn, bordering Covent Garden, has some of those big, old-establishment hotel dining rooms, as well as a big, bright elegant shining star in The Delaunay on the Aldwych.

Master Wei

$ | **CHINESE** | **FAMILY** | Deepest Bloomsbury might be the last place to expect superior Chinese street food, but think again. Tucked down an alleyway just off Southampton Row, this unpretentious eatery features the spicy, surprising cuisine of Xi'an, the city in northwest China that's home to the famed Terracotta Army statues (pictures of which hang above the bar). **Known for:** flat, wide biang biang noodles, served in a variety of sumptuous broths and sauces; authentic, fresh, and flavorful Chinese cuisine; prompt, efficient service. *Average main: £11* *13 Cosmo Pl., Bloomsbury* *020/7209–6888* *www.masterwei.co.uk* *Russell Sq.*

Noble Rot

$$$ | **BRITISH** | There's an old Amsterdam coffeehouse vibe at this dark and creaky wine bar and restaurant on historic Lamb's Conduit Street in Bloomsbury. Run by two wine buffs and cult wine magazine publishers, you'll find deceptively simple ingredient-driven British dishes like Whitstable oyster and Cornish turbot braised in oxidized 1998 Bâtard-Montrachet Grand Cru. **Known for:** paradise for oenophiles; unpretentious seasonal British and French wine-friendly fare; neat combos like leeks vinaigrette and Brixham crab. *Average main: £26* *51 Lamb's Conduit St., Bloomsbury* *020/7242–8963* *www.noblerot.co.uk* *Closed Sun.* *Holborn.*

Hotels

Celtic Hotel

$ | **HOTEL** | This is a solid, dependable budget choice in an otherwise expensive district (close to the West End and British Museum). **Pros:** free Wi-Fi; good location; bargain rates. **Cons:** no-frills approach means few extras; no elevator; not all rooms have private bathrooms. *Rooms from: £100* *62 Guilford St., Bloomsbury* *020/7837–6737* *www.stmargaretshotel.co.uk* *35 rooms* *Free breakfast* *Russell Sq.*

Grange Blooms Hotel

$ | **HOTEL** | Located just around the corner from the British Museum, all the rooms in this Georgian town-house hotel are fully en-suite and come with flat-screen TVs and complimentary Wi-Fi. **Pros:** great location; good value; excellent rates if you book early through the website. **Cons:** guests can be bumped to sister hotel if fully booked; no air-conditioning; street noise in some rooms. *Rooms from: £99* *7 Montague St., Bloomsbury* *020/7323–1717* *www.grange-hotels.com* *26 rooms* *No meals* *Russell Sq.*

Harlingford Hotel

$$ | **HOTEL** | The most contemporary of the hotels around Bloomsbury's Cartwright Gardens offers sleek, quiet, and comfortable bedrooms and perfectly appointed public rooms. **Pros:** good location; free Wi-Fi; private garden. **Cons:** rooms are small; no air-conditioning; no elevator. *Rooms from: £140* *61–63 Cartwright Gardens, Bloomsbury* *020/7387–1551* *www.harlingfordhotel.com* *43 rooms* *Free breakfast* *Russell Sq.*

Jesmond Hotel

$ | **B&B/INN** | This friendly family-run hotel is great value given the location: a short walk from the British Museum in one direction, and Soho and Covent Garden in the other. **Pros:** great location; friendly, helpful staff; free Wi-Fi. **Cons:** some rooms are very small; nearly half have shared bathrooms; no elevator. *Rooms from: £90* *63 Gower St., Bloomsbury* *020/7636–3199* *www.jesmondhotel.org.uk* *15 rooms* *Free breakfast* *Goodge St., Euston Sq., Warren St., Russell Sq.*

Megaro

$$ | **HOTEL** | Directly across the street from St. Pancras International Station, the snazzy, well-designed, modern rooms here surround guests with startlingly contemporary style and amenities that range from power showers and espresso machines to smart TVs and Bluetooth speakers. **Pros:** comfortable beds; great location for Eurostar travelers; short hop on Tube to city center. **Cons:** neighborhood isn't interesting; situated on a busy road, so it can get noisy; interiors may be a bit stark for some. *Rooms from: £200* *Belgrove St., King's Cross* *020/7843–2222* *www.hotelmegaro.co.uk* *57 rooms* *Free breakfast* *King's Cross St. Pancras.*

The Ridgemount Hotel

$ | **B&B/INN** | Mere blocks away from the British Museum and London's West End theaters, this handsomely fronted guesthouse has clean, neat, and plainly decorated rooms at bargain rates. **Pros:** free Wi-Fi; helpful staff; family rooms (accommodating up to five) are excellent value. **Cons:** decoration is basic; no elevator; cheapest rooms have shared bathrooms. *Rooms from: £102* *65–67 Gower St., Bloomsbury* *020/7636–1141* *www.ridgemounthotel.co.uk* *32 rooms* *Free breakfast* *Goodge St.*

★ **St. Pancras Renaissance**

$$$ | **HOTEL** | This stunningly restored Victorian landmark—replete with gingerbread turrets and neo-Gothic flourishes—started as a love letter to the golden age of railways, and now it's one of London's most sophisticated places to stay. **Pros:** unique and beautiful; faultless service; close to the train station. **Cons:** very crowded bar and restaurant; streets outside are busy 24/7; free Wi-Fi only in the lobby and public areas. *Rooms from: £270* *Euston Rd., King's Cross* *020/7841–3540* *www.marriott.com/hotels/travel/lonpr-st-pancras-renaissance-hotel-london* *245 rooms* *No meals* *King's Cross St. Pancras. National Rail: Kings Cross, St. Pancras.*

 Nightlife

The gorgeous pubs of Bloomsbury attract tourists in the daytime and huge crowds of after-work drinkers in the early evening. They tend to quiet down as the night advances, making this a great spot for a relaxing night out. The redevelopment of the area around King's Cross St. Pancras Station has especially invigorated the nightlife scene here. Fitzrovia, meanwhile, manages to blend sophistication, informality, and a certain edginess that's not found elsewhere in the center of town.

Exmouth Market and Upper Street are the main nightlife hot spots in Islington, just north and east of central London. The fun informal bars here make it a reliable choice for going out.

PUBS

Bloomsbury Tavern

BARS/PUBS | **FAMILY** | Located between the British Museum and the West End, this pretty Victorian-era pub and its stained glass windows and varnished wooden floors and paneling is the perfect place for a pitstop. Legend says it was the final watering hole for condemned criminals en-route to the gallows at Marble Arch. There's a good selection of pub fare and beers on tap. *236 Shaftesbury Ave., Holborn* *020/7379–9811* *www.*

bloomsburytavern.co.uk Ⓜ *Holborn, Tottenham Court Rd.*

The Lamb

BARS/PUBS | **FAMILY** | Charles Dickens and his contemporaries drank here, but today's enthusiastic clientele make sure this intimate and eternally popular pub avoids the pitfalls of feeling too old-timey. One interesting feature: for private chats at the bar, you can close a delicate etched-glass "snob screen" to the bar staff, opening it only when you fancy another pint. ✉ *94 Lamb's Conduit St., Bloomsbury* ☎ *020/7405–0713* 🌐 *www.thelamblondon.com* Ⓜ *Russell Sq.*

The Queens Larder

BARS/PUBS | **FAMILY** | Queen Charlotte, the wife of "mad" King George III, is said to have stored food for him here in the basement while he was being treated nearby. The interior of this tiny pub preserves its antique feel, with dark wood and old posters, and in the evenings fills up quickly with office workers, pediatricians, and students. In good weather, you might prefer to grab one of the seats outdoors. ✉ *1 Queen's Sq., Bloomsbury* ☎ *020/7837–5627* 🌐 *www.queenslarder.co.uk* Ⓜ *Russell Sq., Holborn.*

Performing Arts

Once the heart of fashionable literary London, there's still an air of refinement about this neighborhood. A handful of small theaters with links to the colleges with campuses in the area create a vibrant small-scale performance scene with theater, dance, and stand-up comedy.

The Place

DANCE | This is London's only theater dedicated solely to contemporary dance, and with tickets often under £20, it's good value, too. The Resolution Festival, held in January and February, is the United Kingdom's biggest platform event for new choreographers. There's also an excellent bar and café. ✉ *17 Duke's Rd., Bloomsbury* ☎ *020/7121–1100* 🌐 *www.theplace.org.uk* 🎫 *From £10* Ⓜ *Euston.*

Shopping

ACCESSORIES

★ James Smith & Sons Ltd.

JEWELRY/ACCESSORIES | This has to be the world's ultimate umbrella shop (it is definitely Europe's oldest), and a must for anyone interested in real Victorian London. The family-owned shop has been in this location on a corner of New Oxford Street since 1857 and sells every kind of umbrella, parasol, cane, and walking stick imaginable (including some containing a small flask or a corkscrew, or that fold out into a seat). The interior is unchanged since the 19th century; you will feel as if you have stepped back in time. Umbrellas range from about £40 for a folding umbrella to more than £400 for a classic blackthorn root-knob solid stick umbrella, and thousands for bespoke items. If the umbrella prices are too steep, there are smaller accessories like an oxhorn shoehorn or salt spoon that make perfect gifts. ✉ *Hazelwood House, 53 New Oxford St., Bloomsbury* ☎ *020/7836–4731* 🌐 *www.james-smith.co.uk* 🕓 *Closed Sun.* Ⓜ *Tottenham Court Rd., Holborn.*

BOOKS

Gay's the Word

BOOKS/STATIONERY | Open since 1979, this is London's leading gay and lesbian bookshop. Thousands of titles, from literature and thoughtful nonfiction to erotica and prodiversity children's books, fill the shelves. The shop is a well-loved fixture on the scene (it features prominently in the 2014 movie *Pride*) and often hosts discussion groups, readings, and other events. ✉ *66 Marchmont St., Bloomsbury* ☎ *020/7278–7654* 🌐 *www.gaystheword.co.uk* Ⓜ *Russell Sq.*

★ Maggs Bros. Ltd

BOOKS/STATIONERY | How could any book lover resist a shop with such a

Dickensian name? Resembling the library of a bibliophilic gentleman more than a commercial enterprise, Maggs has been selling rare antiquarian books and manuscripts since 1853 and is one of the world's oldest and largest such dealers (it also deals in autographs). The staff—with specialists in early British and early European works, travel, and Japanese photography—are expert enough to advise important collectors, but are friendly and helpful to all interested visitors. Maggs also has a tradition of carrying works on counterculture, subversion, punk, the occult, and more. There are occasional themed exhibitions featuring manuscripts and rare editions, and there's an annex shop on Curzon Street in Mayfair. ✉ *48 Bedford Sq., Bloomsbury* ☎ *020/7493–7160* 🌐 *www.maggs.com* ⏲ *Closed weekends* Ⓜ *Goodge St., Tottenham Court Rd.*

★ **Persephone Books**

BOOKS/STATIONERY | A must for all lovers of fiction and nonfiction by women writers, Persephone is a gem of a bookshop specializing in its own reprints of mostly neglected 20th-century works from predominately female authors. Exquisitely decorated endpapers make these books perfect gifts for your bibliophile friends. ✉ *59 Lamb's Conduit St., Bloomsbury* ☎ *020/7242–9292* 🌐 *www.persephonebooks.co.uk* Ⓜ *Russell Sq., Holborn.*

SPECIALTY STORES

Blade Rubber

SPECIALTY STORES | This unique shop near the British Museum specializes in rubber stamps, with everything from businesslike "Paid" stamps to *Alice in Wonderland* characters, Egyptian gods, VW Beetles, flying saucers, and more. Get a custom-made personal stamp—a great gift for a young person—or bring back stamps of British icons like a double-decker bus, the Tower of London, or a bust of Shakespeare as souvenirs. It also carries crafting supplies and scrapbooking materials, and has friendly knowledgeable staff on hand to advise. ✉ *12 Bury Pl., Bloomsbury* ☎ *020/7831–4123* 🌐 *www.bladerubberstamps.co.uk* Ⓜ *Holborn.*

Holborn

Southeast of Bloomsbury and west of The City, Holborn may appear to be little more than a buffer zone between the two—but although it may lack the panache of its neighbors, don't underestimate this varied slice of the capital. Home to legal London and the impressive Inns of Court, this is also Charles Dickens territory, with the Old Curiosity Shop snug within its borders and the Dickens museum close by. Add to that its fair share of churches and quirky places of interest, and you'll soon discover that Holborn can be a rewarding place to while away an hour or three. Holborn's massive Gothic-style **Royal Courts of Justice** ramble all the way to the Strand, and the **Inns of Court**—Gray's Inn, Lincoln's Inn, Middle Temple, and Inner Temple—are where most British trial lawyers have offices to this day. Geographically, Holborn's borders are probably best defined as: west, Kingsway; north, Theobald's Road; east, Gray's Inn Road; south, where the Strand becomes Fleet Street.

Sights

Gray's Inn

BUILDING | Although the least architecturally interesting of the four Inns of Court and the one most heavily damaged by German bombs in the 1940s, Gray's still has romantic associations. In 1594 Shakespeare's *Comedy of Errors* was performed for the first time in the hall, which was restored after World War II and has a fine Elizabethan screen of carved oak. You must make advance arrangements to view the hall, but the secluded and spacious gardens, first planted by Francis Bacon in 1597, are open to the public. The four Inns of the Court—Gray's Inn, Lincoln's Inn, Middle Temple, and Inner Temple—are where most British trial lawyers have offices to this day. In the 14th century, the inns were lodging houses where barristers lived so that people would know how to easily find them (hence, the label "inn"). ✉ *Gray's Inn Rd., Holborn* ☎ *020/7458–7800* 🌐 *www.graysinn.org.uk* 🎫 *Free* 🕐 *Closed weekends* Ⓜ *Holborn, Chancery La.*

Lincoln's Inn

BUILDING | There's plenty to see at one of the oldest, best preserved, and most attractive of the Inns of Court—from the Chancery Lane Tudor brick gatehouse to the wide-open, tree-lined, atmospheric Lincoln's Inn Fields and the 15th-century chapel remodeled by Inigo Jones in 1620. The chapel and the gardens are open to the public, but to see more you must reserve a place on one of the official tours. But be warned: they tend to prefer group bookings of 15 or more, so it's best to check the website or call for details. ✉ *Chancery La., Holborn* ☎ *020/7405–1393* 🌐 *www.lincolnsinn.org.uk* 🎫 *Free* 🕐 *Closed weekends* Ⓜ *Chancery La.*

Royal Courts of Justice

GOVERNMENT BUILDING | Here is the vast Victorian Gothic pile of 35 million bricks containing the nation's principal law courts, with 1,000-odd rooms running off 3½ miles of corridors. This is where the most important civil law cases—that's everything from divorce to fraud, with libel in between—are heard. You can sit in the viewing gallery to watch any trial you like, for a live version of Court TV; the more dramatic criminal cases are heard at the Old Bailey. Other sights are the 238-foot-long Great Hall and the compact exhibition of judges' robes. Guided tours must be booked online and in advance, and include a chance to view original court documents relating to a certain Guy Fawkes. ✉ *The Strand, Holborn* 🌐 *www.theroyalcourtsofjustice.com* 🎫 *Free, tours £13* 🕐 *Closed weekends* Ⓜ *Temple, Holborn, Chancery La.*

Temple Church

RELIGIOUS SITE | As featured in *The Da Vinci Code,* this church was built by the Knights Templar in the late 12th century. The Red Knights held their secret initiation rites in the crypt here. Having started poor, holy, and dedicated to the protection of pilgrims, they grew rich from showers of royal gifts until, in the 14th century, they were stripped of their wealth, charged with blasphemy and sodomy, and thrown into the Tower. ✉ *King's Bench Walk, The Temple, Holborn* ☎ *020/7353–3470* 🌐 *www.templechurch.com* 🎫 *£5* 🕐 *Closed weekends Aug. and Sept.* Ⓜ *Temple.*

Restaurants

★ The Delaunay

$$$ | **AUSTRIAN** | **FAMILY** | It's all *fin de siècle* Vienna at this evocative art deco–style grand café on the Aldwych near Covent Garden. Dishes on the majestic 60-item menu would do the Austro-Hungarian Empire proud—think Wiener schnitzel, Hungarian goulash, beef Stroganoff, and wonderful *würstchen* (frankfurters and hot dogs), served with sauerkraut and onions. **Known for:** elegant old-world Austro-Hungarian haunt; proper Holstein schnitzel and frankfurters; excellent wine list. 💲 *Average main: £25* ✉ *55 Aldwych, Holborn* ☎ *020/7499–8558* 🌐 *www.thedelaunay.com* Ⓜ *Covent Garden, Holborn.*

Hotels

Rosewood London

$$$$ | **HOTEL** | So striking it was featured in the movie *Howards End,* this landmark structure (originally built by the Pearl Assurance Company in 1914) now houses a luxurious hotel with a clubby atmosphere, elegant decor and furnishings, and huge comfortable beds. **Pros:** gorgeous romantic space; excellent restaurant; great spa. **Cons:** luxury comes at a price; the area can be quiet on weekends; the rooms can't quite match the splendor of the public areas. *Rooms from: £500* ✉ *252 High Holborn, Holborn* ☎ *020/7781–8888, 888/767–3966 in U.S.* 🌐 *www.rosewoodhotels.com/en/london* *306 rooms* *No meals* Ⓜ *Holborn.*

The Hoxton

$$ | HOTEL | FAMILY | The emphasis here is on modest-size rooms elegantly appointed and decorated with a chic eye for detail. **Pros:** good value for money; great location close to West End and the British Museum; friendly, helpful staff. **Cons:** the all-inclusive breakfast is a rather meager affair; smallest rooms are on the tiny side; hotel lobby becomes a co-working space during the day and can get noisy. *Rooms from: £140* ✉ *199–206 High Holborn, Holborn* ☎ *020/7661–3000* 🌐 *www.thehoxton.com* *174 rooms* *Free breakfast* Ⓜ *Holborn.*

SACO Holborn

$$ | RENTAL | FAMILY | Down a quiet backstreet a 10-minute walk from the British Museum, these serviced one- and two-bedroom apartments (some of the latter sleep up to six people) are spacious, modern, and well equipped, including kitchens with dishwashers and washing machines. **Pros:** more independence than hotels; pleasant and spacious accommodations; on-site parking. **Cons:** exterior is dated; responsible for your own dining; the area is empty on weekends. *Rooms from: £250* ✉ *Spens House, 72–84 Lamb's Conduit St., Holborn* ☎ *0330/202–0505* 🌐 *www.sacoapartments.co.uk* *32 apartments* *No meals* Ⓜ *Russell Sq.*

Nightlife

BARS

★ Scarfes Bar

BARS/PUBS | FAMILY | The Rosewood's impossibly glamorous Scarfes Bar is one part Edwardian gentleman's club to two parts *Downton Abbey* drawing room. Recline on sofas by a roaring log fire or sink into velvet armchairs and explore the bar's impressive collection of fine wines, cocktails, and spirits (there's more than 180 single malt whiskies alone to choose from). Bar snacks are restaurant-standard dishes and there's complimentary nightly jazz. Be sure to check out London-born artist (and the bar's namesake) Gerald Scarfe's paintings and political cartoons adorning the walls. ✉ *The Rosewood, 252 High Holborn, Holborn* ☎ *020/3747–8670* 🌐 *www.scarfesbar.com* Ⓜ *Holborn.*

PUBS

Museum Tavern

BARS/PUBS | FAMILY | Across the street from the British Museum in Bloomsbury, this friendly and classy Victorian pub makes an ideal resting place after the rigors of the culture trail. Karl Marx unwound here after a hard day in the British Museum Library. If he visited today, he could spend his *kapital* on its excellent selection of craft beers and spirits. ✉ *49 Great Russell St., Bloomsbury* ☎ *020/7242–8987* 🌐 *www.greeneking-pubs.co.uk/pubs/greater-london/museum-tavern* Ⓜ *Tottenham Court Rd., Holborn.*

Princess Louise

BARS/PUBS | FAMILY | This fine popular pub is an exquisite museum piece of a Victorian interior, with glazed tiles and intricately engraved glass screens that divide the bar area into cozy little annexes. It's not all show, either. There's a good selection of excellent-value Yorkshire real ales from Samuel Smith's brewery. ✉ *208 High Holborn, Holborn* ☎ *020/7405–8816* 🌐 *www.princesslouisepub.co.uk* Ⓜ *Holborn.*

Performing Arts

Peacock Theatre

DANCE | Sadler's Wells's West End annex, this modernist theater near the London School of Economics (which sometimes uses it as a lecture hall during the day) focuses on younger companies and features popular dance genres like flamenco, tango, and hip-hop. ✉ *Portugal St., Holborn* ☎ *020/7863–8222* 🌐 *www.peacocktheatre.com* 🎫 *From £15* Ⓜ *Holborn.*

Shopping

ANTIQUES

London Silver Vaults

ANTIQUES/COLLECTIBLES | Originally built in 1876 as Britain's first safe deposit building, this extraordinary underground space five floors beneath ground level has been converted to more than 30 small shops housing silver (plus a few jewelry) dealers, the majority of which are family businesses. Products range from 16th-century items to contemporary pieces (with everything in between), and from the spectacularly over-the-top costing thousands to smaller items—like teaspoons, candlesticks, or a set of Victorian cake forks—at £25. ✉ *53–64 Chancery La., Holborn* ☎ *020/7242–3844* 🌐 *www.silvervaultslondon.com* ⏲ *Closed Sun.* Ⓜ *Chancery La.*

Fitzrovia

To the north of Soho, on the other side of Oxford Street, is Fitzrovia, famed for its dining and drinking. It is known affectionately by some as "Noho." Like its brasher southern sibling, it has some excellent bars and restaurants (especially on Charlotte Street) but more breathing space and fewer crowds. Its name most likely derives from nearby Fitzroy Square. Originally designed by the Adam brothers, the square and its environs quickly became fashionable for haute bohemia; George Bernard Shaw and James McNeill Whistler lived here. To the west, Great Portland Street separates it from Marylebone, while Tottenham Court Road marks its eastern border, beyond which is Bloomsbury. Busy Euston Road (and the Circle Line beneath it) is its northern extent.

Restaurants

Berners Tavern

$$$ | **MODERN BRITISH** | **FAMILY** | All the cool cats swing by this grand brasserie at Ian Schrager's insanely trendy London Edition hotel near Tottenham Court Road. Enter the monumental Edwardian dining salon, where you might swoon over a light lunch of hot smoked Loch Duart salmon or an evening dinner of Herdwick lamb rump with maitake mushrooms and salsa verde. **Known for:** knock-out dining salon; cool back-lit cocktail bar; legendary Buccleuch Estate beef tartare. $ *Average main: £30* ✉ *The London Edition, 10 Berners St., Fitzrovia* ☎ *020/7908–7979* 🌐 *www.bernerstavern.com* Ⓜ *Oxford Circus, Tottenham Court Rd.*

Bonnie Gull Seafood Shack

$$$ | **SEAFOOD** | It almost feels like you're seaside here at London's top seafood shack, where awesome fresh seafood (from Brixham brill to Shetland mussels) takes diners on a tour of the British Isles. Look up, and you'll spot an old ship's bell and captain's hat; a mini–raw bar of iced Palourde clams and Jersey oysters are even stashed inside an antique sea chest. **Known for:** fresh day-boat fish from around the British Isles; passionate service; popular Looe plaice with samphire and clams. $ *Average main: £24* ✉ *21A Foley St., Fitzrovia* ☎ *020/7436–0921* 🌐 *www.bonniegull.com* Ⓜ *Oxford Circus, Goodge St.*

★ **Clipstone**

$$$ | **FRENCH** | Flavorful, inventive dishes elevate this hipster casual joint to the top rank of London's mid-range gastro titans. With a focus on in-house curing, pickling, smoked meats, and heritage vegetables, expect a cavalcade of unlikely combinations and classic gastronomy specialties. **Known for:** fine dining without the fuss; lots of house-made, pickled, fermented, or cured extras; good value set lunches. $ *Average main: £28* ✉ *5 Clipstone St., Fitzrovia* ☎ *020/7637–0871* 🌐 *www.*

clipstonerestaurant.co.uk ⏲ Closed Sun. Ⓜ Great Portland St., Warren St.

★ **Portland**

$$$ | **MODERN EUROPEAN** | Consistently brilliant modern European fare in a low-key setting characterizes this restaurant located just northeast of Oxford Circus. Marvel at the chef's brigade in the open kitchen busily turning the inventive seasonal produce–driven menu into delicious reality. **Known for:** vegetarian and vegan friendly menu; a masterpiece game pithivier (pastry pie); good value lunch and dinner tasting menus. $ *Average main: £30* ✉ *113 Great Portland St., Fitzrovia* ☎ *020/7436–3261* 🌐 *www.portlandrestaurant.co.uk* ⏲ *Closed Sun.* Ⓜ *Oxford Circus.*

Hotels

★ **Charlotte Street Hotel**

$$$ | **HOTEL** | Superstar London hotel designer Kit Kemp has taken the fabled Bloomsbury Group as her inspiration for this super stylish boutique hotel, which, if anything, feels more like a private members' club. **Pros:** elegant and luxurious; great attention to detail; excellent, lively location. **Cons:** the popular bar can be noisy; reservations essential for the restaurant; some rooms are small considering the price. $ *Rooms from: £320* ✉ *15–17 Charlotte St., Fitzrovia* ☎ *020/7806–2000, 888/559–5508 in U.S.* 🌐 *www.firmdalehotels.com* *52 rooms* *No meals* Ⓜ *Goodge St.*

★ **The London Edition**

$$$ | **HOTEL** | Style and image are the draw at the London Edition Hotel, where Michelin-starred chefs and hip bars complement the boutique property's sleek, contemporary design. **Pros:** very trendy; great bars; beautifully designed bedrooms. **Cons:** rooms may feel small to some; lobby can get crowded with trendsetters descending upon the bars; can at times feel more like an events space than a hotel. $ *Rooms from: £333* ✉ *10 Berners St., Fitzrovia* ☎ *020/7781–0000* 🌐 *edition-hotels.marriott.com/london* *173 rooms* *Free breakfast* Ⓜ *Oxford Circus.*

Sanderson Hotel

$$$ | **HOTEL** | Originally designed by French designer Philippe Starck, the style of this fashionable, quirky hotel is part surrealist baroque, part pure *Alice in Wonderland*; sleigh beds are positioned in the middle of bedrooms at playful angles, and so are the freestanding bath tubs and wash basins–indeed, everything is off-center. **Pros:** excellent design; your every whim gratified; unique afternoon tea. **Cons:** glass walls and sheer curtains are all that separate the bathroom in some rooms; bar and restaurant are so exclusive it's hard to get in; you need to book far in advance to get lower rates. $ *Rooms from: £290* ✉ *50 Berners St., Fitzrovia* ☎ *020/7300–1400* 🌐 *www.sandersonlondon.com* *150 rooms* *No meals* Ⓜ *Oxford Circus, Tottenham Court Rd.*

Nightlife

BARS

★ **Artesian**

BARS/PUBS | They don't take reservations at this jewel box of a cocktail bar at the Langham hotel, but you can order a drink while you wait for a chic mirror-top table surrounded by some of London's most beautiful people. The innovative, creative cocktails involve exotic ingredients like sandalwood and fragrant African zalotti blossom, and are simply unforgettable, if pricey. Service is also top-notch, making this a nightlife treat. ✉ *The Langham, 1C Portland Pl., Fitzrovia* ☎ *020/7636–1000* 🌐 *www.artesian-bar.co.uk* Ⓜ *Oxford Circus, Goodge St.*

★ **The London Edition bars**

BARS/PUBS | Visitors to Ian Schrager's London Edition hotel are spoiled for choice when it comes to bars. High ceilings, eclectic artwork, and innovative cocktails can be found at the all-day Berners Tavern and in the Lobby Bar, which opens in the evening. You'll need a reservation to get into the cozy wood-paneled and open-fire Punch Room, but the bar's reinventions of traditional punches (the type favored by pirates and privateers) and the exemplary service are well worth the extra effort. ✉ *10 Berners St., Fitzrovia* ☎ *020/7781–0000* 🌐 *www.editionhotels.com/london* Ⓜ *Tottenham Court Rd., Oxford Circus.*

Shopping

CLOTHING

★ So Tiny London

SPECIALTY STORES | This small store has loads of imaginative gifts for babies and young children, such as distinctive onesies and T-shirts emblazoned with Union Jacks, "Darth Vader Is My Father," "Baby Gaga," and logos of rock bands like David Bowie, Motörhead, and the Rolling Stones. You'll also find pretty dresses with an English Rose print, dragon costumes for dress-up, Jellycat plush toys (favorites of the current royal little ones), and child-friendly joke items like a knitted gold crown. ✉ *64 Great Titchfield St., Fitzrovia* ☎ *020/7636–3501* 🌐 *www.sotinylondon.com* Ⓜ *Oxford Circus.*

Clerkenwell

Once home to medieval religious orders such as the Knights of the Hospitallers of St. John of Jerusalem, Clerkenwell later became an epicenter of the industrial revolution in the capital and, subsequently, of political radicalism (a young Joseph Stalin is said to have met a young Vladimir Lenin at the Crown Tavern pub in Clerkenwell Green). The monks are long gone—so, too, the communists—and the neighborhood's warehouses and factory floors are now home to cutting-edge design agencies, new media start-ups, and ubertrendy apartments. With its fashionable boutiques, bars, and restaurants, Clerkenwell can be a pleasant place to spend a few hours. Like its neighbor immediately to the east, The City, this area can be quite deserted on weekends.

Sights

Exmouth Market

PEDESTRIAN MALL | At this charming pedestrianized thoroughfare, trendy clothing boutiques, jewelers, beauty salons, gift shops, and even a tattoo parlor, all jostle for space with Exmouth Market's excellent cafés and restaurants, many of which offer outdoor seating. At its southern end is the 19th-century Church of Our Most Holy Redeemer, the only Italian basilica–style church in London. There's also a vibrant food market on weekdays serving gourmet street food. Look out for the brilliantly-named barber shop Barber Streisand. ✉ *Exmouth St., Clerkenwell* 🌐 *www.exmouth.london* Ⓜ *Farringdon, The Angel.*

Museum of the Order of St. John

MUSEUM | This fascinating museum tells the story of the Knights Hospitallers of St. John, from the Order's 11th-century Crusader origins in Jerusalem to its present-day incarnation as the St. John Ambulance service. The museum is spread across two adjacent sites: the arched St. John's Gatehouse, which dates back to 1504, and the Priory Church with its atmospheric Norman crypt. An excellent interactive display explores the Order's past, both as a military force and a religious institution that cared for sick pilgrims, and the eclectic variety of objects on display reflects that colorful history: from antique medicinal jars and medical equipment to pieces of armor worn by the Knights when they defended Malta from the Ottomans in the 16th century, as well as a bronze cannon given by Henry VIII before he dissolved the Order altogether a few years later. ✉ *St. John's Gate, St. John's La., Clerkenwell* ☎ *020/7324–4005* 🌐 *www.*

museumstjohn.org.uk Free, guided tours £5 (suggested donation) Closed Sun. Oct.–June Farringdon.

Restaurants

Anglo

$$ | **MODERN BRITISH** | Modern British bistronomy takes a giant leap forward at chef-patron Mark Jarvis's unprententious fine dining mecca in the historic Hatton Garden jewelry quarter in Farringdon. Feast on the Brit-sourced seasonal foodie creations here, which are offered à la carte or as five- or seven-course tasting menus at lunch or dinner. **Known for:** well-priced tasting menus for lunch and dinner; signature grated cheese and onion on malt toast; inventive desserts like frozen chocolate and water mousse with apple chips. *Average main: £19 30 St Cross St., Clerkenwell 020/7430–1503 www.anglorestaurant.com Closed Sun. and Mon. Farringdon.*

Berber & Q - Shawarma Bar

$ | **ISRAELI** | **FAMILY** | Every night feels as bustling as downtown Tel Aviv at Exmouth Market's superb and hip shawarma bar. Enjoy challah toast with tahini-rich mezze before delving into slow-cooked, harissa-heavy lamb shawarmas and the best *mejadera* (rice with lentils and onions) this side of the Middle East. **Known for:** Tel Aviv–style trendy hangout; wondrous char-grilled lamb and beef shawarmas; unmissable BBQ-ed cauliflower shawarma. *Average main: £14 45 Exmouth Market, Clerkenwell 020/7837–1726 www.shawarmabar.co.uk Closed Sun. Farringdon.*

★ Luca

$$$$ | **MODERN ITALIAN** | This winning mix of modern Italian classics is made from the very best in British seasonal produce. Add to that the super-chic setting—from the art deco–esque dining salon to the marble-top bar and the stunning glass-walled conservatory—and this popular Clerkenwell haunt is very much a case of both style *and* substance. **Known for:** edgy Italian pastas; cool and glamorously designed brasserie; to-die-for fluffy parmesan fries. *Average main: £32 88 St John St., Clerkenwell 020/3859–3000 www.luca.restaurant Closed Sun. Farringdon.*

Moro

$$$ | **MEDITERRANEAN** | **FAMILY** | Exmouth Market is a magnet for fine indie-spirited restaurants like this one. Lovingly nurtured since 1997 by husband-and-wife chefs Sam and Sam Clark, the menu includes a mélange of Spanish, Moroccan, and Moorish North African flavors. **Known for:** loud and buzzy dining room with booming acoustics; expressive Moorish delights; house yogurt cake with pistachios and pomegranate. *Average main: £25 34–36 Exmouth Market, Clerkenwell 020/7833–8336 www.moro.co.uk Farringdon, Angel.*

★ St. John

$$ | **MODERN BRITISH** | **FAMILY** | Global foodie fanatics join Clerkenwell locals for the pioneering nose-to-tail cuisine at this high-ceilinged, converted smokehouse near Smithfield Market. Here the chef uses all scraps of a carcass—from tongue and cheeks to tail and trotters—so brace for radically stark signatures like bone-marrow-and-parsley salad. **Known for:** ground zero of influential Modern British nose-to-tail dining; great wine list; crispy pig's-skin appetizer. *Average main: £23 26 St. John St., Clerkenwell 020/7251–0848 www.stjohnrestaurant.com No dinner Sun. Farringdon, Barbican.*

★ The Rookery

$$ | **HOTEL** | A stylish period masterpiece in the heart of laid-back Clerkenwell, the Rookery is a luxury boutique hotel with a hefty dollop of *Downton Abbey* charm. **Pros:** charming decor; free Wi-Fi; good deals in the off-season. **Cons:** breakfast

costs extra; no restaurant in the hotel; the resident cat might put off guests with allergies. *Rooms from: £240* *12 Peter's La., at Cowcross St., Clerkenwell* *020/7336–0931* *www.rookery-hotel.com* *33 rooms* *No meals* *Farringdon.*

★ The Zetter

$$ | HOTEL | The five-story atrium, art deco staircase, and slick European restaurant hint at the delights to come in this converted warehouse—a breath of fresh air with its playful color schemes, elegant wallpapers, and wonderful views of The City from the higher floors. **Pros:** huge amounts of character; big rooms; free Wi-Fi. **Cons:** rooms with good views cost more; the contemporary style won't appeal to everyone; the property's best bar is across the street at the Zetter Townhouse. *Rooms from: £140* *86–88 Clerkenwell Rd., Clerkenwell* *020/7324–4444* *www.thezetter.com* *59 rooms* *Free breakfast* *Farringdon.*

Nightlife

Café Kick

BARS/PUBS | Perfect for a mid-afternoon pick-me-up or late-night drinks, this quirky, friendly bar has a continental feel and a football (that's soccer to the Americans) vibe. Football memorabilia and bank notes from across the globe line the walls while formica furniture and not one, but two, foosball fill out the space. World beers and cocktails are the drinks of choice (the caipirinhas are legendary), and simple but tasty pub fare is served up at lunchtime. *43 Exmouth Market, Clerkenwell* *020/7837–8077* *www.cafekick.co.uk* *Farringdon, Angel.*

Craft Beer Co

BARS/PUBS | FAMILY | With 37 beers on tap and 350 more in bottles (one brewed exclusively for the Craft Beer Company), the main problem here is knowing where to start. Luckily, friendly and knowledgeable staff are happy to advise or give tasters—or why not sign up for a guided tasting session? A huge chandelier and a mirrored ceiling lend antique charm to the interior, and a smattering of tourists and beer pilgrims break up the crowds of Leather Lane workers and locals. *82 Leather La., Clerkenwell* *020/7404–7049* *www.thecraftbeerco.com* *Closed Sun.* *Chancery La.*

★ Jerusalem Tavern

BARS/PUBS | FAMILY | Loved by Londoners and owned by the well-respected St. Peter's Brewery in Suffolk, the Jerusalem Tavern is one-of-a-kind: small, historic, atmospheric, and endearingly eccentric. Antique Delft-style tiles meld with wood and concrete in a converted watchmaker and jeweler's shop dating back to the 18th century. The beer, both bottled and on tap, is some of the best available anywhere in London. It's often busy, especially after work, but it's closed on weekends. *55 Britton St., Clerkenwell* *020/7490–4281* *www.stpetersbrewery.co.uk/london-pub* *Closed weekends* *Farringdon.*

Islington

Islington is one of the most fashionable of London's villagelike neighborhoods. Upper Street, with its high-street stores, independent boutiques, and myriad restaurants and bars, is where most of the action takes place. But wander off the main drag and you'll discover elegant residential streets and squares, as well as bustling charming markets. You'll also find a handful of top-flight Off West End theaters and music venues in the area, including the Almeida, the hugely atmospheric Union Chapel, and—down on Islington's border with Clerkenwell—the renowned contemporary dance venue, Sadler's Wells.

Sights

Camden Passage

NEIGHBORHOOD | A pretty pedestrian thoroughfare just off Upper Street, Camden Passage is famous for its many antiques shops selling everything from vintage furniture to period jewelry to timeless timepieces. In recent years, a sprinkling of independent boutiques, delis, and cafés has given the passage an eclectic vibrant feel. Check out the antiques market held on Wednesday and from Friday through Sunday. ✉ *Islington* 🌐 *www.camdenpassageislington.co.uk* Ⓜ *The Angel.*

Chapel Market

NEIGHBORHOOD | Chapel Market is what Islington used to be: an unpretentious, working-class enclave. There's a lively food market that runs for half the length of the street every day except Monday—just listening to the stallholders advertising their wares can be entertainment enough. Although trendy eateries are beginning to pop up here and there, it is still home to London's oldest eel, pie, and mash shop, M. Manze's, with its marble tables and tiled interior largely untouched since it was established in 1902. ✉ *Chapel Market, Islington* Ⓜ *The Angel.*

Victoria Miro Gallery

MUSEUM | This large, important commercial gallery, in a former furniture factory, has exhibited some of the biggest names on the British contemporary art scene: Grayson Perry, Chris Ofili, the Chapman Brothers, Peter Doig, and many others. Some exhibitions spill out into the gallery's garden. It also brings in exciting talent from abroad. There's another branch in Mayfair. ✉ *16 Wharf Rd., Islington* ☎ *020/7336–8109* 🌐 *www.victoria-miro.com* 🎫 *Free* 🕒 *Closed Sun. and Mon.* Ⓜ *Old St., Angel.*

Restaurants

Oldroyd

$$ | **ITALIAN** | This tiny neighborhood bistro's perennial popularity is all thanks to the sensational Italian food and the warm and friendly service. Well-priced,with the focus firmly on seasonal ingredients. **Known for:** jam-packed space; earthy Italian fare like osso buco; buzzy atmosphere. $ *Average main: £17* ✉ *344 Upper St., Islington* ☎ *020/8617–9010* 🌐 *www.oldroydlondon.com* Ⓜ *Angel.*

Ottolenghi

$ | **CAFÉ** | **FAMILY** | Captivating foodie window displays and a funky modern interior characterize this North African, Middle Eastern, and Mediterranean deli-bakery-café set in Islington's main Upper Street drag. Dig into exceptionally inventive, tasty, and healthy veg-centric dishes along with cult Ottolenghi fresh salads, soups, flaky pastries, and artisanal cakes. **Known for:** zingy veg-centric Middle Eastern salad combos; fabulous meringue-filled window displays; weekend brunches. $ *Average main: £13* ✉ *287 Upper St., Islington* ☎ *020/7288–1454* 🌐 *www.ottolenghi.co.uk* Ⓜ *Angel.*

Nightlife

BARS

69 Colebrooke Row

BARS/PUBS | This elegant faux speakeasy must be London's tiniest cocktail lounge. Book one of the handful of tables or a seat at the diminutive bar to sample perfectly made twists on classic cocktails, like the panettone bellini, which uses a purée of the sweet Italian bread instead of peach. ✉ *69 Colebrooke Row, Islington* ☎ *07540/528–593* 🌐 *www.69colebrookerow.com* Ⓜ *Angel.*

LIVE MUSIC

Union Chapel

MUSIC CLUBS | **FAMILY** | The beauty of this sublime old chapel and its impressive multicultural not-for-profit programming make this spot one of London's best musical venues, especially for acoustic shows. A variety of star names have played here in recent years (including Kris Kristofferson, Björk, and Beck) alongside alternative country, world music, and jazz performers. There's also poetry and literary events, film screenings, and stand-up comedy gigs. Tickets are only available online. ✉ *Union Chapel, Compton Terr., Islington* ☎ *020/7226–1686 for venue (no box office; ticket sales numbers vary with each event)* 🌐 *www.unionchapel.org.uk* *Free–£40* Ⓜ *Highbury & Islington.*

 Performing Arts

Close to central London, yet with its own unique atmosphere, this neighborhood is home to a handful of renowned theaters and music venues that make the short journey northeast well worth the effort.

DANCE

★ Sadler's Wells

DANCE | FAMILY | If you're into leading classical and contemporary dance companies, head to this purpose-built complex, which opened in 1998 and is the sixth theater on this site in its 300 year history. Choreographers like Matthew Bourne and Hofesh Shechter often bring their work here. The little Lilian Baylis Studio hosts avant-garde work. ✉ *Rosebery Ave., Islington* ☎ *020/7863–8000* 🌐 *www.sadlerswells.com* *From £12* Ⓜ *Angel.*

THEATER

Almeida Theatre

THEATER | This Off West End venue, helmed by director Rupert Goold, premiers excellent new plays and exciting twists on the classics, often featuring high-profile actors. There's a good café and a licensed bar that serves "sharing dishes," as well as tasty main courses. ✉ *Almeida St., Islington* ☎ *020/7359–4404* 🌐 *www.almeida.co.uk* *From £10* Ⓜ *Angel, Highbury & Islington.*

King's Cross Station 

Sick of living in the shadow of its sumptuously renovated next-door neighbor, St. Pancras Station, King's Cross—and the area behind it—has undergone a major makeover of its own, with bars, restaurants, shops, cultural venues, and a stunning fountain display for all to enjoy. It's also a place dear to Harry Potter fans everywhere, because it was from the imaginary platform 9¾ that our hero boarded the *Hogwarts Express* (the station has helpfully put up a sign for platform 9¾ if you want to take a picture there).

Little Angel Theatre

PUPPET SHOWS | FAMILY | Innovative puppetry performances for children and adults have been taking place in this adorable former temperance hall since 1961. ✉ *14 Dagmar Passage, Islington* ☎ *020/7226–1787* 🌐 *www.littleangeltheatre.com* *From £7* Ⓜ *Angel, Highbury & Islington.*

 Shopping

HOUSEHOLD GOODS

★ TwentyTwentyOne

HOUSEHOLD ITEMS/FURNITURE | This furniture, lighting, and accessories store is a must-see if you're into mid-century and modernist design. It carries an enormous selection of 20th-century classics, including pieces from Eames, Noguchi, Wegner, Aalto, Prouvé, Saarinen, and the husband-and-wife team Robin and Lucienne Day, both in the form of original pieces and licensed reissues. You can also find contemporary products from modern masters like Tom Dixon, Thomas Heatherwick, and Marc Newson. The kids' line is particularly cool, with items like a record-lookalike frisbee by playful British artist, David Shrigley. Small accessories

Centered on the train station made most famous as the fictional gateway to Hogwarts, King's Cross has seen a bevy of new dining and nightlife openings in the past few years.

like tote bags and bathmats will easily fit into your luggage. ✉ *274–275 Upper St., Islington* ☎ *020/7288–1996* 🌐 *www.twentytwentyone.com* Ⓜ *Highbury & Islington.*

King's Cross

Once upon a time, King's Cross was a byword for sleaze and street crime, but after a multibillion-pound redevelopment—actually, make that transformation—it's become a lively urban quarter. On what was once postindustrial wasteland and railroad yards, the 67-acre site is now home to bars, restaurants, street-food vendors, and shops. What's more, with the capital's premier art college, the University of the Arts in London, having relocated to Granary Square, alongside a raft of cultural venues, this spot now has a certain air of artistic credibility about it, too. If all that weren't enough, by courtesy of the Regent's Canal, this bustling quarter even has the occasional peaceful oasis of calm as well.

Sights

Granary Square

PLAZA | The heart of the new King's Cross, Granary Square is one of London's liveliest open spaces. Pride of place is given to the ever-changing 1,000-strong fountain display, which is even more spectacular by night when lights accompany the choreography. The immense, six-story granary building—designed in 1852 to store wheat for London's bakers—now houses the University of the Arts in London, as well as a selection of excellent bars and eateries. The square's south-facing steps double as an amphitheater for site-specific arts events; at times, the steps themselves become the installation—such as when they're covered with carved pumpkins at Halloween or a blanket of flowers in spring. ✉ *King's Cross* Ⓜ *King's Cross St. Pancras.*

London Canal Museum

MUSEUM | **FAMILY** | This quirky museum, dedicated to the rise and fall of London's once-extensive canal network, is based in the former warehouse of ice-cream maker Carlo Gatti (hence it also partly features the ice-cream trade as well as London's canals). Children enjoy the activity zone and learning about Henrietta, the museum's horse. Outside, on the Battlebridge Basin, you'll find the painted narrowboats of modern canal dwellers—a stone's throw from the hustle and bustle of the King's Cross redevelopment. You can walk to the museum along the towpath from Camden Lock; download a free audio tour from the museum's website to accompany the route. ✉ *12–13 New Wharf Rd., King's Cross* ☎ *020/7713–0836* 🌐 *www.canalmuseum.org.uk* 🎫 *£5* ⏲ *Closed Mon.* Ⓜ *King's Cross.*

Performing Arts

Kings Place

ART GALLERIES—ARTS | The cultural jewel of the King's Cross transformation, this airy concert venue is the headquarters of the London Sinfonietta. Its resident orchestra, Aurora Orchestra, is the world's first professional orchestra to perform whole symphonies by the likes of Mozart and Beethoven without sheet music. There's a varied cultural calendar here, including jazz, comedy, folk, and political and literary lectures, plus two gallery spaces. ✉ *90 York Way, King's Cross* ☎ *020/7520–1490* 🌐 *www.kingsplace.co.uk* 🎫 *Free–£70* Ⓜ *King's Cross.*

Chapter 7

THE CITY

Updated by
Ellin Stein

Sights ★★★★★ | Restaurants ★★★☆☆ | Hotels ★★★☆☆ | Shopping ★☆☆☆☆ | Nightlife ★★☆☆☆

THE CITY SNAPSHOT

TOP REASONS TO GO

St. Paul's Cathedral: Although the cathedral is increasingly surrounded by skyscrapers, the beauty of Sir Christopher Wren's 17th-century masterpiece nevertheless remains undiminished.

The Millennium Bridge: Travel from past to present on this promenade between St. Paul's and Tate Modern—and get a great river view, too.

The Tower of London: This medieval complex is home to atmospheric towers, the dazzling Crown Jewels, and hundreds of years of history.

The Museum of London: From skimpy leather briefs dating to Roman times and Queen Victoria's crinolines to Selfridges's art deco elevators and a diorama of the Great Fire (including sound effects and flickering flames), this gem of a museum has got it all.

GETTING THERE

The City is well served by a concentration of Tube stations—St. Paul's and Bank on the Central Line, and Mansion House, Cannon Street, and Monument on the District and Circle lines. Liverpool Street and Aldgate border The City's eastern edge, while Chancery Lane and Farringdon lie to the west. Barbican and Moorgate provide easy access to the theaters and galleries of the Barbican, and Blackfriars, to the south, leads to Ludgate Circus and Fleet Street.

MAKING THE MOST OF YOUR TIME

The City is also known as the "Square Mile," which hints at how compact it is with little distance between points of interest. For full immersion in the Tower of London, set aside half a day, especially if seeing the Crown Jewels is a priority. Allow an hour minimum each for the Museum of London, St. Paul's Cathedral, and Tower Bridge. On weekends, without the workers who make up 90% of the daytime population, The City is nearly deserted and many affordable lunch places are closed—and yet this is when the major attractions are at their busiest.

QUICK BITES

■ **City Càphê** This unpretentious but charming family-run Vietnamese street-food café offers delicious quick bites and takeout dishes for lunch. Try the pho, banh mi, or spring rolls. ✉ *17 Ironmonger La., City of London* 🌐 *www.citycaphe.com* ⏲ *Closed weekends* Ⓜ *Mansion House, Bank.*

■ **White Mulberries** This friendly coffee shop at St. Katharine Docks serves outstanding breakfast (with fresh juices and baked goods) plus homemade soups, cakes, and light bites for lunch. ✉ *D3 Ivory House, St. Katharine Docks, City of London* ☎ *07507/572600* 🌐 *www.whitemulberries.com* Ⓜ *Tower Hill, Tower Gateway (DLR).*

■ **Ye Olde Cheshire Cheese** This wonderfully higgledy-piggledy, multilevel inn on Fleet Street was built in 1667, but the basement bar is centuries older, lending credence to its claim as London's oldest pub. The list of famous people who've imbibed here is like a "who's who" of London history, including the likes of Samuel Pepys, Charles Dickens, and Samuel Johnson. ✉ *145 Fleet St., City of London* ☎ *020/7353–6170* Ⓜ *St. Paul's.*

The capital's fast-beating financial heart, The City is associated with power and pomp, embodied in the three institutions at its epicenter: the Bank of England, the Royal Exchange, and Mansion House. The site of the original Roman settlement from which all of London grew, the "Square Mile" has statement skyscrapers cheek-by-jowl with some of London's most iconic historic buildings, from Wren's uplifting St. Paul's Cathedral to the Tower of London, a royal fortress, prison, and jewel house surrounded by a moat.

Home to both the latest financial high-tech and the descendants of medieval guilds, The City is where the historic past and fast-moving present collide. Begin your explorations on **Fleet Street,** the site of England's first printing press and the undisputed seat of British journalism until the 1980s. Nestled behind Fleet Street is **Dr. Johnson's House,** where the noted lexicographer, famous for asserting "when a man is tired of London, he is tired of life," compiled the original *Dictionary of the English Language*. Nearby **St. Bride's,** a Wren gem recognizable by its tiered-wedding-cake steeple, is still known as "the journalists' church" while to the east is Wren's masterpiece of the English baroque, **St. Paul's Cathedral.** Legacies of London's past are everywhere: at the **Central Criminal Court,** better known as The Old Bailey (and, in its various incarnations, the venue for many of London's most notorious criminal trials); the soaring Victorian **Smithfield Market,** built on a site where livestock has been sold since the 14th century and where a dusk-to-dawn wholesale meat market—the largest in Britain—still operates; the Romanesque church **St. Bartholomew the Great** and next to it **St. Bartholomew's Hospital,** both begun in 1123 at the eastern end of Smithfield; the **Guildhall,** from whose Gothic Great Hall The City was governed and where you can see recently excavated remains of the only Roman amphitheater in London; the church of **St. Mary-le-Bow,** home of the "Bow Bells," of which true Cockneys are supposedly born within earshot; and the maze of charmingly old-fashioned, narrow streets around **Bow Lane.**

To the south is another Wren edifice, the **Monument,** begun in 1671 to commemorate the Great Fire of London five years earlier, while farther east is the historically rich **Tower of London,** which has dominated the riverbank for over a thousand years. Looking towards the river, you'll immediately spot the Victorian Gothic **Tower Bridge,** one of London's most recognizable landmarks. You can put all this history into context at the **Museum of London,** where the archaeological displays include a segment of the **Roman Wall** that ringed The City when it was known to Romans as "Londinium."

The City is also home to some of London's most distinctive contemporary architecture. To the north of Smithfield is the **Barbican Centre,** a Brutalist concrete complex of arts venues and apartments that was controversial when it was built between 1965 and 1976, but has since become an indispensable part of the London streetscape. A plethora of distinctive new structures now tower over The City, not all of which are popular; bold designs such as **20 Fenchurch Street** (aka The Walkie Talkie) and **30 St Mary Axe** (The Gherkin) are almost as contentious today as the Barbican was 40 years ago (but several have top-floor restaurants, where you can take in superb views). They all add to the mix in this constantly evolving area, and whenever you return—whether in months or years—The City is guaranteed not to be the same as when you saw it last.

Sights

Bank of England

BANK | Since its establishment in 1694 as England's central bank, the role of the "Old Lady of Threadneedle Street" (a political cartoon caption that stuck) has grown to include managing foreign exchanges, issuing currency, storing the nation's gold reserves, and regulating the United Kingdom's banking system. Since 1997, it has had operational responsibility for Britain's monetary policy, most visibly setting interest rates (similar to the Federal Reserve in the United States). The 3-acre site is enclosed in a massive, neoclassical curtain wall designed by Sir John Soane. This 1828 windowless outer wall is all that survives of Soane's original Bank building, which was demolished in 1925. You can discover more about the bank's history in the surprisingly varied Bank of England Museum (the entrance is around the corner on Bartholomew Lane). In addition to the bank's original Royal Charter, there's a lively program of special exhibitions, plus interactive displays (you can even try your hand at controlling inflation). The most popular exhibit remains the solid-gold bar in the central trading hall that you can actually hold—but before you get any ideas, there's security everywhere. ✉ *Threadneedle St., City of London* ☎ *020/3461–4878* 🌐 *www.bankofengland.co.uk* 🎟 *Free* 🕑 *Closed weekends and bank holidays* Ⓜ *Bank, Monument.*

Dr. Johnson's House

HOUSE | Built in 1700, this elegant Georgian residence, with its restored interiors, paneled rooms, and period furniture, is where Samuel Johnson lived between 1748 and 1759, compiling his landmark *A Dictionary of the English Language* in the garret as his health deteriorated. There's a research library with two early editions on view, along with other mementos of Johnson and his friend and biographer, James Boswell, one of literature's greatest diarists. After your visit, enjoy more 17th-century atmosphere around the corner in Wine Office Court at the venerable pub **Ye Olde Cheshire Cheese,** once Johnson and Boswell's favorite watering hole. ✉ *17 Gough Sq., City of London* ☎ *020/7353–3745* 🌐 *www.drjohnsonshouse.org* 🎟 *£7* 🕑 *Closed Sun. and bank holidays* ☞ *Admission is cash-only* Ⓜ *Holborn, Chancery La., Temple.*

A Brief History of London

Although there is evidence of scattered Celtic rural settlements on the north bank of the Thames, London truly begins with the Romans, who established an outpost of the empire called Londinium (which was about the size of Hyde Park) in 47 AD. In 60 AD, the warrior queen Boudicca led an uprising of the native Iceni, burning the city to the ground, but the Romans soon regained control, adding a defensive wall. Not much is known of what happened to the city after the Romans left in the 5th century (while England as a whole suffered successive invasions by the Angles, Saxons, Jutes, and Vikings), beyond the establishment of a 7th-century cathedral dedicated to Saint Paul (the famous one now stands on the same site). After the Norman invasion of 1066 and William the Conqueror's building of the fortress-cum-castle that became known as the Tower of London, the city started to prosper again within those old Roman walls. By the early 13th century, King John acknowledged the city's importance by granting it the right to elect a Lord Mayor. During the Middle Ages, powerful guilds took root that helped nurture commerce, and in the Tudor era, London became the center of both government and trade, reaching a population of some 200,000 people. Dockyards were built to service the British ships that plied lucrative new trade routes, both to the New World and India, laying the foundations for London's role as the world's premier city for the next three centuries.

After the Restoration of 1660, London immediately faced two disasters: the Great Plague of 1665, which killed almost a quarter of the city's population, and then, in 1666, the Great Fire, which destroyed most of its old medieval wood structures. However, the reconstruction gave rise to buildings created by one of Britain's greatest architects, Sir Christopher Wren. He, along with John Nash in the 18th century, gave shape to much of the city we see today. Subsequent Regency and Victorian expansion created the characteristic look of new neighborhoods to the west and north like Kensington, Notting Hill, Camden, and Hampstead. Another disaster befell London, particularly in the East End and The City, when Luftwaffe bombs rained down relentlessly during World War II (a destruction equalled by, some argue, the unimaginative urban planners of the 1960s and 1970s). However, as the plethora of shiny new skyscrapers attest, the capacity for reinvention that has enabled this city to thrive for 2,000 years remains undimmed.

Guildhall

BUILDING | For centuries, this building has been the administrative and ceremonial base of the Corporation of London, the world's oldest continuously elected municipal governing authority (the Corporation still oversees The City's civic administration but now in a more modern building). Built between 1411 and 1440, it is The City's only surviving secular medieval building, and although it lost roofs to both the Great Fire of 1666 and the Blitz of 1940, its Gothic Great Hall has remained intact. Adding to the Hall's period atmosphere are the colorful coats of arms and banners of the 110 City Livery Companies, descendants of medieval trade guilds, which still officially elect the Lord Mayor of London. These range from older Companies originally formed

Walking over the Millennium Bridge takes you to St. Paul's Cathedral, the Sir Christopher Wren–designed masterpiece that is one of the most beautiful cathedrals in England.

by trades of yesteryear to new ones representing modern activities like information technology, along with several that remain eternally relevant (e.g., carpenters, upholsterers, and fishmongers).

The Hall has been the site of several historic trials, including that of "the Nine Day Queen" Lady Jane Grey in 1553 and the landmark *Zong* case (1783), which helped end Britain's involvement in the slave trade. Even more ancient are the 11th Century East and West Crypts, survivors of the original Saxon Hall and the largest remaining medieval crypts in London. To the right of Guildhall Yard is the Guildhall Art Gallery, which includes portraits of notables, cityscapes, and a slightly cloying pre-Raphaelite section. The construction of the gallery in the 1980s led to the exciting discovery of London's only Roman Amphitheater, which had lain undisturbed for more than 1,800 years. Visitors can walk through the excavation, although most of the artifacts are now at the Museum of London. There are 75-minute guided tours on select Thursdays when the city council meets at 10:45 am (advance booking required); check the website for dates. ✉ *Off Guildhall Yard, Gresham St., City of London* ☎ *020/7332–1313* 🌐 *www.cityoflondon.gov.uk* 🎫 *Guildhall tours £10* ⏲ *Closed Aug.* Ⓜ *St. Paul's, Moorgate, Bank, Mansion House.*

The Monument

MEMORIAL | Designed by Sir Christopher Wren and Dr. Robert Hooke to commemorate 1666's "dreadful visitation" of the Great Fire of London (note the gilded orb of flame at the column's pinnacle), the world's tallest isolated stone column offers spectacular views of the city from the viewing platform 160 feet up. The two architects were asked to erect the monument as close as possible to where the fire began, and so it's located exactly 202 feet from the alleged point of origin, Farrier's baking house on Pudding Lane. Built between 1671 and 1677, the fluted Doric column also stands 202 feet tall, so if climbing the 311 steps of the beautiful spiral staircase to the public balcony seems too arduous, you can watch a live view from the platform played on a screen at the entrance. ✉ *Monument St., City of London* ☎ *020/7403–3761* 🌐 *www.themonument.info* 🎫 *From £5* ☞ *Admission is cash only* Ⓜ *Monument.*

★ **Museum of London**

MUSEUM | FAMILY | This fascinating museum reveals London in its many incarnations, from its first days as a Roman settlement around AD 50 (and even before, with finds going back to 450,000 BC) up to the present. The more than 7,000 objects encompass everything from Queen Victoria's crinolines and Selfridges's original art deco elevators to grim Georgian iron doors from the city's infamous Newgate Prison and Thomas Heatherwick's cauldron from the 2012 London Olympics. Permanent galleries are devoted to nearly every era of English history, including the current globalized megalopolis period. The Roman London collection contains some extraordinary gems, including an astonishingly well-preserved floor mosaic uncovered just a few streets away; don't miss the extraordinary Bronze Age and Roman artifacts unearthed during construction of the new Crossrail underground railway. There are also themed temporary exhibitions, themed walking tours (such as "Hogarth's London"), and an offshoot branch near Canary Wharf devoted to the history of the area and the River Thames. ✉ *150 London Wall, City of London* ☎ *020/7001–9844* 🌐 *www.museumoflondon.org.uk* 🎫 *Free* Ⓜ *Barbican, St. Paul's.*

The Old Bailey

GOVERNMENT BUILDING | Visitors are allowed into the public galleries of the 16 courtrooms at London's **Central Criminal Court** (universally known as "the Old Bailey," a reference to the street where it's located, which follows the line of the original fortified city wall, or "bailey" in Middle English). Historically it has been the venue for many of Britain's most famous criminal trials. It was here that Oscar Wilde was condemned for "gross indecency" in 1895, where notorious murderers like the Kray twins in the 1960s and the Yorkshire Ripper in the 1980s were convicted, and, more recently, where high-profile terrorism cases have been tried. Originally the site of a medieval courthouse destroyed in the Great Fire, a courthouse was built here next to the grim Newgate Prison, the poor man's version of the Tower, in 1673. The building went through two more incarnations before the present Edwardian baroque building opened in 1907 (it was rebuilt again after the Blitz). Until 1868, executions were held on the street outside (a great public attraction) and you can still see the "Dead Man's Walk" along which condemned prisoners were taken from their cells to the gallows under a series of ever-narrowing arches. Note the 12-foot gold leaf statue of Lady Justice at the top of the dome, not wearing a blindfold as she is usually portrayed.

Visitors are only allowed access to the public galleries to view trials; there is no visitor access to the rest of the building. Trials take place from 10 am to 1 pm and 2 pm to 4:30 pm. There are security restrictions, and children under 14 and overly casual dress are not allowed. ✉ *The Old Bailey, City of London* ☎ *020/7248–3277* 🌐 *www.cityoflondon.gov.uk* 🎫 *Free* ⏲ *Closed weekends, bank holidays, and when court not in session.* Ⓜ *St. Paul's.*

★ **St. Bartholomew the Great**

RELIGIOUS SITE | Originally founded in 1123 as part of an Augustinian monastery, this is one of the oldest churches in London and one of the city's few surviving Norman buildings. Although much of the church has been destroyed or demolished over the centuries, with restoration only beginning in the mid-19th century (it even saw use as a stable and a factory in the interim), it nevertheless remains perhaps the best preserved example of

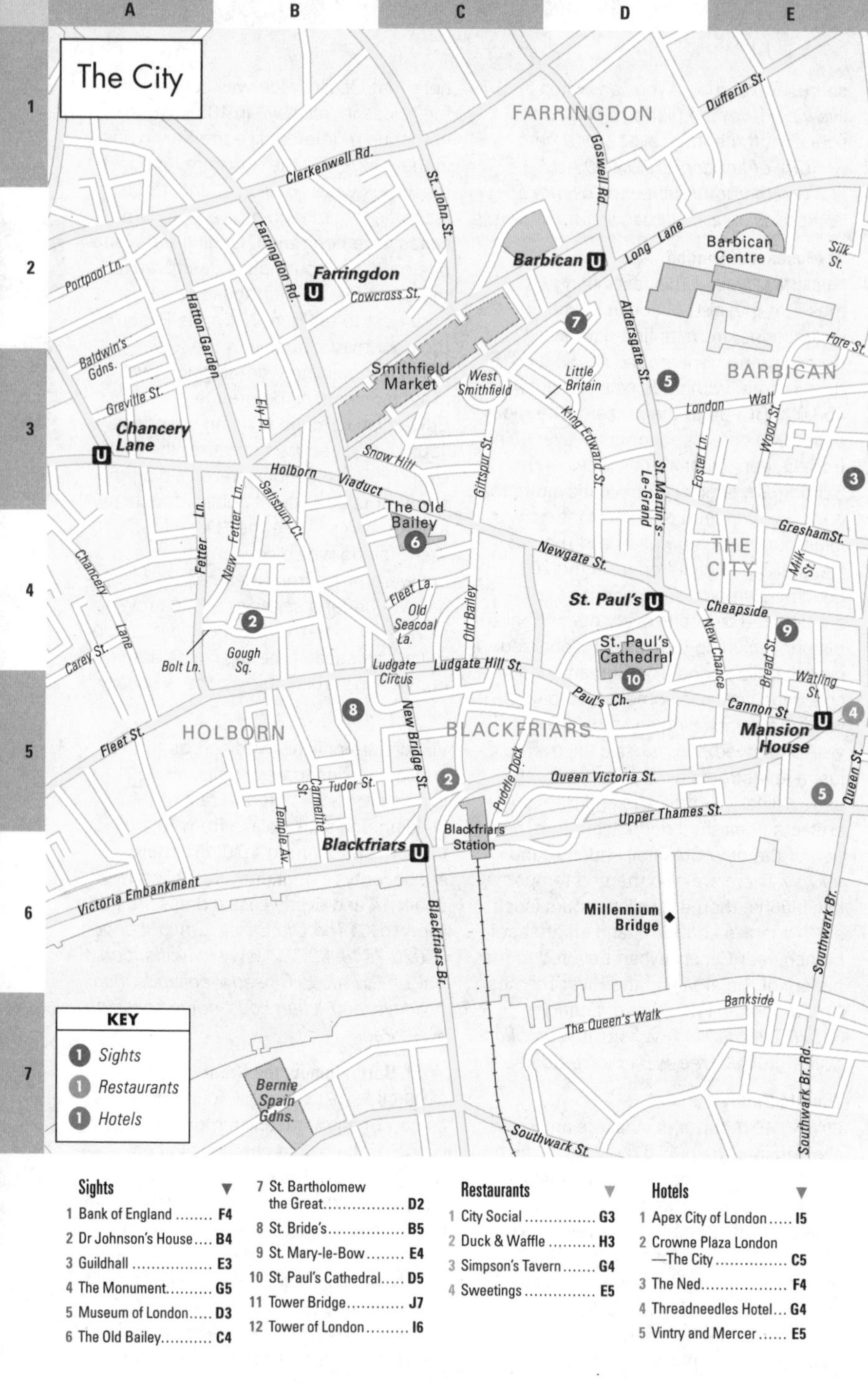

Sights ▼

1 Bank of England F4
2 Dr Johnson's House B4
3 Guildhall E3
4 The Monument.......... G5
5 Museum of London..... D3
6 The Old Bailey........... C4
7 St. Bartholomew the Great................ D2
8 St. Bride's............... B5
9 St. Mary-le-Bow........ E4
10 St. Paul's Cathedral..... D5
11 Tower Bridge........... J7
12 Tower of London......... I6

Restaurants ▼

1 City Social G3
2 Duck & Waffle H3
3 Simpson's Tavern....... G4
4 Sweetings E5

Hotels ▼

1 Apex City of London..... I5
2 Crowne Plaza London —The City C5
3 The Ned.................. F4
4 Threadneedles Hotel... G4
5 Vintry and Mercer E5

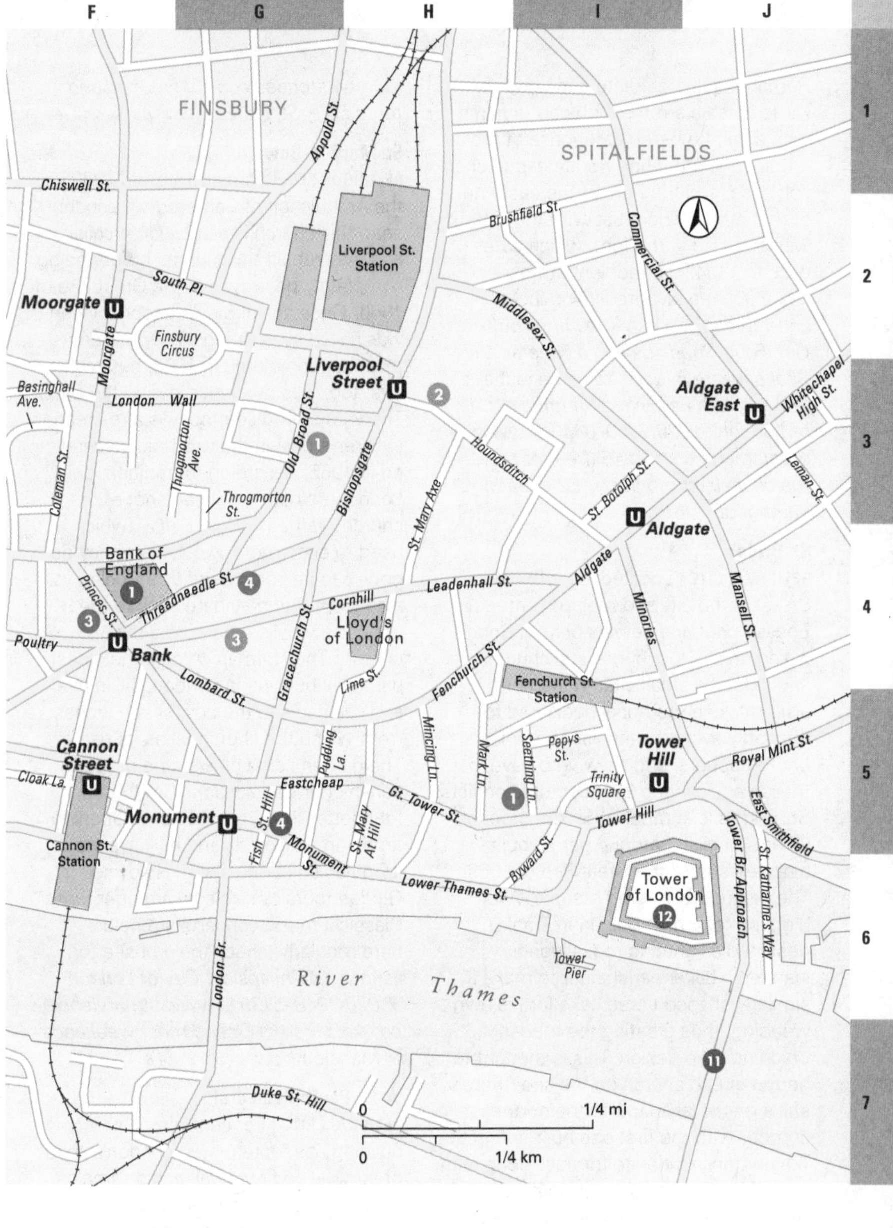

F
G
H
I
J
1
2
3
4
5
6
7
FINSBURY
SPITALFIELDS
Chiswell St.
Appold St.
Liverpool St. Station
Brushfield St.
Commercial St.
South Pl.
Moorgate
Moorgate
Finsbury Circus
Middlesex St.
Liverpool Street
Aldgate East
Whitechapel High St.
Basinghall Ave.
London Wall
Old Broad St.
Houndsditch
Coleman St.
Throgmorton Ave.
Throgmorton St.
Bishopsgate
St. Mary Axe
St. Botolph St.
Leman St.
Aldgate
Bank of England
Threadneedle St.
Princes St.
Cornhill
Leadenhall St.
Aldgate
Minories
Mansell St.
Poultry
Bank
Gracechurch St.
Lloyd's of London
Lombard St.
Lime St.
Fenchurch St.
Fenchurch St. Station
Cannon Street
Cloak La.
Pudding La.
Eastcheap
Mincing Ln.
Mark Ln.
Seething Ln.
Pepys St.
Tower Hill
Trinity Square
Royal Mint St.
Monument
Fish St. Hill
Monument St.
St. Mary At Hill
Gt. Tower St.
Tower Hill
Byward St.
East Smithfield
Cannon St. Station
Lower Thames St.
Tower of London
Tower Br. Approach
St. Katharine's Way
Tower Pier
River Thames
London Br.
Duke St. Hill
0
1/4 mi
0
1/4 km

Romanesque architecture in London. Most notable are the 13th-century arch with a half-timbered gatehouse at the entrance and the fine Romanesque chancel, apse, and triforium at the east end of the interior. The artist William Hogarth was baptized in the font, which dates back to 1404. The redolent atmosphere has made it a favorite filming location, and you can see it in *The Other Boleyn Girl, Four Weddings and a Funeral,* and *Shakespeare in Love,* to name just a few. ✉ *Cloth Fair, West Smithfield, City of London* ☎ *020/7600–0440* 🌐 *www.greatstbarts.com* 🎟 *£5 (free for prayer in the chapel), photography £2* Ⓜ *Barbican, Farringdon.*

St. Bride's

RELIGIOUS SITE | Located just off Fleet Street in the city's former epicenter of English print and newspaper, St. Bride's is known as "the journalists' church," and indeed a small altar in the north aisle marks a memorial dedicated to the sadly ever-growing list of reporters, photographers, and crew who have lost their lives covering 21st-century conflicts. St. Bride's is another of Sir Christopher Wren's English baroque gems, built nine years after the Great Fire of 1666. The distinctively tiered steeple, Wren's highest, for which Benjamin Franklin designed a lightning rod, allegedly inspired a baker parishioner to make a similarly shaped tiered cake for his own wedding, thus creating the modern wedding cake design. This is thought to be the eighth church on the site (there's still a medieval chapel in the northeast corner), with the first one built during the 7th century. Evidence for this, along with a section of a Roman mosaic sidewalk, was discovered in the crypt, where you can now see the many archaeological finds unearthed from the thousands of coffins there. Ninety-minute guided tours are held on Tuesday afternoon starting at 2:15 pm; the church also hosts regular free lunchtime concert recitals. ✉ *Fleet St., City of London* ☎ *020/7427–0133* 🌐 *www.stbrides.com* 🎟 *Free; guided tours £6* Ⓜ *St. Paul's, Blackfriars.*

St. Mary-le-Bow

RELIGIOUS SITE | Founded around 1080 as the Archbishop of Canterbury's London seat, this church is a survivor; it collapsed and was rebuilt three times before being completely destroyed in the Great Fire of 1666. Once again, Sir Christopher Wren was called in, creating a new building that was completed in 1673, but sadly this, too, was destroyed during the Blitz. The version you see today is a re-creation of Wren's design that was reconsecrated in 1965. According to tradition, only Londoners born within earshot of the church's famous "Bow Bells" (which used to echo more widely than they do now) can be considered true Cockneys, a concept that may date back to the 9 pm curfew bells rung during the 14th century. The Norman crypt is the oldest parochial building in London still in use, and you can see the bow-shape arches from which the church takes its name. The garden contains a statue of former parishioner Captain John Smith, the founder of the Virginia Colony. Opening times on weekends and holidays are irregular, so calling ahead is advised. Guided tours available by arrangement. Classical music concerts are held here regularly; check the website for listings. ✉ *Cheapside, City of London* ☎ *020/7248–5139* 🌐 *www.stmarylebow.co.uk* 🎟 *Free* ⏲ *Closed most weekends* Ⓜ *Mansion House, St. Paul's.*

★ St. Paul's Cathedral

RELIGIOUS SITE | For centuries, this iconic building has represented London's spirit of survival and renewal, and it remains a breathtaking structure, inside and out. Sir Christopher Wren started planning the current cathedral in 1666, immediately after the previous medieval building, founded in 1087, was destroyed in the Great Fire, hence the word "resurgam" ("I shall rise again") inscribed on the pediment of the south door. St. Paul's again became a symbol of the city's resilience during the Blitz, when local volunteers risked death to put out a blaze on the dome (despite these efforts, much of the cathedral's east end and its high altar were destroyed). It has often been the scene of great state occasions, such as Winston Churchill's funeral and the wedding of Prince Charles and Princess Diana.

Construction started in 1675 and took 35 years to finish. It was actually Wren's third design: the first was rejected for being too modern; the second for being too modern *and* too Italian, that is, Catholic (you can see the 20-foot "Great Model" of this design in the crypt). Despite mollifying the Anglican clergy with the promise of a traditional English spire, Wren installed a neoclassical triple-layered dome, the second-largest cathedral dome in the world after St. Peter's in Rome.

The interior is a superb example of the English baroque. Climb 257 steps up the Geometric Staircase, a perfectly engineered stone spiral, to the Whispering Gallery, so named because a whisper against one wall can be heard on the wall 112 feet opposite. Another 119 steps up is the Stone Gallery, which encircles the exterior of the dome and provides panoramic views over London. If you have a head for heights, tackle another 152 steps to the small Golden Gallery, an observation platform at the dome's highest point. At 278 feet above the cathedral floor, it offers even more spectacular vistas. Back on the ground, in the south choir aisle, you'll find the grave of John Donne, the poet who was dean of St. Paul's from 1621 until his death in 1631. His marble effigy is the oldest memorial in the cathedral and one of the few to survive the Great Fire. The intricate lively figures on the choir-stall nearby are the work of master carver Grinling Gibbons, who also embellished the Wren-designed great organ. Behind the high altar is the American Memorial Chapel, dedicated to the 28,000 American GIs stationed in the United Kingdom during World War II. Among the notables buried in the crypt are the Duke of Wellington, Admiral Lord Nelson, Sir Joshua Reynolds, Henry Moore, and Wren himself. The Latin epitaph above his tomb fittingly reads, "Reader, if you seek his monument, look around you."

Free, introductory 20-minute talks are offered regularly throughout the day. Free 90-minute guided tours take place Monday through Saturday at 10, 11, 1, and 2; reserve a place at the welcome desk when you arrive. ■ **TIP→ Save £3 per ticket and get fast-track entry by booking online.** ✉ *St. Paul's Churchyard, City of London* ☎ *020/7246–8350* 🌐 *www.stpauls.co+.uk* 🎟 *£20* ⏲ *Closed Sun. except for services* Ⓜ *St. Paul's.*

Tower Bridge

BRIDGE/TUNNEL | Despite its medieval appearance, London's most iconic bridge was actually built at the tail end of the Victorian era in the then-popular neo-Gothic style, first opening to traffic in 1894. With a latticed steel construction clad in Portland stone, the bridge is famous for its enormous bascules—the 1,000-ton "arms" that open to allow ships taller than its normal 28-foot clearance to glide beneath. The steam-powered bascules were a marvel of Victorian engineering when they were created (you can still visit the Engine Room, now with explanatory films and interactive displays), and required 80 people to raise and lower. Initially, heavy river traffic meant this happened 20 to 30 times a day, but it's now reduced to a number of days per month, with greater frequency depending on the time of year (see the bridge's website for a schedule).

The family-friendly **Tower Bridge Exhibition** includes the ground-level Engine Room, displays in the North Tower documenting the bridge's history, access to the east and west walkways that run alongside the road between the turrets and provide views over the river and city, and for those untroubled by vertigo, a transparent walkway 138 feet up between the towers that lets you look down on the traffic or, if the bascules are raised, the ships below. ✉ *Tower Bridge Rd., City of London* ☎ *020/7403–3761* 🌐 *www.towerbridge.org.uk* 🎫 *From £10* Ⓜ *Tower Hill.*

★ **Tower of London**

CASTLE/PALACE | FAMILY | Nowhere else does history seem so vividly alive as in this minicity begun by the Normans more than 1,000 years ago. In its time, the Tower has been a fortress, a mint, a palace, an archive, and the Royal Menagerie (which formed the kernel of the London Zoo). Most of all, however, it has been known as a place of imprisonment and death. Thousands of unfortunate souls, including numerous aristocrats and even a few sovereigns (some notorious traitors, some complete innocents), spent their last days here, several etching their final recorded thoughts onto their cell walls, and pints of royal blood have been spilled on its stones. Executions at the Tower were reserved for the nobility, with the most privileged beheaded in the privacy of **Tower Green** instead of before the mob at Tower Hill. In fact, only seven people received this dubious "honor," among them Anne Boleyn and Catherine Howard, two of Henry VIII's six wives. The **White Tower** , the oldest building in the complex (which is actually made up of 20 towers, not just one) is also its most conspicuous. Begun by William the Conqueror in 1078 and whitewashed (hence the name) by Henry III (1207–72), it contains the **Armouries,** a splendid collection of arms and armor. Across the moat to the right is the riverside **Traitors' Gate,** to which the most famous prisoners were rowed to bring them to their impending doom.

Opposite is the **Bloody Tower,** where the "little princes in the Tower"—the uncrowned boy king Edward V and his brother—were consigned by their wicked uncle, who then took the crown for himself, thus becoming Richard III. The boys were never seen again, widely assumed to have been murdered in their tower prison. Also not-to-be-missed are the gorgeous **Crown Jewels** in the Jewel House. The original crown, orb, and scepter, symbols of monarchial power, were destroyed during the English Civil War; the ones you see here date back to after the Restoration in 1661. The most impressive gems were added only in the 20th century, when their countries of origin were part of the British Empire. Free 60-minute tours of the Tower depart every half hour or so (until mid-afternoon) from the main entrance. They are conducted by the Yeoman Warders, more popularly known as Beefeaters, who have guarded the Tower since Henry VII appointed them in 1485. Veterans of Britain's armed forces, they're easy to spot in their resplendent navy-and-red Tudor uniforms (scarlet-and-gold on special occasions). Keep an eye out for the ravens upon whose residency of the Tower, legend has it, the safety of the kingdom depends. **■TIP→ Avoid lines by buying a ticket in advance online, by phone, or from the automatic kiosks on Tower Hill. For free tickets to the 700-year-old Ceremony of the Keys (the locking of the main gates, nightly between 9:30 and 10), write several months in advance; check the Tower website for details.** ✉ *Tower Hill, City of London* ☎ *020/3166–6000* 🌐 *www.hrp.org.uk* 🎫 *£28 (£25 online)* Ⓜ *Tower Hill.*

Restaurants

The City caters overwhelmingly to traditional business-focused dining.

City Social

$$$$ | MODERN BRITISH | A largely corporate crowd comes here for the Manhattan-esque views of The City and chef Jason Atherton's masterful but straightforward cuisine. Impressed diners look out from level 24 of Tower 42 on a majestic

Continued on page 204

THE TOWER OF LONDON

The Tower is a microcosm of the city itself—a sprawling, organic hodgepodge of buildings that inspires reverence and terror in equal measure. See the block on which Anne Boleyn was beheaded, marvel at the Crown Jewels, and pay homage to the ravens who keep the monarchy safe.

An architectural patchwork of time, the oldest building of the complex is the fairytale White Tower, conceived by William the Conqueror in 1078 as both a royal residence and a show of power to the troublesome Anglo-Saxons he had subdued at the Battle of Hastings. Today's Tower has seen everything, as a palace, barracks, a mint for producing coins, an armoury, and the Royal menagerie (home of the country's first elephant). The big draw is the stunning opulence of the Crown Jewels, kept on-site in the heavily fortified Jewel House. Most of all, though, the Tower is known for death: it's been a place of imprisonment, torture, and execution for the realm's most notorious traitors as well as its martyrs. These days, unless you count the killer admission fees, there are far less morbid activities taking place in the Tower, but it still breathes London's history and pageantry from its every brick and offers hours of exploration.

TOURING THE TOWER

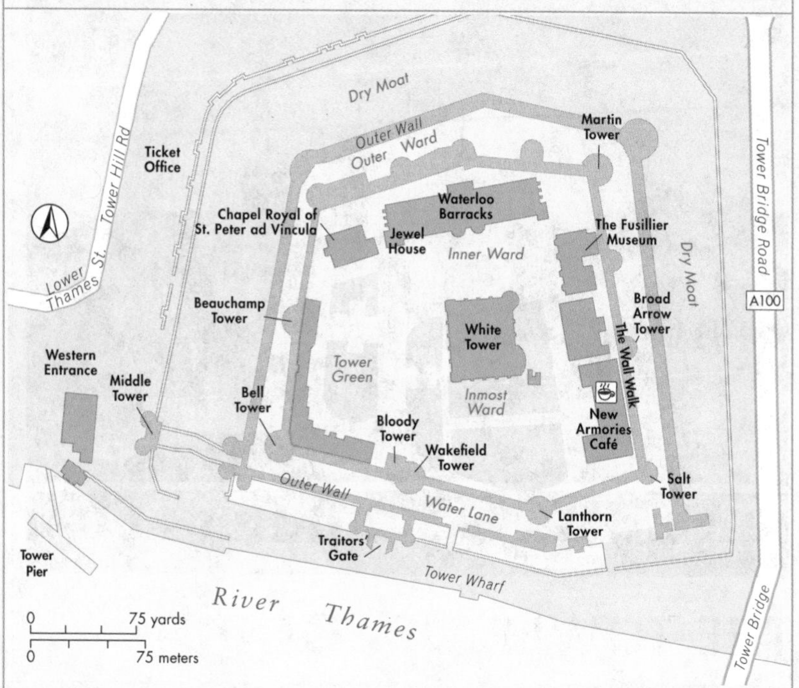

Entry to the Tower is via the **Western Entrance** and the **Middle Tower,** which feed into the outermost ring of the Tower's defenses.

Water Lane leads past the dread-inducing **Traitors' Gate,** the final point of entry for many Tower prisoners.

Toward the end of Water Lane, the **Lanthorn Tower** houses by night the ravens rumored to keep the kingdom safe, and by day a timely high-tech reconstruction of the Catholic Guy Fawkes's plot to blow up the Houses of Parliament in 1605.

The **Bloody Tower** earned its name as the apocryphal site of the murder of two young princes, Edward and Richard, who disappeared from the Tower after being put there in 1483 by their uncle, Richard III. Two little skeletons (now in Westminster Abbey) were found buried close to the White Tower in 1674 and are thought to be theirs.

The **Beauchamp Tower** housed upper-class miscreants: Latin graffiti about Lady Jane Grey can be glimpsed today on its walls.

Like a prize gem set at the head of a royal crown, the **White Tower** is the centerpiece of the complex. Its four towers dominate the Inner Ward, a fitting and forbidding reminder of Norman strength at the time of the conquest of England.

GOLD DIGGER?

Keep your eyes peeled as you tour the Tower: according to one story, Sir John Barkstead, goldsmith and Lieutenant of the Tower under Cromwell, hid £20,000 in gold coins here before his arrest and execution at the Restoration of Charles II.

Tower of London exterior

ROYAL BLING

The Crown of Queen Elizabeth, the Queen Mother, from 1937, contains the exotic 105-carat Koh-i-Noor (mountain of light) diamond.

TIME KILLERS

Some prisoners managed to keep themselves plenty amused: Sir Walter Raleigh grew tobacco on Tower Green, and in 1561 suspected sorcerer Hugh Draper carved an intricate astronomical clock on the walls of his Salt Tower cell.

Once inside the White Tower, head upstairs for the **Armouries,** where the biggest attraction, quite literally, is the suit of armor worn by a well-endowed Henry VIII. There is a matching outfit for his horse.

Other fascinating exhibits include the set of Samurai armor presented to James I in 1613 by the emperor of Japan, and the tiny set of armor worn by Henry VIII's young son Edward.

The **Jewel House** in **Waterloo Block** is the Tower's biggest draw, perfect for playing pick-your-favorite-crown from the wrong side of bulletproof glass. Not only are these crowns, staffs, and orbs encrusted with heavy-duty gems, they are invested with the authority of monarchical power in England, dating back to the 1300s.

Outside, pause at **Tower Green**, permanent departure point for those of noble birth. The hoi polloi were dispatched at nearby Tower Hill. The Tower's most famous female victims—Anne Boleyn, Margaret Countess of Salisbury, Catherine Howard, and Lady Jane Grey—all went this "priviledged" way.

Behind a well-kept square of grass stands the **Chapel Royal of St. Peter ad Vincula**, a delightful Tudor church and final resting place of six beheaded Tudor bodies.

TIP→ Visitors are welcome for services and can also enter after 4:30 pm daily.

The **Salt Tower**, reputedly the most haunted corner of the complex, marks the start of the **Wall Walk**, a bracing promenade along the stone spiral steps and battlements of the Tower that looks down on the trucks, taxis, and shimmering high-rises of modern London.

The Wall Walk ends at the **Martin Tower**, former home of the Crown Jewels and now host to the crowns and diamonds exhibition that explains the art of fashioning royal headwear and tells the story of some of the most famous stones.

On leaving the Tower, browse the **gift shop,** and wander the wharf that overlooks the Thames, leading to a picture-postcard view of Tower Bridge.

WHO ARE THE BEEFEATERS?

First of all, they're Yeoman Warders, but probably got the nickname "beefeater" from their position as Royal Bodyguards which entitled them to eat as much beef as they liked. Part of the "Yeoman of the Guard," started in the reign of Edmund IV, the warders have formed the Royal Bodyguard as far back as 1509 when Henry VIII left a dozen of the Yeoman of the Guard at the Tower to protect it.

Originally, the Yeoman Warders also served as jailers of the Tower, doubling as torturers when necessary. (So it would have been a Beefeater tightening the thumb screws, or ratchetting the rack another notch on some unfortunate prisoner. Smile nicely.) Today 36 Yeoman Warders (men and women since 2007), along with the Chief Yeoman Warder and the Yeoman Gaoler, live within the walls of the Tower with their families, in accommodations in the Outer Ward. They stand guard over the Tower, conduct tours, and lock up at 9:53 pm every night with the Ceremony of the Keys.

■ TIP→ **Free tickets to the Ceremony of the Keys are available by writing several months in advance; check the Tower Web site for details.**

HARK THE RAVENS!

Legend has it that should the hulking black ravens ever leave, the White Tower will crumble and the kingdom fall. Charles II, no doubt jumpy after his father's execution and the monarchy's short-term fall from grace, made a royal decree in 1662 that there should be at least six of the carrion-eating nasties present at all times. There have been some close calls. During World War II, numbers dropped to one, echoing the precarious fate of the war-wracked country. In 2005, two (of eight) died over Christmas when Thor—the most intelligent but also the largest bully of the bunch—killed new recruit Gundolf, named after the Tower's 1070 designer. Pneumonia put an end to Bran, leaving lifelong partner Branwen without her mate.

■ DID YOU KNOW? **In 1981 a raven named Grog, perhaps seduced by his alcoholic moniker, escaped after 21 years at the Tower. Others have been banished for "conduct unbecoming."**

The six that remain, each one identified by a colored band around a claw, are much loved for their fidelity (they mate for life) and their cheek (capable of 440 noises, they are witty and scolding mimics). It's not only the diet of blood-soaked biscuits, rabbit, and scraps from the mess kitchen that keeps them coming back. Their lifting feathers on one wing are trimmed, meaning they can manage the equivalent of a lop-sided air-bound hobble but not much more. In situ they are a territorial lot, sticking to Tower Green and the White Tower, and lodging nightly by Wakefield Tower. They've had free front-row seats at all the most grisly moments in Tower history—Anne Boleyn's execution included.

■ TIP→ **Don't get too close to the ravens: they are prone to pecking and not particularly fond of humans, unless you are the Tower's Raven Master.**

AND WHAT ARE THEY WEARING?

Anyone who refers to this as a costume will be lucky to leave the Tower with head still attached to body: this is the ceremonial uniform of the Yeoman Warders, and it comes at a cool £13,000 a throw.

A **pike** (or halberd), also known as a partisan, is the Yeoman Warder's weapon of choice. The Chief Warder carries a staff topped with a miniature silver model of the White Tower.

The black Tudor **bonnet** is made of velvet; the blue undress consists of a felt top hat, with a single Tudor rose in the middle.

This **Tudor-style ruff** helps date the ceremonial uniform, which was first worn in 1552.

Insignia on a Yeoman Warder's upper right arm denote the rank he carried in the military.

The **medals** on a Yeoman Warder's chest are more than mere show: all of the men and women have served for at least 22 years in the armed forces.

This version of the **royal livery** bears the insignia of the current Queen ("E" for Elizabeth) but originally dates from Tudor times. The first letter changes according to the reigning monarch's Christian name; the second letter is always an "R" for *rex* (king) or *regina* (queen).

Slits in the **tunic** date from the times when Beefeaters were expected to ride a horse.

Red socks and **black patent shoes** are worn on special occasions. Visitors are more likely to see the regular blue undress, introduced in 1858 as the regular working dress of the Yeoman Warders.

The **red lines down the trousers** are a sign of the blood from the swords of the Yeoman Warders in their defense of the realm.

(IN)FAMOUS PRISONERS OF THE TOWER

Anne Boleyn Lady Jane Grey Sir Walter Raleigh

Sir Thomas More. A Catholic and Henry VIII's friend and chancellor, Sir Thomas refused to attend the coronation of Anne Boleyn (Henry VIII's second wife) or to recognize the multi-marrying king as head of the Church. Sent to the Tower for treason, More was beheaded in 1535.

Anne Boleyn. The first of Henry VIII's wives to be beheaded, Anne, who failed to provide the king with a son, was accused of sleeping with five men, including her own brother. All six got the chop in 1536. Her severed head was held up to the crowd, and her lips were said to be mouthing prayer.

Margaret, Countess of Salisbury. Not the best-known prisoner in her lifetime, she has a reputation today for haunting the Tower. And no wonder: the elderly 70-year-old was condemned by Henry VIII in 1541 for a potentially treacherous bloodline (she was the last Plantagenet princess) and hacked to death by the executioner after she refused to put her head on the block like a common traitor and attempted to run away.

Queen Catherine Howard. Henry VIII's fifth wife was locked up for high treason and infidelity and beheaded in 1542 at age 20. Ever eager to please, she spent her final night practicing how to lay her head on the block.

Lady Jane Grey. The nine-days-queen lost her head in 1554 at age 16. Her death was the result of sibling rivalry gone seriously wrong, when Protestant Edward VI slighted his Catholic sister Mary in favor of Lady Jane as heir, and Mary decided to have none of it.

Guy Fawkes. The Roman Catholic soldier who tried to blow up the Houses of Parliament and kill the king in the 1605 Gunpowder plot was first incarcerated in the chambers of the Tower, where King James I requested he be tortured in ever-worsening ways. Perhaps unsurprisingly, he confessed. He met his seriously grisly end in the Old Palace Yard at Westminster, where he was hung, drawn, and quartered in 1607.

Sir Walter Raleigh. Once a favorite of Elizabeth I, he offended her by secretly marrying her Maid of Honor and was chucked in the Tower. Later, as a conspirator against James I, he paid with his life. A frequent visitor to the Tower (he spent 13 years there in three stints), he managed to get the Bloody Tower enlarged on account of his wife and growing family. He was finally executed in 1618 in Old Palace Yard, Westminster.

Josef Jakobs. The last man to be executed in the Tower was caught as a spy when parachuting in from Germany and executed by firing squad in 1941. The chair he sat in when he was shot is preserved in the Royal Armouries' artifacts store.

FOR FURTHER EVIDENCE . . .

A trio of buildings in the Inner Ward, the **Bloody Tower, Beauchamp Tower,** and **Queen's House,** all with excellent views of the execution scaffold in Tower Green, are the heart of the Tower's prison accommodations and home to a permanent exhibition about notable inmates.

TACKLING THE TOWER (WITHOUT LOSING YOUR HEAD)

MAKING THE MOST OF YOUR TIME: Without doubt, the Tower is worth two to three hours. A full hour of that would be well spent by joining one of the Yeoman Warders' tours (included in admission). It's hard to better their insight, vitality, and humor—they are knights of the realm living their very own fairytale castle existence.

The Crown Jewels are worth the wait, the White Tower is essential, and the Medieval Palace and Bloody Tower should at least be breezed through.

■ TIP→ **It's best to visit on weekdays, when the crowds are smaller.**

WITH KIDS: The Tower's centuries-old cobblestones are not exactly stroller-friendly, but strollers are permitted inside most of the buildings. If you do bring one, be prepared to leave it temporarily unsupervised (the stroller, that is—not your child) outside the White Tower, which has no access. There are baby-changing facilities in the Brick Tower restrooms behind the Jewel House. Look for regular free children's events such as the Knight's school where children can have a go at jousting, sword-fighting, and archery.

■ TIP→ **Tell your child to find one of the Yeoman Warders if he or she should get lost; they will in turn lead him or her to the Byward Tower, which is where you should meet.**

IN A HURRY? If you have less than an hour, head down Wall Walk, through a succession of towers, which eventually spit you out at the Martin Tower. The view over modern London is quite a contrast.

TOURS: Tours given by a Yeoman Warder leave from the main entrance near Middle Tower every half-hour from 10–4, and last about an hour. Beefeaters give occasional 30-minute talks in the Lanthorn Tower about their daily lives. Both tours are free. Check website for talks and workshops panorama that takes in iconic buildings like The Gherkin and The Walkie Talkie. **Known for:** majestic panoramas of The City; gutsy steak and fish standards; suited financiers and corporate deal-maker crowd. *Average main: £34 Tower 42, 25 Old Broad St., City of London 020/7877–7703 www.citysociallondon.com Closed Sun. No lunch Sat. Liverpool St.*

Duck & Waffle

$$ | **MODERN BRITISH** | **FAMILY** | Zoom up to the 40th floor of 110 Bishopsgate and head straight for the cult signature dish of confit duck leg, Belgium waffle, fried duck egg, and mustard maple syrup for a taste of foodie bliss. Open 24/7, with spectacular panoramas of The City, you might satisfy the munchies with a foie gras breakfast, served all day, alongside streaky bacon and homemade Nutella or an Elvis PB&J waffle with banana brûlée. **Known for:** rare-to-London 24-hour service; awe-inspiring panoramas of London's skyline; eponymous duck-and-waffle dish. *Average main: £19 Heron Tower, 110 Bishopsgate, City of London 020/3640–7310 www.duckandwaffle.com Liverpool St.*

Simpson's Tavern

$ | **BRITISH** | **FAMILY** | The City's oldest tavern and chop house was founded in 1757 and undoubtedly is every bit as raucous now as the day it opened. Approached via a cobbled alleyway, it draws diners who revel in the old boarding school surroundings and are eager to down oodles of claret and English tavern-style grub. **Known for:** lots of history, with past diners from diarist Samuel Pepys to Charles Dickens; signature stewed cheese on toast; charming but old-fashioned service. *Average main: £12 Ball Court, 38½ Cornhill, City of London 020/7626–9985 www.simpsonstavern.co.uk Closed weekends. No dinner Bank.*

Sweetings

$$$ | **SEAFOOD** | Established in 1889 not far from St. Paul's Cathedral, little seems to have changed since the height of the British Empire at this quirky eatery. Although there are some things Sweetings doesn't do (dinner, reservations, coffee, or weekends), it does, mercifully, do great seafood. **Known for:** fresh Billingsgate fish served at raised linen-covered counters; tankards of "Black Velvet" Guinness and champagne; popular potted shrimp and Dover sole. *Average main: £30 39 Queen Victoria St., City of London 020/7248–3062 www.sweetingsrestaurant.co.uk Closed weekends. No dinner Mansion House.*

Hotels

Apex City of London

$$ | **HOTEL** | At this sleek modern branch of the small Apex chain near the Tower of London, bedrooms are reasonably spacious, with contemporary color schemes, 40-inch flat screen TVs, and little sofas. **Pros:** great location; helpful staff; good advance-booking discounts. **Cons:** geared more to business than leisure travelers; price can rise sharply during busy times; the neighborhood is hardly the most buzzing on weekends. *Rooms from: £170 1 Seething La., City of London 020/7702–2020 www.apexhotels.co.uk 209 rooms No meals Tower Hill.*

Crowne Plaza London—The City

$$ | **HOTEL** | Don't let the hotel's all-business appearance put you off: it's a polished operation, with stylish minimalist rooms, just steps from the Blackfriars Tube and train station in one direction and bustling Fleet Street in the other. **Pros:** good rates available with advance booking; devices in each room that allow access to streaming services; two excellent dining options. **Cons:** neighborhood is super busy during the day and empty at night; breakfast not included in the price of rooms; short Tube ride from

main neighborhood sights. $ *Rooms from: £170* ✉ *19 New Bridge St., City of London* ☎ *0871/942–9190* 🌐 *www.cplondoncityhotel.co.uk* *204 rooms* 🍴 *No meals* Ⓜ *Blackfriars.*

★ **The Ned**

$$ | HOTEL | Bursting with eye-catching art deco design and achingly hip interiors, the Ned is as close to the glamour of the 1920s Jazz Age as you'll find in contemporary London. **Pros:** amazing variety of bars and restaurants, all of high quality; rooftop pool with views of St. Paul's Cathedral; beautiful interiors in all rooms. **Cons:** location in The City means public spaces get very busy after work; neighborhood is deserted on weekends; also doubles as a private members' clubs, so the vibe can get snooty. $ *Rooms from: £195* ✉ *27 Poultry, City of London* ☎ *020/3828–2000* 🌐 *www.thened.com* *252 rooms* 🍴 *No meals* Ⓜ *Bank.*

Threadneedles Hotel

$$ | HOTEL | The elaborate building housing this grand hotel in the financial district is a former bank, and the vast old banking hall—beautifully adapted as the lobby, with luxurious marble and mahogany panels—really sets the scene. **Pros:** lap of luxury; excellent service; a good variety of drinking and dining options. **Cons:** a bit stuffy for some tastes; can be at least three times more expensive weekdays; neighborhood is quiet at night. $ *Rooms from: £212* ✉ *5 Threadneedle St., City of London* ☎ *020/7657–8080* 🌐 *www.hotelthreadneedles.co.uk* *74 rooms* 🍴 *No meals* Ⓜ *Bank.*

Vintry and Mercer

$$ | HOTEL | Located close to the London Stock Exchange, merchant banks, hedgefunds, and the City's oldest guilds, the luxury boutique hotel Vintry and Mercer offers a nod to tradition then proceeds to deliver a chic, colorful, and contemporary experience that stands out in this neighborhood. **Pros:** rooms with gorgeous fabrics and chic wallpapers; excellent on-site izakaya restaurant; some rooms have stunning views of the City. **Cons:** predominantly business crowd dominates the bar and restaurant; neighborhood is extremely quiet on weekends; slightly removed from the sights of the West End. $ *Rooms from: £191* ✉ *19–20 Garlick Hill, City of London* ☎ *020/3908–8088* 🌐 *www.vintryandmercer.com* *92 rooms* 🍴 *No meals* Ⓜ *Monument.*

Nightlife

Workers from The City's many finance firms pour into the neighborhood's pubs at the end of the day, but by 8 pm the party is pretty much over and you'll have no trouble finding a place to sit. It's always worth ducking down a side street, as this is where some of the area's most interesting drinking establishments can be found.

PUBS

★ **The Blackfriar**

BARS/PUBS | FAMILY | A step from Blackfriars Tube station, this spectacular pub has an Arts and Crafts interior that is entertainingly, satirically ecclesiastical, with inlaid mother-of-pearl, wood carvings, stained glass, and marble pillars all over the place. Under finely lettered temperance tracts on view just below the reliefs of monks, fairies, and friars, there is a nice group of ales on tap from independent brewers. The 20th-century poet Sir John Betjeman once led a successful campaign to save the pub from demolition. ✉ *174 Queen Victoria St., City of London* ☎ *020/7236–5474* 🌐 *www.nicholsonspubs.co.uk* Ⓜ *Blackfriars.*

Ye Olde Mitre

BARS/PUBS | FAMILY | Hidden off the side of 8 Hatton Gardens (and notoriously hard to find), this cozy pub's roots go back to 1546, though it was rebuilt around 1782. Originally built for the staff of the Bishop of Ely, whose London residence was next door, it remained officially part of Cambridgeshire until the 20th century. Elizabeth I was once spotted dancing round a cherry tree here with a dashing young beau. Now it's a friendly little labyrinthine place, with a fireplace, well-kept ales, wooden beams, and traditional bar snacks. ✉ *1 Ely Ct., City of London* ✣ *Off 8 Hatton Gardens* ☎ *020/7405–4751* 🌐 *www.yeoldemitreholburn.co.uk* ⏲ *Closed weekends* Ⓜ *Chancery La.*

Ye Olde Watling

BARS/PUBS | FAMILY | This busy corner pub has been rebuilt at least three times since 1666. One of its incarnations was as the drawing office for Sir Christopher Wren, who used it while building nearby St. Paul's Cathedral. The ground floor is a laid-back pub, while the upstairs houses an atmospheric restaurant, complete with wooden beams and trestle tables, and offering a basic English pub menu, such as fish-and-chips, and Gloucester old-spot sausages. ✉ *29 Watling St., City of London* ☎ *020/7248–8935* 🌐 *www.nicholsonspubs.co.uk* Ⓜ *Mansion House.*

Performing Arts

It may seem at first glance like the denizens of London's financial center are far too busy to take time out for culture, but look a little closer: arts events are taking place all over, courtesy of a number of acclaimed annual festivals. Art exhibits in empty offices and chamber performances in historic churches are regular occurrences.

★ **Barbican Centre**

ART GALLERIES—ARTS | FAMILY | Opened in 1982, the Barbican is an enormous Brutalist concrete maze that Londoners either love or hate—but its importance to the cultural life of the capital is beyond dispute. At the largest performing arts center in Europe, you could listen to Elgar, see 1960s photography, and catch German animation with live accompaniment, all in one day. The main concert hall, known for its acoustics, is most famous as the home of the London Symphony Orchestra. The Barbican is also a frequent host to the BBC Symphony Orchestra. Architecture tours take place several times a week. ✉ *Silk St., City of London* ☎ *020/7638–8891* 🌐 *www.barbican.org.uk* 🎫 *Art exhibits free–£15, cinema from £6, theater and music from £10, tours £13* Ⓜ *Barbican.*

Bridge Theatre

THEATER | This gleaming theater on the banks of the River Thames by Tower Bridge is the brainchild of director Nicholas Hytner and producer Nick Starr, who together oversaw a golden age at the National Theatre before handing over the reins to current artistic director Rufus Norris. The program at this totally adaptable space is a blend of the classics (Hytner's *Julius Caesar* was a huge hit in 2018) and riskier new works through big-name actors (e.g., Ben Whishaw, Laura Linney) are a constant. ✉ *3 Potters Fields Park, London Bridge* ☎ *033/3320–0051* 🌐 *www.bridgetheatre.co.uk* 🎫 *From £15* Ⓜ *London Bridge, Tower Hill.*

Chapter 8

EAST LONDON

Updated by
Jo Caird

Sights	Restaurants	Hotels	Shopping	Nightlife
★★★☆☆	★★★★☆	★★★☆☆	★★★★☆	★★★★★

EAST LONDON SNAPSHOT

TOP REASONS TO GO

Dennis Severs' House: The atmospheric set-pieces in this Georgian town house use visuals, sounds, and aromas to evoke the lives of its fictional previous inhabitants.

Broadway Market: Check out more than 100 (mainly) foodstalls here on Saturday, offering everything from cheeses to oysters.

London's hottest art scene: Edgy galleries mix with large collections.

Jack the Ripper: Track Britain's most infamous serial killer through streets that were part of a major slum area in Victorian times.

The ArcelorMittal Orbit: This enormous sculpture offers great views over London and a rush of adrenaline if you take the quick route back down to Earth via the slide.

GETTING THERE

The London Overground, with stops at Shoreditch High Street, Hoxton, Whitechapel, Dalston Junction, Dalston Kingsland, London Fields, Hackney Central, and Hackney Wick is the easiest way to reach East London. Alternatively, the best Tube stations to use are Old Street on the Northern Line, Bethnal Green on the Central Line, and Liverpool Street on the Metropolitan and Circle lines.

MAKING THE MOST OF YOUR TIME

To experience East London at its most lively, visit on the weekend. Spitalfields Market bustles all weekend, while Brick Lane and Columbia Road are best on a Sunday morning and Broadway Market on Saturday. If you're planning to explore East London's art galleries, pick up a free map at the Whitechapel Art Gallery. As for the area's booming nightlife scene, there's no time limit: you'll find people partying Wednesday through Sunday.

QUICK BITES

■ **E5 Bakehouse** This bakery, which supplies bread to many of East London's top eateries, has a friendly café and deli on-site, where you can sample some of the tastiest toasted sandwiches in the city, plus pizzas on Sunday. ✉ *Mentmore Terr., Arch 395, Dalston* ☎ *020/8986–9600* 🌐 *www.e5bakehouse.com* ⏲ *No dinner* Ⓜ *Overground: London Fields.*

■ **Poppies of Spitalfields** Poppies of Spitalfields strikes a balance between trendy and traditional with retro-diner style and efficient service. The specialty is fish-and-chips, but if fish isn't your thing, try the free-range grilled chicken. ✉ *6–8 Hanbury St., Spitalfields* ☎ *020/7247–0892* 🌐 *www.poppiesfishandchips.co.uk* Ⓜ *Shoreditch High St.*

SAFETY

■ Around Shoreditch, Spitalfields, and Brick Lane, streets are largely safe during daylight hours. Be cautious on the rougher streets of Whitechapel, Bethnal Green, and Hackney at night.

Made famous by Dickens and infamous by Jack the Ripper, East London is one of London's most enduringly evocative neighborhoods, rich in popular history, architectural gems, and artists' studios. Since the early 1990s, hip gallerists, designers, and new-media entrepreneurs have colonized its handsome Georgian buildings and converted industrial lofts. Today, this collection of neighborhoods lays claim to being the city's hippest area.

The British equivalent of parts of Brooklyn, East London is a patchwork of districts encompassing struggling artists, multicultural enclaves, and upscale professionals occasionally teetering, like its New York equivalent, on the edge of self-parody. The vast area ranges from gentrified districts like Spitalfields, where bankers and successful artists live in desirable renovated town houses, to parts of Hackney, where seemingly derelict, graffiti-covered industrial buildings are hives of exciting creative activity. It remains a little rough around the edges, so stick to busier streets at night.

At the start of the new millennium, Hoxton, an enclave of Shoreditch, became the glossy hub of London's buzzing contemporary art scene, which accelerated the gentrification process. Some artists, such as Tracey Emin and Gilbert & George, long-term residents of Spitalfields' handsome Georgian terraces—and successful enough to still afford the area—have remained.

One such residence, **Dennis Severs' House,** was transformed two decades ago by the eponymous American artist into a unique "living house museum" that evokes how past generations of a fictional Huguenot family might have lived there. Not far away, **Spitalfields Market** offers an ever-changing selection of crafts and funky clothes stalls under a glass roof in what was once a Victorian produce market. Across from the market, **Christ Church, Spitalfields,** Nicholas Hawkmoor's masterpiece, soars above Fournier Street.

In the last decade, streets around the Old Street roundabout (as well as converted warehouses in Hackney and Dalston) have flourished with start-ups, with attendant stylish boutiques (especially on Redchurch Street), destination restaurants, and hipster bars as part of a government initiative to attract IT-oriented businesses to the neighborhood. Old and new Shoreditch meet on **Brick Lane,** the heart of the Bangladeshi community, lined with innumerable curry houses and

The East End's Famous Streets

Brick Lane and the narrow streets running off it offer a paradigm of East London's development. Its population has moved in waves: communities seeking refuge, others moving out in an upwardly mobile direction.

Brick Lane has seen the manufacture of bricks (during the 16th century), beer, and bagels, but nowadays it's primarily known as the heart of Banglatown—Bangladeshis make up one-third of the population in this London borough, and you'll see that the names of the surrounding streets are written in Bengali—where you find many kebab and curry houses along with shops selling DVDs, colorful saris, and stacks of sticky sweets. On Sundays, cars aren't allowed on the upper section of the street. Shops and cafés are open, and several stalls are set up, creating a companion market to the one on nearby **Petticoat Lane.**

Fournier Street contains fine examples of the neighborhood's characteristic Georgian terraced houses, many of them built by the richest of the early-18th-century Huguenot silk weavers (note the enlarged windows on the upper floors to maximize light for the intricate work). Most of those along the north side of Fournier Street have since been restored.

Wilkes Street, with more 1720s Huguenot houses, is north of Christ Church, Spitalfields; and neighboring **Princelet Street** was once important to East London's Jewish community. Where No. 6 stands now, the first of several thriving Yiddish theaters opened in 1886. **Elder Street,** just off Folgate, is another gem of original 18th-century houses. On the south and east side of Spitalfields Market are yet more time-warp streets that are worth a wander, such as **Gun Street,** where artist Mark Gertler (1891–1939) was born, at No. 16.

glittering sari shops, plus vintage-clothing emporia. Here you'll also find the **Old Truman Brewery,** an East London landmark converted into a warren of street fashion and pop-up galleries. On Sunday, the Columbia Road Flower Market to the north of Brick Lane becomes a colorful, fragrant oasis of greenery.

As property prices have climbed, up-and-coming artists have sought more affordable studio spaces in former industrial buildings eastward toward Whitechapel and Bethnal Green, where there are also some notable galleries. Here you'll find the **Whitechapel Gallery,** a leading center for contemporary art, and—a design connoisseur's favorite—the **Geffrye Museum,** a collection of domestic interiors through the ages that occupies a row of early-18th-century almshouses (although the museum is closed for renovations until spring 2020).

Probably the best start to an East London tour is via the London Overground, getting off at Shoreditch High Street Station. Immediately northwest of the station, on the west side of Shoreditch High Street, is the heart of the neighborhood that aspires to be the U.K. equivalent to Silicon Valley. To the northeast is Shoreditch's boutique, gallery, and restaurant zone. The subneighborhood of Hoxton is located just above Shoreditch, north of the Old Street roundabout. To the southeast of the station are the handsome Georgian streets of Spitalfields. Bethnal Green is due east, past busy Brick Lane. Whitechapel, formerly Jack the Ripper's

On Sunday, additional clothing and craft stalls surround Spitalfields covered market.

patch, is to the south of Spitalfields. All of these neighborhoods are within what is traditionally referred to as the "East End," although East London extends farther to the north and east.

Sights

Bevis Marks Synagogue

RELIGIOUS SITE | This is Britain's oldest synagogue still in use and is certainly its most splendid. It was built in 1701, after the Jews, having been expelled from England in 1290, were allowed to return under Cromwell in 1656. Inspired by the Spanish and Portuguese Great Synagogue of Amsterdam, the interior is embellished with rich woodwork, seven hanging brass candelabra (representing the seven days of the week), and 12 trompe-l'oeil wood columns painted to look like marble. The magnificent Ark, which contains the sacred scrolls of the five books of Moses, is modeled on contemporary Wren neoclassical altarpieces, with oak doors and Corinthian columns. In 1992 and 1993 the synagogue was seriously damaged by IRA bombs, but was subsequently completely restored. It's closed to visitors during Jewish holidays so check the website before visiting. ✉ *Bevis Marks, Whitechapel* ☎ *020/7621–1188* 🌐 *www.sephardi.org.uk/bevis-marks* 🎟 *£6* ⏲ *Closed Sat. and bank holiday Mon.* Ⓜ *Aldgate, Liverpool St.*

★ **Christ Church, Spitalfields**

RELIGIOUS SITE | This is the 1729 masterpiece of Sir Christopher Wren's associate Nicholas Hawksmoor, one of his six London churches and an example of English baroque at its finest. It was commissioned as part of Parliament's 1711 "Fifty New Churches" Act, passed in response to the influx of immigrants with the idea of providing for the religious needs of the "godless thousands"—and to help ensure they joined the Church of England, as opposed to such nonconformist denominations as the Protestant Huguenots. (It must have worked; you can still see gravestones with epitaphs in French in the crypt.) As the local silk industry declined, the church fell into disrepair, and by 1958 the structure was crumbling, with the looming prospect of demolition. But after 25 years—longer than it took to build the church—and a huge local fund-raising effort, the structure was meticulously restored and is a joy to behold, from the colonnaded Doric portico and tall spire to its soaring, heavily ornamented plaster ceiling. Its excellent acoustics make it a superb concert venue. Tours that take you "backstage" to the many hidden rooms and passages, from the tower to the vaults, are offered by appointment. There's also a café in the crypt. ✉ *Commercial St., Spitalfields* ☎ *020/7377–2440* 🌐 *www.ccspits.org* 🎫 *Free, tours £50 per hr* ⏲ *Closed Sat.* Ⓜ *Overground: Shoreditch High St.*

★ Dennis Severs' House

HOUSE | The remarkable interiors of this extraordinary time machine of a house are the creation of Dennis Severs (1948–99), a performer-designer-scholar from Escondido, California, who dedicated his life to restoring this Georgian terraced house. More than that, he created "still-life dramas" using sight, sound, and smell to evoke the world of a fictitious family of Huguenot silk weavers, the Jervises, who might have inhabited the house between 1728 and 1914. Each of the 10 rooms has a distinctive compelling atmosphere that encourages visitors to become lost in another time, deploying evocative design details like rose-laden Victorian wallpaper, Jacobean paneling, Georgian wing-back chairs, baroque carved ornaments, rich "Catholic" wall colors downstairs, and more sedate "Protestant" shades upstairs. The Silent Night candlelight tour offered Monday, Wednesday, and Friday evenings, a stroll through the rooms with no talking allowed, is the most theatrical and memorable way to experience the house. The Exclusive Silent Night visits, which conclude with champagne or mulled wine by the fire and a chat with the curators, are available one night per month (more frequently near the Christmas holiday), and private group visits can also be arranged. ✉ *18 Folgate St., Shoreditch* ☎ *020/7247–4013* 🌐 *www.dennisseversshouse.co.uk* 🎫 *£10 Sun. and Mon., £15 Mon., Wed., and Fri. evenings* ⏲ *Closed Tues., Thurs., and Sat.* Ⓜ *Overground: Shoreditch High St.*

Maureen Paley Gallery

MUSEUM | Inspired by the DIY punk aesthetic and the funky galleries of New York's Lower East Side, Maureen Paley started putting on exhibitions in her East End home back in 1984, when it was virtually the only gallery in the area. Since then, this American artist and gallerist has shown such respected contemporary artists as Gillian Wearing, Helen Chadwick, Jenny Holzer, Peter Fischli, and Wolfgang Tillmans and, today, is considered the doyenne of East End gallerists. The petite gallery has been in its current home, a converted warehouse in Bethnal Green, since 1999. ✉ *21 Herald St., Bethnal Green* ☎ *020/7729–4112* 🌐 *www.maureenpaley.com* 🎫 *Free* ⏲ *Closed Mon. and Tues.* Ⓜ *Bethnal Green.*

Old Truman Brewery

PEDESTRIAN MALL | **FAMILY** | The last old East End brewery still standing—a handsome example of Georgian and 19th-century industrial architecture, and in late Victorian times the largest brewery in the world—has been transformed into a cavernous hipster mall housing galleries, record shops, fashion-forward boutiques, bars, clubs, and restaurants, along with an array of international street-food vendors. The retailers are at street level with offices and studios on the upper floors. Events include fashion shows for both new and established designers, excellent sample sales, art installations, and, on weekends, a food hall and a vintage clothes fair. The brewery itself shut down in 1989. ✉ *91 Brick La., Spitalfields* ☎ *0207/770–6000* 🌐 *www.trumanbrewery.com* Ⓜ *Overground: Shoreditch High St.*

★ Queen Elizabeth Olympic Park

CITY PARK | FAMILY | Built for the London 2012 Olympic and Paralympic games, this 560-acre parkland still boasts some of the city's best sporting arenas. The Stadium, site of the London 2012 athletics competitions, is now home to local soccer team Westham United; it also hosts major athletic events. In addition, it's open for behind-the-scenes tours; check the website for dates. You can try four types of cycling (track, road-racing, BMX, and mountain-biking) at the Lee Valley VeloPark or go for a swim in the magnificent pool within the London Aquatics Centre. The ArcelorMittal Orbit, an enormous sculpture, is well worth a visit—the views across London from the top are terrific. Thrill-seekers have a couple of options when it comes to getting back down: a gasp-inducing slide that twists its way around the outside of the structure (art buffs might recognize it as the work of Belgian artist Carsten Höller) or via vertical rappelling (available on selected dates, advance booking essential). ✉ *East End* ☎ *080/0072–2110* 🌐 *www.queenelizabetholympicpark.co.uk* 🎫 *From £13, stadium tours £19* Ⓜ *Stratford, Hackney Wick, Pudding Mill Lane, Leyton.*

★ Regent's Canal

BODY OF WATER | The 19th-century waterway known as Regent's Canal officially starts in Little Venice in West London, but you'll find this quirky section east of City Road Basin. Join the towpath, where horses once walked as they pulled barges carrying all manner of cargo, at Wharf Road in Islington (N1) then head east on foot or by bike to experience the East End from an unusual perspective. What was once a no-go area is now a route lined with trendy cafés, floating bookshops, and a distinct community of water-dwelling Londoners. The Regent's Canal runs through Hackney, before heading south through Bethnal Green and Mile End, ending up at Limehouse Basin and the River Thames. Or you can continue eastward by turning off along the Hertford Union Canal at Victoria Park, a route that eventually leads to the Queen Elizabeth Olympic Park. ✉ *East End.*

Royal London Hospital Museum

MUSEUM | Located in the crypt of a Victorian church, the Royal London Hospital Museum uses exhibits of historic medical equipment, surgical instruments, and archives to document the history of this East London institution from its foundation in 1740 to the present day. Highlights include a forensic medicine section with documentation and original materials connected to the Jack the Ripper murders and the RLH surgeon who helped investigate them. There are also artifacts and documents relating to Joseph Merrick (aka the Elephant Man) who spent his final years in the hospital, and a set of dentures worn by George Washington. Opening hours are subject to change on short notice, so call ahead. ✉ *St. Augustine with St. Philip's Church, Newark St., Whitechapel* ☎ *020/7377–7608* 🌐 *www.bartshealth.nhs.uk/the-royal-london-hospital-museum-and-archives* 🎫 *Free* 🕓 *Closed Sat.–Mon.* Ⓜ *Whitechapel.*

Spitalfields City Farm

FARM/RANCH | FAMILY | An oasis of rural calm in an urban landscape, this little community farm raises a variety of animals, including some rare breeds, to help educate city kids about life in the country. A tiny farm shop sells freshly laid eggs, along with organic seasonal produce. ✉ *Buxton St., Spitalfields* ☎ *020/7247–8762* 🌐 *www.spitalfieldscityfarm.org* 🎫 *Free* 🕓 *Closed Mon.* Ⓜ *Overground: Shoreditch High St.*

Sutton House

HOUSE | FAMILY | Built by a courtier to King Henry VIII, this Tudor mansion has since been home to merchants, Huguenot silk weavers, and, in the 1980s, a group of arty squatters. The house dates back to 1535, when Hackney was a village on the outskirts of London surrounded by

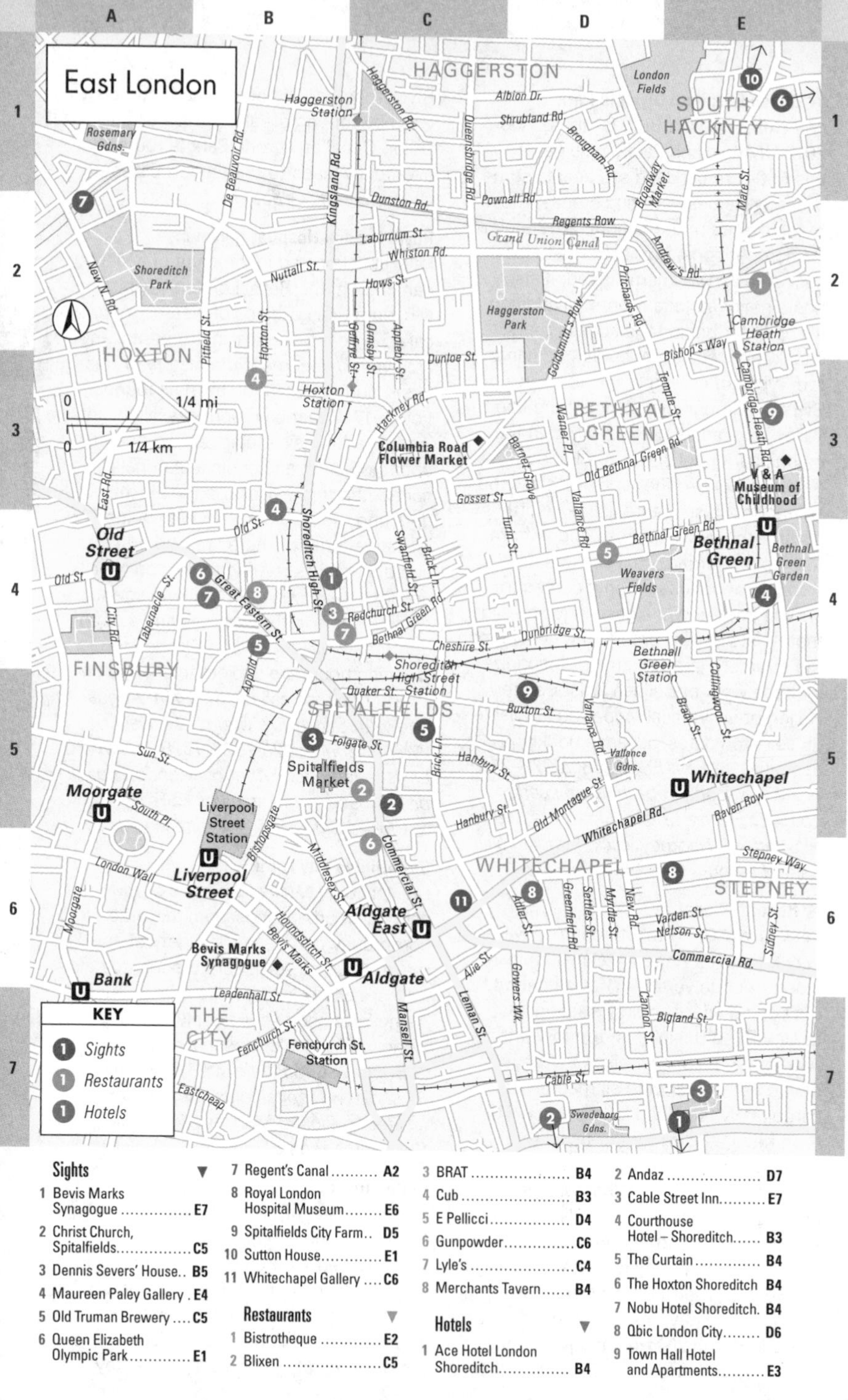

Sights

1 Bevis Marks Synagogue E7
2 Christ Church, Spitalfields............... C5
3 Dennis Severs' House.. B5
4 Maureen Paley Gallery . E4
5 Old Truman Brewery C5
6 Queen Elizabeth Olympic Park............ E1
7 Regent's Canal A2
8 Royal London Hospital Museum........ E6
9 Spitalfields City Farm.. D5
10 Sutton House............. E1
11 Whitechapel Gallery C6

Restaurants

1 Bistrotheque E2
2 Blixen C5
3 BRAT B4
4 Cub B3
5 E Pellicci................. D4
6 Gunpowder............... C6
7 Lyle's C4
8 Merchants Tavern...... B4

Hotels

1 Ace Hotel London Shoreditch.............. B4
2 Andaz D7
3 Cable Street Inn.......... E7
4 Courthouse Hotel – Shoreditch...... B3
5 The Curtain B4
6 The Hoxton Shoreditch B4
7 Nobu Hotel Shoreditch. B4
8 Qbic London City........ D6
9 Town Hall Hotel and Apartments.......... E3

fields. Later, in 1751, it was split into two self-contained houses. Its oak-paneled rooms, tranquil courtyard, and adorable café are an unexpected treat in an area that's yet to entirely shake off its grit. Guided tours (£10) are available by appointment. *✉ 2–4 Homerton High St., Hackney ☎ 020/8986–2264 🌐 www.nationaltrust.org.uk/sutton-house 🎫 £8 ⏲ Closed Mon. and Tues. Ⓜ Overground: Hackney Central.*

★ **Whitechapel Gallery**

MUSEUM | Founded in 1901, this internationally renowned gallery mounts exhibitions that rediscover overlooked masters and showcase tomorrow's legends. Painter and leading exponent of abstract expressionism Jackson Pollock was exhibited here in the 1950s as was pop artist Robert Rauschenberg in the 1960s; the 1970s saw a young David Hockney's first solo show. The exhibitions continue to be on the cutting edge of contemporary art. The gallery also hosts talks, film screenings, workshops, and other events; tours of local galleries take place on the first Thursday of every month. Pick up a free East London art map to help you plan your visit to the area. *✉ 77–82 Whitechapel High St., Whitechapel ☎ 020/7522–7888 🌐 www.whitechapelgallery.org ⏲ Closed Mon. Ⓜ Aldgate East.*

Restaurants

An invasion of hipsters and foodies has transformed the once-bleak East End food scene into the city's most daring dining zone. Seek out new British breakout stars like BRAT or Lyle's in Shoreditch, or hunt down a nighttime food truck for an irreverent taste of the foodie underground.

Bistrotheque

$$$ | **MODERN EUROPEAN** | **FAMILY** | You'll need some help finding this East End fashionista headquarters located down a side alley in hipster Bethnal Green.

East End Tours 

The two-hour **Jack the Ripper Walk** (🌐 *www.walks.com*) departs from Tower Hill Tube station daily at 7:30 pm, plus Saturday at 3. **Street Art London** (🌐 *www.streetartlondon.co.uk*) offers two-hour walking tours of East London's street art on Tuesday, Thursday, and Saturday at 10 am.

Once inside, check out the striking loft dining space and the Manchichi bar in its post-industrial chic setting, before polishing off light French and English dishes. **Known for:** classic choices like steak tartare and Croque Madame; weekend brunch with pancakes and maple syrup; resident pianist at brunch. *$ Average main: £25 ✉ 23–27 Wadeson St., Bethnal Green ☎ 020/8983–7900 🌐 www.bistrotheque.com Ⓜ Bethnal Green.*

Blixen

$$ | **BRASSERIE** | **FAMILY** | Within a magnificent Kew Gardens–style tropical garden and plant conservatory, you'll find this stylish brasserie backing out onto Old Spitalfields Market. Housed in a converted former Victorian bank, Blixen offers evergreen European comfort food. **Known for:** captivating, palm-filled tropical conservatory; great cocktails in the basement bar; popular weekend brunches. *$ Average main: £17 ✉ 65A Brushfield St., Spitalfields ☎ 020/7101–0093 🌐 www.blixen.co.uk Ⓜ Liverpool St.*

★ **BRAT**

$$$ | **SPANISH** | Welsh chef Tomos Parry brings his signature wood-grilled, whole roast Cornish turbot to this Basque-inspired hipster restaurant. Expect other live fire smashes like aged Jersey beef chops and seared leeks. **Known for:** meat-heavy dishes grilled in a variety of ways; noisy hipster atmosphere; heritage Welsh grain flour breads. *$ Average main:*

£26 ✉ *1st fl., 4 Redchurch St., Shoreditch* 🌐 *www.bratrestaurant.com* ⏲ *No dinner Sun.* Ⓜ *Liverpool St., Overground: Shoreditch High St.*

Cub

$$$$ | BRITISH | This tiny Hoxton joint is helmed by leading cocktail impresario Ryan Chetiyawardana (aka "Mr Lyan"), who turns his innovative, seasonal-focused hand to food in a truly exciting fashion. The largely plant-based set menu includes highly original dishes, drinks, and snacks that will get you thinking differently about the way we cook, eat, and drink. **Known for:** house-made ferments; unusual foraged ingredients such as chickweed; involved dining experience that won't suit those who prefer to be left alone to their meals. $ *Average main: £67* ✉ *153 Hoxton St., Hoxton* ☎ *020/3693–3202* 🌐 *www.lyancub.com* ⏲ *Closed Sun.–Tues.* Ⓜ *Overground: Hoxton.*

E. Pellicci

$ | CAFÉ | FAMILY | It's all Cockney banter and full English breakfasts at this tiny family-run café and onetime gangsters' lair near Brick Lane and Columbia Road markets. A rowdy hole-in-the-wall, E. Pellicci serves the greasy fry ups Londoners still adore. **Known for:** full cast of East End Cockney characters; copious full English breakfasts and builders' brew tea; cash-only cheap dishes. $ *Average main: £8* ✉ *332 Bethnal Green Rd., Bethnal Green* ☎ *020/7739–4873* 🌐 *www.epellicci.com* 💳 *No credit cards* ⏲ *Closed Sun. and Aug. No dinner* Ⓜ *Bethnal Green.*

Gunpowder

$ | INDIAN | Eschew the myriad copy-and-paste curry houses of Brick Lane and opt instead for this broom cupboard–size Spitalfields restaurant serving flawless small plate Indian cuisine. The charming waitstaff are happy to offer guidance when it comes to the menu, with its highly original takes on authentic flavor combinations from the subcontinent. **Known for:** ingredients not normally found on Indian menus, such as duck or seabass; lines out the door, thanks to the no-reservations policy; rasam ke bomb snack, a puff of spiced potato served atop a flavorful Bloody Mary–style shot. $ *Average main: £11* ✉ *11 White's Row, Spitalfields* 🌐 *www.gunpowderlondon.com* ⏲ *Closed Sun.* Ⓜ *Liverpool St.*

★ Lyle's

$$ | MODERN BRITISH | Globally acclaimed Brit chef and co-owner James Lowe forsakes heavy sauces and sorcery at this stripped-back, informal British dining mecca in Shoreditch. Stark but highly inventive locally sourced dishes may include house-cured cod with radiant nasturtium flowers or 24-hour Cornish Helford Estuary monkfish with wood sorrel and pick-your-own East Sussex greengages. **Known for:** highly modern and airy dining space; serious new-wave British neo-bistronomy; excellent cheese plates and wines by the glass. $ *Average main: £19* ✉ *Tea Bldg., 56 Shoreditch High St., East End* ✥ *Entrance on Bethnal Green Rd.* ☎ *020/3011–5911* 🌐 *www.lyleslondon.com* ⏲ *Closed Sun. and bank holiday Mon.* Ⓜ *Shoreditch High St.*

Merchants Tavern

$$ | MODERN EUROPEAN | FAMILY | The legend on the front of this Hoxton restaurant reads "Merchants of Good Fortune," which neatly sums up the exceptional, smart-casual dining experience you'll encounter within. Seasonal, veg-focused hits from France, Italy, and Britain emerge from the open-counter kitchen housed in a former Victorian warehouse and onetime apothecary. **Known for:** eclectic Modern European cuisine; 1960s-style interior and open kitchen; rare-pink venison with Alsace bacon. $ *Average main: £20* ✉ *38 Charlotte St., Hoxton* ☎ *020/7060–5335* 🌐 *www.merchantstavern.co.uk* ⏲ *No dinner Sun.* Ⓜ *Old St.*

The East End Art Scene

Banksy, the Bristol-based artist and provocateur who has maintained his anonymity despite works that now command six figures, is widely credited with making Londoners see street art as more than mere vandalism. He first came to public attention in the East End in the late '80s, and the area continues to attract new talent from around the globe today. Unfortunately, much of Banksy's early work has been lost, either from being covered over by local councils and building owners, defaced by other graffiti artists, or removed by profiteers. Currently murals remain at Rivington Street near Old Street (in the garden of Cargo bar and nightclub), and Stoke Newington Church Street. **Street Art London** (🌐 *www.streetartlondon.co.uk*) offers a knowledgeable, insider view on the ever-changing scene, taking you through the history of street art and graffiti in this area and highlighting the best of Banksy's successors. Take the Saturday tour to avoid the noise of weekday traffic.

Today, East London is a global hotbed of contemporary art, but its avant-garde roots go way back. **Shoreditch's** cheap industrial units and Georgian–Victorian terraced streets have attracted artists since the 1960s, when op-art pioneer Bridget Riley established a service to find affordable studio space for her contemporaries. In the early '90s it gained new notoriety when Young British Artists Sarah Lucas and Tracey Emin began selling their own and their friends' work in The Shop, joining Maureen Paley's influential Bethnal Green gallery, and the long-established Whitechapel Art Gallery, where many leading abstract expressionists and pop artists had their first U.K. shows. **Hoxton** truly became a destination for well-heeled collectors when Jay Jopling, the most important modern-art dealer in town, set up his White Cube gallery in 2000 (it's now in Bermondsey, with a second location at Mason's Yard in Westminster), followed by Kate MacGarry's gallery in 2002.

Priced out by the area's fashionability, the emerging artists themselves have relocated farther off the beaten path to edgier neighborhoods such as **Hackney**, with several trendsetting galleries found clustered around **Cambridge Heath Road** and **Vyner Street.**

Hotels

What was once a lodging no-man's land is fast becoming the hippest place to stay in London. Hotels tend to be quirky and design-led, attracting a crowd keen to make the most of the excellent food and drink, culture, and shopping opportunities available in the East End.

Ace Hotel London Shoreditch
$$ | **HOTEL** | The first European outlet of the superhip Ace hotel chain fits right into the scenery in achingly cool Shoreditch, surrounded by galleries and on-trend boutiques every bit as style conscious as its own creatively minimalist interiors. **Pros:** extremely fashionable; large and comfortable bedrooms; great bar. **Cons:** not everyone will enjoy being surrounded by hipsters; street noise can be a problem; frustrating online booking system. *Rooms from: £170* ✉ *100 Shoreditch High St., Shoreditch* ☎ *020/7613–9800* 🌐 *www.acehotel.com* *258 rooms* *No meals* Ⓜ *Shoreditch High St.*

Andaz

$$ | HOTEL | Swanky and upscale, this hotel sports a modern masculine design, and novel check-in procedure—instead of standing at a desk, guests sit in a lounge while a staff member with a tablet takes their information. **Pros:** nice attention to detail; no standing in line to check in; complimentary "healthy minibars" are stocked with nuts, fruit, and yogurt. **Cons:** sparse interior design is not for all; rates rise significantly for midweek stays; busy, sometimes hectic neighborhood. *Rooms from: £240* ✉ *40 Liverpool St., East End* ☎ *020/7961–1234, 800/492–8804 in U.S.* *www.andaz.hyatt.com* *282 rooms* *No meals* *Liverpool St.*

★ **Cable Street Inn**

$$ | B&B/INN | Wonderful modern art lines the walls of this former Victorian pub a mile east of the Tower of London, which has been beautifully restored and converted into a modern B&B. **Pros:** true one-of-a-kind place; beautiful art; wonderful host. **Cons:** 20-minute journey by DLR then Tube to the center; historic nature of the building makes it unsuitable for those with mobility problems; with only three rooms, availability can be low. *Rooms from: £130* ✉ *232 Cable St., East End* ☎ *020/7790–4019* *www.cablestreet-inn.co.uk* *3 rooms* *Free breakfast* *DLR: Shadwell.*

Courthouse Hotel – Shoreditch

$$ | HOTEL | Housed within a beautifully restored former courthouse, this hip Shoreditch hotel contributes its own contemporary flair to the grand architectural style of the original building, with chic rooms that provide the perfect base to explore the surrounding trendy neighborhood. **Pros:** great views over neighboring rooftops from the terrace; lively bar; excellent facilities including cinema and bowling alley. **Cons:** not all rooms are located in the historic former courthouse; a 20-minute Tube ride into central London; the size and scope of the public spaces can lead to some areas feeling deserted. *Rooms from: £179* ✉ *335–337 Old St., Shoreditch* ☎ *020/3310–5555* *www.shoreditch.courthouse-hotel.com* *128 rooms* *No meals* *Old St.*

The Curtain

$$$ | HOTEL | For a classic hip Hoxton stay, it would only be right to choose a hotel crammed with exposed brick, heavy doses of industrial chic, and stylish loft living appeal—a combination that The Curtain presents from its location on the border of Shoreditch and The City. **Pros:** rooftop pool great for summertime hangs; rooms feel spacious and some come with terraces with great views; very trendy basement bar and restaurant. **Cons:** bar and restaurant areas can get overcrowded; some guests will find the industrial style a turnoff; area is renowned for nightlife so don't expect quiet nights. *Rooms from: £290* ✉ *45 Curtain Rd., Shoreditch* ☎ *020/3146–4545* *www.thecurtain.com* *120 rooms* *No meals* *Overground: Shoreditch High St.*

★ **The Hoxton Shoreditch**

$$ | HOTEL | The design throughout this trendy East London lodging is contemporary—but not so modern as to be absurd; in keeping with a claim to combine a country-lodge lifestyle with true urban living, a fire crackles in the lobby. **Pros:** cool vibe; neighborhood known for funky galleries and boutiques; huge weekend discounts. **Cons:** price skyrockets during the week; away from major tourist sights; cheapest rooms are called "shoeboxes" for a reason. *Rooms from: £149* ✉ *81 Great Eastern St., East End* ☎ *020/7550–1000* *www.thehoxton.com* *210 rooms* *Free breakfast* *Shoreditch High St.*

Nobu Hotel Shoreditch

$$ | HOTEL | Nobu's first European hotel combines ravishing design (think soothing Japonism-inspired patterns and palettes alongside bold statements of industrial chic) with slick service, in a back street location in the heart of Shoreditch. **Pros:** double-height basement bar exudes Bond villain cool; luxury feel rarely encountered outside central London; on-site spa and gym has his and hers steam rooms. **Cons:** rooms on the lower floors don't have a lot of natural light ; not all rooms have desks; in-room lighting and air conditioning is unnecessarily complicated. *Rooms from: £220* *10–50 Willow St., Shoreditch* *020/7683–1200* *www.nobuhotelshoreditch.com* *148 rooms* *No meals* *Old St.*

Qbic London City

$ | **HOTEL** | A contrast to the superexpensive business hotels that proliferate in this part of the East End on the edge of The City, the Qbic is a modern and surprisingly affordable option in a trendy corner of town. **Pros:** free bike rentals; great value for money; environmentally friendly. **Cons:** a bit out of the way; not everyone will love the style; cheapest rooms have no windows. *Rooms from: £68* *42 Adler St., East End* *020/3021–1440* *www.qbichotels.com* *183 rooms* *Free breakfast* *Aldgate East.*

Town Hall Hotel and Apartments

$$$ | **HOTEL** | An art deco town hall, abandoned in the early 1980s and turned into a chic hotel 30 years later, is now a lively and stylish place, with the best of the building's elegant original features intact. **Pros:** beautifully designed; lovely staff; big discounts on weekends. **Cons:** the area is far from the major sights; a 15-minute Tube ride from central London; some rooms choose style over function. *Rooms from: £198* *Patriot Sq., Bethnal Green, East End* *020/7871–0460* *www.townhallhotel.com* *98 rooms* *Free breakfast* *Bethnal Green, Overground: Cambridge Heath.*

Nightlife

East London's bar scene is ever evolving, with the trendy hipster crowd constantly pushing farther east in search of the next big thing. Shoreditch has bars and clubs to suit nearly all tastes these days, while Dalston, the neighborhood to its north, attracts an edgier, younger clientele. In historic neighborhoods such as Spitalfields and Wapping, there's a cozy old drinking den around practically every corner.

BARS

Callooh Callay

BARS/PUBS | Cocktails are tasty, well-executed classics, and there's also a selection of unique instant-classics at this eccentric Hoxton bar where the bells and whistles are left to the decor. *65 Rivington St., Hoxton* *020/7739–4781* *www.calloohcallaybar.com* *Old St.*

Crate Bar and Pizzeria

BARS/PUBS | Enjoy canalside craft beer and pizza at the busiest of a handful of grown-up bars in this ubertrendy area of East London. Rub shoulders with the locals—the community still has its share of artists who made their way east following rent hikes in Shoreditch—as well as visitors who come for late-night raves in the area's many warehouses. There's a warm atmosphere inside, with quirky upcycled interior design and DJs playing on weekend evenings. The beer comes from the on-site brewery, while thin-crust pizzas emerge from the open kitchen. *Unit 7, Queens Yard, Hackney* *020/8533–3331* *www.cratebrewery.com* *Overground: Hackney Wick.*

Nightjar

BARS/PUBS | The feel is moody, Prohibition-era '20s Chicago at this fabulously low-lit tin-tiled ceiling speakeasy and basement jazz cocktail bar in Shoreditch. Book a table or chance it on the door at this no-standing venue, where live jazz and swing bands nightly keeps things lively. *129 City Rd., Hoxton*

☎ *020/7253–4101* 🌐 *www.barnightjar.com* 🎫 *£5 music cover charge* Ⓜ *Old St.*

Untitled

BARS/PUBS | One of London's leading bartenders, Tony Conigliaro has crafted a cocktail menu featuring some downright bizarre ingredients at this superhip, stripped-back Dalston bar—think white clay and chalk in a vodka-based Snow or leather in a Champagne-based Cuir de Russie. It all somehow works, and the Japanese food served alongside the drinks is delicious. ✉ *538 Kingsland Rd., Dalston* ☎ *078/4102–2924* 🌐 *www.untitled-bar.com* Ⓜ *Overground: Dalston Junction.*

LIVE MUSIC

★ Cafe Oto

MUSIC CLUBS | A relaxed café by day, and London's leading venue for experimental music by night, Cafe Oto is a Dalston institution. Its programming of free jazz, avant-garde electronica,,and much more is enough of a draw that it regularly sells out, with music fans steaming up the windows and spilling out onto the pavement and road outside to smoke during breaks. Healthy Persian-inspired food is served in the daytime, before customers are kicked out at 5 pm to make way for sound checks. It's open as a bar (no cover) on nights when no concerts are taking place. ✉ *18–22 Ashwin St., Dalston* 🌐 *www.cafeoto.co.uk* Ⓜ *Overground: Dalston Junction.*

★ EartH

MUSIC CLUBS | East London's newest, and coolest, performing arts venue occupies two huge spaces (one standing, one with unallocated bench seating) in an old art deco movie theater. Original architectural details add to the shabby-hib feel of the place, while in EartH Kitchen, the bar and restaurant on the venue's second floor, you'll find Scandi-modern styling (along with reasonably priced modern British cuisine and delicious cocktails). The wide-ranging and very much on-trend program runs from world music and hip-hop to country and folk, with stand-up comedy and free sets by leading DJs in the bar. ✉ *11–17 Stoke Newington Rd., Dalston* ☎ *020/7422–7505* 🌐 *www.earthackney.co.uk* Ⓜ *Overground: Dalston Kingsland, Dalston Junction.*

PUBS

★ Prospect of Whitby

BARS/PUBS | **FAMILY** | Named after a collier ship, this is one of London's oldest riverside pubs, dating to around 1520. Although a regular for Dickens, Pepys, Samuel Johnson, and the American artist James Whistler, once upon a time it was called the Devil's Tavern because of the lowlifes—sailors, smugglers, footpads, and cutthroats—who congregated here. With a 400-year-old flagstone floor and ornamented with pewter ware and nautical objects, this much-loved boozer has a terrace with views of the Thames, from where boat trips often point it out. ✉ *57 Wapping Wall, East End* ☎ *020/7481–1095* 🌐 *www.greeneking-pubs.co.uk/pubs/greater-london/prospect-of-whitby* Ⓜ *Wapping. DLR: Shadwell.*

The Ten Bells

BARS/PUBS | **FAMILY** | Although the number of bells in its name has varied between 8 and 12, depending on how many bells were used by neighboring Christ Church, Spitalfields, this pub retains it original mid-Victorian interior and original tiles, including a frieze depicting the area's French Huguenot silk weaving tradition on the north wall and particularly fine floral tiling on two others. Urban legend says that Jack the Ripper's third victim, Annie Chapman, had a drink here before meeting her gory end. The pub is also depicted in Alan Moore's acclaimed graphic novel *From Hell.* ✉ *84 Commercial St., Spitalfields* ☎ *020/7247–7532* 🌐 *www.tenbells.com* Ⓜ *Liverpool St.*

Performing Arts

Artists and other creative types, no longer able to afford central London rents, have been making their way eastward for years. It began in Shoreditch, but as rents increased there, too, neighborhoods farther and farther out have taken on these new residents. Go gallery hopping in Vyner Street in Bethnal Green or catch a hip band in action at one of Shoreditch's myriad music venues.

PERFORMING ARTS CENTERS

★ Wilton's

CONCERTS | Arguably London's most atmospheric cultural space, Wilton's has been entertaining the crowds since 1743, first as an alehouse, then as a music hall. It now hosts gigs, talks, theater performances, movie screenings (often with live scores), and swing-dance evenings. The cozy Mahogany Bar, the oldest part of the building, serves a good range of quality local ales, along with snacks and meals that change according to what's playing in the theater. There's a cocktail bar upstairs, in what was once the artists' green room. ✉ *Graces Alley, East End* ☎ *020/7702–2789* 🌐 *www.wiltons.org.uk* Ⓜ *Aldgate East, Tower Hill.*

THEATER

Hackney Empire

DANCE | **FAMILY** | The history of this treasure of a theater is drama in its own right. Charlie Chaplin is said to have appeared at Hackney Empire during its days as a thriving variety theater and music hall in the early 1900s. The theater now hosts traditional family entertainment and variety shows, opera, music, musical theater, dance, and drama, often with a multicultural slant. Its annual Christmas pantomime show is legendary. ✉ *291 Mare St., Hackney* ☎ *020/8985–2424* 🌐 *www.hackneyempire.co.uk* Ⓜ *Overground: Hackney Central.*

Shopping

CLOTHING

Beyond Retro

CLOTHING | The more than 10,000 vintage items for men and women here—from cowboy boots to bowling shirts to prom dresses—include the largest collection of American retro in the United Kingdom. There's another outpost in Dalston and one in Soho. ✉ *110–112 Cheshire St., Spitalfields* ☎ *020/7297–9001* 🌐 *www.beyondretro.com* Ⓜ *Whitechapel. Overground: Shoreditch High St.*

★ Blue Mountain School

CLOTHING | It's hard to think of somewhere more East London than Blue Mountain School, a building that comprises a fashion, furniture, and accessories archive (the focus at the boutique is slow fashion and homewares by the likes of Anecho, Geoffrey B. Small, and Amy Revier); a gallery with changing contemporary exhibits; a listening room; and a tiny chef's table restaurant from Nuno Mendes, of Chiltern Firehouse fame. Around the corner at 28 Old Nichol Street is Hostem, a more traditional format boutique selling men's and women's garments and footwear by brands such as P.R. Patterson, Casey Casey, and Visvim. This might all sound offputtingly hip, but give it a chance; it's a beautifully curated shopping experience, albeit one that will make considerable demands on your wallet. The store also operates a three-bedroom guesthouse in a converted Georgian town house in Whitechapel. ✉ *9 Chance St., Shoreditch* ☎ *020/7739–9733* 🌐 *www.bluemountain.school* Ⓜ *Overground: Shoreditch High St.*

Rokit

CLOTHING | Magazine and music stylists love these two premises along Brick Lane that carry everything from handbags and ball gowns to jeans, military garb, and Western wear. The ever-changing stock spans the 1930s to the 1990s. There are also branches in Camden and

Did You Know?

The Columbia Road Flower Market opens at 8 am on Sunday. Arrive early to see the photogenic market at its best and to find the freshest selection. The road is lined with funky shops selling antiques, vintage clothing, horticultural accessories, and more.

Covent Garden. ✉ *101 and 107 Brick La., Spitalfields* ☎ *020/7375–3864* 🌐 *www.rokit.co.uk* Ⓜ *Overground: Shoreditch High St.*

69b Boutique

CLOTHING | This petite boutique claims to be London's first store dedicated to socially and environmentally sustainable fashion, with a strict transparency and accountability policy that all its brands must adhere to. So you can happily indulge in the likes of Marimekko, Happy Haus, and Frieda Sand, plus accessories from Aspiga, Elk, and Kavat entirely guilt-free. ✉ *69b Broadway Market, Dalston* ☎ *020/7249–9655* 🌐 *www.69bboutique.com* Ⓜ *Overground: London Fields.*

★ **Sunspel**

CLOTHING | This British firm has been making fine men's underwear since the mid-19th century and it's still its specialty, along with luxury basics such as knitwear, outerwear, polo shirts, and swimwear. Prince Charles is a real-life customer and James Bond, a cinematic one (he wore their shorts in *Thunderball* and polo shirt in *Quantum of Solace*). The spy's creator, Ian Fleming, was another client. Sunspel also carries elegant, minimalist T-shirts, sweaters, and sweats for women. There are other branches in Marylebone, Notting Hill, St. James's, and Soho. ✉ *7 Redchurch St., Shoreditch* ☎ *020/7739–9729* 🌐 *www.sunspel.com* Ⓜ *Overground: Shoreditch High St.*

HOUSEHOLD GOODS

Botany

HOUSEHOLD ITEMS/FURNITURE | Loyal customers flock to this plant, homewares, and natural beauty boutique from all over the world, picking up specially commissioned ceramic pieces, stocking up on hand-made organic skincare products, and attending craft workshops. Its eclectic set-up reflects the diverse interests of the creative community that lives in this area close to buzzy Chatsworth Road. ✉ *5 Chatsworth Rd., Hackney* ☎ *020/3759–8191* 🌐 *www.botanyshop.co.uk* ⏲ *Closed Mon.–Wed.* Ⓜ *Overground: Clapton.*

Labour & Wait

HOUSEHOLD ITEMS/FURNITURE | Although mundane items like colanders and clothespins may not sound like ideal souvenirs, this shop (something of a hipster heaven selling both new and vintage items) will make you reconsider. The owners are on a mission to revive retro, functional British household goods, such as enamel kitchenware, genuine feather dusters, bread bins, bottle brushes, and traditional Welsh blankets. ✉ *85 Redchurch St., Shoreditch* ☎ *020/7729–6253* 🌐 *www.labourandwait.co.uk* ⏲ *Closed Mon.* Ⓜ *Overground: Shoreditch High St.*

MARKETS

Brick Lane

OUTDOOR/FLEA/GREEN MARKETS | The noisy center of the Bangladeshi community is a hubbub of buying and selling on Sunday. Stalls have food, hardware, household and electrical goods, bric-a-brac, secondhand clothes, spices, and traditional saris. Some of the CDs and DVDs are pirated, and the bargain iron may not have a plug, so check carefully. Shoppers nevertheless flock to the market to enjoy the buzz, sample curries and Bangladeshi sweets, or indulge in salt beef on a bagel at Beigel Bake—London's 24-hour bagel bakery, a survivor of the neighborhood's Jewish past. Brick Lane's activity spills over into nearby Petticoat Lane Market, where there are similar goods but less atmosphere. ✉ *Shoreditch* 🌐 *www.visitbricklane.org* ⏲ *Market closed Mon.–Sat.* Ⓜ *Aldgate E. Overground: Shoreditch High St.*

★ **Broadway Market**

SHOPPING NEIGHBORHOODS | This parade of shops in hipster-centric Hackney (north of Regent's Canal) is worth visiting for the specialty bookshops, independent boutiques, organic cafés, neighborhood restaurants, and even a traditional (but now rare) pie-and-mash shop. But wait for Saturday (9–5), when it really comes into its own with a farmers' market and more than 100 street-food and produce stalls rivaling those of south London's famed Borough Market. Artisanal breads, cheeses, pastries, organic meats, waffles, fruit and vegetables, seafood, and international food offerings: this is foodie heaven. There are also stalls selling vintage clothes, crafts, jewelry, and more. ✉ *Broadway Market, Hackney* 🌐 *www.broadwaymarket.co.uk* Ⓜ *London Fields.*

★ Columbia Road Flower Market

OUTDOOR/FLEA/GREEN MARKETS | London's premier flower market is about as pretty and photogenic as they come, with more than 50 stalls selling flowers, shrubs, bulbs, and trees—everything from bedding plants to 10-foot banana trees—as well as garden tools, pots, and accessories at competitive prices. The stallholders' patter is part of the fun. It's on Sunday only, and it's all over by 3 pm. Columbia Road itself is lined with 60 interesting independent shops purveying art, fashion, furnishings (most of which are only open on weekends), and the local cafés are superb. ✉ *Columbia Rd., Hoxton* 🌐 *www.columbiaroad.info* 🕒 *Market closed Mon.–Sat.* Ⓜ *Old St. Overground: Hoxton.*

Old Spitalfields Market

OUTDOOR/FLEA/GREEN MARKETS | Once the East End's wholesale fruit and vegetable market and now restored to its original architectural splendor, this fine example of a Victorian market hall is at the center of the area's gentrified revival. The original building is largely occupied by shops (mostly upscale brands like Rag & Bone, Lululemon, and Superga, but some independents like trendy homeware-and-fashion purveyor The Mercantile), with traders' stalls in the courtyard. A modern shopping precinct under a Norman Foster–designed glass canopy adjoins the old building and holds approximately 70 traders' stalls. You may have to wade through a certain number of stalls selling cheap imports and tacky T-shirts to find the good stuff, which includes vintage and new clothing, handmade rugs and jewelry, hand-carved toy trains, vintage maps, unique baby clothes, rare vinyl, and cakes. Thursday is for antiques; Friday for a biweekly record fair; while weekends offer a little of everything. The Kitchens, 10 central dining venues showcasing small, independent chefs and restaurants, provide fresh takes on Mexican, Japanese, and other world cuisines. There are also indie street food stalls and some superior chain outlets. ✉ *16 Horner Sq., Brushfield St., Spitalfields* 🌐 *www.oldspitalfieldsmarket.com* Ⓜ *Liverpool St. Overground: Shoreditch High St.*

MUSIC

Rough Trade East

MUSIC STORES | Although many London record stores are struggling, this veteran indie-music specialist in the Old Truman Brewery seems to have gotten the formula right. The spacious surroundings are as much a hangout as a shop, complete with a stage for live gigs and a café. There's another branch on Talbot Road in Notting Hill. ✉ *Dray Walk, Old Truman Brewery, 91 Brick La., Spitalfields* ☎ *020/7392–7788* 🌐 *www.roughtrade.com* Ⓜ *Liverpool St. Overground: Shoreditch High St.*

Chapter 9

SOUTH OF THE THAMES

Updated by
Ellin Stein

Sights	Restaurants	Hotels	Shopping	Nightlife
★★★★★	★★★☆☆	★☆☆☆☆	★★☆☆☆	★★★★☆

SOUTH OF THE THAMES SNAPSHOT

TOP REASONS TO GO

Shakespeare's Globe: See one of Shakespeare's plays in this historically accurate replica of the Elizabethan theater where they were first performed.

The Tate Modern: One of the world's great collections of post-1900 modern art, the centerpiece of this Tate branch is the huge renovated electric turbine hall, now an exhibition space used for large installations.

Sunset on Waterloo Bridge: This is one of London's most romantic views, with St. Paul's to the east and the Houses of Parliament to the west.

The London Eye: One of the city's tallest structures, this observation wheel gives you a bird's-eye view of some of the city's most iconic sights.

GETTING THERE

For the South Bank, use Embankment on the District, Circle, Northern, and Bakerloo lines and walk across the Golden Jubilee Bridges; or Waterloo on the Northern, Jubilee, and Bakerloo lines, from where it's a 10-minute walk. London Bridge on the Northern and Jubilee lines is five minutes from Borough Market and Southwark Cathedral. The station also serves Bermondsey Street, although, confusingly, the next stop on the Jubilee Line is called Bermondsey. Brixton has its own stop on the Victoria Line.

MAKING THE MOST OF YOUR TIME

Don't attempt to visit the area south of the Thames in one go. Tate Modern alone deserves a whole afternoon, especially if you want to do justice to both the temporary exhibitions and the permanent collection. The Globe requires about two hours for the exhibition theater tour and two to three hours for a performance. Finish with drinks at the Oxo Tower or one of the Shard's restaurants, with their spectacular views. You can return across the river to central London via Southwark on the Jubilee Line from Tate Modern, although it's a good walk to the station.

QUICK BITES

■ **Pieminister** In the art-and-design shopping enclave of Gabriel's Wharf, you'll find this branch of Pieminister, which began life in Borough Market. Have a meat pie made with ingredients like free-range chicken with bacon and tarragon (vegetarian alternatives are also available). ✉ *Gabriel's Wharf, 56 Upper Ground, South Bank* ☎ *020/7928–5755* 🌐 *www.pieminister.co.uk* ⏲ *No dinner* Ⓜ *Waterloo.*

■ **Wahaca** This canteen-style outpost of the eco-conscious chain serves mildly spiced Mexican food like marinated grilled chicken or tostadas with Devon crab, plus the usual burritos, quesadillas, tacos, and salads. ✉ *119 Waterloo Rd., South Bank* ☎ *020/3697–4140* 🌐 *www.wahaca.co.uk* Ⓜ *Waterloo.*

This area is a magnet for tourists and residents alike, with attractions that include the IWM London, the Southbank Centre (Europe's largest arts center), and the gastronomic delight that is Borough Market.

The most important sights are clustered around the South Bank and in Bankside and Southwark, but the surrounding neighborhoods of Bermondsey and Lambeth are rising rapidly, with galleries, shops, and restaurants opening constantly. And the formerly drab Nine Elms area (near Vauxhall) is in the process of being totally transformed, with luxury high-rises and shops proliferating in the wake of the huge, fairly new U.S. embassy in the area.

A borough of the City of London since 1327, Southwark first became well known for its inns (the pilgrims in Chaucer's *A Canterbury Tale* set off from one), theaters, prisons, tanneries, and brothels, as well as entertainments such as cockfighting. For four centuries, this was a sort of border town outside the city walls (and jurisdiction) where Londoners went to let their hair down and behave badly. Originally, you were just as likely to see a few bouts of bearbaiting at the Globe as you were Shakespeare's most recent work. But now that south London encompasses a world-class museum, high-caliber art, music, film, and theater venues, as well as an aquarium, a historic warship, two popular food markets, and greatly improved transportation links, this neighborhood has become one of London's leading destinations.

Today, you can walk the **Thames Path** along the river from the London Eye all the way to Greenwich. The segment beside the South Bank is alive with skateboarders, secondhand-book stalls, and street entertainers. At one end the **London Eye,** a 21st-century landmark that became an instant favorite with both Londoners and out-of-towners, rises next to the **London Aquarium** and the **Southbank Centre,** home to the **Royal Festival Hall,** the **Hayward Gallery,** the **BFI Southbank,** and the **National Theatre.** Farther east you'll come to a reconstruction of Sir Francis Drake's 16th-century ship the ***Golden Hinde***; **Butler's Wharf,** where some notable restaurants occupy what were once shadowy Dickensian docklands; **the Shard,** the tallest building in the EU, which offers spectacular views over the city; and, next to **Tower Bridge,** the massive headlight-shape **City Hall.** Nearby Bermondsey Street (from "Beormund's Eye," as it was known in Saxon times) is home to the bright yellow Fashion Museum, the White Cube Gallery, and lots of trendy shops, restaurants, and cafés. Meanwhile, younger visitors will enjoy the **London Dungeon** and **HMS *Belfast,*** a decommissioned Royal Navy cruiser, while food lovers should make a straight line to London's oldest food market, **Borough Market,** where the independent stallholders sell farm-fresh produce, artisanal bread and cheese, and specialty fish and meat.

Even from the Shard's lofty viewing platform 1,016 feet up, the area south

The restaurant at Tate Modern has some of the best views in London. Here you can see St. Paul's Cathedral in the distance.

of the Thames still isn't one of London's most beautiful; but you'll be able to see how this patchwork of neighborhoods fits together. The heart is the South Bank, which extends east from the London Eye to Blackfriars Bridge, with the river to the north and Waterloo Station to the south. From Blackfriars Bridge east to London Bridge is Bankside, where you'll find the Globe and Tate Modern. Moving east from London Bridge is Borough, with its cobbled streets and former factories now turned into expensive lofts. Next, southeast of Borough, is buzzy, urban Bermondsey, while leafy Dulwich, with its renowned gallery and charming period streets, is quite a distance to the south. Returning up the river to the west of the South Bank is Lambeth and then Vauxhall, with the imposing IWM London (formerly the Imperial War Museum), a thriving gay scene, and scary through-traffic routes. It's a rapidly changing district, thanks to a regeneration spearheaded by the opening of the U.S. Embassy in adjacent Nine Elms and a slew of upscale riverside residential developments. South of here is Brixton, long the heartland of London's Afro-Caribbean community—with a lively club scene—and now attracting young families priced out of nearby Clapham.

Sights

Bankside Gallery

MUSEUM | Two artistic societies—the Royal Society of Painter–Printmakers and the Royal Watercolour Society—have their headquarters in this gallery next to Tate Modern. Together they mount exhibitions of current members' work, which is usually for sale, along with art books, making this a great place for finding that unique, not too expensive gift. There are also regular themed exhibitions. ✉ *48 Hopton St., Southwark* ☎ *020/7928–7521* 🌐 *www.banksidegallery.com* 🎫 *Free* Ⓜ *Mansion House, Southwark, St. Paul's.*

★ **Borough Market**

MARKET | There's been a market in Borough since Roman times, and this latest incarnation, spread under the arches and railroad tracks leading to London Bridge Station, is where some of the city's best artisanal food producers set up stalls. Fresh coffees, gorgeous cheeses, chocolates, and baked goods complement the organically farmed meats, fresh fish, condiments, fruits, and vegetables.

Don't make any other lunch plans for the day; this is where celebrity chef Jamie Oliver's scallop man cooks them up fresh at Shellseekers, and Ginger Pig's rare-breed sausages sizzle on grills, while for the sweets lover there are chocolates, preserves, and Whirld's artisanal confectionery, as well as 18 restaurants and cafés, most above average. The Market Hall hosts workshops, tastings, and demonstrations, and also acts as a greenhouse. The market is open Wednesday and Thursday 10–5, Friday 10–6, and Saturday 8–5, with only stalls for hot food and produce on Monday and Tuesday 10 – 5.

On weekends, a separate, highly regarded market specializing in produce and street food operates on nearby Maltby Street. It was originally established by eight breakaway Borough Market traders. Stalls include African Volcano, purveyors of Mozambique-style hot sauces and marinades, and Raclette Brothers' superb melted cheese. ✉ *8 Southwark St., Borough* ☎ *020/7402–1002* 🌐 *www.boroughmarket.org.uk* 🕓 *Closed Sun.* Ⓜ *London Bridge.*

The Clink Prison Museum

MUSEUM | **FAMILY** | This attraction devoted to re-creating life in a medieval prison is built on the site of the original "Clink," the oldest of Southwark's five prisons and the reason why the "clink" is now slang for jail. Owned by the Bishops of Winchester from 1144 to 1780, it was the first prison to detain women, many for prostitution. Because of the bishops' relaxed attitude toward the endemic trade—they decided to license prostitution rather than ban it—the area within their jurisdiction was known as "the Liberty of the Clink." Inside, you'll discover how grisly a Tudor prison could be, operating on a code of cruelty, deprivation, and corruption. The prison was only a small part of Winchester Palace, a huge complex that was the bishops' London residence. You can still see the remains of the early 13th-century Great Hall, with its famous rose window, next to Southwark Cathedral. ✉ *1 Clink St., Borough* ☎ *020/7403–0900* 🌐 *www.clink.co.uk* 🎫 *£8* Ⓜ *London Bridge.*

★ **Dulwich Picture Gallery**

MUSEUM | Famed for its collection of more than 600 paintings, including many Old Masters, the Dulwich (pronounced "Dull-ich") Picture Gallery, designed by Sir John Soane, was the world's first purpose-built art museum when it opened in 1811 (the recent extension was designed by Rick Mather). The permanent collection includes landmark works by Rembrandt, Van Dyck, Rubens, Poussin, and Gainsborough, and the museum also hosts three or so major temporary exhibitions each year. Check the website for its schedule of family activities; there's a lovely café here, too. While you're in the area, take a short wander and you'll find a handful of cute clothing and crafts stores and the well-manicured Dulwich Park, which has lakeside walks and a fine display of rhododendrons in late May. Development in Dulwich Village is tightly controlled, so it feels a bit like a time capsule, with old-fashioned street signs and handsome 18th-century houses on the main street. ✉ *Gallery Rd., Dulwich* ☎ *020/8693–5254* 🌐 *www.dulwichpicturegallery.org.uk* 🎫 *£17* 🕓 *Closed Mon.* Ⓜ *Brixton Station, then Bus P4. National Rail: West Dulwich from Victoria or North Dulwich from London Bridge.*

Fashion and Textile Museum

MUSEUM | The bright yellow-and-pink museum (it's hard to miss) designed by Mexican architect Ricardo Legorreta features changing exhibitions devoted to developments in fashion design, textiles,

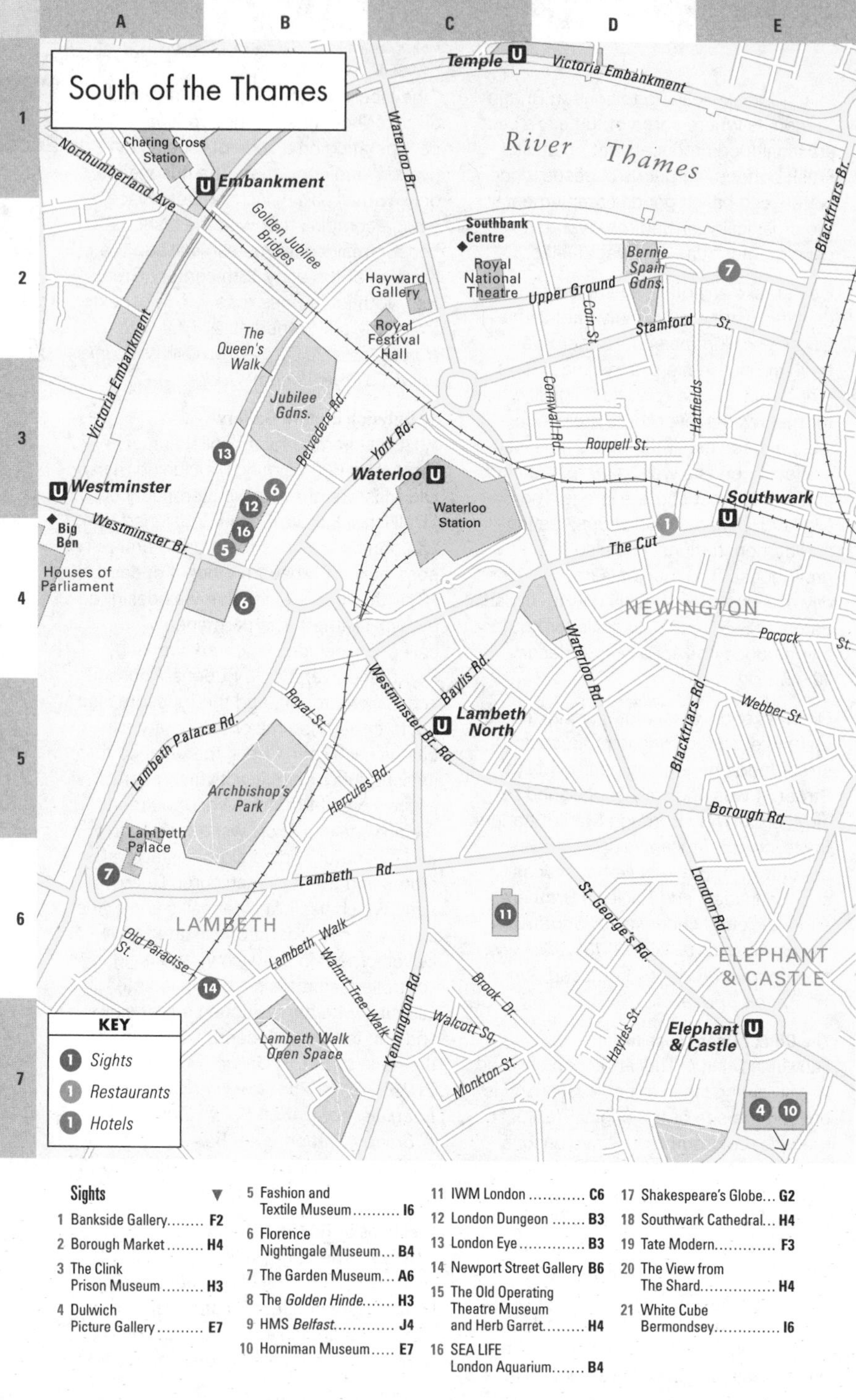

Sights

1 Bankside Gallery........ F2
2 Borough Market........ H4
3 The Clink Prison Museum......... H3
4 Dulwich Picture Gallery.......... E7
5 Fashion and Textile Museum.......... I6
6 Florence Nightingale Museum... B4
7 The Garden Museum... A6
8 The *Golden Hinde*....... H3
9 HMS *Belfast*............ J4
10 Horniman Museum..... E7
11 IWM London............ C6
12 London Dungeon....... B3
13 London Eye.............. B3
14 Newport Street Gallery B6
15 The Old Operating Theatre Museum and Herb Garret......... H4
16 SEA LIFE London Aquarium....... B4
17 Shakespeare's Globe... G2
18 Southwark Cathedral... H4
19 Tate Modern............. F3
20 The View from The Shard................ H4
21 White Cube Bermondsey............... I6

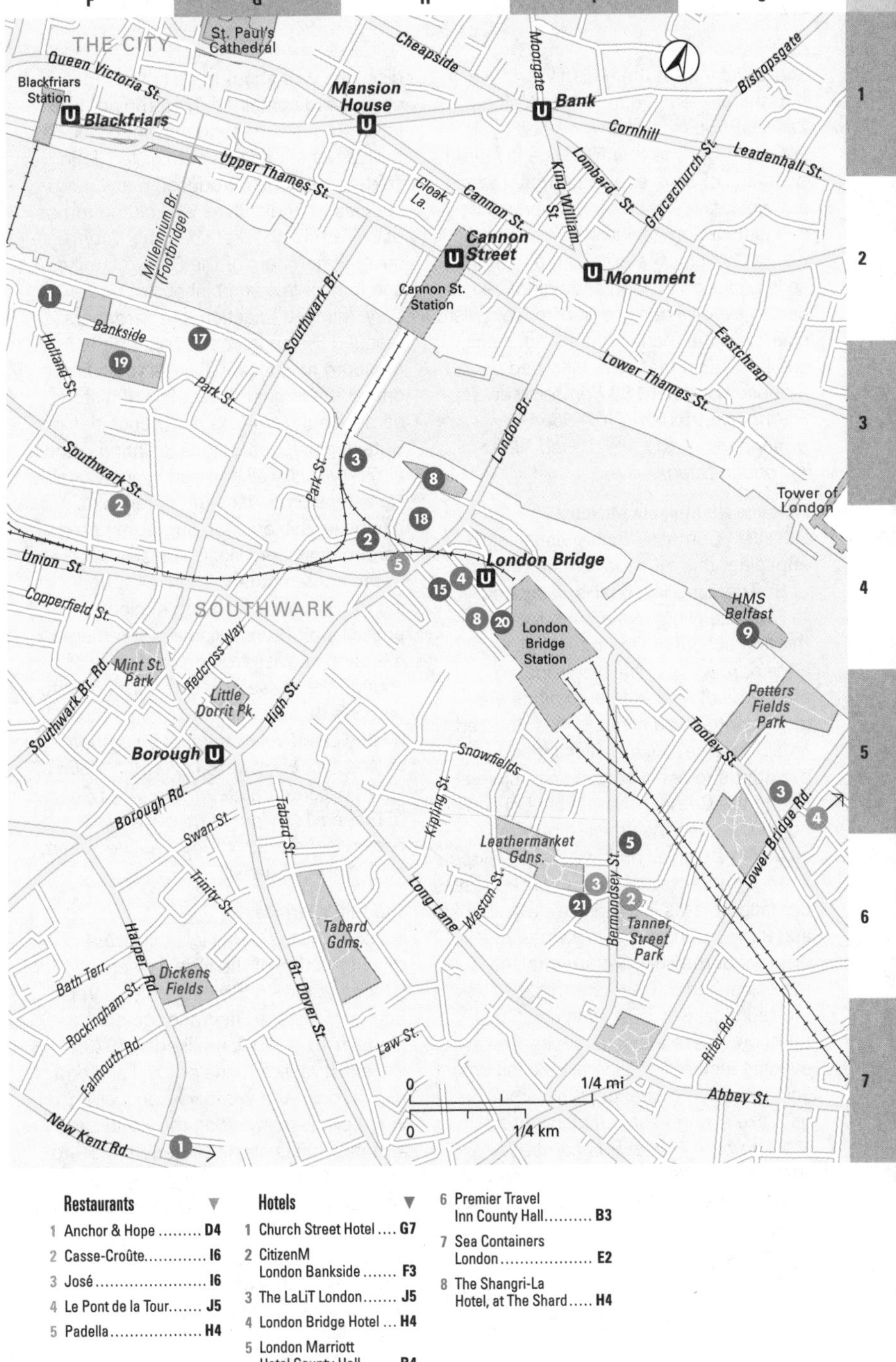

Restaurants

1 Anchor & Hope **D4**
2 Casse-Croûte............ **I6**
3 José **I6**
4 Le Pont de la Tour....... **J5**
5 Padella.................... **H4**

Hotels

1 Church Street Hotel **G7**
2 CitizenM London Bankside **F3**
3 The LaLiT London....... **J5**
4 London Bridge Hotel ... **H4**
5 London Marriott Hotel County Hall **B4**
6 Premier Travel Inn County Hall.......... **B3**
7 Sea Containers London.................. **E2**
8 The Shangri-La Hotel, at The Shard..... **H4**

and jewelry from the end of World War II to the present. Founded by designer Zandra Rhodes, and now owned by Newham College, the FTM is a favorite with fans of style and costumes. There are weekday fashion-based workshops and lectures on design and aspects of fashion history; the excellent gift shop sells books on fashion and one-of-a-kind pieces by local designers. After your visit, check out the many restaurants, cafés, and boutiques that have bloomed on Bermondsey Street. ✉ *83 Bermondsey St., Bermondsey* ☎ *020/7407–8664* 🌐 *www.ftmlondon.org* 🎫 *£9* 🕑 *Closed Mon.* Ⓜ *London Bridge.*

Florence Nightingale Museum

MUSEUM | Compact, highly visual, and engaging, this museum on the grounds of St. Thomas's Hospital is dedicated to Florence Nightingale, who founded the first school of nursing and played a major role in establishing modern standards of health care. Exhibits are divided into three areas: one is devoted to Nightingale's Victorian childhood, the others to her work tending soldiers during the Crimean War (1854–56) and her subsequent health-care reforms, including a display on how she developed a program for training nurses. The museum incorporates Nightingale's own books and famous lamp as well as interactive displays of medical instruments and medicinal herbs. There are free 15-minute tours daily at 3:30, with additional tours on weekends at 11:30, as well as evening lectures, temporary exhibitions, and a shop with unexpectedly amusing gifts like syringe-shaped highlighters. ✉ *2 Lambeth Palace Rd., Lambeth* ☎ *020/7620–0374* 🌐 *www.florence-nightingale.co.uk* 🎫 *£8* Ⓜ *Waterloo.*

The Garden Museum

GARDEN | This celebration of one of England's favorite hobbies was created in the mid-1970s after two gardening enthusiasts came upon a medieval church, which, they were horrified to discover, was about to be bulldozed. The churchyard contained the tombs of two adventurous 17th-century plant collectors, a father and son both called John Tradescant, who introduced many new species to England, as well as the tombs of William Bligh, captain of the *Bounty,* several members of the Boleyn family, and quite a few archbishops of Canterbury. Inspired to action, the gardeners rescued the church, and created the museum now inside it. Here you'll find one of the largest collections of historic garden tools, artifacts, and curiosities in Britain, plus photographs, paintings, and films—virtually all donated by individuals. An extension houses temporary exhibitions on subjects ranging from noted garden designers like Charles Jencks to the contemporary Guerilla Gardening movement (cultivating neglected public land). There's also a green-thumb gift shop, a glass-fronted café, and, of course, the museum's own four beautiful gardens that are maintained year-round by dedicated volunteers. ✉ *5 Lambeth Palace Rd., Lambeth* ☎ *020/7401–8865* 🌐 *www.gardenmuseum.org.uk* 🎫 *£10* 🕑 *Closed 1st Mon. of month and for occasional events; check website* Ⓜ *Lambeth North, Vauxhall.*

The *Golden Hinde*

MARINA | **FAMILY** | This is a full-size reconstruction of the little galleon in which the famed Elizabethan explorer Sir Francis Drake circumnavigated the globe in 1577–80. Launched in 1973, the exact replica made one full and one partial round-the-world voyage, calling in at ports—many along the Pacific and Atlantic coasts of the United States—to do duty as a maritime museum. Now berthed at the St. Mary Overie Dock, the ship continues its educational purpose, complete with a "crew" in period costumes and three decks of artifacts. The puppet show and pirate training sessions are especially popular with younger visitors. Call for information on guided tours. ✉ *St. Mary Overie Dock, Cathedral St.,*

Bankside ☎ *020/7403–0123* 🌐 *www.goldenhinde.co.uk* 🎫 *£5* Ⓜ *London Bridge.*

HMS *Belfast*

MILITARY SITE | FAMILY | At 613½ feet, this large light cruiser is one of the last remaining big-gun armored warships from World War II, in which it played an important role in protecting the Arctic convoys and supporting the D-Day landings in Normandy; the ship later saw action during the Korean War. This floating museum has been moored in the Thames as a maritime branch of **IWM London** since 1971. A tour of all nine decks—including an engine room 15 feet below sea level, the admiral's quarters, mess decks, bakery, punishment cells, operations room, and more—gives a vivid picture of life on board the ship, while the riveting interactive gun-turret experience puts you in the middle of a World War II naval battle. ✉ *The Queen's Walk, Borough* ☎ *020/7940–6300* 🌐 *www.iwm.org.uk* 🎫 *£18* Ⓜ *London Bridge.*

Horniman Museum

GARDEN | FAMILY | Set amid 16 acres of gardens, this eclectic museum is considered something of a well-kept secret by the residents of south London—perhaps because of its out-of-the-way location. You can explore world cultures, natural history, and a fine collection of some 1,300 musical instruments (including a giant tuba) here. The emphasis is on fun and a wide range of activities, including London's oldest nature trail that features domesticated creatures such as sheep, chickens, and alpacas, and an aquarium stocked with endangered species. It's also home to comically overstuffed taxidermied walrus who serves as the museum's unofficial mascot. It's a 15-minute bus ride from here to the Dulwich Picture Gallery; Bus P4, heading toward Brixton, takes you from door to door. ✉ *100 London Rd., Forest Hill, London* ☎ *020/8699–1872* 🌐 *www.horniman.ac.uk* 🎫 *Free (small charge for temporary exhibitions and aquarium)* Ⓜ *Overground: Forest Hill.*

★ **IWM London**

MUSEUM | FAMILY | Despite its name, the cultural venue formerly known as the Imperial War Museum (one of five IWM branches around the country) does not glorify either Empire or bloodshed but emphasizes understanding through conveying the impact of 20th- and 21st-century warfare on citizens and soldiers alike. A dramatic six-story atrium at the main entrance encloses an impressive amount of hardware—including a Battle of Britain Spitfire, a German V2 rocket, the remains of a car blown up in post-invasion Iraq, tanks, guns, and submarines—along with accompanying interactive material and a café. The First World War galleries explore the wartime experience on both the home and fighting fronts, with the most comprehensive collection on the subject in the world—some 1,300 objects ranging from uniforms, equipment, and weapons to letters and diaries. Three permanent exhibitions in the Second World War galleries shed light on that conflict: an extensive and haunting Holocaust exhibition; *A Family In Wartime,* which documents the story of one London family living through the Blitz; and *Turning Points 1934–1945,* which relates key moments in the conflict to objects on display. *Peace and Security 1945–2015* looks at more contemporary hostilities, including the Cold War, Iraq, Afghanistan, and Kosovo. Other galleries are devoted to works relating to conflicts from World War I to the present day by painters, poets, documentary filmmakers, and photographers. James Bond fans won't want to miss the intriguing Secret War Gallery, which charts the work of secret agents. ✉ *Lambeth Rd., South Bank* ☎ *020/7416–5000* 🌐 *www.iwm.org.uk* 🎫 *Free (charge for special exhibitions)* Ⓜ *Lambeth North.*

London Dungeon

LOCAL INTEREST | FAMILY | Saved by a keen sense of its own borderline ridiculousness, this gory attraction is full of over-the-top tableaux depicting the bloody

Built at the site of the original theater where Shakespeare's plays were performed, the modern-day Globe is a painstaking reconstruction of an open-air theater.

demise of famous figures alongside the torture, murder, and ritual slaughter of lesser-known victims, all to a sound track of screaming, wailing, and agonized moaning. There are lively dramatizations about the Great Plague, Henry VIII, (the fictional) Sweeney Todd, and (the real) Jack the Ripper, to name a few, with costumed characters leaping out of the gloom to bring the information to life and add to the fear and fun. Perhaps most shocking are the crowds of children baying to get in: most kids absolutely love this place, although those with more a sensitive disposition may find it too frightening (that goes for adults as well). Expect long lines on weekends and during school holidays. There are also adults-only evening tours that include drinks. ■ **TIP→ Tickets bought online and in advance can be up to 30% less than walk-up prices**. ✉ *Riverside Bldg., County Hall, Westminster Bridge Rd., South Bank* ☎ *0207/654–0809* 🌐 *www.thedungeons.com/london* 🎫 *From £24* Ⓜ *Waterloo.*

★ London Eye

VIEWPOINT | FAMILY | To mark the start of the new millennium, architects David Marks and Julia Barfield devised this instant icon that allows Londoners and visitors alike to see the city from a completely new perspective. The giant Ferris wheel was the largest cantilevered observation wheel ever built at the time, and remains one of the city's tallest structures. The 25-minute slow-motion ride inside one of the enclosed passenger capsules is so smooth you'd hardly know you were suspended over the Thames. On a clear day you can see up to 25 miles, with a bird's-eye view of London's most famous landmarks as you circle 360 degrees. If you're looking for a special place to celebrate, Champagne can be arranged ahead of time. ■ **TIP→ Buy your ticket online to avoid the long lines and get a 15% discount. For an extra £10, you can save even more time with a Fast Track flight (check in 15 minutes before your "departure").** You can also buy a combination ticket for the Eye and other London attractions (check online for details) or combine with a river cruise for a 40-minute sightseeing voyage on the Thames. In December, there's a scenic ice rink just below the wheel. ✉ *Jubilee Gardens, South Bank* ☎ *0871/781–3000* 🌐 *www.londoneye.com* 🎫 *From £27; cruise package from £39 (online only)* Ⓜ *Waterloo.*

Newport Street Gallery

MUSEUM | Putting the seal on Vauxhall's status as an up-and-coming neighborhood, business-savvy artist Damien Hirst opened this gallery in a cavernous space that was formerly a Victorian scenery-painting workshop. It currently houses a rotating selection from his large private collection of contemporary art that includes works by Francis Bacon, Banksy, Picasso, Jeff Koons, Richard Hamilton, and Tracey Emin, to name just a few, along with six-month-long solo shows for emerging artists. There's also a shop selling artists' books, limited-edition prints, and sculptures, while snacks and drinks are available from Pharmacy 2, which takes its name and some artwork from Hirst's fashionable (and now-closed) millennium-era Notting Hill watering hole. ✉ *Newport St., London* ☎ *020/3141–9320* 🌐 *www.newportstreetgallery.com* 🎫 *Free* ⏲ *Closed Mon.* Ⓜ *Vauxhall, Lambeth North.*

The Old Operating Theatre Museum and Herb Garret

MUSEUM | This rare example of a 19th-century operating theater, the oldest surviving one in Europe, dates back to 1822, when part of the large herb garret in the roof of the 17th-century St. Thomas's Church was converted for surgical use. The English baroque church was part of St. Thomas's Hospital, which was founded in the 12th century as a monastery that looked after the sick. In 1862, the hospital moved to its present Lambeth location and the operating theater was closed. It remained abandoned until 1956, when it was restored and turned into a medical museum. Today you can see the artifacts of early-19th-century medical practice: the wooden operating table under a skylight; the box of sawdust underneath used for absorbing blood; and the surrounding banks of seats where students crowded in to observe operations. On weekends at 11 and 4, there are demonstrations of pre-anesthetic surgical practices incorporating the knives, pliers, and handsaws that were the surgeons' tools back in the day (not for the fainthearted or small children). Next door is a re-creation of the 17th-century **Herb Garret,** with displays of the medicinal herbs St. Thomas's apothecary would have used, along with Sunday-afternoon "gore tours," a hands-on survey of Victorian surgical instruments, at 2. ⚠ **Access is by a 52-step spiral staircase, although disabled access by elevator is available by prior arrangement.** ✉ *9A St. Thomas St., Lambeth* ☎ *020/7188–2679* 🌐 *www.oldoperatingtheatre.com* 🎫 *£7* Ⓜ *London Bridge.*

SEA LIFE London Aquarium

ZOO | **FAMILY** | The curved, colonnaded, neoclassical former County Hall that once housed London's municipal government is now home to a superb three-level aquarium where you can walk above sharks and stingrays and view more than 600 other aquatic species, both common and rare. There are also hands-on displays. It's not the biggest aquarium you've ever seen, but the educational exhibits are particularly well arranged, with 17 themed zones for different oceans, water environments, and climates, ranging from a stunning coral reef to a seahorse colony to a rain forest. Regular feeding times and free talks are offered throughout the day. There are also special experiences that include behind-the-scenes tours and feeding (or, for the brave, snorkeling with) sharks at an extra charge. ■ **TIP→ Admission at peak periods is by 15-minute timed entry slot, but for an additional £10 you can purchase flexible priority-entry tickets that also avoid the long lines.** ✉ *County Hall, Westminster*

Designed by renowned architect Renzo Piano, the Shard punctures the London skyline with its record-breaking height and spectacular modernity.

Bridge Rd., South Bank ☎ 0871/663–1678 🌐 www.visitsealife.com 💷 From £27 Ⓜ Westminster, Waterloo.

★ Shakespeare's Globe

ARTS VENUE | FAMILY | This spectacular theater is a replica of Shakespeare's open-roof, wood-and-thatch Globe Playhouse (built in 1599 and burned down in 1613), where most of the Bard's greatest works premiered. American actor and director Sam Wanamaker worked ceaselessly for several decades to raise funds for the theater's reconstruction 200 yards from its original site, using authentic materials and techniques, a dream that was finally realized in 1997. "Groundlings" (patrons with £5 standing-only tickets) are not allowed to sit during the performance, but you get the best view of the stage and the most authentic viewing experience. Fortunately, you can reserve an actual seat on any one of the theater's three levels, but you will want to rent a cushion for £2 (or bring your own) to soften the backless wooden benches (cushions must be booked when you book your tickets). The show must go on, rain or shine, warm or chilly, so come prepared for anything. Umbrellas are banned, but you can bring a raincoat or buy a cheap Globe rain poncho, which doubles as a great souvenir. In the winter months, the Sam Wanamaker Playhouse, a 350-seat re-creation of an indoor Jacobean theater lighted by candles, offers plays and concerts in a less exposed though still atmospheric setting. Some Wanamaker benches are backless, and there are fixed standing positions in the theater's upper gallery. Forty-minute tours of the theater are offered every half-hour most days until 5 pm (unless there's a matinee performance or other major event, when they're offered until noon). There are also special kid-friendly tours (two adults, three children) for £46. Tours of the Wanamaker Playhouse are offered on an occasional basis and must be arranged directly with the theater; availability varies and is subject to change depending on performances and other events. You can also book a tour of the surrounding Bankside area, which emphasizes places Shakespeare would have frequented, including the archaeological remains of the nearby Rose Theatre, the oldest theater in Bankside. ✉ *21 New Globe Walk, Bankside* ☎ *020/7401–9919 general info* 🌐 *www.shakespearesglobe.com* 🎫 *Globe Theatre tour £17; Bankside tour £14; Wanamaker tour £14; Globe performances £5 (standing), from £19 (seated); Wanamaker performances £10 (standing), from £20 (seated)* ⏲ *No Globe performances mid-Oct.–mid-Apr.; no Wanamaker Playhouse performances mid-Apr.–mid.-Oct.* Ⓜ *London Bridge; Mansion House, then cross Southwark Bridge.*

Southwark Cathedral

RELIGIOUS SITE | Pronounced "Suthuck," this is the oldest Gothic church in London, parts of it dating back to the 12th century. It remains off-the-beaten track, despite being the site of some remarkable memorials and a concert program that offers free half-hour organ recitals at 1:10 pm every Monday (except in August and December) and classical music at 3:15 pm every Tuesday during the school year. Originally the priory church of St. Mary Overie (as in "over the water," on the South Bank), it became a palace church under Henry VIII (when it became known as St Saviour's) until some merchant parishioners bought it from James I in 1611. It was only promoted to cathedral status in 1905. Look for the vivid 15th-century roof bosses (small ornamental wood carvings); the gaudily renovated 1408 tomb of John Gower, Richard II's poet laureate and a friend of Chaucer's; and the Harvard Chapel, where John Harvard, a local butcher's son who went on to found the American university, was baptized. Another notable buried here (between the choir stalls) is Edmund Shakespeare, brother of William. Free 45-minute tours are offered on Tuesday at 2 and 3 pm, Wednesday at 3 pm, Thursday at 11:30 am, and Friday at 11 am and 3 pm. ✉ *London Bridge, Bankside* ☎ *020/7367–6700* 🌐 *cathedral.southwark.anglican.org* 🎫 *Free (suggested donation £4)* Ⓜ *London Bridge.*

★ **Tate Modern**

MUSEUM | This spectacular renovation of a mid-20th-century power station is one of the most-visited museums of modern art in the world. Its great permanent collection, which starts in 1900 and ranges from modernist masters like Matisse to the most cutting-edge contemporary artists, is arranged in eight areas by theme (for example, "Media Networks," about artists' responses to mass media) rather than by chronology. Its blockbuster temporary exhibitions have showcased the work of individual artists like Gauguin, Rauschenberg, Modigliani, Picasso, and O'Keefe, among others. Other major temporary exhibitions have a conceptual focus, like works created in response to the American Black Power movement or by Soviet and Russian artists between the Revolution and the death of Stalin.

The vast **Turbine Hall** is a dramatic entrance point used to showcase big audacious installations that tend to generate a lot of publicity. Past highlights include Olafur Eliasson's massive glowing sun, Ai Weiwei's porcelain "sunflower seeds," and Carsten Holler's huge metal slides.

On the ground floor of a 10-story addition, you'll find The Tanks, galleries devoted to various types of new art, including moving image, performance, soundscapes, and interactive works, while at the top is a roof terrace offering spectacular views of the London skyline. In between are three exhibition floors offering more room for large-scale installations, for art from outside Europe and North America, and for digital and interactive projects. The Start Display (Level 2) provides an introduction to the collection, highlighting art from various countries, cultures, and periods, all linked by color. Not to be missed in the original building is the collection of Rothko murals, originally created for the

Four Seasons restaurant in New York, and displays devoted to Gerhard Richter (both on Level 2), Antony Gormley, Jenny Holzer, and video pioneer Nam June Paik (Level 4).

Head to the restaurant on Level 9, the café on Level 1, or the Espresso Bar on Level 3 for stunning vistas of the Thames. The view of St. Paul's from the Espresso Bar's balcony is one of the best in London. Near the café you'll find the Drawing Bar, which lets you create work on one of several digital sketch pads and then project your result on the gallery wall.

You can join free 45-minute guided tours, each covering a different gallery: The Artist and Society at 11, In the Studio at noon, Performer and Participant at 1, Materials and Objects at 2, and Media Networks at 3. If you plan to visit Tate Britain too, take advantage of the Tate Boat, which takes visitors back and forth between the two Tates every 40 minutes. ✉ *Bankside* ☎ *020/7887–8888* 🌐 *www.tate.org.uk/modern* 🎫 *Free (charge for special exhibitions)* Ⓜ *Southwark, Blackfriars, St. Paul's.*

The View from the Shard

BUILDING | At 800 feet, this addition to the London skyline currently offers the highest vantage point in Western Europe. Designed by the noted architect Renzo Piano, it has attracted both admiration and disdain. While the building itself is generally highly regarded, many felt it would have been better sited in Canary Wharf (or perhaps Dubai), as it spoils views of St. Paul's Cathedral from traditional vantage points such as Hampstead's Parliament Hill. No matter how you feel about the building, there's no denying that it offers a spectacular 360-degree view over London (extending 40 miles on a clear day) from viewing platforms on level 69, and the open-air skydeck on level 72—almost twice as high as any other viewpoint in the city. Digital telescopes provide information about 200 points of interest. There's a weather guarantee that lets you return on a more clement day if visibility is seriously impeded, and various themed events like silent discos or early morning yoga classes are offered at an extra charge. Admission is by timed ticket only. If you find the price as eye-wateringly high as the viewing platforms, there's a less dramatic but still very impressive (and free) view from the lobby of the Shangri-La hotel on the 35th floor, or, in the evenings, the hotel's chic Gong bar on the 52nd floor (over-18s only). ✉ *Railway Approach, Borough* ☎ *0344/499–7222* 🌐 *www.theviewfromtheshard.com* 🎫 *From £32* Ⓜ *London Bridge.*

White Cube Bermondsey

MUSEUM | When the United Kingdom's highest-profile commercial gallery moved to this huge converted 1970s-era warehouse on Bermondsey Street, it sealed the area's reputation as a rising art-scene hot spot. This is the home gallery of some of today's top contemporary artists, including Tracey Emin, Gilbert and George, Georg Baselitz, Antony Gormley, Gabriel Orozco, Harland Miller, Anselm Kiefer, and several other artists with international reputations. An antiseptic central cuboid gallery, the "white cube"—also called 9 x 9 x 9 (meters, that is)—rests between two other spaces that host smaller exhibitions. There is also a bookshop and auditorium. ✉ *144–152 Bermondsey St., Bermondsey* ☎ *0207/930–5373* 🌐 *whitecube.com* 🕒 *Closed Mon.* Ⓜ *London Bridge.*

Restaurants

First mentioned in 1276 and believed to have existed in Roman times, Borough Market is a forever favorite with tourists, chefs, and foodies alike. Located under the Victorian wrought-iron railway arches near London Bridge, here you'll find food lovers eager to pick up produce, cheese, organically farmed meats, fresh fish, baked goods, condiments, pastries, and chocolates from the more than 120 stalls operated by some of the city's best artisanal food producers. A breakaway market on Maltby Street offers stalls that are smaller in number, but equally high in quality. Pubs, bars, restaurants, and specialty shops fill the surrounding streets, while a new restaurant row has sprung up on nearby Bermondsey Street, just south of the Shard.

Anchor & Hope

$$ | **MODERN BRITISH** | Exceptional Brit-focused fish and meat dishes at wallet-friendly prices fly out of the open kitchen at this permanently packed, no-reservations (apart for Sunday lunchtime) gastropub in Southwark. Pot-roast duck, braised pigs' cheeks, steamed Scottish haddock fillet, and beetroot with horseradish and watercress keep the British flag flying and punch above their weight in terms of taste and tenderness. **Known for:** innovative gastropub cuisine; buzzy and informal atmosphere; large crowds so prepare to wait and maybe share a table. *Average main: £18 36 The Cut, Southwark 020/7928–9898 www.anchorandhopepub.co.uk No dinner Sun.; no lunch Mon. Waterloo, Southwark.*

★ Casse-Croûte

$$ | **BISTRO** | This bistro on Bermondsey Street near the Shard is as French as a pack of Gauloises, from the yellow walls and red-and-white checked tablecloths to the perfectly executed classics like *lapin à la moutarde* (rabbit in a creamy mustard sauce), *suprême de volaille aux mousserons* (chicken breast stuffed with mushrooms), quiche Lorraine, and Paris-Brest (decadent choux pastry stuffed with praline and whipped cream). The daily changing menu offers three reasonably-priced options per course and the wine list (French, of course) goes off-the-beaten path with discoveries from small local producers. **Known for:** beautifully prepared bistro classics; authentic French atmosphere in tight quarters; reservations necessary for dinner. *Average main: £20 109 Bermondsey St., Bermondsey 020/7407–2140 www.cassecroute.co.uk No dinner Sun. London Bridge.*

José

$$ | **TAPAS** | Renowned chef José Pizarro has managed to re-create an authentic, slightly rustic Spanish tapas-and-sherry bar. With just 30 seats and no reservations, it's always packed after 6 pm, but it's worth the wait for remarkably fresh, perfectly prepared classic tapas plates like *patatas bravas, croquetas,* flash-fried prawns with chili and garlic, and razor clams with chorizo. **Known for:** notoriously long waits and large crowds; daily changing menu of authentic tapas; unique sherry menu. *Average main: £20 104 Bermondsey St., Southwark 020/7403–4902 www.josepizarro.com/jose-tapas-bar Borough, London Bridge.*

Le Pont de la Tour

$$$ | **FRENCH** | Formerly a temple to French haute cuisine, the restaurant has a new chef who has adopted a more innovative approach fused with Modern British touches, with dishes like hand-picked Devon crab with an apple and celeriac remoulade or Tournedos Rossini with seared duck foie gras and a truffle mash. Standards, like the prices, remain high, and the swanky dining room takes inspiration from the art deco liner the SS *Normandie*. **Known for:** stunning views of Tower Bridge and the Thames; outside terrace dining in nice weather; destination and celebration meals. *Average main: £32 36D Shad Thames, Bermondsey 020/7403–8403 www.lepontdelatour.co.uk London Bridge, Tower Hill.*

★ Padella

$ | **ITALIAN** | Sit at the galley kitchen counter and you can watch the chefs toss hot pans of authentic handmade Italian pasta, generally considered among the best in London. The acclaimed but amazingly affordable dishes include a ravioli with

Neal's Yard ricotta and sage butter, burrata with Puglian olive oil, papardelle with a slow-cooked beef-shin ragù, or Dorset crab tagliarini with chili and lemon. **Known for:** low priced, high-quality handmade Italian pasta; papardelle with eight-hour beef-shin ragù; no reservations and waits can be long. *Average main: £7 6 Southwark St., Borough www.padella.co Borough, London Bridge.*

Hotels

★ Church Street Hotel

$ | **HOTEL** | Like rays of sunshine in gritty south London, the rooms at this Camberwell hotel are decorated in rich colors that evoke Mexico, a theme enhanced by authentic touches like elaborately painted crucifixes, tiles handmade in Guadalajara, and homemade iron bed frames. **Pros:** individual and fun vibe; great breakfasts; closer to central London than it might appear. **Cons:** location very urban and busy; a mile from a Tube station (though bus connections are handier); some rooms have shared bathrooms. *Rooms from: £115 29–33 Camberwell Church St., Camberwell, South East London 020/7703–5984 www.churchstreethotel.com 31 rooms Free breakfast Oval St.*

CitizenM London Bankside

$$ | **HOTEL** | High-concept, high-tech, and supertrendy, this Dutch budget boutique minichain has a unique selling point—nearly everything at the hotel is self-service, and that includes check-in and breakfast. **Pros:** free Wi-Fi and free movies; stylish and modern decor; 24-hour self-service canteen. **Cons:** only really qualifies as "budget" on certain nights (price is higher midweek); might be too much technology for some; rooms are compact. *Rooms from: £126 20 Lavington St., Bankside 020/3519–1680 www.citizenm.com/destinations/london/london-bankside-hotel 192 rooms No meals Southwark.*

The LaLiT London

$$$ | **HOTEL** | A stone's throw from City Hall and just down the road from the Shard, this luxurious hotel (the first international expansion from the India-based LaliT chain) harks backs to the building's former incarnation as a Victorian grammar school, designating bedrooms as different types of classrooms and meeting rooms as laboratories. **Pros:** decor combines English heritage with Indian warmth and color; lots of Indian dining options; complimentary minibar (and stuffed elephant toys) in all rooms. **Cons:** basic rooms are much smaller than their more expensive counterparts; location a bit out of the way and dead on weekends; theme might be too in-your-face for some. *Rooms from: £329 181 Tooley St., London Bridge 020/3765–0000 www.thelalit.com/the-lalit-london 70 rooms No meals London Bridge.*

London Bridge Hotel

$$ | **HOTEL** | Steps away from the London Bridge rail and Tube stations, and handy for the South Bank, this thoroughly modern stylish hotel is popular with business travelers, but leisure travelers find it just as appealing. **Pros:** helpful concierge; free Wi-Fi; good deals available online in the off-season. **Cons:** small bedrooms; prices rise by £100 or more midweek; area is filled with crowds on evenings and weekends. *Rooms from: £190 8–18 London Bridge St., Southwark 020/7855–2200 www.londonbridgehotel.com 141 rooms No meals London Bridge.*

London Marriott Hotel County Hall

$$ | **HOTEL** | This grand hotel on the Thames enjoys perhaps the most iconic view in the city—right next door is the London Eye, and directly across the Thames are the Houses of Parliament and Big Ben. Until the 1980s this building was the seat of London's government, and the public areas are suitably grand, full of pedimented archways, bronze doors, and acres of polished mahogany.

Pros: handy for South Bank arts scene, the London Eye, and Westminster; great pool; good weekend discounts. **Cons:** executive level lounge not up to usual standard; rooms facing the river cost extra; high summer midweek rates are just ridiculous. *Rooms from: £250 London County Hall, Westminster Bridge Rd., South Bank 020/7928–5200, 888/236–2427 in U.S. www.marriott.com/hotels/travel/lonch-london-marriott-hotel-county-hall 206 rooms No meals Westminster, Waterloo. National Rail: Waterloo.*

Premier Travel Inn County Hall
$$ | HOTEL | FAMILY | The small but nicely decorated rooms at this budget choice are in the same County Hall complex as the fancier London Marriott Hotel County Hall, and, though it lacks the spectacular river views and facilities are more basic, it has the same convenient location at a fraction of the price. **Pros:** fantastic location for the South Bank; bargains to be had if you book in advance; kids (sharing with adults) stay free. **Cons:** limited services; cookie-cutter chain-hotel atmosphere; on a busy road. *Rooms from: £129 County Hall, Belvedere Rd., South Bank 0871/527–8648 www.premierinn.com 318 rooms No meals Westminster, Waterloo. National Rail: Waterloo.*

Sea Containers London
$$$ | HOTEL | The achingly hip Sea Containers started life as part of London's docklands, and is now a fun callback to the area's history. **Pros:** excellent bars and restaurants; beautiful river views; short riverside walk to Tate Modern and Shakespeare's Globe. **Cons:** river-view rooms are pricey (of course); public areas can be noisy; standard rooms are small. *Rooms from: £256 Sea Containers House, 20 Upper Ground, Southwark 020/3747–1000 www.seacontainerslondon.com 359 rooms No meals Blackfriars, Southwark.*

★ **The Shangri-La Hotel, at The Shard**
$$$$ | HOTEL | With its floor-to-ceiling windows, the city's highest cocktail bar and infinity pool, and unrivaled views of the London skyline from 1,016 feet above the South Bank of the Thames, the Shangri-La has become one of London's most chic addresses. **Pros:** perhaps the best views in the city; great infinity pool and spa; superb restaurants and cocktail bar. **Cons:** design flaw allows some guests to see into neighboring rooms at night; decor may be too understated for some; restaurant, bar, and elevator can be crowded due to popularity of the view. *Rooms from: £468 31 St. Thomas St., South Bank 0207/234–8000 www.the-shard.com/shangri-la 202 rooms No meals London Bridge Station.*

Nightlife

Recent years have seen an explosion in south London nightlife, as Brixton becomes more gentrified, artists flock to Peckham, and the gay scene in Vauxhall remains thriving. Head to the area around Borough Market—one of London's oldest neighborhoods—for lively historic pubs where locals and tourists jostle for craft ales and gourmet snacks.

BARS

Aqua Shard
BARS/PUBS | This sophisticated bar on level 31 of the iconic Shard is worth a visit for the phenomenal views alone. The cocktail list is pretty special, too—big on fruit purees and unusual bitters. No reservations are taken in the bar, so be prepared to wait during busy periods. *The Shard, 31 St. Thomas St., Level 31, London Bridge 020/3011–1256 www.aquashard.co.uk London Bridge.*

Royal Vauxhall Tavern
CABARET | This former Victorian pub near the cricket grounds has been hosting drag acts since the days of World War II, with Princess Diana reportedly visiting

in the late 1980s disguised as a man and accompanied by Freddy Mercury. LBGT-oriented entertainment is still its mainstay, with the long-running avant garde club night Duckie providing "queer heritage, performance art, and honky-tonk" every Saturday night. Other favorites are a bingo-cabaret night and traditional drag performance extravaganzas, some featuring RuPaul Drag Race alums. The atmosphere is welcoming, inclusive, and fun. ✉ *372 Kennington Ln., London* ☎ *020/7820–1222* 🌐 *www.vauxhalltavern.com* Ⓜ *Vauxhall.*

Three Eight Four

BARS/PUBS | Epitomizing a new breed of Brixton bar, Three Eight Four is known for its innovative cocktails and tapas-style shared plates. The cocktail menu changes seasonally but always involves artisinal spirits and unusual mixing techniques—try the Nightshade, which comes with a pipette that you use to add the final ingredient (crème de cassis) yourself. The bare lightbulbs and stripped brick walls are a bit of a hipster bar cliché, but this place manages it with particular panache. ✉ *384 Coldharbour La., Brixton* ☎ *020/3417–7309* 🌐 *www.threeeightfour.com* Ⓜ *Brixton.*

PUBS

George Inn

BARS/PUBS | Not every pub is also a Grade I-listed, National Trust property, but this is London's last surviving galleried coaching inn. Dickens once frequented the inn's Coffee Room (now the Middle Bar), and name-checked The George in *Little Dorrit.* The gallery overlooks a cobblestone courtyard where plays may have been performed in Elizabethan times (galleried inns were frequently used as production venues), although the current building dates back only to 1677 after the original was destroyed in a fire. The interior is a maze of 18th-century low-ceilinged rooms replete with wood-panel walls and period features. The cozy Parliament Bar, where passengers would have waited for the coach, is on the ground floor, while a restaurant is upstairs on the galleried level. Luckily the pub is not just a museum piece—it also has modern amenities like a beer garden and Wi-Fi. ✉ *77 Borough High St., South Bank* ☎ *020/7407–2056* 🌐 *www.greeneking-pubs.co.uk/pubs/greater-london/george-southwark* Ⓜ *London Bridge.*

The Market Porter

BARS/PUBS | If you find yourself craving a drink at 6 am, this traditional London pub is for you. The early opening hour is not because it caters to alcoholics but for the Borough Market stallholders, who have already put in several hours come open time. The S-shape Victorian-era bar, with its walls and ceiling covered in pump badges and beer mats, is packed when the market is busy but calms down during off-peak hours. There are 12 real ales on draught and decent pub grub using seasonal produce from the market is served in the restaurant upstairs. The pub also provided the location for the "Third Hand Emporium" in the movie version of *Harry Potter and the Prisoner of Azkaban.* ✉ *9 Stoney St., Borough* ☎ *020/7407–2495* 🌐 *www.themarketporter.co.uk* Ⓜ *London Bridge.*

The Mayflower

BARS/PUBS | With a solid claim to being the oldest pub on the Thames, this deeply atmospheric riverside inn dates back to the mid-16th century (although it was rebuilt in the 17th) and comes with exposed beams, mullioned windows, open fires, and nautical design touches. You can sit outside on the heated jetty, which overlooks the original mooring of the *Mayflower*; it was here that Captain Christopher Jones took on 65 passengers who were to become some of the original Pilgrims when the ship sailed for America in 1620 (Jones is buried in the nearby church of St. Mary's in Rotherhithe). The Mayflower, formerly known as the Spread Eagle, is also the only pub licensed to sell U.S. and U.K. postage

Contemporary Art: London Today

In the 21st century, the focus of the city's art scene has shifted from the past to the future. Helped by the prominence of Tate Modern, London's contemporary art scene has never been so high profile. In publicly funded exhibition spaces like the Barbican Gallery, the Hayward Gallery, and the Institute of Contemporary Arts, London now has a modern art environment on par with that of Bilbao and New York. The so-called Young British Artists (YBAs, although no longer that young) Damien Hirst, Tracey Emin, and others are firmly planted in the public imagination. The celebrity status of British artists has a lot to do with the annual Turner Prize, which always stirs up controversy in the media during the display of the work, usually at Tate Britain.

Depending on who you talk to, the Saatchi Gallery is considered to be either the savior of contemporary art or the wardrobe of the emperor's new clothes. After a couple of moves it is now ensconced in the former Duke of York's barracks off Chelsea's King's Road.

The South Bank's Tate Modern may house the giants of modern art, but east London is where the innovative action is. There are dozens of galleries in the fashionable spaces around Old Street, and the truly hip have already moved even farther afield, to areas such as Bethnal Green, to the east, and Peckham, to the south. The Whitechapel Art Gallery and Jay Jopling's influential White Cube, with branches in Bermondsey and St. James's, remain essential parts of the new art establishment and continue to show exciting work by emerging British artists.

On the first Thursday of every month, more than 130 museums and galleries in east London stay open late and host talks, workshops, and other events (more information at 🌐 *www.first-thursdays.co.uk*).

stamps (inquire at the bar), a tradition dating back to the 1800s when time-pressed sailors were able to order a pint and a postage stamp at the same time. ✉ *117 Rotherhithe St., South East London* ☎ *020/7237–4088* 🌐 *www.mayflowerpub.co.uk* Ⓜ *Overground: Rotherhithe.*

Performing Arts

The South Bank and its easterly near neighbor Bankside together make up one of the richest areas in London when it comes to arts and entertainment. Whether you want to watch a play, hear a concert, or see an art exhibit, you won't have to wander far to find something top class. Venture a little farther into south London for a sprinkling of fringe theaters that act as incubators for the capital's mainstream theater scene.

FILM

BFI London IMAX Cinema

FILM | FAMILY | The British Film Institute's glazed drum-shape IMAX theater (now, confusingly, operated by Odeon) has the largest screen in the United Kingdom (approximately 75 feet wide and the height of five double-decker buses). It shows state-of-the-art 2-D and 3-D films. ✉ *1 Charlie Chaplin Walk, South Bank* ☎ *0330/333–7878* 🌐 *www.bfi.org.uk/imax* 🎟 *From £15* Ⓜ *Waterloo.*

BFI Southbank

FILM | With the best repertory programming in London, the four movie theaters here are effectively a national film center run by the British Film Institute. More than 1,000 titles are screened each year, with art-house, foreign, silent, overlooked, classic, noir, and short films favored over recent Hollywood blockbusters. The center also has a gallery, bookshop, and "mediatheque" where visitors can watch film and television from the National Archive for free (closed Monday). The Riverfront Bar and Kitchen offers dining with views while the Benugo BFI Bar and Kitchen is informal and buzzy. This is one of the venues for the BFI London Film Festival; throughout the year there are minifestivals, seminars, and guest speakers. ✉ *Belvedere Rd., South Bank* ☎ *020/7928–3232* 🌐 *www.bfi.org.uk* 🎟 *From £10* Ⓜ *Waterloo.*

PERFORMING ARTS CENTERS

The Scoop at More London

CULTURAL FESTIVALS | FAMILY | This 800-seat open-air amphitheater next to City Hall hosts free musical performances in July, theater productions in August (often family-friendly retellings of classic Greek plays, with post-show chats taking place on select dates), and film screenings in September (including live relays from the Royal Opera House) as well as talks every night during all three months, plus circus and dance workshops. The emphasis is on community accessibility and family-friendly programming. ✉ *Queens Walk, London Bridge* ☎ *020/7403–4866* 🌐 *www.londonbridgecity.co.uk/events* 🎟 *Free* Ⓜ *London Bridge, Tower Hill.*

★ **Southbank Centre**

ART GALLERIES—ARTS | FAMILY | The general public has never really warmed to the Southbank Centre's hulking concrete buildings (beloved by architecture aficionados), products of the Brutalist style popular when the center was built in the 1950s and '60s—but all the same, the masses flock to the concerts, recitals, festivals, and exhibitions held here, Europe's largest arts center. The **Royal Festival Hall** is truly a People's Palace, with seats for 2,900 and a schedule that ranges from major symphony orchestras to pop stars. The smaller **Queen Elizabeth Hall** is more classically oriented. It contains the **Purcell Room,** which hosts lectures and chamber performances. For art, head to the **Hayward Gallery**, which hosts shows on top contemporary artists such as Antony Gormley and Cy Twombly. The center's riverside street level has a terrific assortment of restaurants and bars, though you'll need to head to The Cut, just south of here, for independent eateries. ✉ *Belvedere Rd., South Bank* ☎ *020/3879–9555* 🌐 *www.southbankcentre.co.uk* 🎟 *Free–£120* Ⓜ *Waterloo, Embankment.*

THEATER

★ **Battersea Arts Centre** *(BAC)*

ARTS CENTERS | Battersea Arts Centre has a reputation for producing innovative new work as well as hosting top alternative stand-up comics. Performances take place in quirky spaces all over this atmospheric former town hall. Check out Scratch events, low-tech theater where the audience provides feedback on works-in-progress. Entry for Scratch events is pay-what-you-can (minimum £3). The bar, which serves snacks and sharing plates, is open all day. ✉ *176 Lavender Hill, Battersea* ☎ *020/7223–2223* 🌐 *www.bac.org.uk* 🎟 *Pay what you can (£3 suggested)–£30* Ⓜ *National Rail: Clapham Junction.*

Menier Chocolate Factory

THEATER | This converted industrial space has become celebrated for its inspired reworkings of classic musicals, with several of its productions eventually transferring to the West End and even winning Tonys on Broadway. It's not unusual for shows to feature top British talent and stars-of-tomorrow like Sharon Horgan and Tom Hollander before they become famous. It also hosts comedy nights and there's an excellent Modern British restaurant on-site. ✉ *53 Southwark St., London* ☎ *020/7378–1713* 🌐 *www.menierchocolatefactory.com* 🎫 *From £38* Ⓜ *London Bridge.*

★ National Theatre

THEATER | FAMILY | When this complex designed by Sir Denys Lasdun opened in 1976, Londoners were slow to warm-up to the low-rise Brutalist block, with Prince Charles describing it as "a clever way of building a nuclear power station in the middle of London without anyone objecting." But whatever you think of the outside, the inside offers generally superb theatrical experiences at (relatively) friendly prices—several of which (like *War Horse* or *One Man, Two Guvnors*) have gone on to become long-running Broadway hits. Interspersed with the three theaters—the 1,150-seat Olivier, the 890-seat Lyttelton, and the 450-seat Dorfman—is a multilayered foyer with exhibitions, bars, restaurants, and free entertainment. Musicals, classics, and plays are performed by top-flight professionals, who you can sometimes catch giving foyer talks as well. Backstage, costume, and architecture tours are available daily at 9:45 am except Sunday. The Clore Learning Centre offers courses and events on different aspects of theater production, and you can watch staff at work on set building and scenery painting from the Sherling High-Level Walkway. Each weekend in August, the free outdoor River Stage Festival presents live music, dance, family workshops, and DJ sets in front of the theater. ✉ *Belvedere Rd., South Bank* ☎ *020/7452–3000* 🌐 *www.nationaltheatre.org.uk* 🎫 *From £15, tours £13* Ⓜ *Waterloo.*

The Old Vic

THEATER | In 2015, Matthew Warchus, the director behind *Matilda the Musical,* took over as artistic director of this grand old theater, where stage legends like John Gielgud, Vivien Leigh, Peter O'Toole, Richard Burton, and Judi Dench once trod the boards. Today, it still produces some of the best shows in London, some featuring contemporary stars like Andrew Scott and Claire Foy. ✉ *The Cut, Southwark* ☎ *0844/871–7628* 🌐 *www.oldvictheatre.com* 🎫 *From £10* Ⓜ *Waterloo, Southwark.*

Unicorn Theatre

THEATER | FAMILY | Dedicated to innovative work for young audiences, this modern theater hosts plays, musicals, and interactive theater for everyone from toddlers on up. Inclusivity is a major focus, with performances for those with visual and hearing and other impairments taking place regularly. ✉ *147 Tooley St., Borough* ☎ *020/7645–0560* 🌐 *www.unicorntheatre.com* 🎫 *From £12* Ⓜ *London Bridge.*

Young Vic

THEATER | Just down the road from its elder sibling The Old Vic, this offshoot hosts big names performing alongside emerging talent, often in daring innovative productions of both new and classic plays that appeal to a more diverse audience than is traditionally found on the London scene. Good food is served all day at the bustling bar. ✉ *66 The Cut, Waterloo, South Bank* ☎ *020/7922–2922* 🌐 *www.youngvic.org* 🎫 *From £10* Ⓜ *Southwark, Waterloo.*

Shopping

ART

Oxo Tower Wharf

CRAFTS | The artisans creating fashion, jewelry, home accessories, textiles, prints and photographs, furniture, and other design items have to pass rigorous selection procedures to set up shop in these prime riverside studios, where they make, display, and sell their work. The Oxo Tower Restaurant & Brasserie on the top floor is expensive, but with its fantastic view of London, it's worth popping up for a drink. There's also a public terrace where you can take in the view. ✉ *Oxo Tower Wharf, Bargehouse*

St., South Bank ☎ 020/7021–1686 24-hr info 🌐 www.coinstreet.org ⏲ Closed Mon. Ⓜ *Waterloo.*

MARKETS

Bermondsey Square Antiques Market
ANTIQUES/COLLECTIBLES | The early bird catches the worm at this Friday market, so come before dawn (flashlight recommended) to bag a bargain at London's largest antiques market. Dealers also arrive before dawn to snap up the best curios and silver, paintings, objets d'art, and furniture. The early start grew out of a loophole in the law (dating from when the market began on the site in 1885) that said stolen goods bought during the hours of darkness could not be prosecuted as the origin of the goods could not be determined. While stolen goods are no longer welcome here, the market has expanded to some 200 stalls, including food, clothing, and crafts. It finishes at 2 pm. ✉ *Long La. and Bermondsey Sq., Bermondsey* 🌐 *www.bermondseysquare.net* ⏲ *Closed Sat.–Thurs.* Ⓜ *London Bridge.*

Chapter 10

KENSINGTON, CHELSEA, KNIGHTSBRIDGE, AND BELGRAVIA

Updated by
Ellin Stein

Sights ★★★★☆ | Restaurants ★★★★☆ | Hotels ★★★★☆ | Shopping ★★★★★ | Nightlife ★★☆☆☆

KENSINGTON, CHELSEA, KNIGHTSBRIDGE, AND BELGRAVIA SNAPSHOT

TOP REASONS TO GO

The V&A Museum: The Victoria & Albert is the world's best decorative arts museum, with millions of objects to dazzle you.

The Natural History Museum: With panels depicting creatures both living and extinct, this is one of the world's most impressive natural history collections; keep an eye out for the animatronic *T. rex*.

Kensington Palace: The public areas and gardens of this royal family home show off some of the beauty enjoyed by its past and present residents, including Queen Victoria, Princess Diana, and the Duke and Duchess of Cambridge (William and Kate) and their children.

Hyde Park: Explore one of London's largest green spaces by walking, cycling (free docked bikes are available at several locations), or rowing on the Serpentine, the tranquil lake that snakes through the park.

The Serpentine Galleries: Expand your cultural horizons at one of London's foremost showcases for modern art, or just have a bite at the café in the extension to the Serpentine Sackler Gallery, designed by famed architect Zaha Hadid and a work of art in itself.

GETTING THERE

Several Tube stations are nearby: Sloane Square and High Street Kensington on the District and Circle lines; Knightsbridge and Hyde Park Corner on the Piccadilly Line; and South Kensington, and Gloucester Road on the District, Circle, and Piccadilly lines.

MAKING THE MOST OF YOUR TIME

You could fill three or four days in this borough, especially if you enjoy museums. Give yourself at least a half day for the Victoria & Albert Museum, a half day for Kensington Palace, and a half day for either the Natural History Museum or the Science Museum.

QUICK BITES

■ **Duke of York Square Farmers' Market** West London's answer to Borough Market, this Saturday open-air market is in a pedestrian-only plaza off Duke of York Square, a chic shopping precinct. It hosts 40 stalls purveying artisanal and locally produced products from more than 150 small producers. Like Borough Market, this is a grazer's paradise, giving you the chance to sample fresh oysters and cooked sausages as well as yummy hot snacks from countries ranging from Brazil to Thailand. ✉ *Duke of York Sq., Chelsea* ☎ *020/7823–5577* 🌐 *www.dukeofyorksquare.com* ⊗ *Closed Sun.–Fri.* Ⓜ *Sloane Sq.*

■ **Stick and Bowl** This hole-in-the-wall restaurant, a neighborhood favorite for more than 20 years, is an amazing bargain for this pricey part of town, serving good basic Chinese food at reasonable prices. Standouts on the extensive menu include baked fried chicken and rice, crispy pork belly, and seafood hor-fun. ✉ *31 Kensington High St., Kensington* ☎ *020/7937–2778* ▭ *No credit cards* Ⓜ *High St. Kensington.*

The Royal Borough of Kensington & Chelsea (or K&C, as the locals call it) is where you'll find London at its richest, and not just in the moneyed sense. South Kensington offers a concentration of great museums near Cromwell Road, with historic Kensington Palace and Kensington Gardens nearby in Hyde Park. Once-raffish Chelsea, where the Pre-Raphaelites painted and Mick Jagger partied, is now a thoroughly respectable home for the discreetly wealthy, while flashier Knightsbridge has become a haven for international plutocrats, with shopping to match their tastes.

Kensington

Kensington comprises the area along the southern edge of Hyde Park from Exhibition Road (where the big museum complex is) and the area to the west of the park bordered by leafy Holland Park Avenue on the north and traffic-heavy Cromwell Road on the south. This more westerly zone includes the satellite neighborhood of Holland Park, with its serenely grand villas and charming park, as well as local shopping mecca Kensington High Street and the antiques shops on Kensington Church Street.

The area's green lung is the 350-acre **Hyde Park,** an oasis offering rolling lawns, ancient trees, boating on a meandering lake, swimming, formal gardens, a playground, a leading contemporary art gallery, and even a palace.

Kensington's first royal connection was created when King William III became fed up with the dampness arising from the Thames, so he bought a country place there in 1689 and converted it into **Kensington Palace.** Surrounding the palace are the formal **Kensington Gardens,** originally laid out in the 17th century by William III. Also part of the Gardens is the children's playground dedicated to Diana, Princess of Wales, and, to the north (Bayswater) side, the Italian Gardens, an ornamental water garden with four main fountains, originally proposed by Queen Victoria's consort, Prince Albert and modeled on the gardens he introduced at Osborne House. The profits from the Great Exhibition of 1851, organized by Prince Albert, were used, at Albert's urging, to buy the land which became the site of a complex of colleges and museums that would eventually include the **Victoria & Albert Museum (V&A)**, the **Science Museum**, and the **Natural History Museum**. Posthumous tributes to the prince in the area include the **Royal Albert Hall**, with bas-reliefs that make it resemble a giant, redbrick Wedgwood teapot, and the small but lavish **Albert Memorial**.

Turn into Derry Street or Young Street and enter **Kensington Square**, one of the most complete 17th-century residential squares in London. **18 Stafford Terrace**, the perfectly preserved family home of a well-to-do, aesthetically inclined Victorian household, is nearby.

Sights

Albert Memorial

MEMORIAL | This gleaming, neo-Gothic shrine to Prince Albert created by Sir Gilbert Scott epitomizes the Victorian era. After Albert's early death from typhoid in 1861, his grieving widow, Queen Victoria, had this elaborate confection erected to the west of where Albert's brainchild, the Great Exhibition of 1851, had been held a decade before. A 14-foot gilt-bronze statue of the prince rests on a 15-foot-high pedestal, along with other statues representing his passions and interests. ✉ *Kensington Gardens, Kensington* Ⓜ *S. Kensington, High St. Kensington.*

Design Museum

MUSEUM | Located in the former Commonwealth Institute, this museum was the first in the United Kingdom to place everyday contemporary objects in a social and cultural context and to consider their role in the history of design. A free, permanent exhibition displays some 1,000 examples of 20th- and 21st-century design—from furniture, fashion, and domestic products to digital technology, architecture, and engineering. The temporary exhibitions may be focused on leading individual designers, such as Charles and Ray Eames, Isamu Noguchi, Terence Conran, or David Adjaye, on themes such as the global influence of Californian design or the role of design in related art forms, like an exhibition devoted to the work of director Stanley Kubrick. There's also a design library and archive, two shops, a café, and a restaurant. ■ **TIP→ Young designers ages 5–11 may enjoy the free, drop-in "Create and Make" workshops held the last Sunday of every month.** ✉ *224–238 Kensington High St., Kensington* ☎ *020/3862–5900* 🌐 *www.designmuseum.org* 💷 *Free (charge for temporary exhibitions)* Ⓜ *High St. Kensington.*

18 Stafford Terrace

HOUSE | The home of *Punch* cartoonist Edward Linley Sambourne in the 1870s, this charming house is a rare example of the "Aesthetic interior" style; it displays delightful Victorian and Edwardian antiques, fabrics, and paintings, as well as several samples of Linley Sambourne's work for *Punch*. The Italianate house was the scene for society parties when Sambourne's granddaughter Anne Messel was in residence in the 1940s. This being Kensington, there's inevitably a royal connection: Messel's son, Antony Armstrong-Jones, was married to the late Princess Margaret, and their son has preserved the connection by taking the title Viscount Linley. On Wednesday and weekends, 75-minute guided tours are given in the morning (reservations required)—with Saturday tours given by costumed actors—but in the afternoons, you are free to wander at will. There's also a costumed evening tour the third Wednesday of every month. ✉ *18 Stafford Terr., Kensington* ☎ *0207/602–3316* www.rbkc.gov.uk/linleysambourne-house £9, morning tour £12, evening tour £20 Closed Mon., Tues., Thurs., and Fri. High St. Kensington.

★ Hyde Park

CITY PARK | **FAMILY** | Along with the smaller St. James's and Green parks to the east, the 350-acre Hyde Park grew out of Henry VIII's hunting grounds. Along its south side runs Rotten Row, once Henry's royal path to the hunt—the name is a corruption of *Route du Roi* (Route of the King). It's still used by the Household Cavalry, who live at the Hyde Park Barracks, a high-rise and a low, ugly red block to the left. You can see the Guardsmen in full regalia leaving on horseback for guard duty at Buckingham Palace at about 10:30 (or come at noon when they return). Hyde Park is wonderful for strolling, cycling, or just relaxing by the Serpentine, the long body of water near its southern border. On the south side, the Lido Café and Bar by the 1930s Serpentine Lido is a good spot to refuel, and close-by is the Princess Diana Memorial Fountain. On Sunday, you'll find the uniquely British tribute to free speech, Speakers' Corner, close to Marble Arch. Though not what it was in the days before people could use the Internet to vent their spleen, it still offers a unique assortment of passionate, if occasionally irrational, advocates literally getting up on soapboxes. Summer sees giant pop concerts with top artists while during the Christmas season the park hosts a "Winter Wonderland" amusement park, Christmas market, and ice rink. *Hyde Park 030/0061–2114 www.royalparks.org.uk Free Hyde Park Corner, Knightsbridge, Lancaster Gate, Marble Arch.*

★ Kensington Gardens

GARDEN | **FAMILY** | Laid out in 1689 by William III, who commissioned Sir Christopher Wren to build Kensington Palace, the gardens are a formal counterpart to neighboring Hyde Park. Just to the north of the palace itself is the Dutch-style **Sunken Garden .** Nearby, the 1912 bronze statue *Peter Pan* commemorates the boy in J. M. Barrie's story who lived on an island in the Serpentine and who never grew up. Kids will enjoy the magical **Diana, Princess of Wales' Memorial Playground,** whose design was also inspired by Barrie's book. The **Elfin Oak** is a 900-year-old tree trunk that was carved with scores of tiny elves, fairies, and other fanciful creations in the 1920s. The **Italian Gardens,** an ornamental water garden commissioned by Prince Albert in 1860, comprise several ornamental ponds and fountains (there's also a nice café on-site), while the **Round Pond** attracts model-boat enthusiasts. *Kensington 030/0061–2000 www.royalparks.org.uk Free High St. Kensington, Lancaster Gate, Queensway, South Kensington.*

★ Kensington Palace

CASTLE/PALACE | **FAMILY** | This is a rare chance to get a glimpse into the more domestic and personal side of royal life. Neither as imposing as Buckingham Palace nor as charming as Hampton Court, Kensington Palace is something of a Royal Family commune, with various close relatives of the Queen occupying large apartments in the private part of the palace. Bought in 1689 by Queen Mary and King William III, it was converted into a palace by Sir Christopher Wren and Nicholas Hawksmoor, and royals have been in residence ever since. Princess Diana lived here with her sons after her divorce, and this is where Prince William now lives with his wife, Catherine, Duchess of Cambridge, and their three children. Prince Harry also shared his cottage on the grounds with Meghan Markle before their marriage.

The State Apartments are open to the public. The Queen's State Apartments are the private quarters of Queen Mary II, who ruled jointly with her husband, William II. By contrast, the lavish King's

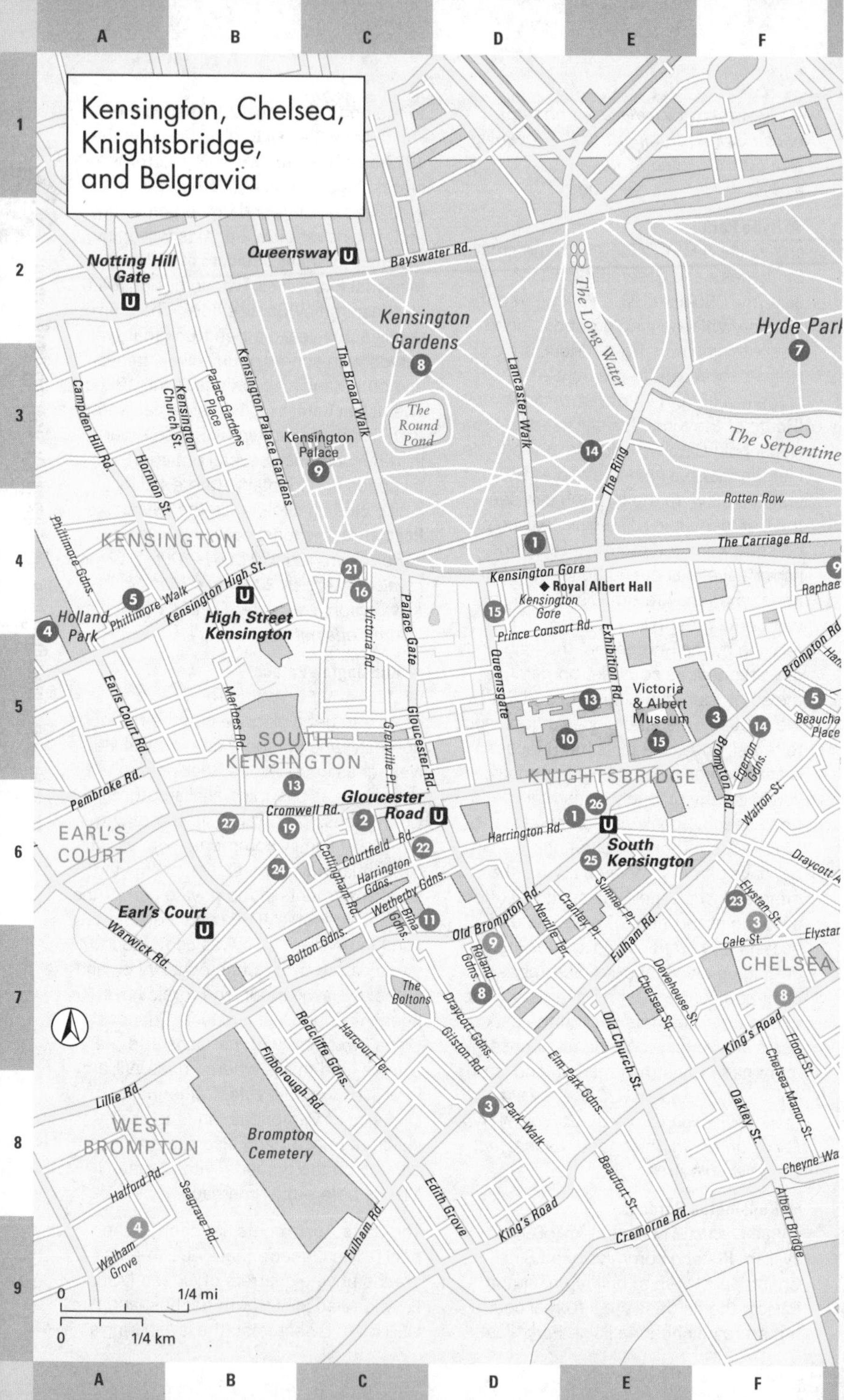
Kensington, Chelsea, Knightsbridge, and Belgravia
Notting Hill Gate
Queensway
Bayswater Rd.
Kensington Gardens
Hyde Park
The Long Water
The Round Pond
Kensington Palace
The Serpentine
Rotten Row
The Carriage Rd.
Kensington Gore
Royal Albert Hall
KENSINGTON
High Street Kensington
Holland Park
Prince Consort Rd.
Victoria & Albert Museum
SOUTH KENSINGTON
KNIGHTSBRIDGE
Gloucester Road
South Kensington
EARL'S COURT
Earl's Court
CHELSEA
WEST BROMPTON
Brompton Cemetery
The Boltons
Cromwell Rd.
Harrington Rd.
Old Brompton Rd.
Fulham Rd.
King's Road
Lillie Rd.
Cremorne Rd.
Albert Bridge
1/4 mi
1/4 km

Sights ▼

1 Albert Memorial D4
2 Belgrave Square........ H4
3 Brompton Oratory F5
4 Design Museum A4
5 18 Stafford Terrace..... A4
6 Harrods G5
7 Hyde Park................. F2
8 Kensington Gardens..... C3
9 Kensington Palace C3
10 Natural History Museum E5
11 Royal Hospital Chelsea H7
12 Saatchi Gallery.......... G6
13 Science Museum........ E5
14 Serpentine Galleries E3
15 Victoria & Albert Museum E5

Restaurants ▼

1 Bar Boulud G4
2 Dinner by Heston Blumenthal............. G4
3 Elystan Street F6
4 The Harwood Arms..... A9
5 Mari Vanna............. G4
6 Marcus.................. H4
7 Pétrus.................... H4
8 Rabbit..................... F7
9 Yashin Ocean House ... D7

Hotels ▼

1 Ampersand............... E6
2 Ashburn Hotel........... C6
3 At Home Inn Chelsea... D8
4 B&B Belgravia............ I6
5 The Beaufort............ F5
6 Belmond Cadogan Hotel...................... G5
7 The Berkeley........... H4
8 Blakes Hotel............ D7
9 Bulgari Hotel London... G4
10 The Capital Hotel G4
11 The Cranley Hotel....... D6
12 The Draycott G6
13 easyHotel South Kensington....... B6
14 Egerton House F5
15 The Gore Hotel.......... D4
16 Kensington House Hotel...................... C4
17 The Lanesborough...... H4
18 Lime Tree Hotel I6
19 London Marriott Kensington B6
20 Mandarin Oriental Hyde Park............... G4
21 The Milestone Hotel..... C4
22 Millennium Gloucester............... C6
23 myhotel Chelsea F6
24 The Nadler Kensington B6
25 Number Sixteen.......... E6
26 The Pelham Hotel........ E6
27 The Rockwell........... B6
28 San Domenico House G6
29 Studios@82................ I6

Ice-skaters outside the Natural History Museum in South Kensington

State Apartments, originally built for George I, are a stage set, a circuit of sumptuous rooms where Georgian monarchs received and entertained courtiers, politicians, and foreign dignitaries. Look for the King's Staircase, with its panoramic trompe-l'oeil painting, and the King's Gallery, with royal artworks surrounded by rich red damask walls, intricate gilding, and a beautiful painted ceiling. One permanent exhibition, *Victoria Revealed,* is devoted to the private life of Queen Victoria, who was born and grew up here. Another exhibition is devoted to designer sketches for gowns worn by Princess Diana.

Outside, the grounds are almost as lovely as the palace itself. There are free, history-oriented tours of the gardens on Tuesday, Thursday, and Saturday at noon and 2 pm from May through September. They also make a fine location for a picnic on one of the benches—or head for the delightful café (busy during peak hours) in the Kensington Palace Pavilion, near the Sunken Garden (the café's usual home, the Orangery, is closed for renovations until 2021). An extension adjoining the Orangery is planned to house an educational center. At the Pavilion, you can also indulge in a formal afternoon tea. ✉ *The Broad Walk, Kensington Gardens, Kensington* ☎ *0207/482–7799 for advance booking in U.K., 0203/166–6000* 🌐 *www.hrp.org.uk* 🎟 *£18* Ⓜ *Queensway, High St. Kensington.*

★ Natural History Museum

MUSEUM | FAMILY | Originally built to house the British Museum's natural history collection and bolstered by samples provided by Britain's great 19th-century explorers and scientists—notably Charles Darwin—this enormous Victorian cathedral of science is one of the world's preeminent museums of natural history and earth sciences. As might be expected given its Darwin connection, the emphasis is on evolution and conservation. The terra-cotta facade is embellished with relief panels depicting living creatures to the left of the entrance and extinct ones to the right (although some species have subsequently changed categories). Most are represented inside the museum, which contains more than 70 million different specimens. Only a small percentage is on public display, but you could still spend a day here and not come close to seeing everything.

The skeleton of a giant blue whale dominates the vaulted, cathedral-like entrance hall. Meanwhile, similarly huge dino bones can be found in the Dinosaur Gallery (Blue Zone), along with fossils and some extremely long iguanodon teeth. You'll also come face-to-face with a virtual Jurassic sea dragon and a giant animatronic *T. rex* that's programmed to sense when human prey is near and "respond" in character. When he does, you can hear the shrieks of fear and delight all the way across the room.

An escalator takes you into a giant globe in the Earth Galleries, where there's a choice of levels to explore. Don't leave without checking out the earthquake simulation in the Volcanoes and Earthquake Gallery. The Darwin Centre houses some 80 million items the museum itself doesn't have room to display, including "Archie," a 28-foot giant squid. If you want to see Archie and some of the other millions of animal specimens preserved in spirit (including some acquired on Darwin's *Beagle* voyage), you'll need to book one of the low-cost behind-the-scenes Spirit Collection tours (around £15). These 45-minute tours take place at 11:30, 12:30, and 1:30, plus 3:30 on weekends, and can be booked on the same day (space is limited, so come early). The center's interactive Cocoon Experience is a free 45-minute tour that reveals how the museum stores, preserves, and uses specimens from its plant and insect collections. In the David Attenborough Studio, there are free, half-hour drop-in talks (usually on Friday and Saturday afternoon) given by scientists and curators, covering a wildly eclectic range of subjects. Night owls might prefer one of the evening talks or spending an entire night in the museum at one of the "Dino Snores" events.

The museum also has an outdoor ice-skating rink October through January, and a popular Christmas fair. ✉ *Cromwell Rd., South Kensington* ☎ *0207/942–5000* 🌐 *www.nhm.ac.uk* 🎫 *Free (some fees for special exhibitions)* Ⓜ *South Kensington.*

★ Science Museum

MUSEUM | FAMILY | With attractions ranging from entertaining yet educational exhibits—like the Wonderlab interactive gallery, where kids can perform their own scientific experiments, to an exhibition on the fight against superbugs—the Science Museum brings the subject alive for visitors of all ages. Highlights include *Puffing Billy,* the oldest steam locomotive in the world; Watson and Crick's original DNA model; and the Apollo 10 capsule. The Information Age gallery, devoted to communication networks from the telegraph to the Internet, was opened in 2014 by Queen Elizabeth, who marked the occasion by sending her first tweet. The Winton Gallery, all about mathematics and its applications, has more than 100 math-related objects, such as a 17th-century Islamic astrolabe and an early version of Alan Turing's Enigma machine. Overshadowed by a three-story blue-glass wall, the Wellcome Wing is an annex to the rear of the museum, devoted to contemporary science and technology. It contains a 450-seat theater (where you can visit the ocean floor or the Hubble space telescope via IMAX) and the Legend of Apollo—an advanced 3-D motion simulator that combines seat vibration with other technology to re-create the experience of a moon landing. Another popular space-related immersive experience is the 360-degree VR recreation of traveling back to Earth from the International Space Station in a Soyuz capsule with astronaut Tim Peake as your guide. If you're a group of at least five, you might be able to get a place on one of the popular monthly Science Night sleepovers by booking well in advance. ✉ *Exhibition Rd., South Kensington* ☎ *0870/870–4868* 🌐 *www.sciencemuseum.org.uk* 🎫 *Free (charge for special exhibitions, IMAX, Wonderlab, and simulator rides)* Ⓜ *South Kensington.*

Serpentine Galleries

MUSEUM | Taking its name from the artificial recreational lake that curves its way through Hyde Park, the Serpentine Gallery, housed in a brick 1930s tea pavilion in Kensington Gardens, is one of London's foremost showcases for contemporary art. Just about everyone who's anyone has exhibited here: Louise Bourgeois, Jeff Koons, Marina Abramovic, and Gerhard Richter, to name a few. A permanent work on the gallery's grounds, consisting of eight benches and a carved stone circle, commemorates its former patron, Princess Diana. The Serpentine Sackler Gallery, a second exhibition space that's in a small Georgian gunpowder storeroom just across a small bridge, has a dramatic extension designed by Zaha Hadid as well as a stylish restaurant. If you're in town between May and September, check out the annual Serpentine Pavilion, where each year a leading architect is given free rein to create a temporary pavilion of their choosing—always with imaginative results. Past designers have included Frank Gehry, Daniel Libeskind, and Jean Nouvel. ✉ *Kensington Gardens, Kensington* ☎ *020/7402–6075* 🌐 *www.serpentinegalleries.org* 🎫 *Free* ⊙ *Closed Mon.* Ⓜ *Lancaster Gate, Knightsbridge, South Kensington.*

★ Victoria & Albert Museum

MUSEUM | **FAMILY** | Known to all as the V&A, this huge museum with more than 2 million items on display in 145 galleries is devoted to the applied arts of all disciplines, all periods, and all nationalities. First opened as the South Kensington Museum in 1857, it was renamed in 1899 in honor of Queen Victoria's late husband and has since grown to become one of the country's best-loved cultural institutions, with high-profile temporary exhibitions alongside an impressive permanent collection. Many collections at the V&A are presented not by period but by category—textiles, sculpture, jewelry, and so on. ■ **TIP→ It's a tricky building to navigate, so use the free map.**

Nowhere is the benefit of the categorization more apparent than in the Fashion Gallery (Room 40), where formal 18th-century court dresses are displayed alongside the haute couture styles of contemporary designers. The museum has become known for high-profile temporary exhibitions exploring fashion icons such as Alexander McQueen, Balenciaga, and Christian Dior, as well as pop legends including David Bowie and Pink Floyd.

The British Galleries (Rooms 52–58 and 118–125) survey British art and design from 1500 to 1900 and are full of rare and beautiful artifacts such as the Tudor Great Bed of Ware (immortalized in Shakespeare's *Twelfth Night*) and silks woven by Huguenot refugees in Spitalfields. Among the series of actual rooms that have been painstakingly reconstructed piece by piece are the glamorous rococo Norfolk House Music Room and the serenely elegant Henrietta St. Drawing Room, originally designed in 1722.

The Asian Galleries (Rooms 44–47) are full of treasures, but among the most striking items on display is a remarkable collection of ornate samurai armor in the **Japanese Gallery** (Room 44). Works from China, Korea, and the Islamic Middle East have their own displays. Also of note is a gallery thematically grouped around Buddhist sculpture from different regions and periods. The Europe Gallery (Rooms 1–7) brings together more than 1,100 objects created between 1600 and 1815, while the Medieval and Renaissance galleries, which document European art and culture from 300 to 1600, have the largest collection of works from the period outside of Italy. An entrance off Exhibition Road offers access through the U.K.'s first porcelain-tiled public courtyard that also serves as a venue for contemporary installations and a glass-fronted café. A photography center, houses books, photo equipment, and more than 270,000 prints formerly held by the Royal Photographic Society, joining the more than 500,000 photos already in the museum's collection. A room in the center has been named the Elton John and David Furnish Gallery after the couple donated some 7,000 photographs by 20th-century masters.

As a whirlwind introduction, you could take a free one-hour Introductory tour. Occasional public lectures during the week are delivered by bigwigs from the art and fashion worlds in addition to free lectures throughout the week given by museum staff. **TIP→ Whatever time you visit, the spectacular sculpture hall will be filled with artists, both amateur and professional, sketching the myriad artworks on display there. Don't be shy; bring a pad and join in.** *Cromwell Rd., South Kensington 020/7942–2000 www.vam.ac.uk Free (charge for some special exhibitions, from £5) South Kensington.*

Restaurants

Kensington is a Victorian residential neighborhood with a wide range of restaurants, from French bistros to funky Persian hideaways.

Yashin Ocean House

$$$ | **JAPANESE** | Here at one of London's top Japanese restaurants, head chef and cofounder Yasuhiro Mineno creates fresh, colorful, and exquisite sushi, sashimi, salads, and carpaccios. Tofu-topped miso cappuccino comes in a Victorian cup and saucer, while *nigiri* might include signature flourishes such as truffle shavings on fatty tuna. **Known for:** exquisite sushi and sashimi with creative twists; 5- to 15-piece chef-decides omakase sets; head-to-tail seafood dishes. *Average main: £30 117–119 Old Brompton Rd., Kensington 020/7373–3990 www.yashinocean.com High St. Kensington.*

Hotels

From cheap and cheerful hostels for students and gleaming, efficient hotels aimed at business travelers to Victorian mansions converted to comfortable, elegant boutique hotels, this tourist-heavy part of London has accommodations to suit all tastes.

Ampersand

$$ | **HOTEL** | A sense of style emanates from every surface of this stylish hotel in the heart of Kensington, and the playful vintage vibe lends the property a refreshingly down-to-earth feel in a neighborhood that can feel stodgy. **Pros:** flawless design; great service; good restaurant. **Cons:** ground-floor rooms can be noisy; breakfast is not included in the price of a room; the area swarms with tourists visiting the museums on weekends. *Rooms from: £234 10 Harrington Rd., Kensington 020/7589–5895 www.ampersandhotel.com 111 rooms No meals Gloucester Rd.*

Ashburn Hotel

$$ | **HOTEL** | A short walk from Gloucester Road Tube station and within walking distance of Harrods and the Kensington museums, the Ashburn is one of the better "boutique" hotels in this part of town. **Pros:** friendly atmosphere; free Wi-Fi; different turndown gift every night. **Cons:** summer prices sometimes hike the cost; some rooms on the small side; on very busy road. *Rooms from: £144 111 Cromwell Rd., Kensington 020/7244–1999 www.ashburn-hotel.co.uk 38 rooms Free breakfast Gloucester Rd.*

Blakes Hotel

$$$ | **HOTEL** | Located in a set of adjoining Victorian town houses, this boutique hotel—one of London's first—puts design, luxury, and glamour front and center, and consequently has always attracted visiting rock and movie stars. **Pros:** glamorous, sexy atmosphere; imaginative design; lovely outdoor courtyard. **Cons:** over-the-top look may not be for everyone; elevator is slow and tiny; high prices not reflected in quality of rooms. *Rooms from: £340* *33 Roland Gardens, Kensington* *020/7370–6701* *www.blakeshotels.com* *45 rooms* *No meals* *South Kensington.*

The Cranley Hotel

$$ | **HOTEL** | Old-fashioned British propriety is the overall feeling at this small, Victorian town house hotel, where high ceilings, huge windows, and a deep Regency color scheme flood the bedrooms with light. **Pros:** good-size rooms; attractively decorated; free evening treats (and Champagne) are a nice touch. **Cons:** steep stairs into lobby; some elements of the decor feel a little tired; prices rise in midsummer. *Rooms from: £175* *10–12 Bina Gardens, South Kensington* *020/7373–0123* *www.cranleyhotel.com* *39 rooms* *Free breakfast* *Gloucester Rd.*

easyHotel South Kensington

$ | **HOTEL** | London's original "pod hotel" has tiny rooms with a double bed, private shower room, and little else—each brightly decorated in the easyGroup's trademark orange and white (to match their budget airline easyJet). **Pros:** amazing rates; safe and decent-enough space; good location. **Cons:** not for the claustrophobic—rooms are truly tiny and most have no windows; six floors and no elevator; Wi-Fi is not included in the price of rooms. *Rooms from: £48* *14 Lexham Gardens, Kensington* *07951/440134* *www.easyhotel.com* *34 rooms* *No meals* *Gloucester Rd.*

★ **The Gore Hotel**

$$ | **HOTEL** | This gorgeous hotel with old-school attentive service has a mixture of the comfortable and the extraordinary. **Pros:** gorgeously designed and spacious rooms; outstanding attentive service; air-conditioning in all rooms. **Cons:** slow Wi-Fi; bar can be noisy; some rooms are dark. *Rooms from: £198* *190 Queen's Gate, Kensington* *020/7584–6601, 888/757–5587 in U.S* *www.starhotelscollezione.com/en/our-hotels/the-gore-london* *50 rooms* *Free breakfast* *Gloucester Rd.*

Kensington House Hotel

$ | **HOTEL** | A short stroll from High Street Kensington and Kensington Gardens, this refurbished 19th-century town house has streamlined contemporary rooms with large windows letting in plenty of light and comfortable beds with luxurious fabrics and soft comforters. **Pros:** attractive design; relaxing setting; free Wi-Fi. **Cons:** rooms are on the small side; bathrooms are minuscule; room decor might feel quite plain to some. *Rooms from: £120* *15–16 Prince of Wales Terr., Kensington* *020/7937–2345* *www.kenhouse.com* *41 rooms* *Free breakfast* *High St. Kensington.*

London Marriott Kensington

$$ | **HOTEL** | A big favorite with the business crowd, this pleasant modern outpost of the Marriott megachain is just one of several big-name hotels on busy Cromwell Road. **Pros:** friendly efficient service; good neighborhood; one-minute Tube ride to Kensington museums. **Cons:** business ambience feels impersonal; bedrooms are on the small side; unattractive location on busy Cromwell Road. *Rooms from: £190* *147 Cromwell Rd., Kensington* *020/7973–1000* *www.marriott.com/hotels/travel/lonlm-london-marriott-hotel-kensington* *216 rooms* *Free breakfast* *Earl's Ct., Gloucester Rd.*

★ **The Milestone Hotel**

$$$ | **HOTEL** | This pair of intricately decorated Victorian town houses overlooking Kensington Palace is an intimate luxurious alternative to the city's more famous high-end hotels, offering thoughtful hospitality and opulent distinctive rooms full of antiques. **Pros:** beautiful and elegant; big rooms, many with park views; excellent location. **Cons:** actual room rate discounts are rare; luxury and elegance comes at a high price; some guests might find the decor a little over-the-top. *Rooms from: £345 ✉ 1 Kensington Ct., Kensington ☎ 020/7917–1000 🌐 www.milestonehotel.com 62 rooms 🍴 Free breakfast Ⓜ High St. Kensington.*

Millennium Gloucester

$$ | **HOTEL** | Located next to a conference center and opposite a Tube station, this is very much a business hotel. **Pros:** great location; good business facilities; good deals available if you book in advance. **Cons:** lighting in some bedrooms is a bit too subtle; bathrooms are relatively small; rather bland decor will appeal more to business travelers. *Rooms from: £131 ✉ 4–18 Harrington Gardens, Kensington ☎ 020/7373–6030 🌐 www.millenniumhotels.co.uk 610 rooms 🍴 Free breakfast Ⓜ Gloucester Rd.*

The Nadler Kensington

$$ | **HOTEL** | Known as an "aparthotel," this creamy white Georgian town house on a garden square offers a useful compromise between full-service hotel and the freedom of self-catering in the form of comfortable rooms with a stylish modern look and tiny kitchenettes. **Pros:** handy minikitchens; helpful staff; televisions can stream content from your tablet or phone. **Cons:** basic rooms are small; breakfast is served to the room only with extra charge; not close to many sights. *Rooms from: £130 ✉ 25 Courtfield Gardens, South Kensington ☎ 020/7244–2255 🌐 www.nadlerhotels.com 65 rooms 🍴 No meals Ⓜ Earl's Ct.*

★ **Number Sixteen**

$$$ | **HOTEL** | Rooms at this lovely boutique hotel just around the corner from the Victoria & Albert Museum, look like they come from the pages of *Architectural Digest*, and the delightful garden is an added bonus. **Pros:** just the right level of helpful service; interiors are gorgeous; the afternoon tea is excellent. **Cons:** no restaurant; elevator doesn't go to third floor; intimacy of a small boutique hotel may not be for everyone. *Rooms from: £336 ✉ 16 Sumner Pl., South Kensington ☎ 020/7589–5232, 888/559–5508 in U.S. 🌐 www.firmdale.com 41 rooms 🍴 Free breakfast Ⓜ South Kensington.*

The Pelham Hotel

$$ | **HOTEL** | One of the first boutique hotels ever in London, this still-stylish choice is just a short stroll away from the Natural History, Science, and Victoria & Albert museums. **Pros:** great location for museum-hopping; elegant interior design; lovely staff. **Cons:** taller guests will find themselves cursing the top-floor rooms with sloping ceilings; some rooms are on the small side given the price; some suites are only accessible via the stairs. *Rooms from: £200 ✉ 15 Cromwell Pl., South Kensington ☎ 020/7589–8288, 888/757–5587 in U.S. 🌐 www.starhotelscollezione.com/en/our-hotels/the-pelham-london 52 rooms 🍴 Free breakfast Ⓜ South Kensington.*

The Rockwell

$ | **HOTEL** | Despite being on the notoriously traffic-clogged Cromwell Road, the Rockwell is one of the best boutique hotels in this part of London—and windows have triple-soundproofing. **Pros:** large bedrooms; good value for neighborhood; helpful staff. **Cons:** on busy road; no bathtubs; decor a bit tired in places. *Rooms from: £108 ✉ 181 Cromwell Rd., South Kensington ☎ 020/7244–2000 🌐 www.therockwell.com 40 rooms 🍴 Free breakfast Ⓜ Earl's Ct.*

Performing Arts

These refined neighborhoods just west of central London have a wide variety of galleries and performance spaces, with several located within the area's large public green spaces.

CLASSICAL MUSIC

Cadogan Hall

CONCERTS | Once a church, this spacious venue is home to the Royal Philharmonic Orchestra, and the English Chamber Orchestra performs here regularly. The hall also hosts a wide range of choral and chamber concerts, plus the occasional folk, rock, and world-music gig. ✉ *5 Sloane Terr., Kensington* ☎ *020/7730–4500* 🌐 *www.cadoganhall.com* 🎫 *Free–£100* Ⓜ *Sloane Sq.*

★ Royal Albert Hall

CONCERTS | Opened in 1871, this splendid iron-and-glass-domed auditorium hosts everything from pop and classical headliners to Cirque du Soleil, awards ceremonies, and sumo wrestling championships, but it is best known for the annual July–September BBC Promenade Concerts. Bargain-price standing-room (or promenading or sitting-on-the-floor) tickets for "the Proms" are sold on the night of the concert. The circular 5,272-seat auditorium has a terra-cotta exterior surmounted by a mosaic frieze depicting figures engaged in cultural pursuits. The hall is open most days for daytime guided tours and Tuesday through Sunday for afternoon tea. ✉ *Kensington Gore, Kensington* ☎ *0207/589–8212* 🌐 *www.royalalberthall.com* 🎫 *From £7; tours £14* Ⓜ *South Kensington.*

Shopping

HOUSEHOLD GOODS

The Conran Shop

HOUSEHOLD ITEMS/FURNITURE | This is the brainchild of Sir Terence Conran, who has been a major influence on British taste since he opened Habitat in the 1960s, with its then-groundbreaking concept of advanced design at an affordable price. Although he is no longer associated with Habitat, his Conran Shops remain bastions of similarly clean, unfussy modernist design. Housewares from furniture to lighting, stemware, and textiles—both handmade and mass-produced, by famous names and emerging designers—are housed in a building that is a modernist landmark in its own right. Both the flagship store and the branch on Marylebone High Street are bursting with great gift ideas. ✉ *Michelin House, 81 Fulham Rd., South Kensington* ☎ *020/7589–7401* 🌐 *www.conranshop.co.uk* Ⓜ *South Kensington.*

Mint

HOUSEHOLD ITEMS/FURNITURE | Owner Lina Kanafani has scoured the globe to curate an eclectic mix of conceptual statement furniture, art, ceramics, glassware, textiles, and home accessories. Mint also showcases avant-garde works by an international selection of up-and-coming designers and sells plenty of specially commissioned limited edition and one-off pieces, for a price. If you don't want to ship a couch home, consider a miniature flower vase or a hand-painted plate. ✉ *2 North Terr., at Alexander Sq., South Kensington* ☎ *020/7225–2228* 🌐 *www.mintshop.co.uk* 🕙 *Closed Sun.* Ⓜ *South Kensington.*

JEWELRY

Butler & Wilson

JEWELRY/ACCESSORIES | Specialists in bold costume jewelry and affordable glamour, Butler & Wilson attracts fans including the Duchess of Cambridge. Semiprecious stones have been added to its foundation diamanté, colored rhinestone, and crystal collections. The British sense of humor is reflected in items like Champagne-bottle earrings or crystal studs in the shape of an eye. ✉ *189 Fulham Rd., South Kensington* ☎ *020/7352–3045* 🌐 *www.butlerandwilson.co.uk* 🕙 *Closed Sun.* Ⓜ *South Kensington.*

Chelsea

Chelsea was settled before the Domesday Book was compiled and already fashionable when two of Henry VIII's wives lived there in the 16th century. On the banks of the Thames are the vast grounds of the **Royal Hospital,** designed by Christopher Wren. A walk along the riverside embankment will take you to **Cheyne Walk,** a lovely street dating back to the 18th century. Several of its more notable residents—from J. M. W. Turner and Henry James to Laurence Olivier and Keith Richards—are commemorated by blue plaques on their former houses.

The **Albert Bridge,** a sherbet-color Victorian confection of a suspension bridge, provides one of London's great romantic views, especially at night. Leave time to explore the tiny Georgian lanes of pastel-color houses that veer off King's Road to the north—especially **Jubilee Place** and **Burnsall Street,** leading to the hidden "village square" of **Chelsea Green.** On Saturday there's an excellent farmers' market up from the Saatchi Gallery in Duke of York's Square selling artisanal cheese and chocolates, local oysters, and organic meats, plus stalls serving international food.

Residential Chelsea extends along the river from the Chelsea Bridge west to the Battersea Bridge and north as far as the Old Brompton Road.

Sights

Royal Hospital Chelsea

HISTORIC SITE | Charles II founded this residence for elderly and infirm soldiers in 1682 to reward the troops who had fought for him in the civil wars of 1642–46 and 1648. No sick people are treated here today; it's more of a history-packed retirement home. A creation of three of England's greatest architects—Wren, Vanbrugh, and Hawksmoor—this small enclave of brick and Portland stone set in expansive manicured grounds (which you can visit) surrounds the Figure Court (the figure being a 1682 gilded bronze statue of Charles II dressed as a Roman general). The beautiful Wren-designed chapel (a working church) and the Great Hall (the Hospital's dining room) are open to the public at certain times during the day. There is a small museum devoted to the history of the resident "Chelsea Pensioners," but the real attraction, along with the building, is the approximately 300 pensioners themselves. Recognizable by their traditional scarlet frock coats with gold buttons, medals, and tricorne hats, they are all actual veterans, who wear the uniform, and the history it represents, with a great deal of pride. On Sundays mornings (10:45) in April through November, you can see groups of pensioners in full uniform on parade in the Figure Court. Individuals can visit the grounds, chapel, Great Hall, and museum for free. On weekdays, you can go on a 90-minute guided tour for groups of 10 or more (from £180 per group; must be booked a month in advance) led by one of the pensioners. ✉ *Royal Hospital Rd., Chelsea* ☎ *020/7881–5298* 🌐 *www.chelsea-pensioners.co.uk* 🎫 *Free* 🕐 *Closed Sun. and bank holidays. Museum closed weekends* Ⓜ *Sloane Sq.*

Saatchi Gallery

MUSEUM | Charles Saatchi, who made his fortune in advertising, is one of Britain's canniest collectors of contemporary art, credited with discovering the likes of Damien Hirst and Tracey Emin. His current gallery, still largely devoted to contemporary art by emerging artists, is in the former Duke of York's HQ, just off King's Road. Built in 1803, its grand period exterior belies an imaginatively restored modern interior transformed into 15 exhibition spaces of varying size and shape. There is no permanent collection other than a few ongoing site-specific installations; at any one time, there are between one and three concurrent, imaginatively curated exhibitions that normally run for up to six months. There's also an excellent café, which is open late. *Duke of York's HQ Bldg., King's Rd., Chelsea 020/7811–3070 www.saatchigallery.com Free Sloane Sq.*

Restaurants

In Chelsea, once the epicenter of 1960s Swinging London, today restaurants here range from top chefs' passion projects to trendy cafés perfect for a catch-up, a glass of fizz, and a no-carb bite on the go.

★ Elystan Street

$$$ | **MODERN BRITISH** | Chef Phil Howard is committed to seasonality, bringing together well-matched ingredients in this relaxed, loftlike space that leans toward the modernist and minimalist. The dishes are deeply flavored and accomplished, earning the restaurant a Michelin star (the vegetarian game is especially strong). **Known for:** Michelin-level cuisine in a relaxed setting; roast grouse with celeriac and pear puree; convivial vibe enhanced by a smart wine list. *Average main: £30 43 Elystan St., Chelsea 020/7628–5005 www.elystanstreet.com South Kensington.*

The Harwood Arms

$$$$ | **MODERN BRITISH** | Despite a Michelin star and a co-owner who's also the chef at one of Britain's (and indeed the world's) top restaurants, this is a relaxed neighborhood gastropub with an unusually fine kitchen. It specializes in British produce, wild food, and especially game, with dishes like crab royale with peas and lovage and game pie with Somerset cider jelly, all served via set menus only. **Known for:** Michelin-starred food in a gastropub setting; seasonal venison from the pub's own hunting estate; good value set menus. *Average main: £38 27 Walham Grove, Chelsea 020/7386–1847 www.harwoodarms.com No lunch Mon. Fulham Broadway.*

The Chelsea Flower Show

Run by the Royal Horticultural Society, the Chelsea Flower Show, the year's highlight for thousands of garden-obsessed Brits, is held every May (usually the third week). The huge showcase for garden design and horticultural innovation takes up all of the Royal Hospital's large grounds. You can buy all manner of gardening supplies and accessories from the many exhibitors, and the end of the last day sees a scrimmage for discount plants from the displays. For more information, check out the website at *www.rhs.org.uk*.

Rabbit

$$ | **MODERN BRITISH** | **FAMILY** | Owned by three brothers who grew up on a farm (which supplies the restaurant with its produce and livestock), Rabbit introduces a note of rusticity to one of London's glitziest areas. The emphasis is on locality and sustainability, and the menu changes daily, depending on what's in season and available. **Known for:** fresh game including rabbit served marinated in a bone marrow sauce and enclosed in large ravioli; shared plates with all seasonal and local ingredients; English wines from owners' vineyard. *Average main: £17 172 Kings Rd., London 020/3750–0172 www.rabbit-restaurant.com No dinner Sun. No lunch Mon. Sloane Sq.*

Hotels

At Home Inn Chelsea

$$ | **B&B/INN** | **FAMILY** | King's Road and the rest of superrich Chelsea is just a short stroll from this delightfully informal B&B, and you'd be hard-pressed to find a better room in this neighborhood for the price. **Pros:** picturesque top-floor

terrace; central Chelsea location; can be booked as a whole apartment. **Cons:** only accessible via the owners' own apartment's main entrance; few extras; one bathroom shared between both rooms. *Rooms from: £125 ✉ 5 Park Walk, Chelsea ☎ 07790/844–008 ⊕ www.athomeinnchelsea.com ⇆ 2 rooms 🍴 Free breakfast Ⓜ Fulham Broadway.*

Belmond Cadogan Hotel
$$$$ | **HOTEL** | This elegant hotel in spread out over five town houses and features luxurious decor that incorporates sculptural lighting and modern art while retaining nods to the hotel's Edwardian past (it was the infamous site of Oscar Wilde's arrest for gross indecency with a young man). **Pros:** luxurious but not stuffy; garden access; free Wi-Fi. **Cons:** rooms are quite small; expensive rates; old-school clubhouse decor not for everyone. *Rooms from: £458 ✉ 75 Sloane St., Chelsea ☎ 020/7235–7141 ⊕ www.cadogan.com ⇆ 54 rooms 🍴 Free breakfast Ⓜ Sloane Sq.*

★ **The Draycott**
$$$ | **HOTEL** | **FAMILY** | This elegant yet homey boutique hotel near Sloane Square is the stuff London dreams are made on—if your dream is to live like a pleasantly old-fashioned, impeccably mannered, effortlessly stylish Chelsea lady or gentleman. **Pros:** lovely traditional town house; attentive service; access to garden square. **Cons:** no restaurant or bar; single rooms are very small; elevator is tiny. *Rooms from: £286 ✉ 26 Cadogan Gardens, Chelsea ☎ 020/7730–0236 ⊕ www.draycotthotel.com ⇆ 35 rooms 🍴 Free breakfast Ⓜ Sloane Sq.*

myhotel chelsea
$$ | **HOTEL** | Rooms at this small chic charmer—tucked away down a side street in an upscale neighborhood—are tiny but sophisticated, with colorful pastel throws atop crisp white down comforters. **Pros:** stylish rooms made for relaxation; good neighborhood; healthy dining options. **Cons:** tiny rooms; not much food variety at on-site café; relaxed style not for everyone. *Rooms from: £167 ✉ 35 Ixworth Pl., Chelsea ☎ 020/7225–7500 ⊕ www.myhotels.com ⇆ 54 rooms 🍴 Free breakfast Ⓜ South Kensington.*

★ **San Domenico House**
$$$ | **HOTEL** | Discreet, beautiful, and exceptionally well run, this converted Chelsea town house makes for a restful hideaway. **Pros:** unique and beautiful design; great neighborhood, with the King's Road and Saatchi Gallery a short walk away; exceptional service. **Cons:** no bar or restaurant on-site; no breakfast included for the (still pretty expensive) cheapest rates; only some rooms have bathtubs. *Rooms from: £288 ✉ 29–31 Draycott Pl., Chelsea ☎ 020/7581–5757 ⊕ www.sandomenicohouse.com ⇆ 19 rooms 🍴 Free breakfast Ⓜ Sloane Sq.*

Nightlife

The pages of society magazines are crammed with photographs of gorgeous young people dancing the night away at clubs located in these famously swanky neighborhoods. Dress up and be prepared to splurge—if you can get in (many are members-only). Pubs here range from classy modern affairs with impressive wine lists and shared plates to tiny local institutions guaranteed to make you feel like you've stepped back in time.

JAZZ AND BLUES

606 Club
MUSIC CLUBS | This Chelsea jazz club has been doing things speakeasy-style since long before it became a nightlife trend. Buzz the door near the far end of King's Road and you'll find a basement venue showcasing mainstream and contemporary jazz by well-known U.K.-based musicians. You must eat a meal in order to consume alcohol, so allow for an extra £30. Reservations are advisable. Lunchtime jazz takes place on select Sundays; call ahead. *✉ 90 Lots Rd., Chelsea*

☎ *020/7352–5953* 🌐 *www.606club.co.uk* 🎫 *From £10 music charge added to bill* Ⓜ *Fulham Broadway. Overground: Imperial Wharf.*

PUBS

The Anglesea Arms

BARS/PUBS | The front patio and wood-paneled bar of this traditional pub next door to Charles Dickens' former residence is invariably crowded, especially after work, but the restaurant to the rear is comfortable and more peaceful. Dishes range from traditional pub classics like burgers or fish and chips to more sophisticated offerings like pan-fried seabass. Standards, both of the cooking and the selection of beer and wines, are high. Service is friendly, if occasionally erratic. ✉ *15 Selwood Terr., Chelsea* ☎ *020/7373–7960* 🌐 *www.angleseaarms.com* Ⓜ *South Kensington.*

Performing Arts

Royal Court Theatre

THEATER | For decades, the Royal Court was one of Britain's leading showcases for exciting new theatrical voices and premieres of ground-breaking works, and it still continues to produce important British and international dramas. For some productions, four 10-pence standing tickets go on sale one hour before each performance (but the view is severely restricted), and £12 tickets are available at 9 am Mondays for that night's performance. Monthly backstage and building tours are offered occasionally (check website for more information). ✉ *Sloane Sq., Chelsea* ☎ *020/7565–5000* 🌐 *www.royalcourttheatre.com* 🎫 *From £12; tours £10* Ⓜ *Sloane Sq.*

Shopping

ACCESSORIES

Anya Hindmarch

JEWELRY/ACCESSORIES | Exquisite leather bags and personalized, printed canvas totes are what made Hindmarch famous, and this store sells her complete collection of bags, several with a whimsical motif. You can also order a custom piece like the "Be A Bag," a wash bag imprinted with your chosen photo. There are branches around the corner on Pont Street in Knightsbridge, Bond Street in Mayfair, and in Notting Hill. ✉ *157–158 Sloane St., Chelsea* ☎ *0207/730–0961* 🌐 *www.anyahindmarch.com* Ⓜ *Sloane Sq.*

BOOKS

John Sandoe (Books) Ltd.

BOOKS/STATIONERY | This atmospheric warren that crams some 25,000 titles into an 18th-century building off King's Road is the antithesis of a soulless chain bookstore, so it's no surprise it has attracted equally idiosyncratic customers like Tom Stoppard and Keith Richards. Staff members are wonderfully knowledgeable (don't try to figure out how the stock is organized without their help), and there are a lot of them per customer—if a book isn't in stock, they will try to find it for you, even if it is out of print. ✉ *10 Blacklands Terr., Chelsea* ☎ *020/7589–9473* 🌐 *www.johnsandoe.com* Ⓜ *Sloane Sq.*

CLOTHING

Brora

CLOTHING | The knitwear is cozy, but the style is cool in this contemporary Scottish cashmere emporium for men, women, and kids. There are stylish pullovers, wraps, cardigans, and adorable baby ensembles, as well as noncashmere items such as T-shirts and jersey or linen dresses. Other branches are in Marylebone and Covent Garden; plus there's a clearance store farther down King's Road. ✉ *6–8 Symons St., Chelsea* ☎ *020/7730–2665* 🌐 *www.brora.co.uk* Ⓜ *Sloane Sq.*

Hackett

CLOTHING | If Ralph Lauren isn't preppy enough for you, try Hackett, with additional branches in St. James's and Canary Wharf. Originally a posh thrift shop recycling cricket flannels, hunting pinks, Oxford brogues, and other staples of a British gentleman's wardrobe, Hackett now creates its own line and has become a genuine—and very good—men's outfitter. The look is traditional and classic best buys include polo shirts, corduroys, and striped scarves. There's also a boys' line for the junior man-about-town. ✉ *137–138 Sloane St., Chelsea* ☎ *020/7730–3331* 🌐 *www.hackett.com* Ⓜ *Sloane Sq.*

Jigsaw

CLOTHING | The quality of fabrics and detailing belie the reasonable prices here, where clothes are classic yet trendy and elegant without being dull—and where cuts are kind to the womanly figure. The style is epitomized by the Duchess of Cambridge, who, as Kate Middleton before her marriage, was a buyer for the company. Although there are numerous branches across London, no two stores are the same. Preteens have their own line, Jigsaw Junior. ✉ *The Chapel, 6 Duke of York Sq., Chelsea* ☎ *020/730–4404* 🌐 *www.jigsaw-online.com* Ⓜ *Sloane Sq.*

DEPARTMENT STORES

★ Peter Jones

DEPARTMENT STORES | This tasteful department store has been a beloved local institution since it opened in 1937, and the poet John Betjeman remarked that come the end of the world he would like to be in the haberdashery department of Peter Jones, "because nothing bad could ever happen there." It's the traditional default wedding-list option of Kensington & Chelsea brides, thanks to its outstanding selection of bed and bath linens (many provided by John Lewis, the store's parent company), flatware, ceramics, and glassware, with offerings at all price points. There's also an extensive and eclectic beauty department, as well as kitchenware and appliances, tech stuff, a florist, clothing, shoes, and accessories for the whole family, and pretty much everything else you can think of, along with a restaurant and a Clarins spa. ✉ *Sloane Sq., Chelsea* ☎ *020/7730–3434* 🌐 *www.johnlewis.com/our-shops/peter-jones* Ⓜ *Sloane Sq.*

FOOD

L'Artisan du Chocolat

FOOD/CANDY | Praised by top chefs Gordon Ramsay and Heston Blumenthal, L'Artisan raises chocolate to an art form. "Couture" chocolates are infused with fruits, nuts, and spices (including such exotic flavorings as Szechuan pepper and tobacco). This is one of the few chocolate shops in the world that makes liquid salted caramels. There are other branches in West Hampstead, Borough Market, and Kensington. ✉ *89 Lower Sloane St., Chelsea* ☎ *0845/270–6996* 🌐 *www.artisanduchocolat.co.uk* Ⓜ *Sloane Sq.*

HOUSEHOLD GOODS

Designers Guild

HOUSEHOLD ITEMS/FURNITURE | Tricia Guild's exuberantly patterned fabrics, wallpapers, paints, furniture, and bed linens have decorated design-conscious British homes for several decades, and her soft-furnishings book has taught many budget-conscious do-it-yourselfers how to reupholster a sofa or make lined draperies. The shop also stocks contemporary furniture, wallpapers, and home accessories by other designers like Christian Lacroix. There's another branch in Marylebone. ✉ *267–277 King's Rd., Chelsea* ☎ *020/351–5775* 🌐 *www.designersguild.com* ⏲ *Closed Sun.* Ⓜ *Sloane Sq.*

SHOES

★ Manolo Blahnik

SHOES/LUGGAGE/LEATHER GOODS | Blink and you'll miss the discreet sign that marks fashionista footwear central. Blahnik, the man who single-handedly managed to revive the sexy stiletto, has been trading out of this small shop on a Chelsea side street since 1973. It's a must for shoe lovers with generous budgets. If you decide to wear your new Manolos, hop on Bus No. 11 or 22 or grab a cab—the nearest Tube station is about a 20-minute totter away. ✉ *49–51 Old Church St., Chelsea* ☎ *020/7352–8622* 🌐 *www.manoloblahnik.com* ⏲ *Closed Sun.* Ⓜ *Sloane Sq., South Kensington.*

SPECIALTY STORES

Green & Stone Art Materials

SPECIALTY STORES | Relocated from its original fabulous cave on King's Road, this treasure trove of artists' materials, papers, art books, easels, and mannequins began life in 1927 as part of the Chenil Gallery, run by a distinguished group that included the artist Augustus John and the playwright George Bernard Shaw. Subsequent customers have included luminaries like David Hockney, Damien Hirst, Francis Bacon, and Lucian Freud. The shop also has a framing service, antique paint boxes, and craft supplies. ✉ *251–253 Fulham Rd., Chelsea* ☎ *020/7352–0837* 🌐 *www.greenandstone.com* Ⓜ *Sloane Sq.*

Knightsbridge

There's no getting away from it. With two world-famous department stores, **Harrods** and **Harvey Nichols,** a few hundred yards apart; numerous boutiques selling the biggest names in international luxury and expensive jewelry; and a summer influx of supercars like Maseratis imported from the Gulf states, London's wealthiest enclave will appeal most to those who enjoy conspicuous consumption.

Posh Sloane Street is lined with top-end designer boutiques such as Prada, Dior, and Tods. If it all starts to become a bit generic (expensive generic), **Beauchamp Place** (pronounced "Beecham") is lined with equally luxe one-off boutiques, which tend to be more distinctive and less global.

Knightsbridge is located to the east of Kensington, bordered by Hyde Park on the north and Pont Street just past Harrods on the south.

Sights

Brompton Oratory (*London Oratory*)

RELIGIOUS SITE | This is a late product of the mid-19th-century English Roman Catholic revival led by John Henry Cardinal Newman (1801–90), who established the oratory in the 1840s and whose statue you see outside. Architect Herbert Gribble was an unknown 29-year-old when he won a competition to design the church, bringing a baroque exuberance to his concept for the vast, incredibly ornate interior. It's punctuated by treasures far older than the church itself, like the giant Carrara marble *Twelve Apostles* in the nave, sculpted by Giuseppe Mazzuoli in the 1680s for Siena's cathedral. The Oratory is known for the quality of its organs and choir, with exceptional music being an integral part of services here. ✉ *Brompton Rd., Knightsbridge* ☎ *0207/808–0900* 🌐 *www.bromptonoratory.com* 🎫 *Free* Ⓜ *South Kensington.*

Harrods

STORE/MALL | With an encyclopedic assortment of luxury brands, this Knightsbridge institution, currently owned by the Qatar Investment Authority, has more than 300 departments and 25 eating and drinking options, all spread over 1 million square feet on a 4½-acre site. Now populated more by window-shopping tourists and superrich visitors from abroad than by the bling-averse natives, Harrods is best approached as the world's largest, most upscale and expensive mall. After a two year redesign of the food hall, you can now find a variety of dining options on-site, including sushi, Indian, pasta, and more; all have counter seating so you can watch the chefs at work. At the center is the Wine Bar, with over a hundred wines by the glass and food by Caviar House and Prunier. There's also a giant coffee roasting station, ceiling-high shelves of fresh bread at the Bakery, a vegetable butchery, and an expanded deli counter. In addition, the revamped

World-famous Harrods has been luring shoppers with its classic wares since 1834.

Beauty Hall now offers cult brands, innovative "Magic Mirrors" that allow shoppers to instantly see a new make-up look via digital technology, beauty master classes, and over 46,000 different lipsticks, as well as 13 treatment rooms where you can try on make-up in private. ✉ *87–135 Brompton Rd., Knightsbridge* ☎ *020/7730–1234* 🌐 *www.harrods.com* Ⓜ *Knightsbridge.*

Restaurants

You can dine like a king in Knightsbridge, as long as you're prepared to spend on a regal scale and don't mind a similar level of formality. The world-class restaurants are mostly found in the area's platinum-class hotels. Come here for a celebratory dining experience, but don't expect bargains (unless it's lunchtime).

Bar Boulud

$$ | BRASSERIE | New York–based French superchef Daniel Boulud combines French brasserie classics like escargot, salade nicoise, and poule au pot with American-style gourmet burgers at this sophisticated but casual restaurant located within the Mandarin Oriental. The excellent grazing menu has something for everyone, and the professional but informal waitstaff enhance the convivial vibe. **Known for:** excellent foie gras/beef/short rib burgers; affordable set meals from noon until 6:30; superb take on French brasserie classics. $ *Average main: £25* ✉ *Mandarin Oriental Hyde Park, 66 Knightsbridge, Knightsbridge* ☎ *020/7201–3899 for reservations only* 🌐 *www.barboulud.com/london* Ⓜ *Knightsbridge.*

★ Dinner by Heston Blumenthal

$$$$ | BRITISH | Medieval English cuisine meets molecular gastronomy in this reassuringly luxurious, two Michelin star Blumenthal flagship within the Mandarin Oriental. Try the signature "Meat Fruit" appetizer (last popular in the 16th century), a ball of ultrasmooth chicken liver parfait encased in a citrus-flavored gel "peel" or the much-more-appetizing-than-it-sounds "Rice and Flesh", a

15th-century dish of yellow saffron rice with veal sweetbreads and wild smoked eel. **Known for:** handsome dining room with Hyde Park views; creative reinterpretations of historical dishes; pineapple Tipsy cake for dessert. *Average main: £44* *Mandarin Oriental Hyde Park, 66 Knightsbridge, Knightsbridge* *020/7201–3833* *www.dinnerbyheston.com* *Knightsbridge.*

Marcus

$$$$ | **MODERN BRITISH** | A former Gordon Ramsay protegé who is now a celebrity chef in his own right, Marcus Wareing left behind Ramsay and opened this restaurant, which already has a Michelin star. Wareing's Modern British cooking uses the freshest ingredients to create innovative and delicious flavor combinations like duck with pistachio, apricot, and wild nettle or a buttermilk parfait with lavender glazed peach and grapefruit donuts. **Known for:** sophisticated, seasonal dishes; excellent wine list; slightly less formal vibe than other celebrity chef restaurants. *Average main: £90* *1 Wilton Pl., London* *207/7235–1200* *www.marcusrestaurant.com* *Closed Sun.* *Hyde Park Corner.*

Mari Vanna

$$ | **RUSSIAN** | London's sizeable, well-heeled Russian community flocks to this maximalist evocation of a pre-Revolution *babushka*'s living room, overflowing with vintage chandeliers, porcelain figurines, tapestries, and nested Russian dolls. The menu leans toward traditional old-country comfort food like Siberian *pelmeni* (dumplings) filled with pork and beef, smoked salmon blinis, creamy beef Stroganoff with wild mushrooms, and, of course, borscht, finished off with a 12-layer honey cake. **Known for:** over-the-top nostalgic Russian décor; borscht, blinis, and beef Stroganoff; flavored vodka shot selection. *Average main: £24* *The Wellington Court, 116 Knightsbridge, Knightsbridge* *020/7225–3122* *www.marivanna.ru/london* *Knightsbridge.*

Hotels

The Beaufort

$$ | **HOTEL** | This gracious boutique hotel appears in the little black books of many fashionistas—Harrods and Harvey Nicks are just a short walk from the front door. **Pros:** attractive, well-designed decor; friendly and professional staff; complimentary daily afternoon tea. **Cons:** standard doubles are much smaller than the price might indicate; soundproofing could be better; no restaurant on-site. *Rooms from: £230* *33 Beaufort Gardens, Knightsbridge* *020/7584–5252* *www.thebeaufort.co.uk* *22 rooms* *Free breakfast* *Knightsbridge.*

★ **The Berkeley**

$$$$ | **HOTEL** | **FAMILY** | Convenient for Knightsbridge shopping, the very elegant Berkeley is known for its excellent restaurants, splendid rooftop swimming pool and garden, and an excellent, if pricey, Bamford spa. **Pros:** lavish and elegant; attentive service; great drinking and dining options. **Cons:** you'll need your best designer clothes to fit in; even the cheapest rooms are expensive; while beautiful, the style is very traditional luxury. *Rooms from: £450* *Wilton Pl., Knightsbridge* *020/7235–6000, 800/637–2869 in U.S.* *www.the-berkeley.co.uk* *190 rooms* *Free breakfast* *Knightsbridge.*

Bulgari Hotel London

$$$$ | **HOTEL** | This luxury hotel checks all the Knightsbridge boxes (top-of-the-range everything, ultra-fashionable design, a haven for the international rich) and brings the same attention to detail and Italian high style to the decor as it does to its eponymous jewelry line. **Pros:** luxurious decor and ambience; excellent service; lovely spa and pool. **Cons:** somewhat anonymous atmosphere of wealth; restaurant not quite worth the price; extremely expensive. *Rooms from: £800* *171 Knightsbridge, Knightsbridge* *020/7151–1010* *www.*

bulgarihotels.com/en_US/london/the-hotel/overview 85 rooms No meals Knightsbridge.

The Capital Hotel
$$$ | **HOTEL** | Nothing is ever too much at this elegant hotel that was formerly a private house; mattresses are handmade, sheets are 450-thread count, bathrooms are marble, and everything is done in impeccable taste. **Pros:** beautiful space; handy for shopping at Harrods; excellent restaurant. **Cons:** breakfast is expensive; cheaper rooms are small for the price; neighborhood can be pricey. *Rooms from: £295 22–24 Basil St., Knightsbridge 020/7589–5171, 800/926–3199 in U.S. www.capitalhotel.co.uk 49 rooms No meals Knightsbridge.*

★ **Egerton House**
$$$ | **HOTEL** | **FAMILY** | This welcoming boutique hotel is an oasis of understated country house chic in glitzy Knightsbridge, with guest rooms that don't stint on design touches, like bold, rich textiles. **Pros:** personalized, attentive service; luxurious but comfortable design; striking art. **Cons:** some may find rooms over-decorated; the traditional elegance won't appeal to everyone; on the pricier side. *Rooms from: £330 17–19 Egerton Terr., Knightsbridge 020/7589–2412, 877/955–1515 in U.S. www.redcarnationhotels.com 29 rooms Free breakfast Knightsbridge, South Kensington.*

★ **The Lanesborough**
$$$$ | **HOTEL** | Beautiful, traditional, and luxurious, the Lanesborough is like a gilded cocoon for the seriously wealthy that exudes Regency splendor, from the design-magazine perfection of the bedrooms to the magnificent 19th-century antiques. **Pros:** beautiful and historic; great service, including a team of personal butlers; everything—rooms, food, spa—is top-notch. **Cons:** prices are extraordinary; might be too fancy for some; Hyde Park Corner is often clogged with heavy traffic. *Rooms from: £635 Hyde Park Corner, Knightsbridge 020/7259–5599, 800/999–1828 in U.S. www.lanesborough.com* No credit cards *95 rooms Free breakfast Hyde Park Corner.*

★ **Mandarin Oriental Hyde Park**
$$$$ | **HOTEL** | Following an extensive postfire renovation, this ultraluxe hotel on the edge of Hyde Park welcomes you with one of the most exuberantly Edwardian facades in town, then fast-forwards you to high-trend modern London, thanks to striking and luxurious guest rooms filled with high-tech gadgets. **Pros:** several rooms have balconies or terraces overlooking Hyde Park; spacious rooms and bathrooms; excellent service. **Cons:** nothing comes cheap; rooms on lower floors on Knightsbridge side may have traffic noise; street outside often very busy. *Rooms from: £720 66 Knightsbridge, Knightsbridge 020/7235–2000 www.mandarinoriental.com/london 181 rooms Free breakfast Knightsbridge.*

Nightlife

The Blue Bar at the Berkeley Hotel
BARS/PUBS | With its Lutyens blue walls, Edwardian plasterwork, white onyx bar, and black crocodile-print leather floor, this hotel bar oozes sultry sophistication. Immaculate service, an excellent seasonal cocktail list, and a glass extension make this an ideal spot for a romantic tête-à-tête, complete with a background soundtrack of lounge and deep house music. *The Berkeley, Wilton Pl., Knightsbridge 020/7235–6000 www.the-berkeley.co.uk Knightsbridge, Hyde Park Corner.*

Shopping

CLOTHING

Egg
CLOTHING | Tucked away in a residential mews, this spartan shop in a former Victorian dairy is the brainchild of Maureen

Doherty, once Issey Miyake's assistant who still shares his relaxed but cutting-edge aesthetic. More than half the minimalist, unstructured styles for men and women—in natural luxury fabrics such as silk, cashmere, and antique cotton—are handmade. Garments may be casually hung on hooks or folded on wooden tables, but the price tags are anything but unassuming. The clientele includes the likes of Donna Karan and former British PM Theresa May. One-of-a-kind ceramics and jewelry are also on display. ✉ *36 Kinnerton St., Knightsbridge* ☎ *020/7235–9315* 🌐 *www.eggtrading.com* 🕓 *Closed Sun.* Ⓜ *Knightsbridge.*

Rachel Riley

CLOTHING | FAMILY | Specializing in traditional English style for boys and girls, Riley's luxurious, vintage-inspired collection includes classics like duffel coats and hand-smocked floral dresses. Mothers who love the Riley look (including the Duchess of Cambridge, who has put her royal offspring in Riley clothes) can pick up 1950s-inspired coordinating outfits for themselves here or at the Marylebone High Street location. ✉ *14 Pont St., Knightsbridge* ☎ *020/7259–5969* 🌐 *www.rachelriley.co.uk* 🕓 *Closed Sun.* Ⓜ *Knightsbridge.*

Rigby & Peller

SPECIALTY STORES | Many of London's most affluent women find their luxury lingerie (plus swimwear) here because the quality is excellent and the service impeccably knowledgeable—and perhaps because it's the Queen's favored underwear supplier and has provided maternity wear to the Duchess of Cambridge. Despite the upscale clientele, it's much friendlier than you might expect. Brands include Primadonna and Aubade as well as R&P's own line, and if the right fit eludes you, there's a made-to-measure service that starts at around £300. There are also branches in Mayfair, Chelsea, St. John's Wood, and The City. ✉ *2 Hans Rd., Knightsbridge* ☎ *020/7225–4760* 🌐 *www.rigbyandpeller.com* Ⓜ *Knightsbridge.*

DEPARTMENT STORES

Harvey Nichols

DEPARTMENT STORES | While visiting tourists flock to Harrods, local fashionistas shop at Harvey Nichols, aka "Harvey Nicks." The womenswear and accessories departments are outstanding, featuring top designers like Tom Ford, Loewe, Roland Mouret, Valentino, Tory Burch, and just about every fashionable name you can think of. The furniture and housewares are equally gorgeous (and pricey), although they become somewhat more affordable during the biannual sales in January and July. The Fifth Floor bar is the place to see and be seen, but if you're in search of food, the same floor also has an all-day Modern European café, a branch of Burger & Lobster, the carnivore-friendly Zelman Meats, or sushi-to-go from Yo! Sushi. To keep you looking as box-fresh as your purchases, the Beauty Lounge features a rotating menu of treatments from brands such as Elemis, La Mer, and Dermalogia, plus makeovers, LED facials, IV vitamin infusions, and blow-dry, nail, and brow bars. ✉ *109–125 Knightsbridge, Knightsbridge* ☎ *020/7235–5000* 🌐 *www.harveynichols.com* Ⓜ *Knightsbridge.*

Belgravia

Steps away from the roaring traffic of Hyde Park Corner, lying just to the east of Kensington and Chelsea, is quiet, fashionable Belgravia, one of the most impressive set pieces of 19th-century urban planning. Street after street is lined with grand, cream-color stucco terraces, once aristocrats' town houses and most still part of the Grosvenor estate owned by the Duke of Westminster. Many buildings are leased to embassies or organizations, but a remarkable number around **Lowndes Square, Eaton Place,** and **Eaton Square** remain in the hands of private owners, whether old money or new oligarchs who put their security guards in the attached mews houses. Some people consider the area near **Elizabeth Street** to be southern Belgravia; others call it Pimlico-Victoria. Whatever its name, here small, unique stores specialize in baked goods, wine, gifts, and stationery.

Sights

Belgrave Square

PLAZA | This is the heart of Belgravia, once the preferred address for the gentry's London town houses, although it's now mostly occupied by organizations, embassies, and the international rich. The Square and the streets leading off it share a remarkably consistent elegant architectural style thanks to all being part of a Regency redevelopment scheme commissioned by the Duke of Westminster and designed by Thomas Cubitt with George Basevi. The grand, cream-color stucco terraced houses were snapped up by aristocrats and politicians due to their proximity to Buckingham Palace just around the corner, and still command record prices on the rare occasions when they come onto the market. The private garden in the center is open to the public once a year. Walk down Belgrave Place toward Eaton Place and you pass two of Belgravia's most beautiful mews: Eaton Mews North and Eccleston Mews, both fronted by grand rusticated entrances right out of a 19th-century engraving. **■ TIP→ Traffic can really whip around Belgrave Square, so be careful.** ✉ *Belgravia* Ⓜ *Hyde Park Corner.*

Restaurants

Pétrus

$$$$ | **MODERN FRENCH** | Now in its third location, this Gordon Ramsay flagship offers fine dining to the max without being overly stuffy or cautious. The cooking combines superb technique with creativity, blending complex and intricate flavors in dishes like Orkney scallops with kombu, bacon and sabayon; rich turbot with leeks in a seaweed beurre blanc; or Dorset beef in a charcuterie sauce. **Known for:** Gordon Ramsay's flagship London restaurant; seasonal British ingredients with a French twist; "preferred" business-casual dress code. *$ Average main: £35* ✉ *1 Kinnerton St., Belgravia* ☎ *020/7592–1609* 🌐 *www.gordonramsayrestaurants.com/petrus* Ⓜ *Knightsbridge, Hyde Park Corner.*

Hotels

B&B Belgravia

$$ | **B&B/INN** | At this contemporary guesthouse near Victoria Station, minimalist décor, Scandinavian Modern furniture, and a lounge where a fire crackles away in the winter are all geared to homey comforts. **Pros:** nice extras like 24-hour complimentary tea and coffee; bike hire included; superb value for money in a pricey area. **Cons:** rooms and bathrooms are small; some decor and mattresses tired; no elevator. *$ Rooms from: £194* ✉ *64–66 Ebury St., Belgravia* ☎ *020/7259–8570* 🌐 *www.bb-belgravia.com* *17 rooms* *Free breakfast* Ⓜ *Sloane Sq., Victoria.*

Lime Tree Hotel

$$ | **HOTEL** | In a central neighborhood where hotels veer from wildly overpriced at one extreme to grimy bolt-holes at the other, the Lime Tree gets the boutique style just about right—and at a surprisingly reasonable cost for the neighborhood. **Pros:** lovely and helpful hosts; great location; rooms are decent size. **Cons:** cheaper rooms are small; some are up several flights of stairs and there's no elevator; lack of amenities. *$ Rooms from: £205* ✉ *135–137 Ebury St., Belgravia* ☎ *020/7730–8191* 🌐 *www.limetreehotel.co.uk* *28 rooms* *Free breakfast* Ⓜ *Victoria, Sloane Sq.*

Studios@82

$$ | RENTAL | A side operation from B&B Belgravia located eight doors down from the mothership (where you check in), these self-contained, serviced studio apartments with kitchenettes offer great value for the location. **Pros:** great rates; central but quiet location; all the independence of self-catering. **Cons:** lots of stairs and no elevator; no major amenities; can be subject to street noise. *Rooms from: £180* *82 Ebury St., Belgravia* *020/7259–8570* *www.bb-belgravia.com* *9 apartments* *Free breakfast* *Knightsbridge.*

Nightlife

PUBS

The Grenadier

BARS/PUBS | Tucked away on a quiet mews, this 1720 building was originally the officers' mess for the First Royal Regiment of Foot Guards whose barracks were next door. Opened as a pub in 1818 and renamed after the Grenadier Guards, it's now adorned with antique Guards cartoons and memorabilia, and might just be haunted by a subaltern named Cedric, a young soldier who was beaten to death after allegedly cheating at cards. The money on the ceiling has been hung by visitors trying to pay his debt. Turn up on the annual Regimental Remembrance Day for a colorful army veterans' gathering. There are traditional bar snacks, more substantial seasonal main courses like roast partridge, and a notable selection of cask ales. *18 Wilton Row, Belgravia* *020/7235–3074* *www.grenadierbelgravia.com* *Knightsbridge, Hyde Park Corner.*

Shopping

ACCESSORIES

★ **Philip Treacy**

JEWELRY/ACCESSORIES | Magnificent hats by Treacy are annual showstoppers on Ladies' Day at the Royal Ascot races and regularly grace the glossy magazines' party and catwalk pages. Part Mad Hatter, part Cecil Beaton, Treacy's creations always guarantee a grand entrance and are favorites with everyone from Lady Gaga to Kate Middleton. In addition to the extravagant, haute couture hats handmade in the atelier, less flamboyant ready-to-wear hats are also for sale, as are some bags. *69 Elizabeth St., Belgravia* *020/7730–3992* *www.philiptreacy.co.uk* *Sloane Sq.*

SPECIALTY STORES

Mungo & Maud

SPECIALTY STORES | If you don't want to leave London without buying something for your pet, Mungo & Maud have something for your furry friend. Pick up a well-designed coat, leash, harness, bowl, toy, or comfortable bed that will make your dog the snazziest pooch in town (some collars are hand-stitched), or select from baskets, suede collars, and blankets for your cat. Even owners get a nod with luxurious merino throws (soon to be covered in pet hair), pet-themed jewelry, and leather "poop bag" pouches. *79 Elizabeth St., Belgravia* *020/7467–0823* *www.mungoandmaud.com* *Sloane Sq.*

Chapter 11

NOTTING HILL AND BAYSWATER

Updated by
James O'Neill

Sights	Restaurants	Hotels	Shopping	Nightlife
★★☆☆☆	★★★☆☆	★★★☆☆	★★★★☆	★★★☆☆

NOTTING HILL AND BAYSWATER SNAPSHOT

TOP REASONS TO GO

Portobello Road: The early bird can catch considerably more than the worm; go before 10 am on Saturday to hook the good stuff at London's world-famous antiques market, or come during the week for a leisurely browse.

Holland Park: An often-overlooked gem, this is arguably London's most romantic green space, complete with woodland walks, a Jacobean mansion, open-air theater, and opera in the summer; there's even a gorgeous Japanese-style garden with a waterfall.

Notting Hill's picturesque streets and squares: From the grandeur of Lansdowne Road and Stanley Crescent to the west of Kensington Park Road, to the pastel-colored hues of Chepstow Villas to the east, this is residential London at its finest and most seductive.

GETTING THERE

For Portobello Market and environs, the best Tube stops are Ladbroke Grove and Westbourne Park (Hammersmith and City Line); ask for directions when you emerge. The Notting Hill Gate stop on the District, Circle, and Central lines enables you to walk the length of Portobello Road while going slightly downhill.

MAKING THE MOST OF YOUR TIME

Saturday is the most exciting day for shopping, eating, and drinking here. The market gets crowded by noon in summer, so come early if you are serious about shopping. Head south from the north end of Portobello Road, using the parks to take a break on the way. On Sunday, the Hyde Park and Kensington Gardens railings along Bayswater Road are lined with artists displaying their work, which may slow your progress.

QUICK BITES

■ **The Prince Bonaparte** A laid-back, airy, art deco–inspired gastropub serving up quality Modern British food, the Prince Bonaparte offers a fine selection of artisanal ales and carefully chosen wines. A stone's throw from Portobello Market, it's the perfect place for a drink or a bite to eat. ✉ *80 Chepstow Rd., Bayswater* ☎ *020/7313–9491* 🌐 *www.theprincebonapartew2.co.uk* Ⓜ *Notting Hill Gate, Royal Oak.*

■ **The Tabernacle** The Victorian Gothic interior of this bar, café, and arts center combo hosts intimate music gigs, literary events with the likes of *Tales of The City*'s Armistead Maupin, and 15-minute talks with speakers such as historian Niall Ferguson. The food is Caribbean-influenced, and the atmosphere, especially in the outdoor courtyard, is relaxed. ✉ *34–35 Powis Sq., Notting Hill* ☎ *020/7221–9700* 🌐 *www.tabernaclew11.com* 🕒 *Closed Sun.* Ⓜ *Notting Hill Gate.*

SAFETY

■ At night, avoid straying from the main streets north of Westbourne Park Road toward Ladbroke Grove's high-rise estates (projects) and the surrounding areas.

The center of London's West Indian community from the 1950s through the '70s, Notting Hill these days is the address of choice for the well-heeled, be they bankers, rock stars, media and advertising types, or rich hippies.

Teeming with trendy restaurants, cool bars, and buzzing street markets, the area is also studded with some of London's most handsome historic residences, crescents, and terraces. Every weekend, the hordes descend on Portobello Road to go bargain-hunting at one of the world's great antiques markets. Holland Park, to the west, has even grander villas, while Bayswater (to the east) has excellent world-cuisine restaurants.

Notting Hill

Notting Hill as we know it emerged in the 1840s when the wealthy Ladbroke family developed a small suburb to the west of London. Before then, the area had the far less glamorous name of "the Potteries and the Piggeries," after the two industries it was best known for: ceramics and pig farming.

During the 1980s, Notting Hill transformed from a lively but down-at-heel and sometimes dangerous West Indian enclave to a supertrendy fashionable neighborhood. Nowadays, one of the joys of visiting this neighborhood is the opportunity it gives you to explore some of the capital's most charming squares and thoroughfares.

The area's Caribbean legacy persists, however, not least in the form of the annual Notting Hill Carnival in late August. The new millennium saw Notting Hill's fame go global thanks to the hit rom-com of the same name, though the movie itself was criticized by locals for downplaying the area's cultural diversity. For the Notting Hill of the silver screen, head for fashionable **Westbourne Grove** and **Ledbury Road,** lined with eclectic independent boutiques offering highly desirable designer goods for the home and family, as well as contemporary art—prices and taste levels are high.

For less rarefied shopping, try **Portobello Road**; the famous Saturday antiques market and shops are at the southern end. A little farther southwest lies the elegant splendor of **Holland Park,** at the end of which you'll find the exotic delights of the **Leighton House Museum.**

Sights

Graffik

MUSEUM | Not everyone thinks graffiti can be a bonus to the urban landscape, but those who do should head for this leading gallery of contemporary street art. The big name here is Banksy, but there are works for sale by several other artists in the same vein such as Trust.iCON and CODE FC, who are more concerned with social commentary than tagging. This is one gallery experience that really appeals to young people, especially if the visit coincides with one of Graffik's two-hour weekend workshops. ✉ *284 Portobello*

Within Holland Park, you'll find the tranquil Kyoto Garden and its Japanese maple trees, dahlias, and a koi carp pond.

Rd., Notting Hill ☎ *020/8354–3592* 🌐 *www.graffikgallery.com* 🎫 *Free* Ⓜ *Notting Hill Gate, Ladbroke Grove.*

Holland Park

CITY PARK | FAMILY | Formerly the grounds of a 17th-century aristocrat's manor house and open to the public only since 1952, Holland Park is an often-overlooked gem in the heart of London. The northern "Wilderness" end offers woodland walks among native and exotic trees first planted in the early 18th century. Foxes, rabbits, and hedgehogs are among the residents. The central part of the park is given over to the manicured lawns—still stalked by raucous peacocks—one would expect at a stately home, although Holland House itself, originally built by James I's chancellor and later the site of a 19th-century salon frequented by Byron, Dickens, and Disraeli, was largely destroyed by German bombs in 1940. The east wing was reconstructed and has been incorporated into a youth hostel, while the remains of the front terrace provide an atmospheric backdrop for the open-air performances of the April–September Holland Park Opera Festival (🌐 *www.operahollandpark.com).* The glass-walled Orangery garden ballroom now hosts events and art exhibitions, as does the Ice House, while an adjoining former granary has become the upscale Belvedere restaurant. In spring and summer the air is fragrant with aromas from a rose garden, great banks of rhododendrons, and an azalea walk. Garden enthusiasts will also not want to miss the tranquil, traditional Kyoto Garden with its pretty waterfall, a legacy of London's 1991 Japan Festival. The southern part of the park is devoted to sport and play: cricket and soccer pitches; a golf practice area; tennis courts; a well-supervised children's Adventure Playground (with a zipline!); and a giant outdoor chess set. ✉ *Ilchester Pl., West Holland Park* 🌐 *www.rbkc.gov.uk/leisure-and-culture/parks/holland-park* Ⓜ *Holland Park, High St. Kensington.*

★ Leighton House Museum

MUSEUM | Leading Victorian artist Frederic (Lord) Leighton lived and worked in this building on the edge of Holland Park, spending 30 years (and quite a bit of money) transforming it into an opulent "private palace of art" infused with an orientalist aesthetic sensibility. The interior is a sumptuous Arabian Nights fantasy, with walls lined in peacock-blue tiles designed by Leighton's friend, the ceramic artist William de Morgan, and beautiful mosaic wall panels and floors, marble pillars, and gilded ceilings. The centerpiece is the Arab Hall, its marble walls adorned with even more intricate murals made from 16th- and 17th-century ceramic tiles imported from Syria, Turkey, and Iran, surmounted by a domed ceiling covered in gold leaf with a gold mosaic frieze running underneath. You can also visit Leighton's studio, with its huge north window and dome; the house is filled with paintings, several of his own along with works by other Pre-Raphaelites. ⊠ *12 Holland Park Rd., West Holland Park* ☎ *020/7602–3316 weekdays, 020/7471–9160 weekends* ⊕ *www.rbkc.gov.uk/subsites/museums/leightonhousemuseum1.aspx* 🎫 *£9* ⏲ *Closed Tues.* Ⓜ *Holland Park, South Kensington.*

Museum of Brands, Packaging and Advertising

MUSEUM | This fascinating museum explores how advertising and marketing has come to pervade our lives. Curios from the 1800s to the present day include branded toys, clothes, games, and domestic goods such as World War II–era toilet paper (brand name: Nasti toilet roll) that has Hitler's face on every sheet. ⊠ *111–117 Lancaster Rd., Notting Hill* ☎ *020/7243–9611* ⊕ *www.museumofbrands.com* 🎫 *£9* Ⓜ *Ladbroke Grove.*

Portobello Road Market

MARKET | Looking for a 19th-century snuff spoon? Perhaps a Georgian salt cellar? What about a 1960s-era minidress? Then head to Portobello Road's famous Saturday market—and arrive at about 9 am to avoid the giant crowds. Stretching almost 2 miles from Notting Hill, the market is made up of four sections, each with a different emphasis: antiques, fresh produce, household goods, and a flea market. The antiques stalls are packed in between Chepstow Villas and Westbourne Grove, where you'll also find almost 100 antiques shops plus indoor markets, which are open on weekdays, when shopping is much less hectic. Where the road levels off, around Elgin Crescent, youth culture and a vibrant neighborhood life kicks in, with a variety of interesting small stores and food stalls interspersed with a fruit-and-vegetable market. On Friday and Saturday the section between Talbot Road and the Westway elevated highway becomes one of London's best flea markets, specializing in discounted new household goods, while north of the Westway you'll find secondhand household goods and bric-a-brac. Scattered throughout, but especially under the Westway, are vendors selling a mishmash of designer, vintage, and secondhand clothing, together with jewelry, custom T-shirts, and assorted junk. There's a Trinidad-style Carnival centered on Portobello Road on the late August bank-holiday weekend, a tribute to the area's past as a center of the West Indian community. ⊠ *Notting Hill* ⊕ *www.portobelloroad.co.uk* Ⓜ *Notting Hill Gate, Ladbroke Grove.*

Restaurants

Ever since Hugh Grant and Julia Roberts starred in *Notting Hill* and put the area on the global map, Notting Hill's had a reputation as London's most glamorous neighborhood, with its myriad boutiques, chic cafés, pâtisseries, restaurants, bars, pubs, and the famous Portobello Road Market's collection of antiques shops, vintage-clothing stands, and food stalls. Portobello is one of London's most popular street markets, so get there

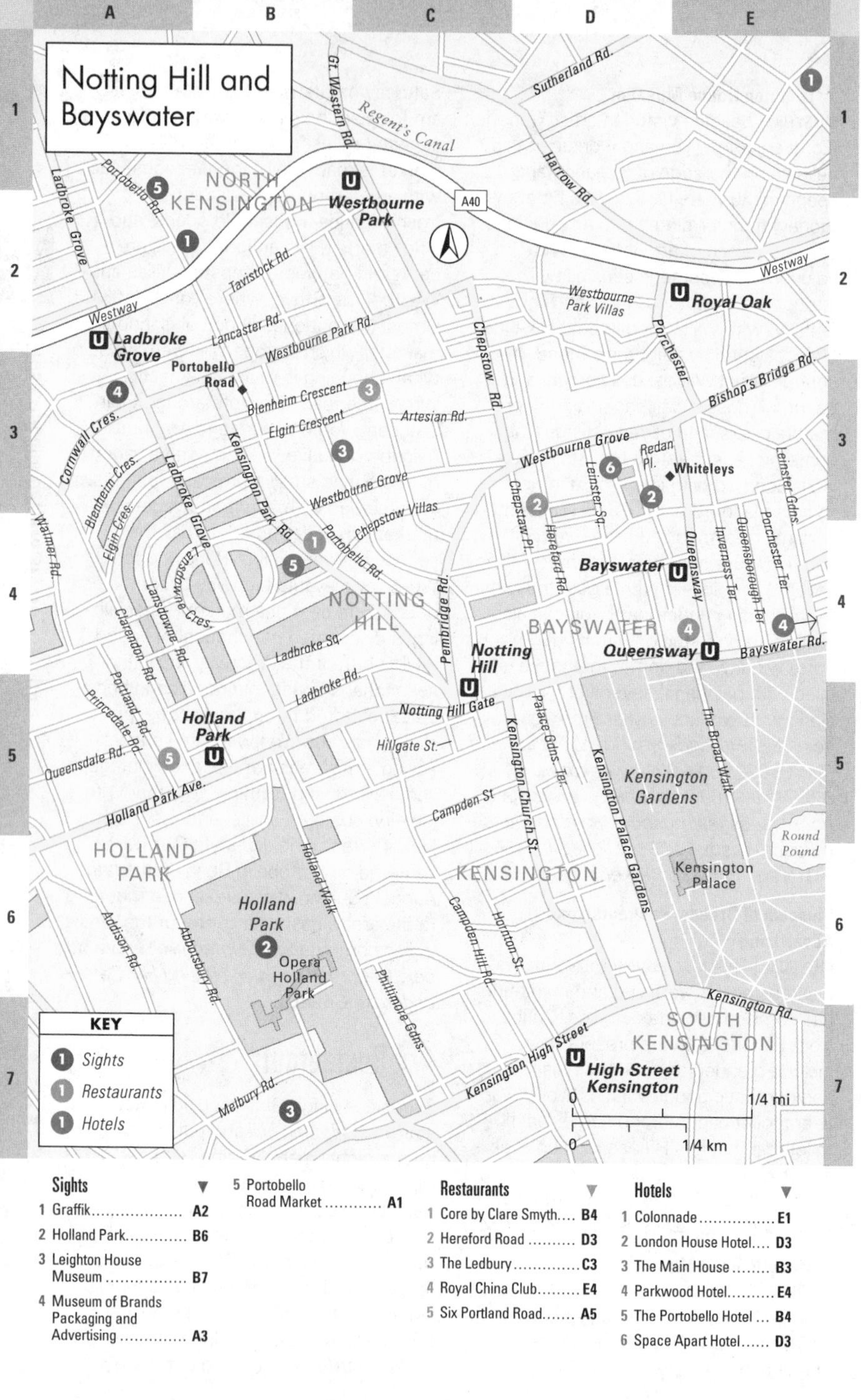

Sights

1 Graffik A2
2 Holland Park B6
3 Leighton House Museum B7
4 Museum of Brands Packaging and Advertising A3
5 Portobello Road Market A1

Restaurants

1 Core by Clare Smyth B4
2 Hereford Road D3
3 The Ledbury C3
4 Royal China Club......... E4
5 Six Portland Road....... A5

Hotels

1 Colonnade E1
2 London House Hotel.... D3
3 The Main House B3
4 Parkwood Hotel.......... E4
5 The Portobello Hotel ... B4
6 Space Apart Hotel...... D3

early on Saturday morning (the market is open 9–7) to beat the crowds. Peruse the antiques and vintage clothes stalls, and when you want to eat, head to the north end where you'll find fresh fruit-and-veg stalls, artisan bakeries, and rare Spanish olive and French cheese purveyors, plus numerous hot-food stalls peddling savory crêpes, gourmet hamburgers, spicy German chicken rolls, paella, Moroccan kebabs, and Malaysian noodles.

★ Core by Clare Smyth

$$$$ | MODERN BRITISH | FAMILY | With two Michelin stars above the door, chef Clare Smyth's casual fine dining extravaganza in Notting Hill offers must-try dishes like skin-on potato cooked in red seaweed and topped with smoked trout, herring roe, edible flowers, and fermented mini salt-and-vinegar crisps. Watch the kitchen through a floor-to-ceiling glass partition as they cook up some culinary magic. **Known for:** brilliant vegetable and fish dishes elevated to the highest levels; relaxed, smart, casual dining experience; three-course à la carte or nine-course tasting menus. *$ Average main: £40 ✉ 92 Kensington Park Rd., Notting Hill ☎ 020/3937–5086 🌐 www.corebyclaresmyth.com ⏲ Closed Sun. and Mon. Ⓜ Notting Hill Gate, Labroke Grove.*

★ The Ledbury

$$$$ | MODERN FRENCH | FAMILY | Aussie chef Brett Graham wins hearts, minds, and some serious accolades at this upbeat modern French (with Pacific and British hints) dining landmark. Global gourmands will struggle to find a more inventive vegetable dish than Graham's white beetroot baked in clay with goat's cheese and hazelnuts, and it's impossible to best his ultrapretty, precise, and complex mains. **Known for:** creative vegetable dishes like white asparagus soup with lemon, grapes, and ricotta; excellent game like Berkshire muntjac with endive cooked in grilled oil; signature brown sugar tart with stem ginger ice cream for dessert. *$ Average main: £40 ✉ 127 Ledbury Rd., Notting Hill ☎ 0207/7792–9090 🌐 www.theledbury.com ⏲ No lunch Mon. and Tues. Ⓜ Westbourne Park, Ladbroke Grove.*

A Good Walk in Notting Hill

Almost directly opposite Notting Hill Tube station is a small enclave of pretty streets that are well worth a detour. Hillgate Street (just past the Gate Cinema) is the entry point to this little village in the heart of the city. Just four blocks wide—from Jameson Street to the east and Farm Place to the west—and one block deep, you can spend a lovely afternoon zigzagging your way through these charming multicolor residential terraces.

★ Six Portland Road

$$ | FRENCH | FAMILY | The ultimate neighborhood restaurant in west London's wealthy Holland Park section draws diners with its brilliant-but-understated French and Mediterranean classics, relaxed service, and interesting, largely French Caves de Pyrene–sourced wines. Treat yourself to sea trout with romesco and saffron or some superdelicate nettle and ricotta ravioli. **Known for:** intimate seating; unpretentious but pitch-perfect service; winning boutique wine list. *$ Average main: £22 ✉ 6 Portland Rd., Notting Hill ☎ 020/7229–3130 🌐 www.sixportlandroad.com ⏲ Closed Sun. No lunch Sat. Ⓜ Holland Park.*

★ The Main House

$$ | B&B/INN | This wonderfully welcoming boutique hotel is a little gem. **Pros:** elegant and peaceful oasis in the heart of the city; charming and helpful owners; room prices decrease for longer stays.

Cons: not for those who like the hustle and bustle of a big hotel; few in-house services; small number of rooms means availability can be limited. *Rooms from: £130* *6 Colvile Rd., Notting Hill* *020/7221–9691* *www.themainhouse.com* *4 rooms* *No meals* *Notting Hill Gate.*

The Portobello Hotel

$$ | **HOTEL** | One of London's quirkiest hotels, the little Portobello (formed from two adjoining Victorian houses) has attracted scores of celebrities to its small but stylish rooms over the years, and the decor reflects these hip credentials with joyous abandon. **Pros:** stylish and unique; pets are allowed; guests have use of nearby gym and pool. **Cons:** all but the priciest rooms are quite small; may be too eccentric for some; a continental breakfast is included in the price but cooked breakfasts are extra. *Rooms from: £195* *22 Stanley Gardens, Notting Hill* *020/7727–2777* *www.portobellohotel.com* *21 rooms* *Free breakfast* *Notting Hill Gate.*

Nightlife

The focus is more on bars than clubs in this west London neighborhood, although late-night fun is on offer at a few notable exceptions. In general, you can expect a young moneyed crowd making this their first stop on a wild night out elsewhere. The line between pub and bar is frequently blurred here, with an emphasis on good—often haute—food, sleek style, and extensive wine lists.

BARS

★ Beach Blanket Babylon

BARS/PUBS | In a Victorian mansion house close to Portobello Market, this always-packed bar is distinguishable by its eclectic indoor–outdoor spaces with Gaudí-esque curves and snug corner spaces—like a candlelit fairy-tale grotto, folly, or a medieval crypt. A sister restaurant-bar-gallery offers a slightly more modern take on similar themes in an ex-warehouse in Shoreditch (*19–23 Bethnal Green Road; 020/7749–3540*). *45 Ledbury Rd., Notting Hill* *020/7229–2907* *www.beachblanket.co.uk* *Notting Hill Gate.*

Electric Diner

BARS/PUBS | **FAMILY** | A huge selection of bottled beers and quirky twists on classic cocktails (Courvoisier, mint, and champagne anyone?) are the attractions at this bar and diner next to Notting Hill's famed Electric Cinema on Portobello Road. Run by the people behind the members-only Soho House, the place exudes the same effortless mixture of posh and cool, but it is open to anyone and everyone. Sit in the window and watch the world go by along Portobello, or opt for one of the luxury takes on classic diner fare at a booth in the moody, vaulted interior. *191 Portobello Rd., Notting Hill* *020/7908–9696* *www.electricdiner.com* *Ladbroke Grove.*

PUBS

The Cow

BARS/PUBS | **FAMILY** | This boho-chic Irish pub is all about the Guinness and the seafood, whether you're enjoying it in the unpretentious downstairs saloon bar or the more formal dining rooms upstairs. The pub food is all excellent, though pricey, with lots of oysters, steaks, and generous seafood platters. The atmosphere's always warm, welcoming, and buzzing. *89 Westbourne Park Rd., Notting Hill* *020/7221–0021* *www.thecowlondon.co.uk* *Westbourne Park, Royal Oak.*

Performing Arts

This cosmopolitan west London neighborhood, shown to advantage in the 1999 film of the same name, is best known for the Notting Hill Carnival, a lively music-focused street festival that takes over the wider area on the final weekend of August each year. There's a year-round culture scene, too, catering mainly to the neighborhood's trendy young professionals.

FILM

The Electric Cinema

FILM | FAMILY | This refurbished Portobello Road art house screens mainstream and international movies. The emphasis is on comfort, with leather sofas for two, armchairs, coffee tables for your wine and appetizers, and even double beds in the front row. The Electric also has another movie theater in east London on Redchurch Street, with sofas and wine coolers. ✉ *191 Portobello Rd., Notting Hill* ☎ *020/7908–9696* 🌐 *www.electriccinema.co.uk* 🎫 *From £18* Ⓜ *Ladbroke Grove, Notting Hill Gate.*

OPERA

Opera Holland Park

OPERA | FAMILY | In summer, well-loved operas and imaginative productions of lesser-known works are presented under a spectacular canopy against the remains of Holland House, one of the first great houses built in Kensington. The company has successfully branched out into opera for families in recent years, too. There are 1,200 tickets offered free to those ages 7–18 every season. Tickets go on general sale in April (earlier for members). After the opera season is over in August, the venue hosts under-the-stars showings of recent movies on a giant screen. ✉ *Holland Park, Kensington High St., Kensington* ☎ *0300/999–1000 for box office (opens Apr.), 020/3846–6222 for inquiries* 🌐 *www.operahollandpark.com* 🎫 *From £20* Ⓜ *High St. Kensington, Holland Park.*

Shopping

BOOKS

★ Books for Cooks

BOOKS/STATIONERY | It may seem odd to describe a bookshop as delicious-smelling, but on several days you can't but notice the aromas wafting out of the tiny café in the back of the shop—where the resident chef cooks a three-course set lunch for only £7, served from noon to 1 pm Tuesday through Friday (but be sure to get there early). The dishes are drawn from recipes in the 8,000 cookbooks on the shelves. Just about every world cuisine is represented, along with a complete lineup of works by celebrity chefs. Before you come to London, visit the shop's website to sign up for a specialized cooking workshop in the upstairs demonstration kitchen. ✉ *4 Blenheim Crescent, Notting Hill* ☎ *020/7221–1992* 🌐 *www.booksforcooks.com* Ⓜ *Notting Hill Gate, Ladbroke Grove.*

CLOTHING

Aimé

CLOTHING | French-Cambodian sisters Val and Vanda Heng-Vong launched this shop to showcase the best of French clothing and designer housewares. Expect to find cult French labels like Isabel Marant, Forte Forte, and Michel Vivien, along with housewares and a well-chosen collection of ceramics. Petit Aimé, next door, sells children's clothing. There's also a Shoreditch branch. ✉ *32 Ledbury Rd., Notting Hill* ☎ *020/7221–7070* 🌐 *www.aimelondon.com* Ⓜ *Notting Hill Gate.*

Caramel Baby & Child

CLOTHING | FAMILY | This is the place for adorable yet understated clothes for children six months and up: handcrafted Peruvian alpaca cardigans in sherbet colors, floral cotton dresses for girls; check shirts and earth-tone tees for boys; comfortable pants in twill, corduroy, and cotton for both; and merino cashmere sweaters for extremely fashionable babies, plus shoes and accessories. A range of Mom-size clothing is offered in a similar vein. Caramel also sells a small selection of children's books and traditional toys, as well as decorative-functional items like sleeping bags, lamps, and quilts. Prices are no bargain, but the quality is superb. On Monday, Tuesday, and Saturday the shop offers a hair salon for little customers. There's another branch in South Kensington and outlets in Selfridges and Harrods. ✉ *77 Ledbury Rd., Notting Hill* ☎ *020/7727–0906* 🌐 *www.caramel-shop.co.uk* Ⓜ *Westbourne Park, Notting Hill Gate.*

The Cross

CLOTHING | One of the first "lifestyle boutiques" and still one of the best, this west London favorite carries luxury casual fashion by in-the-know favorites like Vanessa Bruno, Velvet, and Chinti & Parker, plus accessories, jewelry, housewares, and kids' clothes. The emphasis is on feminine and quirky boho chic. ✉ *141 Portland Rd., Notting Hill* ☎ *020/7727–6760* 🌐 *www.thecrossshop.co.uk* 🕓 *Closed Sun.* Ⓜ *Holland Park.*

Raey

CLOTHING | This affordable in-house offshoot line of high-end designer destination 🌐 *matchesfashion.com* has quickly become a fashion editor favorite thanks to Raey's minimalist, wearable styles for men and women that use luxurious fabrics and superb cuts far above their price points (cotton jersey T-shirts start at £85 going up to shearling jackets for £1,200). This is the brand's first standalone store. Matches Fashion itself has boutiques next door and farther down the road. ✉ *83 Ledbury Rd., Notting Hill* ☎ *020/7221–1120* 🌐 *www.matchesfashion.com* Ⓜ *Notting Hill Gate.*

Rellik

CLOTHING | Now in the modernist landmark known as the Trellick Tower and favored by the likes of Kate Moss, Rellik began as a stall in the Portobello Market. Vintage hunters looking to splurge can find a selection of YSL, Dior, Pierre Cardin, and Ossie Clark as well as items from lesser-known designers. ✉ *Trellick Tower, 8 Golborne Rd., Notting Hill* ☎ *020/8962–0089* 🌐 *www.relliklondon.co.uk* 🕓 *Closed Sun. and Mon.* Ⓜ *Westbourne Park.*

MUSIC

Music & Video Exchange

MUSIC STORES | This store is a music collector's treasure trove, with a constantly changing stock refreshed by customers selling and exchanging as well as buying. The ground floor focuses on rock, pop, indie, and punk, both mainstream and obscure, in a variety of formats ranging from vinyl to CD, cassette, and even minidisk. Don't miss the classical music in the basement and the soul, jazz, house, techno, reggae, and more upstairs. Like movies? There's a wide variety of Blu-ray and DVD box sets, as well as bargain classic and cult films. Keep an eye out for rarities—including first pressings and one-offs—in all departments. Similar exchanges for comics (No. 32) and books (No. 30) are on nearby Pembridge Road (also a destination for vintage clothing for men [No. 34] and women [No. 20], plus more clothing, accessories, and retro homewares [No. 28]). Note: Stock depends on what customers bring in to exchange, so you'll surely find many more DVDs with European (PAL) formatting than the North American–friendly NTSC format, but the store does get the latter occasionally. ✉ *38 Notting Hill Gate, Notting Hill* ☎ *020/7243–8573* 🌐 *www.mgeshops.com* Ⓜ *Notting Hill Gate.*

SHOES

Emma Hope

SHOES/LUGGAGE/LEATHER GOODS | The signature look of the footwear here is elegant and feminine, with pointed toes and kitten heels, often ornamented with bows, lace, crystals, or exquisite embroidery (such craftsmanship doesn't come cheap, unfortunately). Ballet flats and sneakers in velvet or animal prints provide glamour without sacrificing comfort. Alternatively, there's small but perfectly formed handbags, as well as shoes and accessories for men. ✉ *207 Westbourne Grove, Notting Hill* ☎ *020/7313–7493* 🌐 *www.emmahope.com* Ⓜ *Notting Hill Gate.*

Bayswater

East of Notting Hill Gate Tube station, Notting Hill turns into Bayswater, characterized by wide streets lined with imposing white stucco terraced houses. Traditionally given over to cheap bed-and-breakfasts, many are being converted back to private homes as the area continues to gentrify. The eastern end of Westbourne Grove and the streets around it are known for their excellent restaurants, particularly Chinese, Lebanese, and Greek.

Nearby **Paddington Station** is as well known for its association with the world's most famous marmalade fan, Paddington Bear, as it is for being one of London's more handsome rail terminals.

Restaurants

Hereford Road

$ | **MODERN BRITISH** | **FAMILY** | A Bayswater favorite with the well-connected Notting Hill set, Hereford Road is renowned for its pared-down, pomp-free, and ingredient-driven seasonal British fare, with an emphasis on well-sourced regional British produce. Work your way through uncluttered combos like steamed mussels with cider and thyme, lemon sole with roast cauliflower and capers, or chilled English rice pudding with a dollop of strawberry jam. **Known for:** pared-back Modern British nose-to-tail dining; deceptively simple-sounding dishes like duck livers with green beans; famously affordable two- and three-course set lunches. *Average main: £15 ✉ 3 Hereford Rd., Bayswater ☎ 020/7727–1144 🌐 www.herefordroad.org ⊙ No lunch Mon.–Wed. Ⓜ Bayswater, Queensway.*

Royal China Club

$$ | **CANTONESE** | **FAMILY** | This busy Cantonese restaurant has become something of an institution over the years, and locals insist it serves the best dim sum in London. From succulent crab and spinach steamed dumplings to delicate honey-glazed pork puffs, each dim sum is a parcel of pure perfection. **Known for:** traditional dim sum (meaning it's served only during lunchtime); authentic, delicious Cantonese fare for dinner; elegant, comfortable surroundings. *Average main: £20 ✉ 13 Queensway, Bayswater ☎ 020/7221–2535 🌐 www.royalchina-group.co.uk/restaurants/queensway Ⓜ Queensway, Bayswater.*

Hotels

Colonnade

$$ | **HOTEL** | Near a canal filled with colorful "narrowboats" in the Little Venice neighborhood, this lovely town house offers individually styled rooms, some of which are split-level; others have balconies filled with rich brocades, velvets, and antiques. **Pros:** beautifully decorated; unique and little-known part of London by the Regent's Canal; free Wi-Fi. **Cons:** you have to go through shoddier parts of town to get here; rooms are small; not the closest location for visiting major sights. *Rooms from: £130 ✉ 2 Warrington Crescent, Bayswater ☎ 020/7286–1052 🌐 www.colonnadehotel.co.uk 43 rooms Free breakfast Ⓜ Warwick Ave.*

London House Hotel

$ | **HOTEL** | Set in a row of white Georgian town houses, this excellent budget option in hit-or-miss Bayswater is friendly, well run, and spotlessly clean. **Pros:** friendly and efficient; emphasis on value; good location. **Cons:** basement rooms lack sunlight; smallest rooms are tiny; the area isn't quite as vibrant as neighboring Notting Hill. *Rooms from: £110 ✉ 81 Kensington Garden Sq., Bayswater ☎ 020/7243–1810 🌐 www.londonhouse-hotels.com 103 rooms No meals Ⓜ Queensway, Bayswater.*

Parkwood Hotel

$$ | **B&B/INN** | Just seconds from Hyde Park in one of London's swankiest enclaves, this sweet little guesthouse

is an oasis of value, with warm and helpful hosts and bright guest rooms that are simply furnished with pastel color schemes and reproduction antique beds. **Pros:** fascinating but ghastly nearby history; free Wi-Fi; hotel guarantees to match or beat rate of any other hotel of its class in the area. **Cons:** often booked up in advance; no elevator and no ground-floor bedrooms; front-facing rooms can be noisy. $ *Rooms from: £130* ✉ *4 Stanhope Pl., Bayswater* ☎ *020/7402–2241* 🌐 *www.london-parkwood.com* *16 rooms* 🍴 *Free breakfast* Ⓜ *Marble Arch.*

Space Apart Hotel

$$ | RENTAL | These studio apartments near Hyde Park are done in soothing tones of white and gray, with polished wood floors and attractive modern kitchenettes equipped with all you need to make small meals. **Pros:** especially good value; the larger suites have space for four people; handy location. **Cons:** no in-house restaurant or bar; two-night minimum stay; standard apartments are small. $ *Rooms from: £140* ✉ *36–37 Kensington Gardens Sq., Bayswater* ☎ *020/7908–1340* 🌐 *www.aparthotel-london.co.uk* *30 rooms* 🍴 *No meals* Ⓜ *Bayswater.*

Chapter 12

REGENT'S PARK AND HAMPSTEAD

Updated by
Ellin Stein

Sights	Restaurants	Hotels	Shopping	Nightlife
★★★★☆	★★☆☆☆	★★☆☆☆	★★★☆☆	★★★☆☆

REGENT'S PARK AND HAMPSTEAD SNAPSHOT

TOP REASONS TO GO

Hampstead Heath: Londoners adore the Heath for providing an escape to the countryside without leaving the city.

Keats House: Visit the rooms where one of England's greatest poets wrote some of his major works, inspired by his love for the girl-next-door, Fanny Brawne.

Regent's Park: Cycle past Nash's grand neoclassical stucco terraces or walk up Primrose Hill for a great view over the city.

Kenwood House: See one of Britain's best art collections at this 18th-century gentleman's estate largely designed by Robert Adam.

The London Zoo: A VIP ticket will let you get up close and personal with the penguins at the city's zoo.

GETTING THERE

To get to Hampstead by Tube, take the Northern Line (the Edgware branch) to Hampstead or Golders Green Station, or take the London Overground to Hampstead Heath Station. The south side of Hampstead Heath can also be reached by the London Overground Gospel Oak Station. To get to Regent's Park, take the Bakerloo Line to Regent's Park Tube station or, for Primrose Hill, the Chalk Farm stop on the Northern Line. Little Venice is reachable by the Warwick Avenue stop on the Bakerloo Line and St. John's Wood has its own stop on the Jubilee Line.

MAKING THE MOST OF YOUR TIME

Regent's Park, Primrose Hill, and Hampstead can be covered in a day. Spend the morning in Hampstead, with a brief foray onto the Heath, then head south to Regent's Park in the afternoon so that you're closer to central London come nightfall, if that is where your hotel is located. (You'll also be heading downhill instead of up.) You can always return to Hampstead another day for a long walk across the Heath or to head west to Little Venice's canals.

FEELING PECKISH?

■ **Ginger and White** Family-friendly and thoroughly modern, Ginger and White is a delightful fusion of continental-style café and traditional British "caff"—all bound up with a sophisticated Hampstead vibe. ✉ *4A–5A Perrins Ct., Hampstead* ☎ *020/7431–9098* 🌐 *www.gingerandwhite.com* ⏲ *No dinner* Ⓜ *Hampstead.*

■ **Marine Ices** Near the Camden Lock market, this family-owned ice cream parlour serves its own brand of artisanal gelato and sorbet that's one of London's best. ✉ *Old Dairy Mews, 61 Chalk Farm Rd., Camden Town* ☎ *020/7428–9990* 🌐 *www.marineices.co.uk* Ⓜ *Chalk Farm.*

SAFETY

■ Avoid Hampstead Heath, Primrose Hill, and Regent's Park at night unless there's an event; all are perfectly safe during the day. Also to be avoided after dark: the canal towpath in Primrose Hill and Camden.

Regent's Park, Primrose Hill, Belsize Park, and Hampstead are four of London's prettiest and most genteel neighborhoods. The city becomes noticeably calmer and greener as you head uphill from Marylebone Road through Regent's Park to the refreshing greenery of Primrose Hill and the handsome Georgian houses and Regency villas of Hampstead. To the west, the less bucolic but equally elegant St. John's Wood and Little Venice also provide a taste of moneyed London.

Leaving the park at the London Zoo, walk up adjoining **Primrose Hill** for one of the most picturesque views of London. Long a magnet for the creative (though these days within reach of only the most well-heeled creatives), this is the kind of neighborhood where the local library's screening of *The Madness of King George* is introduced by its writer, long-time resident Alan Bennett. Peel off from the Hill to explore Regent's Park Road and its attractive independent shops and cafés, as well as the surrounding streets with their pastel Victorian villas.

Alternatively, continue hugging the Hill heading north along Primrose Hill Road. This will take you to Belsize Park, itself a celebrity hot spot (Tim Burton and Hugh Laurie have houses here) with a mixture of Victorian, Arts and Crafts, and art deco buildings. Turn right onto England's Lane, another street full of independent shops and nice cafés, then left onto Haverstock Hill and head farther uphill. At the corner of Pond Street you will see two enormous Victorian Gothic buildings: one, St. Stephen's Church, is now a community arts center. The other, AIR Studios, founded by the Beatles' producer, Sir George Martin, is where scores for movies, including *Iron Man 3, Paddington 2,* and *Dunkirk,* have been recorded.

Turn right onto Pond Street and go downhill past the unlovely Royal Free Hospital to South End Green and the entrance to **Hampstead Heath.** Or go straight to stay on Rosslyn Hill and then Hampstead High Street, the neighborhood's main drag. Turn left onto Church Row, with its unspoiled early Georgian terraced houses leading to **St. John's-at-Hampstead,** where the painter John Constable is buried. To the northeast of Hampstead Heath is Highgate, another upscale north London "village" with a large concentration of Georgian and early Victorian buildings, particularly around The Grove (home to Kate Moss [who lives in Samuel Taylor Coleridge's former residence] and Jude Law).

To reach **Little Venice,** go to the west entrance of Regent's Park by the gold-domed London Central Mosque and then north past **Lord's Cricket Ground** to the St. John's Wood Tube stop. Turn left onto Grove End Road, which will bring you to the famous Abbey Road crosswalk featured on the Beatles' album of the same name. Head southwest for Little Venice, known as the Belgravia of north London due to its stucco terraces (found on streets such as Randolph Avenue, Clifton Avenue, and Randolph Road) that are very similar to the other neighborhood's. The "Venice" comes from its proximity to a picturesque stretch of the Grand Union Canal along Blomfield Road, where highly decorative houseboats are moored. If you happen to be here on the second Sunday in May, you'll be able to see houseboats from all over London's canals gather here in Paddington Basin for the Blessing of the Boats.

Regent's Park with Primrose Hill and Camden Town

Commissioned by his patron the Prince Regent (later George IV) to create a master plan for this part of London, formerly a royal hunting ground, London's great urban planner and architect John Nash laid out the plans for the 410-acre Regent's Park in 1812. Bordered by grand neoclassical terraces, the park holds many attractions, including the London Zoo and the summer display of more than 400 varieties of rose in Queen Mary's Gardens.

Sights

Cecil Sharp House

ARTS VENUE | The home of the English Folk Dance and Song Society, this soaring building from 1930 hosts concerts by artists ranging from Mumford & Sons and Laura Marling to the Ukulele Orchestra of Great Britain, as well as family barn dances and *céilidhs* (Irish barn dances). Meet the locals at one of the drop-in dance classes offering everything from Regency and Victorian ballroom dancing and tango to English, Irish, and American folk dancing. There are also temporary exhibitions on British folk art, a café and bar, and an outstanding specialist library with an extensive collection of recordings, manuscripts, sheet music, and images relating to British folk song, dances, and regional cultures in general. ✉ *2 Regent's Park Rd., Primrose Hill* ☎ *020/7485–2206* 🌐 *www.cecilsharphouse.org* 🎫 *Free, classes from £4* ⏲ *Library closed Aug., Mon., and 2nd and 4th Sat. of each month* Ⓜ *Chalk Farm, Camden Town.*

Jewish Museum

MUSEUM | This fascinating museum tells the story of Britain's Jewish community through a combination of art, religious artifacts, photographs, manuscripts, and interactive displays. Its permanent exhibitions include an exploration of Jewish history in Britain from 1066 to today, including the period between the 13th and 17th centuries when Judaism was outlawed in England. It also features a recreation of a Jewish East End street from the Victorian era and displays relating to refugees from Nazism, including the 10,000 Jewish Kindertransport children who came to Britain as World War II loomed. Other permanent exhibitions include the story of a Britain-based Holocaust survivor and a medieval *mikveh* (ritual bath) excavated a few miles from here in 2001. A free overview of the museum can be found on the ground floor, along with rotating temporary exhibitions and a collection of personal diaries, letters, medals, uniforms, and souvenirs from Jewish soldiers who served in the British military. ✉ *Raymond Burton House, 129–131 Albert St., Camden Town* ☎ *020/7284–7384* 🌐 *www.jewishmuseum.org.uk* 🎫 *£9* ⏲ *Closed major Jewish holidays* Ⓜ *Camden Town.*

Lord's Cricket Ground & Museum

MUSEUM | The spiritual home of this most English of games—and the headquarters of the MCC (Marylebone Cricket Club)—opens its "behind the scenes" areas to visitors during a 100-minute tour. Highlights include the beautiful Long Room, a VIP viewing area where portraits of cricketing greats are on display (you can also book a traditional Afternoon Tea here); the players' dressing rooms; and the world's oldest sporting museum, where cricket's 400-year progress from gentlemanly village-green game to worldwide sport is charted via memorabilia, equipment, trophies, and footage of memorable performances. Don't miss the prize exhibit: the urn known as the Ashes—allegedly the remains of a cricket bail (part of the wicket assembly) presented to the English captain in 1883 by a group of Australian women, a jokey allusion to a newspaper's satirical obituary for the death of English cricket published after a resounding defeat. It's been a symbol of the two nations' long-running rivalry ever since. They still play for possession of the Ashes—an official (as opposed to joke) trophy only since 1998—every two years. A Waterford crystal version changes hands these days, although the winners still hold a replica of the original urn aloft. There is no separate nontour admittance to the museum, except for match ticket holders. All tours must be booked in advance, and are not available during matches. Tour itineraries can change due to grounds maintenance. ✉ *St. John's Wood Rd., St. John's Wood* ☎ *020/7616–8595* 🌐 *www.lords.org* 🎫 *Tour £25; museum £5 with county match ticket, free with major match ticket* ⏲ *Closed late Dec.; no tours Apr.–Sept. on major match days, preparation days, and event days; limited availability on other match days* Ⓜ *St. John's Wood.*

★ Primrose Hill

CITY PARK | **FAMILY** | More conventionally parklike than Hampstead Heath, the rolling lawns of Primrose Hill, the northerly extension of Regent's Park, rises to 213 feet and provides outstanding views over the city to the southeast, encompassing Canary Wharf and the London Eye. Formerly the site of boxing matches and duels but now filled with families and picnickers in nice weather, it has been featured in several books—it was here that Pongo engaged in "twilight barking" in *The Hundred and One Dalmatians* and the Martians set up an encampment in H.G. Wells's *The War of The Worlds*. It's also been mentioned in songs by Blur, Madness, and Paul McCartney, among others, and served as a location for films including *Bridget Jones: The Edge of Reason*, and *Paddington*. ✉ *Regent's Park Rd., Regent's Park* ☎ *0300/061–2300* 🌐 *www.royalparks.org.uk* 🎫 *Free* Ⓜ *Chalk Farm.*

★ Regent's Park

CITY PARK | **FAMILY** | One of London's principal charms is to find the formal cultivated serenity of Regent's Park—more country-house grounds than municipal amenity—just on the edge of the intensely urban West End, a world away from the traffic-clogged surrounding roads. The 395-acre park, with the largest grass area for sports in central London, draws the athletically inclined from around the city.

At the center of the park, **Queen Mary's Gardens,** created in the 1930s, are a fragrant 17-acre circle containing some 30,000 individual specimens and more than 400 varieties of roses. Unsurprisingly, it's a favorite spot for weddings. Just to the east of the Gardens is the **Regent's Park Open-Air Theatre** and the **Boating Lake,** the latter best explored by renting a pedalo (paddleboat) or rowboat.

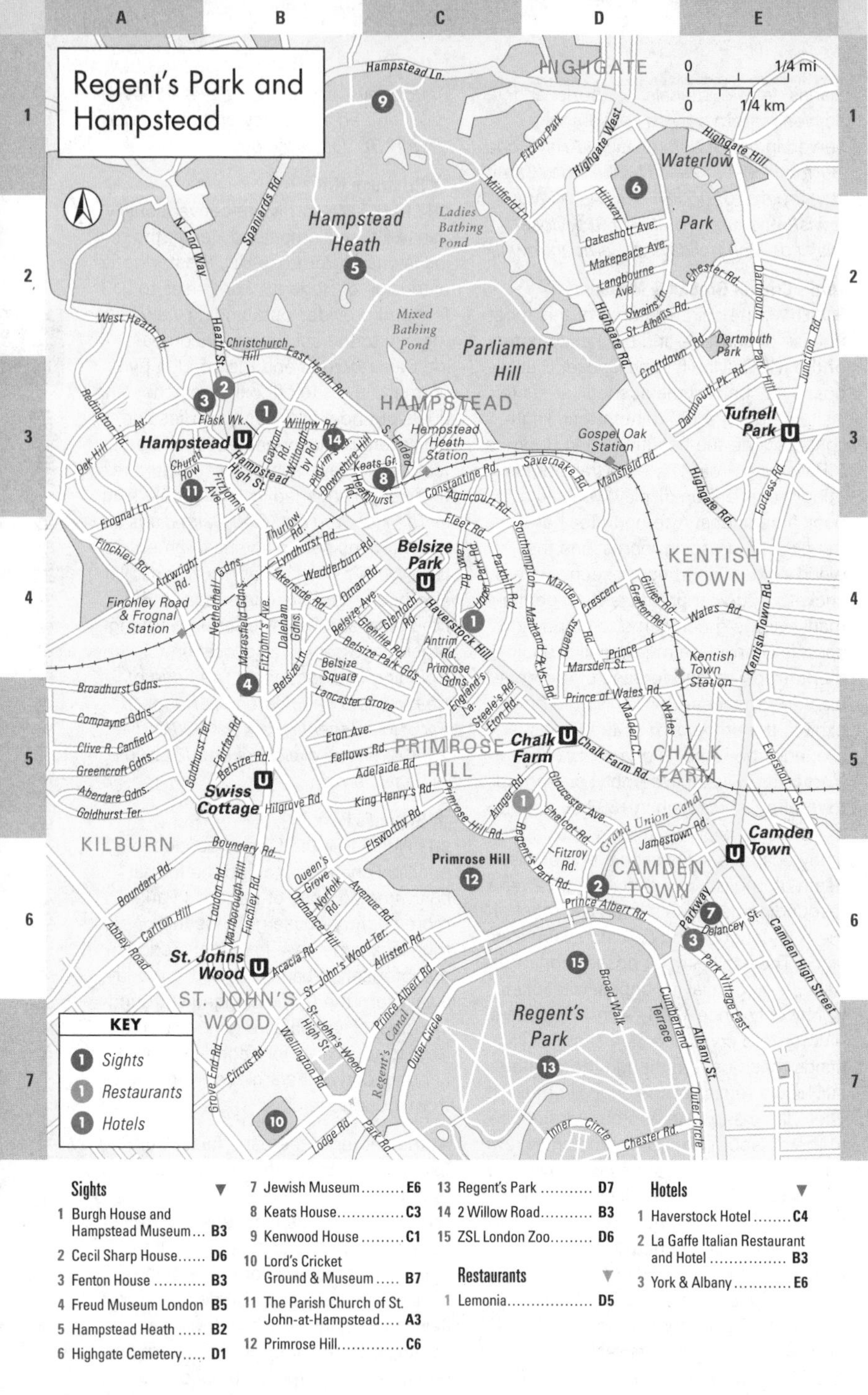

Sights

1 Burgh House and Hampstead Museum... B3
2 Cecil Sharp House...... D6
3 Fenton House B3
4 Freud Museum London B5
5 Hampstead Heath B2
6 Highgate Cemetery..... D1
7 Jewish Museum......... E6
8 Keats House.............. C3
9 Kenwood House C1
10 Lord's Cricket Ground & Museum B7
11 The Parish Church of St. John-at-Hampstead.... A3
12 Primrose Hill.............. C6
13 Regent's Park D7
14 2 Willow Road........... B3
15 ZSL London Zoo......... D6

Restaurants

1 Lemonia.................. D5

Hotels

1 Haverstock Hotel........ C4
2 La Gaffe Italian Restaurant and Hotel B3
3 York & Albany E6

Heading east from the rose gardens along Chester Road past the **Broad Walk** brings you to Nash's iconic white stucco **Cumberland Terrace,** with its central Ionic columns surmounted by a triangular Wedgwood-blue pediment (home to artist Damien Hirst). At the north end of the Broad Walk you'll find the **London Zoo,** while to the northwest of the central circle is **The Hub**, London's largest outdoor sports facility that has changing rooms, exercise classes, and a café with 360-degree views of the surrounding sports fields, used for soccer, rugby, cricket, field hockey, and softball. There are also tennis courts toward the park's southeast (Baker Street) entrance, and the park is a favorite north–south route for cyclists. **■ TIP→ Regent's Park also hosts two annual events: the prestigious Frieze Art Fair, and the Taste of London, a foodie-oriented extravaganza.** ✉ *Chester Rd., Regent's Park* ☎ *0300/061–2300* 🌐 *www.royalparks.org.uk* 🎟 *Free* Ⓜ *Baker St., Regent's Park, Great Portland St.*

★ ZSL London Zoo

ZOO | FAMILY | With an emphasis on education, wildlife conservation, and the breeding of endangered species, London Zoo offers visitors the chance to see tigers, gorillas, meerkats, and more in something resembling a natural environment rather than a cage. Operated by the nonprofit Zoological Society of London, the zoo was begun with the royal animals collection, moved here from the Tower of London in 1828; the zoo itself did not open to the public until 1847. Big attractions include Land of the Lions, a walk-through re-creation of an Indian forest where you can see three resident Asiatic lions relaxing at close range; Gorilla Kingdom, which provides a similar re-created habitat (in this case an African rain forest) for its colony of six Western Lowland Gorillas; and the Attenborough Komodo Dragon House, renamed to honor the renowned naturalist. The zoo also offers the chance to get up close and personal with 15 ring-tailed lemurs. The huge B.U.G.S. pavilion (Biodiversity Underpinning Global Survival) is a self-sustaining, contained ecosystem for 140 less-cuddly species, including invertebrates such as spiders and millipedes, plus some reptiles and fish. Rainforest Life is an indoor tropical rain forest (complete with humidity) inhabited by the likes of armadillos, monkeys, and sloths. A special nighttime section offers glimpses of nocturnal creatures like slow lorises and bats. The Animal Adventures Children's Zoo allows kids to closely observe coatis, as well as to interact with llamas, donkeys, small pigs, sheep, and goats. Two of the most popular attractions are Penguin Beach, especially at feeding time (1:30 and 4:30), and meerkat snack time (11:15), where you can see the sociable animals keeping watch over their own sandy territory.

If you're feeling flush, try to nab one of the six daily "Meet the Penguins" VIP tickets (1:45 pm) that offer a 20-minute guided close encounter with the locals (£54); there are similar VIP encounters with giraffes, meerkats, and various denizens of the rain forest. Other zoo highlights include Butterfly Paradise and Tiger Territory, an enclosure for four beautiful endangered Sumatran tigers (including two cubs born at the zoo). Adults-only Zoo Nights held Friday nights in June and July offer street food, alcoholic drinks, and entertainment. You can also experience the zoo after-hours by booking an overnight stay in one of the cozy cabins near (not *in*) the lion enclosure. Check the website or the information board out front for free events, including creature close encounters and "ask the keeper" sessions. ✉ *Outer Circle, Regent's Park* ☎ *0844/225–1826* 🌐 *www.zsl.org* 🎟 *From £27* Ⓜ *Camden Town, then Bus 274.*

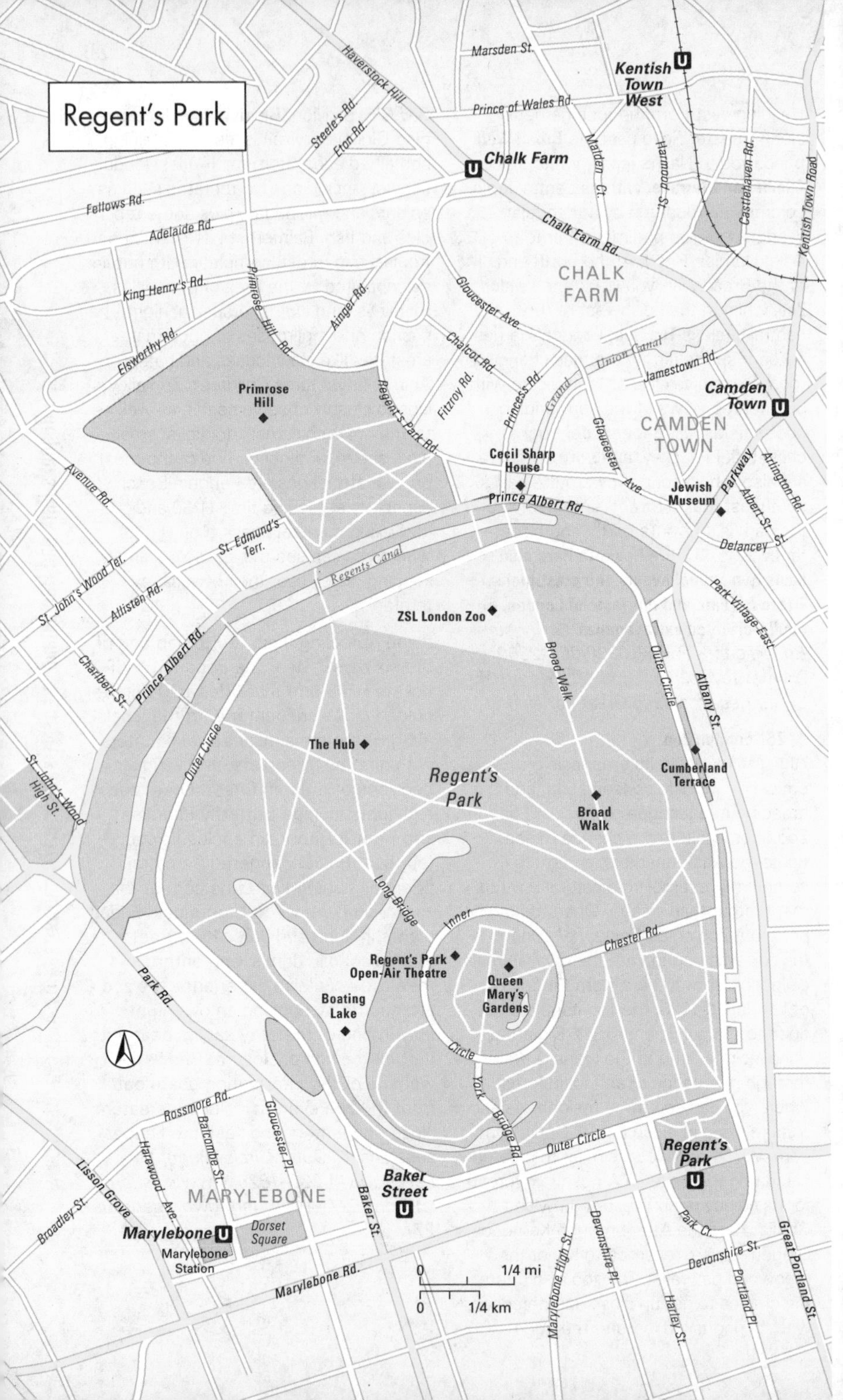
Regent's Park
Marsden St.
Kentish Town West
Haverstock Hill
Prince of Wales Rd.
Steele's Rd.
Eton Rd.
Chalk Farm
Malden Ct.
Harmood St.
Castlehaven Rd.
Kentish Town Road
Fellows Rd.
Adelaide Rd.
Chalk Farm Rd.
CHALK FARM
King Henry's Rd.
Primrose Hill Rd.
Ainger Rd.
Gloucester Ave.
Elsworthy Rd.
Chalcot Rd.
Grand Union Canal
Jamestown Rd.
Primrose Hill
Regent's Park Rd.
Fitzroy Rd.
Princess Rd.
Camden Town
CAMDEN TOWN
Gloucester Ave.
Cecil Sharp House
Parkway
Arlington Rd.
Avenue Rd.
Jewish Museum
Albert St.
Prince Albert Rd.
St. Edmund's Terr.
Delancey St.
Regents Canal
St. John's Wood Ter.
Allisten Rd.
Park Village East
ZSL London Zoo
Prince Albert Rd.
Broad Walk
Outer Circle
Albany St.
Charlbert St.
Outer Circle
The Hub
Cumberland Terrace
Regent's Park
St. John's Wood High St.
Broad Walk
Long Bridge
Inner
Chester Rd.
Regent's Park Open-Air Theatre
Queen Mary's Gardens
Park Rd.
Boating Lake
Circle
York Bridge Rd.
Rossmore Rd.
Gloucester Pl.
Balcombe St.
Harewood Ave.
Outer Circle
Regent's Park
Lisson Grove
Baker Street
MARYLEBONE
Baker St.
Broadley St.
Marylebone
Dorset Square
Marylebone Station
Park Cr.
Devonshire Pl.
Marylebone High St.
Devonshire St.
Great Portland St.
Marylebone Rd.
0
1/4 mi
0
1/4 km
Harley St.
Portland Pl.

Restaurants

The high-profile but low-key residents of Primrose Hill love the unpretentious, family-friendly neighborhood restaurants like Lemonia. Meanwhile farther north, leafy Hampstead is known for its cozy, atmospheric pubs converted from 17th-century coaching inns, with wood beams, open fireplaces, and hearty Sunday roast lunches.

Lemonia

$$ | **GREEK** | **FAMILY** | This consistently popular, family-run, taverna-style restaurant has been serving local families and celebrities alike in its large, vine-decked premises for more than 40 years. Besides a large selection of Greek Cypriot small-dish meze dips, hot breads, and starters, there are rustic mains like moussaka or slow-baked *kleftiko* lamb in lemon. **Known for:** Greek taverna-style atmosphere; meze, moussaka, and grilled sea bass; great weekday set lunches. *Average main: £16* *89 Regent's Park Rd., Primrose Hill* *020/7586–7454* *www.lemonia.co.uk* *No dinner Sun.* *Chalk Farm.*

Hotels

You'll find a few outposts of the mega-chains in North London, but accommodations with character are surprisingly hard to find in this area otherwise so laden with it.

York & Albany

$$ | **HOTEL** | Located on the northern edge of Regent's Park opposite the zoo entrance, this town house hotel with stylish, individually decorated rooms is owned by noted chef Gordon Ramsay, who also operates the restaurant on the ground floor. **Pros:** location close to Regent's Park and Camden town; excellent restaurant on-site; charming decor that is both traditional and modern. **Cons:** some traffic noise from outside road; hotel located at busy intersection; rooms not spacious for the price. *Rooms from: £210* *127–129 Parkway, London* *207/387–5700* *www.gordonramsay-restaurants.com/york-and-albany* *9 rooms* *No meals* *Camden Town.*

Nightlife

London's villagelike northern neighborhoods all boast fantastic local pubs where you can easily while away an afternoon. Camden Town has more of a buzz and attracts a younger international crowd with its dance clubs and music venues. Every genre is covered, from folk and indie to jazz and world music, with interesting gigs taking place every night of the week. In short, the spirit of the area's most well-known musical daughter, Amy Winehouse, is still venerated here.

DANCE CLUBS

KOKO

DANCE CLUBS | Once known as the Camden Palace, this legendary venue has lush red decor and gilt-trimmed boxes that recall its past as a Victorian theater, but now packs the dance floor with genres from punk and acid house to funky house, club classics, and indie. Headliners who have performed "secret" gigs here include Madonna, Prince, Kanye West, Bruno Mars, Skepta, The Red Hot Chili Peppers, and Amy Winehouse. A recent renovation expanded the space into two adjoining buildings, adding five more performance areas, three restaurants, and a roof terrace; its reopening will occur in spring 2020. *1A Camden High St., Camden Town* *020/7388–3222* *www.koko.uk.com* *From £6* *Mornington Crescent.*

LIVE MUSIC

The Camden Assembly

MUSIC CLUBS | At one of the finest small clubs in the capital, punk, indie guitar, and new metal rock attract a nonmainstream crowd. Weekend club nights upstairs host DJs (and live bands) who rock the decks. ✉ *49 Chalk Farm Rd., Camden Town* ☎ *020/7424–0800 for venue, 020/7424–0800 for tickets* 🌐 *www.camdenassembly.com* 🎟 *Free–£14* Ⓜ *Chalk Farm.*

The Dublin Castle

MUSIC CLUBS | Run by the same family for nearly three decades, The Dublin Castle has hosted almost every British rock group you care to name, from Madness to Coldplay. With four bands on the bill almost every night, and DJs taking over afterward on Friday and weekends, there's something for most tastes at this legendary venue. ✉ *94 Parkway, Camden Town* ☎ *07949/575–149* 🌐 *www.thedublincastle.com* 🎟 *From £4* Ⓜ *Camden Town.*

★ Jazz Café

DANCE CLUBS | A long-standing hotbed of cool in Camden, the Jazz Café hosts top acts in mainstream jazz as well as hip-hop, funk, world music, soul, and Latin fusion. On Saturday nights a DJ plays disco, house, and soul. Book ahead if you want a table in the balcony restaurant overlooking the stage; otherwise you'll standing (and probably dancing). ✉ *5 Parkway, Camden Town* ☎ *020/7485–6834 for venue info, 020/7485–6834 for tickets (Ticketmaster)* 🌐 *www.thejazzcafelondon.com* 🎟 *From £5* Ⓜ *Camden Town.*

Roundhouse

MUSIC CLUBS | This 1840s former railway terminus and onetime gin warehouse in Chalk Farm now hosts a varied program of circus, theater, contemporary dance, the occasional art installation, and even a bit of Lucha Libre (Mexican wrestling). Usually there's a genre-busting assortment of new and familiar musical acts, most of them cult favorites ranging from world and electronica to indie and emo. Standing tickets offer good value. There's a nice restaurant on the first floor, and in the summer, the terrace bar is transformed into a popular "urban beach," complete with sand, a retro bar, palm trees, and outdoor film screenings. ✉ *Chalk Farm Rd., Chalk Farm* ☎ *0300/6789–222* 🌐 *www.roundhouse.org.uk* 🎟 *From £5* Ⓜ *Chalk Farm.*

O2 Forum Kentish Town

MUSIC CLUBS | The best up-and-coming and medium-to-big-name music acts (recent bookings have included Lizzo, The Specials, Primal Scream, and So Solid Crew) consistently play at this 2,000-capacity club. It's a converted 1920 art deco movie theater, with a balcony (the only area with seats) overlooking the grungy dance floor. ✉ *9–17 Highgate Rd., Kentish Town* ☎ *0844/477–2000 for tickets* 🌐 *www.academymusicgroup.com/o2forumkentishtown* 🎟 *From £12* Ⓜ *Kentish Town.*

Performing Arts

Leafy north London has long been a stomping ground for the capital's cultural elite—stroll through Primrose Hill and you're practically guaranteed to spot a film star or musician—but there's diversity here, too. Camden Town is justifiably famous for its indie music scene, as well as leading stand-up comedy venues.

THEATER

Open Air Theatre

THEATER | **FAMILY** | Works by Shakespeare have been performed here every summer (from mid-May to mid-September) since 1932, with casts including luminaries such as Vivien Leigh, Dame Judi Dench, and Damien Lewis. Today the theater also mounts productions of classic plays, musicals, and shows for family audiences among its four annual productions. *A Midsummer Night's Dream* is the one to catch, if it's on—never has that enchanted Greek wood been better evoked, especially when enhanced by genuine birdsong and a rising moon. There's a covered restaurant for pretheater dining, an informal café, and, of course, a bar. You also can order picnic hampers in advance. The park can get chilly, so bring a blanket. Performances proceed rain or shine (umbrellas aren't allowed) with refunds only in case of a very heavy downpour. ✉ *Inner Circle, Regent's Park* ☎ *0844/826–4242* 🌐 *www.openairtheatre.com* 🎫 *From £25* Ⓜ *Baker St., Regent's Park.*

Shopping

HOUSEHOLD GOODS

Graham & Green

HOUSEHOLD ITEMS/FURNITURE | Combining style with practicality and a whimsical twist, this delightful interiors shop carries a broad but carefully curated selection of faux-fur throws, elegant lamps and lampshades, embroidered cushions, sheepskin rugs, agate or Venetian glass doorknobs, folding deck chairs (as found in the Royal Parks), shabby-chic sofas, ceramics and cutlery, dinosaur string lights, and more. There are branches in Notting Hill and Bayswater. ✉ *164 Regent's Park Rd., Primrose Hill* ☎ *020/7586–2960* 🌐 *www.grahamandgreen.co.uk* Ⓜ *Chalk Farm.*

MARKETS

The Camden Markets

OUTDOOR/FLEA/GREEN MARKETS | Begun in the early 1970s, when weekend stalls sold the output of nearby craft workshops, Camden Lock Market later expanded to four markets: Camden, Camden Lock, The Stables, and the Canal Market, all grouped around two locks on the Regent's Canal. Though much of the merchandise is targeted at young street-fashion aficionados as well as aging hippies, anyone with a taste for alternative culture will also find plenty that appeals. This shopping experience is best suited to those who don't mind large crowds and a boisterous atmosphere (i.e. teenagers), especially on weekends. For many years, the markets have hosted more than 1,000 stalls offering a wide-ranging array of merchandise—vintage and new clothes, antiques and junk, rare vinyl, vintage board games, ceramics, Indian bedspreads, fetishwear, obscure band memorabilia, and toys.

The outdoor Camden Market on Camden High Street mainly sells cheap jeans, secondhand clothes, and tacky pop-culture paraphernalia; Camden Lock Market is the place to go for crafts, clothes, and jewelry, plus loads of street food stalls; and The Stables Market, which has expanded into the so-called Catacombs (Victorian brick arches), has more than 700 shops and stalls and is where you go for furniture and vintage items. The former Canal Market is now known as Hawley Wharf, a mixed-use development with luxury apartment buildings plus retail and dining outlets, a canal-side farmer's market, and an arthouse cinema. The other three markets are currently ear-marked for further redevelopment, so more gentrification is in the cards—if the original scrappy, bohemian atmosphere of the area appeals to you, enjoy it while you can. ✉ *Camden High St. to Chalk Farm Rd., Camden Town* 🌐 *www.camdenmarket.com* Ⓜ *Camden Town, Chalk Farm.*

SHOES

Spice

SHOES/LUGGAGE/LEATHER GOODS | Touring London requires a lot of walking, so if your feet are crying out for mercy, stop in at this long-established boutique that specializes in spiffy but comfortable shoes, sandals, and boots for men and women from brands like Coccinelle, Arche, and Chie Mihara, as well as from its own Spice line. ✉ *162 Regent's Park Rd., Primrose Hill* ☎ *020/7722–2478* 🌐 *www.spiceshu.co.uk* Ⓜ *Chalk Farm.*

Hampstead

Back in 1818, even impoverished Romantic poet John Keats could afford to live in **Hampstead.** His former residence, now known as **Keats House,** is a pretty Regency villa where he spent two years and wrote several of his most famous works. These days Hampstead's bohemian past is long gone, although several distinguished writers, actors, and musicians still live here. Artisanal food shops and boutiques cluster along Hampstead High Street, where upscale high-street chains proliferate the closer you get to Hampstead Tube station. Be sure to leave the beaten path to explore the numerous narrow charming roads, like Flask Walk, Well Walk, and New End Road. Also hidden among Hampstead's winding streets are **Fenton House,** a Georgian town house with a lovely walled garden, and Burgh House, the oldest (1704) house in the village and a repository of local history.

Hampstead's biggest claim to fame, however, is **Hampstead Heath** (known locally as "The Heath"), 791 acres of verdant open space, woods, spring-fed swimming ponds, and some of Europe's oldest oaks. It's also home to one of London's highest vantage points (321 feet), Parliament Hill. On the Highgate end of Hampstead Heath, you'll find **Kenwood House,** an 18th-century mansion that was designed by Robert Adam and is noted for its remarkable art collection and grounds.

Sights

Burgh House and Hampstead Museum

HOUSE | One of Hampstead's oldest buildings, Burgh House was built in 1704 to take advantage of the natural spa waters of the then-fashionable Hampstead Wells. A private house until World War II, it was saved from dereliction in the 1970s by local residents, who have maintained it ever since. The building is a fine example of the genteel elegance common to the Queen Anne period, with brick frontage, oak-paneled rooms, and a terraced garden that was originally designed by Gertrude Jekyll. Today the house contains a small but diverting museum on the history of the area, and also hosts regular talks, concerts, and recitals. The secluded garden courtyard of the café is a lovely spot for lunch, tea, or a glass of wine on a summer's afternoon. ✉ *New End Sq., Hampstead* ☎ *020/7431–0144* 🌐 *www.burghhouse.org.uk* 🎫 *Free* 🕒 *Closed Mon., Tues., and Sat.* Ⓜ *Hampstead.*

Fenton House

GARDEN | This handsome 17th-century merchant's home, Hampstead's oldest surviving house, has fine collections of porcelain, Georgian furniture, and 17th-century needlework. The 2-acre walled garden, with its rose plantings and apple orchard, has remained virtually unchanged for 300 years; there are free garden tours led by the head gardener on Thursday at 2 pm, from May through September. International musicians give recitals on the important collection of early keyboard instruments throughout the week; check the website for details. ✉ *Hampstead Grove, Hampstead* ☎ *020/7435–3471* 🌐 *www.nationaltrust.org.uk* 🎫 *£9; £15 combination ticket with 2 Willow Rd.* 🕒 *Closed Mon. and Tues.* Ⓜ *Hampstead.*

Freud Museum London

MUSEUM | The father of psychoanalysis lived here with his family for a year, between his escape from Nazi persecution in his native Vienna in 1938 and his death in 1939. His daughter Anna (herself a pioneer of child psychoanalysis) remained in the house until her own death in 1982, bequeathing it as a museum to honor her father. The centerpiece is Freud's unchanged study, containing his remarkable collection of antiquities and his library. Also on display is the family's Biedermeier furniture—and, of course, the couch. As well, there are lectures, study groups, and themed exhibitions, in addition to a psychoanalysis-related archive and research library. Looking for a unique souvenir for the person who has everything? The gift shop here sells "Freudian Slippers." ✉ *20 Maresfield Gardens, Swiss Cottage*

The more residential neighborhoods of London, like Hampstead, are marked by rows of colorful houses called terraces.

☎ 020/7435–2002 🌐 www.freud.org.uk 🎫 £9 ⏲ Closed Tues. year-round and Mon. Oct.–Feb. Ⓜ Swiss Cottage, Finchley Rd.

★ Hampstead Heath

NATURE PRESERVE | FAMILY | For generations, Londoners have headed to Hampstead Heath to escape the dirt and noise of the city, and this unique 791-acre expanse of *rus in urbe* ("country in the city") is home to a variety of wildlife and habitat: grassy meadows, woodland, scrub, wetlands, and some of Europe's most venerable oaks. Be aware that, aside from the Parliament Hill area to the south and Golders Hill Park in the west, it is more like countryside than a park, with signs and amenities in short supply. Pick up a map at Kenwood House or at the "Enquiries" window of the Staff Yard near the tennis courts off Highgate Road, where you can also find details about the history of the Heath and its flora and fauna. An excellent café near the Edwardian bandstand serves Italian food.

Coming onto the Heath from the Savernake Road entrance on the southern side, walk past the **Playground** and **Paddling Pool** and head uphill to the top of **Parliament Hill.** At 321 feet above sea level, it's one of the highest points in London, providing a stunning panorama over the city. On clear days you can see all the way to the Surrey Hills beyond the city's southern limits. Keep heading north from Parliament Hill to find the more rural parts of the Heath.

If you keep heading east from the playground instead, turn right past the Athletics Track and you'll come to the **Lido,** an Olympic-size outdoor unheated swimming pool that gets packed on all-too-rare hot summer days. More swimming options are available at the Hampstead ponds, which have been refreshing Londoners for generations. You'll find the "Mens" and "Ladies" ponds to the northeast of Parliament Hill, with a "Mixed" pond closer to South End Green. A £2 donation is requested.

■ TIP→ Golders Hill Park, on the Heath Extension to the northwest, offers a good café, tennis courts, a duck pond, a croquet lawn, and a walled flower garden, plus a Butterfly House (May–September) and a small zoo with native species including muntjac deer, rare red squirrels, and a Scottish wildcat. ✉ *Hampstead* ☎ *020/7332–3322* 🌐 *www.cityoflondon.gov.uk/hampstead* 🎫 *Free* Ⓜ *Overground: Hampstead Heath for west of Heath or Gospel Oak for south and east of Heath and Lido; Northern Line: Golders Green, then Bus 210 or 268 to Whitestone Pond for north and west of Heath and Golders Hill Park.*

Highgate Cemetery

CEMETERY | Highgate is not the oldest cemetery in London, but it is probably the best known, both for its roster of famous "inhabitants" and the quality of its funerary architecture. After it was consecrated in 1839, Victorians came from miles around to appreciate the ornate headstones, the impressive tombs, and the view. Such was its popularity that 19 acres on the other side of the road were acquired in 1850, and this additional East Cemetery is the final resting place of numerous notables, including the most visited, Karl Marx (1818–83), as well as George Eliot and, a more recent internment, George Michael. At the summit is the **Circle of Lebanon,** a ring of vaults built around an ancient cypress tree, a legacy of the 17th-century gardens that formerly occupied the site. Leading from the circle is the **Egyptian Avenue,** a subterranean stone tunnel lined with catacombs, itself approached by a dramatic colonnade that screens the main cemetery from the road. Both sides are impressive, with a grand (locked) iron gate leading to a sweeping courtyard built for the approach of horses and carriages. By the 1970s the cemetery had become unkempt and neglected until a group of volunteers, the Friends of Highgate Cemetery, undertook the huge upkeep. Tours are conducted by the Friends, who will show you the most interesting graves among the numerous statues and memorials once hidden by overgrowth. The West side can only be seen during a one-hour tour. Booking is essential for weekdays but not permitted for weekends; tours of the East side on Saturday are first-come, first-served. You're expected to dress respectfully, so skip the shorts and the baseball cap; children under eight are not admitted and neither are dogs, tripods, or video cameras. Note that unless you book online in advance, admission and tour fees are cash-only. ✉ *Swains La., Highgate* ☎ *020/8340–1834* 🌐 *www.highgatecemetery.org* 🎫 *East Cemetery £4, tours £8; West Cemetery tours £12, includes admission to East Cemetery* Ⓜ *Archway, then Bus 210, 271, or 143 to Waterlow Park; Belsize Park, then Bus C11 to Brookfield Park.*

Keats House

HOUSE | It was while living in this house between 1818 and 1820 that the leading Romantic poet John Keats (1795–1821) fell in love with girl-next-door Fanny Brawne and wrote some of his best-loved poems. (Soon after, ill health forced him to move to Rome, where he died the following year.) After a major refurbishment to make the rooms more consistent with their original Regency style, the house now displays all sorts of Keats-related material, including portraits, letters, many of the poet's original manuscripts and books, the engagement ring he gave to Fanny, and items of her clothing. A pretty garden contains the plum tree under which Keats supposedly composed *Ode to a Nightingale.* There are free, half-hour guided tours daily at 1:30 pm and 3 pm, plus evening poetry readings, concerts, and special events featuring local literary luminaries. The ticket gives you entry for a full year, so you can come back as often as you like. Picnics can be taken onto the grounds during the summer. ✉ *10 Keats Grove, Hampstead* ☎ *020/7332–3868* 🌐 *www.cityoflondon.gov.uk/things-to-do/keats-house* 🎫 *£8* ⏲ *Closed Mon. and Tues.* Ⓜ *Overground: Hampstead Heath.*

The fabled cover of the Beatles' album *Abbey Road*, with the world's most famous traffic crossing

★ Kenwood House

HOUSE | This largely Palladian villa offers an escape to a gracious country house with a magnificent collection of Old Masters and beautiful grounds, all within a short Tube ride from central London. Originally built in 1616, Kenwood was expanded by Robert Adam starting in 1767 and later by George Saunders in 1795. Adam refaced most of the exterior and added the splendid library, which, with its vaulted ceiling and Corinthian columns, is the highlight of the house's interior. A major renovation restored four rooms to reflect Adam's intentions as closely as possible, incorporating the furniture he designed for them and his original color schemes. Kenwood is also home to the **Iveagh Bequest,** a world-class collection of some 60 paintings that includes masterworks like Rembrandt's *Self-Portrait with Two Circles* and Vermeer's *The Guitar Player,* along with major works by Reynolds, Van Dyck, Hals, Gainsborough, Turner, and more. The grounds, designed by Humphry Repton and bordered by Hampstead Heath, are equally elegant and serene, with lawns sloping down to a little lake crossed by a trompe-l'oeil bridge. All in all, it's the perfect home for an 18th-century gentleman. In summer, the grounds host a series of popular and classical concerts, culminating in fireworks on the last night. The Brew House café, occupying part of the old coach house, has outdoor tables in the courtyard and a terraced garden. ✉ *Hampstead La., Highgate* ☎ *0870/333–1181* 🌐 *www.english-heritage.org.uk/visit/places/kenwood* 🎫 *Free, house and estate tour £18* Ⓜ *Golders Green or Archway, then Bus 210. Overground: Gospel Oak.*

The Parish Church of St. John-at-Hampstead

RELIGIOUS SITE | There has been a church here since 1312, but the current building—consecrated in 1747 and later extended in 1877—is a fine example of neoclassical serenity, enhanced by Ionic columns and vaulting arches. Also known as the Hampstead Parish Church, it stands at the end of Church Row, a narrow street lined with flat-fronted brick

A Trip to Abbey Road

The black-and-white crosswalk (known as a "zebra crossing") near the Abbey Road Studios at No. 3, where the Beatles recorded their entire output from "Love Me Do" onward, is a place of pilgrimage for Beatles' fans from around the world, many of them teenagers born long after the band split up. They converge here to re-create the cover of the Beatles' 1969 *Abbey Road* album, posing on the crossing despite the onrushing traffic. **TIP→ Be careful if you're going to attempt this; traffic on Abbey Road is busy.** One of the best ways to explore landmarks in the Beatles' story is to take one of the excellent walking tours offered by **Original London Walks** (*020/7624–3978* *www.walks.com*). Try **The Beatles In-My-Life Walk** (Saturday and Tuesday at 11 am outside Marylebone Railway station) or **The Beatles Magical Mystery Tour** (Wednesday at 2 pm and Thursday except for December and January and Sunday at 11 am, at Underground Exit 1, Tottenham Court Road).

Georgian houses that gives you a sense of what Hampstead was like when it truly was a rural village as opposed to a traffic-clogged north London neighborhood. Many local notables are buried in the picturesque churchyard, including painter John Constable (some of whose most famous works depict the Heath), John Harrison (the inventor of the marine chronometer at the heart of the book *Longitude*), members of the artistic Du Maurier family, Jane Austen's aunt, and comedy god Peter Cook. *Church Row, Hampstead 020/7794–5808 www.hampsteadparishchurch.org.uk Free* *Hampstead.*

2 Willow Road

HOUSE | Among the many artists and intellectuals fleeing Nazi persecution who settled in the area was noted architect Erno Goldfinger, who built this outstanding and influential modernist home opposite Hampstead Heath in 1939 as his family residence. (His plans drew the ire of several local residents, including novelist Ian Fleming, who supposedly named a Bond villain after his neighbor to get revenge.) As well as design touches and building techniques that were groundbreaking at the time, the unique house, a place of pilgrimage for 20th-century architecture enthusiasts, also contains Goldfinger's impressive collection of modern art and self-designed innovative furniture. Between 11 am and 2 pm, admission is by first-come, first-served hourly tour only, but you can visit independently after 3. *2 Willow Rd., Hampstead 020/7435–6166 www.nationaltrust.org.uk From £8 Closed Mon. and Tues.* *Overground: Hampstead Heath.*

Hotels

Haverstock Hotel

$$ | HOTEL | Just down the hill from Hampstead Village is this stylish boutique hotel located in a converted pub. **Pros:** cool, minimalist decor; convenient to Hampstead, Belsize Park, and Primrose Hill; free Wi-Fi and buffet breakfast. **Cons:** no elevator; rooms on the small side; some rooms can be noisy. *Rooms from: £135 154 Haverstock Hill, Hampstead 020/7722–5097 www.haverstockhotel.com 22 rooms Free breakfast* *Belsize Park.*

La Gaffe Italian Restaurant and Hotel

$ | **B&B/INN** | The name of this unpretentious, family-run restaurant with rooms means "the mistake" in Italian, and it also provides the punchline to the unlikely tale of how the original owners (the parents of the current proprietor) met in the 1950s. **Pros:** unusual place with a cheerful atmosphere; great price; comes with the convenience of a traditional Italian restaurant below. **Cons:** few amenities; no elevator; small rooms. *Rooms from: £110* *107–111 Heath St., Hampstead* *020/7435–8965* *www.lagaffe.co.uk* *18 rooms* *Free breakfast* *Hampstead.*

Nightlife

PUBS

The Holly Bush

BARS/PUBS | A short walk up the hill from Hampstead Tube station, the friendly Holly Bush dates back to the 18th century and retains something of the country pub it was before London spread this far north, thanks to the stripped wooden floors, walls paneled in dark wood, and big open fires. The combination of great ales and organic, free-range gastropub food makes it perennially packed with locals. Try the Cornish crab on toast or the homemade chicken, leek, and mushroom pie, and don't miss the hot cider in the wintertime. *22 Holly Mount, Hampstead* *020/7435–2892* *www.hollybushhampstead.co.uk* *Hampstead.*

The Spaniards Inn

BARS/PUBS | Ideal as a refueling point when you're hiking over Hampstead Heath, this atmospheric oak-beamed pub has been serving customers since 1585 and comes with a gorgeous garden that was immortalized in Dickens's *Pickwick Papers*. Other notable former patrons include infamous highwayman Dick Turpin, local resident Keats, and fellow poets Shelly, Blake, and Byron. Fresh takes on traditional pub food and a wide selection of cask beer ensure a crowd, especially on Sunday. And if you've brought your furry friend along, there's a doggie bath in the garden. *Spaniards Rd., Hampstead* *020/8731–8406* *www.thespaniardshampstead.co.uk* *Hampstead.*

Performing Arts

FILM

Everyman Hampstead

FILM | The antithesis of a noisy, sticky-floored multiplex, the Everyman arthouse chain offers a premium cinema-going experience with ticket prices to match. But many say it's worth it for the large leather armchairs, loveseats, and waitstaff that bring tapas and champagne to your seat. Along with recent releases, the cinema screens live performances from the National Theatre, the Royal Ballet, and the Metropolitan Opera. There's another branch down the hill in Belsize Park. *5 Holly Bush Vale, Hampstead* *0871/906–9060* *www.everymancinema.com* *From £18* *Hampstead.*

THEATER

Hampstead Theatre

THEATER | Located in nearby Swiss Cottage, this handsome theater specializes in commissioning and producing new work. Established names like Mike Bartlett, Terry Johnson, and Joe Penhall debut their creations in the upstairs theater (with several productions eventually going on to the West End), while fresh voices are produced in the downstairs studio theater at friendly ticket prices. It's also known for its productions of recent Pulitzer Prize–winning plays imported from the United States. There's a good café that's open all day as well as during performances. *Eton Ave., Swiss Cottage* *207/722–9301* *www.hampsteadtheatre.com* *Swiss Cottage.*

Susan Wainwright

GIFTS/SOUVENIRS | FAMILY | If you're looking for an alternative to the cheesy and the mass-produced, this eclectic shop packs loads of distinctive, stylish, affordable gifts into a small space. The assortment includes handsome gloves and fake-fur accessories, handmade silver jewelry, tweed travel blankets, cashmere shawls, leather handbags, comfy yet attractive robes and pajamas, natural-fiber baby and children's clothes and accessories, retro toys, sophisticated stationery, artisanal creams and lotions, and flasks and leather goods for him. Best of all, prices are reasonable. ✉ *31 South End Rd., Hampstead* ☎ *020/7431–4337* Ⓜ *Overground: Hampstead Heath.*

Chapter 13

GREENWICH

Updated by
Jo Caird

Sights	Restaurants	Hotels	Shopping	Nightlife
★★★★☆	★★☆☆☆	★☆☆☆☆	★★★☆☆	★☆☆☆☆

GREENWICH SNAPSHOT

TOP REASONS TO GO

The Greenwich Meridian Line: At the Royal Observatory—where the world's time is set—you can be in the eastern and western hemispheres simultaneously.

The Queen's House: Sir Inigo Jones's 17th-century building was the first in England to embrace the styles of the Italian Renaissance.

The National Maritime Museum: Discover Britain's seafaring past, and see how Britannia ruled the waves and helped shape the modern world.

***Cutty Sark*:** Take a stroll along the deck of the last surviving 19th-century tea clipper, now shipshape after years of renovation.

GETTING THERE

The Docklands Light Railway (DLR) is a zippy way to get to Cutty Sark Station from Canary Wharf or Bank Tube station in The City. Or take the DLR to Island Gardens and walk the old Victorian Foot Tunnel under the river. (Sitting at the front of a train can be disconcerting, as you watch the controls in the fully automated driver's cab move about as if a ghost were at the helm.) The best way to arrive, however—time and weather permitting—is like a sea captain of old: by water (it takes an hour from central London).

MAKING THE MOST OF YOUR TIME

Set apart from the rest of London, Greenwich is worth a day to itself—those who love maritime history will want to spend two—in order to make the most of walks in the rolling parkland and to immerse yourself in the richness of Greenwich's history, science, and architecture. The boat trip takes about an hour from Westminster Pier (next to Big Ben) or 25 minutes from the Tower of London, so factor in enough time for the round-trip.

NEAREST PUBLIC RESTROOMS

Duck into the Visitor Centre at the Old Royal Naval College, where the loo is free.

QUICK BITES

■ **The Pavilion Café** Healthy snacks and lunches are served at this excellent café next to the Royal Observatory. Homemade soups and sandwiches are good for a quick refuel, or try one of the delicious stone-baked pizzas for something more substantial. ✉ *Charlton Way, Greenwich* ☎ *020/8305–2896* 🌐 *www.royalparks.org.uk* Ⓜ *Cutty Sark, Greenwich.*

■ **The Old Brewery** Right next to Discover Greenwich, the Old Brewery is a relaxed café by day and a sophisticated restaurant at night. The artful, high-ceiling dining room merits a visit, but the Modern British cuisine is also among the best in this part of London—and reasonably priced, too. ✉ *Pepys Bldg., Old Royal Naval College, King William Walk, Greenwich* ☎ *020/3437–2222* 🌐 *www.oldbrewerygreenwich.com* Ⓜ *Cutty Sark, Greenwich.*

■ **Trafalgar Tavern** With its excellent vista of the Thames, there is no more handsomely situated pub in Greenwich than the Trafalgar Tavern. It's still as grand a place as it ever was to have a pint and a quick tasty meal. ✉ *Park Row, Greenwich* ☎ *020/3887–9886* 🌐 *www.trafalgartavern.co.uk* Ⓜ *Cutty Sark, Greenwich.*

About 8 miles downstream (meaning seaward, to the east) from central London, Greenwich is a small borough that looms large across the world. Once the seat of British naval power, it is not only home to the Old Royal Observatory, which measures time for our entire planet, but also the Greenwich Meridian, which divides the world into two—you can stand astride it with one foot in either hemisphere.

Bear in mind that the journey to Greenwich is an event in itself. In a rush, you can take the driverless DLR train, but many opt for arriving by boat along the Thames. This way, you glide past famous sights on the London skyline—there's a guaranteed spine chill on passing the Tower—and ever-changing docklands, and there's usually a chirpy Cock-er-ney navigator enlivening the journey with fun commentary.

A visit to Greenwich feels like a trip to a rather elegant seaside town—albeit one with more than its fair share of historic sites. The grandiose **Old Royal Naval College,** designed by Sir Christopher Wren, was originally a home for veteran sailors. Today it's a popular visitor attraction, with a more glamorous second life as one of the most widely used movie locations in Britain.

Greenwich was originally home to one of England's finest Tudor palaces, and the birthplace of Henry VIII, Elizabeth I, and Mary I. Inigo Jones began what is considered the first "classical" building in England in 1616: the **Queen's House,** which now houses a collection of fine art. Britain was the world's preeminent naval power for more than 500 years, and the excellent **National Maritime Museum** details that history in an engaging way. Its prize exhibits include the coat worn by Admiral Lord Nelson (1758–1805) in his final battle—bullet hole and all. The 19th-century tea clipper ***Cutty Sark*** was nearly destroyed by fire in 2007 but reopened in 2012 after a painstaking restoration. Now it's more pristine than ever and has an impressive visitor center.

Greenwich Park, London's oldest royal park, is still home to fallow red deer, just as it has been since they were first introduced here for hunting by Henry VIII. The **Ranger's House** now houses a private art collection, next door to a beautifully manicured rose garden. Above it all is the **Royal Observatory,** where you can be in two hemispheres at once by standing along the **Greenwich Meridian Line,** before seeing a high-tech planetarium show.

Toward north Greenwich, the hopelessly ambitious Millennium Dome has been successfully reborn as The O2 and now hosts major concerts and stand-up comedy gigs. More adventurous visitors can also go **Up at The O2** on a climbing expedition across the massive domed surface. Meanwhile, those who prefer excursions of a gentler kind may prefer to journey a couple of miles south of the borough, farther out into London's southern suburbs, to the shamefully underappreciated **Eltham Palace,** once a favorite of Henry VIII. Parts of the mansion were transformed into an art deco masterpiece in the 1930s.

Sights

★ *Cutty Sark*

HISTORIC SITE | FAMILY | This sleek, romantic clipper was built in 1869, one among a vast fleet of tall-masted wooden ships that plied the oceanic highways of the 19th century, trading in exotic commodities—in this case, tea. *Cutty Sark* (named after a racy witch in a Robert Burns poem) was the fastest in the fleet, sailing the London–China route in 1871 in only 107 days. The clipper has been preserved in dry dock as a museum ship since the 1950s, but was severely damaged in a devastating fire in 2007. Yet up from the ashes, as the song goes, grow the roses of success: after a major restoration project, the visitor facilities are now better than ever. Not only can you tour the ship in its entirety, but the glittering visitor center (which the ship now rests directly above) allows you to view the hull from below. There's plenty to see here, and the cramped quarters form a fantastic time capsule to walk around in—this boat was never too comfortable for the 28-strong crew (as you'll see). Don't forget to take in the amusing collection of figureheads. The ship also hosts comedy, cabaret, and theater shows. ✉ *King William Walk, Greenwich* ☎ *020/8858–4422* 🌐 *www.rmg.co.uk/cuttysark* 🎫 *From £15* Ⓜ *DLR: Cutty Sark.*

★ Eltham Palace

CASTLE/PALACE | Once a favorite getaway for Henry VIII (who liked to spend Christmas here), Eltham Palace has been drastically remodeled twice in its lifetime: once during the 15th and 16th centuries, and again during the 1930s, when a grand mansion was annexed onto the Tudor great hall by the superwealthy Courtauld family. Today it's an extraordinary combination of late medieval grandeur and art deco masterpiece, laced with an eccentric whimsy—the Courtaulds even built an entire room to be the personal quarters of their beloved pet lemur. The house and its extensive gardens were fully restored when the palace finally entered public ownership in the late 1990s. Be sure to get a glimpse of the Map Room, where the Courtaulds planned their round-the-world adventures, and the reconstruction of a lavish 1930s walk-in wardrobe, complete with genuine dresses from the time period. ✉ *Court Rd., Eltham* ☎ *020/8294–2548* 🌐 *www.english-heritage.org.uk/eltham-palace* 🎫 *£16* 🕓 *Closed Sat.* Ⓜ *Eltham.*

Emirates Air Line

VIEWPOINT | FAMILY | It may not have become the essential commuter route its makers envisioned, but this cable car, which connects Greenwich Peninsula with the Docklands across the Thames, offers spectacular views from nearly 300 feet up. The journey takes about 10 minutes each way and cable cars arrive every 30 seconds. Entrance to the Emirates Aviation Experience, a small exhibition about commercial air travel that includes life-size models of aircraft and flight simulators, is included with "Discovery Experience" round-trip tickets. ✉ *Edmund Halley Way* ☎ *0203/440–7021* 🌐 *www.emiratesairline.co.uk* 🎫 *One-way ticket £5, Discovery Experience £11* Ⓜ *North Greenwich, Royal Victoria.*

Did You Know?

Once sailors could determine their distance from the Greenwich meridian (longitude), maritime navigation was greatly improved. Look for the brass line marking the two hemispheres throughout the cobblestone streets.

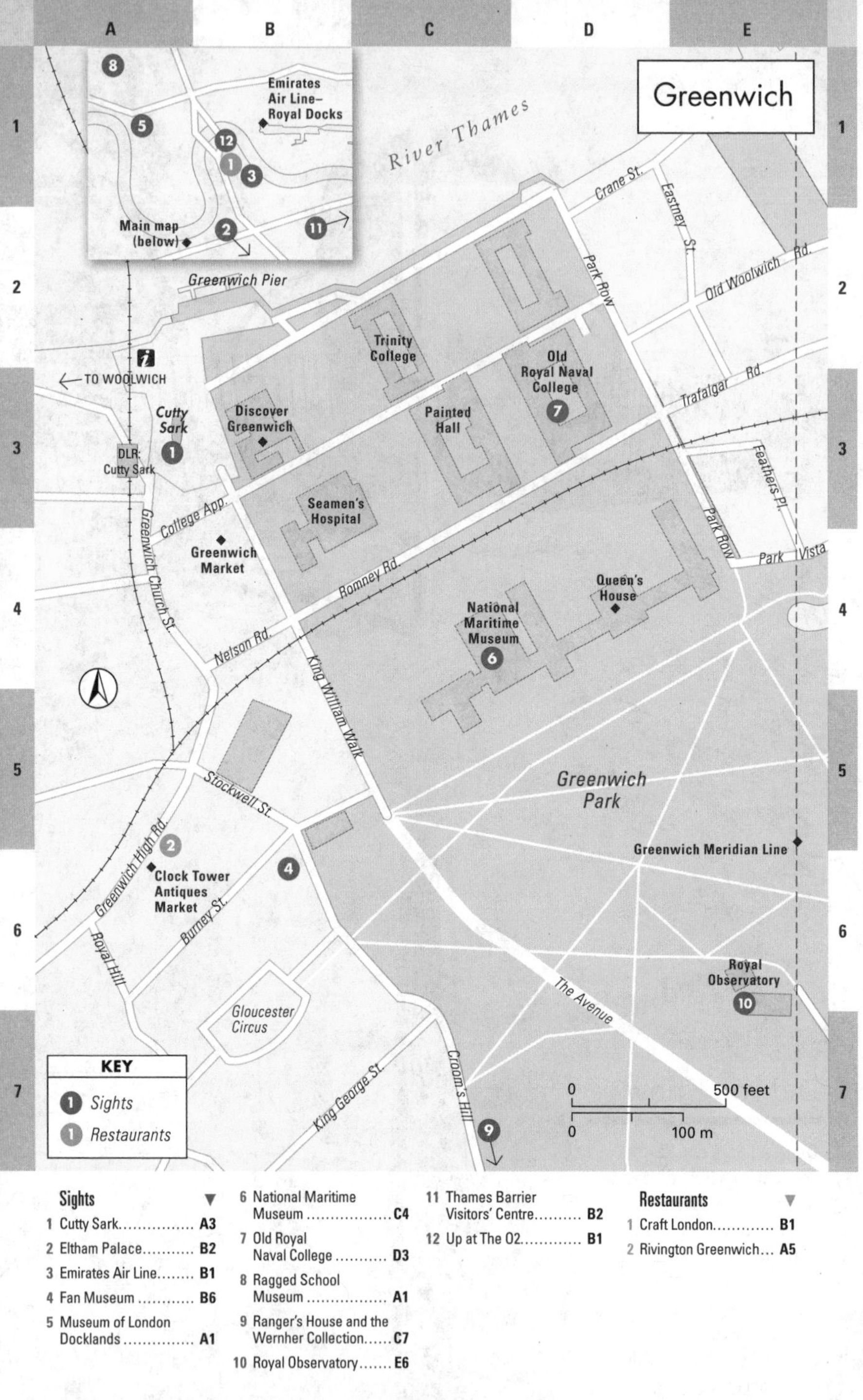

Sights

1 Cutty Sark **A3**
2 Eltham Palace **B2**
3 Emirates Air Line **B1**
4 Fan Museum **B6**
5 Museum of London Docklands **A1**
6 National Maritime Museum **C4**
7 Old Royal Naval College **D3**
8 Ragged School Museum **A1**
9 Ranger's House and the Wernher Collection...... **C7**
10 Royal Observatory....... **E6**
11 Thames Barrier Visitors' Centre.......... **B2**
12 Up at The O2............ **B1**

Restaurants

1 Craft London............ **B1**
2 Rivington Greenwich... **A5**

Fan Museum

MUSEUM | This quirky little museum is as fascinating and varied as the uniquely prized object whose artistry it seeks to chronicle. The simple fan is more than a mere fashion accessory; historically, fans can tell as much about craftsmanship and social mores as they can about fashion. There are 5,000 of them in the collection, dating from the 17th century onward, often exquisitely crafted from ivory, mother-of-pearl, and tortoiseshell. It was the personal vision of Helene Alexander that brought this enchanting museum into being, and the workshop and conservation–study center that she has also set up ensure that this art form continues to have a future. Afternoon tea is served in the café on Tuesday and Friday through Sunday between 12:30 pm and 4 pm. ✉ *12 Crooms Hill, Greenwich* ☎ *020/8305–1441* 🌐 *www.thefanmuseum.org.uk* 🎫 *£5* ⏲ *Closed Mon.* Ⓜ *DLR: Cutty Sark.*

Museum of London Docklands

MUSEUM | This wonderful old warehouse building, on a quaint cobbled quayside near the tower of Canary Wharf, is worth a visit in its own right. With uneven wood floors, beams, and pillars, the museum used to be a storehouse for coffee, tea, sugar, and rum from the West Indies, hence the name: West India Quay. The fascinating story of the old port and the river is told using films, together with interactive displays and reconstructions. Excellent permanent exhibitions include *City and River,* which chronicles the explosion of trade and industry that, by the mid-19th century, had transformed this district into the world's most important port. *Sailortown* is an effective reconstruction of the Wapping district in Victorian times, complete with period shops, a pub, spooky alleys, and costumed guides. Young kids can hunt for treasure and let off some steam in the soft play area in the Mudlarks Gallery. Special events happen year-round; check the museum's website for details. ✉ *No. 1 Warehouse, West India Quay, Canary Wharf* ☎ *020/7001–9844* 🌐 *www.museumoflondon.org.uk/docklands* 🎫 *Free, special exhibitions sometimes extra* Ⓜ *Canary Wharf. DLR: West India Quay.*

★ **National Maritime Museum**

MUSEUM | **FAMILY** | From the time of Henry VIII until the 1940s, Britain was the world's preeminent naval power, and the collections here trace half a millennia of that seafaring history. The story is as much about trade as it is warfare: *Atlantic: Slavery, Trade, Empire* gallery explores how trade in goods (and people) irrevocably changed the world, while *Traders: The East India Company and Asia* focuses on how the epoch-defining company shaped trade with Asia for 250 years. One gallery is devoted to Admiral Lord Nelson, Britain's most famous naval commander, and among the exhibits is the uniform he was wearing, complete with bloodstains, when he died at the Battle of Trafalgar in 1805. Temporary exhibitions here are usually fascinating—those in recent years have included personal accounts of the First World War at sea. Borrow a tablet computer from the front desk and take it to the giant map of the world in the courtyard at the center of the museum; here, a high-tech, interactive app opens up hidden stories and games as you walk between continents. The Ahoy! gallery is filled with interactive fun for kids, where they can learn about polar exploration, pirates, and more. The adjacent **Queen's House** is home to the museum's art collection, the largest collection of maritime art in the world, including works by William Hogarth, Canaletto, and Joshua Reynolds. Permission for its construction was granted by Queen Anne only on condition that the river vista from the house be preserved, and there are few more majestic views in London than Inigo Jones's awe-inspiring symmetry. ✉ *Romney Rd., Greenwich* ☎ *020/8312–6608* 🌐 *www.rmg.co.uk/national-maritime-museum* 🎫 *Free; tours*

Did You Know?

The Docklands Light Railway (DLR) connects former warehouses that have been converted to museums and malls, such as Hay's and Butler's wharves, and the gleaming office buildings of Canary Wharf shown here.

£10; fee for special exhibitions Ⓜ *DLR: Greenwich.*

★ **Old Royal Naval College**

HISTORIC SITE | Built by Sir Christopher Wren between 1696 and 1751 as a rest home for ancient mariners, the college became a naval school in 1873. A small part of the site is still used for classes by the University of Greenwich and the Trinity College of Music, although you're more likely to recognize it as a film location—blockbusters to have made use of its elegant interiors include *Skyfall, Les Misérables,* and *The King's Speech.* Architecturally, you'll notice how the structures part to reveal the **Queen's House** across the central lawns. The **Painted Hall,** the college's dining hall, derives its name from the baroque murals of William and Mary (reigned jointly 1689–94; William alone 1695–1702) and assorted allegorical figures. James Thornhill's frescoes, depicting scenes of naval grandeur with a suitably pro-British note, were painstakingly completed 1707–12 and 1718–26, and were good enough to earn him a knighthood. The hall recently underwent an extensive renovation, reopening looking better than ever alongside the Sackler Gallery, which tells the story of the frescoes. In the opposite building stands the **College Chapel,** which was rebuilt after a fire in 1779 in an altogether more restrained, neo-Grecian style. The free visitor center includes interactive exhibits on the history of Greenwich, plus an assortment of local treasures and artifacts. Most intriguing among them is a 17th-century "witch bottle," once used to ward off evil spirits. High-tech scans have revealed it to contain a mixture of human hair, fingernails, and urine. ✉ *King William Walk, Greenwich* ☎ *020/8269–4747* 🌐 *www.ornc.org* 🎫 *Visitor center and chapel free; grounds tours and Painted Hall £12* Ⓜ *DLR: Greenwich, Cutty Sark.*

Ragged School Museum

MUSEUM | **FAMILY** | In its time, the Ragged School Museum was the largest school in London and a place where impoverished children could get free education and a good meal. The museum re-creates a classroom dating from the 1880s. It's an eye-opener for adults, and fun for kids, who get the chance to learn just like Victorian children did in one of the many organized workshops. If you really want to get into the spirit, visitors of all ages can attend an authentic, 45-minute Victorian school lesson (first Sunday of every month, 2:15 and 3:30), complete with a fully costumed schoolmistress who tests your slate-writing technique—and might give you a dunce hat if you misbehave. ✉ *46–50 Copperfield Rd., Mile End* ☎ *020/8980–6405* 🌐 *www.raggedschoolmuseum.org.uk* 🎫 *Free; £2 donation requested for Victorian lessons* 🕒 *Closed Mon., Tues., Fri., and weekends, except 1st Sun. of month* Ⓜ *Mile End; DLR: Limehouse.*

Greenwich Foot Tunnel

In 1849, Greenwich Hospital bought Island Gardens, on the other side of the Thames, to guard against industrial sprawl and to preserve one of the most beautiful views in London. Take the stone spiral steps down into Greenwich Foot Tunnel and head under the Thames (enjoying the magnificently creepy echo) to Island Gardens, at the southern tip of the Isle of Dogs. Then look back over the river for a magnificent vista: the Old Royal Naval College and Queen's House in all their glory, framed by the verdant green borders of the park.

Ranger's House and the Wernher Collection

HOUSE | This handsome, early-18th-century villa, which was the Greenwich Park ranger's official residence during the 19th century, is hung with Stuart

Without a central support, the Tulip Stairs spiral up to the Great Hall of Queen's House.

and Jacobean portraits, but the most interesting diversion is the Wernher Collection, which contains nearly 700 artworks that were amassed by the diamond millionaire Sir Julius Wernher (1850–1912) and were once housed in his fabulous stately house, Luton Hoo, in Bedfordshire. The collection ranges from Old Master paintings to Renaissance jewelry and assorted pieces of decorative art and curios from the medieval period onward, including the gorgeous *Madonna of the Pomegranates* from the workshop of Sandro Botticelli. The Ranger's House is just under a mile's walk from the DLR station at Greenwich, or you can catch a bus there from Greenwich or Deptford DLR. ✉ *Blackheath, Chesterfield Walk, Greenwich Park, Greenwich* ☎ *020/8294–2848* 🌐 *www.english-heritage.org.uk* 🎫 *£10* ⏲ *Closed Fri., Sat., and Nov.–Mar.* Ⓜ *DLR: Deptford Bridge, then Bus 53; or Greenwich, then Bus 386.*

★ Royal Observatory

MUSEUM | FAMILY | Greenwich is on the prime meridian at 0° longitude, and the ultimate standard for time around the world has been set here at the Royal Observatory since 1884, when Britain was the world's maritime superpower. The observatory is actually split into two sites, a short walk apart: one devoted to astronomy, the other to the study of time. The enchanting **Peter Harrison Planetarium** is London's only planetarium, its bronze-clad turret glinting in the sun. Shows on black holes and how to interpret the night sky are enthralling and enlightening. Even better for kids are the high-technology rooms of the **Astronomy Centre,** where space exploration is brought to life through cutting-edge interactive programs and fascinating exhibits—including the chance to touch a 4½-billion-year-old meteorite.

Across the way is **Flamsteed House,** designed by Sir Christopher Wren in 1675 for John Flamsteed, the first Royal Astronomer. The Time Ball atop Flamsteed House is one of the world's earliest public time signals. Each day at 12:55, it rises halfway up its mast.

At 12:58 it rises all the way to the top, and at 1 exactly, the ball falls. A climb to the top of the house also reveals a **28-inch telescope,** built in 1893 and now housed inside an onion-shape fiberglass dome. It doesn't compare with the range of modern optical telescopes, but it's still the largest in the United Kingdom. Regular wintertime viewing evenings reveal startlingly detailed views of the lunar surface. In the **Time Galleries,** linger over the superb workmanship of John Harrison (1693–1776), whose famous **maritime clocks** won him the Longitude Prize for solving the problem of accurate timekeeping at sea, paving the way for modern navigation. Outside, a brass line laid among the cobblestones marks the meridian. As darkness falls, a green laser shoots out, following exactly the path of the meridian line. The hill that is home to the observatory gives fantastic views across London, topped off with £1-a-slot telescopes to scour the skyline. ✉ *Romney Rd., Greenwich* ☎ *020/8858–4422* 🌐 *www.rmg.co.uk/royal-observatory* 🎫 *Royal Observatory £16, planetarium shows £10; combined ticket with Cutty Sark £27* Ⓜ *DLR: Greenwich.*

Thames Barrier Visitors' Centre

INFO CENTER | Built in the early 1980s, the Thames Barrier is the one of the largest and most high-tech flood defense systems in the world. The barrier, which is raised to protect the city during exceptionally high tides, has a starkly futuristic design—sometimes compared to a row of crashed UFOs, bobbing out of the river. Multimedia presentations, a film about the Thames's history, working models, and views of the barrier itself put the importance of the relationship between London and its river in perspective. It's a treat for science and engineering geeks, but probably too far out of the way if your interest is only casual. ✉ *1 Unity Way, Eastmoor St., Woolwich* ☎ *020/8305–4188* 🌐 *www.visitlondon.com/things-to-do/place/26941-thames-barrier-information-centre* 🎫 *£5* ⏲ *Closed Mon.–Wed. Sept.–July* Ⓜ *North Greenwich, then Bus 161 or 472; National Rail: Charlton (from London Bridge), then Bus 177 or 180.*

Up at The O2

VIEWPOINT | Certainly one of the most original ways to see London, this thrilling urban expedition takes you on a 90-minute journey across the giant dome of the O2 arena. After a short briefing, you're dressed in safety gear and taken in small groups across a steep walkway, running all the way to the summit and down the other side. The high point (literally) is a viewing platform, 171 feet above ground, with magnificent views of the city. On a clear day you can see for 15 miles (that's as far as Waltham Abbey to the north and Sevenoaks to the south). Climbs at sunset and twilight are also available, but the best trips are on nights when London is lit up by fireworks, such as New Year's Eve, Fireworks Night, and Diwali. It's quite an experience, but unsurprisingly there are restrictions: you have to be at least 8 years old, taller than 4 feet, have a waist measurement that's less than 49 inches, weigh less than 286 pounds, and pregnant women can't make the climb at all. Wheelchairs can be accommodated on a few tours. Advance booking is essential. ✉ *Peninsula Sq., London* ☎ *020/8463–2680* 🌐 *www.theo2.co.uk/do-more-at-the-o2/up-at-the-o2* 🎫 *From £36* ⏲ *Closed Mon.–Thurs. in Jan.* Ⓜ *North Greenwich.*

Restaurants

Craft London

$$ | **BRITISH** | Playful modern British cuisine is the order of the day at this surprisingly intimate and atmospheric restaurant on the otherwise rather soulless North Greenwich peninsula. Not all the experimental dishes on the concise seasonal menu are entirely successful, but dining at Craft is an undeniably exciting experience and you can be assured that every element will be flawlessly cooked and presented. **Known for:** house-made ingredients including bread, butter, ferments, and ice creams; weekly "Test Kitchen Tuesday" events where guests are offered an experimental set menu in exchange for feedback on the dishes; gorgeous artisanal crockery. *Average main: £21* ✉ *Peninsula Sq., Greenwich* ☎ *020/8465–5910* 🌐 *www.craft-london.co.uk* ⏲ *Closed Sun.* Ⓜ *North Greenwich.*

Rivington Greenwich

$$ | **BRITISH** | **FAMILY** | This attractive and welcoming neighborhood restaurant is a favorite with Greenwich's well-to-do older set and specializes in British cuisine with a focus on traditional methods, cuts, and ingredients. Generous portions, rich sauces, and persuasive staff recommendations may lead to overindulgence, but you'll have earned those extra calories after a day tramping around the area's various tourist spots and museums. **Known for:** enormous (200-plus) range of gins, including alcohol-free varieties; outdoor seating area for alfresco dining; kids eat for free (two per adult main course) on weekdays. *Average main: £20* ✉ *178 Greenwich High Rd., Greenwich* ☎ *020/8293–9270* 🌐 *www.rivingtongreenwich.co.uk* Ⓜ *Cutty Sark, Greenwich.*

Shopping

Clock Tower Antiques Market

ANTIQUES/COLLECTIBLES | The weekend open-air Clock Tower Antiques Market on Greenwich High Road has vintage shopping, and browsing among the "small collectibles" makes for a good half-hour diversion. Give it a miss in bad weather, when the number of stalls falls dramatically. ✉ *166 Greenwich High Rd., Greenwich* ☎ *079/4091–4204* 🌐 *www.clocktowermarket.co.uk* Ⓜ *Greenwich Rail.*

Greenwich Market

OUTDOOR/FLEA/GREEN MARKETS | Established as a fruit-and-vegetable market in 1700, the covered market now offers around 120 mixed stalls of art and crafts on Monday, Wednesday, Friday, and weekends, and vintage antiques on Tuesday, Thursday, and Friday. You can buy food on each day, although the offerings are usually best on weekends. Shopping for handicrafts is a pleasure here, as in most cases you're buying directly from the artist. ✉ *College Approach, Greenwich* ☎ *020/8269–5096* 🌐 *www.greenwichmarketlondon.com* Ⓜ *DLR: Cutty Sark.*

Music & Video Exchange

MUSIC STORES | This London institution (there are other branches in Notting Hill) carries a remarkable range of secondhand vinyl records, with everything from bargain 25 cent records to treasured first editions costing more than £1,000. ✉ *23 Greenwich Church St., Greenwich* ☎ *020/8858–8898* 🌐 *www.mgeshops.com* Ⓜ *Cutty Sark, Greenwich.*

Chapter 14

THE THAMES UPSTREAM

Updated by
Toby Orton

Sights ★★★★☆ | Restaurants ★★☆☆☆ | Hotels ★☆☆☆☆ | Shopping ★☆☆☆☆ | Nightlife ★★☆☆☆

THE THAMES UPSTREAM SNAPSHOT

TOP REASONS TO GO

Hampton Court Palace: Go ghost hunting or just admire the beautiful Tudor architecture at Henry VIII's beloved home, then lose yourself in the maze as night begins to fall.

Strawberry Hill: The 19th-century birthplace of connoisseur Horace Walpole's Gothic style, this mock-castle is a joyous riot of color and invention.

Kew Gardens: See the earth from above by visiting Kew's treetop walkway at the famous Royal Botanic Gardens.

The River Thames: Enjoy a pint from the creaking balcony of a centuries-old riverside pub as you watch the boats row by on the loveliest stretch of England's greatest river.

GETTING THERE

The District Line is your best Tube option, stopping at Turnham Green (in the heart of Chiswick but a walk from the houses), Gunnersbury (for Syon Park), Kew Gardens, and Richmond. For Hampton Court, overland train is quickest: South West trains run from Waterloo four times an hour, with roughly half requiring a change at Surbiton. There are also regular direct trains from Waterloo to Chiswick Station (best for Chiswick House), Kew Bridge, St Margarets (for Marble Hill House), and Richmond (for Ham House). London Overground trains also stop at Gunnersbury, Kew Gardens, and Richmond.

A pleasant way to go is by river. Boats depart from Westminster Pier, by Big Ben, for Kew (1½ hours), Richmond (2 hours), and Hampton Court (3 hours). The trip is worth taking if you make it an integral part of your day, and know that it gets breezy. Round-trip tickets run £22–£27. For more details contact **Thames River Boats** (☎ *020/7930–2062* ⊕ *www.wpsa.co.uk*).

QUICK BITES

■ **The Original Maids of Honour** This most traditional of old English tearooms is named for a kind of cheese tart invented near here in Tudor times. Legend has it that Henry VIII loved them so much he had the recipe kept under armed guard. **Known for:** using traditional baking techniques that date back over centuries; excellent full English breakfast; nostalgic mock Tudor decor rebuilt following bomb damage during WWII. ✉ *288 Kew Rd., Kew* ☎ *020/8940–2752* ⊕ *www.theoriginalmaidsofhonour.co.uk.*

MAKING THE MOST OF YOUR TIME

■ Hampton Court Palace requires half a day to experience its magic, although you could make do with a few hours for the other attractions. Because of the distance between sights, it's best to focus on one sight, add in some others within the area, then a riverside walk and a pint at a pub.

The upper stretch of the Thames links a string of upmarket districts—Chiswick, Kew, Richmond, and Putney—with winding old streets, horticultural delights, cozy riverside pubs, and Henry VIII's Hampton Court Palace. The neighborhoods along the way are as proud of their villagey feel as of their stately history, witnessed by such handsome estates as Strawberry Hill and Syon House. After the sensory overload of the West End, it's easy to forget you're in a capital city.

Chiswick

On the banks of the Thames just west of central London, far enough out to escape the crush and crowds you're just getting used to, Chiswick is a low-key, upscale district, content with its run of restaurants, stylish shops, and film-star residents. No doubt its most famous son wouldn't approve of all the conspicuous wealth, though; Chiswick was home to one of Britain's best-loved painters, William Hogarth, who tore the fabric of the 18th-century nation to shreds with his slew of satirical engravings. **Hogarth's House** has been restored to its former glory. Incongruously stranded among Chiswick's row houses are a number of fine 18th-century buildings, which are now some of the most desirable suburban houses in London. By far the grandest of all is **Chiswick House,** a unique Palladian-style mansion born from the 3rd Earl of Burlington's love of classical and Renaissance architecture—a radical style at the time.

Sights

★ Chiswick House

HOUSE | Completed in 1729 by the 3rd Earl of Burlington (also known for Burlington House—home of the Royal Academy—and Burlington Arcade on Piccadilly), this extraordinary Palladian mansion was envisaged as a kind of temple to the arts. Burlington was fascinated by the architecture he saw in Italy while on the Grand Tour as a young man and loosely modeled this building on the Villa Capra near Vicenza and the Pantheon in Rome (note the colonnaded frontage and

Did You Know?

Chiswick is the finishing point for the Oxford and Cambridge Boat Race, a famous rowing race held annually since 1856 on the last weekend of March or the first weekend of April between Oxford University and Cambridge University along the River Thames.

the domed roof, which is visible from the inside in the Upper Tribunal).

The sumptuous interiors were the work of William Kent (1685–1748), and it's easy to see how they made such a profound impact at the time; the astonishing Blue Velvet Room, with its gilded decoration and intricate painted ceiling, is an extraordinary achievement, as are the gilded domed apses that punctuate the Gallery (an homage to the Temple of Venus and Roma from the Fora Romana in Rome). Such ideas were so radical in England at the time that wealthy patrons clamored to have Kent design everything from gardens to party frocks.

The rambling grounds are one of the hidden gems of West London. Italianate in style (of course), they are filled with classical temples, statues, and obelisks. Also on the grounds are a café and a children's play area. ✉ *Burlington La., Chiswick* ☎ *020/3141–3350* 🌐 *www.chiswickhouseandgardens.org.uk* 🎫 *£8, grounds free* 🕓 *House closed Nov.–Mar. and Tues., Thurs., and Fri. in summer* Ⓜ *Turnham Green, Chiswick. National Rail: Chiswick.*

Hogarth's House

HOUSE | The satirist and painter William Hogarth (1697–1764), little-known in the rest of the world, is hugely famous in Britain. His witty, acerbic engravings, which railed against the harsh injustices of the time, may be called the visual equivalent of the satires of Jonathan Swift and were no less influential in their time. Unfortunately his beloved house has had an appalling streak of bad luck; as if the decision, in the 1960s, to route one of the nation's busiest highways outside the front gates wasn't ignoble enough, the house was closed after a fire in 2009. Now fully restored, the rooms contain absorbing exhibitions, featuring many of Hogarth's 18th-century prints, together with replica furniture of the period. Look out for the 300-year-old mulberry tree outside; Hogarth and his wife used its fruit to bake pies for destitute children. The original copies of some of Hogarth's most famous works can be seen elsewhere in the city: *A Rake's Progress* at Sir John Soane's Museum; *Marriage A-la-Mode* at the National Gallery; and *Gin Lane*at the British Museum. His tomb is in the cemetery of St. Nicholas's Church on nearby Chiswick Mall. ✉ *Hogarth La., Great West Rd. (A4), Chiswick* ☎ *020/8994–6757* 🌐 *www.hounslow.info/arts/hogarthshouse* 🎫 *Free* 🕓 *Closed Mon.* Ⓜ *Turnham Green. National Rail: Chiswick.*

Kew

A mile or so beyond Chiswick is Kew, a leafy suburb with little to see other than its two big attractions: the lovely **Kew Palace** and the **Royal Botanic Gardens**—anchored in the landscape for several miles around by a towering, mock-Chinese pagoda.

Sights

★ **Kew Gardens**

GARDEN | **FAMILY** | Enter the Royal Botanic Gardens, as Kew Gardens are officially known, and you are enveloped by blazes of color, extraordinary blooms, hidden trails, and lovely old follies. Beautiful though it all is, Kew's charms are secondary to its true purpose as a major center for serious research; more than 200 academics are consistently hard at work here on projects spanning 110 countries. First opened to the public in 1840, this 326-acre site has been supported by royalty and nurtured by landscapers, botanists, and architects since the 1720s. Today the gardens, now a UNESCO World Heritage Site, hold more than 30,000 species of plants, from every corner of the globe.

Architect Sir William Chambers built a series of temples and follies, of which the crazy 10-story **Pagoda,** visible for

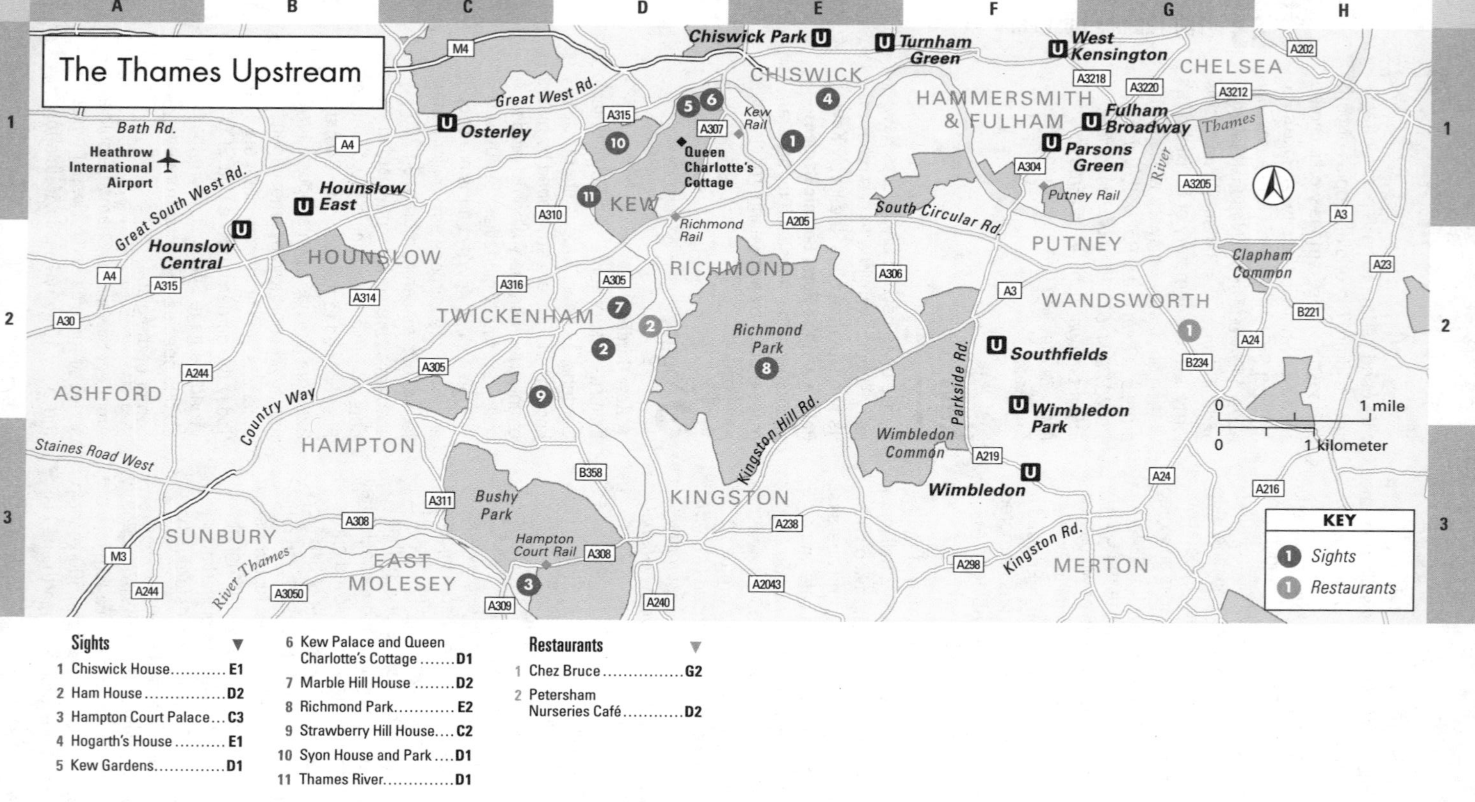

Sights

1 Chiswick House........... E1
2 Ham House................ D2
3 Hampton Court Palace... C3
4 Hogarth's House.......... E1
5 Kew Gardens.............. D1
6 Kew Palace and Queen Charlotte's Cottage D1
7 Marble Hill House D2
8 Richmond Park............ E2
9 Strawberry Hill House.... C2
10 Syon House and Park D1
11 Thames River............. D1

Restaurants

1 Chez Bruce G2
2 Petersham Nurseries Café........... D2

miles around, is the star. The Princess of Wales conservatory houses 10 climate zones, and the Xstrata Treetop Walkway takes you 59 feet up into the air. Two great 19th-century greenhouses—the **Palm House** and the **Temperate House**—are filled with exotic blooms, and many of the plants have been there since the final glass panel was fixed into place, including the largest greenhouse plant in the world, a Chilean wine palm planted in 1846 (it's so big you have to climb the spiral staircase to the roof to get a proper view of it).

To get around the gardens, the Kew Explorer bus runs on a 40-minute, hop-on, hop-off route, starting at the Victoria Gate, every 30 minutes 11–4:30. Free guided tours, run by volunteers, are given daily at 11 and 1:30, plus special seasonally themed tours at other times. Discovery Tours, fully accessible for visitors in wheelchairs, are also available daily with advance booking. ✉ *Kew Rd. at Lichfield Rd., for Victoria Gate entrance, Kew* ☎ *020/8332–5000* 🌐 *www.kew.org* 🎫 *£17, Explorer Land Train £5* Ⓜ *Kew Gardens. National Rail: Kew Gardens, Kew Bridge.*

★ Kew Palace and Queen Charlotte's Cottage

CASTLE/PALACE | The elegant redbrick exterior of the smallest of Britain's royal palaces seems almost humble when compared with the grandeur of, say, Buckingham or Kensington palace. Yet inside is a fascinating glimpse into life at the uppermost end of society from the 17th to 19th century. This is actually the third of several palaces that stood here; once known as Dutch House, it was one of the havens to which George III retired when insanity forced him to withdraw from public life. Queen Charlotte had an *orné* (a rustic-style cottage retreat) added in the late 18th century. In a marvelously regal flight of fancy, she kept kangaroos in the paddock outside. The main house and gardens are maintained in the 18th-century style. Entry to the palace itself is free, but it lies within the grounds of Kew Gardens, and you must buy a ticket to that to get here. ✉ *Kew Gardens, Kew Rd. at Lichfield Rd., Kew* ☎ *020/3166–6000* 🌐 *www.hrp.org.uk/kew-palace* 🎫 *Free with entry to Kew Gardens* ⏲ *Closed Oct.–Apr.* Ⓜ *Kew Gardens.*

A Good Walk in Chiswick

From Chiswick House, follow Burlington Lane and take a left onto Hogarth Lane—which, in reality, is anything but a lane—to reach Hogarth's House. Chiswick's Church Street (reached by a rather unappealing underpass from Hogarth's House) is the nearest thing to a sleepy country village street you're likely to find in London. Follow it down to the Thames and turn left at the bottom to reach the 18th-century riverfront houses of Chiswick Mall, referred to by locals as "Millionaire's Row."

Richmond

Named after the (long-vanished) palace Henry VII started here in 1500, Richmond is still a welcoming suburb with a small-town feel, marred only by choking levels of traffic. Duck away from the main streets to find many handsome Georgian and Victorian houses, antiques shops, a Victorian theater, a grand stately home—and, best of all, the largest of London's royal parks.

Sights

Ham House

HOUSE | To the west of Richmond Park, overlooking the Thames and nearly opposite the memorably named Eel Pie Island, Ham House was built in 1610 and remodeled 60 years later. It's one of the most complete examples in Europe of a lavish 17th-century house, and as such you can get a clear sense of how the English aristocracy really lived during that period (in short: comfortably). The beautiful formal gardens, with their distinctive spherical and conical topiary, have become an influential source for other palaces and grand villas seeking to restore their gardens to how they were in their heyday. The original decorations in the Great Hall, Round Gallery, and Great Staircase have been replicated, and most of the furniture and fittings are on permanent loan from the Victoria & Albert Museum. Note that from January to March, visits are by guided tour only, lasting around 30 minutes (no need to book). A tranquil and scenic way to reach the house is on foot, which takes about 30 minutes, along the eastern riverbank south from Richmond Bridge. ✉ *Ham St., Richmond* ☎ *020/8940–1950* 🌐 *www.nationaltrust.org.uk/hamhouse* 🎫 *£13* Ⓜ *Richmond, then Bus 65 or 371.*

★ **Hampton Court Palace**

CASTLE/PALACE | **FAMILY** | The beloved seat of Henry VIII's court, sprawled elegantly beside the languid waters of the Thames, Hampton Court is steeped in more history than virtually any other royal building in England. The Tudor mansion, begun in 1515 by Cardinal Wolsey to curry favor with the young Henry, actually conceals a larger 17th-century baroque building, which was partly designed by Sir Christopher Wren. The earliest dwellings on this site belonged to a religious order founded in the 11th century and were expanded over the years by its many subsequent residents, until George II moved the royal household closer to London in the early 18th century. After entering through the magnificent Tudor courtyard, start with a look through the **State Apartments,** decorated in the Tudor style, and on to the wood-beamed magnificence of Henry's Great Hall, before taking in the strikingly azure ceiling of the **Chapel Royal.** Watch out for the ghost of Henry VIII's doomed fifth wife, Catherine Howard, who lost her head yet is said to scream her way along the **Haunted Gallery.** (Believe it or not, what is certainly true is that the corridor is prone to sudden drops in temperature—and no one quite knows why.) Latter-day masters of the palace, the joint rulers William and Mary (reigned 1689–1702), were responsible for the beautiful **King's and Queen's Apartments** and the elaborate baroque of the **Georgian Rooms.**

Well-handled reconstructions of Tudor life take place all year, from live appearances by "Henry VIII" to cook-historians preparing authentic feasts in the **Tudor Kitchens.** (Dishes on offer in the adjacent café include a few of these traditional recipes.) The highlight of the formal grounds is undoubtedly the famous maze (the oldest hedge maze in the world), its half mile of pathways among clipped hedgerows still fiendish to negotiate. There's a trick, but we won't give it away here; it's much more fun just to go and lose yourself. Meanwhile, the **Lower Orangery Garden** shows off thousands of exotic species that William and Mary, avid plant collectors, gathered from around the globe. Family ghost tours are given on evenings from October to February. Not only are they entertainingly spooky, but they're a great opportunity to see the older parts of the palace without the crowds. Scarier, adults-only versions last two hours. Note that tours can sell out several weeks in advance. ✉ *Hampton Court Rd., East Molesey* ☎ *020/3166–6000* 🌐 *www.hrp.org.uk/hamptoncourtpalace* 🎫 *£24 palace, maze, and gardens; £5 maze only; £8 maze and gardens* Ⓜ *Richmond, then Bus*

Hampton Court Palace, the seat of Henry VIII's court, is a prime example of a Tudor mansion, and features the oldest hedge maze in the world.

R68. National Rail: Hampton Court, 35 mins from Waterloo (most trains require change at Surbiton).

Marble Hill House

HOUSE | This handsome Palladian mansion is set on 66 acres of parkland on the northern bank of the Thames, almost opposite Ham House. It was built in the 1720s by George II for his mistress, the "exceedingly respectable and respected" Henrietta Howard. Later the house was occupied by Mrs. Fitzherbert, who was secretly (and illegally) married to the Prince Regent (later George IV) in 1785. The house was restored and opened to the public in 1903, looking very much like it did in Georgian times, with extravagant gilded rooms in which Mrs. Howard entertained the literary superstars of the age, including Alexander Pope and Jonathan Swift. A ferry service from Ham House operates during the summer; access on foot is a half-hour walk south along the west bank of the Thames from Richmond Bridge. Note that entry is by guided tour only, run by English Heritage and volunteers from a local history group. ✉ *Richmond Rd., Twickenham* ☎ *037/0333–1181* 🌐 *www.english-heritage.org.uk/visit/places/marble-hill-house* 🎫 *£8* ⏲ *Closed Nov.–Apr. and weekdays* Ⓜ *Richmond. National Rail: St. Margaret's.*

★ Richmond Park

CITY PARK | **FAMILY** | This enormous park was enclosed in 1637 for use as a royal hunting ground—like practically all other London parks. Unlike the others, however, Richmond Park still has wild red and fallow deer roaming its 2,500 acres (three times the size of New York's Central Park) of grassland and heath. Its ancient oaks are among the last remnants of the vast, wild forests that once encroached on London in medieval times. The Isabella Plantation (near the Ham Gate entrance) is an enchanting and colorful woodland garden, first laid out in 1831. There's a splendid protected view of St. Paul's Cathedral from King Henry VIII's Mound, the highest point in the park; find it, and you have a piece

Another highlight of Richmond is the dazzling and bold Strawberry Hill House.

of magic in your sights. The park is also home to White Lodge, a 1727 hunting lodge that now houses the Royal Ballet School. ✉ *Richmond* ☎ *030/0061–2200* 🌐 *www.royalparks.org.uk* 🎫 *Free* Ⓜ *Richmond, then Bus 371 or 65.*

★ Strawberry Hill House

HOUSE | From the outside, this rococo mishmash of towers, crenellations, and white stucco is dazzling in its faux-medieval splendor. Its architect and owner, Sir Horace Walpole (1717–97), knew a thing or two about imaginative flights of fancy; the flamboyant son of the first British prime minister, Robert Walpole, he all but single-handedly invented the Gothic novel with *The Castle of Otranto* (1764). Once you pass through Strawberry Hill's forbidding exterior, you'll experience an explosion of color and light, for Walpole boldly decided to take elements from the exteriors of Gothic cathedrals and move them inside. The detail is extraordinary, from the cavernous entrance hall with its vast Gothic trompe-l'oeil decorations, to the Great Parlour with its Renaissance stained glass, to the Gallery, where extraordinary fan vaulting is a replica of the vaults found in Henry VII's chapel at Westminster Abbey. The gardens have been meticulously returned to their original 18th-century design, right down to a white marble loveseat sculpted into the shape of a shell. Opening days can vary, so call ahead to check times. ✉ *268 Waldegrave Rd., Twickenham* ☎ *020/8744–1241* 🌐 *www.strawberryhillhouse.org.uk* 🎫 *£13* 🕒 *Property closed Jan.–Mar.; house closed Thurs.–Sat. Apr.–Dec.* Ⓜ *Richmond, then Bus 33 or R68. National Rail: Strawberry Hill.*

★ Syon House and Park

HOUSE | **FAMILY** | The residence of the Duke and Duchess of Northumberland, this is one of England's most lavish stately homes. Set in a 200-acre park landscaped by the great gardener "Capability" Brown (1716–83), the core of the house is Tudor—it was one of the last stopping places for Henry VIII's fifth wife, Catherine Howard, and the extremely short-lived monarch Lady Jane Grey before they were sent to the Tower. It was remodeled in the Georgian style in 1762 by famed decorator Robert Adam. He had just returned from studying the sights of classical antiquity in Italy and created two rooms sumptuous enough to wow any Grand Tourist: the entryway is an amazing study in black and white, pairing neoclassical marbles with antique bronzes, and the Ante Room contains 12 enormous verd-antique columns surmounted by statues of gold—and this was just a waiting room for the duke's servants and retainers. The Red Drawing Room is covered with crimson Spitalfields silk, and the Long Gallery is one of Adam's noblest creations. ✉ *Syon Park, Brentford* ☎ *020/8560–0882* 🌐 *www.syonpark.co.uk* 🎟 *£13, £8 gardens and conservatory only* ⏲ *Property closed Nov.–mid-Mar.; house closed Mon., Tues., Fri., and Sat. mid-Mar.–Oct.* Ⓜ *Gunnersbury, then Bus 237 or 267 to Brentlea.*

Thames River

BODY OF WATER | The twists and turns of the Thames through the heart of the capital make it London's best thoroughfare and most compelling viewing point. Every palace, church, theater, wharf, museum, and pub along the bank has a tale to tell, and traveling on or alongside the river is one of the best ways to soak up views of the city. Frequent daily tourist-boat services are at their height April through October. In most cases you can turn up at a pier, and the next departure won't be far away; however, it never hurts to book ahead if you can. The trip between Westminster Pier and the Tower of London takes about 40 minutes, while that between the Tower and Greenwich takes around half an hour. A full round-trip can take several hours. Ask about flexible fares and hop-on, hop-off options at the various piers. ✉ *London.*

Restaurants

Chez Bruce

$$$ | MODERN FRENCH | Top-notch French and Mediterranean cuisine, faultless service, and a winning wine list make this one of London's all-star favorite restaurants. At this cozy haunt overlooking Wandsworth Common, prepare for unfussy grown-up gastro wonders ranging from homemade charcuterie to lighter, simply grilled fish dishes. **Known for:** elegant neighborhood salon; luxe classics like lobster and scallop ravioli; impressive sommelier. $ *Average main: £27* ✉ *2 Bellevue Rd., Wandsworth Common, Battersea* ☎ *020/8672–0114* 🌐 *www.chezbruce.co.uk* Ⓜ *Overland: Wandsworth Common.*

Petersham Nurseries Cafe

$$$ | ITALIAN | Bucolic beauty and rustic Italian cuisine combine wonderfully at Petersham Nurseries Cafe, a delightfully charming and informal dining experience housed within the serene environ of Richmond's poshest garden center. Prices are high, but your farm-fresh dishes do come surrounded by a backdrop of hanging plants, succulents, shrubs, and climbers that create London's most whimsical greenhouse dining room. **Known for:** sustainable ingredients and slow food philosophy; stunning ramshackle interiors filled with plants; relaxed, rustic fine dining. $ *Average main: £28* ✉ *Church La., off Petersham Rd., London* ☎ *020/8940–5230* 🌐 *www.petershamnurseries.com* ⏲ *Closed Mon.* Ⓜ *Richmond Station, 65 bus.*

Nightlife

A pint in a riverside pub is a London must, and the capital's western reaches (including the Richmond and Hammersmith neighborhoods) offer some truly picturesque drinking opportunities. Pick a traditional establishment and you'll feel like you've ventured far from the Big Smoke.

PUBS

★ The Dove

BARS/PUBS | **FAMILY** | Read the list of famous ex-regulars, from Charles II and Nell Gwynn to Ernest Hemingway and Dylan Thomas, as you wait for a beer at this smart, comely, and popular 16th-century Thames riverside pub on the Upper Mall towpath in Hammersmith. If—as is often the case—the Dove is too full, stroll upstream along the bank to the Old Ship or Blue Anchor. ✉ *19 Upper Mall, Hammersmith* ☎ *020/8748–9474* 🌐 *www.dovehammersmith.co.uk* Ⓜ *Hammersmith.*

Roebuck

BARS/PUBS | **FAMILY** | Perched on top of Richmond Hill, the Roebuck has perhaps the best view of any pub in London. The most sought-after seats are the benches found directly across the road, which look out over the Thames as it winds its way into the countryside below. Friendly and surprisingly unpretentious, given its lofty surrounds, it is well worth the long climb up the hill from the center of Richmond. ✉ *130 Richmond Hill, Richmond* ☎ *020/8948–2329* 🌐 *www.greenekingpubs.co.uk* Ⓜ *Richmond.*

Chapter 15

SIDE TRIPS FROM LONDON

Updated by
Toby Orton

Sights ★★★★☆ | Restaurants ★★★☆☆ | Hotels ★☆☆☆☆ | Shopping ★☆☆☆☆ | Nightlife ★☆☆☆☆

Londoners are undeniably lucky. Few urban populations enjoy such glorious—and easily accessible—options for day-tripping. Even if you have only one day to spare, head out of the city. A train ride past hills dotted with sheep, a stroll through a medieval town, or a visit to one of England's great castles could make you feel as though you've added another week to your vacation.

Not only is England extremely compact, but its train and bus networks, although somewhat inefficient and expensive compared with their European counterparts, are extensive and easily booked (though pricing structures can be confusing), making "a brilliant day out" an easy thing to accomplish.

Although you can do the Warner Bros. Harry Potter Studio Tour in a day, many of the towns near London would make for a frenzied day trip. And in summer, heavy crowds make it difficult to sightsee in a relaxed manner, so consider staying for a day or two instead. You'd then have time to explore a different England—one with quiet country pubs, tree-lined lanes, and neat fields.

Planning

Prices

Prices in the reviews are the average cost of a main course at dinner or, if dinner is not served, at lunch. Note: If a restaurant offers only prix-fixe (set-price) meals, it has been given the price category that reflects the full prix-fixe price.

What it Costs

	$	$$	$$$	$$$$
RESTAURANTS	Under £14	£14–£23	£24–£31	Over £31

Getting Around

Normally the towns near London are best reached by train. Bus travel costs less, but can take twice as long. Wherever you're going, plan ahead: check the latest timetables before you set off, and try to get an early start.

Station Tips

You can reach any of London's main-line train stations by Tube. London's bus stations can be confusing for the uninitiated, so here's a quick breakdown:

To Get To ...	TAKE THE TRAIN FROM ...	TAKE THE BUS FROM ...
Cambridge	King's Cross (45–90 minutes, every 10 or 20 minutes); Liverpool St. (80 minutes, every 30 minutes)	Victoria Coach (about 3 hours, every 60–90 minutes)
Oxford	Paddington (55–110 minutes, every 3–20 minutes)	Victoria Coach (100 minutes, every half hour) or Oxford Tube, Buckingham Palace Rd. (100 minutes, every 12–20 minutes)
Stonehenge	Waterloo to Salisbury (90 minutes, every hour)	Victoria Coach to Amesbury (2 hours, about 3 times daily)
Stratford-upon-Avon	Marylebone (2–2½ hours, every 2 hours); or Euston (1½ hours, every 20 or 40 minutes or hourly)	Victoria Coach (3 hours 25 minutes, about 3 times daily)
Warner Bros. Harry Potter Studio Tour	Euston (20 minutes) to Watford, then shuttle bus to attraction	Watford (15 minutes, every 20 minutes), after taking London train from Euston.
Windsor	Paddington (25–50 minutes, every 5–30 minutes) or Waterloo (1 hour 5 minutes, every half hour)	Green Line Coach, Victoria (1 hour 5 minutes, hourly)

Green Line Coach Station is on Bulleid Way and is the departure point for most Green Line and Megabus services.

Victoria Bus Station is where many of the local London bus services arrive and depart, and is directly outside the main exits of the train and Tube stations.

Victoria Coach Station is on Buckingham Palace Road: it's a five-minute walk from Victoria Tube station. This is where to go for coach departures; arrivals are at a different location, a short walk from here.

Cambridge

60 miles northeast of London.

With the spires of its university buildings framed by towering trees and expansive meadows, its medieval streets and passages enhanced by gardens and riverbanks, the city of Cambridge is among the loveliest in England. The city predates the Roman occupation of Britain, but there's confusion over exactly how the university was founded. The most widely accepted story is that it was established in 1209 by a pair of scholars from Oxford, who left their university in protest over the wrongful execution of a colleague for murder.

This university town may be beautiful, but it's no museum. Even when the students are on vacation, there's a cultural and intellectual buzz here. Well-preserved medieval buildings sit cheek-by-jowl with the latest in modern architecture (for example, the William Gates building, which houses Cambridge University's computer laboratory) in this growing city—dominated culturally and architecturally by its famous university, whose students make up around one

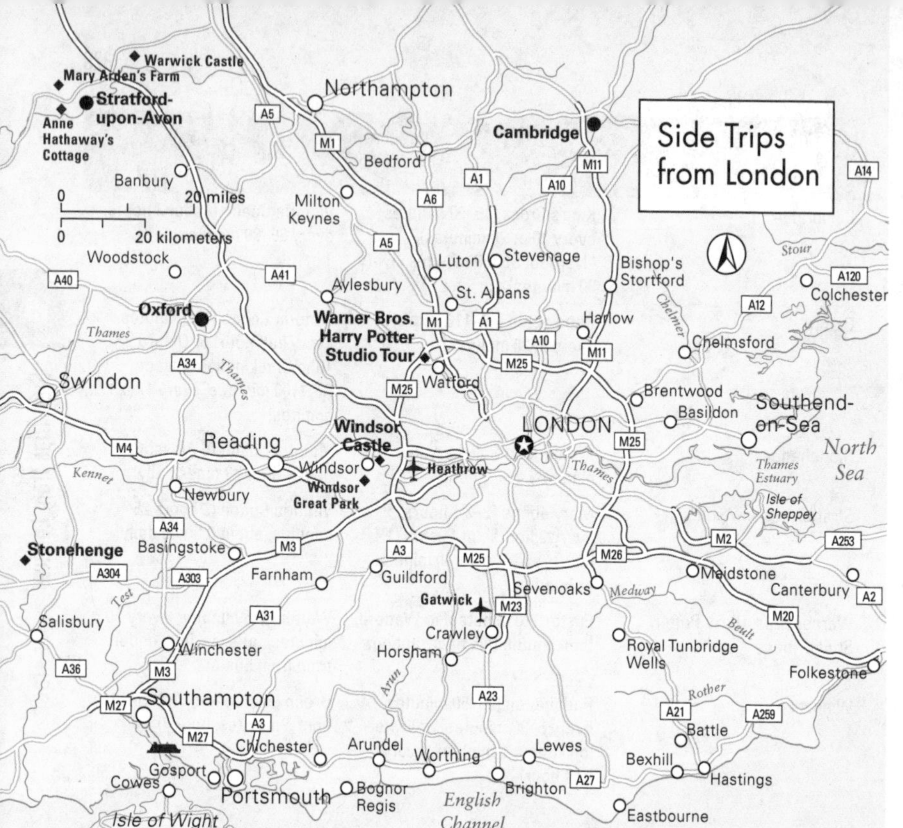

fifth of the city's 109,000 inhabitants, and beautified by parks, gardens, and the quietly flowing River Cam. One quintessential Cambridge pursuit is punting on the Cam (one occupant propelling the narrow, square-end, flat-bottom boat with a long pole), followed by a stroll along the Backs, the left bank of the river fringed by St. John's, Trinity, Clare, King's, and Queens' colleges, and by Trinity Hall.

GETTING HERE AND AROUND

Good bus (three hours) and train (one hour) services connect London and Cambridge. The city center is very amenable to explorations on foot, or you could join the throng by renting a bicycle.

VISITING THE COLLEGES

College visits are certainly a highlight of a Cambridge tour, but remember that the colleges are private residences and workplaces, even when school isn't in session. Each is an independent entity within the university; some are closed to the public, but at others you can see the chapels, dining rooms (called halls), and sometimes the libraries, too. Some colleges charge a fee for the privilege of nosing around. All are closed during exams (usually mid-April–late June), and the opening hours often vary. Additionally, all are subject to closure at short notice (especially King's); check the websites in advance. For details about visiting specific colleges not listed here, contact Cambridge University.

TOURS

City Sightseeing

BUS TOURS | This company operates open-top bus tours of Cambridge, including the Backs, colleges, and Botanic Gardens. Tours can be joined at marked bus stops in the city. Ask the tourist office about additional tours. ✉ *Silver, Street East* ☎ *01789/299123* 🌐 *www.city-sightseeing.com* 🎫 *From £17.*

Visit Cambridge
WALKING TOURS | Walking tours are led by official Blue or Green Badge guides. The 1½- or 2-hour tours leave from the tourist information center at Peas Hill. Hours vary according to the tour, with the earliest leaving at 11 am and the latest at 2 pm. ✉ *The Guildhall, Peas Hill* ☎ *01223/791501* 🌐 *www.visitcambridge.org/official-tours* 🎫 *From £13.*

ESSENTIALS

VISITOR INFORMATION Cambridge Visitor Information Centre ✉ *The Guildhall, Peas Hill* ☎ *01223/791500* 🌐 *www.visitcambridge.org.*

Sights

Emmanuel College
COLLEGE | The master hand of architect Sir Christopher Wren (1632–1723) is evident throughout much of Cambridge, particularly at Emmanuel, built on the site of a Dominican friary, where he designed the chapel and colonnade. A stained-glass window in the chapel has a likeness of John Harvard, founder of Harvard University, who studied here. The college, founded in 1584, was an early center of Puritan learning; a number of the Pilgrims were Emmanuel alumni, and they remembered their alma mater in naming Cambridge, Massachusetts. ✉ *St. Andrew's St.* ☎ *01223/334200* 🌐 *www.emma.cam.ac.uk* 🎫 *Free* 🕓 *Closed during exam periods.*

★ Fitzwilliam Museum
MUSEUM | In a Classical Revival building renowned for its grand Corinthian portico, "The Fitz," founded by the 7th Viscount Fitzwilliam of Merrion in 1816, has one of Britain's most outstanding collections of art and antiquities. Highlights include two large Titians, an extensive collection of French impressionist paintings, and many works by Matisse and Picasso. The opulent interior displays these treasures to marvelous effect, from Egyptian pieces like inch-high figurines and painted coffins to sculptures from the Chinese Han dynasty of the 3rd century BC. Other collections of note here include a fine collection of flower paintings, an assortment of medieval illuminated manuscripts, and a fascinating room full of armor and muskets. ✉ *Trumpington St.* ☎ *01223/332900* 🌐 *www.fitzmuseum.cam.ac.uk* 🎫 *Free* 🕓 *Closed Mon. except bank holidays.*

King's College
COLLEGE | Founded in 1441 by Henry VI, King's College has a magnificent late-15th-century chapel that is its most famous landmark. Other notable architecture includes the neo-Gothic Porters' Lodge, facing King's Parade, which was a comparatively recent addition in the 1830s, and the classical Gibbs building. **TIP→ Head down to the river, from where the panorama of college and chapel is one of the university's most photographed views.** Past students of King's College include the novelist E.M. Forster, the economist John Maynard Keynes, and the World War I poet Rupert Brooke. ✉ *King's Parade* ☎ *01223/331100* 🌐 *www.kings.cam.ac.uk* 🎫 *£9, includes chapel.*

★ King's College Chapel
RELIGIOUS SITE | Based on Sainte-Chapelle, the 13th-century royal chapel in Paris, this house of worship is perhaps the most glorious flowering of Perpendicular Gothic in Britain. Henry VI, the king after whom the college is named, oversaw the work. From the outside, the most prominent features are the massive flying buttresses and the fingerlike spires that line the length of the building. Inside, the most obvious impression is of great space—the chapel was once described as "the noblest barn in Europe"—and of light flooding in from its huge windows. The brilliantly colored bosses (carved panels at the intersections of the roof ribs) are particularly intense, although hard to see without binoculars. An

exhibition in the chantries, or side chapels, explains more about the chapel's construction. Behind the altar is *The Adoration of the Magi,* an enormous painting by Peter Paul Rubens. **■TIP→ The chapel, unlike the rest of King's College, stays open during exam periods.** Every Christmas Eve, a festival of carols is sung by the chapel's famous choir. It's broadcast on national television and considered a quintessential part of the traditional English Christmas. To compete for the small number of tickets available, join the line at the college's main entrance in the early hours—doors open at 7 am. ✉ *King's Parade* ☎ *01223/331212* 🌐 *www.kings.cam.ac.uk* 🎫 *£9, includes college and grounds* 🕓 *Sometimes closed for events; check ahead to confirm.*

★ Polar Museum

MUSEUM | Beautifully designed, this museum at Cambridge University's Scott Polar Research Institute chronicles the history of polar exploration. There's a particular emphasis on the British expeditions of the 20th century, including the ill-fated attempt by Robert Falcon Scott to be the first to reach the South Pole in 1912. Norwegian explorer Roald Amundsen reached the pole first; Scott and his men perished on the return journey, but their story became legendary. There are also collections devoted to the science of modern polar exploration; the indigenous people of northern Canada, Greenland, and Alaska; and frequently changing art installations. ✉ *Scott Polar Research Institute, Lensfield Rd.* ☎ *01223/336540* 🌐 *www.spri.cam.ac.uk/museum* 🎫 *Free* 🕓 *Closed Sun. except 1st Sun. of every month and Mon. except bank holidays.*

Queens' College

COLLEGE | One of the most eye-catching colleges, with a secluded "cloister court" look, Queens' is named after Margaret, wife of Henry VI, and Elizabeth, wife of Edward IV. Founded in 1448 and completed in the 1540s, the college is tucked away on Queens' Lane, next to the wide lawns that lead down from King's College to the Backs. The college's most famed piece of architecture is the wooden lattice Mathematical Bridge, first built in 1749. The original version is said to have been built without any fastenings, though the current bridge (reconstructed in 1902) is securely bolted. ✉ *Queens' La.* ☎ *01223/335500* 🌐 *www.quns.cam.ac.uk* 🎫 *£4* 🕓 *Closed weekends Jan. and Feb. and during exam periods, certain wks Apr.–July; call to confirm.*

A Gift for Science

For centuries Cambridge has been among the country's greatest universities, rivaled only by Oxford. Since the time of one of its most famous alumni, Sir Isaac Newton, it's outshone Oxford in the natural sciences. The university has taken advantage of this prestige, sharing its research facilities with high-tech industries. Surrounded by technology companies, Cambridge has been dubbed "Silicon Fen," a comparison to California's Silicon Valley.

Trinity College

COLLEGE | Founded in 1546 by Henry VIII, Trinity replaced a 14th-century educational foundation and is the largest college in either Cambridge or Oxford, with nearly 1,000 undergraduates. In the 17th-century great court, with its massive gatehouse, is **Great Tom,** a giant clock that strikes each hour with high and low notes. The college's true masterpiece is Sir Christopher Wren's **library,** colonnaded and seemingly constructed with as much light as stone. Among the things you can see here is A. A. Milne's handwritten manuscript of *The House at Pooh Corner.* Trinity alumni include Sir Isaac Newton, William Thackeray, Lord Byron, Lord Tennyson, and 31 Nobel Prize winners. ✉ *St.*

John's St. ☎ *01223/338400* 🌐 *www.trin.cam.ac.uk* 🎫 *£3* ⏲ *College and chapel closed exam period and event days; Wren library closed Sun.*

Restaurants

Loch Fyne

$$ | SEAFOOD | Part of a Scottish chain that harvests its own oysters, this airy, casual place across from the Fitzwilliam Museum is deservedly popular. The seafood is fresh and well prepared, served in a traditional setting with a modern ambience. **Known for:** Bradan Rost smoked salmon; Scottish oysters; great Scotch whisky menu. 💲 *Average main: £17* ✉ *37 Trumpington St.* ☎ *01223/362433* 🌐 *www.lochfyneseafoodandgrill.co.uk.*

★ **Midsummer House**

$$$$ | FRENCH | Beside the River Cam on the edge of Midsummer Common, this gray-brick 19th-century villa holds a two–Michelin star restaurant set in a comfortable conservatory. Fixed-price menus for lunch and dinner (with five to eight courses) present innovative French and Mediterranean-influenced dishes that often include apples from the trees in the garden. **Known for:** great river views; beautiful historic setting; special-occasion dining. 💲 *Average main: £135* ✉ *Midsummer Common* ☎ *01223/369299* 🌐 *www.midsummerhouse.co.uk* ⏲ *Closed Sun.–Tues.*

River Bar Steakhouse & Grill

$$ | MODERN BRITISH | Across the river from Magdalene College, this popular waterfront bar and grill serves delicious steak burgers and pies, plus specialties such as lobster mac and cheese, and salmon steak with molasses and spices. There's an extensive cocktail menu as well. **Known for:** classic British mains; rooftop terrace dining; huge cocktail menu. 💲 *Average main: £23* ✉ *Quayside, 3 Thompsons La., off Bridge St.* ☎ *01223/307030* 🌐 *www.riverbarsteakhouse.com.*

Oxford

55 miles northwest of London.

With arguably the most famous university in the world, Oxford has been a center of learning since 1167, with only the Sorbonne preceding it. It doesn't take more than a day or two to explore its winding medieval streets, photograph its ivy-covered stone buildings and ancient churches and libraries, and even take a punt down one of its placid waterways. The town center is compact and walkable, and at its heart is Oxford University. Alumni of this prestigious institution include more than 50 Nobel Prize winners, 28 British prime ministers, and 28 foreign presidents, along with poets, authors, and artists such as Percy Bysshe Shelley, Oscar Wilde, and W. H. Auden.

Oxford is northwest of London, at the junction of the rivers Thames and Cherwell. The city is more interesting and more cosmopolitan than Cambridge, and although it's also bigger, its suburbs aren't remotely interesting to visitors. The interest is all at the center, where the old town curls around the grand stone buildings, great restaurants, and historic pubs. Victorian writer Matthew Arnold described Oxford's "dreaming spires," a phrase that has become famous. Students rush past on the way to exams, clad with antiquarian style in their requisite mortar caps, flowing dark gowns, stiff collars, and crisp white bow ties. ■ **TIP→ Watch your back when crossing roads, as bikes are everywhere.**

GETTING HERE AND AROUND

Megabus, Oxford Bus Company, and Stagecoach Oxford Tube all have buses traveling from London 24 hours a day; the trip takes between one hour 40 minutes and two hours. In London, Megabus departs from Victoria Coach Station, while Oxford Bus Company and Stagecoach Oxford Tube have pick-up

Radcliffe Camera, an unmissable circular library at Oxford University

points on Buckingham Palace Road; Oxford Tube also picks up from the Marble Arch underground station. Oxford Bus Company runs round-trip shuttle service from Gatwick Airport every hour and Heathrow every half-hour. Trains to Oxford depart from London's Paddington Station for the one-hour trip. Once here, you can easily traverse the town center on foot, but the Oxford Bus Company has a one-day ticket for unlimited travel in and around Oxford.

VISITING THE COLLEGES

You can explore the town's major sights in a day, but it takes more than a day to spend an hour in each of the key museums and absorb the college scene. Some colleges are open only in the afternoons during university terms. When undergraduates are in residence, access is often restricted to the chapels, dining rooms, and libraries, and you're requested to refrain from picnicking in the quadrangles. All are closed certain days during exams, usually mid-April–late June.

TOURS

City Sightseeing

ORIENTATION | This company runs hop-on, hop-off bus tours with 20 stops around Oxford. Your ticket, purchased from the driver, is good for 24 hours. ☎ *01865/790522* 🌐 *www.citysightseeingoxford.com* 🎫 *From £16.*

Oxford Visitor Information Centre

WALKING TOURS | You can find information here on the many guided walks of the city. The best way of gaining access to the collegiate buildings is to take the two-hour university and city tour, which leaves the Tourist Information Centre at 10:45 am and 1 and 2 pm daily from March through October. You can book in advance online. ✉ *15–16 Broad St.* ☎ *01865/686430* 🌐 *www.experienceoxfordshire.org* 🎫 *From £17.*

Sights

★ **Ashmolean Museum**

MUSEUM | What might be Britain's greatest museum outside London is also the oldest public museum in the United Kingdom. "The Ash," as locals call it, displays its rich and varied collections from the Neolithic to the present day over five stunning floors. Innovative and spacious galleries explore connections between priceless Greek, Roman, and Indian artifacts, as well as Egyptian and Chinese objects, all of which are among the best in the country. In the superb art collection, don't miss drawings by Raphael, the shell-encrusted mantle of Powhatan (father of Pocahontas), the lantern belonging to Guy Fawkes, and the Alfred Jewel, set in gold, which dates to the reign of King Alfred the Great (ruled 871–899). ✉ *Beaumont St.* ☎ *01865/278000* 🌐 *www.ashmolean.org* 🎫 *Free.*

The Bodleian Library and Radcliffe Camera

LIBRARY | A vast library, the domed Radcliffe Camera is Oxford's most spectacular building, built in 1737–49 by James Gibbs in Italian baroque style. It's usually surrounded by tourists with cameras trained at its golden-stone walls. The Camera contains part of the Bodleian Library's enormous collection, begun in 1602 and one of six "copyright libraries" in the United Kingdom. Like the Library of Congress in the United States, this means it must by law contain a copy of every book printed in Great Britain. In addition, the Bodleian is a vast repository for priceless historical documents—including a Gutenberg Bible and a Shakespeare First Folio. The collection continues to grow by more than 5,000 items a week. Tours reveal the magnificent Duke Humfrey's Library, which was the original chained library, completed in 1488 (the ancient tomes are dusted once a decade) as well as the spots used to create Hogwarts in the Harry Potter films. Arrive early to secure tickets for the three to six daily tours. The standard tours can be prebooked, as can the extended tours on Wednesday and Saturday; otherwise, tours are first-come, first-served. Audio tours don't require reservations. ✉ *Broad St.* ☎ *01865/287400* 🌐 *www.bodleian.ox.ac.uk* 🎫 *From £6* ⏲ *Sometimes closed for events; call to confirm.*

Christ Church

COLLEGE | Built in 1546, the college of Christ Church is referred to by its members as "The House." This is the site of Oxford's largest quadrangle, Tom Quad, named after the huge bell (6¼ tons) that hangs in the Sir Christopher Wren–designed gate tower and rings 101 times at 9:05 every evening in honor of the original number of Christ Church scholars. The vaulted, 800-year-old chapel in one corner has been Oxford's cathedral since the time of Henry VIII. The college's medieval dining hall contains portraits of many famous alumni, including 13 of Britain's prime ministers, but you'll recognize it from its recurring role in the Harry Potter movies (although they didn't actually film here, the room was painstakingly re-created in a film studio). ■ **TIP→ Plan carefully, as the dining hall is often closed between noon and 2 during term time.** Lewis Carroll, author of *Alice in Wonderland,* was a teacher of mathematics here for many years; a shop opposite the meadows on St. Aldate's sells Alice paraphernalia. ✉ *St. Aldate's* ☎ *01865/276492* 🌐 *www.chch.ox.ac.uk* 🎫 *£8 (£10 in July–Dec.)* ⏲ *Sometimes closed for events; check website to confirm.*

★ **Magdalen College**

COLLEGE | Founded in 1458, with a handsome main quadrangle and a supremely monastic air, Magdalen (pronounced *maud*-lin) is one of the most impressive of Oxford's colleges and attracts its most artistic students. Alumni include such diverse people as P. G. Wodehouse, Oscar Wilde, and John Betjeman. The school's large, square tower is a famous local landmark. ■ **TIP→ To enhance your visit, take a stroll around the Deer Park and along Addison's Walk; then have tea in the Old Kitchen, which overlooks the river.** ✉ *High St.* ☎ *01865/276000* 🌐 *www.*

magd.ox.ac.uk 🎫 £7 ⏲ Closed mornings Oct.–June.

Oxford University Museum of Natural History

MUSEUM | **FAMILY** | This highly decorative Victorian Gothic creation of cast iron and glass, more a cathedral than a museum, is worth a visit for its architecture alone. Among the eclectic collections of entomology, geology, mineralogy, and zoology are the towering skeleton of a *Tyrannosaurus rex* and casts of a dodo's foot and head. There's plenty for children to explore and touch. ✉ *Parks Rd.* ☎ *01865/272950* 🌐 *www.oumnh.ox.ac.uk* 🎫 *Free.*

★ Pitt Rivers Museum

MUSEUM | **FAMILY** | More than half a million intriguing archaeological and anthropological items from around the globe, based on the collection bequeathed by Lieutenant-General Augustus Henry Lane Fox Pitt-Rivers in 1884, are crammed into a multitude of glass cases and drawers. In an eccentric touch that's surprisingly thought-provoking, labels are handwritten, and items are organized thematically rather than geographically—a novel way to gain perspective. Give yourself plenty of time to wander through the displays of shrunken heads, Hawaiian feather cloaks, and fearsome masks. ✉ *S. Parks Rd.* ☎ *01865/270927* 🌐 *www.prm.ox.ac.uk* 🎫 *Free (donations welcome).*

St. John's College

COLLEGE | One of Oxford's most attractive campuses, St. John's has seven quiet quadrangles surrounded by elaborately carved buildings. You enter the first through a low wooden door. This college dates to 1555, when Sir Thomas White, a merchant, founded it. His heart is buried in the chapel (it's a tradition for students to curse as they walk over it). The Canterbury Quad represented the first example of Italian Renaissance architecture in Oxford, and the Front Quad includes the buildings of the old St. Bernard's Monastery. ✉ *St. Giles'* ☎ *01865/277300* 🌐 *www.sjc.ox.ac.uk* 🎫 *Free.*

University Church of St. Mary the Virgin

RELIGIOUS SITE | Seven hundred years' worth of funeral monuments crowd this galleried and spacious church, including the alter-step tombstone of Amy Robsart, the wife of Robert Dudley, who was Elizabeth I's favorite suitor. One pillar marks the site where Thomas Cranmer, author of the *Anglican Book of Common Prayer,* was brought to trial for heresy by Queen Mary I (Cranmer had been a key player in the Protestant reforms). He was later burned at the stake nearby on Broad Street. The top of the 14th-century tower has a panoramic view of the city's skyline—it's worth the 127 steps. The Vaults and Garden Café, part of the church accessible from Radcliffe Square, serves breakfasts and cream teas as well as good lunches. ✉ *High St.* ☎ *01865/279111* 🌐 *www.universitychurch.ox.ac.uk* 🎫 *Church free, tower £4, £5 on weekends.*

University of Oxford Botanic Garden

GARDEN | Founded in 1621 as a healing garden, this is the oldest of its kind in the British Isles. Set on the river, the diverse garden displays 6,000 species ranging from lilies to citrus trees. There is a spacious walled garden, six luxuriant glass houses, including insectivorous and lily houses, and interesting medicinal, rock, and bog gardens to explore. Picnics are allowed, but you must bring your own food and drinks, as there's nowhere to buy them inside. ✉ *Rose La.* ☎ *01865/286690* 🌐 *www.botanic-garden.ox.ac.uk* 🎫 *£6.*

Restaurants

Branca

$ | **ITALIAN** | **FAMILY** | While visitors don't need much persuading to venture out of the town center to the trendy nearby enclave of Jericho, Branca's charming interior, vibrant atmosphere, and solid menu of Italian classics provides yet more allure for the neighborhood. À la carte options inside the rustic, airy corner restaurant include everything from stone-baked pizza to risotto along with a wide selection of meat and fish dishes. Look out for the lunchtime and supper specials and be sure to check out the next-door deli. **Known for:** great lunchtime and dinner set menu deals; popular weekend brunches; deli next door provides perfect picnic food. *$ Average main: £15 ✉ 111 Walton St. ☎ 018/655–5111 🌐 www.branca.co.uk.*

Brasserie Blanc

$$ | FRENCH | Raymond Blanc's sophisticated brasserie in the Jericho neighborhood is the more affordable chain restaurant cousin of Le Manoir aux Quat'Saisons in Great Milton. The changing menu always lists a good selection of steaks and innovative adaptations of bourgeois French fare, sometimes with Mediterranean or Asian influences. **Known for:** French classics like beef bourguignon; affordable prix-fixe lunch menu; good wine selection. *$ Average main: £17 ✉ 71–72 Walton St. ☎ 01865/510999 🌐 www.brasserieblanc.com.*

Gee's

$$ | MODERN BRITISH | With its glass-and-steel framework, this former florist's shop just north of the town center makes a charming conservatory dining room, full of plants and twinkling with lights in the evening. The menu concentrates on the best of Oxfordshire produce and changes daily, but you can expect to find the likes of delicate seafood linguine, farm-fresh roasted vegetables, and wood fired guinea fowl. **Known for:** sophisticated British dishes with local produce; chocolate nemesis and pistachio ice cream dessert; affordable lunch and early dinner menus. *$ Average main: £18 ✉ 61 Banbury Rd. ☎ 01865/553540 🌐 www.geesrestaurant.co.uk.*

Stonehenge

85 miles southwest of London.

Almost five millennia after their construction, these stone circles on the Salisbury Plain continue to pose fascinating questions. How were the giant stones, some weighing as much as 45 tons, brought here, possibly from as far away as Wales? What was the site used for? Why were the stones aligned with the midsummer sunrise and the midwinter sunset? But Stonehenge is more than just the megaliths; the surrounding landscape is dotted with ancient earthworks, remains of Neolithic settlements, and processional pathways, creating a complex of ceremonial structures that testifies to the sophisticated belief system of these early Britons.

GETTING HERE AND AROUND

From London, you need to first take a train or bus to Salisbury or Avebury. Stonehenge Tour buses leave from Salisbury's train and bus stations every half hour from 9:30 to 2:30, and then hourly from 3 to 5, from early June to August; hourly from 10 to 4 from April to early June and September through October; and 10 to 2 in November through March. Tickets cost £16 (bus to site only) or £38 (includes Stonehenge and a visit to Old Sarum). Other options are a taxi or a custom tour. Drivers can find the monument near the junction of A303 with A344.

Sights

★ Stonehenge

ARCHAEOLOGICAL SITE | FAMILY | Mysterious and ancient, Stonehenge has baffled archaeologists, not to mention the general public, for centuries. One of England's most visited monuments (attracting over a million visitors a year) and a UNESCO World Heritage Site, the circle of giant stones standing starkly against the wide sweep of Salisbury Plain still has the capacity to fascinate and move those who view it. Unattractive visitor facilities have been removed to better establish the stones in their original context of grass fields, other nearby monuments, and original processional approach, the Avenue. Although general visitors can no longer enter the stone circle itself (except by special arrangement; call for further information), you can roam free over the surrounding landscape with its Neolithic earthworks, some of which predate the stones. To best experience the awe and mystery of Stonehenge, visit the circle in the early morning or in the evening, when the crowds have dispersed.

Stonehenge was begun as early as 3000 BC with the construction of a circular earthwork enclosure. The nearby Cursus, long rectangular earthwork banks, were also created around this time. The stone circle itself was completed in stages, beginning around 2500 BC with the inner circle of bluestones, and continued to be changed and in use until around 1600 BC. The early inner circle was later surrounded by an outer circle of 30 sarsen stones, huge sandstone blocks weighing up to 25 tons, which are believed to have originated from the Marlborough Down. Within these two circles was a horseshoe-shape group of sarsen trilithons (two large vertical stones supporting a third stone laid horizontally across it) and within that another horseshoe-shape grouping of bluestones. The sarsens used in the trilithons averaged 45 tons. Many of the huge stones were brought here from great distances before the invention of the wheel, and it's not certain what ancient form of transportation was used to move them. Every time a reconstruction of the journey has been attempted, it has failed. The labor involved in quarrying, transporting, and carving these stones is astonishing, all the more so when you realize that it was accomplished about the same time as the construction of Egypt's major pyramids.

Stonehenge (the name derives from the Saxon term for "hanging stones") has been excavated several times over the centuries, but the primary reason for its erection remains unknown. It's fairly certain that it was a religious site, and that worship here involved the cycles of the sun; the alignment of the stones on the axis of the midsummer sunrise and midwinter sunset makes this clear. Viewed from the center of the stone circle, the sun rises adjacent to the Heel Stone at midsummer and sets between the stones of the tallest trilithon at midwinter. The Druids certainly had nothing to do with the construction: the monument had already been in existence for nearly 2,000 years by the time they appeared. Some historians have maintained that Stonehenge was a kind of Neolithic computer, with a sophisticated astronomical purpose—an observatory of sorts—though evidence from excavations in the early 20th century shows that it had once been used as a burial ground. Another possibility is that this Neolithic village was home to those who performed the religious rites at Stonehenge, where people gathered from far and wide to feast and worship.

Without direct access to the stones, it is not possible to closely examine their prehistoric carvings, some of which show axes and daggers, so bring a pair of binoculars to help make out the details on the monoliths. To fully engage your imagination, or to get that magical photo, it's worth exploring all aspects of the site, both near and far. An informative visitor center is located 1½ miles away (access to the stone circle is via a frequent shuttle), with parking, audio guide rental, a café, loads of branded merchandise, and an exhibition of prehistoric objects found at the site. There's also a dramatic display using time-lapse photography that puts you (virtually) in the center of the circle as the seasons change. Next to the visitor center are some re-created Neolithic huts that show how the people who built and used Stonehenge might have lived. Visits are by timed admission slots only. ✉ *Amesbury ✣ Junction of A360 and Airman's Corner* ☎ *0370/333–1181, 0370/333–0605 for stone circle access* 🌐 *www.english-heritage.org.uk* 🎫 *£22 (walk-up); £19 (advance).*

Restaurants

Charter 1227

$$ | BRITISH | Casual and friendly but still upscale, this second-floor restaurant overlooking Market Place offers seasonal menus blending traditional British and European elements. Dishes prepared by the owner-chef include confit duck leg in a sticky plum puree or locally sourced fillet of beef with potato gratin and shallot puree. **Known for:** prix-fixe lunches and early-bird dinners; friendly service; signature dish of crab ravioli. $ *Average main: £20* ✉ *6/7 Ox Row, Market Pl., Salisbury* ☎ *01722/333118* 🌐 *www.charter1227.co.uk* ⏲ *Closed Sun. and Mon.*

Stratford-upon-Avon

104 miles north of London.

Stratford-upon-Avon has become adept at accommodating the hordes of people who stream in for a glimpse of William Shakespeare's world. Filled with distinctive, Tudor half-timber buildings, this is certainly a handsome town, and the Royal Shakespeare Theatre is a don't-miss for those who want to see Shakespeare performed in England. But the town can feel, at times, like a literary amusement park, so if you're not a fan of the Bard, you may want to explore elsewhere.

GETTING HERE AND AROUND

Chiltern Railways serves the area from London's Marylebone Station and takes on average two hours; some trains are direct, but most have one change.

TOURS AND TICKETS

★ **City Sightseeing**

GUIDED TOURS | These double-decker tour buses offer two options: a hop-on, hop-off bus tour that allows you to create your own itinerary around 11 landmarks in and around the town, and a six-hour marathon that takes in all five of the Shakespeare family homes. ☎ *01789/299123* 🌐 *www.city-sightseeing.com/en/100/stratford-upon-avon* 🎫 *From £15.*

★ **Shakespeare Birthplace Trust**

The main places of Shakespearean interest (Anne Hathaway's Cottage, Hall's Croft, Mary Arden's Farm, Shakespeare's New Place, and Shakespeare's Birthplace) are run by the Shakespeare Birthplace Trust, an independent charity that aims to preserve and promote the properties. By far the most economical way to visit the properties is to get a Full Story ticket (£22.50), which gives unlimited access to all five houses for a year. ☎ *01789/204016* 🌐 *www.shakespeare.org.uk.*

Stratford Town Walk

WALKING TOURS | This walking tour runs every day of the year, even on Christmas Day. There are also ghost-themed walks on Saturday nights (booking in advance is essential). The meeting point is by the yellow sign outside the Royal Shakespeare Company, opposite the junction with Sheep Street. ☎ *01789/292478* 🌐 *www.stratfordtownwalk.co.uk* 🎫 *From £6.*

ESSENTIALS

VISITOR INFORMATION Stratford-upon-Avon Tourist Information Centre ✉ *Bridgefoot* ☎ *01789/264293* 🌐 *www.visitstratforduponavon.co.uk.*

Hall's Croft

HISTORIC SITE | One of the finest surviving Jacobean (early-17th-century) town houses in England, this impressive residence (one of the best preserved of the

Stratford-upon-Avon honors Shakespeare's birthday with an annual procession.

Shakespeare family homes) has a delightful walled garden and was once the home of Shakespeare's eldest daughter, Susanna, and her husband, Dr. John Hall. John Hall was a wealthy physician who, by prescribing an herbal cure for scurvy, was well ahead of his time. One room is furnished as a medical dispensary of the period, and throughout the building are fine examples of heavy oak Jacobean furniture, including a child's high chair and some 17th-century portraits. The café serves light lunches and afternoon teas. ✉ *Old Town* ☎ *01789/338533* 🌐 *www.shakespeare.org.uk* 🎫 *£9; Full Story ticket £23 includes Anne Hathaway's Cottage and Gardens, Shakespeare's Birthplace, Shakespeare's New Place, and Mary Arden's Farm.*

Holy Trinity Church

RELIGIOUS SITE | This 13th-century church on the banks of the River Avon is the final resting place of William Shakespeare. He was buried here not because he was a famed poet but because he was a lay rector of Stratford, owning a portion of the township tithes. On the north wall of the sanctuary, over the altar steps, is the famous marble bust created by Gerard Jansen in 1623 and thought to be a true likeness of Shakespeare. The bust offers a more human, even humorous, perspective when viewed from the side. Also in the chancel are the graves of Shakespeare's wife, Anne; his daughter, Susanna; his son-in-law, John Hall; and his granddaughter's first husband, Thomas Nash. Also here is the christening font in which Shakespeare was baptized. ✉ *Old Town* ☎ *01789/266316* 🌐 *www.stratford-upon-avon.org* 🎫 *£4 donation requested.*

★ **Royal Shakespeare Company**

THEATER | One of the finest repertory troupes in the world and long the backbone of England's theatrical life, the Royal Shakespeare Company (RSC) performs plays year-round in Stratford and at venues across Britain. The stunning Royal Shakespeare Theatre, home of the RSC, has a thrust stage based on the original Globe Theater in London. The Swan

Theatre, part of the theater complex and also built in the style of Shakespeare's Globe, stages plays by Shakespeare and his contemporaries such as Christopher Marlowe and Ben Jonson, and contemporary works are staged at The Other Place nearby. Prices start from £5 for rehearsals and previews. ■ TIP→ **Seats book up fast, but day-of-performance and returned tickets are sometimes available.** ✉ *Waterside* ☎ *01789/403493* 🌐 *www.rsc.org.uk* 🎫 *General tickets from £16.*

★ **Shakespeare's Birthplace**

MUSEUM | A half-timber house typical of its time, the playwright's birthplace is a much-visited shrine that has been altered and restored since Shakespeare lived here. Passing through the modern visitor center, you are immersed in the world of Shakespeare through a state-of-the-art exhibition that includes evocative audio and visuals from contemporary stagings of his plays. The house itself is across the garden from the visitor center. Colorful wall decorations and furnishings reflect comfortable, middle-class Elizabethan domestic life; you can view his father's workshop and you can see the very room where Shakespeare was born. Mark Twain and Charles Dickens were both pilgrims here, and you can see the signatures of Thomas Carlyle and Walter Scott scratched into the windowpanes. In the garden, actors present excerpts from his plays. There's also a café and bookshop on the grounds. ✉ *Henley St.* ☎ *01789/204016* 🌐 *www.shakespeare.org.uk* 🎫 *£18; Full Story ticket £23, includes Anne Hathaway's Cottage and Gardens, Hall's Croft, Shakespeare's New Place, and Mary Arden's Farm.*

★ **Shakespeare's New Place**

HOUSE | This is the spot where Shakespeare lived for the last 19 years of his life and where he wrote many of his plays, including *The Tempest*. Though the actual 15th-century building he inhabited was torn down in the 18th century, the site was imaginatively reinterpreted in 2016 as an outdoor space where the footprint of the original house can be traced. Each of his 38 plays is represented by a pennant in the Golden Garden, and his sonnets are engraved into the stone paving. Highlights include a mulberry tree that some believe was given to Shakespeare by King James I and a restored Elizabethan knot garden. A permanent exhibition inside the neighboring Nash's House tells the story of the New House and Shakespeare's family life within it; there's also a roof terrace, which provides views of the gardens. Nash's House was once home to Thomas Nash, the husband of Shakespeare's granddaughter Elizabeth Hall. ✉ *22 Chapel St.* ☎ *01789/338536* 🌐 *www.shakespeare.org.uk* 🎫 *£13; Full Story ticket £23, includes Anne Hathaway's Cottage and Gardens, Shakespeare's Birthplace, Hall's Croft, and Mary Arden's Farm.*

Around Stratford

Two additional stops on the Shakespeare trail are just outside Stratford; also nearby is spectacular Warwick Castle.

★ **Anne Hathaway's Cottage**

BUILDING | The most picturesque of the Shakespeare Birthplace Trust properties, this thatched cottage on the western outskirts of Stratford is the family home of the woman Shakespeare married in 1582. The "cottage," actually a substantial Tudor farmhouse with latticed windows, is astonishingly beautiful. Inside it is surprisingly cozy with lots of period furniture, including the seat where Shakespeare reputedly conducted his courtship, and a rare carved Elizabethan bed. The cottage garden is planted in lush Edwardian style with herbs and flowers. Wildflowers are currently being grown in the adjacent orchard (a nod to what was grown in the garden in the Hathaways' time), and the neighboring arboretum has trees, shrubs, and roses mentioned in Shakespeare's works. ■ TIP→ **The**

best way to get here is on foot, especially in late spring when the apple trees are in blossom. The signed path runs from Evesham Place (an extension of Grove Road) opposite Chestnut Walk. Pick up a leaflet with a map from the tourist office; the walk takes 25–30 minutes. ✉ *Cottage La.* ☎ *01789/338532* 🌐 *www.shakespeare.org.uk* 🎫 *£13; Full Story ticket £23, includes entry to Hall's Croft, Mary Arden's Farm, Shakespeare's New Place, and Shakespeare's Birthplace.*

★ Mary Arden's Farm

HOUSE | FAMILY | This charming working farm was the childhood home of Shakespeare's mother, Mary Arden, and offers great insight into the farming methods employed in Tudor England. The rural heritage attraction, just 3 miles outside Stratford, is great for kids, who can try their hand at basket weaving and gardening, listen as the farmers explain their work in the fields, watch the cooks prepare food in the Tudor farmhouse kitchen, or play in the amazing timber-framed adventure playground. There are also daily falconry and archery displays and opportunities to meet the farm animals, as well as a good café. ✉ *Station Rd., Wilmcote* ☎ *01789/338535* 🌐 *www.shakespeare.org.uk* 🎫 *£15; Full Story ticket £23, includes Anne Hathaway's Cottage and Gardens, Hall's Croft, Shakespeare's New Place, and Shakespeare's Birthplace* ⏲ *Closed Nov.–mid-Mar.*

★ Warwick Castle

CASTLE/PALACE | FAMILY | The vast bulk of this medieval castle rests on a cliff overlooking the Avon River and is considered "the fairest monument of ancient and chivalrous splendor which yet remains uninjured by time," to use the words of Sir Walter Scott. Today the company that runs the Madame Tussauds wax museums owns the castle, and it has become more theme park than authentic heritage site, but it is still a lot of fun. Warwick's two soaring towers, bristling with battlements, can be seen for miles: the 147-foot-high Caesar's Tower, built in 1356, and the 128-foot-high Guy's Tower, built in 1380. Warwick Castle's monumental walls enclose an impressive armory of medieval weapons, as well as state rooms with historic furnishings and paintings. Other exhibits explore the castle's history through the ages, display the sights and sounds of a great medieval household as it prepares for an important battle, and tell the story of a princess's fairy-tale wedding. Be prepared both to play your part and be spooked in the gruesome dungeon experience (50 minutes and not recommended for under-10s) as you travel through scenes of torture, poisonings, and death sentences. Elsewhere, a working trebuchet (a kind of catapult), falconry displays, and rat-throwing (stuffed, not live) games add to the atmosphere. Below the castle, strutting peacocks patrol the 64 acres of grounds elegantly landscaped by Capability Brown in the 18th century. ■ **TIP→ Arrive early to beat the crowds. If you book online, you save 30% on ticket prices.** Lavish medieval banquets take place throughout the year, and plenty of food stalls serve lunch. For the ultimate castle experience, you can "glamp" (glamorously camp) in a medieval tent, stay in a wooden lodge in the Knight's Village, or spend the night in your own luxury suite in the 14th-century Caesar's Tower. ✉ *Castle La. off Mill St., Warwick* ☎ *0871/265–2000* 🌐 *www.warwick-castle.com* 🎫 *Castle £29, £21 in advance; castle and dungeon £34, £26 in advance.*

Restaurants

★ The Black Swan/The Dirty Duck

$ | BRITISH | The only pub in Britain to be licensed under two names (the more informal one came courtesy of American GIs who were stationed here during World War II), this is one of Stratford's most celebrated and consistently rated pubs, attracting actors since the 18th-century days of thespian David

Garrick. Along with your pint of bitter, you can choose from the extensive pub grub menu of fish and chips, steaks, burgers, and grills; there are also good-value light bites. **Known for:** classic English pub atmosphere; reservations-only for dinner; veranda overlooking the river. *Average main: £12 Waterside 01789/297312 www.greeneking-pubs.co.uk.*

Opposition
$$ | **MODERN BRITISH** | Hearty, warming meals are offered at this informal, family-style restaurant in a 16th-century building on the main dining street near the theaters. The English and international dishes—chicken roasted with banana in lime butter and served with curry sauce and basmati rice, for instance—win praise from the locals. **Known for:** historical ambience; plenty of vegetarian and healthy options; summertime crowds. *Average main: £16 13 Sheep St. 01789/269980 www.theoppo.co.uk Closed Sun.*

Warner Bros. Harry Potter Studio Tour

20 miles northwest of London.

Popular and family-friendly, the Warner Bros. Harry Potter Studio Tour has sets and props from the successful films, and plenty of engaging interactive diversions for all ages. The train and a special shuttle bus from Watford get you here.

Sights

★ **Warner Bros. Harry Potter Studio Tour**
MUSEUM | **FAMILY** | Attention all Muggles: this spectacular attraction just outside Watford immerses you in the magical world of Harry Potter for hours. From the Great Hall of Hogwarts—faithfully re-created, down to the finest detail—to magical props beautifully displayed in the vast studio space, each section of this attraction showcases the real sets, props, and special effects used in the eight movies. Visitors enter the Great Hall, a fitting stage for costumes from each Hogwarts house. You can admire the intricacies of the huge Hogwarts Castle model, ride a broomstick, try butterbeer, explore the Forbidden Forest, and gaze through the shop windows of Diagon Alley. The Hogwarts Express section—at a faithfully reproduced Platform 9¾—allows you to walk through a carriage of the actual steam train and see what it's like to ride with Harry and the gang. Tickets, pegged to a 30-minute arrival time slot, must be prebooked online. The studio tour is a 20-minute drive from St. Albans. You can also get here by taking a 20-minute train ride from London's Euston Station to Watford Junction (then a 15-minute shuttle-bus ride; £3 cash only). Via car from London, use M1 and M25—parking is free. *Studio Tour Dr., Leavesden Green 0345/084–0900 www.wbstudiotour.co.uk £45.*

Windsor Castle

21 miles west of London.

The tall turrets of Windsor Castle, one of the homes of the Royal Family, can be seen for miles around. The grand stone building is the star attraction in this quiet town with some remaining medieval elements—although Eton College, England's most famous public school, is also just a lovely walk away across the Thames.

GETTING HERE AND AROUND

Fast Green Line buses leave opposite London's Victoria Coach Station every half hour for the 70-minute trip to Windsor. Trains travel from London Waterloo every 30 minutes, or you can catch more frequent trains from Paddington and change at Slough. The trip takes less than an hour from Waterloo and around 30 minutes from Paddington.

ESSENTIALS

VISITOR INFORMATION Royal Windsor Information Centre ✉ *Old Booking Hall, Windsor Royal Station, Thames St.* ☎ *01753/743900, 01753/743907 for accommodations* 🌐 *www.windsor.gov.uk.*

Sights

★ Eton College

COLLEGE | Signs warn drivers of "Boys Crossing" as you approach the splendid Tudor-style buildings of Eton College, the distinguished boarding school for boys ages 13–18 founded in 1440 by King Henry VI. It's all terrifically photogenic—during the college semester students still dress in pinstripe trousers, swallowtail coats, and stiff collars. Rivaling St. George's at Windsor in terms of size, the Gothic **Chapel** contains superb 15th-century grisaille wall paintings juxtaposed with modern stained glass by John Piper. Beyond the cloisters are the school's playing fields where, according to the Duke of Wellington, the Battle of Waterloo was really won, since so many of his officers had learned discipline and strategy during their school days. Boris Johnson is the most recent of the country's many prime ministers to have been educated here. The **Museum of Eton Life** has displays on the school's history and vignettes of school life. The school gives public tours on Friday afternoon from early April through early September, bookable online. ✉ *Brewhouse Yard, Eton* ☎ *01753/370100* 🌐 *www.etoncollege.com* 🎟 *£10* ⏲ *Closed Sept.–early Apr.*

★ Windsor Castle

CASTLE/PALACE | From William the Conqueror to Queen Victoria, the kings and queens of England added towers and wings to this brooding, imposing castle that is visible for miles, the largest inhabited castle in the world and the only royal residence in continuous use by the British Royal Family since the Middle Ages. Despite the multiplicity of hands involved in its design, the palace manages to have a unity of style and character. The most impressive view of Windsor Castle is from the A332 road, coming into town from the south. Admission includes an audio guide and, if you wish, a guided tour of the castle precincts. Entrance lines can be long in season, and you're likely to spend at least half a day here, so come early.

As you enter the castle, **Henry VIII's gateway** leads uphill into the wide castle precincts, where you're free to wander. Across from the entrance is the exquisite **St. George's Chapel** (closed Sunday). Here lie 10 of the kings of England, including Henry VI, Charles I, and Henry VIII (Jane Seymour is the only one of his six wives buried here). One of the noblest buildings in England, the chapel was built in the Perpendicular style popular in the 15th and 16th centuries, with elegant stained-glass windows; a high, vaulted ceiling; and intricately carved choir stalls. The colorful heraldic banners of the Knights of the Garter—the oldest British Order of Chivalry, founded by Edward III in 1348—hang in the choir. The ceremony in which the knights are installed as members of the order has been held here with much pageantry for more than five centuries. The elaborate **Albert Memorial Chapel** was created by Queen Victoria in memory of her husband.

The **North Terrace** provides especially good views across the Thames to Eton College, perhaps the most famous of Britain's exclusive public schools (confusingly, "public schools" in Britain are highly traditional, top-tier private schools). From the terrace, you enter the **State Apartments,** which are open to the public most days. On display to the left of the entrance to the State Apartments, **Queen Mary's Dolls' House** is a perfect miniature Georgian palace-within-a-palace, created in 1923. Electric lights glow, the doors all have tiny keys, and a miniature library holds Lilliputian-size books written especially for the young queen by famous authors of the 1920s. Five cars, including a Daimler and Rolls-Royce, stand at the ready. In the adjacent corridor are exquisite French couturier–designed costumes made for the two Jumeau dolls presented to the Princesses Elizabeth and Margaret by France in 1938.

Although a fire in 1992 gutted some of the State Apartments, hardly any works of art were lost. Phenomenal repair work brought to new life the **Grand Reception Room,** the **Green and Crimson Drawing Rooms,** and the **State and Octagonal Dining Rooms.** A green oak hammer-beam (a short horizontal beam that projects from the tops of walls for support) roof looms magnificently over the 600-year-old **St. George's Hall,** where the Queen gives state banquets. The State Apartments contain priceless furniture, including a magnificent Louis XVI bed and Gobelin tapestries; carvings by Grinling Gibbons; and paintings by Canaletto, Rubens, Van Dyck, Holbein, Dürer, and Bruegel. The tour's high points are the **Throne Room** and the **Waterloo Chamber,** where Sir Thomas Lawrence's portraits of Napoléon's victorious foes line the walls. You can also see arms and armor—look for Henry VIII's ample suit. A visit October to March also includes the Semi-State rooms, the private apartments of George IV, resplendent with gilded ceilings.

To see the castle come magnificently alive, check out the Changing the Guard, which takes place daily at 11 am April to July, and on alternate days at the same time August to March. Confirm the exact schedule before traveling to Windsor. Note that the State rooms (and sometimes the entire castle) are closed during official state occasions; dates of these closures are listed on the website or you can call ahead to check. ✉ *Castle Hill* ☎ *0303/123–7304 for tickets* 🌐 *www.royalcollection.org.uk* 🎫 *£23 for Precincts, State Apartments, Gallery, St. George's Chapel, and Queen Mary's Dolls' House; £13 when State Apartments are closed.*

Did You Know? 

The Queen uses Windsor often—it's said she likes it much more than Buckingham Palace—spending most weekends here, often joined by family and friends. You know she's in when the Royal Standard is flown above the Round Tower but not in when you see the Union Jack.

★ Windsor Great Park

CITY PARK | The remains of an ancient royal hunting forest, this park stretches for some 5,000 acres south of Windsor Castle. Much of it is open to the public and can be explored by car or on foot. Its chief attractions are clustered around the southeastern section, known (or at least marketed) as the **Royal Landscape.** These include **Virginia Water,** a 2-mile-long lake that forms the park's main geographical focal point. More than anything, however, the Royal Landscape is defined by its two beautiful gardens. **Valley Gardens,** located on the north shore of Virginia Water, is particularly vibrant in April and May, when the dazzling multicolor azaleas are in full bloom. If you're feeling fit, the romantic **Long Walk** is one of England's most photographed footpaths—the 3-mile-long route, designed by Charles II, starts in the Great Park and leads all the way to Windsor Castle.

Divided from the Great Park by the busy A308 highway, the smaller **Windsor Home Park,** on the eastern side of Windsor Castle, is the private property of the Royal Family. It contains **Frogmore House ,** a lavish royal residence. Completed in 1684, Frogmore was bought by George III as a gift for his wife, Queen Charlotte. The sprawling white mansion later became a beloved retreat of Queen Victoria. Today it's home to the Duke and Duchess of

Sussex, otherwise known as Prince Harry and Meghan Markle, and can only be visited by guided tour on a handful of charity days in the summer; see *www.royalcollection.org.uk* more information. *Entrances on A329, A332, B383, and Wick La. 01753/860222 www.windsorgreatpark.co.uk Free; Savill Garden £11(£6 Nov.–Feb.).*

Restaurants

★ Fat Duck

$$$$ | MODERN BRITISH | One of the top restaurants in the country, and ranked by many food writers among the best in the world, this extraordinary place packs in fans of hypercreative, hyper-expensive cuisine, who enjoy it for the theater as much as for the food. Culinary alchemist Heston Blumenthal is famed for the so-called molecular gastronomy he creates in his laboratory-like kitchen and his name has become synonymous with weird and funky taste combinations. **Known for:** creative and immersive dining experience; strict booking process and long waiting list for reservations; famed strange dishes like bacon-and-egg ice cream. *Average main: £325 High St., Bray 01628/580333 www.thefatduck.co.uk Closed Sun. and Mon.*

Two Brewers

$$ | BRITISH | Locals congregate in a pair of low-ceiling rooms at this tiny 17th-century establishment by the gates of Windsor Great Park. Those under 18 aren't allowed inside the pub (although they can be served at a few outdoor tables), but adults will find a suitable collection of wine, espresso, and local beer, plus an excellent menu with dishes like roasted cod with butter sauce and samphire, or steak frites with brandy and peppercorn. **Known for:** classic, adults-only British pub; traditional lunchtime roast on Sunday; historic setting. *Average main: £16 34 Park St. 01753/855426 www.twobrewerswindsor.co.uk.*

Index

D

E

F

G

H

T

U

V

W

X

Y

Z

Photo Credits

Front Cover: EyeEm Premium [Description: Street Amidst Buildings Leading Towards St Paul's Cathedral]. **Back cover, from left to right:** Victor10947/Dreamstime, Gbphoto27/Dreamstime, Mistervlad/Shutterstock. **Spine:** Kim Pin/Shutterstock. **Interior, from left to right:** s4svisuals/Shutterstock (1). Jarek Kilian/iStockphoto (2). photo75/iStockphoto (5). **Chapter 1: Experience London:** Daniel Lange/iStockphoto (6). Mistervlad/Shutterstock (8). Danbreckwoldt/Dreamstime (9). robertharding/Alamy Stock Photo (9). Mariagroth/Dreamstime (10). PA Images/Alamy Stock Photo (10). Alexeyfedoren/Dreamstime (10). Mirohasch/Dreamstime (10). Matt Child/Alamy Stock Photo (11). Ml12nan/Dreamstime (11). Gavin Bates/Dreamstime (12). tony french/Alamy Stock Photo (12). Lucidwaters/Dreamstime (12). Peter D Noyce/Alamy (12). Tupungato/Shutterstock (13). Dan Breckwoldt/Shutterstock (13). Peter Phipp/Travelshots.com/Alamy (14). Lowerkase/Dreamstime (14). tim gartside london/Alamy (14). Ross Brinkerhoff /Fodors Travel (14). Kiev.Victor/Shutterstock (15). Hawksmoor (20). Gordon's Gin (21). Camden Market (22). James Smith & Sons Umbrellas (23). Trustees of the Natural History Museum (24). Kiev.Victor/Shutterstock (24). Victoria and Albert Museum, London (24). Imperial War Museum (25). Plastiques Photography Limited (25). Dean and Chapter of Westminster (26). Vladislav Zolotov/iStockphoto (26). Royal Collection Trust/Courtesy of Her Majesty Queen Elizabeth II 2019 (26). TomasSereda/iStockphoto (26). Historic Royal Palaces (27). asiastock/Shutterstock (27). Afflamen/Shutterstock (27). Vladislav Zolotov/iStockphoto (27). The City of London Corporation (28). stockinasia/iStockphoto (28). Kornelija Cakarun/Shutterstock (28). S.Borisov/Shutterstock (28). I Wei Huang/Shutterstock (29). Courtesy of Historic Royal Palaces (29). Pajor Pawel/Shutterstock (29). I Wei Huang/Shutterstock (29). Roberto Garagarza/Nicholson's Pubs (30). Greene King (30). Annabel Staff (30). CC-by-SA Photo by George Rex (30). TAYO LEE NELSON/Fullers (31). Geffrye Museum (32). Nate Luebbe/Shutterstock (32). Nicole Engelmann Photography (32). Jonathan Reid/Visit London (32). Max Colson (33). **Chapter 3: Westminster and St. James's:** Peter Phipp/Travelshots.com/Alamy (71). Doug Pearson (80-81). Kiev.Victor/Shutterstock (83). Chlodvig/Dreamstime (86). ktylerconk/Flickr, [CC BY 2.0] (90). **Chapter 4: Mayfair and Marylebone:** Derek Croucher/Alamy (101). Benedict Johnson (104). Pawel Libera/Alamy (108). Alex Segre/Shutterstock (114). PCL/Alamy (121). **Chapter 5: Soho and Covent Garden:** Courtesy of Courtauld Gallery (127). British Tourist Authority (143). Ann Steer/iStockphoto (144). **Chapter 6: Bloomsbury and Holborn:** Michael Jenner/Alamy (155). Jarno Gonzalez Zarraonandia/Shutterstock (162). British Museum (163). Grant Rooney/Alamy (164). British Museum (164). British Museum (166). britainonview/McCormick-McAdam (167). Eric Nathan/Alamy (168). Alexey Fedorenko/Shutterstock (183). **Chapter 7: The City:** PSL Images/Alamy (185). Tomas1111/Dreamstime (190). photo75/iStockphoto (197). Tom Hanley/Alamy (199). Petr Kovalenkov/shutterstock (199). HRP/newsteam.co.uk (200). Peter Phipp/age fotostock (201). Mary Evans Picture Library/Alamy (202). Classic Image/Alamy (202). Reflex Picture Library/Alamy (202). Jan Kranendonk/iStockphoto (203). **Chapter 8: East London:** Leklek73/Dreamstime (207). Elly Godfroy/Alamy (211). Jon Arnold (222). **Chapter 9: South of the Thames:** Mike Peel (225). Melba/agefotostock (228). Lance Bellers/Shutterstock (234). piotreknik/Shutterstock (236). **Chapter 10: Kensington, Chelsea, Knightsbridge, and Belgravia:** Cahir Davitt/age fotostock (247). Londonstills.com/Alamy (254). Kiev.Victor/Shutterstock (267). **Chapter 11: Notting Hill and Bayswater:** Roger Cracknell 01/classic/Alamy (273). Robin Nieuwenkamp/Shutterstock (276). **Chapter 12: Regent's Park and Hampstead:** Visit England Images (285). I-Wei Huang/Dreamstime (297). Pictorial Press Ltd/Alamy (299). **Chapter 13: Greenwich:** Michael Booth/Alamy (303). Jon Arnold Images Ltd/Alamy (307). Alicephotography/Dreamstime (310). Mcginnly (312). **Chapter 14: The Thames Upstream:** Mark6138/Dreamstime (315). Terry Harris/Alamy (318). Emotionart/Dreamstime (323). Hilsdon25/Dreamstime (324). **Chapter 15: Side Trips from London:** Andrew Holt/Alamy (327). British Tourist Authority/ Tourism South East (334). John Martin/Alamy (340). **About Our Writers:** All photos are courtesy of the writers except for the following: Ellin Stein, Courtesy of Paul Rider. Alex Wijeratna, Courtesy of Heathcliff O'Malley.

**Every effort has been made to trace the copyright holders, and we apologize in advance for any accidental errors. We would be happy to apply the corrections in the following edition of this publication.*

Notes

Notes

Notes

Notes

Notes

Notes

Notes

Notes

Notes

Notes

Notes

Notes

Fodor's LONDON 2020

Publisher: Stephen Horowitz, *General Manager*

Editorial: Douglas Stallings, *Editorial Director*; Jacinta O'Halloran, Amanda Sadlowski, *Senior Editors*; Kayla Becker, Alexis Kelly, Teddy Minford, Rachael Roth, *Editors*

Design: Tina Malaney, *Director of Design and Production*; Jessica Gonzalez, *Graphic Designer;* Mariana Tabares, *Design & Production Intern*

Production: Jennifer DePrima, *Editorial Production Manager*, Carrie Parker, *Senior Production Editor*, Elyse Rozelle, *Production Editor;* Jackson Pranica, *Editorial Production Assistant*

Maps: Rebecca Baer, *Senior Map Editor*, David Lindroth, Mark Stroud (Moon Street Cartography), *Cartographers*

Photography: Viviane Teles, *Senior Photo Editor;* Namrata Aggarwal, Ashok Kumar, Carl Yu, *Photo Editors;* Rebecca Rimmer, *Photo Intern*

Business & Operations: Chuck Hoover, *Chief Marketing Officer*, Robert Ames, *Group General Manager*, Tara McCrillis, *Director of Publishing Operations;* Victor Bernal, *Business Analyst*

Public Relations and Marketing: Joe Ewaskiw, *Senior Director Communications & Public Relations*; Esther Su, *Senior Marketing Manager*

Fodors.com: Jeremy Tarr, *Editorial Director;* Rachael Levitt, *Managing Editor*

Technology: Jon Atkinson, *Director of Technology;* Rudresh Teotia, *Lead Developer*, Jacob Ashpis, *Content Operations Manager*

Writers: Jo Caird, James O'Neill, Toby Orton, Ellin Stein, Alex Wijeratna

Editors: Amanda Sadlowski (lead editor), Debbie Harmsen

Production Editor: Elyse Rozelle

35th Edition

ISBN 978-1-64097-228-5

ISSN 0149–631X

Library of Congress Control Number 2019952394

SPECIAL SALES

This book is available at special discounts for bulk purchases for sales promotions or premiums. For more information, e-mail SpecialMarkets@fodors.com.

PRINTED IN CANADA

10 9 8 7 6 5 4 3 2 1

About Our Writers

Jo Caird is a travel and arts journalist who writes on theater, visual arts, film, literature, and food and drink, as well as cycling and scuba diving. Her travel stories, city guides, and arts features appear regularly in the *Guardian*, the *Independent*, the *Sunday Telegraph*, the *Economist*, *Condé Nast Traveler*, and *World of Interiors*. Born and raised in London, Caird has an endless fascination for the city, and is delighted to write about it whenever the opportunity arises. For this edition, she updated the Westminster and St. James's; East London; and Greenwich chapters. Follow her on Twitter (🌐 *www.twitter.com/jocaird*) or visit her website (🌐 *www.jocaird.com*).

James O'Neill loves London and—as his work updating our chapters on Bloomsbury and Holborn; Notting Hill and Bayswater; and Travel Smart for this edition proves—loves rediscovering it, too. Although originally from Ireland, he's lived in London for almost 20 years—and still loves it just as much now as he did back then. He has written extensively for TV (BBC and Channel 4), the stage, and the page. He is currently finishing his debut novel, which is set in—where else?—London.

Having studied in London and never left—aside from a brief sojourn in Madrid—**Toby Orton** has experienced everything in the capital from Hackney to Notting Hill, Highgate to Peckham, and still finds it the most inspiring city in the world. He credits the bookshops, bars, galleries, clubs, and streets of London with making him the person he is today. He has written about travel, cycling, food, and drink for a range of websites and publications. He updated the Experience; Mayfair and Marylebone; The City; and The Thames Upstream chapters this edition.

Ellin Stein has written for publications on both sides of the Atlantic, including the *New York Times*, the *Times* (London), the *Guardian*, the *Telegraph*, and *InStyle*, for whom she was European correspondent. Her book *That's Not Funny, That's Sick: The* National Lampoon *and the Comedy Insurgents Who Captured the Mainstream*, was published by W. W. Norton & Co. in 2013. Originally from Manhattan, she has lived in London for two decades. For this edition, she updated our chapters on Kensington, Chelsea, Knightsbridge, and Belgravia; South of the Thames; and Regent's Park and Hampstead.

London restaurant maven **Alex Wijeratna** is permanently blown away by the capital's rocket-fueled restaurant scene. From locavore heroes and street-food gourmet democrats, to global gastro-panjandrums, Alex tickles out the best joints that restaurant-mad London has to offer. Alex has also written for the *Times* (London), the *Guardian*, the *Independent*, the *Daily Mail*, the *Daily Express*, and the *Face*. For this edition, he updated the Soho and Covent Garden chapter.

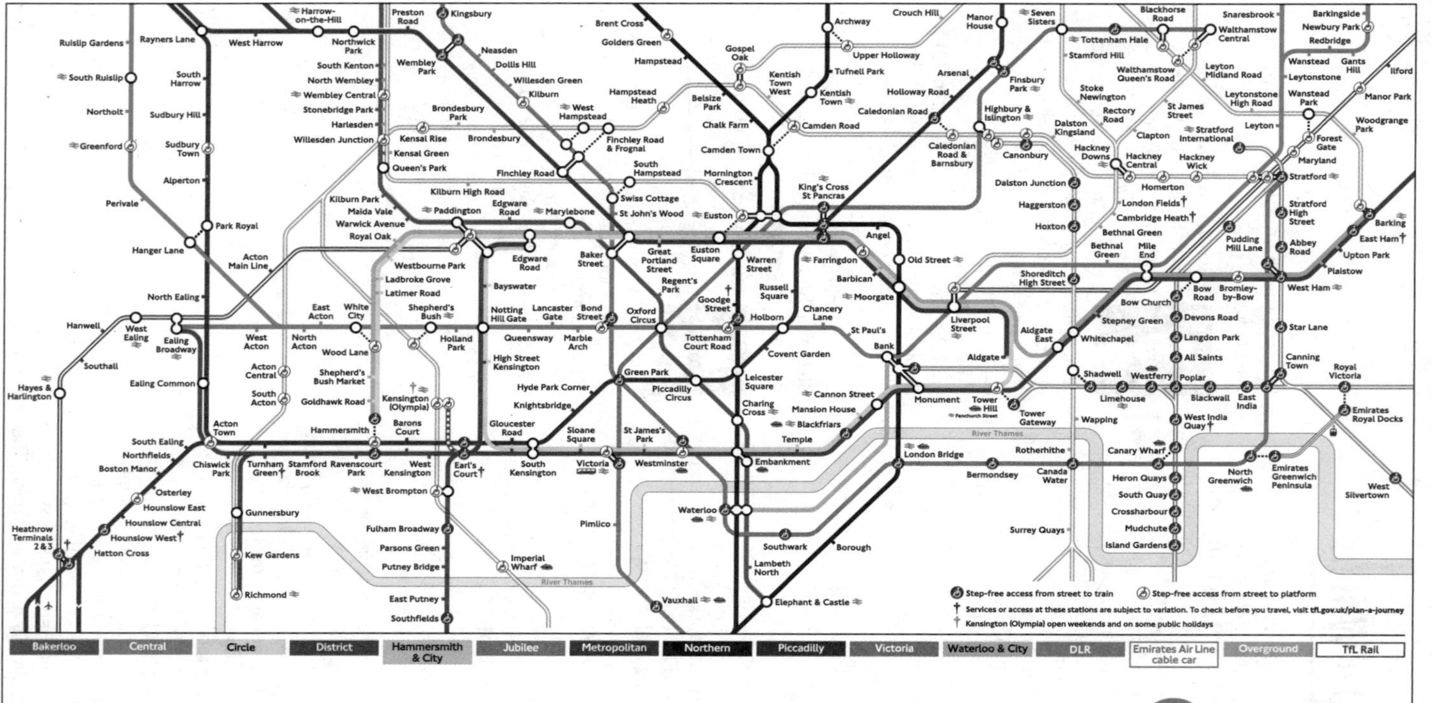
Harrow-on-the-Hill
Preston Road
Kingsbury
Crouch Hill
Manor House
Seven Sisters
Blackhorse Road
Snaresbrook
Barkingside
Newbury Park
Redbridge
Ruislip Gardens
Rayners Lane
West Harrow
Northwick Park
Brent Cross
Golders Green
Archway
Upper Holloway
Tottenham Hale
Walthamstow Central
South Ruislip
South Harrow
South Kenton
North Wembley
Wembley Central
Stonebridge Park
Harlesden
Willesden Junction
Wembley Park
Neasden
Dollis Hill
Willesden Green
Kilburn
Hampstead
Gospel Oak
Kentish Town West
Kentish Town
Tufnell Park
Arsenal
Finsbury Park
Stamford Hill
Walthamstow Queen's Road
Leyton Midland Road
Wanstead
Gants Hill
Leytonstone
Ilford
Northolt
Sudbury Hill
Sudbury Town
Greenford
Alperton
Perivale
Brondesbury Park
Brondesbury
Kensal Rise
Kensal Green
Queen's Park
West Hampstead
Hampstead Heath
Finchley Road & Frognal
Finchley Road
Belsize Park
Chalk Farm
Camden Road
Camden Town
Holloway Road
Caledonian Road
Caledonian Road & Barnsbury
Highbury & Islington
Canonbury
Stoke Newington
Rectory Road
Dalston Kingsland
Hackney Downs
Hackney Central
St James Street
Clapton
Stratford International
Leytonstone High Road
Wanstead Park
Manor Park
Woodgrange Park
Leyton
Forest Gate
Maryland
Stratford
Hackney Wick
Homerton
Dalston Junction
Haggerston
Hoxton
London Fields
Cambridge Heath
Bethnal Green
Mile End
Pudding Mill Lane
Stratford High Street
Abbey Road
Barking
East Ham
Upton Park
Plaistow
West Ham
South Hampstead
Swiss Cottage
St John's Wood
Mornington Crescent
Euston
King's Cross St Pancras
Kilburn High Road
Kilburn Park
Maida Vale
Warwick Avenue
Royal Oak
Paddington
Edgware Road
Marylebone
Park Royal
Hanger Lane
Acton Main Line
Westbourne Park
Ladbroke Grove
Latimer Road
Baker Street
Great Portland Street
Euston Square
Warren Street
Angel
Old Street
Farringdon
Barbican
Moorgate
Liverpool Street
Shoreditch High Street
Bow Church
Bow Road
Bromley-by-Bow
Stepney Green
Devons Road
Langdon Park
All Saints
Star Lane
Canning Town
Royal Victoria
Emirates Royal Docks
North Ealing
East Acton
White City
Shepherd's Bush
Notting Hill Gate
Bayswater
Lancaster Gate
Bond Street
Oxford Circus
Regent's Park
Goodge Street
Russell Square
Chancery Lane
St Paul's
Hanwell
West Ealing
Ealing Broadway
West Acton
North Acton
Wood Lane
Holland Park
Queensway
Marble Arch
Tottenham Court Road
Holborn
Covent Garden
Bank
Aldgate East
Aldgate
Whitechapel
Southall
Acton Central
Shepherd's Bush Market
High Street Kensington
Green Park
Leicester Square
Cannon Street
Monument
Tower Hill
Fenchurch Street
Tower Gateway
Shadwell
Westferry
Poplar
Blackwall
East India
Limehouse
Hayes & Harlington
Ealing Common
South Acton
Goldhawk Road
Kensington (Olympia)
Hyde Park Corner
Knightsbridge
Piccadilly Circus
Charing Cross
Mansion House
Blackfriars
Temple
Wapping
West India Quay
Acton Town
Hammersmith
Barons Court
Gloucester Road
Sloane Square
St James's Park
South Ealing
Northfields
Boston Manor
Chiswick Park
Turnham Green
Stamford Brook
Ravenscourt Park
West Kensington
Earl's Court
South Kensington
Victoria
Westminster
Embankment
London Bridge
River Thames
Rotherhithe
Canary Wharf
North Greenwich
Emirates Greenwich Peninsula
West Silvertown
Bermondsey
Canada Water
Heron Quays
South Quay
Crossharbour
Mudchute
Island Gardens
Osterley
Hounslow East
Hounslow Central
Hounslow West
Heathrow Terminals 2 & 3
Hatton Cross
Gunnersbury
Kew Gardens
Richmond
West Brompton
Fulham Broadway
Parsons Green
Putney Bridge
East Putney
Southfields
Imperial Wharf
Pimlico
Vauxhall
Waterloo
Southwark
Lambeth North
Borough
Elephant & Castle
Surrey Quays
Step-free access from street to train
Step-free access from street to platform
Services or access at these stations are subject to variation. To check before you travel, visit tfl.gov.uk/plan-a-journey
Kensington (Olympia) open weekends and on some public holidays
Bakerloo
Central
Circle
District
Hammersmith & City
Jubilee
Metropolitan
Northern
Piccadilly
Victoria
Waterloo & City
DLR
Emirates Air Line cable car
Overground
TfL Rail
MAYOR OF LONDON
tfl.gov.uk
24 hour travel information
0343 222 1234*
Sign up for email updates
tfl.gov.uk/emailupdates
@TfLTravelAlerts
UNDERGROUND
TRANSPORT FOR LONDON
EVERY JOURNEY MATTERS